NAPOLEON AND THE ART OF LEADERSHIP

NAPOLEON AND THE ART OF LEADERSHIP

HOW A FLAWED GENIUS CHANGED THE HISTORY OF EUROPE AND THE WORLD

William Nester

Foreword by
John Grehan

FRONTLINE
BOOKS

First published in Great Britain in 2020 by

FRONTLINE BOOKS
an imprint of Pen & Sword Books Ltd,
47 Church Street, Barnsley, S.Yorkshire, S70 2AS

Copyright © William Nester 2020

The right of William Nesterto be identified as the author of
this workhas been asserted by him in accordance with the
Copyright, Designs and Patents Act 1988.

ISBN: 978 1 52678 277 9

All rights reserved. No part of this publication may be reproduced,
stored in or introduced into a retrieval system, or transmitted, in any form,
or by any means (electronic, mechanical, photocopying, recording or otherwise)
without the prior written permission of the publisher. Any person who does
any unauthorized act in relation to this publication may be liable to
criminal prosecution and civil claims for damages.

CIP data records for this title are available from the British Library

For more information on our books, please visit
www.frontline-books.com, email info@frontline-books.com
or write to us at the above address.

Printed and bound by TJ Books Limited, Padstow, Cornwall
Typeset by Concept, Huddersfield, West Yorkshire
Pen & Sword Books Ltd incorporates the imprints of Pen & Sword
Archaeology, Atlas, Aviation, Battleground, Discovery,
Family History, History, Maritime, Military, Naval, Politics,
Social History, Transport, True Crime, Claymore Press,
Frontline Books, Praetorian Press,
Seaforth Publishing and White Owl

For a complete list of Pen and Sword titles please contact

OXFORDSHIRE COUNTY COUNCIL	
3303621401	
Askews & Holts	23-Feb-2021
944.05092	

Contents

Acknowledgements		vii
List of Illustrations		ix
Foreword		xi
Maps		xiii
Introduction	Napoleon and the Art of Power	1
Chapter 1	The Rebel	33
Chapter 2	The Master of Italy	50
Chapter 3	The Pharaoh	71
Chapter 4	The Usurper	96
Chapter 5	The Peacemaker	109
Chapter 6	The New World Dreamer	125
Chapter 7	The Great Reformer	138
Chapter 8	The Reluctant Belligerent	144
Chapter 9	The Spymaster	159
Chapter 10	The Emperor	170
Chapter 11	The Sun of Austerlitz	179
Chapter 12	The Ghost of Frederick	197
Chapter 13	The Kingmaker	227
Chapter 14	The Sisyphus of the Peninsula	250
Chapter 15	The Gatekeeper of Vienna	260
Chapter 16	The Antichrist	275

Chapter 17	The Titan	286
Chapter 18	The Lord of the Kremlin	313
Chapter 19	The Dying Gaul	328
Chapter 20	The Odysseus	349
Chapter 21	The Prometheus	368

Endnotes	397
Bibliography	501
Index	517

Acknowledgements

I want to express my deep gratitude and pleasure at having had the opportunity to work with the outstanding Frontline editorial team of Lisa Hoosan, Stephen Chumbley, John Grehan, and Martin Mace, who were always as kind as they were I am especially grateful to Stephen for accenting all the French names and words, and to Martin for finding and captioning all the wonderful illustrations.

I would also like to thank Jason Petho for his wonderful maps.

List of Illustrations

1. Twenty-seven-year-old General Bonaparte would, in less than eight years' time, become Emperor of the French and the most powerful man in Europe.
2. Bianchi's lithograph of a young Captain Bonaparte explaining to senior officers how the Siege of Toulon could be won.
3. *Pont de Lodi, 10 Mai 1796* by Charles Etienne Pierre Motte.
4. Thomas Charles Naudet's drawing of Bonaparte leading his troops across the bridge at Arcole in November 1796.
5. General Bonaparte at Lanato in 1796 by Lordereau.
6. Bonaparte in Egypt.
7. Bonaparte reviewing his Consular Guard.
8. Bonaparte leading his troops at the Battle of Marengo.
9. Bonaparte in his full Consular regalia.
10. The displays erected to celebrate the coronation of Napoleon Bonaparte and Josephine as Imperial majesties.
11. Even Napoleon's divorce from Josephine was an elaborate affair full of poignancy and high drama.
12. A portrait of Napoleon drawn just before he embarked on his disastrous Russian campaign.
13. J. Baillie's *Napoleon and Son*.
14. A scene depicting Napoleon's triumphant return to Paris in March 1815.
15. Napoleon retreating after the Battle of Waterloo.
16. Napoleon on the deck of HMS *Bellerophon* in Plymouth Sound awaiting his banishment to St Helena.

Foreword

Leadership techniques have long been studied and are well known. Indeed, many who will read this book will have attended man-management courses and practised and role-played all manner of workplace and possibly even battlefield scenarios. Yet we have all seen that regardless of how many skills or techniques have been taught and understood, some people are simply, seemingly innately, better leaders than others – and no finer example of this can be found than Napoleon Bonaparte.

Adored by vast numbers who followed him unquestioningly, even enthusiastically, into battle, he was also loathed by many and the royalist flame was never wholly extinguished in some regions of France during his period in power. The imperial crown sat uncertainly upon his far from regal head and remained there only as long as his army stood victorious on the battlefield.

Napoleon, though, certainly had the common touch. He made a point of knowing and remembering, the names of some of his *'grognards'* of the Old Guard which had a tremendous effect on their loyalty, but in the days before the advent of mass communications the only other means by which he could influence people was through the issuing of highly evocative bulletins. Through these he could appeal to the French people's growing spirit of nationalism and of their quest for the ever-elusive *'glorie'*. Of course, not everyone was convinced with Napoleon's stirring calls to arms in the advancement or defence of *'La patrie'* and the phrase 'to lie like a bulletin' was common currency. Yet, by appealing to French hearts rather than French heads, he was able to carry the nation with him, creating, at least in part, a meritocracy which gave perhaps a little more than just a passing nod to liberty, equality and fraternity.

Possibly the most obvious example of this was his creation of the *Légion d'honneur*, the highest award which could be bestowed upon an individual in France which, at least in theory, was open to anyone from whatever rank in the military or society whom it was felt merited such a distinction. The reasoning behind the creation of this order of merit was explained by Napoleon when the value of such medals was questioned: 'You call these baubles, well, it is with baubles that men are led . . . Do you think that you would be able to make men fight by reasoning? Never. That is good only for the scholar in his study. The soldier needs glory, distinctions, rewards.'

Napoleon rose to become the most powerful man in Europe and the methods by which he achieved such a status and how he wielded the power he had amassed, is the subject of William Nester's insightful study. Rather than merely retelling the rise and fall of history's most enigmatic figure, as so many books have in the past, Professor Nestor has undertaken an investigation into not just the methods Napoleon adopted in his quest for power, but how he employed that power as much for the good of the *sans-culottes* as for the perpetuation of the Bonaparte dynasty.

In this study, William Nester makes his case by quoting Napoleon's very own highly revealing words. The Corsican Napoleon struggled to master the French language, his spelling was poor and his handwriting barely legible, yet William Nester has found and pieced together a huge number of the great man's words and those ascribed to him by others.

For those unfamiliar with Napoleon and his place in history who are looking to understand how the son of an Italian lawyer from an island in the Mediterranean became the Emperor of the French and the most feared as well as the most admired man in Europe, there is no better place to look than in here. For those who know that story well, this book is a lavish indulgence – an opportunity to luxuriate in the sharp phrases and the sharp tongue of Napoleon Bonaparte.

John Grehan
Storrington
October 2019

Maps

Map 1. Europe, January 1799.
Map 2. Europe, July 1803
Map 3. Europe, September 1806
Map 4. Europe, March 1810.
Map 5. Europe, May 1812.
Map 6. Europe, June 1815.

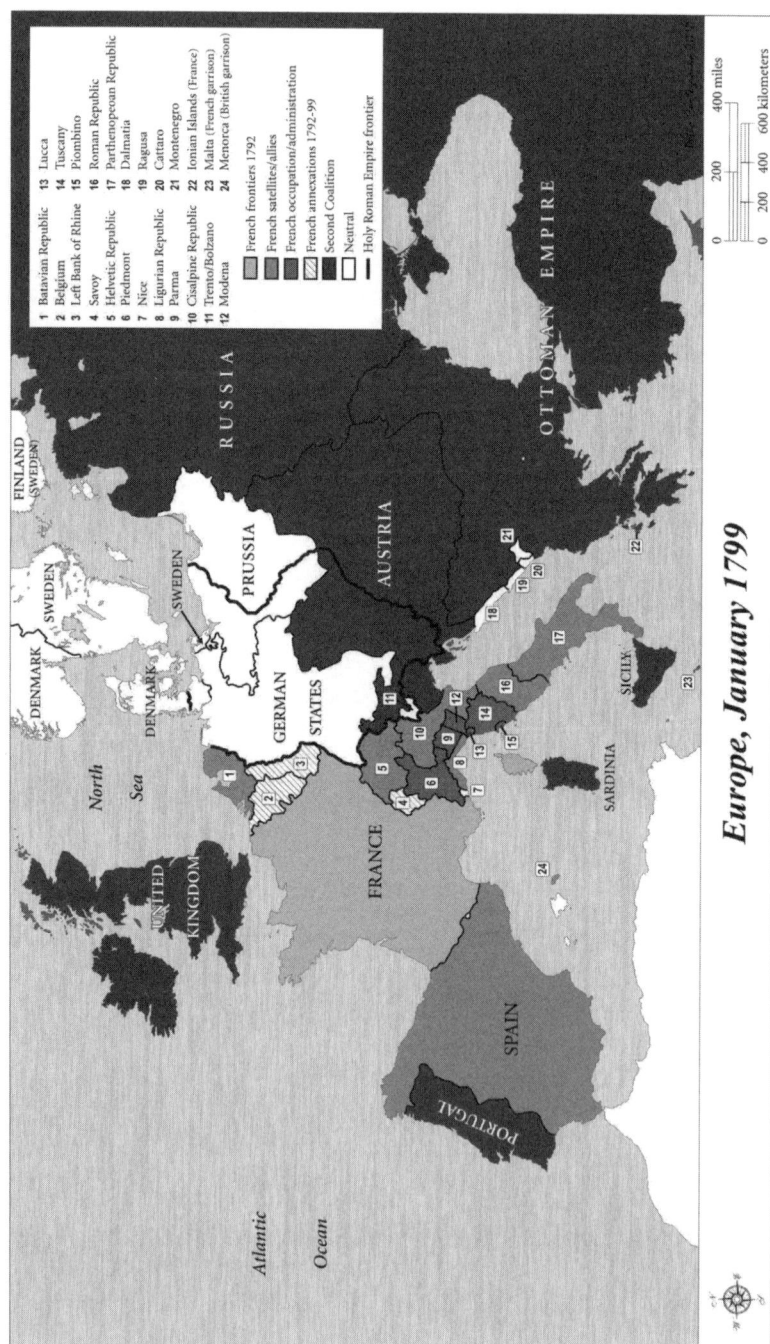

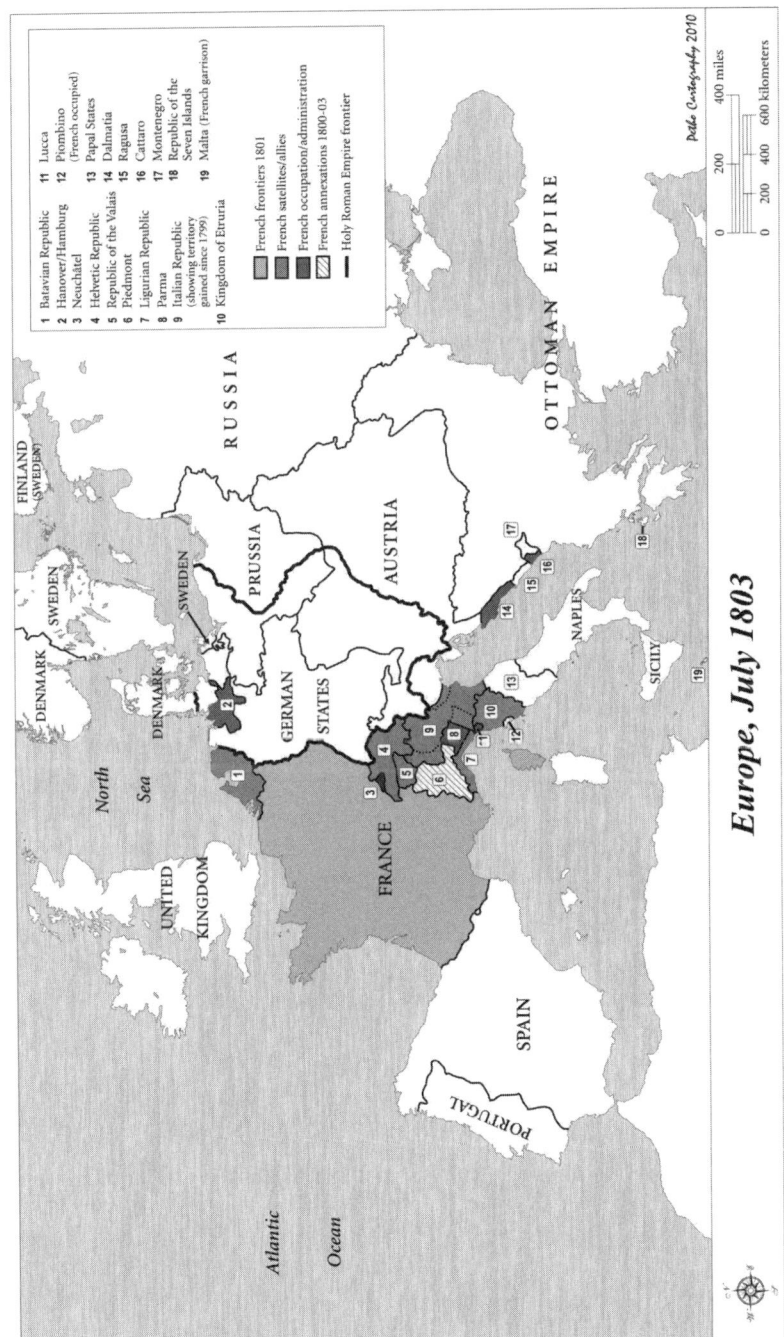

Europe, July 1803

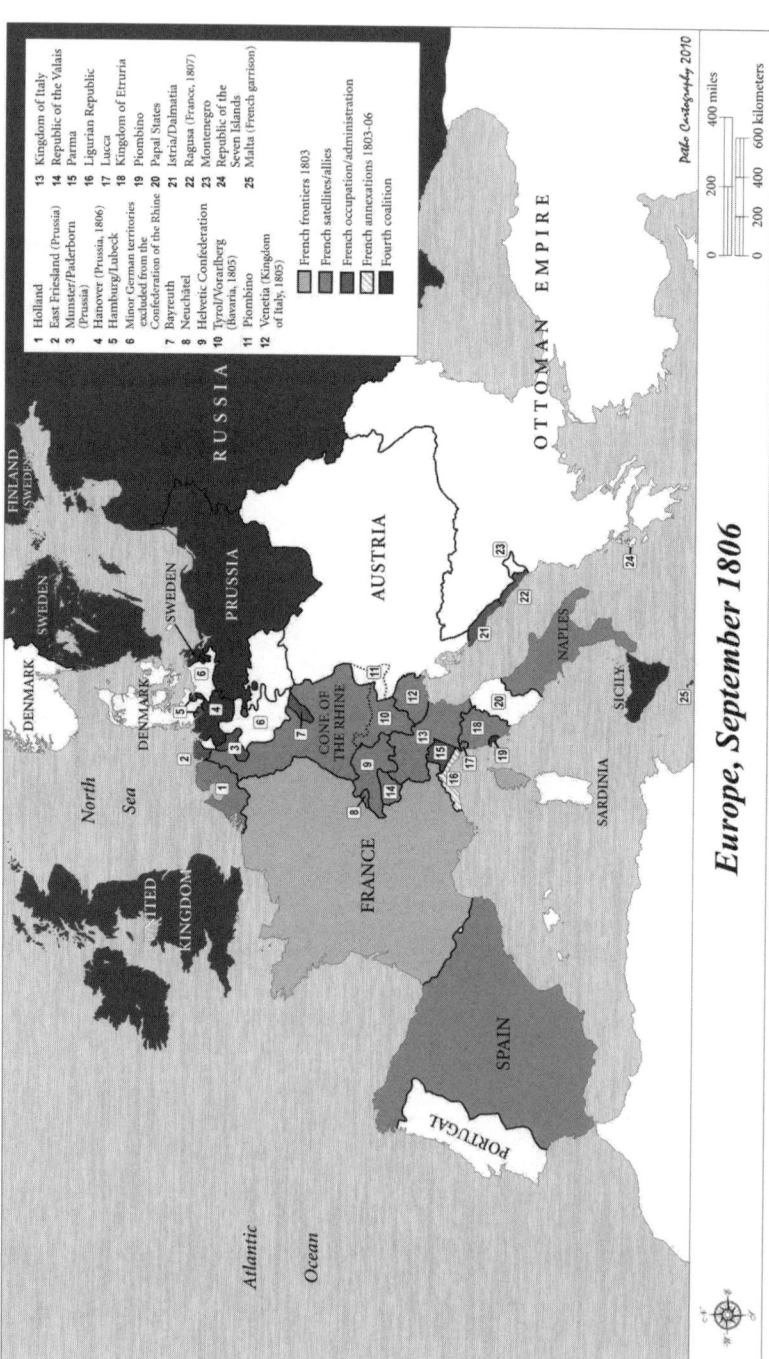

Europe, September 1806

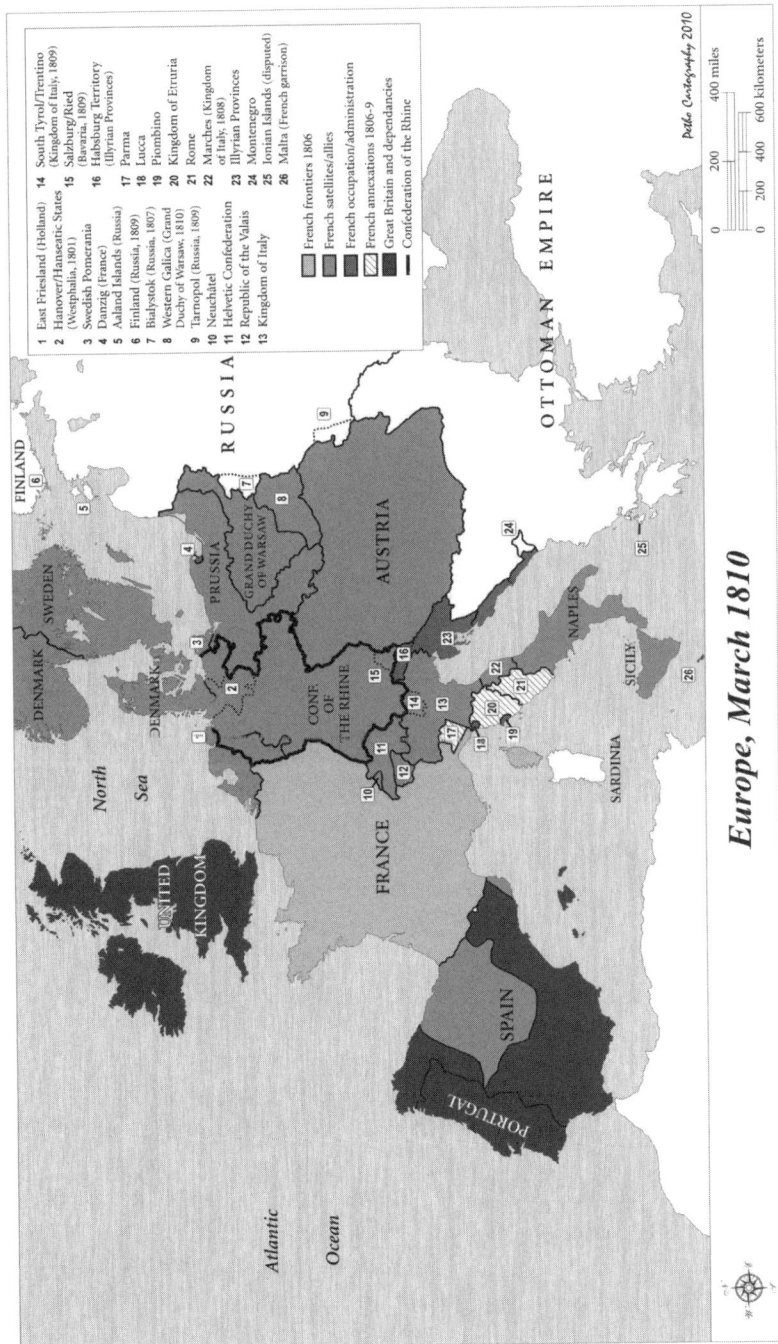

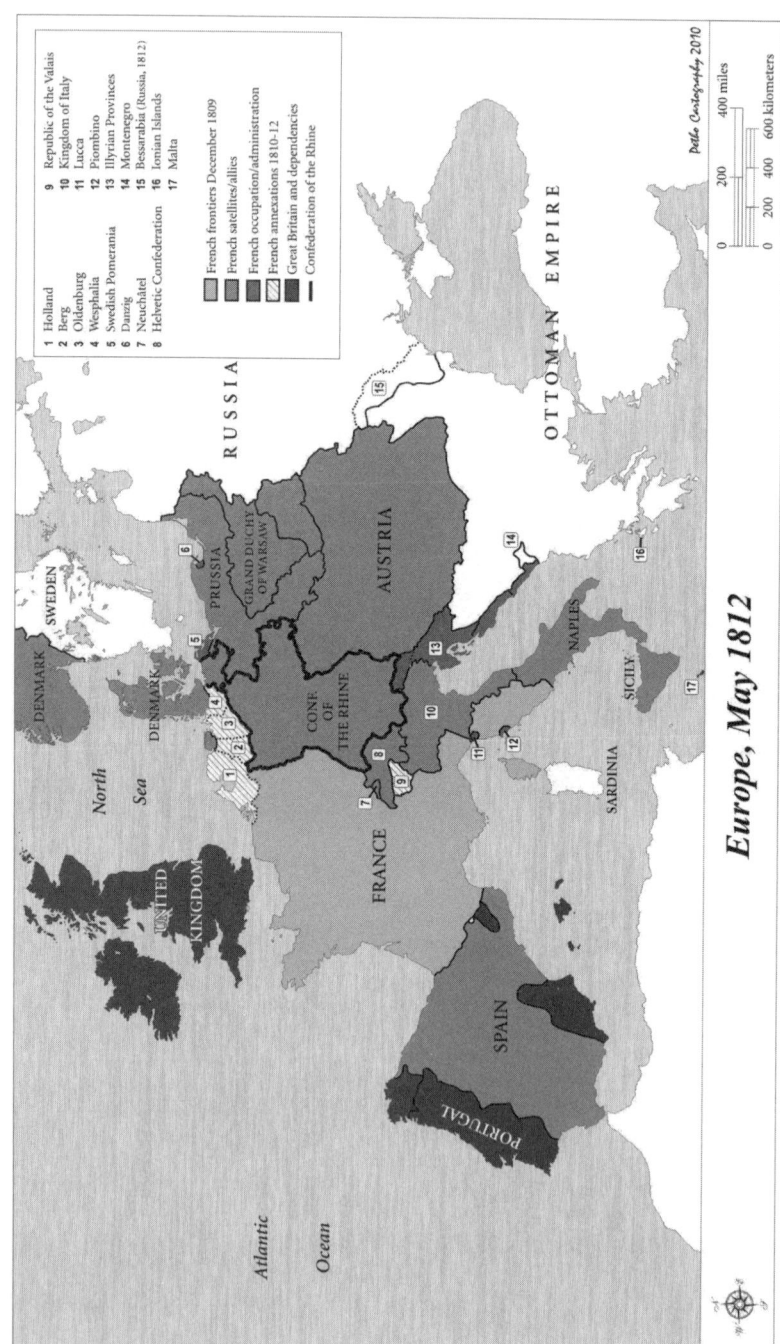

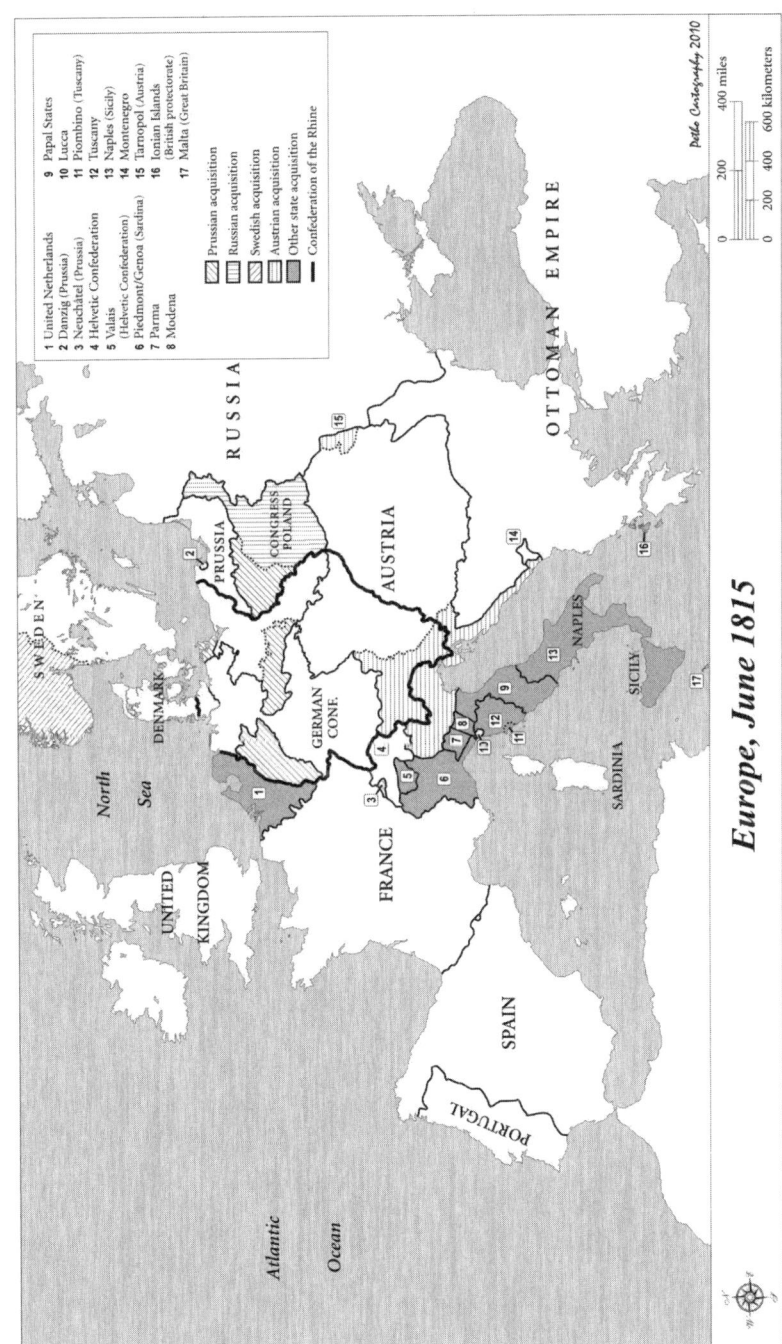

Introduction

Napoleon and the Art of Power

'I was never truly my master, but was always governed by circumstances . . . I was never so foolish as to want to twist events to my system, but instead adapted my system to unforeseen events.'

'The most beautiful title on earth is to be born French . . . I want to raise the glory of the name France so high that it will become the envy of all nations.'

'I wanted deeply to plant our doctrines, our administration and our codes for Europe's regeneration . . . I had vast and numerous projects all calculated for the well-being of humanity . . . I have been condemned for having an iron hand, but that ignores my goal.'

'A statesman's heart must be in his head.'

'The essential secret of lawmaking is knowing how to draw support even from those one intends to regulate.'

'A prince's first duty, without doubt, is do what the people want, but what the people want is nearly never what they say they want.'

'Men who have changed the world have never succeeded by winning over leaders but always by moving the masses. The first way is by resorting to intrigue and only leads to secondary results; the second way is the march of genius and changes the face of the world.'

'When I wanted to set aside an issue, I closed that drawer and I opened another. They did not at all mix and it did not at all fatigue me to go from one to another.'

'I reflect philosophically on the times when I had to do the work of Providence . . . I truly see how often luck entered into the destinies of those who I governed'.

'Peace is an empty word. It is a glorious peace that we want.'

'To conquer is nothing; one must profit from the success . . . The art consists in making one's success in war pay for itself.'

'I lend as much to a manufacturer as his number of workers because they are going to be without work. The vital consequence of this loan must be that the manufacturer stays in business.'

'Diplomacy is inseparable from war.'

'I think that you understand my system of war. England this year borrowed a billion.

We must exhaust their expenses.'

'The smallest circumstances can lead to the greatest events.'

'The truest truths . . . are so hard to obtain for history . . . There are so many truths!'

Power is the ability to get what one wants. One's power rises with the scale of one's ambitions and the ability to realize them versus others with conflicting ends and means. That is the conscious assertion of power. Then there is unintended power. Like the Sorcerer's Apprentice, asserting power can inadvertently set in motion forces that change the world for the better, the worse or some mix of the two. By these measures, Napoleon Bonaparte was among history's most powerful individuals.

No one surpassed Napoleon's understanding and mastery of a virtuous cycle of power composed of interdependent military, economic, administrative, diplomatic, cultural, psychological and, thus, political dimensions. Success in one realm was enhanced by success in others; failure in one by failure in others. For instance, he famously said: 'The art consists in making one's success in war pay for itself' and 'To conquer is nothing; one must profit from the success.'[1] He understood the distinctions and relationships among hard, soft and smart power in which hard power is physical like armies, navies, factories and farms; soft power is psychological like leadership, strategy, tactics, values and beliefs; and smart power is choosing to assert or develop the appropriate sources of hard and soft power to get what one wants.[2] He understood that all power is relative and limited in varying ways and degrees.

Yet, ultimately, Napoleon failed spectacularly at the art of power. The near-absolute power he amassed as emperor and through his dazzling military victories warped him. He believed that he was invincible and could do no wrong and he intimidated into tight-lipped silence anyone in his entourage who suggested otherwise. And for that he is among history's most controversial figures, an inkblot test for the beholders. Admirers applaud his military and administrative genius that advanced the modernization of France and Europe. Critics deplore him as a megalomaniac whose decisions led to devastation or outright death for hundreds of thousands of people. And both are right.[3]

Character and Power

Napoleon was at once a man of his time who eventually transcended it. He was born during the Ancien Régime and came of age during the Revolution. He was a man of thought and action, a progressive and a despot, a builder and a destroyer, cruel and caring, decisive and fatalistic, ruthless and forgiving, rational and sentimental, generous and austere, a cynic and a romantic, a humanist and a brute. At age 25, he described himself as having 'a fiery imagination, a cold mind, a bizarre heart and a melancholy inclination that can shine among men like a meteor then disappear like one'.[4] He exuded a charisma that inspired zealous devotion and sacrifices from his followers. Arthur Wellesley, the Duke of Wellington marvelled that: 'His hat on a battlefield is worth 40,000 men.'[5] To his legions of admirers and himself, he exemplified different symbolic characters from mythology and history as his life unfolded. He was a Young Werther as a lonely precocious teenager, a Hannibal in Italy, an Alexander in Egypt, a Caesar as First Consul, a Charlemagne as emperor, a Sisyphus in the Peninsula, a David in his naval war against Britain, a Xenophon in his Russian retreat, an Odysseus from Elba and a Prometheus on St Helena. Indeed, among his sources of political power was his ability to promote all these glorifying images of himself.[6]

He led a charmed life. He emerged from around fifty battles with three light wounds when all around him men were gunned down or blown to bits. A redcoat bayoneted his thigh at Toulon in 1793; a spent musket ball bruised his ankle at Ratisbonne in 1809; and another spent musket ball bruised his arm at Aspern-Essling in 1809. Over the decades he had eighteen horses killed or wounded under him.[7] His closest brush with death off a battlefield was 'the infernal machine', or cart bomb, that exploded just seconds after his coach bypassed it in 1800. Guards prevented an Austrian patriot from plunging a dagger into him in 1809.

He is certainly among history's most recognizable figures. He was lean and fierce-looking, with penetrating large bluish grey-eyes, shoulder-length dark chestnut hair, high cheekbones, a long straight nose, slightly pursed lips and a jutting jaw as a youth and young man. Then after he seized power in 1799 his body and face steadily fattened while he cut his hair short and combed it over his retreating hairline. Contrary to the legend and complex, he was actually about 5ft 6in, his era's average height. French was his second language and his heavy Corsican accent gradually lightened but never disappeared.[8]

No matter how much power he amassed, he was always an outsider, a Corsican upstart who dared to crown himself emperor. In doing so, he trapped himself in a paradox:

> France badly understands my position. Five or six families share Europe's thrones and they view with unhappiness that a Corsican came to sit among them. I can only maintain myself by force. I can never accustom them to regard me as their equal without holding them under my yoke. My empire is destroyed if I cease being dreaded . . . They do not at all like me, but they fear me and that is sufficient. Anywhere and everywhere I only rule by the fear that I inspire. If I abandon this system I would soon be deposed. There is my system and the motives of my conduct.[9]

He overcompensated for his outsider stigma by asserting every effort to become the ultimate insider as the absolute ruler of an empire that engulfed ever more of Europe.

Even his worst critics might acknowledge that he had some laudable traits. He was among history's most curious men. Indeed, his desire and capacity to absorb knowledge was insatiable. He was obsessed with learning more about anything that interested him, which was pretty much everything. He carefully studied reports and the greater their complexity, the more carefully he scrutinized them: 'I have the habit of often rereading the states of situations. I love to find there information that I looked for.'[10] He insisted to his subordinates that 'it is so important for me to know not just where my battalions are, but also my companies'.[11]

Interior Minister Jean-Antoine Chaptal, who secretly despised him, marvelled that in meetings with experts 'he continually questioned, asking for definitions and meanings of words and provoked discussions until he had formed his opinion'.[12] The Austrian Prince Clemens von Metternich loved talking with Napoleon:

> What at first struck me was the remarkable perspicuity and grand simplicity of his mind and its processes. Conversation with him always had charm for me . . . Seizing the essential points of subjects, stripping them of useless accessories, developing his thought and never ceasing to elaborate till he had made it perfectly clear and conclusive, always finding the fitting word or inventing ones where the image of language had not created it . . . Yet he did not fail to listen to the remarks and objections addressed to him. He accepted them, questioned them or opposed them without . . . overstepping the bounds of a business conversation and I have never felt the least difficulty in saying to him what I believed to be the truth, even when it was not likely to please him.[13]

Few people could ever match his astonishing ability both to grand strategize and micromanage, to connect dots and think outside boxes. He had an equally astonishing ability to compartmentalize: 'When I wanted to set aside an issue, I closed that drawer and I opened another. They did not at all mix and it did not at all fatigue me to go from one to another.'[14] He relaxed by filling his brain with details and statistics then applying them to solve problems. On campaign, he escaped briefly from the horrors of war by spotlighting a faraway time and place to ameliorate. For instance, he generated many of his ideas for promoting the arts and sciences during his military campaigns. Once he decided, he acted decisively.

He was a workaholic. He almost always had to be doing something that he deemed constructive: 'Work is my element. I was born and constituted for work.'[15] Yet, although he drove his key advisors as relentlessly as he drove himself, he recognized that everyone could endure only so much hard labour and stress. He then encouraged them to relax and enjoy themselves after they had fulfilled each day's duties. He gave a family member this advice: 'It was always useful, for all sorts of reasons, to see a little of the world and to indulge oneself . . . and lead a wiser life.'[16]

As for his own entertainment, he enjoyed attending tragic history plays or concerts by renowned singers. Hunting on horseback burned off some of his excess energy. When he was restless at night, he might summon an aide to join him in roaming incognito the streets of Paris or wherever else he was. He was a voracious reader, especially of history, but if something struck him as nonsense, he might toss the book out the window. When he was happy and free from official duties, he sometimes expressed his feelings by whistling or even singing, although he could not carry a tune. He was a maladroit dancer and did not enjoy balls, except for masques where he was quickly spotted striding through the throng, observing everyone, his hands locked behind his back. He adored children and was probably at his happiest romping with them. He was addicted to snuff and frequently paused in whatever he was doing to snort a pinch. He luxuriated in long hot baths followed by vigorous massages. He conformed to the importance of dressing for the occasion, including increasingly elaborate costumes of state as his power swelled, but he preferred wearing a simple dark green *chasseur à cheval*'s jacket over a white shirt, waistcoat and pants on campaign or otherwise a dark blue *grenadier à pied*'s jacket. He was no gourmet; he wolfed down simple meals accompanied by a glass or two of diluted red Chambertin wine. When he laughed it was usually from irony rather than mirth.[17]

Metternich described his dual nature: 'Napoleon had two faces. In private he was easygoing and manageable ... As a statesman he never admitted a single sentiment, decided neither from affection nor hate. He crushed or swept away his enemies without considering anything other than what was necessary for doing so.'[18] His criticisms of those who failed him cut to the bone. Yet, after he vented his anger, he was usually swift to forgive in return for the miscreant's profuse apologies and promises to do better. He amply rewarded and never forgot those who played decisive roles in his political and military victories. For instance, speaking in the third person, he said this of General Charles Augereau who was critical in winning the 1796 Battle of Castiglione: 'That day was the most beautiful in the life of that general. Napoleon has never since wanted to forget it.'[19] He was often gracious and affectionate. Typical were these words to General Henri Clarke, then an envoy to the Kingdom of Etruria: 'I learned that your daughter had married. I wish her happiness in all events.'[20]

Napoleon genuinely felt the pain of others, especially when they suffered the loss of a loved one and he wrote them very moving letters of condolence. To the widow of Admiral François Brueys, killed during the Battle of the Nile, he shared these consoling words:

> Your husband was killed by a cannon shot while fighting aboard his ship. He died without suffering in the sweetest death, that most envied by warriors. I vividly sense your sorrow.

> The moment that we separate ourselves from that which we love is terrible; it isolates us from the earth ... The faculties of the soul are annihilated. All that remains for us in the universe is to cross a nightmare that changes everything. One feels in this situation that nothing obliges us to keep living, that it would be better to die. Yet, after this first thought, one presses one's children to one's heart, with tears, with tender sentiments revived by nature and one lives for one's children. Yes, Madame, you will cry with them, you will raise them from childhood, cultivate their youths, speak to them of their father ... with ... maternal love.[21]

A hyper-awareness of life's mingled sublimity, absurdity and brevity shadowed Napoleon. That aching understanding spurred him to do whatever he could to fulfil his dreams with what time he had; it was mostly exhilarating but at times plunged him into despair. He was especially vulnerable and revealing during his early obsessive love for Josephine. Just before his 1796 Italian campaign, he confessed his 'need to be consoled. It is in writing you ... that I can vent my sorrow. What is our future? What is our past? Where are we now? ... We are born, we live, we die amidst marvels. Is it surprising that priests, astrologers and charlatans profit from this ... singular drive to parade our ideas and assert our wills?' What prompted this bout of existential agony was the death of Felix Chauvet, his commissary chief and close friend. Chauvet literally haunted Bonaparte: 'I see his shadow ... his breath in the air; his soul is in the clouds where my destiny has been determined. Inconsolable I shed tears for our friendship and he tells me that I have already cried enough.' The loss of Chauvet deepened his love and need for Josephine: 'Soul of my existence, send me a letter with each courier. I don't know how otherwise to live.'[22]

War demands that a man bottle up his emotions, that he steel himself against not just witnessing but committing the most horrific acts of killing and maiming or ordering others to do so. Yet, like any human being, Napoleon could not remain unmoved by the gruesome results, especially those inflicted by his decisions. A week after the bloodbath at Eylau, he wrote Josephine that 'the country is covered with dead and wounded ... One suffers and the soul is oppressed to see so many victims.'[23] An experience during his first Italian campaign triggered his pent-up emotions. A battle had raged that day and he could not sleep. It was a beautiful moonlit night. Restless, he asked some aides to stretch their legs with him:

> Suddenly a dog rose beside a cadaver and rushed us howling mournfully then abruptly returned to the cadaver. He licked

his master's face then rushed us again. He was at once trying to revive and avenge his master . . . Nothing on any of my battlefields provoked a similar impression. I stopped unwillingly to contemplate this spectacle. This man, I told myself, had friends . . . and here all had abandoned him except his dog. What a lesson nature gave us with a dog as a medium . . . I had without emotion commanded battles . . . Dry-eyed I had observed manoeuvres that led to great losses among us. Yet I was moved by a dog's cries of sorrow! What is certain is that . . . I better understood Achilles in tears rendering Hector's body to Priam.[24]

Of the array of ways to influence others, one was beyond even Napoleon's protean powers. No nation, even the French with their venomous 'ridicule', came close to matching the British art of lampoon. The British excelled exuberantly at searing and sneering words and cartoons and Napoleon was their bull's eye during his years in power. He was terribly thin-skinned and the ceaseless and merciless barrage of calumnies by Britain's satirical writers and artists infuriated him, compounded by his inability to retaliate.[25] Indeed, to get that monkey off his back, he was even willing to subordinate geopolitics. In 1805, he insisted to the Prussian King Frederick William that 'any peace with England . . . must carry the clause of ceasing to give exile to the Bourbons and the émigrés and to restrain the injuries of its writers. These injuries are reprehensible . . . If one tolerates them in silence they give an exclusive privilege to a nation that knows how to extract privilege from everyone.'[26] Protecting one's power justified these measures because 'ridicule is more fatal to those in authority than their mistakes'.[27]

Where character ends and personality begins is not easily discerned, but Napoleon's latter was far less laudable than his former. Simply put, he was a control freak. It was not easy being around him because he continually sought to manipulate people like pawns. For that 'no one was at ease in Napoleon's society except himself', recalled Chaptal. Indeed, one could not enjoy a true discussion with him because he reacted to those who challenged his views 'with humiliation rather than debate'. He then tried to smooth over any hard feelings 'with a false air of bonhomie'.[28] Louis Bourrienne, a former secretary, was just as critical: 'He had everything required . . . to be a pleasant man, except the wish to do so. He was far too domineering to attract people.' However, Napoleon could, 'when removed from the political world . . . be sensitive, good and capable of showing pity. He liked children very much . . . He could be genial and even most indulgent as far as human weaknesses were concerned.'[29] The saying that no man is a hero to his butler was not true for Napoleon's. Louis Constant usually found his master kind, generous, down-to-earth and fun-loving. At the same time, 'being with the emperor was like living in the middle of a whirlwind succession of rapid, stunning events'.[30]

Napoleon had several deep and enduring friendships with men he had bonded with as a fellow young officer before power warped him, although he was most intimate with his older brother Joseph, who he called 'his best friend'.[31] His closest army friends were Christophe Duroc, Louis Desaix, Jean Bessières, Andoche Junot, Jean Savary and Jean Lannes. Being his friend was a continual series of challenges. First, he outranked them from the time he commanded the Army of Italy and the gap between them widened as he became First Consul and then Emperor; only Duroc continued to use the informal *'tu'* rather than the formal *'vous'* for you. Second, he expected and demanded more from them than from his other subordinates. He especially valued Junot and Savary for their loyalty, zeal and ruthlessness and employed them for special military or diplomatic operations. He did not hesitate to blister them when they failed. A typical letter read: 'I can only see with the greatest pain your conduct in this circumstance . . . You know me well enough to know that I do not at all sin in being too indulgent toward my friends.'[32] War presents the ultimate conflict of interests between friends. A commander must lead or send them to potential death. That duty makes one's sorrow even worse when they are killed. Napoleon wept shamelessly when Desaix, Lannes, Bessières and Duroc died on campaign with him. He tried to assuage his grief by reasoning that: 'To live is to suffer and the true man always struggles to accept that.'[33]

As for women, during his life, Napoleon fell deeply in love with several and in lust with many more. For him 'the ideal happiness was perfect love with each elevated by the other furtively, mysteriously and inexplicably'.[34] He perceived and behaved toward women through a traditional mindset. A woman's role was to provide men with pleasure and care, to lighten life's burdens with her beauty, kindness, sensuality, humour and devotion. He discouraged his sister Pauline from expressing any jealousy with her husband, apparently for his unfaithfulness: 'For a busy man any whining is insufferable. A wife must be good and complaisant and must not demand anything. Your husband is currently truly deserving of the title my brother by the glory he has acquired. Be constantly united by love and tender friendship.'[35] Not surprisingly, given his character and career, he saw romance as a struggle for power that could tilt either way, given the strengths of each person's character and gender. His strategy in love as in war was to attack the other's weakest point, for women, their insecurities: 'To be loved, women must doubt and fear the extent and duration of their empire.'[36] He loved no one more than Josephine:

> It is true that I hate intriguing women beyond anything. I am accustomed to good, sweet and complaisant women, those are the ones I love. If they spoiled me, it is not my fault . . . Throw this letter into the fire so that I will not be condemned as your husband . . . You see that I love good women, naïve and sweet, which you personify.[37]

Although he firmly believed in and practised the double standard toward infidelity, he forgave Josephine for her lovers while he was fighting in Italy and Egypt.

Napoleon profoundly understood psychology. What one did with one's life depended on the dynamic among one's unique character, the circumstances in which one lived and the resulting choices one made:

> Without doubt, each man . . . must develop his character through education, but this must be grounded on what nature has given him. Otherwise he runs the risk of losing those advantages, without obtaining the character that he sought . . . The course of life for each must be, after all, the evident result . . . of his character.[38]

Yet character was not destiny. At times good men make bad decisions and bad men make good decisions. At times self-interest helps others and altruism hurts others. Each choice depends on how one perceives and reacts to complex, changing situations:

> Man hardly ever acts according to his character, but by secret momentary passions that emerge from his heart's deepest recesses . . . What is true is that man is very difficult to know and must be judged by his actions . . . In fact, men have their virtues and vices, their heroism and their perversity and are generally neither good or bad, but . . . each is shaped by his nature, education and fate.[39]

For instance, Napoleon greatly admired George Washington as a general and statesman, yet recognized that Washington's life could not be a model for his own nor his life a model for Washington. What they shared was that each man was the product and eventual master of unique psychological, historic, cultural, economic, strategic and thus political circumstances. Their respective characters and cultures differed so greatly that they could never have changed places:

> After I took power, there were those who wanted me to be a Washington: their words counted for nothing since they were said ignorant of the importance of time, place, men and situations. If I were in America, I would willingly be a Washington and I would have done little good . . . And if he would have found himself in France . . . I would have defied him to be himself . . . For myself I could only have been a crowned Washington.[40]

Belief and behaviour are inseparable. Either we act on our beliefs or pretend that we do. What did Napoleon believe in other than himself? He was driven to find meaning and make his mark on the world with what time he had because 'life is a dream that soon dissolves'.[41] One value surpassed all: 'Death is nothing. But to live vanquished and without glory is to die every day.'[42] He wrote to Admiral Antoine Thevenard that he had the sad duty of informing him that a cannon ball had killed his son, but 'he died without suffering and with honour' which was 'the only consolation to soften a father's sorrow. Death eventually devours each of us . . . Happy are those who die on the field of battle! They will live eternally in the memory of posterity.'[43] Glory was won by committing extraordinary deeds for one's country. Although Napoleon was fiercely Corsican as a youth, he became even more fiercely French from his young manhood. He proudly proclaimed that: 'The most beautiful title on earth is to be born French . . . I want to raise the glory of the name France so high that it will become the envy of all nations.'[44] He came to believe that the destinies of himself and France were inseparable. He most vividly expressed that belief in an extraordinary letter he wrote Foreign Minister Charles Talleyrand in October 1797. He was confident that France 'will be Europe's great nation and arbitrator for a long time . . . We hold the balance of power in Europe; we can tilt that balance as we want and even, if such is our destiny . . . we will achieve great results that only overheated imaginations and enthusiasms can foresee and that one man, cool, constant and reasonable, will achieve that.'[45] By then, he was certain that he knew exactly who that one man would be.

As for religion, he was a deist who believed in a supernatural force that somehow eons ago created the universe but thereafter largely let it run itself by natural forces.[46] Yet for mysterious reasons at times an element of that divinity known as Providence intercedes in human affairs, aiding a select few for great achievements: 'I reflect philosophically on the times when I had to do the work of Providence.' Then there was often another mysterious force that interceded: 'I truly see how often luck entered into the destinies of those who I governed.'[47] Fate in the form of Providence or luck prevailed over an individual's will: 'The truth is that I have never been the master of my actions. I had plenty of plans but I was never free to execute a single one . . . I was never truly my master, but was always governed by circumstances . . . I was never so foolish as to want to twist events to my system, but instead adapted my system to events.'[48] He was constantly aware of the web of relations that entangle each of us in which 'the seemingly smallest event can have the greatest results'.[49] He famously told Talleyrand that: 'From triumph to defeat is but a single step. I saw . . . that a nullity always decided the greatest events.'[50] That reality made acting decisively even more pressing because: 'In politics as in war, the lost moment never returns.'[51]

Tragically, as Napoleon's power rose, his mind closed. At some point after he became emperor, his ministers no longer advised him but merely implemented his decrees. Chaptal explained that:

> Once Bonaparte had an idea, true or false, his opinion ruled his conduct . . . and he no longer consulted anyone or he consulted but no longer took anyone's opinion . . . He sharply mocked those with opinions different from his own . . . Napoleon paralyzed all those who surrounded him. He wanted no one to share his own glory. He believed in no talent but his own . . . He monopolized everything. He attributed everything to himself.[52]

He justified all this by insisting that 'I am not accustomed to finding my political opinions in the advice of others . . . I know more in my little finger than they know in all their heads together.'[53] Hubris was Napoleon's Achilles heel. Victories bloated and twisted his ego until his ambitions exceeded even his astonishing abilities. Then the devastating defeats began and eventually destroyed all that he had created.

Governance and Power

Napoleon is known for his maxims. What is not widely known is that his maxims for governance are as numerous as those for war. His most succinct was this: 'The art of government consists in punishing bad and rewarding good men.'⁵⁴ Good government begins with related values and behaviours: 'It is only with prudence, wisdom and much dexterity that one can overcome all obstacles and achieve great goals; otherwise, one will not achieve anything.'⁵⁵ Although how Napoleon governed was inspired more by Thomas Hobbes's *Leviathan* than Jean Jacques Rousseau's *General Will*, he recognized that ultimately even an emperor must be subject to the law and serve the people: 'To know how to command one must know how to obey.'⁵⁶ The motive for doing so was self-serving rather than altruistic: 'Men who have changed the world have never succeeded by winning over leaders but always by moving the masses. The first way is by resorting to intrigue and only leads to secondary results; the second way is the march of genius and changes the face of the world.'⁵⁷ Ideally there was a balance between liberty and order: 'In France all that is not forbidden is permitted and nothing can be forbidden except by law, by the courts or by the police acting on behalf of morality and public order.'⁵⁸ That still gave authorities plenty of wriggle-room to forbid what they did not like.

No one rules a realm alone. Putting the right people in the right places was critical to his art of governance. His secretary, Agathon Fain, explained: 'A single thought dominated the emperor in his choices, the need to surround himself with useful men.'⁵⁹ The worth of government bureaucracies was inseparable from the worth of the men who ran them. He reminded his officials that 'all institutions have two faces, one beneficial, the other not'.⁶⁰ Good government involved a dexterous rather than heavy hand to strike the proper balance between doing too much or too little: 'The great art consists in doing each year only what must be done.'⁶¹ In dealing with sensitive political matters, generally 'one should treat it softly' and 'not reveal the government's hand'.⁶² And sometimes the best policy was doing nothing. He once issued this advice: 'In affairs of this nature, the great art is to know how to wait.'⁶³ That is no easy task for most people, especially someone as impatient as Napoleon.

The play or role may not have been the only thing, but it was essential. His maxim 'to be a king one must act like a king' applied to any level of leadership.⁶⁴ He understood that all politics involves theatre. Convincingly playing an appropriate role is among the many ways to get what one wants from others. One's audiences expand with one's roles on broader political stages.

Like Machiavelli, he believed that political stability depended more on being feared than loved, although both were vital: 'The people need firm magistrates who know how to inspire esteem and fear.'⁶⁵ As for fear, although he had a short fuse, how he expressed his rage was usually carefully calculated: 'When one of my ministers or some other grand personage made a serious mistake . . . that should truly make me angry . . . I was always careful about how I arranged the scene for the recipient and any witnesses . . . Things work better when a salutary fear circulates in the social body's veins. I can punish less and reap more . . . without having done too much harm.'[66]

A united, efficient, problem-solving government was a vital element of national security. At age 26, then General Bonaparte offered these principles to the struggling Genoan republic:

> You are divided against yourselves and have left the field free for malevolent enemies to attack your liberty. Stifle your hatreds and reunite all your efforts if you want to avoid terrible evils to your country. The kings watch with pleasure and perhaps foment disunion in your government, which ruins your trade, deprives the masses of your nation of equality and establishes privileges and prejudices . . . Never lose sight that if you pit religion against liberty, most people will embrace the former . . . You must not govern with excess just as you must not let yourselves perish with weakness. Enlighten the people . . . Inspire love from your fellow citizens and the esteem of Europe.[67]

Enlisting popular support was critical. How that was done involved 'knowing how to draw support even from those one intends to regulate. And the trinkets given to do so present several advantages. At this point in civilization, it is appropriate to elicit support from the multitude to command one's respect. One can satisfy the vanity of the weak without alienating the strong-minded.'[68] The people's so-called general will was fickle and shallow. This meant that 'a prince's first duty, without doubt, is to do what the people want, but what the people want is nearly never what they think they want'.[69] Spider-like, he wove a powerful and intricate web of personal, legal and institutional relationships that depended on and so obeyed him. His critic Germaine de Staël paid him this grudging tribute: 'Never has a man known how to multiply ties of dependence more cleverly than Bonaparte.'[70]

He greatly respected public opinion's potential power to work for or against him: 'Public opinion is an invisible, mysterious, overwhelming power; nothing is more mobile, vague or strong; and however capricious it may be, it is . . . reasonable and just more often than one thinks.'[71] Indeed he even believed that 'Government founds and propels itself on public opinion . . . that reasons and calculates everything'.[72]

He asserted that 'France was not just a family, not just a feeling, but also an opinion'.[73] Through his secret police, he kept a cupped ear to mutterings in salons, cafes and workshops.

He did not believe in a free press, at least for France and its empire: 'It is too stupid to have newspapers with all the disadvantages of liberty of the press without any advantages and that by malevolence or incompetence, spread rumours that alarm commerce and act on England's behalf.'[74] Then as now the mass public eagerly consumed sensational stories and celebrated charismatic criminals as folk heroes. He despised that dimension of human nature. He repeatedly tried and failed to get newspapers to stop catering to the beetle-browed throng with salacious stories.[75] He sought a more sophisticated press: 'Newspapers today critique nothing in the sense of condemning mediocrity, of ameliorating inexperience, of encouraging budding merit, of re-establishing desire for great models: all that they publish are made to discourage, to destroy. Perhaps the Interior Minister can intervene to remedy that.' Yet he recognized the danger that too much government interference could have the opposite effect, stifling any criticism of anything and falling into 'nothing grander than panegyrism and authors of awful works that already inundate us'.[76] He tried to justify his policy with these partly apologetic, partly Orwellian words to Police Chief Joseph Fouché: 'While I wish that censorship did not exist . . . I am obliged to guard . . . public liberty . . . I do not want censorship . . . but I do not want to be responsible for the stupidities that they can print.'[77] The *Moniteur* became his government's quasi-official newspaper by printing favourable stories along with his army bulletins and other messages.

Public officials should be as honest as they were efficient. He launched periodic crackdowns against those who exploited public resources for private gain: 'I will be pitiless against corrupt agents . . . A man punished severely . . . and delivered to the vengeance of the laws spares the lives of countless people and avoids calamities.'[78] Yet here he did not always practise what he preached. He had an astonishing mind for all kinds of calculations, including finance. He was a very skilled investor both for himself and France. In those days there was no wall of separation between one's private interests and public duties, so he shamelessly enriched himself through insider trading.

In government, there are formal powers of institutions, laws and regulations and then there are informal powers of custom, culture and charisma. The latter often trump the former, as Napoleon was well aware. He was frustrated when his informal powers fell short of his formal powers: 'Intrigues were sometimes so adroit . . . and . . . so closely aligned that my efforts, with the best intentions in the world, had to be a veritable lottery . . . The vice is thus in the nature of one's position, in the force of things.'[79] He paid a grudging tribute to the power 'of women in his court . . . their secret dispositions, their views, their hopes . . . in diverse salons' that undermined his authority by 'deploring the brutality of the emperor's manners, the harshness of his words, the ugliness of his person . . . to ridicule . . . These little advantages conflict much with power.'[80]

Napoleon understood that culture and politics are inseparable. Like individuals, each country has its own unique character, called a culture. The art of governing cultures and characters alike depends on discerning and manipulating the unique features of each. He had some scathing observations about his own nation: 'Much of French character involves exaggerating, complaining and distorting that which discontents them.'[81] Yet he found a key to ruling the French:

> One can obtain anything from France by the lure of danger . . . Valour and the love of glory are instinctively part of being French, a type of sixth sense. How many times in the heat of battle did I stop and contemplate my young conscripts who threw themselves in the fray for the first time. Honour and courage oozed from all their pores.[82]

He forged unity and inspired sacrifices by appealing to their patriotism: 'They knew from me one key question and goal: Do you want to be a good Frenchmen with me? And with the affirmative I led each into a defile without a left or a right, obliging them to march straight ahead for the nation's honour, glory and splendour.'[83]

Then there was the issue of personal security for those who governed. Among his warnings to his brother Joseph, after crowning him the King of Naples, was to guard against being poisoned by his cooks or waiters, to keep his bedroom door guarded and locked at night and to open it only at the voice of his most trusted aide. He cited his own precautions as a model: 'You have followed my private life enough to know how much, even in France, I always keep around me only my most trusted and venerable soldiers.'[84]

Prosperity and Power

Napoleon believed that, ultimately, good governance was about bettering the lives of most people, both their standard of living and quality of life.

That was at once an end and, more vitally, a means to enhance national power. A nation's relative power was critically related to the prosperity or poverty of its people.

As with all other dimensions of power, he was an economic pragmatist rather than theorist.[85] The key question was how to create and distribute more wealth and thus power for individuals and the state. The key answer was to establish a dynamic whereby economic wealth and power steadily enhanced and perpetuated themselves. Determining just how to do that was the priceless challenge. One thing was certain – the state's economic role was essential. States and markets were inseparable. The public and private sectors could both create or destroy wealth. Ideally, they partnered to create wealth. Making money depended on spending it.

He scoffed contemptuously at liberal economic theory personified in Adam Smith's *Wealth of Nations*, published in 1776 and his French disciple Jean-Baptiste Say and his *Treatise on Political Economy* of 1803. His economic views and policies were hardly original, but an elaboration of the mercantilism developed by Maximilien Béthune, duc de Sully under Louis XIII and Jean-Baptiste Colbert under Louis XIV. The real world trumped the notion that free trade, by 'embracing all classes would inspire imaginations and motivate people, is completely identical with equality, would naturally lead to independence and, under this relationship, would uphold much better our modern system'.[86] He deplored the notion that greed is good, that as businessmen gorged at their economic feast, crumbs might trickle down to others. Indeed, he believed that 'business withered the soul'.[87] History revealed that the freer a market, the sooner it self-destructed. Big economic fish gobbled up the smaller fry and then each other, resulting in oligopolies or outright monopolies that gouged consumers with sky-high prices. Greed bloated real estate and stock markets into bubbles that fear popped, impoverishing all except those who bailed out in time. As for international commerce, unilaterally practising free trade was folly's height, a self-destructive form of disarmament that let foreign industries conquer one's own industries and transfer wealth from one's country to that rival country. The British could champion free trade only because their Industrial Revolution churned out cheap products that they dumped in foreign markets to bankrupt competitors.[88]

Napoleon was clearly a man far ahead of his time in knowing that when the private sector self-destructed, the public sector had to spend more to revive the economy. For instance, when the economy faltered in late 1806, he tried to stimulate it 'with subsidies of 500,000 francs each month during 1807 to make work for manufacturing'. He asked Archchancellor Jean Cambacérès 'what manner must be employed to realize my goal which is the least onerous to the public treasury?'[89] He understood and acted on the reality that some businesses were too big to fail and thus the government had to rescue them. During an economic crisis in 1807, he explained to Interior Minister Jean-Baptiste Champagny his criteria for determining who was worthy of emergency loans:

> My goal is not to prevent such a company from bankruptcy . . . but to prevent such a manufacturer from closing . . . I will judge your operations on this principle . . . I lend as much to a manufacturer as his number of workers because they are going to be without work. The vital consequence of this loan must be that the manufacturer stays in business.[90]

A vital government duty was partnering with entrepreneurs to foster the most diverse and dynamic economy possible. He distinguished between investors and speculators and tried to encourage the former who mostly made useful things, while stifling the latter who mostly played financial shell games and bilked the gullible. The key was enticing investments in infrastructure, industries and inventions with various subsidies like grants, low interest loans or tax cuts that enticed private investors. Who got what depended on the economic sector's relative importance to the needs of individuals and the nation, 'first agriculture, then industry, . . . and finally commerce'.[91] To better promote economic development, he established a series of institutions including the Bank of France, Stock Exchange, Court of Accounts, Chamber of Commerce, Land Registry, Statistics Office, Commercial Law Code and Ministry of Manufacturing and Commerce.

To finance public investments, he raised both taxes and efficiency. He generated greater savings and thus money by reorganizing and streamlining government. He created wealth and thus revenue by investing in infrastructure like canals, roads, ports and bridges. These instructions captured his ends and means: 'All that will not demand an immense amount of money. Disorder and waste prevent us from doing anything. The best proclamation that can be made is when people see the work that will be accomplished. But above all we need money. Procure it from a thousand available sources.'[92]

He recognized the importance of Britain's ongoing Industrial Revolution and longed for France to emulate and eventually surpass its rival. However, to succeed, an industrial revolution had to be proceeded by a perceptual revolution: 'Formerly, one only understood property to be land.' Then came related revolutions in how to make and manage things: 'And, for failing to recognize this grand revolution in property, for obstinately closing one's eyes on such truths, one makes such stupidities today and exposes oneself to upheavals. The world has suffered a grand displacement.'[93]

Exports were Britain's engine of economic growth and literally and figuratively the bottom line of its military power and he wanted French exports similarly to serve French power: 'Commercial relations with neutral countries advantage her; she is eager for any way to prosper. Grand, strong and rich, she is satisfied when, by her commerce and that of neutrals, exports can boost her agriculture and manufacturing.'[94] His dream of the day when France exceeded Britain in trade power was impossible as long as the war persisted. France was trapped in a vicious cycle whereby the Royal Navy bottled up both France's war and merchant ships in port, thus leaving French sailors, ships and production to atrophy, while further empowering British merchants to extract wealth from around the world, all of which bolstered the blockade and widened the economic chasm between Britain and France.[95] Ending the war with Britain was critical to French prosperity: 'If we force that government to peace, the advantages that we will procure for our commerce in the two worlds will be a great step toward consolidating our liberty and public good.'[96]

Interior Minister Chaptal, who was otherwise among Napoleon's unrelenting critics, grudgingly gave his economic policies high marks:

> Napoleon rendered grand service to industry. It was under his reign that we attained the degree of prosperity that we enjoy today . . . that for the first time our industrial products for price and quality competed in all the markets of Europe . . . This rapid industrial progress was principally due to the prohibition of foreign products and the severe vigilance with which they were repressed.[97]

The flip side of that progress was Napoleon's one grand delusion when it came to economic policy. He believed that he could bring Britain to its knees by shutting Europe's markets to it with his Continental System. The 'logic' of his belief led him to war against Portugal, Spain and Russia and eventually to his downfall.

Diplomacy and Power

Napoleon provided insights into both pursuits when he declared: 'Diplomacy is inseparable from war.'[98] As in war, he devised grand diplomatic strategies only after immersing himself in a myriad of details.[99] His need to know was insatiable. In early 1806, he wrote to Talleyrand that 'I want to put regularity in my foreign affairs work. Thus, it is suitable that you send me every day, after you have read them, all the letters from my ambassadors and foreign agents, my intention being to read all their correspondence.'[100]

He understood that 'peace is a marriage that depends on a union of wills'.[101] Diplomacy involves developing that will in an opponent who is reluctant to give up. To get what one wants through diplomacy, silence can be as important as talk, emotion as important as reason, concessions as important as threats, symbols as important as substance. Among his repertoire of diplomatic strategies, he wielded one persistently. In diplomacy as in war, he sought to divide and conquer alliances, governments and groups alike. He spotlighted and played off their ancient hatreds and ongoing rivalries. He sowed distrust, dissent and favours. He might extend an olive branch to one minister, faction or country while threatening another. He might give a king a face-saving way to bow to his demands by identifying some pro-English faction in his court that betrayed him and his realm in return for English gold. He offered this advice to one of his ambassadors: 'It is necessary to march softly and with reserve and never do what is not contained in one's instructions because it is impossible for an isolated envoy to appreciate the influence of his operations on the general system. Europe forms a system and all that one does is but a speck linked with others; it is necessary to act in concert.'[102]

His tactical plans to his diplomats, even masters like Talleyrand, were often as intricate as those to his generals. He was adept at bending foreign ambassadors to his will with subtle, persistent psychological pressure. For instance, during peace talks between France and Austria in early 1801, he instructed his brother Joseph to treat Foreign Minister Louis Cobenzl 'like an ordinary minister. In the movements of these negotiations he lacks character . . . He should not be lodged and it would not be suitable if you showed him the same intimacy as during his first visit. He should understand that he should come only to lift all obstacles to conclude the peace and not to gain time.'[103]

He appreciated that diplomacy was a struggle for hearts and minds with one's counterparts for a broader audience that always included the other government and populace along with usually all other key governments and peoples. For instance, as the resumption of war with Britain loomed in May 1803, he cautioned General Jean Lannes, his ambassador in Lisbon, in trying to entice Portugal from its alliance with Britain, 'to display the greatest moderation. Conform to the customs of the country . . . In meeting with the ministers . . . express . . . moderate and pacific sentiments.'[104]

Napoleon was his own most trusted diplomat just as he was his own must trusted general. He loved matching wits with adversaries to talk them into conceding things they treasured. To that end, in what can be called the 'Napoleon treatment', he unleashed a barrage of arguments, promises, threats, reason, emotion and appeals to the loftiest ideals and vilest motives; he persisted until he got what he wanted. Diplomat Armand Caulaincourt described what it was like to deal with him:

> The harder the Emperor found it to persuade me, the more art and persistence he put forth to attain that end. His calculated wiles and the language he used, would have made anyone believe that I was one of the powers whom he was so much concerned to win over . . . He acted so towards all whom he wished to persuade and he was always wanting to persuade someone . . . The success which he was accustomed to obtain . . . must be attributed to his predilection for interviews with sovereigns and his habit of dealing in any particularly delicate and important matter directly with the minsters and ambassadors of foreign powers. When he so wished, there could be a power of persuasion and fascination in his voice, his expression, his very manner, giving him an advantage over his interlocutor as great as the superiority and flexibility of his mind . . . He never failed to shift the centre of argument when he encountered opposition.[105]

He understood and wielded the power of projection, of accusing others of one's own vilest faults. Projection at once lessened public animosities against oneself and heightened them against one's foe. No nation was more adept at projection than Britain: 'in my great struggle with England, its government . . . constantly threw odious attacks against my personality and acts . . . deploring my despotism, egoism, ambition and perfidy; in doing so, they were precisely guilty of their charges against me'.[106]

Espionage is essential not just to diplomacy but to all political conflicts. Intelligence involves gathering, analysing and applying information critical for deciding how best to defend or enhance one's interests.

Counterintelligence involves those measures that prevent others from stealing one's secrets while, ideally, recruiting them as double agents. Not surprisingly, Napoleon was a spymaster both by natural skills and necessity. Indeed, not just his regime but his very life depended on getting timely, accurate intelligence. An intelligence failure took place when a cart-bomb exploded seconds after his coach passed it on the crowded Rue Saint-Nicaise on 24 December 1800. To Joachim Murat, whom he had made the King of Naples, he presented some basic espionage lessons: 'The members of the diplomatic corps are spies who nothing can make happy and who write the most ridiculous reports to their governments. Each month hold a solemn audience with them . . . Never dine alone with any of them. Carry away this principle: the less the diplomatic corps approaches you, the better things go.'[107]

Newspapers could be a good intelligence source. He had Europe's leading newspapers delivered to him and had aides read aloud or translate relevant articles. The challenge was separating fact from exaggeration or outright fiction in the articles by reading between the lines. Rulers, including him, often forced newspapers to print disinformation to fool foes and friends alike. As he put it, 'one must not let newspapers serve spies', they should only serve the state in which they are published.[108] He acted as his empire's editor-in-chief by encouraging newspapers to print favourable and repress unfavourable articles. For instance, he received in late 1808 and early 1809 a series of reports that Austria was preparing to launch a war against France. He responded by having his diplomats and allied governments redouble their efforts to glean more intelligence. He also launched a propaganda war. He had his brother Jérôme, Westphalia's king, 'place clever and dependable men as editors of newspapers to write articles that ridiculed the anti-French and anti-Confederation of the Rhine newspaper articles published in Vienna and Pressburg'. He had his ambassador in Munich pressure the Bavarian King Maximilien Joseph to ensure that his own newspapers similarly countered Austrian propaganda. Finally, he had Police Minister Joseph Fouché get French newspapers in Strasbourg and Mainz on the Rhine to join the war of words.[109] He admonished his brother Joseph, then the King of Naples, for issuing 'proclamations that do not feel masterly enough. You will not succeed by caressing too much the Italian people and in general all people; if they do not at all perceive you to be their master, they are disposed to rebellion and mutiny.'[110]

Talleyrand pointed to a flaw in Napoleon as a statesman: 'He loved to fool people for the sole pleasure of doing so and his instinct forced him to do so to the detriment of his policies. To execute the grand schemes that were always rolling around in his head, artifice was scarcely less important than force.'[111] Most people only allow themselves to be fooled once and never trust the trickster again. That was true for ever more of Europe's monarchs who Napoleon bamboozled. And they turned against him as soon as they could safely do so.

Just as he was the military commander-in-chief, he was also the diplomat-in-chief. Five highly talented men acted as foreign minister during his rule, but he always remained his own foreign minister. As with his military chiefs, with time, he increasingly ignored the advice of his diplomatic chiefs. His foreign ministers, like his generals, simply implemented his commands rather than joined debates over the best strategies and tactics. And that was a major reason for his downfall.

War and Power

Measured by the number of battles and campaigns that he won, Napoleon is history's greatest general. If 'total war' is a government's mobilization of a nation's vital economic, social, cultural, population, political, technological, mass media and military dimensions for war, then the first modern example was Revolutionary France in 1793. Although Napoleon did not invent 'total war', he did master it. The scale of his manpower organization, logistics, campaigns and battles was unprecedented and after Waterloo would be unsurpassed for another century.[112]

Napoleon's rise to and fall from power ultimately depended on his ability to wage war. He certainly rejected the notion of peace at any price: 'Peace is an empty word. It is a glorious peace that we want.'[113] Indeed, 'my principle is that war is better than a weak peace'.[114] Unsurprisingly, his greatest heroes were the greatest conquerors, Hannibal, Alexander, Caesar and Charlemagne along with Turenne and Frederick the Great. His favourites were Caesar and Charlemagne because they were equally brilliant at vanquishing and ruling. Yet, accusations that he was a warmonger angered him: 'There are those who never cease speaking of my love of war, but have I not always been occupied with defending myself? When have I not won a great victory without immediately proposing peace?'[115] His first point is more debatable than his second. He insisted that his way of war was the most moral: 'If you make war, make it with speed and severity; that is the only way of rendering it less long and consequently less deplorable for humanity.'[116] That notion is tough to dispute.

Napoleon did not have a systematic theory of war, but rather a set of maxims that he asserted according to circumstances.[117] In war as in all his other pursuits, he was a pragmatist, not a theorist. He valued what worked and experimented until he got it right or could do no more. He did not invent a new form of waging war, he mastered the simple but critical principles followed by history's greatest military leaders. As for the specifics of contemporary warfare, he culled ideas from Frederick the Great's *Secret Instructions*, Jacques Antoine Hypolite, Comte de Guibert's *Essai Général de Tactique* and *Defense du Systeme de Guerre Moderne*, and Pierre de Bourcet's *Principes de la Guerre des Montagnes*.

Napoleon explained and revealed in his campaigns that great generals have the ability to see and act upon all possible moves as many moves ahead on a geopolitical chessboard whose squares and pieces are morphing, distorted, hidden or mirages. With excellent plans decisively executed 'all the army's operations will succeed when they should succeed'.[118] Yet luck could be as important as strategy in determining events: 'One must be flexible in applying the principles of war' because 'war consisted of a chain of chances. A general must never lose sight of his grand view so that he can profit from accidents.'[119] His campaign and battle plans were guidelines rather than blueprints. He gave his commanders plenty of leeway to react creatively to specific threats or opportunities. The key was keeping the grand view in mind while overcoming throngs of immediate challenges: 'Any man can form a campaign plan, but few are capable of making war because that only belongs to a military genius who conducts himself according to events and circumstances. That is why the best tacticians have so often been bad commanding generals.'[120] Yet another quality was vital: 'It is rare and difficult for a general to bring together all the necessary qualities for greatness . . . We speak of physical and moral courage . . . Moral courage is rarer, that of two hours after midnight . . . the courage to improvise in the face of the most sudden events with the same freedom of spirit, judgment and decisiveness.'[121]

'March separately, attack together' was perhaps his most important maxim. On campaign he manoeuvred his corps far enough apart so they did not impede each other but could mass quickly: 'the art of placing troops is the great art of war. Always place your troops in a way that . . . you can easily reunite them in a few days.'[122] Unity of command was as important as unity of force, expressed by this enduring maxim: 'I would rather fight than join a coalition.' One key edge he enjoyed during his 1796, 1805, 1813 and 1814 campaigns was pitting his protean mind against an alliance of lesser minds. Two other elements must be added to a unified command and troops: 'Secrecy and speed are the grand means for success.'[123] Of the two, the latter was more important: 'One can lose battles but never time.' He once issued this complaint about one of his generals: 'He made me lose a day and the world's fate can depend on a day.'[124] During his first Italian campaign, he asked the French government not to send him any more generals, explaining that: 'Our way of war is so different from others that I cannot confer a division to a general without having tested him in two or three battles . . . It is essential for the army and for the Republic to send me young men who understand how to make a war of movements . . . That is what will gain this army great successes.'[125]

The ideal strategy was to outmanoeuvre the enemy, threaten its supply lines and attack its flank or rear as Napoleon did during the Ulm phase of his 1805 campaign and during the Jena and Auerstadt phase of his 1806 campaign. When the enemy was more numerous and concentrated the best strategy was to split it asunder and defeat each part separately as Napoleon did during his Italian campaign's first phase in 1796 and failed to do during the four-day campaign that ended at Waterloo in 1815. When the enemy was more numerous but divided, the strategy was to capitalize on interior lines and quick-march to defeat each force separately as he did successfully during his Italian campaign from July 1796 to January 1797 and during his 1813 and 1814 campaigns until he was overwhelmed by superior converging armies.

Tactics, like strategy, depend on circumstances. Being able quickly to assess how the enemy was deployed across a landscape was critical to determining how one deployed one's own troops in defence or attack. Ideally one attacked the enemy's flank or rear but that was rarely possible. Defenders sought to anchor the ends of their line with terrain, buildings or streams that impeded movement. Regardless of whether one attacked or defended, winning tactics involved combining infantry, cavalry and artillery in ways that devastated and routed the enemy. Not surprisingly, having been trained as an artilleryman, he favoured that arm. Indeed, he insisted that: 'Artillery today is the veritable destiny of armies and peoples' because 'infantry and cavalry, left to themselves without artillery, cannot bring a decisive result . . . The art consists in converging a grand number of shots on the same critical point', followed by a mass infantry attack to shatter the enemy's line and finally a mass cavalry charge that engulfed and destroyed the fleeing or demoralized troops. 'That', Napoleon insisted, 'is the great secret of tactics.'[126]

Atop that Napoleon maximized the benefits of two recent French army innovations. 'Clouds' of skirmishers screened their own front line and eroded that of the enemy's with musketry. For an attack, a column of troops was easier and faster to manoeuvre than a long line, especially over broken ground. A column's disadvantage was that it lacked firepower while it provided the enemy line with a massive target for musket and cannon fire. He finessed that dilemma with the 'mixed order' of columns and lines whereby a column marched toward a key part of the enemy line as the line advanced along either side and fired musket volleys to deplete and distract the rest of the enemy line.

Military technologies and tactics are inseparable, with critical advances in the former prompting critical changes in the latter. Napoleon benefited from a recent change in the French army. Jean-Baptiste de Gribeauval revamped the artillery arm by reducing the array of cannon types to 12-pounders, 8-pounders, 6-pounders and 4-pounders and capitalizing on new casting techniques to reduce each's weight along with that of their limbers. This let French guns be supplied with more ammunition and pulled a bit further and faster each day by the same number of horses. Eight- and 6-pounders were the standard field guns. Twelve-pounders were kept in reserve to be massed to bombard the enemy line's key point. Horse artillery cantered 4-pounders just beyond musket shot of enemy infantry to pound it or ripped shots through enemy cavalry before one's own cavalry charged. There were three times more foot than horse batteries. Each battery had a howitzer with a short 6in-calibre barrel whose shots could arch high over a wall or hill. In addition to the artillery batteries, each regiment had two 4-pounders with eight-man crews. Ideally his army numbered four guns for every thousand troops.

Infantry was split among line and light regiments, with a ratio of three to one. Light infantry regiments were trained to deploy as skirmishers. Line regiments had six companies, including four regular companies, a light company for skirmishing and a grenadier company of the largest, toughest men for leading attacks. The standard French musket was the .69 calibre 1777 model. It was hard keeping up with demand as muskets were inevitably broken or lost on campaign. For instance, on the eve of his 1809 campaign, Napoleon wrote War Minister Henri Clarke that: 'Since my reserve of 120,000 muskets is going to diminish by the redoubled fighting . . . I think that it is necessary to manufacture 500,000 muskets'.[127] An audit of available muskets found 629,000, including 403,000 French and 111,000 foreign muskets in good condition and 22,000 French and 93,000 needing repairs.[128] Unlike the Austrian and British armies, Napoleon never established rifle regiments or even companies. The reason was simple. He considered muskets a superior battle weapon. A rifle's only advantage was that it shot further and more accurately. Otherwise muskets could be loaded and fired several times a minute;

rifles once a minute. Muskets could mount a bayonet; rifles could not. Muskets cost about one-quarter the price of rifles.

Cavalry was designated either light (hussars, chasseurs and lancers) or heavy (dragoons, cuirassiers and carabiniers). Dragoons carried muskets for fighting on foot along with swords. Cuirassiers and carabiniers wore steel helmets and breastplates. Light cavalry scouted, skirmished and pursued; heavy cavalry charged enemy cavalry, infantry or artillery, ideally already battered. Napoleon tried to keep a ratio of one cavalryman for every five infantrymen. If artillery won battles, cavalry won campaigns: 'It is cavalry that follows up a victory by preventing a beaten enemy from rallying.'[129]

Obviously, tactics and technologies are only as successful as the men who wield them. Napoleon insisted that great generalship begins with war's most elementary component: 'A general's first talent was to understand the spirit of his soldiers and capture their confidence.'[130] Unquestioning obedience of those below to those above was essential: 'The soul of every army and navy is the pure devotion of all parties to their leader.'[131] Yet true respect can only be earned, not commanded. He recalled that before his first Italian campaign, his soldiers naturally regarded their young, newly-appointed general with scepticism. The only way to transform that into devotion was to achieve a dynamic among esteem, drive and triumph. As he led his men to one victory after another, his esteem rose in their eyes and they, in turn, marched and fought harder to raise his esteem for them.[132] Even more sceptical were his officers who he outranked but who exceeded him in age and military experience: 'It was necessary, even indispensable to be able to command men older than me that my conduct be irreproachable, exemplary.'[133] Napoleon was a master of pep talks that spurred his men to greater efforts such as: 'Always remember these three things: fight united, fiercely and resolved to perish with glory.'[134] In trying to fire up Admiral Honoré Ganteaume for a pending naval campaign, he sent him these words: 'I count on your talents, your firmness and your character in so important an endeavour . . . You will avenge six centuries of insults and shame. Never, for a greater goal, have my sea and land soldiers exposed their lives.'[135]

He preferred a conscript to a volunteer army: 'One of conscription's great results was that it rendered the French army the best composed that it ever was. It was an institution eminently national.'[136] The challenge was transforming raw recruits into soldiers. For that 'privations, poverty and misery are the school of the good soldier'.[137] He had his generals 'refrain from fatiguing the troops with useless services and instead employ much of their time in training'.[138] He gave this advice to his stepson Eugène:

> Familiarize yourself with all the details of large-scale infantry manoeuvres. The season will soon begin for exercising your troops; act throughout as if you were actually at war when the first moments are the fiercest and most decisive . . . Inspect often the soldiers in detail . . . Listen to their complaints, examine their arms and assure them that they will lack nothing. Seven or eight hour reviews are very advantageous for building their endurance and confidence while diverting them from tempting dissipations.[139]

In war the quality of troops was more important than their quantity: 'It is not the number of soldiers who make the strength of armies, but their loyalty and spirit.'[140]

Commanding his countrymen demanded a special skill:

> French soldiers are the most difficult of all to lead. They are not at all machines that are simply ordered but reasonable beings who must be directed. French soldiers have an impatient courage and feelings of honour that render them capable of the greatest exertions, but they need a severe discipline and must not be left too long at ease. French soldiers are rational . . . They severely judge their officers' talent and courage . . . Russian, Prussian and German troops guard their posts from duty, French troops from honour. The first are nearly indifferent to a defeat, the second are humiliated.[141]

Among the many reasons why Napoleon's soldiers mostly adored him was his genuine concern for their well-being. Concern, however, is common enough among most military leaders. What is uncommon was his astonishing attention to details and efforts to ensure that his men got what they needed. Countless of his letters concern their well-being, urging his commanders to ensure that they were amply fed, clothed, shoed, sheltered and doctored. Although renowned for saying that an army marches on its stomach, he was just as sensitive to the literal reality that an army marches on its feet: 'Shoes facilitate marches and marches win battles.'[142] For each pending and ongoing campaign, he kept shoemakers busy at their work-benches. For instance, in early 1809 as an Austrian attack became more likely, he ordered the stockpiling of

120,000 pairs of shoes at Mainz, 60,000 at Augsburg, 30,000 at Strasbourg, 10,000 at Magdeburg, 6,000 at Glogau and 5,000 at Kustrin.[143] Among his peacetime priorities for his commanders was this: 'Your principal study must be to place my troops in healthy places; it is because I often followed this practice that I had so few sicknesses.'[144] Yet ultimately his soldiers were pawns that he never hesitated to sacrifice when necessary for what he believed was the greater good, the glory of France.

How to pay for things hovered constantly somewhere in Napoleon's seething labyrinth of a mind, especially when it came to war. Massing men depended on massing money. His campaigns were partly driven by this principle: 'That war pays for itself is one less imposition on the French people.'[145] But forcing a defeated enemy to pay reparations only partly financed the campaign's costs; taxpayers and banks supplied the bulk. Then there were more unsavoury sources. He hated the vulture-like loan sharks, stockjobbers and contractors who peddled and feasted off the carnage of war. When it came to raising and spending money, Britain enjoyed a wide lead over France. He ranted that his victories could bring a lasting peace to Europe if London did not bankroll what eventually became seven coalitions against France. But Britain was only the worst instigator. He recognized that Austrian aggression in 1797, 1800, 1805 and 1809 was nearly as much provoked by 'capitalists who speculated or lent money to Austria' as by British gold.[146]

Napoleon, like any commander, faced a dilemma in keeping his men supplied. An advance would slow to a crawl or halt altogether if long supply trains carried all the army's provisions, munitions and other necessities. An army's pace quickened the more it requisitioned supplies along the way. But local sources rarely had all that was needed. Either they did not exist or could not be willingly purchased. And when soldiers were hungry, they foraged, another name for looting. That in turn could provoke an already alienated population to revolt. And even if that did not happen, marauders made bad soldiers: 'A soldier's discipline weakens the more he pillages until . . . he no longer wants to fight.'[147] To avoid that he insisted that his subordinates follow these guidelines: 'You must think about administration. Foraging during marches becomes impracticable when too many troops concentrate. You must then resort to requisitions and at the same time have a great quantity of provisions brought from neighbouring countries at a fixed price by requisitions legally imposed.'[148]

Napoleon knew well the dilemmas facing a conqueror. If he was too harsh, he proliferated his enemies. If he was too soft, he raised expectations among the subject population that could not be fulfilled.

Either way could provoke a revolt. A conqueror had to wield 'a mix of severity, justice and kindness . . . to have a good effect'.[149] He was always sensitive to the chance of rebellions by people brutalized by his soldiers. He issued strict orders against robbery, rape and murder. Officers 'must take care to maintain the most severe discipline . . . There is no pardon for criminals.' Any guilty soldiers were swiftly tried then publicly executed by firing squads. Yet he also tried to mitigate adverse conditions that led to crime. When some men from regiments who were owed back pay committed robberies, he had '6,000 francs advanced to ensure that the troops had no pretext for vexing the countryside'.[150]

When revolts did erupt, he had his troops crush them promptly and brutally. To his brother Joseph, he wrote 'I see with pleasure that a village of insurgents was burned. Such severe examples are necessary. I imagine that the soldiers pillaged the village. This must be the treatment for villages that revolt. It is the right of war, but it is also a proscribed political duty.'[151] He believed in fighting terror with terror. After capturing a terrorist, justice must be swift, ruthless and widely known: 'It is necessary to publish the sentence before the execution and make a big deal of it; thus imposing terror on others who would commit it.'[152] Overall, 'in a war of this nature, one must be cold-blooded, patient and calculating'.[153]

Soft military power involves not just devising winning strategies and tactics and inspiring one's officers and troops to the greatest efforts and sacrifices. Nearly as important is manipulating the perceptions, hopes and fears of both sides and thus decisions and morale. In this propaganda is critical: 'In war, morale and opinion are more than half the reality.'[154] Napoleon's Bulletins or press releases published by the *Moniteur* were designed to do exactly that. The expression 'lie like a Bulletin' exaggerates the content of a typical issue. Good propaganda must be mostly true to be mostly believed. The one area that Napoleon did consistently falsify were numbers; he always deflated French losses and inflated enemy losses, while inflating French troop numbers and deflating enemy troops. For Napoleon, deception was a critical element of power in general and military power in particular. One continually sought to deceive the enemy about one's ends and means, strengths and weaknesses.

Hubris and Power

One man's vision is another man's delusion. Napoleon envisioned a prosperous, peaceful, just European empire headed by France, with him and his heirs as its emperor: 'I wanted deeply to plant our doctrines, our administration and our codes for Europe's regeneration . . . I had vast and numerous projects all calculated for humanity's well-being . . . I have been condemned for having an iron hand, but that ignores my goal . . . Countless people could have benefited in posterity.'[155]

For a while he came close to achieving that. But, ultimately, Napoleon failed spectacularly at the art of power. He trapped himself in a classic vicious cycle of power. His empire's practical and idealistic goals conflicted. He extracted ever more taxes and troops in the name of modernity, enlightenment, prosperity, equality, justice and order. For his foreign subjects, the harsh realities trumped the abstract ideals; they saw only increasingly brutal exploitation in French rule and they longed for liberation even by those who espoused absolute monarchy. Paradoxically, Napoleon's power became more fragile the more he tried to assert it. The fate of himself and his empire become inseparable. By refusing to share power, he made it more likely that his empire would not survive his own death or even a crushing defeat. He knew well that his empire shook with the slightest ill political wind: 'What confusion, what disorder would not result from the faintest rumour, of the least doubt touching my existence. To my life was attached the fate of a great empire . . . and Europe's destiny.'[156] Bloated with hubris, he eventually self-destructed as his ambitions exceeded even his extraordinary abilities, first with his attempt to conquer Spain which resulted in a six-year quagmire that annually devoured 50,000 or so troops and tens of millions of francs, then his attempt to conquer Russia where he lost half a million troops. He eventually provoked all of Europe to unite against him and fight until he was crushed.

During his exile on St Helena, Napoleon had five years and ten months to mull his litany of blunders that destroyed all his achievements and dreams. During one prolonged discussion with his followers over the nature of history and his role in it, he exclaimed:

> The truest truths . . . are so hard to obtain for history . . . There are so many truths! . . . Even honest men will differ . . . Historical truth, so implored, so earnestly called for, is too often nothing more than a name. It is unobtainable even during events given the heat of colliding passions. And if an accord is later reached, it is self-serving. The contradictions are no more. So, what then is historical truth most of the time? A convenient fable . . . That is history![157]

As with countless other subjects, Napoleon's view of history mixes insights, exaggerations and delusions. He mistook propaganda, of which he was a master, for history. It is possible to write an objective, comprehensive, systematic analysis of any subject, even one as controversial as that of Napoleon Bonaparte. *Napoleon and the Art of Leadership* attempts to do that by scrutinizing as many possible critical sources of information and points of view to reveal who he was and why he did what he did while avoiding the Scylla and Charybdis of vilifying or glorifying him.

Chapter 1

The Rebel

'There was never a social revolution without terror . . . It enriches but does not at all satisfy the poor. It convulses everything. During the first stage it brings unhappiness to all; happiness to none.'

'The wind having freshened the night . . . This spectacle was grand, the striking cannon shots, the shores covered with fires, the sea surging and roaring . . . My soul was between eternity, the ocean and the night . . . I went to sleep feeling I was in a romantic and epic dream.'

'Time reverses empires, destroys the world and changes all our affections. Thus we must anticipate and prejudge the future.'

Napoleon Bonaparte was a born troublemaker, even literally.[1] His mother was attending Mass for the Feast of the Assumption in the cathedral of Ajaccio, Corsica, when the contractions overwhelmed her. Assisted by her family she waddled home to release him to the world on 15 August 1769. He was the second son of Carlo Bonaparte and Letizia Ramolino. He would have seven surviving siblings, one elder, Joseph (1768), then Lucien (1775), Elisa (1777), Louis (1778), Pauline (1780), Caroline (1782) and Jérôme (1784).

His actual name was Napoleone Buonaparte. The island of Corsica where he was born had been a province of the Republic of Genoa from 1284 until 15 May 1768, when France took over in return for annually paying 200,000 livres for ten years.[2] So, although he was born a subject of the French king, rather than French he grew up speaking Genoa's dialect of Italian. His father was absent from much of his early life then died in 1785, when Napoleon was just 16 years old. Carlo apparently lingered at home not much longer than it took to sire another child. He was ambitious, passionate, loquacious and opportunistic, one who advanced by currying favour with powerful patrons. He backed the rebel leader Pasquale Paoli until his defeat then, after the takeover, pledged allegiance to the French king and his governor, Louis Marbeuf.[3] After buying a Pisa University law degree, he returned to become a lawyer for Ajaccio's tribunal court in 1771, a judge assessor and Corsican assemblyman in 1772 and received a royal land grant in 1778. As for Napoleon's mother, Letizia was only about 15 when she began conceiving children; she managed her growing brood with tough rather than affectionate love. Apparently with her husband's acquiescence, she wielded her beauty and body to extract favours for Carlo, herself and her children from Governor Marbeuf. Napoleon later paid her this tribute: 'All that I am, all I have been, I owe to the habits of work I received in my childhood and the good principles given to me by my excellent mother.'[4]

Although Carlo was a sporadic husband and father, he played three decisive roles in laying the foundations for his family's rise to the heights of power, although he would not live to see that ascent. With Marbeuf's intervention, the French government approved two applications from Carlo, in 1771 to be recognized as a French noble and in 1778 to educate his sons in France. On 1 January 1779, Carlo enrolled Joseph and Napoleone, then just 9 years old, at the Jesuit College at Autun. Finally, Carlo made a critical decision on their career paths. Normally the first and second-born sons of nobles become military officers and priests respectively. Carlo reversed the order. He sent his naturally rebellious, aggressive son Napoleone to the military school at Brienne, one of twelve across France, and kept the gentle, quiet son Joseph at Autun. How different history would read had he followed tradition!

Buonaparte studied at Brienne from 15 May 1779 to 17 October 1784. The experience was Spartan. Students attended classes six hours a day from Monday to Saturday in an eleven-month school year. Buonaparte excelled at mathematics and did well in history and geography. When he entered l'Ecole Militaire in Paris on 19 October 1784, he exchanged austerity for extravagance. He recalled that 'we were magnificently nourished, served and treated in all things like officers enjoying a great ease, more grand certainly than most of our families'.[5] Like Brienne, l'Ecole Militaire offered few military studies, let alone training; reading about the lives of famous generals provided an idealized conception of war. Instead, the emphasis was on polishing nobles in etiquette. Instruction in dance was as important as instruction in fencing. Then there were all the attractions of Paris.

Amid these pleasures Buonaparte learned that stomach cancer had killed his father at Montpellier in France on 24 February 1785. The son wrote a moving elegy, in which he did not dilute his bitterness toward God or France. He described his father as 'a zealous enlightened citizen' who 'heaven made die . . . in a foreign country indifferent to his existence, far from all that he held precious', prevented 'from the grand consolation of the joyous sadness' of expiring 'at home with his wife and family'. It was 'the Supreme Being . . . who deprived us of what is most dear but at least left us a few cherished people capable of replacing him in our affections'.[6] With these words Buonaparte at once vented and projected his own angry feelings of being forsaken by his father six years earlier in 'a foreign country indifferent to his fate, far from all that he held precious'. During that time his parents only visited him briefly once and he never left school, although Lucien did join him as a student at Brienne in 1784.

Buonaparte graduated from the l'Ecole Militaire as a second lieutenant on 28 October 1785. Although he was 42nd in a class of 58 students, he squeezed his studies into one year when most others needed two years or more to graduate. His aptitude for mathematics made him a top candidate for the artillery or engineers. He joined the La Fère artillery regiment at Valence on 3 November 1785. He was only 16 years old.

* * *

What was Buonaparte like in those days? His childhood nickname was *'rabulione'*, which means 'rambunctious'. He later described himself as a 'taciturn, sombre and morose' youth. His moods swung from exuberance to indifference to depression, but were mostly melancholic and introspective. At times his alienation pushed him to the edge of the abyss: 'Alone in the midst of mankind, I return to my room to muse and to succumb to all the force of my melancholy . . . Because I have to die anyway, should I not kill myself?'[7] Those natural dispositions were exacerbated by being taken away from his family and native land when he was just 9 years old and being installed in a boarding school where the boys teased him for his accent and puny appearance. A teacher there found him 'quiet, loving solitude, capricious, arrogant, extremely inclined to egoism, speaking little, spirited in his answers, quick and harsh in his replies, having much pride and boundless ambition. This young man deserves to be encouraged.'[8]

He dreamed of escaping the dreary, lonely routine with adventures in exotic faraway places, of escaping his lowly outsider status by becoming a hero, a conqueror and a liberator. As a schoolboy the books he voraciously devoured offered fleeting diversions. He relished tales of great military leaders and was deeply affected by Romanticism, especially Jean Jacques Rousseau's novel *La Nouvelle Héloise*, Johann Wolfgang Goethe's novel *The Sorrows of Young Werther* and James Macpherson's epic poem 'Fingal' by the fictional author 'Ossian'. He enjoyed venting his thoughts and feelings on paper and longed to be renowned as a great writer. He was acutely aware that life was uncertain and fleeting: 'Time reverses empires, destroys the world and changes all our affections. Thus we must anticipate and prejudge the future.'[9] Throughout his life the world's hard realities capped by the horrors of war eroded but never extinguished his youthful romanticism. In July 1804, he penned these words to Josephine after reviewing grand manoeuvres of his army and fleet at Boulogne: 'For four days I have been far from you . . . The wind having freshened the night . . . This spectacle was grand, the striking cannon shots, the shores covered with fires, the sea surging and roaring . . . My soul was between eternity, the ocean and the night . . . I went to sleep feeling I was in a romantic and epic dream.'[10]

As an 18-year-old second lieutenant, he looked ahead at a mostly pleasant, secure, monotonous career probably broken by a war or two. Was that how he wanted to spend his life? He resolved to supplement his military career with a writing career and make a history of Corsica his first book. The peacetime army offered a writer the leisure he needed. He could mull what to write on duty then write it down later. He entered but did not win an essay contest to answer this classic Enlightenment question: 'What principles and institutions instil the greatest possible happiness in man?' That literary venture spurred him to others. Somehow between 1786 and 1793, he squeezed time between his regimental duties in France and his family duties and political ambitions in Corsica to produce an astonishing number of works. In all, he wrote four novels, *Le Comte d'Essex* (1789), *La Masque Prophète* (1789), *La Nouvelle Corse* (1789) and *Clisson et Eugénie* (1795), *Histoire de Corse* (1790), philosophical essays like 'Parallele entre l'Amour de Patrie et l'Amour de la Gloire' (1786), 'Le Discours de Lyon' (1791), 'Le Dialogue de l'Amour' (1796) and political essays like 'Les Corses ont-ils eu le droit de secouer le joug des Genois?' (1786), 'La Constitution de la Calotte du regiment de la Fère' (1789), 'Lettre a Matteo Buttafoco' (1791) and 'Souper de Beaucaire' (1793). Like most budding writers, his works were more precocious and passionate than skilled and profound. With time he might have become a first-rate writer but his career took a very different path.

He had served merely ten months before he wangled leave to go home. He reached Ajaccio in September 1786. He had not seen his family for over seven years. His father was dead and his mother was struggling to raise six children on a limited income from her husband's various investments. Most of his surviving letters from his teens and early twenties concern his family's financial welfare, whose 'sad state . . . afflicts me'.[11] To alleviate that he sought to provide his family additional income by developing a nursery for mulberry plants whose leaves nourished silkworms. He claimed a medical excuse to extend his leave and did not finally leave Corsica until September 1787, a year after arriving. Yet he did not immediately rejoin his regiment, now stationed at Auxonne, but instead sojourned from October to December in Paris, where he received his latest leave. He was back in Corsica in January 1788 and remained until June 1788, when he finally rejoined his regiment. In January 1789, he began an intensive course on artillery under the tutelage of General Jean Pierre Du Teil, who was very impressed with his student.

* * *

As Buonaparte embarked on his career, a series of extraordinary events were shaking France. For several years the realm had teetered on the brink of bankruptcy. Within two previous generations, France had fought the extremely costly Seven Years War and the American War of Independence. The national debt had soared and the government was falling further behind paying its creditors. The king's power was not absolute. France was divided among thirteen regions, each with a *parlement* (parliament) whose chief duty was to register laws and decrees. In November 1787, a political crisis erupted when the Paris Parlement refused to register a loan of 10 million livres that King Louis XVI had submitted to avoid bankruptcy. The king's advisors devised a package of financial reforms that Louis submitted in October 1788, but the Paris Parlement rejected that too. In desperation, Louis called for the Estates General, which last met in 1614, to convene in May 1789. The Estates General was a type of legislature composed of 300 priests, 300 nobles and 600 commoners.[12]

When the king convened the Estates General on 5 May 1789, he and his advisors hoped that the delegates would rubber-stamp the package of financial reforms submitted by Finance Minister Jacques Necker. The commoners, or Third Estate, declared itself the National Assembly on 17 June and called on the other estates to join. When, on 20 June, the National Assembly delegates found themselves locked out of their meeting place, they crowded into a nearby indoor tennis court and vowed to persist until the king recognized the National Assembly. Louis resisted for a few days then ordered the First and Second Estates to join the National Assembly.

And then there was the Parisian mob. Power seesawed between the National Assembly's reformers and the Parisian radicals. The revolution turned increasingly violent, beginning when, on 14 July, Parisians stormed the Bastille, a castle and hated symbol of royal oppression, and equipped National Guard battalions with arms captured there and at other arsenals. The National Assembly asserted a major progressive act by passing the Declaration of the Rights of Man and the Citizen on 26 August. The Parisian mob retook the initiative on 4 and 5 October, when 10,000 mostly women marched the dozen miles to Versailles and intimidated the royal family into returning with them to the Tuileries Palace in the city's centre.

Like millions of other French men and women, Buonaparte was trapped in the whirlwind of revolution and desperately tried to grasp anything to survive.[13] That meant appearing to support whichever faction then held power, while looking for a stronger alternative. For the first few years, he backed the moderates over the radical Jacobins. In June 1792, he derided 'Jacobins as fools who lack common sense'.[14] His loathing for the radicals soared on 10 August 1792, when he gingerly stepped through the blood-soaked, body-strewn Tuileries Palace shortly after a Jacobin-led mob had slaughtered and mutilated hundreds of Swiss Guards. But after the Jacobins took power in April 1793 and unleashed the Terror on their opponents, he affiliated with them to avoid being among their thousands of victims. He later described revolutions as among 'the worst evils' that could afflict humanity. 'There was never a social revolution without terror . . . It enriches but does not at all satisfy the poor. It convulses everything. During the first stage it brings unhappiness to all; happiness to none.'[15]

Meanwhile, Buonaparte's identity and loyalty were torn between being more Corsican or French. Naturally the appeal of his Corsican roots echoed far louder. In comparing the fate of France and Corsica, he wrote that while revolution was bringing a rebirth to France, 'must Corsicans continue to kiss the insolent hand of those who repress them'.[16] That was no exaggeration. Corsica's Genoan and French rulers exploited but never truly conquered the native people. Most Corsicans deeply resented the foreign presence and longed to be free. The outsiders remained a minority that dominated trade, finance and administration in the towns of Bastia, Ajaccio, Corte, Calvi and Bonifacio, while most Corsicans were exploited peasants. The Corsicans revolted in 1733 and declared independence in 1735. Genoa appealed to France for help. The French managed to crush the rebels by 1741. Another revolt erupted in 1741 and was finally suppressed in 1752.

Pasquale Paoli led the Corsican cause from 1755. Under Paoli's brilliant leadership Corsica enjoyed more than two decades of freedom before the French smothered the revolt at the Battle of Ponte Nuovo on 8 May 1769. Paoli fled into exile in London. Thereafter most of Corsica's native elite, including Carlo Buonaparte, collaborated with the French rulers.

For Buonaparte, Paoli symbolized not just a heroic father-figure for Corsica but for himself, who had spent little time with his own father. Indeed he had a slender connection to Paoli as his father had briefly served as his secretary. When Buonaparte was 20, he wrote Paoli an astonishing letter:

> I was born as Corsica was perishing from 50,000 French vomited upon our shores, drowning our throne of liberty in a sea of blood, such was the odious spectacle that came to first strike my views. The cries of the dying, the groans of the oppressed, the tears of the despairing, surrounded the cradle of my birth. You left our island and with you disappeared happiness; slavery was the price of our submission, smothered with soldiers, laws and taxes, our compatriots lived scorned by those who had the power to administer them.[17]

From August 1789 to July 1793, Buonaparte spent more than half his time in Corsica in four separate leaves. During his sojourns Corsica became a laboratory in which he conducted various political and military experiments, of which most failed. He learned from his failures. He also forged a critical alliance and friendship with Antoine Saliceti, a political commissar dispatched by Paris to oversee Corsica.

Buonaparte was among the delegation at Ajaccio that welcomed Paoli back to Corsica in July 1790, after 22 years of exile. Paoli had sworn allegiance to France. Buonaparte and his brothers Joseph and Lucien pledged their support to him and his faction that soon won most seats in Corsica's provincial assembly. In January 1791, Buonaparte zealously expressed his devotion to Paoli in a blistering public letter to Matteo Buttafuoco, who led the opposition royalist faction. He wrote that across Corsica 'there is nothing but a chorus of criticisms of you. Your friends hide themselves, your parents disavow you . . . What are you doing? What are the crimes that can instil such indignation so universal, such a complete abandonment?' He went on to laud Paoli as 'the centre of all the movements of the political corps' who 'in a short while put the affairs of our island in a good system'.[18] With time, however, the Buonaparte clan's support for Paoli turned to opposition.

Buonaparte ran for and won election to be the lieutenant colonel of a National Guard battalion in February 1792. After the French government went to war against Austria and Prussia in April 1792, the National Guard's mission expanded from maintaining order to possible military campaigns against foreign enemies. On 21 September 1792, the Convention elected by the Legislative Assembly abolished the monarchy and the next day declared France a republic and learned that on 20 September at Valmy, the French army had defeated an invasion by a Prussian, Austrian and French royalist army. Emboldened by that victory, the government ordered French armies to invade the Austrian Netherlands. The revolutionary government became increasingly radical. The Convention's delegates put Louis XVI on trial for treason on 3 December, founded him guilty on 15 January 1793 and had him executed on 21 January. Then they declared war against Britain and the Netherlands on 1 February 1793 and shortly thereafter against Piedmont-Sardinia, Spain and Portugal.

Buonaparte's first military campaign was a profound disappointment. Paoli ordered his nephew, General Pierre Colona de Cesari Rocca, to capture Madeleine Island off Sardinia's north coast. Buonaparte commanded one of the expedition's two battalions. After bad weather caused weeks of delay, the flotilla of a half dozen vessels sailed from Bonifacio on 22 February 1793 and the troops disembarked on the tiny island of San Stefano near Madeleine. Buonaparte deployed his two cannons, a mortar and troops for a bombardment that would precede a seaborne assault against the Sardinian fort on Madeleine. His guns opened fire on 24 February. The Sardinian gunners returned fire against the largest French vessel, scored several hits and killed and wounded half a dozen sailors. The crews of that vessel and others refused to sail closer to land the troops. Cesari got cold feet, called off the attack and ordered his troops to re-embark and sail back to Bonifacio. When Buonaparte protested, Cesari not only cut him short but ordered the guns abandoned to facilitate their escape. Buonaparte wrote a formal protest signed by himself and other officers on 28 February and conveyed that along with his explanation of the debacle to Paoli on 2 March. Paoli's support of Cesari's decision was a major step in Buonaparte's disillusionment with his former hero.[19]

Meanwhile, France's revolutionary leaders, fearing that Paoli might lead another independence struggle, ordered General Armand Biron, duc de Lauzun, to assume command over all armed forces in Corsica on 1 February. In Paris on 6 April, the Convention established the Committee of Public Safety to mobilize the nation against all its enemies, foreign and domestic. The Jacobins took control of the Committee and wielded it to purge the Girondins and launch a nationwide Terror in which over 20,000 people were arrested and executed from then to July 1794, when moderates overthrew the Jacobins.[20]

Differences over military strategy, political policies and economic interests between the Buonaparte clan and the Paolistes had steadily worsened over the years. The rupture came on 2 April 1793, when Lucien wrote the Convention a letter condemning Paoli as a traitor. Buonaparte followed this up with his own letter to the Convention. He began by lauding their efforts: 'You are the people's true sovereign organ. The Nation either dictates or immediately ratifies all your decrees. Each of your laws is a benefit and provides you new grounds for posterity to recognize you, which the Republic and the world owe you and date the onset of liberty.' He then argued out that 'only one thing profoundly afflicts the people' and that was Pascal Paoli, an ambitious conspirator who 'gave Corsica to England'.[21]

Paoli reacted by publicly ordering the arrest and secretly the assassination of the Buonapartes. After nearly being captured many times, Buonaparte and his family escaped Corsica and sailed to safety on the mainland in June 1793. That flight eliminated the last vestiges of Buonaparte's Corsican nationalism. From now he would be an increasingly fervent French nationalist. After settling his family in Marseille, he rejoined his regiment, now stationed at Nice, which was also the headquarters for the French forces known as the Army of Italy. Astonishingly, the War Ministry not only overlooked his prolonged absences but actually promoted him to captain. The Army of Italy's commander was General Jean du Teil, the brother of Buonaparte's commander at Auxonne. Teil named Buonaparte his aide-de-camp for artillery.

 Meanwhile, the Convention outlawed Paoli and his supporters on 17 July and ordered Lauzun to seize them. Paoli and most of his followers escaped to England where he died far from his beloved homeland in 1807. As French Revolutionary forces reasserted control over Corsica, they began to lose parts of the mainland. Royalists led revolts in Brittany and Normandy where they were known as Chouans and in the Vendée or region between the Loire and Charente River mouths where they were known as Vendeans. In the Rhône River valley, a coalition of royalists and moderate republicans known as federalists took over Lyon, Avignon, Aix-en-Provence, Marseille and Toulon. Republican armies battled all these revolts. Although the Chouans and Vendeans repelled the forces sent against them, by late August Republican troops were brutally repressing the revolts in Lyon, Avignon, Aix-en-Provence and Marseille.

Toulon's rebel government invited in a hovering British fleet commanded by Admiral Samuel Hood on 23 August. Hood's fleet, along with a recently-arrived Spanish fleet led by Admiral Juan Langara, dropped anchor in Toulon's outer and inner harbours. British and Spanish troops joined the rebel militia in manning the dozen or so forts crowning the surrounding heights. The Allies controlled the French fleet that numbered seventeen operational and fourteen refitting ships-of-the-line and twenty-seven smaller warships, along with warehouses packed with munitions, provisions and naval supplies.[22]

General Jean-Baptiste Carteaux commanded the Republican army ordered to retake Toulon. He began deploying his troops half a dozen miles west of Toulon on 30 August. Du Teil dispatched troops to join Carteaux which reached Toulon's eastern outskirts on 2 September. Du Teil ordered Buonaparte to organize and lead convoys of guns and munitions to reinforce Carteaux's swelling army. By 7 September, Carteaux had massed enough guns, troops and supplies to open the siege of Toulon. Antoine Saliceti, Buonaparte's friend and political ally, was among the army's *commissaires* (political representatives of the government). When Carteaux's artillery commander was wounded on 16 September, Saliceti had Carteaux appoint Buonaparte to that command.

It was during the siege of Toulon that Buonaparte first revealed the dimensions of his genius. He immediately took charge. He fired off flurries of orders to administrative and military leaders across the region to requisition all available artillery, munitions, provisions, drovers, draft animals and wagons.[23] He sent a detailed report of his efforts to the army's ordnance commander, noting that 'real evils joined the imaginary' in overcoming challenges to mustering all that was needed.[24] He lauded the political *commissaires* for assisting him. He was grateful that for 'the law that accorded the artillery separate responsibility . . . for the siege'.[25] He then called for the army to name a general of artillery, with himself the obvious, if unstated, choice. Only that could overcome the prevailing ignorance and prejudice among the infantry commanders for how to conduct a successful siege. He capped his argument with his first recorded military axiom: 'It is artillery that takes a position, assisted by infantry.'[26] Over the next three months Buonaparte erected thirteen batteries to bombard the forts guarding Toulon.

Buonaparte's dynamism and decisiveness sharply contrasted with Carteaux's lethargy. The reports of Saliceti and other *commissaires* convinced Paris to replace Carteaux with General François Doppet on 10 November. Doppet was just as lacklustre and was replaced by General

Jacques Dugommier on the 16th of the same month. What most frustrated Buonaparte about Carteaux and Doppet was their refusal to implement his strategy. He had quickly surmised that the western peninsula that divided the inner and outer harbours was the key to taking Toulon. Three forts guarded that peninsula, Fort Mulgrave at the base and Forts Artigues and Malbousquet at Point Eguillette. If those forts fell the guns could be turned against the enemy fleets in both harbours. He finally went over Doppet's head and submitted a detailed plan to War Minister Jean-Baptiste Bouchotte on 14 November 1793. He revealed his understanding of the decisive role that psychology played in war: 'The capture of Eguillette, the expulsion of the English from the bays and the bombardment' will provoke 'general commotion' and 'fear of falling in our hands and not being able to execute a retreat'.[27] A council of war led by Dugommier approved Buonaparte's plan on 25 November.

By mid-December, over 38,000 French troops formed an arc of entrenchments and batteries around an inner arc of a dozen or so forts and batteries defended by 18,700 Allied troops including British, Spanish, Neapolitans, Sardinians and French federalists. Buonaparte commanded over a hundred guns and over 1,000 artillerymen. Half a dozen batteries bombarded Fort Mulgrave. The Allies launched frequent sorties. The largest came on 23 November, when British General Charles O'Hara led an attack on one of the batteries. Dugommier and Buonaparte led the counter-attack that retook the battery and killed or captured around 500 enemy troops; a wounded O'Hara was among the prisoners.

By the rainy night of 17 December, Buonaparte's batteries had pounded parts of Fort Mulgrave's walls to rubble. Buonaparte commanded the reserve as two columns of troops swarmed through the breaches. When the defenders repulsed those attacks, Buonaparte led the reserves into the fort and they eventually routed the defenders. As Buonaparte slashed his way through, someone plunged a bayonet into his thigh. After daybreak, the French assaulted and captured Forts Malbousquet and Eguillette. The Allied commanders ordered a hasty withdrawal of their troops from the other forts to the fleet and the destruction of the French fleet and supplies in the inner harbour. By 19 December, the French revolutionaries had secured Toulon and the surrounding waters were empty of enemy vessels. Both sides, however, claimed victory. The Allies boasted that they escaped with most of their men, 7,500 civilian refugees and four French ships-of-the-line, seven frigates and five brigs, while burning nine ships-of-the-line; the French argued that they prevented far worse losses.

Saliceti rewarded Buonaparte's brilliant work at Toulon by nominating him for promotion to brigadier general on 22 December and making him inspector of Provence's coastal defences on 26 December. On 7 February 1794, the government promoted him to brigadier general and named him the Army of Italy's artillery commander. At Nice, Buonaparte helped plan a campaign to capture western Liguria and the Maritime Alps from the neighbouring Kingdom of Piedmont and Sardinia. In April the Army of Italy won a limited victory by taking the frontier fortress towns of Oneglia, Tanaro and Saorgio before General Pierre Dumerbion, the commander, called a halt, despite Buonaparte's urgings that he push onward. In July, Dumerbion sent Buonaparte on a three-week diplomatic and intelligence mission to the Genoan Republic to pressure it to remain neutral and ideally become a French ally. Genoa remained neutral. Upon his return, Dumerbion had him plan a campaign to overrun the rest of the region. The French pushed the Piedmontese, backed by Austrian troops, from Savona, Carcare and Dego before Dumerbion ordered a halt, again over Buonaparte's protests. Nonetheless, Dumerbion was generous in praising the young general: 'It is to the talents of the General of Artillery that I owe the clever arrangements which have secured our success.'[28] Yet rather than reward him, the government treated him like a traitor.

In Paris, the Committee of Safety's massacres of opponents alienated ever more members of the Convention. In a coup, moderates arrested Jacobin leader Maximilien Robespierre on 27 July 1794 and executed him the following day. They then began purging the radicals. Buonaparte came under suspicion because he had worked with Robespierre's brother, Augustine, when he was a *commissaire* in the region. Authorities arrested Buonaparte at Nice on 9 August and imprisoned him at the fortress in Antibes. He wrote an indignant letter to his jailors:

> You have suspended my functions, arrested me and declared me a suspect. Here I wither without being judged ... In a revolutionary state, there are two classes, suspects and patriots ... Oppressing the second class shakes public liberties. Public magistrates should only condemn upon ... with a succession of facts that permit nothing arbitrary. To declare a patriot suspect ... uproots that which is most precious, his confidence and esteem. In what class do you place me? Since the revolution began have I not always been attached to its principals? Have I not always been seen amidst the struggle against internal enemies and as a soldier against foreign enemies? ... I have served at

Toulon with some distinction and I contributed laurels for the Army of Italy at the taking of Saorgio, Oneglia and Tanaro.

He then called on the officials to 'destroy the oppression that traps me and restore my esteem among patriots'. He asserted that 'the only idea that may be useful to the country leads me bravely to support the burden'.[29] This powerful appeal worked. He was released on 20 August.

* * *

Buonaparte's traits of curt, no-nonsense decisiveness that inspired followers among men tended to have the opposite effect on the opposite sex. Throughout his life he was maladroit around women, seeking to control them with criticism and demands rather than nurture them with sensitivity and generosity.[30] He did not know how to restrain his volcanic passions and ended up more often repelling than seducing or in bed probably more often disappointed than satisfied them. His only recorded sexual experience before Josephine was with a prostitute that he met at the Palais Royale, although likely there were others. He was 25 years old when he first fell in love.

His object was Désirée Clary, the daughter of a rich merchant in Marseille and the younger sister of Joseph's wife Julie.[31] When they met, she was 16 years old. For well over a year, he besieged Désirée, whom he called Eugenie, with the force of his love but failed to inspire her to love him as profoundly. Their relationship was not just chaste but almost entirely epistolary since his duties kept him far from Marseille. He confessed that: 'Your charms, your character have won insensibly the heart of your lover. You have read my soul.' He complained that while he constantly thought of her, 'she is at an age and sex of inconstancy.'[32] After half a year of courting her, she finally sent him some words of encouragement, but only when he was far away at Avignon.[33] Then he was anguished to learn that she was moving with her family to Genoa. He recognized that her tender youth would soon dissipate any feelings that she might have for him, 'such is the empire of time' so he 'could not accuse her of injustice'. He hoped that one day she will embrace 'the bizarreness of his love for her'. He assured her that he treasured her happiness more than his own.[34] In his desperation, he confided to Joseph that if his love for Désirée remained unrequited, he would become 'an infantry general and go to the Rhine to seek my death'.[35] Yet by August 1795, he was finally getting over her. He informed Joseph that a letter from her failed to rouse his emotions like before.[36] He promised Désirée that he only wanted her happiness, while for himself, 'glory or death are my destiny'.[37] Meanwhile, rather than go to the Rhine, he instead went to Paris.

* * *

Buonaparte received orders in May 1795 to take command of an infantry regiment in the Army of the West that was fighting the Chouan and Vendean rebels. Having no desire to fight in a civil war, he lobbied the War Ministry for a different assignment. On 19 August, he was tapped to head the Topography Bureau which reviewed plans submitted by generals to the Committee of Public Safety. Off duty, he was at once appalled and intrigued to observe that in Paris 'the grand men abandon themselves to pleasures, going to balls, plays and parties and courting women who are the world's most beautiful'. In doing so, 'they dissipate the terror as if it were a dream'.[38] Indeed, to that end, France's government was once again shape-shifting.

The Committee of Public Safety submitted the latest constitution to France's electorate on 23 August 1795. The Directorate would consist of a bicameral legislature with a Council of Five Hundred and a Council of Ancients and a five-man executive, whose Directors the Ancients would choose from a list submitted by the Five Hundred. By late September the votes were counted in a plebiscite that approved the proposed constitution by 1,057,000 to 49,000. Despite that overwhelming support, the Directorate was nearly stillborn.

Buonaparte's life was packed with critical days. One came in early October 1795, when a royalist-led mob of 10,000 Parisians threatened to overthrow the government.[39] On 4 October, the Committee of Public Safety fired the Army of the Interior's commander, General Jacques Menou, when he negotiated with the rebels, placed Paul Barras, a political *commissaire*, in that post and made Buonaparte his deputy. Fortunately Barras, who had little military experience, deferred to his subordinate's advice. Buonaparte asserted that cannons aimed down the central city's key streets would rout any mob. Barras authorized him to collect and position as many cannons as possible. Buonaparte sent his aide, Major Joachim Murat, and a cavalry escort to the artillery park at Sablon a dozen miles from Paris to bring back forty cannons, which Buonaparte then deployed along with 4,500 troops. On 5 October, when the mob surged forward, the gunners opened fire and scattered them. Buonaparte ordered the infantry forward to slaughter any holdouts. Perhaps as many as 1,400 rebels died. The next day, he wrote this terse account: 'The Convention named Barras to command the troops. The committee named me to be the second. We disposed our troops. The enemy came to attack the Tuileries. We killed nearly all of them. They killed 30 and wounded 60 of our men. We have disarmed the sections and all is calm.'[40]

As at Toulon, Buonaparte's decisive leadership at Paris was critical for the victory. Although in his memoires Barras downplayed Buonaparte's role, he rewarded him for that 'whiff of grapeshot' by getting the government to promote him to major general on 16 October and appoint him the Army of the Interior's commander on the 26th. Buonaparte also received a lot of money from various official and other sources, enough to bring his family to Paris and buy for himself a two-storey house with a surrounding garden enclosed by a wall at number 7 Rue Chantereine a mile north of the Seine. It was during this time that Napoleone Buonaparte began signing his letters as Napoleon Bonaparte.[41]

The Directorate was officially inaugurated on 2 November 1795. Barras was among the five Directors chosen and would be the only one who would stay for the next four years.[42] He led a charmed political life, having somehow survived the French Revolution's blood-soaked gauntlet, culminating with the Terror. He was a *commissaire* at Toulon, but served on the opposite side of the siege lines from Bonaparte. Then came their collaboration during the critical events of 4 and 5 October. Barras sought dynamic generals to join his political faction in return for patronage. Bonaparte needed a patron but was contemptuous of the fact that 'Barras had never experienced war; he had quit the service as only a captain; he had no understanding of the military'.[43] In his memoirs, Barras is merciless toward Bonaparte, accusing him of opportunism, cynicism, grandstanding, treachery and ruthlessness; in doing so, he projected onto his one-time protégé characteristics ascribed by a host of others to himself. He did offer this one indisputable view: 'His intellectual ferment always dominated him and made him one of those men capable of achieving the happiest of results, just as his errors were the worst imaginable.'[44] Bonaparte was beholden to Barras not just for a succession of military and financial plums but for aiding his courtship of the love of his life.

* * *

Napoleon and Josephine are among history's most renowned couples.[45] It was in October 1795 that they first met at some salon or soirée, probably introduced by Barras, who knew Josephine intimately. In his memoirs Barras smeared Josephine as essentially a high-priced courtesan who enjoyed the favours of many men including General Lazare Hoche. He neither confirmed nor denied rumours that she was his own mistress. He does concede that she was sweet but was capricious and easily bored.[46] Actually Josephine was what Bonaparte and subsequently history called her. Her real name was Rose Joseph Tascher de La Pagerie. He feminized her second name. Perhaps he renamed her in an attempt to shed her former lovers from her and make her his alone. That failed on every level. Josephine would cheat shamelessly on Bonaparte for years until he took power. She was born into a rich planter family on the Caribbean island of Martinique on 23 June 1763. When she was only 16 years old, she was married off to the aristocrat Alexandre Beauharnais. That was not a happy marriage. He cheated on her and she soon reciprocated, although her two children, Eugène and Hortense, were most likely his. During the Revolution, Beauharnais became the National Assembly's president and a general, before being imprisoned and beheaded for the rout of his army at Mainz. Josephine was also arrested but was eventually released. When she met Bonaparte, she was wielding her charms to rebuild her fortune for herself and her children.

If Barras introduced them, Eugène inadvertently brought them together. He learned that his father's sword was at the Army of the Interior's headquarters. Bonaparte was there when he came to request it. Eugène burst into tears when Bonaparte handed it to him. That in turn touched Bonaparte, who embraced him and tried to comfort him. He paid a call on Josephine to laud her son's bravery and love for his father. She expressed her gratitude with all her feminine allures. Smitten, he sought every chance thereafter to be with her. Hortense's first impression of him was not favourable. During a formal dinner at Luxembourg Palace she was seated between 'my mother and the general, who to talk to her presented himself so vivaciously and persistently that he exhausted me and forced me to withdraw . . . He spoke heatedly and seemed solely occupied with my mother.'[47]

Bonaparte fell passionately in love with Josephine. What did he see in her? She was sensuous, coquettish, sweet and light-hearted, with large, gleaming brown eyes and long curly black hair. Despite having borne two children, her body remained curved and supple. She was acclaimed for her arts in bed, especially for a zigzag rhythm that drove men wild. She loved children, flowers, music and songbirds. Her natural grace put people at ease no matter how formal the occasion. Her worst weaknesses were chronic infidelity and unaffordable shopping sprees. Astonishingly, when she was a young girl in Martinique, a medium foresaw that she would one day become rich and wear a crown.

Romantic love is initially myopic if not blind but with time one's vision clears. On St Helena, Napoleon recalled that 'Josephine had an excessive taste for luxury, disorder and overspending natural to Creoles. It was never possible to balance her accounts . . . There were constant grand quarrels when the moment to pay her debts arrived.'[48] Another fault that Napoleon found with Josephine was her negativity, her refusal to do anything that she disliked even if it was her duty or for her own good. But he never stopped loving her.

She inspired in him an ecstatic, insatiable passion for her:

> I awakened full of you. Your portrait and memory of the intoxicating evening yesterday have taken leave of my senses. Sweet and incomparable Josephine, what bizarre effect you have on my heart . . . You deliver profound feelings that master me. I press your lips, your heart and a flame burns me . . . I am awaiting my sweet love to receive a thousand kisses, but don't give me them because they burn my blood.[49]

Two months later, he was just as besotted:

> Each moment that I am away from you . . . you are the perpetual object of my thoughts. My imagination exhausts itself searching for what you are doing. If I see you sad my heart is torn and my sorrow grows. If you are gay and playful with your friends, I reproach you for soon forgetting our sorrowful separation of three days . . . As you see, I am not easily made happy . . . I feel that natural goodness no longer exists for me.[50]

Barras spearheaded the Directory's decision to appoint Bonaparte the commander of the Army of Italy on 2 March 1796. He then stood witness as Napoleon and Josephine exchanged vows on 9 March. It was hardly a storybook wedding. He wanted to marry her because she was the love of his life. She agreed because he seemed the most likely of her suitors to rise the highest in power and wealth; should he die in battle, she would soon beguile the next on her list. A minor clerk mumbled the civil ceremony's lines. The couple lied about their ages to narrow the gap between them from six years to one. Only her children and none of his family attended. Nor was there much of a honeymoon. He snatched passionate moments from her amidst a whirlwind of preparations. Two days later, he dashed off to his new command.

Chapter 2

The Master of Italy

'Soldiers . . . The government owes you much, but can give you nothing . . . I want to lead you into the world's most fertile plains where rich provinces with great cities will be in your power. There you will find honour, glory and riches.'

'You are the first people in history who became free without factions, without revolutions and without heartbreaks. We have given you liberty. Know how to keep it.'

'I never before bore the belief that I was a superior man. It was only at Lodi that I came to believe that I could become . . . a decisive actor on the political scene. And there was born the first spark of the highest ambition.'

Trepidation filled Napoleon Bonaparte on 26 March 1796, as he strode into the Army of Italy's headquarters at Nice: 'My position was very delicate. I commanded older generals. My task was immense. They jealously watched everything I did.'[1] One of them, Louis Suchet, expressed the prevailing scepticism: 'This Corsican has no other reputation than that of a good gun commander. As a general he is only known by Parisians. This intriguer is supported by nothing.'[2] One by one Bonaparte won over his generals and their subordinates with his vision, brilliance, relentless drive, patriotism, sensitivity and decisiveness. For instance, to General André Masséna, he humbly suggested that 'I could be useful directing the glorious destinies that await this army' which 'lacks many necessary things, but it has courage' and 'is bordering a rich and abundant country. When the moment to march comes, I will find, I hope, in you and in the battalions that you command . . . the devotion to the nation.'[3] His ruthless side worked better on others. General Pierre Augereau admitted: 'Something about that little bastard of a general has scared me since the first time I laid eyes on him!'[4] His most vital relationship was the synergy he developed with his chief-of-staff, Alexandre Berthier, who had two decades of military experience, including America's war for independence. With his mastery of details, dedication to work and loyalty, Berthier tirelessly realized Bonaparte's constantly evolving plans over the next 18 years.

As for his troops, Bonaparte found himself 'very well received . . . a confidence that obliged me to reciprocate'.[5] However, what he commanded was not so much an army as a quasi-mutinous rabble lacking uniforms, arms, provisions, munitions, wagons, draft animals and, above all, morale and order. He soon learned that of the many reasons for the army's disarray, one surpassed all: 'The Directorate promised much, but delivered little.'[6] He informed the Directors that 'the army was not only denuded of everything but was without discipline and in a state of perpetual insubordination. The malcontent was so severe that the worst among them . . . formed a company devoted to the dauphin and sang Chouan and counter-revolutionary songs.' His first step in forging a mob into an army was to order the arrest of two officers who cried 'Vive le Roi!'[7]

As if the grinding duties of commanding an army at war were not onerous enough, there was Josephine. As he readied his men for the looming violence, death and destruction, his mind constantly lurched back to her so far away in Paris: 'I do not pass a night without gripping you between my arms. I do not take a cup of tea without cursing the glory and ambition that distances me from my soulmate. Amidst duties, leading my troops, inspecting the camps, my adorable Josephine possesses my heart, occupies my spirit and absorbs my thoughts.'[8] Her inability to match his ardour tormented him. He lamented that her 'last letter was cold . . . I found no fire there to illuminate your regards . . . The thought of not being loved by Josephine . . . forges my sorrow . . . . You inspired my limitless love for you.'[9]

Bonaparte's army was named for a region famously dismissed as only a geographical expression. Politically the territory that is modern Italy was split among twelve sovereign states. Two of those states – Piedmont-Sardinia and the Two Sicilies – were allied with Austria to war against France, while the others struggled to resist the pressure to take sides. One state bordered France. The House of Savoy ruled the kingdom of Piedmont-Sardinia, with its capital at Turin and two separate territories, the island of Sardinia and the upper Po River valley with the Alps on the north and west and the Maritime Alps on the south; Piedmont had a toehold on the sea at Oneglia, its only port. The Republic of Genoa stretched along the Liguria coast backed by the Maritime Alps or

Apennines from Menton to La Spezia, with its capital at Genoa. Although Genoa remained neutral, its military weakness forced it to accept the Army of Italy's occupation of its coast to Voltri, just a dozen miles from Genoa itself. The Republic of Venetia, with its capital at Venice, sprawled across north-eastern Italy. The Austrians controlled most of north-central Italy, directly with its provinces of Alto Adige and Trentino in the Alps and indirectly through Habsburg family rulers of the Duchies of Lombardy, Mantua and Tuscany with their respective capitals at Milan, Mantua and Florence. The four smallest independent states were the Duchy of Modena, the Duchy of Parma, the Republic of Lucca and the Bishopric of Trent. With its capital at Rome, the Papal States curled from a short stretch of the west coast across the peninsula then up a longer stretch of the east coast. Finally, the House of Bourbon ruled the Kingdom of the Two Sicilies, with its capital at Naples and including southern Italy and the island of Sicily.

The combined Austrian and Piedmont forces numbered 50,000 soldiers. General Jean Beaulieu commanded the 31,000-man Austrian army, split among 19,500 under his immediate command around Dego and 11,500 under General Eugène Argenteau around Acqui. By then Beaulieu had spent 53 of his 70 years as an officer. General Michelangelo Colli-Marchini commanded the 20,000 Piedmontese troops deployed between Delmonte and Cosseria. Like Beaulieu, Colli was a Seven Years War veteran. He had headed Piedmont's army since 1793 and knew the region where the campaign would rage thoroughly.

Compared to the enemy forces, Bonaparte's army was deficient in men, arms and position. He counted only 37,000 troops ready for action, including 32,000 infantry, 5,000 cavalry and 148 guns, split among five divisions led by Generals André Masséna, Pierre Augereau, Jean Sérurier, Amédée Laharpe and Jean-Baptiste Meynier. With their backs to the sea, Bonaparte and his troops faced the Maritime Alps that soared several thousand feet before them. The enemy was deployed in passes leading over those mountains. The French soldiers would have to trudge up the zigzagging, narrow roads leading to those passes and somehow rout the defenders. Ideally, General François Kellermann would simultaneously launch his 9,000-man Army of the Alps over the mountains toward Turin and thus draw off some of the forces facing Bonaparte. That would not happen.

Bonaparte left Nice on 1 April to establish his headquarters first at Albenga on the 5th then Savona on the 9th. On the eve of his campaign, he received a letter from Colli protesting the arrest and treason charges against a French émigré in Piedmont's service. He used the letter as an excuse to deftly launch a psychological attack on his counterpart. In his reply, he first condemned turncoats as 'parricides . . . whose presence dishonours your army'. He then lauded Colli and his brave soldiers. Indeed he so esteemed Colli that he was baffled why 'such a man of honour would unleash a tide of blood' in the pending campaign for which 'you and your army will be responsible in the eyes of Europe'.[10] Whether those lines adversely affected Colli's subsequent actions can never be known but their intent were to sow doubt and indecision.

As for asserting soft power, Bonaparte undoubtedly was more successful with this proclamation to his own army: 'Soldiers, you are nude, malnourished; the government owes you much, but can give you nothing. Your patience . . . is admirable, but it will not bring you glory. I want to lead you into the world's most fertile plains where rich provinces with great cities will be in your power. There you will find honour, glory and riches.'[11] And that is exactly what he did.

Bonaparte's plan was simple.[12] He sought to drive a wedge between the Allied armies and destroy each separately before it could withdraw north of the Po River. On 10 April, he ordered his divisions to advance up the steep roads leading to the Maritime Alps passes. He later recalled the sublime spectacle that awaited them on top. Stretching northward were Piedmont's plains crossed from west to east by the Po and into which drained smaller serpentine rivers from north and south; far in the distance the vast jagged wall of the snowcapped Alps stretched from the west across the north. In awe, he turned to his staff and said, 'We've surpassed them!'[13]

Over the next couple of weeks his troops racked up a rapid-fire series of victories, defeating the Austrians at Monte-Legino on 11 April and Montenotte on the 12th and the Piedmontese at Millesimo on 13th and at Cosseria and Dego the next day, then at Dego again on the 15th, Ceva on the 19th and Mondovi on the 21st. By 26 April, he had united the divisions of Masséna, Augereau and Sérurier at Alba between the Austrian and Piedmont armies.

Bonaparte attributed his success to 'the rapidity of the movements, the impetuosity of the troops and especially the art of always fighting an enemy with numbers at least equal and often superior to ourselves'.[14] He lauded his troops which in turn inspired them to even greater exertions: 'Soldiers! You have in fifteen days achieved six victories, taken twenty-one flags, fifty-five cannons, several fortified positions and conquered Piedmont's richest region. You have made fifteen thousand prisoners and killed or wounded more than ten thousand men.'[15] He sent his aide Jean Junot to the Directorate to present 'twenty-one flags taken from the Austrians and Piedmontese at the battles of Montenotte,

Millesimo, Dego and Mondovi, of which four are flags of Sardinia's royal guard corps'.[16]

Bonaparte was well aware that political victories consolidated military victories. He sought to win over a resentful, often ravaged population with stirring words: 'People of Italy! The French army has come to break your chains. The French people are the friends of all peoples. Come with confidence to us. Your property, your religion and your customs will be respected. We are making war against our common enemies and we only want to free you from tyrants.'[17] Meanwhile, he struggled to protect Italy's people from its supposed liberators. His soldiers sacked Ceva and Mondovi and sporadically murdered, robbed, raped and destroyed as they marched. He was appalled by the crimes his troops committed 'that make one ashamed to be a man', and he swore to 'either restore order or I will cease to command these brigands'.[18] He had anyone caught committing a crime immediately tried and executed on the spot. Gradually these tough measures began to work:

> The pillage was diminishing. The first thirst of an army lacking everything is satiated. The discontent was understandable. After having suffered three years atop the Alps, they arrived in the Promised Land and they wanted to gorge themselves. I had to have three of them shot . . . Tomorrow some soldiers and a corporal will be shot for stealing vases from a church.[19]

Bonaparte rejected Colli's first call for an armistice. He asserted that 'the military and morale position of the two armies renders impossible any suspension of arms'. He informed Colli that the only way to stop 'the useless flow of blood' was for the king immediately to announce his realm's neutrality, surrender the fortresses of Coni, Alexandria and Tortona, withdraw his army's remnants toward Turin and let French forces freely cross his country to pursue the Austrians. Those measures would lead to formal peace negotiations.[20] Victor Amadeus sent an envoy to Bonaparte on 27 April, asking for a ceasefire based on Bonaparte's terms. Under the Armistice of Cherasco, signed the next morning, Piedmont quit the coalition, ceded Nice and Savoy to France, withdrew its army to Turin and let French troops occupy Ceva, Coni and Tortona and traverse their territory. These terms were codified by a treaty between Piedmont and France signed in Paris on 15 May.

* * *

At this stage, Bonaparte worried that he might be ruffling feathers in Paris by conducting the related arts of war and diplomacy on his own terms rather than those of the Directors. His sensitivity to their egos and outlooks would diminish steadily with each new triumph over the next few years. Accompanying his ceasefire deal that he sent to Paris was this soothing message: 'If I have not fulfilled your goal and did something contrary to your plan, this would be . . . the worst thing that I can imagine. I have, during this time, foreseen this possibility and asked for instructions; I received word that I should act as events demanded in unexpected circumstances.' He assured them that if they insisted, he would overthrow Piedmont's king and impose a republic, but he strongly discouraged that. Not only would that obviously complicate and impede the campaign against Austria, France's most formidable enemy, but Piedmont was 'not considered ripe for revolution. The only thing . . . in our interests there is peace.'[21] He explained that 'the war in Italy at this moment is half military and half diplomacy'. Victory depended on vigorously asserting both. Neutralizing Piedmont let him concentrate on crushing Austria; securing his rear, obtaining free passage and gathering provisions from Piedmont, all 'crucial to the grand art of war in Italy'.[22] He informed the Directors that 'my columns are on the march; Beaulieu flees; I hope to trap him; I will extract several million in contributions from the Duke of Parma . . . As for Genoa, I believe that you should demand 15 million in indemnities.'[23]

And then there was his other worry in Paris. As if the ceaseless duties, exertions and dangers of leading a campaign were not burdensome enough, there was the love of his life. Josephine could have lightened her husband's load with a stream of cheerful, affectionate, reassuring letters. Instead, she wrote rarely and perfunctorily. He complained that 'when you write me a few words, your style is never that of profound sentiment. You love me as a light caprice; you already feel how ridiculous it is to have seized my heart. It seems that you know who you will replace me with. I wish you happiness.'[24] He asked if she was too busy to write, then just what was she doing. He claimed to be worried rather than jealous but he was obviously both. He implored her to join him on campaign.[25] But she had no intention of leaving the pleasures of Paris and her lover Hippolyte Charles. Rumours of the affair reached him. In desperation, he wrote Director Paul Barras that 'his wife was not coming' because 'she has a lover who keeps her in Paris'.[26] He wrote Joseph that 'I am in despair . . . Reassure me, speak true. You know my heart . . . You know that I have never loved anyone before, that Josephine is the first women that I adore.'[27] Eventually she wrote him a lie that she could not travel because she was pregnant, news that deepened Bonaparte's love for her.[28]

* * *

Beaulieu and Bonaparte raced their armies eastward on opposite sides of the Po.[29] Beaulieu had the few bridges burned or blown up to prevent Bonaparte from crossing to the north side. The footsore advanced division under General Claude Dallemagne finally edged ahead at Piacenza on 3 May. Although Beaulieu soon learned of the crossing, his 20,000 troops were scattered and he could not concentrate them to attack the rapidly swelling French forces on the north bank. He was torn between withdrawing north to Milan or eastward toward Mantua.

Bonaparte's advance guard caught up with Beaulieu's rearguard of 6,500 troops at Lodi on the Adda River on 10 May. The Austrians had evacuated the town, crossed the bridge and deployed along the east bank. The Austrian artillery and infantry opened fire as Bonaparte quickly assessed the situation and issued orders. He cantered his cavalry up the road northward alongside the river to search for a ford, had guns wheeled into place and massed infantry to return fire and prepare to charge across the bridge. Soon a courier galloped up and shouted that the cavalry had found a ford a half mile upstream and were crossing. The stone bridge was narrow and nearly 50 yards long. Austrian and French troops were exchanging volleys from opposite ends. Bonaparte ordered his grenadiers to charge across the bridge. Austrian artillery and musket fire cut down several score of the attackers and they fell back in terror. Bonaparte and his staff rallied the grenadiers then led them across just as the French cavalry attacked the Austrian right flank. The Austrians broke and fled, leaving over 2,000 dead, wounded and prisoners along with a dozen guns behind; the French suffered about 500 casualties. This battle was a decisive turning point for Bonaparte's psyche if not for the campaign. Much later he explained that: 'I never before bore the belief that I was a superior man. It was only at Lodi that I came to believe that I could become . . . a decisive actor on the political scene. And there was born the first spark of the highest ambition.'[30]

Bonaparte fanned out his divisions in pursuit, aiming Augereau toward Peschiara, Masséna toward Verona and Sérurier toward Castel Nuova then Mantua, while those of Laharpe and Meynier deployed in guarding the lengthening lines of communication. Beaulieu did not dare to turn and fight but instead retreated with most of his army up the Lake Garda toward Trento, while detaching 12,000 troops to defend Mantua.

Bonaparte triumphantly led his troops into Milan on 15 May. He set up an administration composed of trusted aides and Italian liberals. He had the city's vast stockpiles of munitions and provision distributed to his far-flung divisions. The city was not completely secure as 2,500 Austrian troops held out in the citadel; they surrendered on 29 June.

He sent his latest batch of captured battle flags to Paris along with the promise to 'display on all occasions my esteem and devotion to the constitution and the government' for which he was 'always be prepared to die'.[31] He was doing his best to follow the Directorate's specific instructions but 'the rapidity of events, the force of circumstances and the distance' from Paris forced him to take 'some initiatives with the greatest repugnance but entirely persuaded that it was what you would have wanted me to do . . . In military operations I consult only myself.'[32]

The Directors did indeed fear that Bonaparte was becoming too powerful and sought to hobble him. They informed him that they would split the Italian front between him and General Kellermann who would soon arrive; Bonaparte would march with part of the army to conquer the Kingdom of Naples while Kellermann pursued the Austrians. An infuriated Bonaparte threatened to resign if they 'made me play a secondary role'.[33] He argued that while he respected Kellermann, 'I cannot willingly serve with a man who believes himself to be Europe's premier general and anyway I believe that it is better to have one bad general than two good ones; war is like government, it is a business of tact'.[34] He insisted that 'I can only render the nation essential services on my own'.[35] The Directors backed off and assured Bonaparte that he could retain sole command over the Italian front.

This crisis was the turning point in Bonaparte's attitude toward the government. He would continue to pledge support while secretly looking for an opportunity to take power: 'I felt the difference . . . between me and other men . . . I was . . . more capable than them of governing . . . From that moment I glimpsed the goal and I marched toward it.'[36] He would eventually win this goal, but only after an epic long march of two and a half years, with a long detour to Egypt.

* * *

With the Austrians on the run and his troops in pursuit, Bonaparte complied with his orders to make the campaign pay for itself. He had already imposed onerous demands on Lombardy and now targeted the duchies of Tuscany and Parma for shakedowns. Although both states were officially neutral, they leaned toward the Austrians. He explained to the Directors that 'these little princes need some guidance. They would more greatly respect a note from our army than our diplomats; only fear can render them honest and respectful to what we tell them.'[37] Tuscany and Parma protested but ultimately yielded to Bonaparte's demands for money, provisions, artworks, saddled and harnessed horses, free passage for French troops and French garrisons.

Meanwhile, Bonaparte's heavy impositions on Lombardy combined with the depredations of his soldiers provoked revolts in Milan, Pavia, Como and Binasco.[38] He swiftly gathered what rear-echelon troops were available, marched against the rebels and ruthlessly crushed them: 'Midway to Pavia, we encountered a thousand peasants at Binasco and routed them. After killing a hundred, we burned the village, thus setting a terrible but effective example. Within the hour we will march on Pavia where it is said that they still resist us.' He told Berthier to make light of the revolts in the newspapers.[39] He ordered General Hyacinthe Despinoy, the French commander in Milan, to 'have shot without formalities the two leaders . . . that were arrested; they are known to be the rebellion's instigators'.[40]

The horrors unleashed by the revolt and the means vital to crushing it left Bonaparte 'sadly affected'. At Pavia, after routing the rebels and rescuing the garrison, 'three times the order to burn the city expired on my lips'. Instead, he warned that 'if the blood of another Frenchman is shed, I would have erected on Pavia's ruins a column on which I would have written, "Here was the city of Pavia". I had the mayor shot and arrested three hundred hostages that I sent to France. Today all is tranquil and I don't doubt that this lesson will serve to rule the Italian peoples.'[41] He knew that if he failed to follow severity with clemency, the next revolt was only a matter of time. As he appeared before captured rebels, 'they threw themselves on their knees and asked for mercy with great cries', to which he replied in Italian: 'I am the friend of all the Italian peoples and especially of Rome. I am here for your well-being. Return to your families. Tell them that the French support religion order and poor people.'[42] Recognizing the priests' role in instigating the rebellion, he sought to subdue them with generosity rather than severity. He issued a proclamation that the French would protect all monasteries, monks and priests.

He sought to deter other states from revolting. He sternly warned Genoa's senate to 'purge from its territory the assassins that fill it. If you fail to do so, I will . . . I have had cities and villages burned in which a single Frenchman was assassinated . . . The cadaver of a murdered Frenchman will bring sorrow to the communes who did not protect him.'[43] To Novi's governor, he declared: 'You harbour rebels... I command you to have arrested all . . . imperial agents found in your territory . . . I will have the cities and the houses burned that harbour murderers or do not arrest them.'[44] His worst fear was that the revolts would inspire the Piedmontese to tear up their peace treaty and attack his rear. He fired off a letter to General Victor Amadeus de la Tour, Piedmont's new army commander, expressing his 'relief . . . at the solid peace that assures the repose of your brave nation. One must hope that . . . Europe will have a peace equally vital to all nations.'[45]

One Italian state after another signed armistice treaties with Bonaparte, Parma on 9 May, Modena on 17 May, Naples on 5 June and the Papal States on 26 June. Each agreement let French troops occupy key places and cross that state's territory, while the government yielded treasure and art to the conqueror. Milan paid 20,000,000 livres, Modena 10,000,000 livres, Genoa 8,000,000 livres and Parma 2,000,000 livres. As for paintings, Bonaparte's art experts collected 110, including 15 from Parma, 20 from Modena, 25 from Milan, 40 from Bologna and 10 from Ferrara and that was just the initial haul. Bonaparte extracted the most from Rome: 24 million livres in coin, 34 million livres' worth of provisions, 200 guns and 8,000 muskets, along with the papal legates of Bologna, Ferrara and Ravenna and cities of Ancona, Urbino and Macerata. On 4 June, he met a Venetian delegation that promised their republic would remain neutral.[46]

As if extracting enormous amounts of cash and art from Italy was not enough, Bonaparte also sought to inspire a brain drain back to Paris. In a letter to the Italian astronomer Barnaba Oriani, he lauded 'the sciences, which honour the human spirit, the arts which embellish life and transmit grand actions to posterity', and thus 'must be especially promoted by free governments'. He then intruded a nationalistic note that 'all men of genius, all those who have obtained distinguished ranks in the republic of letters, are French'. That, however, could change as 'thought has become free in Italy' which no longer suffers under the yoke of 'the inquisition, intolerance or despots. I invite the savants to join me and propose ways that they can . . . enliven the sciences and beaux arts . . . The government will acclaim all those who go to France. The French people attach greater worth to acquiring a brilliant mathematician, a reputed painter and a distinguished savant . . . than the richest and most populous city.'[47]

* * *

Meanwhile the Austrian threat swelled as reinforcements arrived. Vienna replaced Beaulieu with General Dagobert Wurmser. The Austrians fielded more troops than the French, with 67,000 to 44,000; both armies were scattered. Mantua with its 12,000 defenders was now behind French lines. The fortress city was on an island connected by causeways to far shores. On 4 June, Bonaparte had Sérurier open a siege of Mantua by erecting fortifications and batteries at each causeway's end.[48] He had French forces occupy Livorno, in Tuscany and Porto Ferraio on the island of Elba, to seize any British vessels, cargoes and subjects in those ports. He had Augereau march into Bologna, Ferrara and Modena with lists of onerous requisitions. By late June, he could proudly write the Directorate that 'today France dominates Italy. With a mediocre army it was vital to overcome everything: to repel the Austrian armies, to besiege fortresses, to guard our rear, to impose ourselves on Genoa, Venice, Tuscany, Rome and Naples. It was vital to wield force everywhere . . . to burn and execute to establish terror. Yet . . . diplomacy truly accompanies force in Italy.'[49]

Wurmser launched an offensive on 29 July, with three columns, two marching south on opposite sides of Lake Garda and another marching south-west across Venetia's territory. His strategy was to overwhelm the French, join forces with Mantua's defenders, then head west to liberate Lombardy. As the Austrian columns punched through the French advanced forces, Bonaparte had Sérurier abandon the siege of Mantua and hasten to join the main army. Bonaparte led his men to victory over the Austrians at Lonato on 3 August and Castiglione on the 5th, and retook Verona on the 7th. As the Austrians retreated, he had Sérurier lay siege to Mantua again.

Bonaparte had won the third round of the war for northern Italy. Looking back, he explained that he 'ceaselessly improvised manoeuvres against' Wurmser's plan which was 'conceived on bad foundations. The worst fault was having the corps act separately without communication between them against a concentrated army.'[50] By taking advantage of interior lines, Bonaparte massed his troops to rout one approaching Austrian army then quick-marched across the countryside to rout the next enemy force. The carnage of war haunted him. He recalled 'entering the convent of San Bonifacio; the church served as a hospital for 400 or 500 wounded packed together, most already dead. The odour of cadavers pervaded everything . . . Two wounded French soldiers lay three days amidst the dead without having eaten, without having been bandaged . . . but they revived on seeing their general.'[51]

In early September, Bonaparte sought to carry the war to the Austrians by marching up the Adige valley. He defeated the Austrians at Roveredo on 4 September and captured the Austrian depot at Bassano on the 9th, before withdrawing down the valley. Meanwhile Wurmser turned his back on Bonaparte and succeeded in marching into Mantua on 12 September, but, rather than liberate the garrison he locked himself and his men into that trap; more than 30,000 Austrians were existing on half-rations as disease killed dozens of them daily.[52]

Bonaparte followed up his victorious campaign with diplomacy. He wrote to Francis, the sovereign of both the Austrian and German empires:

> Your Majesty, Europe wants peace. This disastrous war has lasted far too long. I have the honour of informing Your Majesty that, if you don't send envoys to Paris to open peace negotiations, the Directorate ordered me to overwhelm Trieste and devastate your Adriatic establishments . . . I desire that Your Majesty will be sensitive to the sorrows that menace your subjects and render relief and tranquillity to the world.[53]

He got no response.

* * *

Despite Bonaparte's efforts, the war was not self-financing. By early November, he lamented that 'we are entirely out of money; all our treasure chests are empty'.[54] He warned the Directors that the army's 'inferiority and exhaustion' left France 'on the brink of losing Italy'. He had only 18,000 unpaid, malnourished, scarecrow-like troops fit for duty, who faced the combined forces of 50,000 Austrians. He would not be held responsible for Italy's likely loss: 'I did my duty. The army did its duty. My soul is torn, but my conscience is calm.' The Directorate alone could stave off the pending calamity by immediately sending him much more money and men.[55]

Meanwhile, General Joseph Alvinczy, the latest commander of Austria's army in Italy, launched an offensive that nearly succeeded.[56] He defeated Bonaparte at Bassano on 6 November, while other Austrian troops routed General Claude Vaubois at Calliano on the 7th. But Bonaparte rallied his troops and led them to victory at Caldiero on 11 November and Sérurier blunted an attempt by Wurmser to break out of Mantua on the 23rd. The decisive battle between Bonaparte and Alvinczy raged at Arcole from 25 to 27 November; the French eventually routed the Austrians in a seesaw struggle.

Bonaparte wrote to the Directors that 'I am so harassed with fatigue . . . that I cannot explain all the military movements that preceded the battle of Arcole which just decided Italy's fate'.[57] He then lauded all the generals and regiments that played decisive roles in that victory. Alas, as usual his tormented love for disinterested, unfaithful Josephine complicated his challenges. In late November, he wrote that:

> You don't write me at all, you don't love your husband . . . What affair is so important that you can't tear yourself away to write a few words . . . Josephine, take care, one fine night you will find the doors burst open and me in your bed . . . I hope that soon I will take you in my arms and cover you with a million burning kisses.[58]

The Venetian government sent Bonaparte a letter complaining of French atrocities on its soil. In reply, he insisted that his troops respected the property, values and religions of the lands through which they marched and blamed Austrian troops for any violations. He demanded to know whether Venice was formally declaring war against France. Rather than threaten Venice, he cited his treaties with Naples, Genoa and Piedmont as examples of French generosity in return for peace. Venice's government was well aware that actually each of those and other realms that signed treaties with France at gunpoint paid heavily for the subsequent peace, yet dared not war against him.[59]

The final Austrian offensive opened on 7 January 1797, when Alvinczy launched columns down Lake Garda's east bank and the Adige River valley and another from Padua toward the French rear.[60] Bonaparte massed his army at Rivoli on a plateau between Lake Garda and the Adige River and defeated repeated attacks by Alvinczy on 13 and 14 January. The French suffered 3,200 casualties but killed or wounded 4,000 Austrians and captured 8,000 on the field, then took another 11,000 as they hounded the retreating enemy. Other French forces defeated the third Austrian column near Mantua on 16 January and Wurmser finally surrendered Mantua on 2 February. Ten months after invading Italy, Bonaparte finally expelled the Austrians after fighting six distinct campaigns in which he faced superior forces in each.

Bonaparte informed the Directorate that he intended to march against Vienna, but warned that his campaign would most likely succeed if the two French armies along the Rhine crossed it and marched toward Austria's capital.[61] Archduke Charles now led the 44,000-strong Austrian army in Italy.[62] Bonaparte launched his campaign on 16 March, by leading his 40,000 troops across the Talgiamento River. His troops defeated the Austrians at Gradisca on 19 March, Ocksay on the 20th and Pontebba on the 21st, then captured Trieste on 23 March and Klagenfurt on the 28th. Although he was now just 80 miles from Vienna, his army was overextended and vulnerable since the French armies along the Rhine were still in their winter camps west of that river.

As usual, as his victorious army advanced Bonaparte asserted soft power against both the enemy leaders and people. He wrote to Charles that 'the brave soldiers who make war want peace' for a war 'that had lasted six years'. He asked whether 'we had killed enough and committed enough evils to fill humanity with sorrows'. He pointed out that all of Europe had once united against France but now only Austria fought on. He insisted that he would be happy to forgo any more 'sad glories' won by his army if he could save the life of a single soldier by forging peace.[63] He had a proclamation distributed with this message: 'The French Republic imposes the right of conquest upon you, which will disappear with a reciprocal contract . . . You will furnish my army's needs . . . I will protect your property . . . All the taxes that you are accustomed to paying the emperor will serve to compensate for an army's march and pay for what you furnish.'[64]

Bonaparte negotiated with the Austrians from 31 March to 7 April, when the truce of Judenburg was signed. Negotiations for a preliminary peace treaty began at Leoben on 13 April, when the Austrian envoys General Johann von Merveldt de Courelles and Marzio Mastrilli, Marquis de Gallo, reached Bonaparte's headquarters. Within five days, Bonaparte and the Austrians forged the broad outlines of the preliminary treaty of Leoben that they signed on 18 April. They agreed to negotiate the permanent treaty at Udine. That was the easy part. The devil would be in the details. The haggling would grind on intermittently for the next six months.[65]

* * *

As Bonaparte subdued one enemy in his front, another rose in his rear. Venetia's revolt could not have been more ill-timed and was swiftly crushed.[66] It began on 17 April, when a mob murdered 400 French soldiers convalescing at Verona. When Bonaparte learned of the massacre, he fired off a warning to Ludovico Manin, Venice's Doge, that he would avenge 'the blood of my brothers in arms' and demanded that he immediately suppress the rebels or suffer the consequences of allying with them against France.[67] He instructed General Charles Kilmaine how to overrun

Venetia. He had General Barthelemy Joubert withdraw from the Tyrol back to north-eastern Italy to support Kilmaine and Bonaparte's main army. When the Doge failed to suppress the worsening revolt, Bonaparte declared war on the Venetian republic on 2 May.[68]

The French routed the Venetian forces. The Doge pleaded for peace. Bonaparte led his troops into Venice on 15 May. Under the Treaty of Venice, signed on 16 May, he won for France 'four ships-of-the-line, two frigates, 20 paintings, 900 manuscripts, 5 million livres in cash and 3 million livres worth of naval equipment'.[69] He got the Directors to dispatch Admiral François Brueys with six ships-of-the-line and two frigates from Toulon to Venice to assert control over all that loot.

The Austrians took advantage of the revolt to invade and conquer Venice's provinces of Istria and Dalmatia on the Adriatic's eastern shore. Bonaparte vainly protested. He wrote to Brueys that 'your presence . . . can only have a good effect on negotiations' with Austria and instructed him to spread word that his mission was to gather Venetian naval and army forces to help them retake Dalmatia from the Austrians.[70] In September, he informed Brueys that 'it is indispensable for the Army of Italy's operations that I am absolutely the master of the Adriatic'.[71]

* * *

Napoleon Bonaparte was a creator as well as a destroyer. In between campaigns and sometimes amidst them, he somehow found time to help organize two republics, one south and the other north of the Po River and eventually mesh them into one Italian state.[72] He proposed that the leaders of Modena, Bologna, Reggio and Ferrara establish a Cispadane Republic. During the Congress of Reggio, those states signed on 27 December 1796 a treaty whereby they would form the Cispadane Republic on 1 January 1797 and promulgate its constitution on 27 March 1797. He lauded their efforts to unify and lead Italy to its proper place among the European powers and he assured them that the French people supported their fellow Italian republicans. He helped organize and equip the Cispadane Republic's army, donating French-style uniforms but with green rather than dark blue coats and armed with captured Austrian muskets and cannons. He just as decisively helped transform Lombardy into the Cisalpine Republic, including its flag with vertical bands of green, white and red and its 25,000-man Lombard Legion. He issued this advice to its Congress: 'If Italy wants to be free, what can prevent that? It is not enough for states to unite; they must assert fraternal ties among all classes of each state.' They must also crush any counterrevolutionaries that threatened Italian unity and reforms. And for that, Italy's patriots could expect the French army's support.[73] He supervised the writing of its French-style constitution and picked its president, Galeazzo Serbelloni, five Directors and many of its 180 lawmakers. The Cisalpine Republic was declared on 29 June 1797. The Cispadane Republic subsumed itself to the Cisalpine Republic on 9 July. He praised the Cisalpine Republic's founders: 'You are the first people in history who became free without factions, revolutions and heartbreaks. We have given you liberty. Know how to keep it.'[74]

Bonaparte was also instrumental in the Genoan Republic's transformation into the Ligurian Republic.[75] After installing a provisional government in Genoa on 14 June 1797, he advised its leaders to 'stifle all ferment of hatred that begin to divide your government. Guard against disunity. Liberty has enough enemies in your country without increasing them by a misplaced defiance.'[76] On 11 November, he gave a line-by-line critique of the proposed Genoan constitution and encouraged them to strengthen sections dealing with religious freedom, taxation, legislation and justice.[77] Yet even as he encouraged the Ligurian Republic he envisioned a quite different future for it. He advised the Directorate that 'most Genoans want to be French. That would be a useful acquisition for us and we should not lose sight of that.'[78]

A year and a half of enduring war, diplomacy and politics in Italy had disabused Bonaparte of the ideals he once harboured for the Italians. In October 1797, he fired off a stern reply to a letter from Foreign Minister Charles Talleyrand who urged him to accelerate Italian unity and republicanism: 'You don't understand the peoples here. They are not worth risking the lives of 40,000 Frenchmen.' Talleyrand should abandon his 'false hypothesis that imagines that liberty can squeeze great things from a spineless, superstitious . . . and lazy people. You want me to conjure up miracles and I don't know how . . . Don't let yourself be tricked by a bunch of Italian adventurers in Paris . . . French public opinion is deceived when it comes to Italians.' Yet, 'little by little the people of the Cispadane republic are more enthusiastic about liberty, little by little they are organizing themselves'. As for an army, he hoped that within five years they might field 30,000 troops but 'it would take a very clever leader to get them accustomed to arms'. In all, the Italians were 'an irritating and unreliable nation'. Only a small, weak minority of Italians are genuinely devoted to liberty and equality.'[79]

* * *

Meanwhile, the Papal States, abetted by Austrian and Neapolitan agents, were increasingly restless under French domination. Bonaparte issued in late October 1796, this warning to Cardinal Alessandro Mattei, who was Pope Pius VI's right-hand man:

> The Roman court . . . has broken the armistice and suspended execution of its conditions. It arms. If it wants war, it will have it. But . . . I owe my nation, humanity and myself a last attempt to bring the Pope to his senses. You know . . . the forces and power of the army that I command. To destroy Rome's temporal authority I need simply will it . . . War, so cruel for people, has terrible results for the vanquished; avoid terrible sorrows for the Pope.[80]

Yet Rome persisted in violating the armistice terms. In late January 1797, Bonaparte condemned 'the foreigners who influence the court of Rome' and 'stifle the message of peace that I have sent you'. He warned that 'this ridiculous comedy' was reaching its 'denouement' and insisted on 'my desire to spare you the horrors of war. The pope can rest unworried in Rome as long as he does not join his army to France's enemies.'[81]

When Rome again ignored his warning, Bonaparte sent General Claude Victor's division into the Papal States then joined him on 1 February. The war did not last long.[82] The French routed the Papal troops at Castle Bolognese on 3 February and captured Ancora on the 9th. Pius sent a plea for peace. Under the Treaty of Tolentino, signed on 19 February, Rome ceded Avignon, Comtat Venaissin, 30 million francs, 500 manuscripts and a hundred works of art to France, ceded Bologna, Ferrara and Romagna to the Cispadane Republic, and closed its ports to France's enemies.

Peace negotiations between France and Austria opened at Udine on 31 May 1797, between Henri Clarke and Merveldt and Gallo. From his Milan headquarters, Bonaparte skilfully directed Clarke's strategy toward his counterparts.[83] He swiftly learned that Austria's negotiating position was torn between Foreign Minister Johann Thugut, who 'was ill-intentioned, bad-humoured and opposed to peace', and former foreign minister Johann Philippe Cobenzl, who wanted to end the war. Emperor Francis was too 'lazy and inexperienced' to resolve the tug-of-war one way or the other. Vienna's failure to forge a common diplomatic strategy reduced the envoys to presenting vague platitudes rather than concrete negotiable positions. Bonaparte worried that Francis had succumbed to Thugut's hard line and was putting up a diplomatic smokescreen to mask his army's build-up for the next round of war. He was stunned that Vienna 'searched for all pretexts to give birth to obstacles that stymied the conclusion of peace'.[84] He had Clarke warn Austria's envoys that if Francis was negotiating in 'bad faith' and 'ruptured the preliminaries, he would be responsible, in the eyes of Europe, for the disastrous consequences for humanity'.[85] To resolve these uncertainties, he had Clarke insist that Gallo journey to Vienna and receive clear diplomatic powers and positions from Thugut himself; his aide, Auguste Marmont would accompany Gallo to learn first-hand Vienna's genuine intentions, diplomatic and military.

The impasse persisted even after Gallo and Marmont returned from Vienna. In late July, Bonaparte went to Udine to supersede Clarke. At first, he communicated by letter. He warned Francis that war would resume if no progress was made by late August. He sent long letters to Gallo and Merveldt, systematically exposing all the examples of Vienna's bad faith that would inevitably lead to war unless they began sincerely negotiating for peace.[86]

* * *

Amid the talks Bonaparte received a stunning intelligence and political windfall. Louis de Launay, Count d'Antraigues, was a key agent in the British and royalist counterrevolutionary web. French troops arrested him at Venice on 21 May 1797. Among his papers was evidence that exposed General Charles Pichegru, then president of the Council of Five Hundred, as a traitor. Bonaparte had Antraigues brought to Milan where he interrogated him during the night of 31 May/1 June. He threatened to have him hanged as a spy unless he revealed all, but promised good treatment and hinted at his release if he became a double agent. Antraigues yielded lists of royalist agents and operations in France and beyond. Bonaparte rewarded him by giving him comfortable quarters in the fortress, letting his wife stay with him and even permitting him to stroll in the city on parole. During one of his outings, Antraigues broke his parole and escaped.[87]

Bonaparte shared the intelligence with the Directors and urged them to act decisively against Pichegru and his cabal or be overthrown in a coup.[88] He sent Augereau to Paris, ostensibly to take care of his personal affairs but to protect the government. The Directorate finally acted with mass arrests on 4 September. Eventually Pichegru and 163 other suspects were found guilty of treason and sent to the 'dry guillotine' of Guyana.[89]

The Directors had a strange way of showing their appreciation. Bonaparte learned that they suspected Henri Clarke of conspiring against them. He eventually convinced them of Clarke's loyalty.[90] Then he discovered that he was among their suspects. He fired off a letter to Director Barras expressing his deep resentment and asking to be dismissed,

> because no power on earth can make me continue in the service after the government's horrible mark of ingratitude . . . For a long time great power has been entrusted to my hands. I have served continuously in all circumstances only for the nation's good . . . My recompense is in my conscience and the opinion of posterity . . . Rest assured that whenever the country is imperilled, I will be in the first rank to defend liberty and the constitution.[91]

Barras replied with soothing words and refused to accept Bonaparte's resignation.[92]

* * *

Meanwhile the peace talks dragged on. On 27 August, Bonaparte moved his headquarters to the chateau of Manin in Passariano, ten miles from Udine. The talks alternated between the two towns. Thugut continued to veto any Austrian concessions necessary for a treaty. Bonaparte rattled the sabre by demanding that Vienna choose war or peace.[93] That did the trick. In late September, Francis replaced Thugut with Cobenzl and assigned his brother, Louis von Cobenzl, to negotiate with Bonaparte. After their first lively exchange, Bonaparte observed that Cobenzl was 'unaccustomed to discourse', 'lacks reason' and chatted for hours.[94] Nonetheless, Bonaparte forged a good working relationship with him.

Bonaparte and Cobenzl signed the Treaty of Campo Formio on 18 October 1797. For France, Bonaparte won Austria's recognition of France's acquisition of the Austrian Netherlands (Belgium), a Rhine frontier from Switzerland to above Cologne, including the fortress-city of Mainz and the Ionian Islands in the lower Adriatic Sea. Austria also recognized the Cisalpine and Ligurian Republics. In return, France recognized Austria's acquisition of Venetia east of the Adige River including Friuli, Istria and Dalmatia. Overall, France gained 4 million people and Austria lost 1.5 million people. More importantly, Austria geopolitically shifted eastward. A congress of the Holy Roman Empire at Rastadt would ratify the treaty.

THE MASTER OF ITALY

Symbolically, Bonaparte tapped his chief of staff Louis Berthier and the scientist Gaspard Monge to convey the treaty to the Directorate. They reached Paris on 26 October. In his letter accompanying the treaty, he assured the Directors that 'if, in all my calculations, I made mistakes, my heart and intentions were pure; I silenced any interest in my glory, my vanity and my ambition. I saw only the nation and government . . . Now I must resume my place in the crowd . . . like Cincinnatus.'[95] He wrote to Talleyrand that 'without doubt critics will denigrate the treaty that I just signed. However, all those who understand Europe and are sensitive to worldly affairs will be well convinced that it would have been impossible to reach a better treaty without battering and conquering two or three Austrian provinces.'[96] He later summarized the significance of the Treaty of Campo Formio: 'France was restored to its Gaullish heritage; she had reconquered her natural limits. The First Coalition, which threatened to smother the Republic in its cradle, was vanquished and broken up. England alone remained at war. She profited from the calamities on the continent by seizing the two Indies and asserted a tyranny at sea.'[97]

Bonaparte felt mingled elation and relief at the treaty's signature. A year and a half of nearly nonstop war, diplomacy and politics had exhausted him. To Barras, he confessed that although 'my health is considerably weakened and my morale not less affected . . . I remain in command. I will not relax my lively interest . . . for the republic's prosperity and liberty.'[98] He was eager to get home but was forced to take a long detour. The Directorate appointed him to lead France's delegation to Rastadt, where he arrived on 26 November. The Congress of Rastadt included delegations from Austria, Bavaria, Baden, Mainz, Würzburg, Augsburg, Frankfurt, Hanover, Saxony and Darmstadt, ten states elected by the Diet in October 1795 to represent the Holy Roman Empire. The Congress ratified the treaty on 30 November.

* * *

Bonaparte returned wearily to Paris on 5 December and immediately went into seclusion at his house on Rue Chantereine, which would soon be renamed Rue de la Victoire in his honour.[99] For weeks thereafter he politely fended off the hero-worshiping public's attempts to celebrate him with parades and adoring or fearful political leaders to acclaim him at banquets. He roused himself for only three meetings.

The day after his arrival, Bonaparte met Charles Maurice Talleyrand-Perigord for the first time. They had corresponded since July when their letters crossed in the post. Bonaparte's congratulated Talleyrand for being named foreign minister. Talleyrand's introduced himself and lauded Bonaparte's achievements. Each recognized in the other someone whose intellect and vision complimented his own. For the next half-dozen years they shared outlooks and interests then their relationship unravelled to the point where Talleyrand did everything he could get away with to undermine Bonaparte's rule.[100]

Bonaparte and the Directors had decidedly mixed feelings about each other. He was contemptuous of their venality and incompetence, while they feared he might overthrow them. The Directorate named Bonaparte commander of the Army of England on 9 December and received Bonaparte for an awkward meeting at the Luxembourg Palace on the 10th.

On 25 December 1797, the Institute of France voted by 305 to 7 to make him a member. Bonaparte could not have received a more cherished Christmas present. In his acceptance letter, he wrote that: 'True conquests, the only ones that leave no regret, are those made against ignorance. A nation's most honourable and useful occupation is to help extend humanitarian ideals. Hereafter the French republic's true power must consist of not permitting a single new good idea to exist without realizing it.'[101]

Despite all the accolades, capped by his induction, Bonaparte worried that his celebrity was rapidly fading and he would soon become irrelevant. He confided to his secretary, Louis Bourrienne that: 'No one remembers anything in Paris. If I do nothing for too long, I am lost.'[102] He would soon get the Directorate's approval for a campaign whose ambitions exceeded even what he achieved in Italy.

Chapter 3

The Pharaoh

'The time is not far when . . . to destroy England, we must seize Egypt. The vast Ottoman empire, which decays daily, obliges us . . . to seize the means to conserve our trade with the Levant.'

'From the heights of those pyramids, forty centuries looks down upon you.'

'The biggest thing that we have to fear is terror'.

'I must find myself where my presence can be the most useful. Animated by these sentiments, I will wrap myself in my cloak and leave by ship.'

Emulating one day the conquests of his heroes Alexander the Great and Julius Caesar had gleamed in Napoleon Bonaparte's churning mind from his schooldays at Brienne. Surreal visions enchanted him of exploring the ruins of ancient civilizations engulfed by vast merciless deserts. As a child of the Mediterranean, he envisioned a French empire that eventually embraced the entire basin and the Orient beyond, just like the Roman Empire.[1]

He first partly shared his vision with the Directorate in February 1797: 'Ancona is a very good port . . . I had its fortress put into the best state of repair. We must keep . . . Ancona in a general peace and it must always remain French. That will give us a grand influence on the Ottoman Porte and make us masters of the Adriatic' and eventually beyond. In August 1797 he elaborated his vision:

> It would be better to restore Italy to Austria and keep the four [southern Adriatic] islands which are a source of wealth and

prosperity for our commerce . . . and positions us to undertake different possibilities . . . The time is not far when . . . to destroy England, we must seize Egypt. The vast Ottoman empire, which decays daily, obliges us . . . to seize the means to conserve our trade with the Levant.[2]

Bonaparte was not the only prominent Frenchmen who advocated the conquest of Egypt. Talleyrand made the same argument in two lectures before the French Institute in July 1797. Three days after becoming Foreign Minister on 29 July, he shared his views on Egypt with the Directorate. In August, introductory and congratulatory letters between Bonaparte and Talleyrand crossed in the post. They soon discovered their mutual vision for Egypt's conquest and vowed to work together to realize it. In a letter of 13 September, Bonaparte capped an analysis of French interests and advances in the Adriatic and broader Mediterranean by asking Talleyrand 'to appraise information in Paris and let me know how the Porte would react to our expedition to Egypt'.[3] Bonaparte eyed Malta as the Mediterranean's strategic hinge and a springboard to Egypt. In November 1797, he informed the Directors that he had sent a spy to Malta to gather intelligence for 'the project we have for that island'.[4] That project was its conquest.

The Directorate, however, pointed Bonaparte in the opposite direction as his first assignment after he returned to Paris. He spent nearly six weeks in January and February 1798 inspecting the army and naval forces earmarked to invade England, weighing them against the British warships and regiments that would oppose them. In the report that he submitted on 23 February, he explained that 'invading England without mastery of the sea would be the . . . most difficult operation that could be undertaken'. Doing so depended on hundreds of small boats packed with soldiers, artillery and supplies somehow evading Britain's Channel Fleet for the eight hours or so vital to crossing during the night. He concluded that 'the expedition to England does not appear to be possible' at this time, 'perhaps forever'.[5] With varying degrees of disappointment or relief, the Directors concurred.

With that chimera exposed, Bonaparte and Talleyrand concentrated on talking the Directorate into approving their vision. On 5 March, Bonaparte presented an elaborate campaign plan to conquer Malta and Egypt. The Directors unanimously approved the plan with varying degrees of enthusiasm and trepidation. They were risking an army, fleet and France's best general on a gamble that might yield nothing more than an empty title to a desert land filled with impoverished, rebellious Muslims that devoured ever more troops and treasure, if the Royal Navy did not destroy the armada en route.[6]

Ideally adroit diplomacy would mitigate those risks. The Directors dispatched envoys to Constantinople to talk Sultan Selim III into accepting France's conquest of Egypt, while Bonaparte sought to reconcile key Ottoman governors. During his preparations at Toulon, he wrote to Ali Pasha of Janina, Ibrahim Pasha of Scutari, Djezzar-Pacha of Palestine and the Bey of Tunis, asking each for peaceful relations. One of those letters survives, that to Ibrahim of Scutari, which bordered the Ragusa Republic. He showered Ibrahim with oriental-style flattery and assured him that France remained committed to its alliance with the Ottoman Empire. To further sweeten their long-distance relationship, four crates of muskets accompanied his letter.[7] That diplomatic offensive failed. Selim would declare war against France after learning of the invasion of Egypt.

Bonaparte had two months to organize the expedition before its departure in early May.[8] It was critical to get to Egypt as soon as possible before the burning summer engulfed it. Even more critical was French naval superiority for convoying, protecting and resupplying the expedition. He urged the Directors to allocate 'forty or fifty million livres to reorganize our navy'. Meanwhile, 'England is making immense preparations that are ruining its finances, destroying its commercial spirit and absolutely changing the constitution and people's values . . . England will exhaust itself in an immense effort that cannot prevent our invasion . . . . We must always keep ourselves masters of the Mediterranean.'[9] He explained to Admiral François Brueys d'Aigalliers, the expedition's naval commander, that 'our . . . success or failure depends on the navy'. He issued this key instruction: 'The moment that the enemy is spotted, form a line of battle . . . that protects the convoy to guard its preservation.' He emphasized how vital frigates were for screening the convoy and discovering enemy warships or fleets: 'All subsequent events depend on their first glance and first reports.'[10]

Secrecy was just as essential to pulling off the expedition. Fear of foreign spies in one's midst was, as always, a concern. In a letter to Benoit Georges de Najac, Toulon's marine ordnance commissioner, Bonaparte explained: 'You must keep a grand secret. Spread the rumour that the marine minister is going to Toulon and in consequence prepare lodging which will be for me.' He lauded Najac for 'the fleet that will sail from Toulon is due to the zeal that you have shown in all circumstances'.[11]

* * *

Bonaparte and his colleagues would embark on their expedition worried that war would erupt behind them. The peace with Austria appeared increasingly tenuous. On 13 April 1798, a mob stormed Ambassador Jean-Baptiste Bernadotte's residence in Vienna and tore to shreds the French flag flying over it. Bernadotte promptly left Vienna for Paris. The Congress of Rastadt had no sooner ratified the Treaty of Campo Formio on 28 April 1798, than rogue Austrian hussars waylaid and murdered two French envoys as they left for Paris.

Bonaparte wrote to Louis Cobenzl, Austria's envoy at Rastadt, that 'Austria's government certainly appears to want to resume the war' and warned that Vienna must 'disperse all these clouds and clearly explain whether it would consolidate the peace or decide on war'. He called for high-level talks to discuss the worsening situation. He took this opportunity to express to 'Europe and His Imperial Majesty France's desire to avoid the horrors of a war that will inflict such incalculable evils on our poor continent . . . This peace must endure . . . since I see nothing in the interests of our two nations that should make it end.' He asked Cobenzl to convey to Francis 'how calm the French government was in such a critical circumstance . . . It should be easy enough for us to set aside our passions, destroy all our suspicions, reconcile our interests, foil the intrigues of foreign powers that wish to harm the continent and search only, no matter what it takes, to forge peace.'[12] He suggested that he meet with Cobenzl in Rastadt and try to resolve the array of conflicts pushing their nations to war.

Bonaparte informed Brueys that 'some troubles have come from Vienna . . . that necessitates my presence in Paris; that will have no effect on the expedition'.[13] He told General Louis Caffarelli du Falga that 'I might have to go to Rastadt to negotiate with Cobenzl then, if all goes well, return from Rastadt to Toulon'.[14] He did not end up going to Rastadt but had the politician François de Neufchâteau take his place.

* * *

'All the obstacles that opposed the expedition have been overcome', Bonaparte triumphantly declared on 2 May, then set forth from Paris.[15] He reached Toulon on the 9th and in ten whirlwind days completed his campaign's preparations. His army included 24,300 infantry, 4,000 cavalry, 3,000 artillerymen with 60 field and 40 siege guns, and 1,000 civilians or 32,300 men altogether. The provisions included 4,000 bottles of wine from Burgundy and 400 from Ambassador Joseph Bonaparte's cellar in Rome.[16]

General Alexandre Berthier was the chief of a staff that most prominently included Generals Joachim Murat, Jean Lannes, Louis Davout, Auguste Marmont, Jean Junot and Victor Leclerc and Captains Eugène Beauharnais and Louis Bonaparte. Louis Caffarelli du Falga headed the engineers, Eleazar Dommartin the artillery, Thomas Dumas the cavalry, Simon Sucy de Clisson the ordnance and Jean Larrey the surgeons. Generals Louis Desaix, Jean-Baptiste Kléber, Jacques Menou, Jean Reynier and Louis Bon each commanded a division. Desaix and Kléber proved to be the best field commanders. Bonaparte recalled Desaix as 'the army's most distinguished officer: active, quick, loving glory for itself. He was short and not physically imposing but highly capable both of planning and executing an operation's details.' Kléber 'was the army's handsomest man . . . and loved glory as the road to joy. He was a man of spirit, courage, knowledge of war and was capable of great things.'[17]

The expedition was as much as a cultural as a military operation. Bonaparte intended to bring the Enlightenment to a land that he believed had wallowed in darkness since the fall of the Roman Empire. He conveyed the Enlightenment to Egypt with 167 savants, most prominently mathematician and physicist Gaspard Monge, chemist Claude Berthollet, engineer Jean-Baptiste Lancret, orientalist Jean de Paradis, artist Dominique Denon, astronomer Pierre Beauchamp, architect Jean-Baptiste Lepère, architect Charles Norry, engineer Nicolas Conté, geographer Nicolas Nouet, naturalist Étienne Saint Hilaire, musicologist Guillaume Villoteau, poet François Perceval and painter Henri Redouté. He tracked down and requisitioned a printing press with Arab characters along with Arab speakers who could help him compose proclamations and letters.[18]

At seven o'clock on the morning of 19 May, Bonaparte informed the Directors that 'the light squadron had sailed, the convoy was filing out to sea and we raised our anchor with beautiful weather'. Intelligence reports indicated that while 'there were several English fleets in the Mediterranean, they did not appear to be a position to threaten us'.[19] Starting that day or the next five French flotillas sailed with a combined strength of 232 transports: 106 with 20,500 troops from Toulon; 30 with 3,200 troops from Marseille; 20 with 1,200 troops from Ajaccio; 35 with 3,100 troops from Genoa; and 41 with 4,300 troops from Civitavecchia. A fleet of thirteen ships-of-the-line and seven frigates sailed from Toulon and one or two smaller warships guarded the other transport flotillas until they rendezvoused with the main fleet.[20] Each fleet's commander opened his sealed orders to discover that the destination was Malta.

The appearance of the combined French fleet before Valletta, Malta's capital, on June 9, threw the leaders and population into turmoil. Bonaparte sent word to Ferdinand von Hompesch, Malta's ruler and the Grand Master of the Knights of Saint John, that he sought water and food for his fleet. Hompesch replied that he would let only two vessels at a time inside Valletta's harbour, a number only half that permitted British vessels. At that rate the fleet's 280 vessels would take weeks to draw needed provisions. Bonaparte used that as an excuse to conquer Malta. On the morning of 22 June, he led 3,000 troops with artillery ashore and deployed them across the base of the peninsula on which Valletta was sited. The bombardment began that evening.

The exchange of artillery fire was largely symbolic, a face-saving way for Hompesch honourably to surrender. The following morning, he sent word that he desired a truce. Bonaparte granted a 24-hour cease-fire during which Hompesch accepted his terms. Under the treaty signed on 12 June, Bonaparte essentially bought the rights to Malta: Hompesch received 300,000 francs from Malta's treasury to underwrite his retirement in Trieste, while 300,000 francs paid off Malta's debt and 100,000 francs paid off the expedition's debt to Strasbourg financiers. As for the 332 other knights, those 60 or more years old could stay with annual 700-franc pensions, those younger than 26 years old were enlisted in the French army and the rest were dispatched to their distant countries of origin.[21] Bonaparte boasted that France 'now had in the Mediterranean's centre the most fortified place in Europe which would cost dearly anyone who tried to dislodge us'.[22]

French troops marched into Valletta on 24 June, to seize the forts and '2 ships-of-the-line, 1 frigate, 4 galleys, 1,200 cannons, 1.5 million pounds of gunpowder and 40,000 muskets'.[23] Just as important, his officials eventually extracted 7 million francs from Malta's treasury, churches and subjects, sent most to Paris and used the rest for the expedition's expenses.[24] Bonaparte had water, forage and other vital provisions distributed as needed among his armada's vessels. Worried that the Maltese might revolt, he issued a proclamation 'that the French had come neither to change their mores nor religion; that the severest discipline would be maintained; and that all priests are especially protected . . . All Maltese arms would be gathered in a single place . . . Hostages would be taken from any villages that appeared threatening.'[25] To the bishop, he expressed

> his true pleasure . . . to learn of the good conduct and welcome you have displayed to the French troops. You can assure your

parishioners that the Catholic religion . . . will be respected . . . I desire that you show yourself in the city of Malta and use your influence to maintain calm and tranquillity among the people. I will join you this evening . . . and I would like you to present me to the priests and other heads of orders in the city of Malta and the surrounding villages.[26]

Typically Bonaparte's decisive actions belied his reassuring words. He imposed a modern revolution from above on Malta by abolishing feudalism, slavery and the monasteries, freeing political prisoners, establishing a governing council of liberals, proclaiming freedom of worship for all faiths, and ordering the construction of hospitals, wells, street lights and pavements, all in six hectic days. He left General Charles Vaubois's brigade of 3,053 men to garrison Malta, along with any sick soldiers or sailors.[27]

The surrender bore a diplomatic catch with enormous geopolitical consequences. Russian Tsar Paul I was the Knights of Saint John's official protector and would be elected the Grand Master to replace Hompesch. He would declare war against France after learning that Bonaparte had dissolved the order. Bonaparte could do nothing about that. What he did do was to have France's ambassador in Constantinople inform Selim that the hated Knights of Saint John no longer existed. He sent that same message to the governors of Albania, Scutari, Janina, Algiers, Tunis and Tripoli, adding that he was liberating and repatriating 2,000 Muslim galley slaves to their various countries.[28] His hope that somehow such gestures would convince Selim and the governors to accept France's conquest of Egypt was severely misplaced.

Only after the armada sailed from Malta did Bonaparte reveal its ultimate destination. On 22 June, he issued a proclamation to his men with these stirring words: 'Soldiers! You are undertaking a conquest with incalculable effects on civilization and world commerce. You will inflict a . . . sharp blow to England . . . We will make fatiguing marches. We will win battles. We will succeed in all our endeavours. Destiny is with us . . . We will find at each step exciting memories.' He cautioned his men to respect the Muslim religion and women and forbad any looting or anything else that violated French honour and turned the Egyptians against them.[29]

* * *

The armada dropped anchor at Marabout half a dozen miles west of Alexandria toward evening on 1 July. Bonaparte immediately ordered his army to disembark. The surf was rough. The light faded to pitch dark until a full moon rose from the horizon. The troops were weighed down with muskets, cartridge boxes and packs. Nineteen drowned before reaching the beach. By the morning of the 2nd, only 4,500 of his 32,000 men were ashore; it would take days to empty the transports of the remaining men, horses and supplies. Nonetheless, he recalled his thrill 'after a long perilous journey to find myself on the soil of ancient Egypt, inhabited by oriental nations, completely alien to our customs and religion'.[30]

Bonaparte assigned Desaix with 600 troops to guard the landing and seize nearby Fort Marabout defended by only a few men. He advanced toward the city, with Menou's 1,800 on the left, Kléber's 900 in the centre and Bon's 1,200 on the right. Although he led only 3,900 men forward, he hoped that the sight of nearly 300 ships off shore would sap the defenders' will. That hope dissolved when Alexandria's commander, Seid Mohammed el-Koraim, refused to surrender. Egyptian horsemen appeared and harassed the French flanks but were driven off by skirmishers deployed in groups of four, with two firing and two reloading. Bonaparte assigned each general a different gate to assault. No cannons were yet ashore so sappers armed with axes had to rush forward and smash down the gates as light infantry fired at defenders on the wall above and the rest of the men waited impatiently in column to charge. Each column fought its way through its assigned gate into the maze of streets and eventually converged at the central square. With as many as 800 of his men killed or wounded, Koraim ordered the survivors to lay down their arms. The French suffered about 300 casualties, a relatively light cost for such a critical victory.

Bonaparte met with Koraim and the other religious, military and political leaders on 4 July. He explained that he had come to liberate them from the despotism of the Mamelukes, Egypt's ruling elite of 470 beys or chiefs, each with his band of armed men, and bring them justice and prosperity while respecting their faith, customs and property. In return he asked them to pledge allegiance to and cooperate with the administration he would establish. The vanquished leaders had no choice but to sign the treaty of submission that he presented. Meanwhile the 700 now well-fed, clothed and grateful Egyptian slaves that he had freed from the Maltese galleys appeared in Alexandria as living proof of the conqueror's good intentions.

He learned the disturbing news that a British fleet of thirteen ships-of-the-line and a frigate, commanded by Admiral Horatio Nelson, had appeared off Alexandria on 28 June, then sailed eastward searching for the French armada. At some point Nelson's fleet would undoubtedly reappear. Bonaparte had Brueys deploy his warships to protect the transports as the remaining troops, horses and supplies were disembarked. With that crucial task done, he told Brueys either to squeeze his fleet into Alexandria's small port or sail to distant Corfu.[31]

Ideally any fighting would end with the battle for Alexandria. He wrote to Abou Kekr, Cairo's pasha, explaining that the Directorate had authorized him to punish Egypt's Mameluke rulers for decades of depredations against French commerce. He cited as precedent previous French strikes against the provinces of Tunis and Algiers for their piracy. He claimed that Sultan Selim himself supported that punishment since the Mamelukes were 'capricious and greedy, deaf to the principles of justice and committed unauthorized outrages against his good and ancient friends, the French'. He called on the pasha to join him in deposing Egypt of its cursed rulers.[32] He wrote to France's ambassador at Constantinople, instructing him to express to Selim 'our hope that the Porte will view with pleasure the punishment of men who fail to recognize [the sultan's] power and that He will not be blind to his true interests that we are supporting'. The ambassador should 'report in great detail all that passes in Constantinople' along with the rest of 'that vast empire'.[33] He was counting on Foreign Minister Talleyrand to fulfil his promise to build upon the diplomatic foundations he was laying by journeying to Constantinople and negotiating directly with the sultan. He would later learn that Talleyrand had broken his promise, the first of many betrayals that Bonaparte would suffer from him.

He left Kléber in charge of Alexandria's garrison and established a mobile force under General Jean-Baptiste Dumuy at nearby Aboukir. He had Kléber set up two hospitals and have the wells cleaned of filth. Above all, he should collect 'good intelligence on the Arabs' and respect 'the country's muftis and principal sheiks . . . Little by little he should accustom the population in our manners and ways of thinking, while leaving them great latitude in their interior affairs, all being founded on their divine laws expressed by the Koran.'[34]

He ordered Menou to march his division eastward to Rosetta, a small city at the mouth of the west branch of the River Nile. Menou was to administer Rosetta guided by the essential understanding that success depended on maintaining the goodwill of 'the muftis, imams, religion and backing the principle chiefs who rule the masses of the population', while disarming those who might oppose the occupation. He was to gather into a militia youths from 16 to 20 years old, 'half by free will, half by force, under the pretext of teaching them the profession of arms but for serving as hostages the instant that circumstances demand'. Menou would convene the chiefs, listen to their views, explain the purpose of French rule and send the three most prominent leaders to Bonaparte's headquarters where they would serve as advisors or hostages according to circumstances.[35]

Bonaparte then led 21,000 troops on what became a hellish five-day, 57-mile march across the desert toward the Nile, while a flotilla of fifteen gunboats packed with 600 marines and led by Admiral Jean-Baptiste Perrée ascended the river's west branch. Although he marched his troops at night and rested them during the day, nothing sheltered them from the blazing summer sun. Their thirst grew more agonizing. There were two oasis towns along the way but the lead troops swiftly drained the wells, leaving not a drop for those who followed. The men did slake some of their thirst by devouring melons in the surrounding fields.

Arab horsemen shadowed the army like wolves to prey on the weak. The army fought off charges by 600 of them at Damanhur. The fate of stragglers was horrific. Those the Arabs did not immediately kill were often gang-raped, mutilated or tortured to death; some were released to stumble back to the army and spread terrifying stories. Bonaparte attributed Arab cruelty 'to the miserable lives they lead, exposed all day to the burning sands and the relentless sun, without drinking water. They are pitiless . . . the most hideous species of savage man conceivable.'[36] He found that 'the interior population is composed of a different species, all accustomed to beating or being beaten, tyrannizing or being tyrannized'.[37]

The French finally reached the Nile at El Rahmenieh where the flotilla awaited them on 10 July. There Mourad Bey, Egypt's army commander, attacked with about 3,000 cavalry and 2,000 infantry. Bonaparte had his regiments form squares and pour volleys into the charging horsemen who soon dispersed. Mourad Bey and his men withdrew up the Nile valley as the French plodded wearily after them, while the flotilla accompanied them on the river. The French repelled an attack at Chobrakhyr on 13 July.

Bonaparte found 'the Mamelukes extremely brave and form an excellent corps of light cavalry, richly dressed, armed with great care and mounted on horses of the best quality'.[38] He admired how the 'warriors of this intrepid cavalry come to die in their ranks, after having mass fired . . . muskets and pistols at the heads of our men. Some, with their horses killed beneath them, slip forward on their bellies beneath our bayonets and cut the legs of our soldiers.'[39] Yet even the greatest bravery could not overcome the French army's discipline and tactics:

> Squares are not formed with more than three ranks and on heights often only two ranks. Officers order two ranks to fire

when the cavalry is within 120 feet . . . Skirmishers always march by fours when facing Bedouins or Mamelukes then form a square . . . Mamelukes fight without order; they form a whirlwind on the flanks and throw themselves on the rear of the line.[40]

Despite winning every battle, the army's morale was near rock bottom. Bonaparte recalled 'the army's disgust, discontent and desperation after reaching Egypt'.[41] The men hated everything about Egypt, the featureless, oven-like desert, the barbarous enemy, the wretched peasants, the filthy towns, the crocodiles guarding the Nile, the bland food and foul water, the unavailability of the women and the lack of wine. They longed to return to France. As he could do was urge them onward toward eventual glory and riches.

To the excitement of Bonaparte and his troops, the Pyramids appeared on the southern horizon on July 19. He rested his men for a day then led them forward on 21 July. The Pyramids rose slowly before them on the west bank along with Cairo's minarets on the east bank. Then 12,000 cavalry and 20,000 infantry led by Ibrahim Bey, Egypt's governor, and Mourad Bey appeared before them. Although the Pyramids were still miles away, Bonaparte was inspired to call out to his men that 'From the heights of those pyramids, forty centuries looks down upon you'.[42] He ordered his regiments to form squares with artillery in the gaps between them. The massed musket and cannon volleys decimated the repeated charges. He then ordered his troops to rout the demoralized enemy. The Egyptians lost perhaps 2,000 men killed or wounded in the fighting, drowned trying to escape across the river or captured. The French suffered about 300 casualties. As in previous battles, the French looted every enemy prisoner or corpse they could reach, including some cadavers fished from the Nile before crocodiles could devour them. Ibrahim Bey withdrew with the remnants of his followers eastward to Gaza while Mourad Bey led his men south up the Nile valley.

The following morning, Bonaparte wrote to Cairo's 'sheiks and notables', assuring them of his good will and urging them not to worry 'because no one desires more to contribute to your happiness than me'. He informed them that during the battle 'most Mamelukes had been killed or captured and I am pursing the rest'. He called on them to send over a delegation and enough large boats to convey his army across the Nile, while preparing bread, meat and forage to feed his troops and animals.[43]

The authorities surrendered Cairo on 24 July. Bonaparte deployed his troops to key positions in the city or in camps on the outskirts and set up his headquarters in the citadel. He confiscated most Mameluke mansions to serve as barracks for his men and sold the contents to raise money. However, he ensured that the palaces and harems of Mourad Bey and Ibrahim Bey were guarded, at once preventing looting and rape while holding the women, children and slaves hostage. He had a dozen cannons and four mortars placed on the citadel's walls so that they could 'batter the city and all the principal avenues'.[44] To transport and supply his troops, he gathered as many horses, camels, mules and donkeys and as much wheat, rice, fruit and vegetables as possible. He took over Cairo's gunpowder and cartridge factory and tasked his scientists to improve its quality and quantity.[45]

Elsewhere he deployed troops to occupy Egypt's six lower provinces and assigned each a French commander, an intendant and an administrative commission to work with a diwan or council of leading Muslim clerics and Coptic priests.[46] He had Desaix and Leclerc pursue Mourad Bey and Ibrahim Bey, respectively, but hoped to entice both chiefs into submitting peacefully; neither replied to his entreaties. Leclerc's column failed to catch its elusive foe. Mourad Bey turned on Desaix at Sediman on 7 October, but was driven off after losing 400 to 143 French casualties.[47] Thereafter Mourad Bey in Upper Egypt and Ibrahim Bey in Gaza waited patiently like vultures perched near a dying animal.

Amidst the elation of his conquest, Bonaparte was devastated to learn that Josephine chronically cheated on him. His reluctant informant was Junot, whose lover was had been one of Josephine's maids. Berthier confirmed what was common knowledge. The news plunged Bonaparte into a deep depression that caused him to question everything. To Joseph, he wrote: 'I am disillusioned with human nature. I need solitude and isolation. Grandeur bores me. My feelings are desiccated. Glory has faded.'[48] Then came even more gut-wrenching news.

* * *

Amid his array of actions and worries Bonaparte had little time to think of the French fleet until he 'received several letters from the admiral and I was astonished that he was still there at Aboukir'. He wrote Brueys urging him 'not to lose an hour either entering Alexandria or sailing to Corfu . . . It seems that Admiral Brueys had not wanted to go to Corfu before being certain that he could not enter the port of Alexandria and the army, of which he had no news for a long time, was in a position of not needing to retreat.'[49] Engineers discovered that larger warships with 74 or more guns could be got into the harbour only by removing their ordnance. On 27 July, Bonaparte wrote Brueys that 'I don't doubt that by now you will be in the port with all your fleet'.⁵⁰ On the 30th, he urged Brueys either 'to quickly enter the port of Alexandria or . . . transport yourself to the port of Corfu . . . In the second case be sure to leave . . . the frigates at Alexandria.'⁵¹ The failure of Brueys to do either would have catastrophic consequences.

Brueys had anchored his warships bow to stern with about 150 yards of water between each in Aboukir Bay a dozen miles east of Alexandria. He had failed to post frigates as pickets a dozen or so miles out at sea. Around half of each crew was ashore late on the afternoon of 1 August, when Nelson's fleet appeared and immediately attacked. Of the thirteen French ships-of-the-line, Nelson's fleet sank two and captured nine; only two escaped. Although nearly all the British ships were badly battered, none sank. British gunners and marines killed over 1,700 French, wounded 1,500 and captured 3,305, while suffering only 218 dead and 678 wounded.⁵²

News of the catastrophe shook Bonaparte profoundly and he struggled to find meaning and hope in it: 'If, in this disastrous event, [Brueys] made mistakes, he atoned for them by dying a glorious death. The fates wanted, in this event like so many others, to prove that, if they had given us great predominance on the continent, they gave the empire of the seas to our rival.'⁵³ He appointed Admiral Honoré Ganteaume to command the remnants of the fleet and issued him this veiled rebuke and challenge: 'The situation in which you find yourself . . . is horrible. When you have not perished in this circumstance, it then destined for you to avenge our navy and our friends.'⁵⁴

Vengeance, however, was impossible. With just a few frigates, Ganteaume was powerless before the enemy blockade. On the night of 8 October, thirty-eight Tuscan and Neapolitan merchant ships tried to sail from Alexandria through the blockade. British warships captured and burned twenty-eight of them. Beginning on 24 October, the combined British, Russian and Turkish fleet bombarded Aboukir's fort, the defenders repelled a landing by British troops. In November, Egyptian forces, supplied by the British, harassed Alexandria and cut its water supply. Kléber responded by sending out expeditions to repair the canal and chase the raiders.

* * *

The news of Aboukir Bay at once devastated the morale of the French who were now marooned in Egypt and lifted the spirits of the Egyptians who hoped to destroy their conquerors. The blockade severed nearly all contact with France. That silence exacerbated homesickness among the French, including its commander, in an alien land. Bonaparte ended his 17 December letter to the Directorate by writing that 'we await news from France and Europe; it's a lively need for our souls because, if the nation's glory needs us, we are inconsolable for not being there'.[55] He tried to inspire his troops with this proclamation: 'We have the duty to achieve grand things. We will do them. We will establish a great empire. Although we do not master the sea and are separated from our country, no seawater divides Africa and Asia.'[56]

Bonaparte redoubled his efforts to forge good relations with the Egyptians. The key was the Diwan or governing council. As his commissioners to the Diwan, he tapped scientists Gaspard Monge and Claude Berthollet, charging them with having him 'make the populace . . . understand how essential it was to ignore . . . perfidious and baseless rumours' that excite them to revolt. Instead, the populace should 'swear obedience, live harmoniously with the French and unite their efforts to repress the Arab thieves in their devastating campaigns'. The Egyptians must understand that the French 'are just people; that we are committed only to the country's good and establishing a reign of justice'.[57] He convened a national Diwan with 177 delegates from the thirteen provinces. When he addressed the Diwan on 5 October, he shared his hope eventually to transform it into a national assembly through which to govern Egypt. He was the first of a seemingly endless procession of Westerners who believe that democracy is the salvation for the Arab world's mass poverty, corruption, incompetence and brutality.

He found trying to govern, let alone reform, Egypt a dismaying challenge: 'It is difficult to find a land more fertile and the people more miserable, ignorant and brutalized.'[58] He was determined to change all that. Sooner or later he thought of nearly everything vital for ruling Egypt. He wanted each province's administration to pay for itself by 'promoting commerce and opening new sources of wealth and prosperity'.[59] He established an efficient system of collecting taxes. To both raise additional revenues and punish the enemy, all Mameluke property, including slaves, was confiscated and sold. He imposed 383,448 francs' worth of taxes on the Sultan's leading officers, raised by squeezing more taxes from the subjects they ruled; 785,328 francs on the cities, with the four largest being Alexandria with 237,897 francs, Suez with 214,146 francs, Cairo with 152,094 francs and Damietta with 81,769 francs; land taxes of 15,242,654 francs; business taxes of 383,448 francs; industrial and consumer taxes of 785,328 francs; and taxes on non-Muslims of 88,503 francs that would have gone to the Sultan. These taxes soared because the enemy blockade reduced revenue from international trade to a trickle. The taxes only partly paid for French expenses of 17,092,049 francs in 1798, 25,278,486 francs in 1799 and 6,810,428 francs in 1800 respectively or 57,504,463 francs in total.[60]

He devoted a portion of his revenues to making Egypt more prosperous and habitable. He had the streets cleared of filth and fresh wells dug. He had transportation and irrigation canals refurbished. He assigned a team of engineers to find the best route for a canal linking the Nile and the Red Sea. Although he established a quarantine station at Alexandria, plague broke out there in December 1798 and would kill many of his troops and subjects. He ordered a crackdown on crime and was ruthless in suppressing those committed by Frenchmen and Egyptians alike. In January 1799, two soldiers were convicted and publicly hanged for murdering three Egyptian women.[61]

Most importantly, Bonaparte established the Institute of Egypt, with Monge its first president, on 22 August 1798. The Institute's thirty-six members were split among four sections, literature and art, political economy, physics, and mathematics; Bonaparte was the vice president and a member of the mathematics section. The Institute's purpose was twofold, to support the French administrative, military and economic missions and to research and publish reports on all dimensions of the country. Scholars accompanied each military expedition to study any ruins along the march. He spent several days with a team of scientists camped beside the Pyramids to measure and explore them.

Napoleon later recalled these as his halcyon days:

> The seductions of an oriental conquest turned me aside from thoughts of Europe more than I would have believed . . . In Egypt I found myself freed from the obstacles of an irksome civilization. I was full of dreams . . . I saw myself founding a religion, marching into Asia, riding an elephant, a turban on my head and in my hand a new Koran that I would have composed to my own needs. In my undertakings I would have combined the experiences of the two worlds, exploiting for my own profit the threat of all history . . . The time I spent in Egypt was my life's most beautiful.[62]

Like many foreign visitors over the centuries, Bonaparte observed dismal character flaws in most Egyptians, Muslim and Christian alike: 'We are constantly harassed by swarms of Arabs who are the worse thieves and villains on earth.'[63] The Christian Copts were 'mischievous and shameful . . . but we have to care for them because they are the only ones who have any semblance of ably governing the country'.[64] On 7 December 1798, he approved a Copt petition that let them 'publicly exercise their faith as in Europe' and 'arm themselves'. He promised to severely punish villages that, in their revolts, murdered Copts. In all, he intended 'to restore to the Copt nation their dignity and rights inseparable from being human, that had been lost'.[65]

He was always well aware that he had hearts and minds to cultivate far beyond Egypt itself. He had copies of his proclamations distributed across North Africa, the Holy Land and Turkey. His most important audience was in Constantinople. He wrote to Vizier Nassif Pasha, Sultan Selim's right-hand man, proclaiming that he had liberated Egypt from the Mamelukes and wanted peace with the Ottoman Empire: 'I beg Your Excellency, to send someone armed with plenipotentiary powers to Cairo.'[66] He wrote to Syria's governor, Abdallah Pasha, assuring him that 'we are not enemies of the Muslims and that the only reason we are in Egypt is to punish the beys and avenge the outrages that they had made against our commerce. Thus I desire that you will be persuaded that I want the most perfect friendship to prevail between us.'[67] He asked France's envoy at Tripoli to inform the Bey that 'tomorrow we celebrate the Prophet's birthday with the grandest pomp' and that the French army would protect all caravans bound for Mecca across Egypt.[68] He assured Mecca's Sharif that 'we are the friends of Muslims and the religion of the prophet; we desire to do all that can please and favour the religion'.[69] He sent Pierre Beauchamp, an astronomer and diplomat, on a peace mission to Constantinople; Selim ordered Beauchamp imprisoned in the Castle of Seven Towers along with other French diplomats and merchants.[70]

Ahmed Djezzar, ominously nicknamed 'the Butcher', was Palestine's governor with his capital at Acre. Bonaparte first wrote to him on 22 August 1798, explaining that he came to Egypt to war against the Mamelukes, not against Islam. Indeed, after capturing Malta, he had liberated 2,000 Muslim galley slaves and in Egypt he protected Muslims and celebrated Mohammad's birthday. He sought good diplomatic and trade relations with Palestine.[71] Djezzar replied indirectly by having French merchants in Jaffa robbed and imprisoned.[72] After receiving a plea for help from them, Bonaparte fired off a letter to Djezzar, expressing his 'surprise' that Arab officials were arresting French merchants while he welcomed and protected Muslim merchants. He then attributed the story to 'misinformation', which he assured himself 'would not last and that the governors, listening better to their interests, would assure the tranquillity of the people under their rule'.[73]

To the Directorate, he vented his frustration that neither Selim nor Djezzar 'had replied to a single overture that I had made . . . and that Ottoman officials had arrested French consuls and merchants'. Atop that 'I don't know where Talleyrand is'. He insisted that Talleyrand's diplomatic mission to Constantinople was essential for promoting French interests and that he 'must be held to his word and sent there'. He wondered whether English warships had intercepted his letters.[74] It would be months before he learned that Talleyrand had never set forth to Constantinople while Selim had the French envoy Pierre Ruffin imprisoned in the notorious Castle of Seven Towers on 2 September.

Nothing came from any of his diplomatic initiatives. Nonetheless, he reported on 8 September to the Directorate that:

> . . . all goes perfectly well here. The country is pacified and trade expands for us. The rest is the work of time. All the institutions that can accelerate progress are doing so. The country generates all the money needed to pay the army . . . Never has a colony offered more advantages . . . Master of Egypt, France will eventually be the master of India. The government of England knows that. I have no doubt this will be the means of guaranteeing a general peace.[75]

Bonaparte's report glossed over a vicious circle in which the invaders had trapped themselves. The Egyptians longed to purge the foreign infidels from their country. Sporadic resistance continued mostly with the murder of stray Frenchmen. Bonaparte imposed the rule of collective responsibility on districts, villages and tribes: 'If a Frenchman is killed and the tribe does not arrest the murderers, all the tribe will be held responsible.'[76] But French retaliation against neighbourhoods or villages where murders occurred only provoked those communities to seek vengeance.

The violence escalated. In words that echo louder today than then, Bonaparte warned Kléber that 'the biggest thing that we have to fear is terror'.[77] He felt compelled to fight terror with terror: 'It is necessary to take a tone suitable to make the people obey; and to obey, for them, is to fear.' Thus 'each day I have five or six heads cut off in the streets of Cairo'.[78] He had a proclamation issued that expressed 'to the inhabitants that I am very discontented with their conduct . . . I will entirely disarm them . . . and at the slightest problem I will . . . burn their villages.'[79] He took the twenty-five most prominent leaders as hostages to ensure the good behaviour of their respective clans. These harsh measures 'were the only way to master this country'.[80] He wrote to Murat that 'if the Arabs that you attacked are those who murdered our people . . . I intend to destroy them; let me know the force necessary to do so, study the position they occupy, then . . . envelope and give a terrible example to the country.'[81] Hostages were held in Cairo's citadel. Yet he also recognized that the carrot was as important as the stick. He approved the amnesty that Dugua had given a town and told him 'to take all measures to gain the population's confidence and let them re-establish their commerce'.[82] French officials granted amnesty to those who pledged allegiance.

Muslim clerics mobilized their congregations to gather arms and await word to rid Egypt of the infidels. Shortly after daybreak on 21 October, a mob murdered General Dominique Dupuy, Cairo's commander, and his escort. That ignited a general revolt with attacks on isolated French contingents and twenty-one sick soldiers whose throats the Egyptians cut. The quarter surrounding the Grand Mosque and al-Azhar University were the revolt's epicentre. The Muslims emplaced a dozen or so cannons on its walls and barricaded the maze of narrow streets leading to it.

Bonaparte was across the Nile inspecting an arsenal at Giza when he learned of the revolt. He sent orders for his commanders in and around Cairo to converge toward the centre of resistance. The French fought their way through the city, slaughtering anyone who resisted and many who did not. Cannons were wheeled into place to bombard the mosque and university. It was a typically lopsided victory. In crushing the revolt, the French killed at least 2,500 people, while suffering around 300 casualties. He had hundreds of Egyptians rounded up, imprisoned and interrogated with these questions: Why have they been arrested? Why did they pillage their city? Why did they take up arms against the French? Who armed them? What were their professions? Where were their homes? Where were they during the revolt?[83] What he did not order was torture. Indeed, for practical and thus moral reasons, he outlawed the practice of beating prisoners until they confessed: 'It has been well known for all time that . . . torturing prisoners never does any good.'[84]

He called on the clerics to condemn the revolt and to support French rule. A proclamation was circulated with the same message in Arabic and Turkish. He summoned the head imams and sheikhs to tell them: 'I know that many of you have been weak, but I want to believe that none of you is a criminal; what the Prophet especially condemned was ingratitude and rebellion . . . The el-Azhar mosque has been taken by assault; blood has flowed. Go and purify it . . . Those who are dead have satisfied my vengeance. Tell the people of Cairo that I want to continue to be merciful . . . I pardon everyone.'[85] He redoubled his efforts to convince

Egypt's leaders and masses alike that he 'loved the Koran and the Prophet and that he was sincerely devoted to making the Arab people happy'.[86] To Mecca's sharif and all other Muslims he proclaimed that 'There is no other god but God and Muhammad is his prophet'.[87] In doing so, Bonaparte tried to give the impression that he was a Muslim.

The surviving rebels fled to Suez. Bonaparte and General Bon's division pursued them; 400 camels carried their supplies. At Suez the French routed the rebels who fled to join Ibrahim Bey in Palestine. Bonaparte garrisoned Suez and had his engineers study the possibility of digging a canal north to link the Red Sea and the Mediterranean. During one scouting trip, Bonaparte and his escort nearly drowned from a fast rising tide. Scores of Mamelukes lingered to harass French patrols.

* * *

Bonaparte spent a lot of time gazing north-eastward, trying to imagine the enemy forces massing in the Holy Land a couple of hundred or so miles beyond the horizon. His army's occupation of Egypt would never be secure as long as an enemy army could march against him from that direction. He would have to invade Palestine if he could not convince Djezzar to submit to French rule. On 19 November, he wrote Djezzar a letter shorn of the flowery verbiage favoured by Arabs and instead asserted blunt choices:

> I don't want to war against you if you are not my enemy, but it is time that you explain yourself. If you continue to give refuge to Ibrahim Bey on the Egyptian frontier, I will regard that as a mark of hostility toward me. If you want to live in peace with me, distance Ibrahim Bey forty leagues from the Egyptian frontier and free commerce between Damietta and Syria. Then I promise you I will respect your states and free entirely commerce between Egypt and Syria, by land and by sea.[88]

When Djezzar again replied with contemptuous silence, Bonaparte felt that he had no choice but to conquer the Holy Land and depose him. On 9 December 1798, he ordered General Caffarelli to put his engineer division to work mapping, improving the route, digging or deepening wells and fortifying and stockpiling supplies at key points from Cairo across the Sinai Peninsula to Gaza.[89]

Strategically Bonaparte peered far beyond the Middle East. In late January 1799, he fired off his latest volley of letters to Muslim leaders, trying to justify France's conquest of Egypt and forge good relations.[90] His most intriguing letter was to Mysore's Sultan Tippoo-Sahib, then warring against British India: 'You have already been informed of my arrival on the Red Sea's shore with a numerous and invincible army, filled with desire to liberate you from England's iron yoke.' He asked Tippoo to send him an envoy with whom to confer.[91]

The campaign's build-up took three and a half months until early February 1799, when Bonaparte led 13,150 troops across the Sinai desert.[92] The first enemy resistance was the 2,300-man garrison at El Arish. The French took the town but not the castle on 9 February. The artillery train arrived and was deployed to bombard the castle. The garrison finally surrendered on the 19th and was allowed to march away after promising to fight no more in that campaign. Gaza's garrison surrendered without a fight on 25 February. He paroled Gaza's defenders then had the fort repaired, filled with supplies and garrisoned with 250 men.[93]

Bonaparte and his men were now in the Holy Land. Acre lay 100 miles north along the coast. While he found Palestine 'a very beautiful country', the weather literally dampened his excitement at invading Asia, as it was as rainy, chilly and blustery as a Parisian winter.[94] Yet he could take cold comfort that the same nasty weather inhibited British naval operations. As usual, he tried to enlist local chiefs and their sullen peoples in his cause with proclamations in Arabic that those few who were literate could read to the others. He accused Djezzar of starting the war and vowed to free the Palestinians from his despotic rule. He promised to protect their religion and property. He boasted that 'human efforts are useless against me' and that 'all good comes from God; God is behind all victories'. He insisted that 'I am terrible against my enemies and I am good to my friends and especially forgiving and charitable toward poor people'.[95] He demanded that the Arabs choose peace or war; 'if they want peace, they must chase the Mamelukes from their land and be loyal to me'.[96]

He anticipated that the campaign would climax with the siege of Acre, Djezzar's capital. The siege artillery and its ammunition were so heavy that they had to be conveyed by sea. Somehow those vessels had to slip past the British blockade and sail to Jaffa, which, after the French captured it, would serve as the advanced port to besiege Acre. With the threat posed by the British fleet, he devoted March to securing the route to Jaffa. He opened the siege of Jaffa on 3 March and sent in two envoys with a message to surrender. Jaffa's commander had the envoys decapitated and the heads displayed. On the 9th, after his gunners breached the wall, Bonaparte ordered an assault. His troops captured Jaffa after five hours of fierce hand-to-hand combat, then sacked the town.

Although Bonaparte lamented that his troops had committed 'all the horrors of war that never appeared to me more hideous', he committed his own war crime.[97] Among the 2,500 or so troops who surrendered were around 900 who he had previously paroled. Enraged, he issued this order: 'Conduct all the gunners and other Turks taken with arms in their hands at Jaffa to the seaside and have them shot, doing so in a manner that no one escapes.'[98] Late that day, he casually mentioned that 'the garrison have all perished either during the assault or by being put to the sword'.[99] He justified the slaughter in legal, practical and moral terms. He argued that the soldiers legally merited execution for violating their promise not to fight the French. More importantly, he insisted that the Muslim way of war was utterly merciless, that Muslims respected the ruthless and scorned the soft-hearted. Thus to defeat Muslims one had to match them in cruelty. His immediate intent was to intimidate Djezzar into surrendering. As his troops massacred the prisoners, he wrote to Djezzar with a choice of peace or war to the death:

> My intention was never to make war; my only goal was to chase the Mamelukes; you have not responded to a single overture that I made you . . . I desire that you distance Ibrahim Bey from Egypt's frontiers . . . The provinces of Gaza, Ramleh and Jaffa are in my power. I have treated with generosity those of your troops who put themselves in my hands. I have been severe toward those who have violated the laws of war . . . You have no real reason to be my enemy . . . My friend, be the enemy of the Mamelukes and the English . . . I can provide you so much good and I can inflict upon you so much evil . . . The 24th of this month I will march on Saint Jean of Acre; it is necessary that I receive a response from you before that.[100]

Djezzar replied by ordering the beheading of the courier who brought Bonaparte's letter.

All along the French lived off the land, slaughtering and grilling dogs, donkeys and camels. They suffered terribly from the lack of water, with wells either non-existent, dry or poisoned. The capture of El Arish, Gaza and Jaffa with warehouses filled with provisions alleviated some of army's hunger for a while. Arab, Armenian and Greek Christians helped the French army mostly by establishing hospitals for the sick and wounded; the Muslims would massacre many of them after Bonaparte's army returned to Egypt.[101]

The French pulverized an Ottoman army before Haifa and took that port on 15 March. Haifa is at the south end of a bay with Acre on the north side at a peninsula's tip. Bonaparte deployed his army across that peninsula's base and opened his siege on 18 March. It would last nearly two months and it would fail. One man above all prevented Bonaparte's army from taking Acre, Captain Sidney Smith. Of Bonaparte's countless antagonists throughout his life, none irritated him more than Smith.[102]

Smith arrived with two ships-of-the-line at Acre on 18 March 18. He landed 800 marines, sailors and gunners, munitions and dozens of guns to line the tops of Acre's walls. His engineers, led by the French royalist émigré Louis Phéllippeaux, supervised strengthening the city's defences. His ships-of-the-line captured the vessels carrying the siege artillery as they approached Haifa on 22 March. He even conducted biological warfare; under a flag of truce he landed French prisoners afflicted with the plague, which spread rapidly. To top it off, he cheekily challenged Bonaparte to a duel. Bonaparte was just as cheeky in his reply. He dismissed Smith as his inferior and 'would not come forth to a duel unless the English could fetch Marlborough from his grave'.[103]

The French faced a swelling threat to their rear. Word arrived that Pasha Abdullah of Damascus was marching with 10,000 infantry and 2,500 cavalry to Acre. Bonaparte dispatched troops under Murat, Kléber, Junot and Bon to attack the enemy's advanced forces, then he joined them for the decisive battle near Mount Tabor on 16 April. Although outnumbered ten to one, the French attacked and slaughtered the Syrians. He later admitted that 'the battle of Mount Tabor re-established their reputation a bit obscured by Acre's siege'.[104]

Bonaparte led his victorious troops back to Acre. Without heavy artillery to batter down Acre's walls, he had his troops dig a mine beneath a key tower and pack it with 3,000lbs of gunpowder. The mine was detonated on 24 April but the explosion caused limited damage. Nonetheless, Bonaparte ordered an assault on the high, narrow breach. The defenders repelled it, killing, wounding and capturing hundreds of French. The bombardment resumed to chip away at Acre's walls. That was the first of nine assaults with the final on launched on 10 May.

When that attack failed, he bitterly broke off the siege. To the Directorate, he justified that decision because 'the season is too advanced, the goal that I had sought has been fulfilled and Egypt calls me'. He claimed to have 'reduced Acre to a pile of stones'. In all, 'I have been perfectly happy with the army in all the events and in this type of war so new to Europeans. It revealed the true courage and talents of warriors who were unfazed by everything and overcame every type of deprivation.'[105]

THE PHARAOH

Bonaparte and 11,133 troops marched or rode back to Egypt. The campaign cost his army around 500 killed in battle, 700 killed from disease, 200 mortally wounded, 1,500 wounded who rejoined their units and 85 amputees. Bonaparte had a surgeon give opium overdoses to those who could not be evacuated and would likely suffer a worse fate at the hands of the Arabs.[106]

Turning his back on the Orient profoundly disappointed Bonaparte. He later insisted that had he taken Acre, he would have gone on to conquer India and reign there because 'only the Orient awaited such a man'.[107] That, of course, was pure fantasy. The Royal Navy prevented a French expedition by sea and a gauntlet of heavily-armed empires along the way any march by land. Indeed Smith, a fellow existentialist, issued just such a warning in a taunting farewell letter:

> This last word ought not to escape my mouth – I who ought not to love you . . . but circumstances remind me to wish that you would reflect on the instability of human affairs . . . Believe me, General, adopt sentiments more moderate; that a man will not be your enemy who shall tell your that Asia is not a theatre made for your glory. This letter is a little revenge that I give myself.[108]

Bonaparte dismissed Smith as 'a young fool who wants to make his fortune and tries to show off. The best way to punish him is never to respond to him.'[109]

Actually Bonaparte now was obsessed not with Asia but with returning to France as soon as possible. During talks with Phéllippeaux over a prisoner exchange, he learned of the disasters that France's armies had suffered since he had embarked on his own campaign. The worst was a combined Austrian and Russian army that had overrun all his Italian conquests. Suddenly his Egyptian conquest seemed not just a sideshow but a dead-end and he longed 'to throw himself in the ocean of events that presented themselves in his thoughts'.[110]

* * *

Bonaparte returned to Cairo on 14 June 1799. He hoped but could not know that he had only a couple months left in Egypt.[111] Word of his reverse in Palestine reached Egypt ahead of his army. Revolts in Cairo and elsewhere erupted but were brutally crushed. He tried to cement that victory with his latest public relations campaign. He had the Diwan spread the word that he sought for Egyptians 'only their happiness and prosperity and, if the Nile is the first river of the East, the people of Egypt, under my government, must be the first of peoples'.[112] He repeatedly echoed to Muslim leaders their faith's central tenet that 'there is no god but God and Muhammad is his prophet'.[113] He went so far as to tell them that he shared their condemnation of Christians, at least the English and Russian versions, for believing in three gods, the Father, Son and Holy Spirit. He insisted that God himself backed his efforts to transform Egypt from despotism, poverty and chaos to prosperity, order and justice. All those who opposed him also opposed God and thus committed blasphemy and betrayed Islam.[114] How many Muslims actually believed this is impossible to say. Bonaparte's words were belied by the mostly Christian soldiers that he led and all the death and destruction they had inflicted since they had stepped ashore.

Captain Sidney Smith remained Bonaparte's nemesis. As he and his two ships-of-the-line shadowed Bonaparte's retreat from Palestine, he sent messages via small vessels to Pasha Hussein Mustafa, who commanded the Turkish army at Rhodes, urging him to invade Egypt. Smith joined the blockade off Alexandria. Bonaparte was with a scientific team at the Pyramids on 15 July, when a courier galloped up with word that a Turkish flotilla of 60 vessels had disembarked 8,000 troops under Mustafa at Aboukir Bay four days earlier.[115] He immediately ordered all his forces except skeleton garrisons in Lower Egypt to quickmarch to El Rahmenieh; Desaix was to evacuate Upper Egypt.

Mustafa camped his army on the beach at Aboukir Bay to await Bonaparte's inevitable onslaught. Fearing that Bonaparte would strike his rear and sever his supply line to the Turkish fleet, he did not march his troops a dozen miles westward and besiege Alexandria. All the Turks did was capture the small castle with sixty defenders at Aboukir Bay.

Bonaparte deployed 8,000 troops to face the invading army on 25 July. His plan was simple. Massed artillery blasted the Turkish lines for an hour before the infantry and cavalry charged to rout the remnants. The Turks probably lost 3,500 killed or drowned in the surf trying to escape, while Mustafa and 1,000 or so of his men along with 50 flags and 18 guns were captured and 2,500 or so crowded into Aboukir castle. The French suffered perhaps 220 dead and 750 wounded. When Aboukir surrendered on 2 August, virtually the entire invading force had been captured or killed.[116]

Bonaparte followed up his crushing victory with a long letter to Vizier Youssef Pasha, detailing his army's destruction of the Turkish army and calling for negotiations that would not just lead to peace but an alliance against the Russians and British who were the Ottoman Empire's true enemies. While he awaited a reply from Youssef that never came, Smith gleefully sent him newspapers detailing French defeats in Europe and the loss of all that he had gained in Italy. That infuriated Bonaparte and he became stir-crazy to get back to France at the first chance.[117]

Before Bonaparte returned to Cairo, he secretly had Admiral Ganteaume prepare in Alexandria's harbour two frigates and two smaller warships to lift anchor and unfurl sails at a moment's notice. On 19 August, he received a message from Ganteaume that Smith's two ships-of-the-line had vanished, leaving just a handful of small Turkish warships behind; Smith had gone to Cyprus to replenish his water and food supplies. Bonaparte quietly informed his inner circle, including Berthier, Murat, Bessières, Marmont, Monge, Berthollet, Denon, Perceval, his stepson Eugène, his brother Louis and a company of his Guides or elite troops, to pack their bags because they were going home. They reached Alexandria harbour on 22 August.

General Menou, Alexandria's commander, was incensed when Bonaparte explained that he and his entourage were leaving. Bonaparte handed Menou a long letter to forward to General Kléber, giving him Egypt's command along with detailed military and diplomatic instructions.[118] He had a proclamation printed and distributed to his soldiers that explained: 'News from Europe decided me to leave for France . . . It is painful to part with soldiers that I love, but this absence will only be momentary.'[119] He sent the Directory a letter explaining why he was returning to Paris: 'I must find myself where my presence can be the most useful. Animated by these sentiments, I will wrap myself in my cloak and leave by ship.'[120] The four vessels set sail on 23 August. He had few regrets about leaving Egypt, believing that he had accomplished all that was possible there. It was now time to step boldly upon the latest stage of his destiny.

Chapter 4

The Usurper

'The Revolution's fault is to have destroyed much and built nothing . . . Who will end the revolution? That's a problem that time keeps secret.'

'In what state had I left France and in what state have I found it! I left you in peace and found you at war! I left you with conquests and the enemy passes our frontiers!'

After forty-five anxious days and nights, the flotilla dropped anchor near Antibes on 9 October 1799. Napoleon Bonaparte's Oriental adventure had lasted nearly a year and a half. He stepped ashore eager to return to the heart of French power. Countless people rejoiced to learn that their hero had returned. Archchancellor Jean Cambacérès recalled that: 'The general's march was a veritable triumph. Everywhere he was received amidst applause and acclamations of universal joy.'[1]

Bonaparte and his entourage entered Paris on 16 October and dispersed to their homes. His first priority was to confront Josephine with allegations of her infidelity. She threw herself at his feet and begged forgiveness. With his anger spent, his love for her re-emerged and he tearfully embraced her. She then stunned him with a bill for 325,000 francs for the lovely chateau called Malmaison seven miles west of Paris that she had purchased in April 1799. He would eventually pay off that debt along with the mountain of others that she had accumulated. Intriguing news alleviated some of the anguish and anger that Josephine's capriciousness inflicted on him. Joseph and Lucien informed him that a plot was forming to overthrow the Directorate and was looking for a general to lead it.[2]

He was then just 30 years old but had packed a lifetime of adventures and achievements into his previous dozen years. Although he had been not just a fervent republican but even a Jacobin for a while during the

Revolution, the Terror purged most of his idealism. In July 1797, he penned these blunt lines: 'The Revolution's fault is to have destroyed much and built nothing . . . Who will end the revolution? That's a problem that time keeps secret.'[3] He elaborated his views a couple of months later: 'Despite our pride, our thousand and one pamphlets, our harangues . . . and our boasts, we are very ignorant of political morality. We have not defined the proper powers for the executive, legislature and judiciary.'[4] Now Bonaparte now determined to impose his own designs upon France's government and governance.

* * *

So just what was so bad about the Directorate?[5] It was reviled for its corruption and incompetence, for soaring prices and joblessness, plunging wages and trade and defeats in 1798 and 1799 that lost most of what Bonaparte had won with his stunning Italian campaign capped by the Treaty of Campo Formio in October 1797. Bonaparte scorned the system and those who ran it: 'The five Directors and their families shared Luxembourg palace . . . They formed five little courts placed side by side and agitated by the passions of the women, the children and the valets . . . A Director was neither a minister, nor a prefect, nor a general, he was only a fifth of an executive.'[6]

The Directors lived in fear of being overthrown. They had crushed a proto-communist conspiracy led by François Babeuf in November 1796 and a royalist coup led by Generals Charles Pichegru and Balthazar Barthélemy in September 1797. They had good reason to believe that another attempt was only a matter of time. The army was split between regular and National Guard regiments. Discontent mostly afflicted regular regiments that were usually posted at the front. The troops and their leaders blamed government ineptness and greed for the infuriating shortages of provisions and munitions along with the humiliating defeats that they suffered. The Directors hoped that the relatively well-fed and unbloodied National Guard regiments in Paris would remain loyal and thus deter a coup.

A coup would only be the latest change of government. In the decade since Louis XVI convened the Estates General in May 1789, France had had an absolute monarchy, a constitutional monarchy, a republic, a terrorist dictatorship and, for the past four years, the Directorate. It had been a blood-soaked decade from the storming of the Bastille in 1789, the wars since 1792 and the prolonged terror from April 1793 to July 1794, with sporadic massacres before and since. Revolutionaries had executed or slaughtered at least 30,000 people during those ten years.[7] France's latest constitution passed the legislature on 22 August 1795 and was approved by a plebiscite on 23 September 1795. The government consisted of a five-man executive called the Directorate and a bilateral legislature with a 250-member Council of Ancients and a Council of Five Hundred. The Five Hundred elected Directors from a ten-man list submitted by the Ancients. A new Director was annually elected to replace one drawn by lot to resign. Ideologically the members of the two councils ranged from Jacobins to royalists, but most were moderates. The Five Hundred was the more radical council with only about seventy members supporting the government.[8]

The current Directors included Paul Barras, Louis Gohier, Jean Moulin, Pierre Ducos and Emmanuel Sieyès. With one exception those Directors were more or less determined to uphold the current system. It was Sieyès who was furtively looking for 'a sword' with which to purge and transform the government. In this he was not alone but was the most prominent figure among a loose-knit coterie that included Charles Talleyrand, Jean Cambacérés, Pierre Roederer, Joseph Fouché, Michel Regnaud and Pierre Real along with Joseph and Lucien Bonaparte. Talleyrand described Sieyès as being 'cold-hearted, pusillanimous, inflexible, methodical, prideful and impassioned only to take power and assert his ideas'.[9] Sieyès was also lucky. He was among the few revolutionary leaders who had survived the violence of the past decade. He first came to prominence in January 1789 with his pamphlet, 'What is the Third Estate?' Since then he had served in a variety of high positions, most recently president of the Five Hundred from November 1797 until 9 June 1798, when he was elected a Director.[10]

Besides Bonaparte, five other generals – Jean Moreau, Jean-Baptiste Jourdan, Étienne Macdonald, Charles Augereau and Jean-Baptiste Bernadotte – had enough popularity and ambition to be tempted to overthrow the government. Yet, aside from a fear of being executed if they failed, they largely believed in a republican form of government and sought better leaders and institutions rather than a dictatorship. When Sieyès asked Moreau to be his sword, the general pointed to Bonaparte and replied: 'There is your man. He will make your coup better than me.'[11]

Barras was the only Director who had served since the Directorate was established four years earlier. Barras and Bonaparte owed each other a lot. Barras had been Bonaparte's patron, appointing him to command first the Army of the Interior then the Army of Italy. Politically, Bonaparte earned those appointments first by helping Barras crush the October 1795 royalist uprising, then by sending Augereau to Paris with word of an imminent coup in September 1797. This time Bonaparte would work against rather than for Barras.

The unexpected appearance of Bonaparte and his entourage of hardened generals transformed the political climate. Bonaparte was popularly hailed as the hero of the Italian and Egyptian campaigns rather than a general who had recently abandoned his army. Police Minister Fouché spotted the phenomena's underside, those who viewed Bonaparte with fear and scepticism: 'Already all the parties seemed immobile and expectant before him. His return, his charisma, his renown, his huge following and his immense impact on public opinion provoked worry among those who loved liberty and the Republic.'[12]

Bonaparte attended a meeting of the Institute on the morning of 22 October, then visited Luxembourg Palace for talks with Directors Gohier, Moulin, Sieyès and Ducos; Barras pleaded poor health for staying home. By then Sieyès had talked Ducos into joining the coterie. On 24 October, Sieyès and Ducos visited Bonaparte at his home. The plot began to coalesce as they discussed how to take power and divide it between them. Bonaparte got them to agree that he would be in charge and they would assist him. With the addition of Bonaparte and his followers the cabal numbered around twenty civilian and military leaders. Their first major gathering was at Joseph's home of Mortefontaine on 29 October. The cabal secretly solicited the backing of key financiers and received at least 300,000 livres in loans to buy off any opponents.[13]

The plot faced opposition by Directors Moulin, Gohier and Barras, who adamantly opposed any political change, let alone a coup. Bonaparte assumed that they could easily be sidelined. He worried more about the reaction of the Council of Ancients and especially the more volatile Council of Five Hundred, with its hundreds of Jacobin or royalist members. Pierre Lermercier, the president of the Ancients, appeared sympathetic to notions of a change. Although Lucien was the Five Hundred's president, Bonaparte feared that his brother might have trouble manipulating that tumultuous body. His worst fear was military opposition. In assessing his most formidable possible opponents, he concluded: 'I well believe that I will have Bernadotte and Moreau against me. But I do not fear Moreau. He is soft, listless . . . But Bernadotte! He has a moor's blood in his veins. He is enterprising and bold . . . He does not like me.'[14]

The plan was for the councils to appoint Bonaparte to command the 7,000 troops in or around Paris. Then the councils would vote to move to Saint-Cloud Palace half a dozen miles from Paris to escape an alleged plot inside the city. Once the councils were isolated at Saint-Cloud, the cabal would convince them to abolish the five-man Directorate and approve a three-man Consulate headed by Bonaparte, Sieyès and Ducos. They scheduled the coup for 9 November.[15]

Two evenings before the coup, the councils hosted a banquet honouring Generals Moreau and Bonaparte for their victories. The rivals were wary, cold to each other. Anticipating the critical events that lay ahead, Bonaparte could not hide his nervousness. His fellow conspirators at the gathering also struggled to keep calm and resolute. Afterward, Talleyrand, Fouché, Joseph and Real visited Barras at his home to get him to back the transfer of power, but he refused. However, after they left, he did not sound the alarm for fear of what might happen to him if he did. During the morning of 8 November, Bonaparte tried talking Moreau, Bernadotte and Jourdan into backing him. Bernadotte and Jourdan adamantly refused, Moreau equivocated. Bonaparte then met Barras to press his case but again met with rejection. That afternoon Talleyrand and Bruix literally and figuratively paid Barras yet another visit; this one worked thanks to a 2,000,000-franc golden parachute.[16]

After the councils convened on 9 November, each learned of a possible coup. Votes named Bonaparte the Paris region's commander and authorized the move to Saint-Cloud for protection. Troops escorted the legislators there. Once they assembled, the Ancients in the Gallery of Apollo and the Five Hundred in the Orangerie, each president proposed voting to dissolve the Directorate and replace it with a Consulate. Heated debates ensued. In mid-afternoon a courier arrived with word that four of the five Directors had resigned. Actually only Sieyès, Barras and Ducos had done so; Gohier and Moulin remained defiant. Bonaparte had 300 troops surround Luxembourg Palace to ensure that Gohier and Moulin did not escape and rally opposition. Augereau and Jourdan now joined the conspirators. Yet neither council was prepared to vote for the change. The Jacobins and royalists alike hated Bonaparte and his coterie. The moderates grudgingly or willingly would approve a Consulate but were a minority. Late that day the councils agreed to adjourn for the night and resume the debate the next day.

It was undoubtedly a mistake for the plotters to let them do so. The events of 9 November had shaken and exhausted the legislators. Forcing them to continue debating until they reached a decision, while surrounded by troops, would likely have eventually produced favourable votes. Instead the coterie gave the legislators a long respite to think about what they were being pressured to do. Although probably few got a good night's sleep, most legislators returned on 10 November either resistant or reluctant to authorize the transformation.

THE USURPER

The debates resumed in each council and persisted hour after hour. Bonaparte's impatience and nervousness swelled. Around two o'clock that afternoon, he could no longer restrain himself. He strode into the Ancients' hall and began to harangue them. The vehement incoherence of his words briefly stunned then outraged most delegates who shouted back, 'Long live the constitution! Down with the dictator!' He left that hall and hurried to the Five Hundred where he launched a heated diatribe that began: 'In what state had I left France and in what state have I found it! I left you in peace and found you at war! I left you with conquests and the enemy passes our frontiers!'[17] Several delegates rushed him, shouting 'Death to the tyrant!' They scuffled.

Lucien saved the day. He summoned several huge grenadiers into the hall to push aside the delegates and rescue Bonaparte. Once they were all safely outside, he then called on General Murat to clear the hall. Murat ordered a company of grenadiers to fix bayonets then led them inside. That had the desired effect. Most of the Five Hundred fled while the rest submitted. The Ancients watched in disbelief and many of them also took to their heels. Lucien and Lermercier eventually rounded up enough delegates from each council to form rump quorums that voted for the change. Bonaparte, Sieyès and Ducos swore allegiance to the Republic at five o'clock on the morning of 11 November. Although Bonaparte and his coterie had seized power without gunfire or bloodshed, ultimately they had forced the issue with bayonets.

* * *

First Consul Napoleon Bonaparte then began governing.[18] He met with his Administrative Council on Monday and Saturday, his State Council on Tuesday and Friday, his Council of Ministers on Wednesday and his Public Buildings and Works Council on Thursday. He committed a powerful symbolic act on 19 February 1800, when he moved his residence and executive office from the Luxembourg Palace to an elaborate suite of rooms in the Tuileries.

With mingled awe and resentment, Sieyès characterized the First Consul: 'He wants to do everything. He wants to know everything. He can do everything.'[19] Sieyès was wrong about his last assertion. Bonaparte could not do everything he wanted to do but that did not stop him from trying. Indeed the number of issues that Bonaparte and his government tackled was staggering, from 911 in 1800 to 3,365 in 1804![20] In 14-hour working days, he was a whirlwind of action. He dictated dozens of letters and decrees to relays of four furiously scribbling scribes. He surrounded himself with experts and constantly picked their brains. He questioned, disputed, cajoled and energized his colleagues to better understand and fulfil their respective duties. He played devil's advocate during policy debates. He did not stop until he was satisfied that his advisors had exhausted themselves in exhausting all possibilities. He then pronounced a decision and dismissed them to implement it. All that was the relatively easy part. The First Consul's powers were never absolute. Indeed, he fumed at how often bureaucrats delayed, diluted or even dismissed his decisions. Regardless, no one could keep up with his work habits. He needed just four or so hours sleep each night and a five-minute or so power nap each day before arising rejuvenated to tackle the endlessly packed and shifting agenda. He did enjoy prolonged baths but dictated letters or had reports read to him as he soaked. He was notorious for spending no more than twenty minutes at dinner. Somehow, he managed to sit still for a concert or play a few nights each week.

Bonaparte had Sieyès draft a constitution to establish what would essentially be a one-man dictatorship masquerading as a republic headed by a triumvirate. After receiving the draft on 13 December 1799, he scrutinized it line by line, enhancing his own powers and eviscerating those of his fellow consuls and other institutions. Having done that, he arranged for a plebiscite to approve it. Interior Minister Lucien Bonaparte conducted the plebiscite that lasted from late December to late January. By 7 February, the votes had been counted and Lucien announced the stunning results: an overwhelming 3,011,007 citizens approved and a mere 1,562 opposed the new constitution; four out of ten eligible voters had exercised their right to vote. Although Lucien and his underlings apparently achieved those results by stuffing ballot boxes with yes votes and purging no votes, officially at least the constitution and thus the new regime appeared to reflect the people's 'general will', and thus enjoyed legitimacy.[21] Over the next 14 years, the 1800 constitution remained the foundation for Napoleon Bonaparte's rule with several critical amendments: he was named First Consul for Life on 2 August 1802; he was allowed to name his successor on 4 August 1802; he was named the emperor on 18 May 1804; the Tribunate was abolished on 19 August 1807; and the regency was established on 5 February 1813.

Of the three Consuls, the second and third were simply there to advise the first, whose powers included proposing and executing laws and regulations, appointing or firing ministers, ambassadors and State Council members, directing financial, military and diplomatic affairs, and declaring war and ratifying treaties, subject to the Legislative Corps' approval. Consuls would serve ten-year terms and be chosen by the Senate. Bonaparte soon replaced Sieyès and Ducos with Jean Cambacérès and Charles Lebrun. He did so because Cambacérès and Lebrun were brilliant, unflappable and loyal, while Sieyès was merely brilliant and Ducos displayed none of those qualities. Fortunately Sieyès and Ducos left with tight-lipped rather than voiced bitterness, a compliance bought with golden parachutes into Senate seats. Bonaparte trusted and respected Cambacérès so much that he left him in charge when he was away from Paris, confident that his wisdom, gravitas and decisiveness would prevail. Lebrun was a financial expert who Bonaparte tapped to deal with arcane transactions and calculations. The government's ministries included State, Finance, Treasury, Foreign Relations, Justice, Interior, Police, War, War Administration, Marine and Colonies, Cults and Manufacturing and Commerce. The purposes of most of these are evident. The Treasury and War Administrations implemented policies determined by the Finance and War Ministries, respectively. The Cult Ministry oversaw religions. The State Ministry presided over the others and its Secretary chaired the Council of Ministers.

The constitution established a ponderous system of four legislatures, the State Council, Senate, Tribunate and Legislative Corps, designed to give the appearance rather than reality of a genuine republican government. Although all male citizens at least 21 years old had the right to vote, the chance to do so was confined either to voting in plebiscites or for commune electors who would vote for department electors who would vote for national notables, whose 8,000 members would be eligible for Senate appointment to the Tribunate or Legislative Corps.

Although each legislature had a role in lawmaking, the First Consul and later the Emperor actually determined the agenda and content. The State Council drafted laws and regulations that the First Consul wanted. The Senate acted like a constitutional court by reviewing proposals to ensure that they did not violate legal principles and suggesting revisions if they did. The Tribunate debated proposals but could not vote on them. The Legislative Corps voted on proposals but could not debate them. Bonaparte appointed the Senate's sixty members, who had to be at least 40 years old. Not surprisingly, the Senate largely rubber-stamped State Council measures with little debate let alone dissent. Bonaparte unveiled his list of Senators on 24 December 1799. Over the next 14 years, the Senate expanded as France annexed more territory, eventually peaking at 141 members. The Senate appointed the Tribunate's 100 members (reduced to 50 in 1802), who had to be at least 35 years old and the Legislative Corps' 300 members, who had to be at least 25 years old.

As for their respective locations, the State Council met at Tuileries Palace, the Senate at Luxembourg Palace and the Tribunate and the Legislative Corps at Bourbon Palace.

The State Council was the government's workhorse. Its forty-five members, all picked by Bonaparte, examined critical issues and decided ways to manage or resolve them that the appropriate ministry or ministries would implement. It drafted laws that the Senate, Tribunate and Legislative Corps each had a hand in approving. Finally it was the highest appeal body for complaints against lower officials and it considered petitions submitted by private citizens and groups. Most work was done in one of the five sections, legislative, interior, financial, army and naval affairs. But twice a week the entire State Council convened to discuss the ongoing agenda. A decree devised by the State Council and rubberstamped by the Senate was known as a senatus-consultum.

For years, State Council discussions flowed freely during which Bonaparte acted like a professor conducting a seminar by playing devil's advocate and provoking genuine debates. Well aware that his overpowering mind and personality could intimidate his lessers, he urged members 'to speak boldly' so that he could carefully consider their views. He described his State Council as 'generally composed of educated, hard working men with good reputations'.[22] He critically assessed each member and assigned him arduous tasks that he was best capable of fulfilling. After he became Emperor the discussions lost their vigour and eventually morphed into his lecturing and hectoring. Second Consul Cambacérès or Third Consul Lebrun, who also served respectively as Archchancellor and Treasurer, presided when he was absent. Regardless, being a State Council member was gruelling work. Interior Minister Jean Chaptal revealed what took place:

> The State Council's functions were as punishing as they were extensive . . . The First Consul daily met with each section . . . Nearly each evening we met . . . to deliberate from ten in the evening until four or five in the morning . . . He carried the discussion with clarity, precision, the power of reason and an expanse of views that astonished everyone. Inexhaustible at work and endlessly resourceful, he connected and coordinated with peerless wisdom scattered facts and opinions across the grand system of administration.[23]

The political system had other important institutions. The highest appeals court was the Court of Cassation composed of forty-eight judges picked by the Senate on Bonaparte's recommendations. He set up a special police prefecture for Paris and named Louis Dubois to head it on 8 March 1800. The next day, he named the mayors for Paris's dozen arrondissements or districts. Beyond Paris, on 17 February 1800, he reorganized the departments with enhanced powers for the prefects or governors, then on 2 March picked ninety-eight prefects who were at once competent, honest and loyal to the new government. The number of departments would rise from 98 with 30 million people when he took power in 1799 to 134 with 44 million people in 1812. Departments were divided into communes which rose from 45,768 to peak at 60,000 during those same years. He appointed the mayors who headed each commune or arrondissement in Paris and other large cities.

The First Consul was determined 'to re-establish morality and render true dignity to the national character'.[24] Specifically he sought to purge corruption and incompetence from public affairs and to promote patriotic virtue and efficiency. He definitely squeezed the most possible work from the existing bureaucracy. He streamlined the government, slicing employee ranks from 7,000 to 4,000, although that was still far more than the 1,000 officials when the Revolution began.[25]

Like any ruler in that revolutionary age, Bonaparte figuratively kept a wary eye and ear on his realm's squares, taverns and salons. He had a network of agents who literally did so. He issued orders to various ministers and generals to crack down on spies and revolutionaries in their midst. The Police Ministry, Interior Ministry and Paris Prefect of Police competed to issue him the most comprehensive reports on the public mood and any prominent dissident groups or voices.

Had Bonaparte confined his crusade to purging those who were corrupt, inept and disloyal he would have earned nearly universal acclaim. But he cast a very broad anti-subversive net in his crusade. On 17 January 1800, he revoked the publishing licences of sixty of the seventy-three French newspapers, charging that they undermined national security and solidarity; the survivors were to ensure that they printed nothing that could be deemed seditious. He justified doing so in purely practical terms: 'If I gave free rein to the press, I would not last three months in power.'[26] He made one of the remaining thirteen, *Le Moniteur*, his government's official newspaper. Despite these efforts, words that he found noxious slipped through the self-censorship cracks. On 27 September 1803, he decreed the official censorship of non-periodical literature to suppress works deemed politically subversive or morally obscene.[27]

Bonaparte tried to inspire all with a message of unity, moderation and public service. His rousing words to General Louis Saint Hilaire were typical:

> The glory of our army and our navy and all good that can be done for France will make our generation cherished by future generations. All the radical measures that characterize a weak and vacillating government will persist no more . . . Explain often to the National Guard and all citizens that the revolution is over; that for those filled with ambition and hatred who have torn themselves from the social pact, the state's reins are in firm hands accustomed to surmounting all obstacles. Repeatedly explain that in these hard circumstances, contempt for the public good is deplorable, while moderation is the great virtue of man.

He emphasized how vital winning the local population's hearts and minds was: 'Enlighten the people, make all citizens feel that the time has come to tear themselves from the past . . . In your region, the people are hot-headed; you must transform this fervour into re-establishing commerce.'[28]

* * *

France's worst internal challenge was the royalist rebellion that had raged across swathes of Brittany, Normandy and Vendée for nearly a decade.[29] To end that, Bonaparte was willing to forgive the rebels, known as the Chouans and Vendeans. On 28 December 1799, he issued a proclamation to the western departments ravaged by civil war, offering amnesty and freedom of religion for those who pledged loyalty to the government. He even extended amnesty 'to all the soldiers who deserted in the interior because of their discontent' with fighting a brutal war against fellow citizens; they would be pardoned if they returned to serve in one of the Reserve Army regiments at Dijon.[30] He was always eager to reward exemplary behaviour. For instance, in July 1800, he asked the Vendée's prefect to send to Paris the dozen most prominent leaders who had resisted the British and the rebels during the civil war. He intended to publicly honour 'such brave and good French' to inspire others to similar courageous acts.[31]

Bonaparte ordered General Gabriel Hedouville, who commanded the 20,000-man Army of the West, to wage war and forge peace as circumstances dictated.[32] Hedouville got most rebel leaders to lay down their arms, but Georges Cadoudal stayed defiant. Bonaparte replaced Hedouville with General Guillaume Brune and ordered him to secure the major cities that still harboured rebels. He was to be conciliatory to those who surrendered and brutal toward those who resisted. Indeed he 'should not spare the communes that conducted themselves badly. Burn farms and villages . . . to make a few examples.'[33] Pardoned leaders should be dispatched to talk Cadoudal and others into coming in from the cold. To Bonaparte, Cadoudal was 'truly an English agent' and 'our most dangerous enemy'. He spurred Brune either to crush Cadoudal or force him to surrender and come to Paris for his pardon. He warned Brune that he was 'in a delicate situation where a lost day could decide a military operation'.[34] Brune's army routed Cadoudal and his men at Grand Champ on 25 January 1800.

Devastated by defeat and enticed by the promise of mercy, the remaining rebel leaders and their followers surrendered, with Cadoudal signing his oath of loyalty on 14 February. In early March, Cadoudal reached Paris, where Bonaparte twice received him. After their first meeting, he mused that Cadoudal 'was a fat Breton who might be co-opted for the nation's common interests'.[35] Yet he failed to talk Cadoudal into returning to England and serving as a double agent among the expatriate community there. By 1 May, he realized that Cadoudal had betrayed his trust and called for his arrest before he escaped to England.[36] But that order came too late. Cadoudal slipped across the Channel. He would eventually return.

* * *

During this time, Bonaparte received an extraordinary letter from Louis, Count of Lille and Provence, the would-be King Louis XVIII.[37] Louis asked Bonaparte to help him mount the French throne. Bonaparte deliberately kept him waiting half a year before he replied. His message was blunt: 'I thank you for your frank words. You must not desire to return to France; to do so would mean marching over the bodies of 100,000 cadavers. Sacrifice your interest to France's relief and happiness. History will reward you for that. I am not insensible to your family's sufferings. I would be happy to help you in your retirement's sweet tranquillity.'[38]

Josephine pressed her husband to let all those who had fled France since the Revolution began, known as émigrés, return. Bonaparte took the first step toward a general amnesty in July 1800, when he formed a commission to screen applicants who pledged loyalty to his government. On 26 April 1802, he decreed that all but 1,000 of the 100,000 listed émigrés were eligible for amnesty if they reappeared within six months. Around 45,000 of them returned to their country if not their homes, most of which were now firmly in other hands. With varying degrees of fatalism, rancour, hope and fear, each adult swore allegiance to the latest version of the Revolution that had convulsed his or her life. Most honoured their oath and devoted themselves somehow to building a new life in a land at once familiar and alien. Some either came as royalist agents or joined the counterrevolutionary underground. Police agents struggled to distinguish these differences.

* * *

Bonaparte met with Cambacérès, Joseph and Lucien on 8 May 1802, to map out just how to engineer an extraordinary expansion of the First Consul's power. Within the next forty-eight hours they talked all the key players into accepting their role. On 10 May, the State Council submitted a plebiscite to French voters on whether Napoleon Bonaparte should be Consul for Life. On 12 May, all the Senate and Tribunate members and all but three Legislative Corps members approved Bonaparte's lifelong tenure as Consul. On 2 August, the Senate proclaimed Napoleon Bonaparte Consul for Life legitimized by the plebiscite 'results' of 3,655,600 for and 9,272 against. On 4 August, the Senate approved a constitutional amendment that incorporated that life-long tenure. That event was celebrated as a national holiday and a Te Deum in Notre-Dame Cathedral on his birthday, 15 August 1802. Having talked the Senate into taking that extraordinary step, within two years Bonaparte would just as easily convince the Senate to name him emperor.

Chapter 5

The Peacemaker

'The Republic's goal is make war lead to peace.'

'Drying Europe's tears does not depend on me, but on a general peace and a general order ending the revolutions and wars.'

'I have tried for the last twelve months to give relief and tranquillity to Europe. I have not succeeded and the fighting senselessly continues, instigated by English policy.'

First Consul Napoleon Bonaparte's priority was peace.[1] Indeed all the projects to modernize France that he envisioned depended on it. Yet France remained at war with Austria on land and Britain at sea. The nation's strategic situation could have been far worse but Spain, Prussia, Naples and Bavaria were at peace with France, while Russia was estranged from but had not yet broken with the coalition. Bonaparte hoped to convert the hawks of Vienna and London into doves.

To that end, on Christmas Day 1799, he sent them two priceless gifts. To the Austrian Emperor Francis, he wrote: 'Stranger to all sentiment of vain glory, my first vow is to stop the effusion of blood'. He lauded the emperor's reputation for having a good character and insisted that 'I foresee the possibility of reconciling the interests of our two nations'.[2] He had Talleyrand simultaneously write to Foreign Minister Johann Thugut, condemning those who wanted to continue rather than end the war.[3] Bonaparte's letter to George III was more expansive. He asked whether the war that had ground on for eight years must be eternal and how Europe's two most enlightened countries could sacrifice their prosperity and the happiness of families for vain ideas of glory. He called for their two nations 'to end a war that had embraced the entire world'.[4]

Neither monarch lowered himself to respond directly to the upstart general with his dubious noble lineage.[5] Instead, each handed that task to his foreign minister to send to Talleyrand. Bonaparte directly replied to the British rejection, refuting each point, with his central argument that 'as soon as the French Revolution was declared, nearly all of Europe united for its destruction', but now France was willing to forgive that foreign aggression for a lasting peace founded 'on each nation's right to choose its own form of government'. He called on Britain's leaders to hear 'everywhere the voices of people imploring an end to a war already disastrous enough but whose prolongation threatened Europe with universal disruptions and evils without remedy'. He called for an immediate ceasefire followed by peace talks.[6] But the British spurned Bonaparte's pleas to negotiate at any level for any reason, including prisoner exchanges.[7]

With his diplomatic strategy dead, Bonaparte expressed his only option: 'The Republic's goal is to make war lead to peace.'[8] That was clear enough. The question, of course, was how.

* * *

As the coalition's paymaster, Britain was the key.[9] The coalition would collapse if Britain were defeated. But was Britain invincible? That nation of seafarers and shopkeepers certainly appeared to be invulnerable on its own soil and nearly so on the high seas. Since 1066, either the English or the incompetence of the would-be invaders had defeated every attempted conquest. For nearly as long, the English fleet had won almost every large-scale naval battle. Bitter experience made Bonaparte especially sensitive to both realities. In early 1798, he had commanded the Army of England but reported to the Directorate that its mission of invading, let alone conquering, Britain was impossible. In August 1798, Nelson's fleet destroyed Brueys's fleet at Aboukir Bay, stranding Bonaparte's Army of Egypt in the African desert.

Yet Britain certainly was not invincible. As recently as 1783, Britain lost its war to crush American independence and defeat the Americans' direct ally France and indirect allies Spain and Holland. Somehow Bonaparte had to knit together a similar alliance of money, markets, armies and navies to steadily grind down Britain's ability to fight. If invading Britain was virtually impossible while the Royal Navy's fleets ruled the waves, then perhaps Britain could be defeated indirectly, on its fringe rather than on its own soil or the raging seas.[10]

Bonaparte somehow had to rack up his own collection of trophies that exceeded that of Britain and then trade them until France emerged from the war with significant spoils. In January 1800, he ordered two large naval operations. Admiral Eustache Bruix, who commanded nine ships-of-the-line and seven frigates at Brest, was 'to proceed as promptly as possible to Egypt' where 'he would stay but three days' to discharge vital supplies and gather as much information as possible about the situation. The fleet would then sail to Toulon. Bonaparte had of course not forgotten his nemesis. If the fleet encountered Captain Sidney Smith along the way, Bruix should attack and destroy him.[11] Admiral Jean Lacrosse was to lead his squadron of five ships-of-the-line and two frigates, packed with supplies and 4,600 troops, first down the Atlantic coast to Lisbon, then westward to Madeira, capturing whatever British vessels crossed his path. From there, the squadron would sail to the West Indies, with frigates screening in advance beyond the horizon to reduce the chance of any British warships spotting his main body. They were to call at Martinique and Saint Domingue, with supplies and troops unloaded and intelligence gathered at each. He would return via Havana, Cuba, then through the Bahama straits up America's east coast as far as New England, where he would head back to France.[12]

Issuing orders is meaningless if they are not carried out. Bonaparte grew increasingly impatient as week after week passed with Bruix's fleet still anchored at Brest. On 22 February, he gently but firmly spurred him to 'unfurl his sails as soon as possible'. He elaborated his previous instructions, noting the obvious hard reality that Bruix first had to chase away the British fleet blockading Brest. He was then to stop at Ferrol and Cadiz, where fifteen Spanish warships commanded by Admiral Charles Gravina would join him. His mission's third stage was to drive the British naval blockade from Malta and drop supplies at La Valletta. Only then was the fleet to proceed to Alexandria, ideally to trap and destroy the British blockading squadron. Finally, he was to sail with the French fleet to Toulon while Gravina's Spanish warships returned to their home port. Just how Bruix realized his succession of challenges was entirely up to him, as 'the First Consul is not entering into a single detail' on that and instead 'relies on his talents and zeal for the French navy's glory . . . The season and fortune will favour the French squadron if Admiral Bruix takes advantage of all the opportunities that he is offered and loses not an hour.'[13] Bonaparte sent just as motivating a letter to Gravina, in which he 'counted on his distinguished talents and the love of glory and bravery so natural to the Spanish nation'.[14]

Alas, the best motivational words are useless if the recipients lack the skills and character to get the job done or the mission itself is impossible to realize. Bonaparte was well aware that Bruix and Gravina might be the wrong men for that mission. But, given each navy's ponderous seniority system, he was stuck with them. That prompted him to issue detailed instructions to Bruix, including sailing and anchoring times at key places. But this simply compounded the problems of a mission that Bruix was incapable of fulfilling.[15] Bonaparte got just as frustrated during the time that Lacrosse took to ready his fleet for action. It was not until May that Lacrosse's fleet, packed with 4,000 troops, left Brest but, battered by storms, it was forced back to port. And there the flotilla lay anchored for another year.

Serious problems plagued the navy.[16] Corruption, incompetence, red tape and petty jealousies snarled up the Marine Ministry. Officials signed lucrative contracts with businessmen in return for kickbacks; usually any subsequent 'supplies' were either deficient or non-existent and 'work' was shoddy and tardy if it was done at all. Warships could not put to sea because they lacked such essentials as provisions, munitions, ropes and sails. Officers abandoned their vessels for the pleasures of Paris. Vessels were undermanned because seamen either evaded conscription or deserted. Sailing and gunnery skills eroded because the British blockade prevented their practice. In July 1800, Bonaparte ordered Marine Minister Pierre Forfait to eliminate the corruption and incompetence plaguing his bureaucracy. That, of course, was far easier ordered than implemented.[17]

If Britain was beyond attack, Austria was not. The First Consul threw himself into 14-hour days of preparations to crush the Austrians.[18] The first step was to overhaul the French army which the Directorate had left in disarray, with related deficiencies in money, supplies and morale. He first had Louis Berthier head the War Ministry, then, on 2 April, replaced him with Lazare Carnot; the latter brilliantly realized the reforms that the former initiated. On 8 January, Bonaparte had issued Finance Minister Martin Gaudin an 8.5 million franc army budget and ensured that each field army had enough surgeons, engineers, sappers, miners, horse artillery, pontooneers, rations, shoes and munitions to last the campaign. On 3 January, he established the Consular Guard which would consist of 2,000 of the toughest, bravest, tallest veterans. It would accompany Bonaparte on his Italian campaign and fight heroically at Marengo. It would be renamed the Imperial Guard on 18 May 1804 and expand in numbers and types of units. The Imperial Guard peaked in power on the eve of Napoleon's 1812 campaign against Russia.[19]

By early 1800, France's armies were largely confined to the 'natural frontiers' of the Pyrenees, Rhine and Alps, with one exception. General André Masséna's 40,000 troops were deployed along the Ligurian coast between Nice and Genoa. Facing Masséna was General Michael Melas with 97,000 troops spread across northern Italy. With 130,000 troops defending the upper Rhine River front, General Jean Moreau commanded the largest army. Facing Moreau was General Paul Kray with 120,000 troops along the Rhine's eastern bank. France enjoyed a significant strategic edge over Austria. The Helvetian or Swiss Republic was allied with France and would allow French troops to march through its territory, an advantage that Bonaparte would decisively exploit. The Austrians suffered another handicap, this one self-imposed – they made war by committee, namely the 21-member Aulic Council in Vienna.

Bonaparte ordered a secret 50,000-man Reserve Army formed first at Lyon on 5 December 1799, then at Dijon on 25 January 1800. He intended to command that army during the 1800 campaign even though the constitution prevented the First Consul from doing so; he would finesse that law by putting Berthier nominally in charge on 2 April.[20]

Bonaparte's initial plan of campaign had Moreau attack Kray across the Rhine while Bonaparte led the Reserve Army through Switzerland into the upper Danube Valley, thus cutting off the Austrian army and forcing it to surrender. The victorious French army would then march down the Danube valley to dictate terms in Vienna. Masséna, meanwhile, would try to hold off Melas in Liguria and retreat if necessary. But once Kray was cut off and destroyed, Melas would have to withdraw swiftly to protect Vienna. That was an ingenious plan. Unfortunately, Bonaparte did not yet enjoy complete unity of command. When Moreau bluntly refused to serve directly under him and threatened to resign if he insisted on it, Bonaparte yielded. The First Consul feared that his grip on power was still too uncertain to risk accepting Moreau's resignation then having him and his coterie in Paris plotting a coup against him while he was on campaign.

Bonaparte's second plan was less strategically promising. Moreau's army would fight its way across the Rhine, through the Black Forest and down the Danube valley. Meanwhile Bonaparte would cross the Alps at the Saint Bernard Pass and attack the Austrian army's rear as Masséna held out before them. After forcing Melas to surrender, Bonaparte's army would march north-east on the long road to Vienna as Moreau's army paralleled him north of the Alps.[21] Two weaknesses haunted this plan. One was whether Masséna could last long enough to divert Melas and be rescued. Bonaparte wrote Masséna that he was 'extremely concerned by the awful position in which you find yourself; but I count on your zeal and skills' to prevail. Nonetheless, if he 'had to evacuate Genoa, he should withdraw to Savona'.[22] The plan's other weakness was Moreau himself. Although his army was three times larger than Bonaparte's Reserve Army, Moreau lacked drive.

Masséna split his 36,000-man army between a right wing under General Nicolas Soult and left wing under General Louis Suchet; Masséna was with Soult. Melas's 97,000-man army included 86,000 infantry and 14,000 cavalry but about half those troops were scattered to garrison key cities in northern Italy and Tuscany. Melas launched his offensive on 5 April, defeated Masséna and Soult in several battles then pursued them to Genoa, which he laid siege to on 21 April. Other Austrian forces crossed the Maritime Alps to capture Savona and forced Suchet to retreat beyond the Var and even evacuate Nice.[23]

Bonaparte was becoming increasingly anxious as he received reports of the Austrian onslaught against Masséna in Liguria while Moreau dithered along the Rhine. Yet politically he felt compelled to treat Moreau with kid gloves. On 22 April, he gently encouraged him to take the field: 'The season is beautiful. Your troops are numerous and skilfully lead. Our confidence in you is total. Send us soon the enemy's flags and take many prisoners. Do not stop striking until you have obtained results that surpass our losses.'[24] Two days later he wrote more pointedly that 'I hope the hour has come that you have crossed the Rhine'.[25]

Moreau did not launch his campaign until 25 April, when most of the army under his immediate command crossed the Rhine. Corps led by Generals Claude Lecourbe and Laurent Gouvion St Cyr crossed over the next week. Moreau's plan was to converge and destroy Kray's army between them. The generals together or separately racked up a series of victories against the Austrians at Stockach and Engen on 3 May, Moesskirch on the 5th, Biberach on the 9th and Memmingen on the 10th. With the French in hot pursuit, the remnants of Kray's army withdrew down the Danube valley. The French caught up and defeated the Austrians at Kirchberg on 5 June, then with a cluster of victories at Hochstädt, Launingen, Gundelfingen, Dilligen and Schewennigen on the 14th. That same day Bonaparte won one of his most critical victories.

* * *

The First Consul was unable to wrap up his affairs and secretly leave Paris until the night of 6 May. He explained to Josephine that 'I must travel incognito . . . because I don't want anyone to know what I am going to do'.[26] Three days later he was in Geneva, where his Reserve Army numbered 50,000 troops, including 44,000 infantry, 4,000 cavalry and 2,000 artillerymen with 48 guns, with accumulating reserves that would reach 8,000 infantry and 3,000 cavalry. His Consular Guard included 200 cavalry, 400 grenadiers, 120 guides or light infantry and a six-gun battery with 60 gunners.[27] His infantry division commanders included Generals Jean Lannes, Claude Victor, Philibert Duhesme, Adrien Moncey and Louis Thurreau, while Joachim Murat led the cavalry.

Bonaparte ordered his army on the long arduous march toward Italy. Lannes led the advance over the Saint Bernard pass on 14 May and seized Aosta two days later but stalled before Fort Bard high above the narrow canyon through which the Dora Baltea River flowed with a road alongside. He eventually sneaked his troops past the fort at night and marched on to besiege Ivrea further down the valley. It took another nine days for the rest of the army to surmount the pass, but by 23 May, the troops were either marching down the Aosta valley, slipping around Fort Bard at night or with Lannes at the front. Lannes's troops captured Ivrea on 24 May, then repelled the Austrians at La Chiusella and Romano near Turin two days later. After emerging from the Aosta valley onto the plains of Lombardy, Murat swiftly led his cavalry to mop up Austrian detachments and depots and routed an Austrian force at Turbigo on 31 May. Two days later, Murat and his men clattered unopposed into Milan and seized 300 artillery pieces (half field and half siege guns), 10,000 muskets, 200,000lbs of gunpowder and a huge store of supplies.[28]

Bonaparte and his entourage entered Milan later that day. He announced on 3 June the Cisalpine Republic's rebirth after the Austrian and Russian armies had abolished it in 1799: 'The French people have for the second time broken your chains . . . Can you be insensible to the pride of forming an independent nation? . . . Cisalpine people, as your territory is delivered from the enemy, the republic will be organized on the solid foundation of religion, liberty, equality and good order. Hasten this moment with your energy.'[29]

Learning of Bonaparte's descent on his rear, Melas split his army, leaving 25,000 troops at Genoa and hurrying north with 40,000 troops. Masséna surrendered his 8,000 troops on 4 June. Suchet, meanwhile, defeated the Austrians at Monte Nave on 6 June. Melas established his headquarters at Alessandria, deployed his divisions northward in an arc and tried to glean intelligence on the enemy's whereabouts. The Po River divided the armies of Bonaparte and Melas. Bonaparte raced Murat and his cavalry to seize the bridge at Placentia on 7 June, while Lannes and Victor led the way across below Pavia. Lannes and Victor defeated General Peter Ott at Montebello on the 9th. By 12 June, most of Bonaparte's army had crossed the Po and advanced within half a dozen miles of Alessandria. The unexpected arrival of Egyptian veteran General Louis Desaix delighted Bonaparte and he gave him command of his reserves.

Then Bonaparte committed a mistake that was nearly fatal. He assumed that the fortress city of Alessandria was lightly held and that Melas was far away, but did not send forward his cavalry to determine if that was true. Instead, he split his army. He sent Desaix to seize Novi. He detached some troops to screen the Austrian-held fortress of Tortona. He camped Victor at Marengo, a few miles east of Alessandria, Lannes and Murat a mile or so behind Victor, then established his headquarters surrounded by his Consular Guard on the road to Tortona. In all he had about 25,000 infantry, 3,000 cavalry and 40 guns within a day's march of each other, but only 22,000 men were around Marengo.

Melas had 25,000 infantry, 5,000 cavalry and 200 guns behind the Bormida River that lay between Alessandria and Marengo. On the morning of 14 June, the Austrians crossed the river, then fanned out to rout Victor then march on to drive off Lannes and Murat. Bonaparte dashed forward with his Consular Guard and some reserves but they too were pushed back. He sent a courier galloping to Desaix to recall him. Fortunately, Desaix heard the distant guns and quick-marched his troops back to Marengo. By mid-afternoon Bonaparte had rallied the remnants of his men several miles from the initial onslaught. The Austrians were massing for a final assault when Desaix appeared and spearheaded the French counter-attack that routed them. In all, the Austrians lost 963 dead, 5,518 wounded and 2,921 prisoners, while about 1,100 French were killed, 3,600 were wounded and 900 captured.[30] For Bonaparte, his army's worst loss was Desaix who was killed by a musket ball as he led his men to victory: 'I am in the deepest sorrow because of the death of the man that I loved and esteemed above all.'[31]

Bonaparte never won a closer victory. He was on the verge of being overwhelmed when Desaix came to the rescue. He was also aided by mistakes that Melas made, including not massing all his available forces and leaving the battlefield for Alessandria when it was not yet won. Bonaparte's army was nearly as devastated by victory as the Austrian army was by defeat. The long marches capped by the desperate battle had riddled most regimental rosters; cartridge boxes and caissons were empty; hunger pinched the soldiers' stomachs as supply wagons fell further behind their rapid advances. For now his troops were incapable of inflicting the coup de grace on the Austrians. Political worries compounded Bonaparte's military weaknesses. The further he distanced himself from Paris, the more nervously his mind glanced back far beyond the north-west horizon to imagined plots in the capital that could rob him of power amidst his latest triumph. He was eager to hurry back to Paris to reassert firm control over France.

The battlefield victory was not decisive. Although the Austrians had suffered twice as many casualties, they were diminished and battered but not broken, let alone destroyed. Bonaparte's diplomacy succeeded where his generalship failed in rendering the Austrian army hors de combat. The day after the battle, Melas asked for an armistice. Bonaparte agreed. Under the Convention of Alexandria, signed on 15 June, Melas agreed to abandon all his guns and munitions that corresponded to French standards, turn over the fortresses of Tortona, Alessandria, Coni, Genoa, Turin, Milan, Pizzighettone, Placentia, Ceva, Savona and Arona, and withdraw his army east beyond the Mincio River. As a sign of esteem and consolation, Bonaparte presented Melas with a sabre that he had carried in Egypt.[32]

The following day, Bonaparte sent Francis his latest plea for peace:

> I have the honour of writing to His Majesty to let him know the French people's desire to end a war that has devastated our countries . . . Thousands of French and Austrians exist no more. Thousands of devastated families have lost their fathers, their husbands, their sons . . . It is on the battlefield of Marengo, surrounded by suffering and around 15,000 cadavers, that I beg Your Majesty to hear the cries of humanity . . . Give relief and tranquillity to the current generation. If future generations are foolish enough to fight each other, so be it, they too will become wise and live in peace.

He pointed out that he could have captured Melas and his army, but sought to end the bloodshed rather than win total victory. Francis could end the war with two decisive acts. First, he must sever his ties with Britain which had instigated and bankrolled the war. Then he must sincerely recommit himself to the Treaty of Campo Formio which he had violated to renew war against France. 'If Your Majesty rejects these proposals, hostilities will recommence and, if you will permit me to speak frankly, in the eyes of the world only you be responsible for the war.'[33]

Bonaparte turned over the command of his army to General Guillaume Brune and journeyed to Milan for a triumphant Te Deum at the cathedral. The glow of victory soon faded with word that Paris was in financial and political turmoil; rumours that he had been killed and his army defeated had caused the stock market to plunge. He hurried back and on 2 July, entered Paris paradoxically as a hero who had to consolidate his shaky hold on power. Meanwhile, French forces in the Danube valley kept hounding the Austrians, defeating them at Nordlingen on 23 June, Harburg on 25 June, Oberhausen on 28 June, Landshut on 7 July and Feldkirch on 13 July. On 14 July, Kray and Moreau signed the Armistice of Parsdorf.

The First Consul welcomed Austrian diplomat Francis Saint Julian at the Tuileries on 21 July, then had Talleyrand open negotiations with him. It only took Talleyrand and Saint Julian a week to hammer out the details of a preliminary peace treaty, which they signed on 28 July 1800. Despite French victories in Italy and Germany, Bonaparte did not demand any significant concessions from Vienna. The new treaty largely followed the tenets of the 1797 Treaty of Campo Formio. The next day, Bonaparte fired off another impassioned peace message to Francis, hand-delivered along with the treaty by his aide Christophe Duroc.[34] Vienna's hardliners, led by Foreign Minister Johann Thugut, kept Francis from ratifying it. They convinced Francis that his alliance with Britain forbad a separate peace in return for huge subsidies. Instead, Thugut proposed a peace congress at Lunéville that would include all interested states.

Bonaparte rejected this notion and insisted that Francis ratify the treaty. He had Carnot ready the army to resume war if the treaty remained unratified on 5 September. That deadline passed but he impatiently waited fruitlessly for peace until 13 September, when he reluctantly authorized Carnot to implement the war plans. Moreau would lead his army down the Danube valley toward Vienna. Brune had more complicated instructions. First, he was to secure Lucca and Livorno in Tuscany and Ferrara and Peschiara eastward in the lower Po valley. After his troops had overrun these far-flung strategic cities, he should capture Legnano, Verona and Vicenza in Venetian territory and drive the Austrians east of the Tagliamento River.[35]

Bonaparte's bargaining power for a general peace diminished significantly after the British captured Malta on 3 September 1800, following a nearly two-year siege. Then the chances for peace with Austria brightened after Francis replaced the hardliner Thugut with the more conciliatory Louis Cobenzl as foreign minister on 25 September. Bonaparte responded by agreeing to send his brother Joseph to negotiate with Cobenzl at Lunéville. Meanwhile he authorized Moreau to extend the armistice, which he did with the Convention of Hohenlinden signed on 30 September. The talks dragged on with no resolution. Bonaparte reluctantly ordered his armies to resume the offensive on 3 November. Moreau's army won a string of victories culminating with Hohenlinden on 3 December, then advanced toward Vienna. Francis agreed to the latest armistice, which was signed at Steyr on Christmas Day. Meanwhile, Brune's army in Italy overran Tuscany as far as Sienna, the Italian Tyrol as far north as Bassano and Venezia as far as east as Castelfranco. Under the Armistice of Trevise, signed on 15 January, the Austrians had to withdraw beyond the Tagliamento.

Joseph and Cobenzl resumed negotiations at Lunéville on 2 January 1801. Mercifully, they haggled free of Britain's long shadow. Austria, along with Russia, had formally quit the coalition on 31 December 1800. Francis also boosted negotiations by agreeing to base a deal on the Campo Formio treaty. The Treaty of Lunéville was signed on 9 February 1801. The Austrians renounced any claims to lands west of the Rhine River and recognized French expansion there. In Italy, Vienna recognized the Cisalpine and Ligurian Republics, while the Grand Duchy of Tuscany would be transformed into the Kingdom of Etruria, with the throne held by Louis, the grandson of Spain's King Charles IV, as soon as the infant came of age; meanwhile, Marie Louise, the baby's mother and Charles's daughter, would serve as regent. Ferdinand, Tuscany's deposed Grand Duke, would be compensated with Salzburg. France recognized Austria's possessions of Venezia in Italy along with Trieste, Istria and Dalmatia on the Adriatic's north-east coast. Once again, Bonaparte had followed up a decisive French defeat of Austria with a conciliatory peace. He would not be so generous the next time that he was forced to end a war that the Austrians began.

Bonaparte's diplomacy was largely responsible for Russia's withdrawal from the coalition. Tsar Paul I had become increasingly enraged by how his allies, Austria and Britain, treated Russia.[36] About 9,000 Russian prisoners languished in French hands because Prime Minister William Pitt rejected Bonaparte's offer to trade them for French prisoners held by the British. Bonaparte learned of Paul's disgruntlement and sought to exploit it.[37] In June 1800, he had Talleyrand write Paul a conciliatory letter, asking for peace talks. In July 1800, he offered Malta to Russia 'as proof of his personal consideration for the Russian emperor'. He promised to return his Russian prisoners to their homeland as 'a mark of the esteem that the First Consul has for the brave Russian army'.[38] His offer to hand Malta to Paul was not so much a generous as a desperate act. Britain's blockade had reduced the garrison and population to semi-starvation rations; Malta's surrender was merely a matter of time. Promising Malta to Russia would worsen animosities between St Petersburg and London. The British would not cede the Mediterranean's strategic linchpin after taking it, even to an ally. That conflict could transform the relationship between them from a cold alliance into a hot animosity.

And that is what happened after Malta surrendered to the British on 5 September 1800.

To Bonaparte's pull on Paul, the British inflicted a series of nasty pushes. British warships and privateers preyed mercilessly on any vessels trading with France. That provoked Russia, Sweden and Denmark to form the League of Armed Neutrality on 16 December 1800; Prussia joined two days later. The alliance's goal was to close the Baltic to the British and deter an attack by uniting their fleets against the Royal Navy. Although France could not be a member since it was currently warring against Britain, Bonaparte tried to nurture the natural alliance among them against a common enemy. He promised 'to do all that was suitable and possible' to help them, then added: 'States never perish except by weakness.'[39]

Paul sent Joram Sprengporten with a handwritten letter to Bonaparte, assuring him that Russia was now hostile to Britain and wanted peace with France. The day after receiving that letter, Bonaparte replied, thanking Paul and expressing his confidence that a bilateral peace treaty could inspire the other great powers to follow. He shared his frustration that 'I have tried for the last twelve months to give relief and tranquillity to Europe. I have not succeeded and the fighting senselessly continues, instigated by English policy.'[40] He received exciting news on 9 February 1801. Not only had Paul publicly announced that Russia was withdrawing from the coalition, he had proposed a secret alliance between Russia and France to take India from Britain. He soon learned that Paul had expelled the would-be Louis XVIII and his entourage from their palace at Mittau; they found their latest refuge in Prussian-controlled Warsaw. Negotiations for an alliance between France and Russia opened in Paris on 6 March.

Then came the stunning news that Tsar Paul was dead, officially from a heart attack on 24 March. But word soon seeped out that a coterie had murdered the despotic Tsar to bring his good-hearted, malleable son Alexander to the throne.[41] That was a double blow to Bonaparte who genuinely esteemed Paul and hoped to realize ambitious plans with him. He wrote a letter of condolence to Alexander and encouraged him to carry on his father's legacy of rapprochement between Russia and France. He also wrote to Danish King Christian VII and Swedish King Gustav IV, calling for closer ties between them.[42]

Then came word that the British fleet had destroyed the Danish fleet anchored at Copenhagen on 2 April. Bonaparte had the *Moniteur* publish a diatribe condemning the British government for the outrage.[43] He dispatched his aide Christophe Duroc to Berlin and St Petersburg to encourage the revival of the League of Armed Neutrality and ideally convert it into a French-led anti-British alliance. Duroc first met Frederick William III and encouraged him to occupy Hanover, the British monarch's ancestral home and an ally. Then in St Petersburg, he learned of the new tsar's political leanings and met some of the cabal that had brutally cleared the throne for him.[44]

Peace was Alexander's priority. His first important act as Tsar was to send London a conciliatory letter asking to restore trade and peace. He signed a treaty with Britain renouncing the League of Armed Neutrality on 17 June 1801. Peace was restored between France and Russian by a treaty signed in Paris on 8 October. In return for Russia's recognition of France's expanded territory, France recognized a joint Russian and Turkish protectorate over the Republic of Seven Islands that included Corfu, Cephalonia, Plaxo, Sainte-Maure, Ithaca, Zante and Cythera.

In ceding the Seven Islands, Bonaparte gave up a critical component of his oriental dream. The last nail in the coffin of that vision came when he learned that on 31 August 1801, General Jacques Menou, who then commanded France's army in Egypt, had surrendered to an overwhelming British and Turkish invasion force. Bonaparte now concentrated on diplomacy that advanced French interests in Europe.[45]

Among Bonaparte's priorities was reconciliation with the Catholic Church which had become embittered during a decade of French revolutionary attacks culminating with the capture of Pope Pius VI and his imprisonment at Valence in France. Pius's captivity ended when he died on 29 August 1799. To choose a new pope, the cardinals opened a conclave at Venice on 30 November. Bonaparte made a series of conciliatory gestures. On 29 November 1799, he allowed deported priests to return if they swore allegiance to the constitution. On 28 December he let Sunday services resume and the 30th he had a plaque honouring Pius placed on his tomb. The Vatican could not acknowledge, let alone reciprocate, these acts because it was consumed with finding a new pope. It was not until 14 March 1800 that the cardinals finally voted to transform Cardinal Barnabe Chiramonte into Pope Pius VII.[46]

The victory at Marengo and armistice in June 1800 gave Bonaparte the chance to launch his next diplomatic initiative. At Vercelli on 25 June, he shared his hopes for reconciliation with Cardinal Carlo Martiniana and asked him to convey them to Rome. The new pope and his court needed months to forge a consensus over how to respond. It was not until late October that Pius dispatched Cardinal Joseph Spina to negotiate. Talks began after Spina reached Paris on 5 November 1800, but soon deadlocked. Foreign Minister Talleyrand bluntly rejected

Spina's demands that all confiscated Church property either be returned or paid for, that Catholicism be the state religion and the sole religion tolerated in France and that laws allowing divorce be revoked. He insisted that any treaty would simply acknowledge that most French people were Catholics. Talleyrand himself was an obstacle to negotiations. Spina expressed his distaste at having to haggle with a defrocked priest who had supported revolutionary excesses against the Church.

Bonaparte sought to finesse the stalemate by replacing Talleyrand with Father Étienne Bernier in talks with Spina, while sending to Rome for direct negotiations with Pius, François Cacault, who had negotiated the Treaty of Tolentino. Cacault reached Rome on 6 April 1801. Meanwhile, Bonaparte was losing his patience. On 12 May, he warned Spina that if Rome did not swiftly accept his terms, he would order General Murat to conquer the Papal States. On 19 May, he publicly recalled Cacault. Those two steps alarmed Pius, who had Cardinal Hercule Consalvi accompany Cacault to Paris and replace Spina as the chief negotiator. On 12 July, Bonaparte asked his brother Joseph to supersede Bernier in the talks. Joseph and Consalvi hit it off, got to work and three days later they signed the Concordat.

Bonaparte got what he wanted. The Papacy recognized France's government and its oversight of the French Church, which was split among six archbishops, 50 bishops and around 3,000 parishes subsidized by the state. The First Consul was empowered to appoint all archbishops and bishops. Rome accepted the nationalization of Church property without compensation. Bonaparte wrote to Pius on 27 July 1801, pledging his support while insisting that: 'Drying Europe's tears does not depend on me, but on a general peace and general order ending the revolutions and wars.'[47] Pius granted Bonaparte a birthday gift when he ratified the Concordat on 15 August 1801. Bonaparte ratified the Concordat on 8 September and exchanged it with Consalvi's version two days later. Sensitive to the still widespread anti-Church feelings, he waited another seven months before actually promulgating the Concordat with a Te Deum in Notre-Dame Cathedral in Paris on Easter Sunday, 5 April 1802.[48] Three days later, he amended the Concordat with seventy-seven articles that regulated the French Catholic Church. He had Justice Minister Claude Regnier issue strict rules to keep peace within and among France's religions to uphold the Constitution's promise of equal protection and rights. The government would not interfere in any disputes over dogma within the Catholic Church or any other religion.[49]

The Concordat with Rome was among Bonaparte's more progressive achievements. Interior Minister Chaptal, usually a scornful critic, gave his religious policy high marks: 'Bonaparte's boldest policy during the first years of his rule was re-establishing the Church on its former foundation. To best judge this enterprise's importance and difficulty, one must understand the epoch's relentless hatred and scorn for the clergy. The idea of re-establishing the pope's jurisdiction defied the public spirit.'[50]

* * *

The possibility of peace between France and Britain improved significantly when hardliner William Pitt resigned on 8 February 1801, after George III rejected his Irish reform proposal. The king tapped conciliatory Henry Addington as the new prime minister.[51] On 21 February, Foreign Secretary Robert Hawkesbury sent word of Britain's interest in peace to Talleyrand. On 28 May, Bonaparte dispatched Louis Otto to London to negotiate with Hawkesbury. Otto was to insist upon the following: Egypt would revert to Turkish rule; Malta would revert to the Order of Saint John; the Republic of Seven Islands would be recognized; French troops would withdraw from all Papal and Neapolitan ports that they occupied; in the West Indies, all possessions would be restored to their previous owners; and the British government would recognize the Batavian, Helvetian, Ligurian and Cisalpine Republics.[52]

Otto and Hawkesbury haggled for months with no breakthrough. On 17 September, Bonaparte threatened to end the talks. That had the desired effect. Under the preliminary treaty, signed on 1 October 1801, Britain promised to restore all its conquests including Malta to the Knights of Saint John, with two exceptions; it would keep Trinidad taken from Spain and Ceylon taken from Holland. France would withdraw its troops from the Kingdom of Naples and the Papal States. Both states recognized the independence of the Republic of Seven Islands and renounced any claims to Egypt. Bonaparte wrote George III, praising the preliminary treaty and expressing hope that the final version would be swiftly negotiated and ratified.[53] The Treaty of Amiens, signed on 25 March 1802, retained the preliminary treaty's major points with minor refinements, most notably that Britain would evacuate Malta within three months after ratifications were exchanged and that Malta would be permanently neutral and its ports open to trade with all countries. France was now finally at peace for the first time since April 1792.

First Consul Bonaparte acted swiftly to fulfil France's duties and opportunities under the Treaty of Amiens. He had French troops withdrawn either from conquests or protectorates as required by the treaty. He had prisoners of war embarked on the long trudge or sail back to their countries. He had expeditions reoccupy French possessions in the Caribbean, Indian Ocean, India and, most urgently, Saint Domingue.[54] Typically, he had a grand vision that he was eager to implement. Talleyrand wrote that, ironically, the Peace of Amiens was when 'moderation began to abandon Bonaparte'.[55]

Chapter 6

The New World Dreamer

'In annihilating the black government of Saint Domingue, I am guided less by trade and financial considerations than by the necessity of smothering . . . black power . . . If black liberty and a legitimate government is recognized in Saint Domingue . . . sooner or later the sceptre of black power will fall into their hands throughout the New World.'

'This succession of territory strengthens forever the power of the United States; I have just given to England a maritime rival that will sooner or later humble her pride.'

First Consul Napoleon Bonaparte wanted not just to restore but to expand France's colonial empire in the Caribbean.[1] Before the Revolution, Saint Domingue was the financial jewel in France's colonial Caribbean crown that also included the islands of Martinique, Guadeloupe, Marie Galante, Destrade, Les Saintes, Saint Martin, Saint Lucia and Tobago, along with Guyana in South America. The most important source of wealth extracted from those colonies was sugar, with Saint Dominque's production of the 'white gold' greater than that of all the other colonies combined. The colonies also produced indigo, cotton, tobacco, cocoa and coffee. Slave plantations were the foundation of this vast wealth. Of the three largest colonies, Saint Domingue's population included 55,000 whites, 30,000 free coloureds and 600,000 slaves, Martinique's 11,000 whites, 5,000 free coloureds and 85,000 slaves, and Guadeloupe 14,000 whites, 3,000 free coloureds and 90,000 slaves.[2]

Not everyone in France accepted slavery as the fate for Africans and their descendants in the colonies. Some argued that if natural rights existed, they should apply to all men. In 1788, a group that prominently included Jacques Brissot, Joseph, Marquis de Lafayette, Henri Gregoire, Antoine Condorcet and Honoré Mirabeau, created Les Amis des Noirs to lobby for slavery's abolition. Those same men would play a leading role in the pending Revolution. The Les Amis des Noirs faced formidable colonial interests that included plantation owners, merchants, shipowners and manufacturers, although they were not then organized into a formal group.

The unfolding Revolution in France inspired similar efforts in Saint Domingue. The colonists created their own assembly in 1789 and unveiled a constitution on 28 May 1790. The constitution gave free mulattoes equal rights with whites, although, for now, slavery persisted. On 22 August 1792, France's National Assembly voted to include thirty-six delegates from the colonies. Of that number only nine reached Paris – three whites, three mulattoes and three blacks. Gregoire led the abolitionist effort in the National Assembly, which voted to end slavery in Saint Domingue on 21 September 1793 and in all the colonies on 4 February 1794.

The result was anarchy and mass violence. In Martinique, Guadeloupe, Guyana and Saint Domingue, the colonists revolted against France while emancipated blacks refused to work and instead robbed, raped and murdered their former owners. Eventually whites and mulattoes crushed black insurrections in Martinique, Guadeloupe and Guyana, but failed in Saint Domingue. These racial wars overlapped with the war between France and Britain. British expeditions picked off French colonies one by one; by 1795, the Union Jack flew over Martinique, Tobago, Saint Lucia, the Saints and, briefly, Guadeloupe before the French retook it. With each loss of a colony, Saint Domingue and Guadeloupe became more potentially precious if order and productivity could be restored. The French did gain some territory. With the Treaty of Basel, signed on 22 July 1795, Spain ceded its eastern half of the island of Saint Domingue to France. Tragically, the horrors in France's half had spread to Spain's half and Madrid was relieved to dump that irrepressible violence.[3]

Incapable of suppressing the bloodbath on Saint Domingue by itself, France's government tried to do so by co-opting a brilliant emancipated slave leader, Pierre Toussaint Louverture, by naming him a general in 1795 and giving him command of French forces in Saint Domingue in 1796. Louverture's army eventually crushed all those who opposed him. Louverture, however, was no progressive. He ordered plantations confiscated and nodded approval as subordinates committed crimes against vulnerable whites, mulattoes and blacks.

The abolition of slavery and the resulting anarchy prompted colonial interests to organize a group in Paris to pressure the government to crush the revolts and re-establish slavery. The colonial lobby had important allies in the government including Charles Talleyrand, Jean Cambacérès, Pierre Forfait and François Barbé-Marbois along with Bonaparte's wife Josephine who was born in Martinique and sympathized with the Creole refugees, many of whom were relatives and family friends. That was a formidable political coalition.

Yet Bonaparte resisted the colonial lobby and sought a compromise that hopefully would appease the major players. In April 1800, he dispatched three commissioners to make peace and reassert control over Louverture. The black general and his followers rejected the initiative. Nonetheless, in August 1800, Bonaparte informed the State Council that for Saint Domingue he would retain abolition on the French half and retain slavery on the Spanish half, although he reserved the right 'to soften and limit slavery where I maintain it and to re-establish order and . . . discipline where I maintain liberty'.[4] He had Marine Minister Forfait devise a plan that co-opted Louverture by making him captain general while restraining his power by promoting other collaborators. Bonaparte respected and appreciated Louverture, who he believed had emerged 'amidst the revolution's ravages and by his prudence and courage had saved France a great and important colony. His virtues merit him the confidence of all parties; his success, the admiration of Europe.' Louverture should be assured of the First Consul's 'unlimited confidence' in him.[5] Nonetheless, the renegade general had to know his place so Bonaparte had his envoy to Louverture 'open talks with a certain hauteur'.[6] He issued a checklist of goals to the officers and officials that he dispatched to Saint Domingue, including informing the residents of Spain's former half of the island that henceforth they would be ruled by France, reassuring all whites that the French government would protect them and their property, and convincing everyone that the government would respect their values and customs.

Despite these conciliatory efforts, Louverture remained defiant. In March 1801, Bonaparte wrote directly to Louverture, assuring him that by naming him captain general 'the government could give him no greater mark of confidence'. As for Louverture's duties, he was 'to employ all your influence to maintain the peace, encourage agriculture and discipline and organize the National Guard . . . so that the government can . . . triumph over our enemies . . . I affectionately salute you.'[7] Louverture replied indirectly but could not have been clearer. He issued on 9 May 1801 a constitution that essentially declared independence. In doing so, he threw down the gauntlet to Bonaparte. When the First Consul reluctantly picked it up, he set in motion forces that would lead to another round of vicious fighting, death and destruction on Saint Domingue.

* * *

Bonaparte was not content merely to reassert control over Saint Domingue. Typically he had something far grander in mind. He dreamed of transforming the Caribbean Sea into a French lake bound by its existing colonies and capped by additional vast territory in North America. However, in trying to do so, he no sooner emerged from one war than he plunged France into two others and nearly a third.

He partly revealed his vision in April 1800, when he informed Talleyrand that he intended to talk Spanish King Charles IV into taking the Grand Duchy of Tuscany on behalf of his son-in-law Louis in return for giving France Louisiana and some other yet-to-be-decided assets. But before he could do that, he had to defeat the Austrians and reassert French domination of northern Italy. His victory at Marengo in June 1800 gave him the vital position of strength to bargain with Madrid. In July 1800, he dispatched a courier to Charles with his swap offer, followed by General Louis Berthier with powers to cut that and other deals. With the Treaty of Ildefonso, signed on 1 October 1800, Bonaparte reacquired for France New Orleans and the Louisiana Territory that Versailles had ceded to Madrid with the 1763 Treaty of Paris that ended the Seven Years War, along with Parma and Elba in return for Tuscany.[8]

The reacquisition of Louisiana certainly raised eyebrows. In stark contrast to Saint Domingue's 'white gold' riches, Louisiana was a colonial backwater whose administrative costs far exceeded what few revenues were gleaned for the Crown. Bonaparte valued Louisiana for strategic purposes. Indeed, for that very reason he had to keep his acquisition secret for now. The British would try to capture New Orleans if they learned that France had retaken its title. The French could only openly assert control over Louisiana after restoring peace with Britain.

To facilitate that, Bonaparte needed victories and bargaining chips against Britain. France's fleet was incapable of defeating Britain's Royal Navy on its own, but it had a fighting chance if it sailed united with Spain's fleet. He sought to entice Charles to ally with him against Britain by dangling the possibility of winning back Minorca from Britain for Spain. In November 1800, he replaced Berthier with his brother Lucien as his point man in Madrid. On 21 March 1801, Lucien and Chief Minister Manuel Godoy signed the Treaty of Aranjuez, which mostly reconfirmed the Treaty of Ildefonso. The biggest change was the transformation of the Grand Duchy of Tuscany into the Kingdom of Etruria, thus making Charles's son-in-law King Louis I.

Bonaparte sought to weaken Britain by either converting or conquering its oldest ally, Portugal. That realm would presumably be an easy picking. Portugal was militarily, economically and politically weak. It had a third-rate army and navy, a second-rate economy despite its far-flung colonial empire, and a faction-ridden government. The king had died and the queen, Marie I went mad in 1792; the vacillating crown prince, who would not become John VI until 1816, had been the regent since 1799.

Bonaparte had Talleyrand open negotiations with Portugal for a peace and trade treaty in April 1800.[9] If Lisbon rejected peace, Madrid would be encouraged to declare war against Portugal, motivated by the potential spoils of Portuguese provinces. He warned Lisbon that if it did not yield to the French and Spanish demands to sever all trade and diplomatic ties with Britain, the resulting war would lead to Portugal's destruction. He dispatched his brother-in-law, General Victor Leclerc, to command France's 15,000-man contingent in the alliance with Spain against Portugal

Spain declared war against Portugal on 27 February 1801. For Madrid, actually fighting a war proved to be far more bewildering than declaring one. As allies went, Spain was among the most frustrating for Bonaparte. Spain was a second-rate power whose generals and admirals seemed mired in sloth. Bonaparte had Talleyrand bluntly inform Madrid 'how shameful it was that the Spanish monarchy let two British warships blockade seven of theirs in Cadiz; what happened to the proud Castilians who conquered the New World and who let themselves be battered to the point of becoming the last nation of the world'.[10] He then proposed another swap. He would attach Lucca to Etruria in return for three frigates at Barcelona and six ships-of-the-line at Cartagena, each packed with three months of provisions and a 600,000 franc loan. Charles agreed.[11]

The war of France and Spain against Portugal was short and indecisive. The campaign opened on 20 May, when the allied army invaded Portugal. After the invaders captured Portugal's frontier fortress of Elvas, Lisbon agreed to negotiate. In the Treaty of Badajoz signed on 6 June 1801, the Portuguese ceded only the town of Olivenza to Spain. Charles deliberately let off Portugal as lightly as possible; he never would have attacked Portugal had Bonaparte not bullied him into it.

Bonaparte was furious when he learned the meagre results of the war and treaty. The French and Spanish generals had inexplicably given up without decisively defeating Portugal and occupying either Lisbon or Oporto, then the French and Spanish diplomats had hastily concluded a treaty that won nothing of substance. Bonaparte blistered Lucien for discarding his checklist of spoils to be picked from Portugal, which most vitally included at least two and ideally three provinces. He reminded him that Portuguese concessions were not important in themselves, but as bargaining chips with which to win concessions from Britain; thus the more won from Portugal, the more later to trade with Britain in return for genuine French interests. Actually the war had ended up diverting and thus diluting French rather than British power. He seared Lucien with these words: 'Affairs of this importance are not toys for children . . . Everything critical in politics demands that a minister must march with extreme caution and never decide anything precipitously . . . Influence the court where you find yourself and do not let them influence you.'[12] Lucien dutifully reopened negotiations. Two treaties were negotiated at Badajoz and signed on 29 September 1801, one between Portugal and France and the other between Portugal and Spain. Portugal agreed to close its ports to British trade and ally and trade freely with Spain and France against Britain.

These treaties also angered Bonaparte for being too weak. Without requiring the occupation of part of Portugal, its government would only comply symbolically with its coerced promises. He sought to convince Charles to resume the war with General Laurent Gouvion St Cyr commanding a Franco-Spanish army in a campaign to capture Oporto. Charles demurred; it was too late, peace reigned once again on the Iberian Peninsula. Indeed, Prime Minister Godoy insisted that France must now withdraw all its troops from Spain since Madrid had fulfilled its treaty obligations to Paris. Godoy's demand angered Bonaparte; he ordered Lucien to rebuke Godoy and request that Charles suppress his anti-French machinations. When Madrid remained obdurate, he fired Lucien and replaced him with St Cyr. But the new ambassador also failed to reverse Spanish peace policy with its neighbour. Bonaparte pointedly kept French troops in Spain until he ratified a peace treaty with Britain.[13]

Without the threat of another invasion, the Portuguese avenged themselves by confiscating French vessels and their goods and pricing French goods out of the market with onerous tariffs. Ambassador Jean Lannes repeatedly demanded that Lisbon revert to the previous lower tariffs then, on 10 August 1802, abruptly left the country. Bonaparte issued the same demand to Regent John, But Lisbon, secretly backed by Madrid, remained defiant. The Portuguese and Spaniards now shared the goal of ridding the Iberian Peninsula of French troops and influence. Bonaparte fumed but could do nothing more. He would inflict a harsh vengeance against Portugal five years later.[14]

* * *

Bonaparte had yet another goal in the New World. He sought to end an undeclared naval war that had raged between France and the United States since 1 August 1799. President John Adams got Congress to fund naval operations against French naval and merchant vessels in retaliation for French depredations against American ships that traded with Britain that resulted in the seizure of $20 million worth of cargoes and ships and the imprisonment of 6,500 sailors. America's largest warships were frigates but they and smaller vessels won nearly every battle they fought against their French equivalents. In all, the small American navy battered and captured one French frigate, twenty-six smaller warships and ninety-seven privateers and recaptured fifteen American merchant ships, while the French took merely one American warship and recaptured one of their own. American merchant losses to French depredations plummeted to one-third and insurance rates to half their pre-war levels. The experience that America's naval captains gained during that war would contribute to similar lopsided victories against first Tripoli and then Britain over the next 15 years.[15]

Bonaparte genuinely admired the United States and its heroic military and political leaders. When he turned his eyes toward America, this is what he saw: 'The United States is an independent country founded in the heart of the New World at the cost of the blood of so many immortal men who perished on the battlefield to throw off the English monarchy's leaden yoke.'[16] George Washington was among Bonaparte's heroes. After learning of his death on 14 December 1799, he had his army go into mourning and held a grand ceremony in the Invalides to honour him. He offered this elegy: 'Washington is dead. This great man fought against tyranny. He consolidated his country's liberty. His memory will always be dear to the French people like all free men of the two worlds and especially to French soldiers who, like him and American soldiers, fight for liberty and equality.'[17]

Most importantly, Bonaparte ordered Talleyrand to generously settle the conflict with three American diplomats, William Murray, Oliver Ellsworth and William Davie, that Adams had dispatched to Paris. Talleyrand tried to shake the envoys down for bribes like he had their three predecessors. When Bonaparte learned of Talleyrand's latest scam, he asked his brother Joseph and Pierre Roederer to take over the negotiations on 4 March. It took half a year of talks before they resolved their differences. Under the Treaty of Mortefontaine signed on 30 September 1800, the two countries declared mutual peace, free trade, fishing rights and the return of confiscated ships, cargos and crews; missing from the treaty was any French compensation for American ships and cargoes that had already been sold in prize courts.

In honour of the American envoys, Bonaparte held a festival that included a banquet, two plays, fireworks and 150 guests at his brother's chateau of Mortefontaine where the treaty was signed. Murray recorded his impressions of Bonaparte. He was 'grave, rather thoughtful, occasionally severe – not inflated, not egotistical – very exact in all his motions, which show at once an impatient heart & methodical head . . . of a most skilful self-possessed fencing master'.[18] The Americans in turn fascinated Bonaparte, especially their scrupulous regard for honesty and propriety. He tested that reputation by handing them a bag of ancient Roman coins as a gift then smiled as they politely refused to accept it.[19]

* * *

Bonaparte could not safely attempt to retake Saint Domingue until he restored peace with Britain. The preliminary treaty in October 1801 let him proceed. He meticulously planned the operation, detailing all the warships and transports, regiments, supplies and embarkation and disembarkation sites. He assumed that the expedition's costs would eventually be recouped by revenues skimmed from Saint Domingue's revived plantation production and trade; that proved to be a delusion. He tapped Admiral Louis Villaret-Joyeuse and his brother-in-law, General Victor Leclerc, who had married his sister Pauline, to lead the expedition's respective naval and land forces. The campaign to retake Saint Domingue was a complex operation involving three major squadrons including Villaret-Joyeuse's sailing from Brest, Admiral Honoré Ganteaume's from Toulon and Admiral Antoine Latouche-Treville's from Rochefort, along with smaller ones from Lorient, Havre, Cadiz, Flushing and Guadeloupe, with combined forces of 19,000 troops. Accompanying the expedition were hundreds of former white inhabitants who Bonaparte promised would retake their property and get positions in the restored government.[20]

Bonaparte had his commanders understand that the expedition's success depended on initially winning over Louverture and his black, mulatto and white followers. At first, they 'must be flattered and well-treated, while diminishing their popularity and power', but, after re-establishing control, the black leaders would be arrested and sent to France, the white leaders to Guyana, the mulattoes to Corsica and 'the white women who have prostituted themselves to the blacks . . . to Europe'. A proclamation would justify Louverture's fate for refusing 'to declare loyalty to France', and thus making himself a traitor and criminal subject to the law's strictest assertion.[21] He tried to lull Louverture into the trap with a long laudatory letter in November 1801, explaining the need to end the rebellion and restore order; assuring him of the great esteem he held for him, his brave followers and the constitution they had made; and asking him to swear allegiance to France in return for recognition and aid. He praised him as 'the first of your colour to attain such great power and . . . so distinguished by bravery and military talents . . . Count without reserve on our esteem and conduct yourself as you must as one of the principal citizens of the greatest country on earth.'[22]

Bonaparte sought cooperation from the British, Spanish and Americans, whose ports could supply French forces and whose warships could block supplies to rebel forces, thus achieving their common interest of 'destroying this black rebellion and hopes for a second one'.[23] He had Talleyrand insist to his foreign counterparts that the time to act was now, that next year the black rebels would be so entrenched in power that Bonaparte 'would be obliged to recognize Toussaint and renounce Saint Domingue' as a French colony. He did not disguise the expedition's primary objective: 'In annihilating Saint Domingue's black government, I am guided less by trade and financial considerations than by the need to smother . . . black power . . . If black liberty and a legitimate government is recognized in Saint Domingue . . . sooner or later the sceptre of black power will fall into their hands throughout the New World.'[24]

At first all went according to plan. Leclerc's expedition sailed from Brest on 14 December 1801 and dropped anchor at Cap François on 29 January 1802. Within months other contingents disembarked troops at Port-au-Prince, Port-de-Paix, Porto Plata, Mole, Fort Dauphin, Cayes, Santo Domingo, Gonaives, Saint Marc and Jeremie, first to assert local control and then link up with each other. Louverture submitted on 6 May, was dragged aboard a ship bound for France on 7 June, arrived on 23 July and was transported to a prison cell in the Fortress de Joux, where he died on 7 April 1803. Bonaparte tried to deprive blacks of the rights and other freedoms they had won. On 27 April 1802, he issued regulations that prevented blacks from being members of colonial delegations in France's legislatures and restricting black rights to vote or hold office. On 20 May 1802, the government passed a law that decriminalized the slave trade although it did not explicitly declare that former slaves were re-enslaved.

Bonaparte congratulated Leclerc for apprehending the black rebel leaders and extraditing them to France. Those blows to the rebellion raised France's stock market by inspiring investors with hopes for future business and profits in Saint Domingue.[25] But two black leaders, Jean Dessalines and Henri Christophe, took Louverture's place and carried on the struggle. The black rebels had an invincible deadly ally, yellow fever, which killed or debilitated virtually all the French troops that set foot on Saint Domingue; Leclerc was among the victims, dying on 2 November 1802. General Jean Rochambeau took over the remnants of the French army and begged for reinforcements to fill his army's steadily depleting ranks. Bonaparte sent replacements along with exhortations like 'nothing interests the nation more that island of Saint Domingue; if you are the one who restores it you can inscribe your name among the few who the French people will never forget and that posterity will revere'.[26] Those proved to be hollow words.

Meanwhile, the French did succeed in crushing a slave revolt on Guadeloupe, an island with a much smaller territory and population than Saint Domingue. A 3,600-man expedition led by General Antoine Richepanse left Brest on 7 January 1802 and reached Guadeloupe on 5 May. The French wiped out the last significant black resistance by 8 June and re-established slavery on 16 June. But, as on Saint Domingue, yellow fever decimated the invaders, with Richepanse himself succumbing on 3 September. Admiral Lacrosse completed the crushing of the black revolt.

The resumption of war with Britain in May 1803 threatened these hard-won gains. A British expedition captured Saint Lucia on 22 June and Tobago on 30 June, then forced Rochambeau's surrender at Cap Française, Saint Domingue on 29 November 1803. The British were not so foolish as to try to conquer Saint Domingue and did France a backhanded favour by eliminating that chimera for Bonaparte. The Republic of Haiti declared its independence on 1 January 1804. Independence was no panacea for Haitians; violence, poverty and corruption has persisted ever since. Looking back from St Helena, Napoleon admitted that: 'It was a great mistake to have wanted to submit it by force. I should have contented myself with governing through the intermediary of Toussaint.'[27] That 'mistake' squandered the lives of more than 54,000 soldiers, sailors and auxiliaries in Saint Domingue and elsewhere in the Caribbean basin along with a hundred million or so francs that could have been deployed or invested to bolster French interests elsewhere; perhaps 100,000 rebels and non-combatants, including 12,000 whites and 8,000 mulattoes, lost their lives in 1802 and 1803.[28]

* * *

Meanwhile tensions arose between France and the United States over American merchants smuggling goods to the black rebels on Saint Domingue. Bonaparte asked Talleyrand to gently rattle the sabre in a letter to Secretary of State James Madison. He was deterred from doing more, not wanting to rile American public opinion against France while he was secretly trying to retake Louisiana. With French military power in the New World sinking deeper into the Saint Domingue quagmire, the last thing he wanted was a war that led to America's conquest of Louisiana.[29] On 21 January 1803, he wrote to President Thomas Jefferson, expressing his desire for better bilateral relations and American prosperity.[30]

Reoccupying Louisiana was a covert action. He explained to Marine Minister Denis Decrès that 'we will take over Louisiana with the least delay . . . in the greatest secrecy'.[31] He dispatched General George Collot to administer Louisiana, but cautioned him 'to make his journey without letting anyone know what he was destined to do'.[32] In July 1802, he had a courier gallop off to Madrid with instructions for Ambassador Saint Cyr to expedite Louisiana's transfer as soon as possible. In February 1803, he was tapping regiments to occupy Louisiana.[33]

Bonaparte no sooner retook Louisiana than he sought to get rid of it. Louisiana was a perennial economic liability that the increasingly likely resumption of war with Britain compounded as a strategic liability. The campaign to reconquer Saint Domingue was an utter debacle. Sooner or later the British would take Saint Domingue and then Louisiana after learning that it had reverted to France. It made much more sense to sell Louisiana to the Americans and recoup some of that lost investment rather than lose all of it to Britain.

Rumours that France had bought Louisiana from Spain began circulating not long after the ink dried on the treaty signed in October 1800.[34] Inevitably those rumours, and eventually hard evidence to substantiate them, reached the White House. Savvy Americans understood the stark contrast between having for a neighbour weak, declining Spain or powerful, expanding France. Jefferson captured the strategic challenge posed by France's takeover of Louisiana to Ambassador Robert Livingston in Paris:

> There is on the globe one single spot, the possessor of which is our natural and habitual enemy. It is New Orleans, through which the

produce of three-eighths of our territory must pass to market and from its fertility will ere long yield more than half of our whole produce and contain more than half of our inhabitants. France, placing herself in that door, assumes to us . . . a point of eternal friction . . . From that moment we must marry ourselves to the British fleet and nation.[35]

Jefferson instructed Livingston to determine the price of buying New Orleans and sent James Monroe, a previous ambassador to France, to Paris to assist in negotiating the purchase. They were to pay no more than $5 million for New Orleans. If the price demanded was exorbitant or Bonaparte was unwilling to sell, then Monroe and Livingston should subtlety warn that the United States would be forced to take what it could not buy. Livingston initiated talks with Talleyrand in February 1802. Talleyrand typically tried to shake Livingston down for a bribe before any talks could proceed. That naturally infuriated Livingston who eventually found a way to let Bonaparte know what chicaneries his foreign minister was committing.

Bonaparte recognized that the Americans could easily seize New Orleans and the rest of Louisiana without paying a penny to the French treasury. On 10 April, during a conference with Foreign Minister Talleyrand, Treasury Minister François Barbé-Marbois and Marine Minister Denis Decrès, Bonaparte decided to sell all of Louisiana for 50 million francs. He assigned the negotiations to Barbé-Marbois who had served in the French embassy in Philadelphia from 1779 to 1785, understood Americans and spoke fluent English. But the next day Talleyrand got to Livingston first and informed him that all of Louisiana was for sale. It was not until 15 April, that Barbé-Marbois conveyed that same message to Livingston at his house, where Monroe had arrived earlier that day.

Although Monroe and Livingston were authorized only to buy New Orleans, they leapt at the chance to pocket the entire Louisiana territory. After weeks of haggling between them and Barbé-Marbois and Talleyrand, they eventually agreed to pay 60 million francs ($11,500,000) for Louisiana and assume 20 million francs ($3,750,000) in American claims against France. In the treaty signed on 2 May 1803, the United States acquired the Louisiana Territory which included all lands that drained eastward into the Mississippi River, some stretching as far west as the Rocky Mountains watershed. The Louisiana Purchase doubled America's territory. Talleyrand offered these kind remarks: 'You have made a noble bargain for yourselves and I suppose you will make the best of it.'[36] Bonaparte boasted of the deal's strategic significance: 'This succession of territory strengthens forever the power of the United States; I have just given to England a maritime rival that will sooner or later humble her pride.'[37] Both men's remarks were prescient.

Chapter 7

The Great Reformer

'With all destroyed, we must now recreate.'

'It is by a great number of precise experiments with the view of reaching the truth...that we have advanced little by little to simple theories, useful for everyone for all aspects of life.'

First Consul Napoleon Bonaparte excelled not just as a general and diplomat, but also as a reformer and innovator. He took power with a vision of completing France's revolutionary transformation from a feudal realm into a modern nation-state. In that he fell short, but he led France several giant steps on that centuries-long violent, jolting journey. He best expressed his outlook in a speech whereby he called for attacking the complacency, lethargy and fatalism afflicting those in power: 'With all destroyed, we must now recreate. A government with powers exists, but what about the rest of the country? . . . We are . . . without system, without unity . . . I am devoted to the Republic's wellbeing, but must focus on its future. If you believe that the Republic is firmly established, you are strongly mistaken.'[1]

He sought to stimulate a renaissance of creativity and innovation in France.[2] He had Lucien, his brother and Interior Minister, compose top-ten lists of painters, sculptors, composers, musicians, architects, actors and 'others in all genres whose talent merit public attention' in September 1800.[3] He had paintings commissioned to commemorate the battles of Rivoli, Marengo, Mosekirch, The Pyramids, Aboukir and Mount Tabor. France's national art museum, the Louvre, had been established by a revolutionary decree on 26 May 1791. On 1 September 1801, Bonaparte made the Louvre the flagship of a national art museum system by establishing branches in Lyon, Marseilles, Bordeaux, Geneva, Nantes, Lille, Strasbourg, Nancy, Dijon, Caen, Toulouse, Mainz and Brussels and tapped Vivant Denon to be the first director. And of course, he enhanced France's art collection by stealing hundreds of works from the countries he overran. Bonaparte inadvertently provoked a style revolution. The prevailing neoclassical style inspired by excavations at Pompeii and Herculean during the mid-eighteenth century was disrupted by the gaudy Egyptomania inspired by Bonaparte's conquest and his savants' discoveries. At least one group appreciated Bonaparte's efforts to promote the arts. He wrote a thank-you letter to Edward Livingstone, the president of New York's Academy of Arts, for naming him an honorary member: 'Let them know that I accept with pleasure and that I appreciate the good opinion that wanted to have me.'[4]

As if the Louvre was not getting crowded enough with looted art works, he established the National Archives there. He had scholars search the archives of conquered countries and send any documents concerning French history back to the Louvre. Eventually he transferred the National Archives to the Tuileries. As for literature, he promoted pragmatic rather than creative works. He commissioned an encyclopaedia that brought together the leading works of literature, history and science.[5] He called on the savant René Hauy to write a mathematics textbook for the national lycées or high schools to promote 'the enlightenment in places so important for human knowledge'.[6] He patronized music primarily for political purposes. On 5 March 1800, he instructed Lucien to get composers like Claude Rouget de l'Isle and Ponce Lebrun of popular songs like the 'Marseillaise', 'Hymn aux Combats' and 'Chant du Depart' to adjust their lyrics to champion 'the idea that, among great peoples, peace comes only after victory'.[7]

He instituted the Legion of Honour on 19 May 1802. His intention was 'to found an institution dedicated to perpetuating . . . sentiments of good and great actions'.[8] Eventually the Legion of Honour had five degrees, with the pension and rank awarded according to the recipient's relative service to France; the highest was the Grand Eagle. By the empire's end, Napoleon had distributed more than 48,000 Legions of Honour, with 87 per cent going to the military and the rest to writers, artists, doctors, inventors, industrialists, officials and other individuals of outstanding merit.[9] He explained that: 'These little devices have an incalculable effect on men, whose calculations are not the result of coolheaded reason and in which each carries the fears and prejudices of his group.'[10] He loved talking both theory and practice with scientists, inventors and builders, then heaping them with honours and stipends to reward their achievements and encourage more. Typical was this message to Benjamin Thompson, Count Rumford: 'It is by a great number of precise experiments with the view of reaching truth and with the talent that you put to that, that we have advanced little by little to simple theories, useful for everyone for all aspects of life.'[11]

Perhaps Bonaparte's greatest contribution to humanity was modernizing French law which became a model for many other countries. He recognized that he held three key political assets for transforming France's 42 hodgepodge regional codes and 14,000 Revolutionary decrees into one rational system: timing, talent and will. He assessed the proper timing, asserted his will and assembled the talent. He formed a committee chaired by Second Consul Cambacérès to revise the Civil Code on 12 August 1800. Cambacérès was the perfect choice because he was a legal expert who had already worked on revising the code in 1793 and so was well aware of its daunting complexity. Progress was, however, slow. The members did not conduct their first session until 23 July 1801 and the government did not promulgate the results until 21 March 1804. Bonaparte did what he could to encourage the committee. He attended 55 of the 106 sessions during which he played devil's advocate by questioning underlying assumptions and procedures. His bottom line for any law was whether it was at once fair, clear and useful. The committee eventually distilled French civil law into 2,281 articles in 493 pages. Appropriately, the revised Civil Code was officially renamed the Code Napoleon in 1807.[12]

Reforming the Civil Code was only the first step. It took years to reform each legal area. Experts began work on the Civil Procedure Code on 22 March 1802 and the result was promulgated on 9 May 1806; the Commercial Code on 3 April 1801 and 20 September 1807; the Criminal Instruction Code on 28 March 1801 and 27 November 1808; the Penal Code on 28 March 1801 and 22 February 1810; the Rural Code on 19 May 1808 and by July 1814, but Louis XVIII shelved it. For each code, his object was to simplify and rationalize, to eliminate contradictions, injustices, anachronisms and elite privileges and to promote legal equality for all. In that he largely succeeded.

A critical element of governing is gathering and dispersing revenues as efficiently as possible. Bonaparte sought to impose fiscal sanity on a country where corruption and incompetence reigned, especially under the Directorate that preceded him. To that end he ensured that able men headed the treasury and finance ministries, with each overseeing, checking and dependent on the other. That creative tension boosted efficiency and minimized corruption. He sent a powerful message to speculators on 26 January 1800, when the financier Gabriel Ouvrand was arrested on a litany of charges. Until the revenue system of taxes and tariffs within France was revamped, the government had to borrow money from abroad. Bonaparte had Talleyrand negotiate loans from Holland and Hamburg.[13]

Bonaparte transformed the Caisse des Comptes into the Bank of France with expanded fiscal powers and duties on 13 February 1800. The Bank of France was a joint public and private venture with an initial offering of 30 million francs' worth of shares; he was the first shareholder. The government used the Bank of France for ever more transactions including lottery and pension deposits and payouts and short-term loans. Unfortunately, bad management and speculation in the autumn of 1805 provoked a financial crisis with runs on the Bank of France and other banks. On 22 April 1806, Napoleon overhauled the Bank of France's statute to curb speculation and encourage investments. He explained that 'I must be the master of all that concerns me, especially that regarding the Bank'.[14]

When Bonaparte took power France's monetary system was a mishmash of different currencies including Ancien Régime livres, franc *mandats* that replaced paper *assignats* which had plummeted to less than one per cent of their printed value, a five-gram silver franc and paper issues from diverse financial institutions, most of dubious value. Bonaparte was determined to establish a currency for France that both reflected and enhanced its power. On 18 March 1803, he established the Franc Germinal, whose gold and silver mix remained unaltered until 1928. He granted the Bank of France a 25-year monopoly on issuing the franc, which slowly, steadily muscled aside other currencies and eventually dominated transactions. He appointed two excellent treasury ministers, François Barbé-Marbois from 1801 to 1806 and Nicolas Mollien from 1806 to 1814. He tapped a financial director for each department and 840 inspectors that the finance minister deployed according to circumstances.[15]

Other economic reforms followed. In February 1801, Bonaparte wrote to Interior Minister Jean Chaptal complaining that 'French iron was inferior to Swedish iron', then asked if 'it would be possible to ameliorate the fabrication'. Chaptal was to 'reveal to the principal manufacturers of this country how' the best iron was made 'and how they can improve their own processes'.[16] In September 1801, he adopted for France a uniform system of weights and measures based on the metric system and initiated the first national industrial exposition and work on the Ourcq Canal. He founded the Society for the Encouragement of National Industry in 1801, the Chamber of Commerce in 1802 and the Chamber of Manufacturing in 1803.

Other projects were ongoing. He had the royal palaces refurbished including Versailles, Fontainebleau, Compiègne, Marly and Rambouillet. He had extensive work done to ensure that Paris's fifty-six fountains gushed day and night, while new ones were built. For large-scale, long-term public works like canals, he had labourers organized into military-style 'pioneer' battalions. After reviewing a report critical of a long-term military construction plan for France, he observed that the engineers appeared to be poorly deployed and overwhelmed: 'Experience proves that the worst general administrative fault is trying to do too much'. He called for devoting 'twenty years to finish the blueprints and plans and thus work for posterity'.[17] He took measures to conserve the empire's forests from the clear-cutting that was destroying the venerable oaks for French warships. He issued orders that forest inspectors be investigated to ensure that logging interests had not corrupted them and that they had the powers necessary to halt the devastation.[18]

Bonaparte's brush with the plague in Egypt that killed hundreds of his men rendered him sensitive to the relationship between personal and civic health. He bathed daily and encouraged his fellow citizens to do likewise. He ordered the filth of centuries scraped up and carted from Paris's streets, alleys and vacant lots. He required each arrondissement to have at least one doctor. On 2 June 1800, he called on the French people to get vaccinated against smallpox and required each department to stockpile enough vaccine for those who wanted it. He established a Society for the Extinction of Smallpox to promote his crusade. Years later he set the example by having his son, the King of Rome, inoculated on 11 May 1811. With these acts he undoubtedly prolonged countless lives.

He took measures to revitalize the French Academy whose ranks the Revolution had devastated. In doing so he carried on the banner of that venerable institution, founded in 1635, to get all people living in France actually to speak standard French. That mission was far from complete even more than a century and a half after its inception. Most people around Paris and in the north-east spoke more or less standard French, albeit with distinct accents, but the further south one ventured, the more dialects morphed into the distinct language of Occitan, with its own array of dialects. Then there were pockets of unrelated languages around France's fringe, with Basque and Catalan at opposite ends of the Pyrenees, Breton in Brittany, Flemish in Picardy and German in Alsace.

He understood the relationship between education and power. Schools should promote not just a literate but a skilled, enterprising and patriotic people. Until he took power, schools mostly were a parochial concern. Most Catholic parishes provided elementary instruction in reading, writing and mathematics for children whose families could afford the fees and spare their labour. Scores of expensive private secular schools also existed. There was a government boarding school for boys at St Cyr and another for girls at St Germain, but they were confined to the elite's brightest children. Although in 1793, the revolutionary government proclaimed the right of children to be educated, it did little to realize that vision. There was no national education system.

Bonaparte was determined to change that. On 1 May 1802, he issued a decree that transformed French education. Each department would organize an elementary school system in each commune and as many secondary schools as needed for brighter, interested students. The national government would establish forty-five lycées or advanced schools for those who passed entrance examinations, as well as l'École Spéciale Militaire for boys aged 16 to 18 years old and interested in becoming army officers. Each year 2,400 scholarships would be distributed to the qualified sons of officers or officials. He wanted to make St Cyr a model for the lycées to be established, but was not pleased by what he found during an inspection in 15 May 1801. He complained to Interior Minister Chaptal that the boys were barely clad and without uniforms, there was no rule or order in the classroom or administration and there was no library where the boys could study. He called for the boys to be unformed, split into companies, drilled by veterans, taught by knowledgeable teachers and the library to be filled with at least 2,000 books, all underwritten by a budget of 600 francs for each student.[19] On 10 March 1803 he founded, l'École Polytechnique as an engineering school which emphasized military affairs including gunnery. The Revolution had repressed the religious schools. On 22 June 1804, he decreed that the Catholic Church could re-establish schools.

Tragically, war overshadowed and mostly consumed Bonaparte's array of truly progressive policies.

Chapter 8

The Reluctant Belligerent

'We seem not to be in peace but only in truce, which is completely the English government's fault.'

'If we were masters of the straits for six hours, we would be masters of the world.'

The Treaty of Amiens was viewed by the governments of France and Britain, along with nearly all other states, as merely a breather before war resumed. That attitude helped fuel a cycle of accusations and aggressions by both Paris and London that fulfilled the prophecy. First Consul Napoleon Bonaparte used that swelling likelihood as both an excuse and an imperative to expand French influence and territory wherever he could.[1]

Dominating Italy was critical to Bonaparte's plan eventually to squeeze Britain from the Mediterranean. In ceding Venetia to Austria in the Lunéville treaty, he hoped to reassert French hegemony over the rest of the Italian Peninsula. He took a decisive step in that strategy on 25 January 1802, when he engineered the Cisalpine Republic's transformation into the Italian Republic. He had convened the Cisalpine Republic's assembly in Lyon, where the members not only approved the name change but by acclamation elected him their president for a ten-year term. The following day, he tapped Francesco Melzi d'Eril to be his vice president and run the Republic based on his instructions. He sought to bolster the Italian Republic's economy by eliminating trade barriers among the former realms that composed it and forming a national bank to finance investments. Building a reliable Italian state, nation and army would take years. For now, the Italian Republic's survival ultimately depended on the presence of 10,000 French troops that would quickly crush any revolt against its development.[2]

Bonaparte was sensitive to the slightest foreign political changes. In June 1802, after Charles Emmanuel IV of Sardinia ceded his throne to his brother who became Victor Emmanuel I, Bonaparte instructed Foreign Minister Talleyrand 'to let our agents in Rome, Naples and Tuscany know that I will not tolerate the Sardinian king's presence in Italy. If the Sardinian king wants to abdicate, wants to live in Rome, he must not maintain any correspondence with any minsters nor have more than five attendants . . . who will be subject to' that military district's supervision.[3] He had nothing subversive to fear from Charles Emmanuel who had abandoned his crown in deep sorrow after his beloved wife died and thereafter sought to isolate himself from all worldly affairs.

Bonaparte then took a series of steps to transform Piedmont into French territory. French troops were deployed at fortresses, mountain passes and cities. French officials pressured local governments to dismiss Piedmontese loyal to the House of Savoy and replace them with pro-French republicans. That pending annexation of Piedmont obviously enraged Victor Emmanuel and his court at Cagliari in Sardinia. Bonaparte put Talleyrand to work getting the king to recognize that annexation in return for annual payments of 500,000 francs to him and his children as long as they lived. In return, France would recognize the monarchy's legitimacy and possession of Sardinia. He acted legally according to the Ildefonso treaty with Spain, when he annexed the island of Elba on 26 August 1802. He committed a blatant act of imperialism when he annexed Piedmont and split it into six departments on 11 September 1802.[4]

Among Napoleon Bonaparte's many sobriquets was kingmaker. The first kingdom that he concocted was that of Etruria, the former Grand Duchy of Tuscany which he traded for Elba.[5] The new king and queen would be Louis, the son of Duke Ferdinand of Parma, and Marie Louise, the daughter of King Charles IV of Spain. They were living in Madrid when word of their promotion reached them. The First Consul invited the new royal couple to spend some time in Paris to observe how France was progressively governed before they proceeded to Florence. Bonaparte and Josephine welcomed Louis and Marie at Malmaison on 3 June 1801, for a visit that dragged on for six weeks. Bonaparte struggled to conceal his disappointment with Louis, who was as weak-minded as he was weak-willed. Instead he or Talleyrand met with the newly-minted royal couple to advise them before Bonaparte finally informed them on 27 July 1801 that their kingdom was ready to receive them. They arrived in Florence in mid-August. Bonaparte assigned Mérédic Moreau Saint-Méry to act as Louis's advisor and help him organize his new realm with a model French-style administration, ensuring that only pro-French Tuscans took key positions.

Louis soon realized Bonaparte's misgivings about him by alienating his realm's leading subjects along with Saint-Méry and French ambassador General Henri Clarke. Bonaparte was perplexed over what to do: 'Without doubt Louis I is king and he has the right . . . to rule as he wishes.' He had Talleyrand discern whether Louis 'was crazy or just sick'.[6] He shared his concerns with Charles IV about his son-in-law and warned him of the possibility that Etruria's government might declare the king insane and depose him in favour of his infant son, with the queen as regent. Meanwhile, he took an almost a paternal interest in Louis by treating him as an apprentice to power with long letters of advice. When Louis's father, Ferdinand, the Duke of Parma, died on 9 October 1802, Bonaparte sent his condolences and eventually joined Parma to Etruria. He did so only after consulting Pius VII over whether it would be better to give Parma to Sardinia's king as compensation for his loss of Piedmont. He finally reasoned that satisfying Charles IV, Louis's father-in-law, enhanced French interests more than giving it to Victor Emmanuel. Then Bonaparte learned that Louis had died on 27 May 1803. His four-year-old son took the throne as Louis II. Bonaparte shifted his letters of advice to the boy's mother and regent, Marie Louise.[7]

The Kingdom of the Two Sicilies, which included the Italian peninsula's southern third and the island of Sicily, was at best a secondary player on Europe's geopolitical stage. Although the realm occupied the Mediterranean basin's core, its government was too corrupt and effete and its people too poverty-stricken and feudalistic to capitalize on that strategic and economic crossroads. Then came the convulsions that shook the peninsula from Bonaparte's conquests in northern Italy in 1796 and 1797, followed by Austria's 1798 counter-conquest, backed by a Russian army. King Ferdinand IV was a naturally timid man, but his outspoken, anti-French queen Maria Carolina, his chief minister and English expatriate John Acton, British ambassador William Hamilton and Admiral Horatio Nelson pressured him into joining the coalition. In September 1799, Ferdinand ordered the 30,000-man Neapolitan army led by General Karl von Mack to invade the Papal States to drive out the French. The Neapolitan army marched into Rome on 29 November, but soon retreated as French General Jean Championnet advanced with 30,000 troops. Rebellions erupted against Bourbon rule in Naples and other cities. The royal family fled to Palermo, Sicily, shortly before Championnet marched into Naples on 21 January 1799 and helped install the Parthenopean Republic. The republic lasted a mere six months after Championnet withdrew his army to Rome. A peasant revolt led by Cardinal Fabrizio Ruffo in Calabria combined with a combined British and Russian fleet led by Admirals Nelson and Fyodor Ushakov, respectively, off Naples, caused the rebels to surrender on 21 June 1799. Ferdinand and Maria Carolina settled uneasily back upon their thrones. In March 1800, newly elected Pius VII ascended the throne, backed by both Papal and Neapolitan troops. Then came Bonaparte's whirlwind campaign capped by Marengo on 14 June 1800. Under the armistice, the remnants of Austria's army withdrew east beyond the Mincio. A second round of fighting that climaxed with Hohenlinden in December led to the Lunéville treaty in February 1801. Bonaparte now shifted his mind southward.

Hegemony over southern Italy and better relations with Rome had long been on Bonaparte's lengthening to-do list. The first step was to force Ferdinand not just to evacuate Rome but let French troops garrison key Neapolitan ports. To raise the pressure, he dispatched General Joachim Murat to Florence to command French troops in Tuscany and mass them on the frontier of the Papal States. Murat's mission was delicate: 'He should treat the Roman court like a friendly power. He must convey on all occasions that the Government highly esteems the Pope. As for Naples, he must make known that the government's intention is not to worry the king of Naples about his realm as long as he evacuates the Roman state and leaves the Pope the master of his own realm.'[8] He explained that 'after the Neapolitans . . . return home we must advance to the Neapolitan kingdom's frontier without giving Rome a single worry . . . We must make the pope understand that whatever happens to Naples results from their obstinate king.'[9] The Neapolitans must agree in writing to French domination of the Papal States and sever all trade with Britain and the British garrison in Malta. The Neapolitans must not only render the fortresses of Taranto, Gallipoli, Otranto and Brindisi to French garrisons, but must pay 500,000 francs each month for their upkeep. The occupation troops would number 7,000 infantry, 1,000 cavalry and 400 sappers. French citizens must be compensated for any losses they suffered from confiscations or riots by Neapolitan officials, troops or mobs. Finally, the Neapolitans must present France with all the art they looted from Rome. And that is exactly what happened. Under the Truce of Foligno of 18 February 1801, reiterated by the Treaty of Florence of 28 March 1801, Ferdinand accepted these concessions if Bonaparte pledged to support his continued rule. News of the humiliating treaty sparked protests in Naples. Ferdinand had the dissent crushed. French troops occupied the designated ports by April 1801.[10]

Diplomatic relations between Paris and Naples remained tense. Bonaparte was well aware that Ferdinand deeply resented these impositions while, atop that, Maria Carolina fiercely hated France whose revolutionaries had dethroned and beheaded her younger sister Marie Antoinette. The queen figuratively wore the trousers in their family; she was as outspoken as her husband was meek. Bonaparte sent them separate letters with similar messages on 28 July 1803. He lauded Ferdinand for hosting French troops and assured him that Naples only owed them lodging, food and firewood, which, by the way, they were far behind in providing. He hoped that the king would fulfil his duty and spurn being swayed by French enemies in his court. He began his letter to Maria Carolina with a nod to her letter imploring him to release them from their obligations to France. He then explained that French policy was to promote peace with its neighbours. Having said that, he castigated her and her husband for letting their administration be headed by a foreigner, Acton, whose true loyalty was to England. Although intervening in another realm's internal affairs was repugnant to him, the kingdom of Naples was geographically and politically too important to France for him to overlook that affront. He hoped that she and her husband would do what was necessary to maintain peace between their countries. The queen and her king ignored Bonaparte's not-so-veiled warnings. They, Acton and other key officials conspired with British agents to undercut French influence not just in their own realms but throughout the Italian peninsula. Bonaparte had French ambassador Charles Alquier convey to Ferdinand, Maria Carolina and Acton, that the First Consul laughed at their machinations, could easily conquer all of Italy if he so desired and indeed, if the provocations persisted, might well overthrow the kingdom of Naples and attach that realm to the Italian Republic. Eventually he would make good on most of that threat.[11]

Bonaparte also sought hegemony over Switzerland, the Helvetian Republic, to bridge the parallel advances of French armies along the Danube and Po River valleys during future wars with Austria. The first step came on 7 January 1801, when, assisted by French agents, Swiss federalists ousted centralists and took power in Berne, the capital. Bonaparte sent General Michel Ney and 40,000 troops into Switzerland to impose order and pressure the Diet to dissolve itself on 26 October 1801. He then arranged to have the pro-French Alois von Reding made the Helvetian Republic's Landammann or prime minster on 21 November 1801. He followed this up on 28 December 1802, with a lengthy letter to representatives of the cantons, advising them on how best to construct an enduring republic. He began by declaring their situation critical as their religious, economic and linguistic differences appeared poised to overwhelm centuries of alliance among them. He called on them to set aside their quarrels and construct a federation that guaranteed equal rights for all cantons and citizens. That meant that some cantons would have to dismantle the oligarchies that ruled them. Finally, he warned them that the French and Italian republics would not tolerate a Swiss government aligned with their enemies. He organized six new cantons, Saint Gall, Grisons, Argovie, Thurgovie, Tessin and Vaud, and added them to the Helvetian Republic. No canton was more strategic than Vaud since it straddled the Simplon Pass leading to Italy. He annexed the French-speaking cantons of Geneva, Mulhouse, Bienne, Neuchatel and Valais which were outside the Helvetian Republic. On 19 February 1803, he presided as representatives of the nineteen cantons signed the Act of Mediation that reconciled centralists and federalists under French protection. He ensured that pro-French Swiss held key government posts in as many cantons as possible, especially in Berne. His man in Berne was Jean Rapp, a tough, smart army officer fluent in German whose critical role was to ensure that most Swiss senators kept their country aligned with France. The other European states naturally feared that the Helvetian Republic, like the Italian Republic, was merely a French puppet that would soon name Bonaparte its president. Bonaparte had Talleyrand spread reassurances to Europe's capitals that he would reject any such offer. Nonetheless France and Switzerland signed a defensive alliance on 27 September 1803.[12]

The resolution of peace with some countries unmasked violent conflicts with others. As great power warships stopped prowling the Mediterranean and sailed back to their respective ports, the Barbary States resumed their piracy against European and American merchant vessels. Algerian pirates were the most voracious despite the peace treaty their government signed with France on 28 December 1801. Twice in July 1802, Bonaparte wrote to Algiers' ruler, demanding that he end the depredations and pay 200,000 piasters in reparations or else France would devastate Algiers as an example to the other Barbary States. Meanwhile he had Talleyrand issue Constantinople with a complaint against Algiers and demand that Sultan Selim order his governor to end the piracy or else the First Consul would reconquer Egypt. The Bey eventually paid up and the other Barbary rulers restrained their predations. French and Tunisian diplomats signed a peace treaty on 23 February 1802. Bonaparte followed this up by dispatching Colonel Horace Sebastiani and two aides first to Tripoli, to get its ruler to recognize the Italian Republic, then to Egypt, Palestine, Smyrna, Zante, Cephalonia and Corfu to assess political and military conditions there before finally returning to France. At each place the key goal was to determine the extent of British influence and how it might be countered both before and during the next war.[13]

Bonaparte wanted to prolong peace for as long as possible even as he took steps that made war more likely. He launched a diplomatic campaign to assure Europe that he was committed to peace, while playing off each country against the others. His effort to reroute all diplomatic roads to Paris did not get far. In July 1802, with mounting foreign criticism over French forces lingering in the Papal States, the Kingdom of Naples and the Helvetian Republic, he had a letter sent to the British, Austrian, Russian, Prussian and Bavarian governments, pledging that those troops would soon withdraw. He tried to entice the Prussian King Frederick William into a defensive alliance against Austria but was rejected. He tried to entice Austrian King Francis into a pact to promote common interests but was rejected. He tried to nurture close ties with young Tsar Alexander by keeping him updated on his compliance with Amiens, his efforts to end Barbary States piracy and his other peaceful initiatives in Germany, Italy and elsewhere. He was disappointed when Alexander snubbed his efforts.[14]

* * *

All along, the biggest strategic thorn troubling Bonaparte was Malta, where the British remained embedded despite being required to leave within three months after the Treaty of Amiens was ratified. He wrote to Pius VII, asking him to name a new Grand Master of the Knights of Saint John as soon as possible to undercut British authority along with Neapolitan claims to the island.[15] In November 1802, he sent Antoine Andreossy as his ambassador to London with a long diplomatic wish list topped by Britain's withdrawal from Malta, but also including the resumption of bilateral trade; the recognition of the Italian, Ligurian and Helvetian Republics; and the ending of support for French counterrevolutionaries.[16] Nearly two months later, the British refusal to yield on any of these issues prompted Bonaparte to observe that 'we seem not to be in peace but only in truce, which is completely the English government's fault'.[17] He complained of Britain's retention of Malta to Charles Whitworth, the new British ambassador, after he arrived on 13 November 1802. The British not only did not budge from Malta but committed other provocative acts. In December 1802, he had Talleyrand inform Whitworth 'how astonished and upset I am to learn that Comte d'Artois', the would-be Louis XVIII's younger brother Charles, had received various honours and hospitality from George III.[18]

Bonaparte launched a diplomatic offensive in early 1803, designed to ally France with 'the peoples and princes suffering with growing impatience under the English yoke'.[19] The message to various courts was that 'the continent needs peace and the only thing that can disturb that are English games'.[20] He sought diplomatic allies, the weightier the better. He wrote to Frederick William complaining that Britain violated the Treaty of Amiens by retaining Malta and asking for his help in pressuring London to comply with its legal and moral obligations.[21]

He saw Russia as the continent's key diplomatic and military power. Geopolitically Russia directly threatened not France but the Central European powers. An alliance between France and Russia would keep those states in line and perhaps push them into a European effort against Britain. So he employed all his diplomatic wiles to keep Alexander neutral and ideally talk him into an alliance. In a March 1803 letter, he proposed that they work together to advance several common interests, including preventing Muslim states from repressing Christian residents, bettering relations with the Ottoman Empire and, especially, pressuring Britain to evacuate Malta. He called on Alexander to become Malta's protector and guarantee its independence. In doing so, he tried to sidestep the Treaty of Amiens that designated the Kingdom of Naples as Malta's protector. He dispatched General Auguste Colbert to Russia as an envoy to nurture relations with Alexander, his younger brother Constantine and other prominent figures in Russia's elite, while gathering intelligence on that country's economic and military might and the extent of British influence at the court. When Alexander expressed his desire to mediate between France and Britain, Bonaparte encouraged him with one caveat. A formidable obstacle to better relations was Ambassador Arkadi Markov, with his belligerent character and virulent hatred of France. Alexander could only act as a diplomatic go-between if he replaced Markov with someone congenial in Paris and stopped listening to anti-French advisors in St Petersburg. Although Alexander did recall Markov and replace him with Peter Oubril, the change in style did not diminish conflicts between France and Russia.[22]

The British had a lengthy list of grievances against Bonaparte just as he did against them. London protested France's annexations of Elba and Piedmont on 26 August and 11 September 1802, respectively, along with Bonaparte's 'mediation' for Switzerland on 30 September 1802, although none of those acts violated the Treaty of Amiens. Nonetheless, on 15 February 1803, Whitworth informed Bonaparte that Britain would keep Malta in retaliation for France's annexation of Piedmont and Elba. Bonaparte angrily insisted that the Treaty of Amiens legally bound

Britain to evacuate Malta and said nothing about Piedmont and Elba.[23] On 9 March, Parliament approved George III's military budget for war preparations.

During a formal reception for the diplomatic corps on 18 March 1803, Bonaparte erupted in wrath against Whitworth. Bonaparte's stepdaughter Hortense recalled that he

> said several words to the women but on finding himself near Lord Whitworth . . . denounced him with scathing words before the assembly. He spoke of treaties the English broke and their cabinet's bad faith . . . with a tone that rendered everyone mute with astonishment and fear . . . After returning to his quarters, the First Consul appeared unburdened of a great weight. His anger had disappeared . . . My mother gently reproached him, 'You made everyone tremble'. . . . `They all actually heard me?' he asked. 'It is true. I was wrong'.[24]

He tried to repair the situation in a private meeting with Whitworth, but the damage was done.

Word of his public tirade empowered London's war hawks. The Addington government rejected his face-saving offer of trading Corfu or Crete for Malta. Instead, on 26 April, Whitworth issued an ultimatum that France withdraw from Holland and Helvetia immediately while accepting Britain's occupation of Malta for a decade. On 4 May, Bonaparte had Talleyrand express to Whitworth his disbelief that such 'a great, powerful, sensible nation could want . . . a war whose results will unleash such terrible evils for such petty reasons'.[25] He insisted that the Treaty of Amiens was and should be inviolable and that the British should evacuate Malta. Whitworth countered by citing Bonaparte's blatant treaty violations by keeping troops in Holland, Switzerland, the Papal States and the Kingdom of Naples.

With both countries on the brink of war, Bonaparte was willing to compromise. He instructed Talleyrand in meeting with Whitworth on 10 May,

> to act cold, aloof and even a little arrogant. If the note is an ultimatum, make him understand that this word means war and that this manner of negotiating is from a superior to an inferior. If the note does not contain this word, act like it is there . . . Frighten him with its consequences. If he is unshakeable', walk out with him and as you part, ask him 'Are Cape Hope and Goree

Island evacuated?' Soften a bit as the meeting ends and invite him to return before writing to his court, so that you can tell him the bad impression he made on me, but that could be diminished with the evacuation of Cape Hope and Goree Island.[26]

The obvious implication was that France would withdraw from Holland and Helvetia if Britain withdrew from Malta, Cape Hope and Goree.

Whitworth spurned this chance to cut a face-saving deal. Instead, the following day, he and his assistants had their belongings packed into his coach and left Paris on the long road to Calais. His departure alarmed Bonaparte who now embraced his fall-back position. He had Talleyrand send Whitworth a face-saving way to avert war. Mutual mistrust caused France and Britain to retain possessions that the Treaty of Amiens required them to evacuate. The way to prevent war and enhance trust was a mutually agreed-upon timetable whereby each complied with the treaty. That timetable could include a decade before Britain evacuated Malta and France evacuated Taranto and Otranto in southern Italy. Meanwhile, he sought to raise the pressure on Britain to deter war and seize a bargaining chip should war resume. At Nijmegen, General Adolphe Mortier should study the best route for marching his division toward Hanover's frontier, taking care to skirt any Prussian territory along the way.[27]

Bonaparte desperately hoped that Whitworth would return. Upon learning that the ambassador had crossed the Channel, he fired off letters to neutral governments, castigating the British for severing talks and asking for their support. For instance, he informed Swiss Landammann Louis d'Affry that 'war between France and England is about to be declared and I want to leave you with no doubt about the reasons and justice of the war that France is obliged to make'.[28] He explained to Prince John, Portugal's regent, that 'I did everything to spare the world this calamity but England refused to fulfil the Treaty of Amiens'.[29] He insisted to Pius VII that 'I am not at all the cause of the war', and asked permission for French troops to cross Papal territory.[30]

With war all but officially declared, the British sought to strike the first blow. On 16 May 1803, George III ordered the Royal Navy to destroy all French and Dutch warships at sea and seize any French and Dutch merchant vessels at sea or docked in British ports. Still hoping for some last-minute offer from London, Bonaparte did not officially inform the Senate until 20 May that the British government had recalled its ambassador. Word that London had launched a naval war against France on 16 May and formally declared war on 18 May, prompted

Bonaparte to order all British subjects arrested and their property confiscated on the 22nd.

* * *

Although France and Britain were again at war, as usual neither had the power decisively to defeat the other. The Royal Navy could sweep the oceans of French shipping; the French could overrun Britain's allies on the Continent; neither could invade the other. Bonaparte wistfully expressed what proved to be an impossible dream: 'If we were masters of the straits for six hours, we would be masters of the world.'[31]

Britain had only one vulnerable territory accessible to French arms. On 27 May 1803, Bonaparte ordered General Adolphe Mortier to invade Hanover, George III's ancestral home. On 11 July, Mortier received Hanover's capitulation. Bonaparte then dangled Hanover as a prize to Frederick William III in return for allying with France against Britain. Frederick William was torn over what to do. Staying neutral certainly made sense. A Prussian takeover of Hanover would trigger a British declaration of war and might also prompt Russia and Austria to ally with Britain against Prussia and France, something that he wanted to avoid at all costs. Yet Berlin and Paris did share an interest in reducing and ideally eliminating British influence in northern Germany. For the next two and a half years, the First Consul and then Emperor failed to convince the Prussian king to ignore his fears and take the plunge into Hanover.[32]

The search for allies seemed to pay off in July 1803, when the Tuileries received a letter from Irish leader Robert Emmett, who was leading a revolt against British rule and asked for French help. That similar efforts in 1796 and 1798 had failed disastrously did not mean that a third was not worth venturing. Ample doses of the right mix of leaders, men, munitions, provisions, vessels and luck might win Ireland's freedom and alliance with France. He had General Louis Berthier interview the array of exile groups in Paris and discern whether any of their schemes merited backing. He had Marine Minister Denis Decrès look into the potential of provoking and arming 25,000 Irish rebels against their British oppressors. Neither Berthier nor Decrès was optimistic about backing such schemes. He assigned General Charles Augereau to lead an Irish expedition later in 1803, but postponed it to 1804 and finally shelved it in the face of Britain's overwhelming blockade of French ports. Meanwhile, the British crushed Emmett and his few hundred followers and executed him on

23 September 1803. That ended the last hope of turning Ireland into an 'English Vendée'.³³

For the foreseeable future the struggle between France and Britain would be little more than a 'phoney war'. All that Bonaparte could do was issue volleys of orders to ensure that regional commanders readied their troops or warships for combat, ambassadors sought to enrol potential French allies and deter potential French enemies and colonial governors undertook all vital preparations for war. He had customs officials seize British vessels, cargoes and crews in ports. He had officials everywhere arrest and intern British subjects. He had letters of marque issued to privateers to prey on British shipping. He instructed Marine Minister Decrès to have a flatboat designed that could carry a hundred soldiers across the English Channel. He had commanders in or near ports exercise their troops with frequent embarkations and debarkations on various vessels and had the soldiers taught how to swim. He had all regiments raised to full strength in numbers, arms, equipment and training. He ensured that all vital provisions, munitions, wagons, cavalry horses, draft animals, forage, tools and spare parts were either in place, en route or ordered. He had commanders keep strict order among their troops and punish any who committed crimes. He had treasury officials ensure that the government's finances were sound and all existing sources of revenue flowing freely into the national coffers. He had the censors insist that newspapers only printed stories that rallied the French people for a long struggle. He calmed the jittery nerves of key officers and officials who feared revolts, spies or outright British invasions. He ran into the usual infuriating array of obstacles to implementing his policies. He complained that the Marine Ministry's failure to fulfil his order three years earlier to fit frigates with carronades kept French warships at a disadvantage in combats with British warships. He was angered to learn that workers employed in various public works in Paris were not being properly paid and insisted that they promptly received all that was due them.³⁴

He brainstormed with his admirals over possible campaigns against the British, but reluctantly concluded 'that France alone could equal England at sea before ten years is a chimera'.³⁵ Just defending French colonies in the West Indies seemed nearly impossible: 'To nourish war in the Indies for several campaigns, we must assume that we will not be masters of the seas and that we can hope for little help from others. It seems difficult that an army corps could long oppose the English without alliances and pressure points.' Any chance of success depended on overcoming those challenges. The best way to do that was to forge an alliance between France, Holland, Spain and Portugal.³⁶

He ordered Admiral Eustache Bruix, who commanded Boulogne's fleet, to take advantage of 'the long nights that have arrived' and 'chose two or three bold and enterprising privateer captains . . . to sail with their vessels overnight to the English coast, seize several boats and even some villagers who can give intelligence on matters that concern us'. That raid would be the first of many that covered the coast, 'revealing to us, league by league, the nature of the beaches, the villages and' the key points of the enemy forces and their means to defend them. 'Send me the report as soon as possible.'[37]

He had the Consular Guard expanded to 5,000 men, with half in grenadier and half in chasseur regiments. The ideal grenadier was huge, tough, courageous and powerful; the ideal chasseur was swift, tough, courageous and powerful. Each company numbered 120 men, with half veterans and half conscripts that met the physical requirements. The Guard artillery included eighteen guns, with many gunners recruited from the navy.[38]

In any war against Britain, Spain was the most critical potential French ally or enemy.[39] Charles IV was willing to ally his realm with France against Britain if Bonaparte underwrote Spain's 100,000-man army. Bonaparte dismissed the notion, arguing that the more France weakened Britain, the more Spain benefited. He had Talleyrand give Madrid a choice of either paying France six million livres a month or allying openly with France and besieging Gibraltar. He followed this up by writing to Charles directly on 18 September 1803, 'praying that he would open his eyes to the sinkhole that English intrigues had dug beneath his throne'. Bonaparte counted Manuel Godoy, the king's chief minister, among those English agents who sought to overthrow him and provoke war between Spain and France. Why could not Charles see that he 'is Spain's true king'? Ultimately, Spain's fate rested on whether the king tolerated or dismissed his traitorous minister.[40] Bonaparte's arguments failed to sway Charles; Godoy would remain his chief minister until Emperor Napoleon deposed the regime five years later.

Nonetheless, Bonaparte got most of what he sought with a bilateral treaty signed on 19 October 1803. Madrid pledged to pay Paris six million livres monthly for the duration of the war against Britain. It had been hard enough to get the Spanish to make that promise; getting them to fulfil it proved impossible. The Spaniards never paid in full and paid ever less money less frequently until they stopped all payments. Bonaparte had Talleyrand issue demands and threats but Madrid pleaded an empty treasury. French merchants complained of suffering discrimination by the Spanish. In March 1803, Bonaparte sent Charles IV a polite but firm request to end the discrimination and strengthen Spain's sea power which was in a perilously decrepit condition.[41]

Bonaparte asked the Portuguese Prince John to resist the pressure by his pro-English advisors, especially Foreign Minister Joao de Almeida de Melo e Castro, to ally with Britain and instead at the very least stay neutral since Britain had clearly broken the Treaty of Amiens and resumed war against France. He also demanded that John end the policy of harassing, arresting and seizing the property of French merchants in his realm. He warned that if such insults and depredations persisted, John risked provoking overwhelming French vengeance. Finally, there was Lisbon's worst aggression of all – giving 200,000 francs to Chouan and Vendean rebels. Portugal pledged to remain neutral, open its ports to French commerce and pay France 16 million francs in a treaty signed with France on 19 March 1804.[42]

The Batavian Republic would be another reluctant ally. Under the Treaty of The Hague, signed on 16 May 1795, France was entitled to keep 25,000 troops in the Netherlands until two years after a peace treaty was ratified with Britain. With the French-style 1798 constitution, Dutch liberals overthrew the Netherlands stadtholder system and transformed the Netherlands into the Batavian Republic ruled by a five-man Directorate. In April 1801, the Directorate complained to Bonaparte that the commander of French troops in their country, General Charles Augereau, was rude and meddled in their civil and political affairs; they asked the First Consul to replace him and reduce French forces to 10,000 troops. Bonaparte tried to smooth things over, sending 'proofs of the goodwill and friendship that link our two peoples'. He turned their complaints against Augereau against themselves, arguing that surely 'they did not want to dishonour the man who had commanded your troops with glory and success and contributed to your independence' by having him recalled. And with that rhetorical flip-flop, he gave them the choice of pressing their petition or enduring the command of someone they loathed.[43] Indirectly he had Talleyrand assure Roger Schimmelpennick, Batavia's ambassador to France that, after a face-saving interval and excuse, he would cut the number of troops and replace Augereau with someone better suited to Dutch interests and sensibilities.[44] And Bonaparte was good to his word. In July 1801 he reduced the troops to 10,000 and replaced Augereau with General Auguste Marmont.[45]

Yet Bonaparte thought nothing of promising one thing and then either blatantly or subtlety doing the opposite. In the spring of 1801, he had Talleyrand reassure the Batavian Directory that he would not meddle in their affairs or pressure them to rewrite their constitution, while submitting to them a list of proposed changes to their political system.[46] However, in this case, the constitutional reform committee actually incorporated a number of his suggestions into their final draft. The next set of demands came in 1803. In the Convention of Paris, signed on 25 June 1803, the Batavian Republic agreed to furnish warships, sailors and naval stores to France.

Bonaparte's diplomacy had succeeded in rounding up Spain, Helvetia and Batavia as reluctant allies with no place for now to go in a phoney war.

Chapter 9

The Spymaster

'We have discovered here a very mysterious plot hatched.'

'Europe must know that they should conspire no more against me.'

Among Napoleon Bonaparte's long list of skills was spymaster.[1] Highly intelligent, creative, suspicious and ruthless, he was naturally gifted at espionage. He wielded his abilities not just to garner critical information from and plant disinformation among enemy, neutral and allied states alike, but also from an array of revolutionary groups that kept trying to murder him and overthrow his government. Not just his regime but his life depended on knowing what his enemies were plotting. He was nearly assassinated twice, first by a cart bomb planted by a terrorist group in December 1800 and then by a young Austrian man who wanted to kill the conqueror of his country in October 1809.

Espionage was a vital part of Napoleon's daily agenda. He informed Police Minister Joseph Fouché that 'the reestablishment of peace would give me more time to spend on police matters so I want to be informed in the greatest detail and work with you at least one and often two hours daily as will be needed'.[2] He imposed the same rational, comprehensive, systematic organization on espionage that he did on all his other endeavours. He had Justice Minister Claude Regnier compose 'a dictionary in alphabetical order with the names of all agents employed by foreigners or the Bourbons who have disturbed France's tranquillity, whose names were compromised or revealed by different means since . . . the Revolution'.[3] The postal service was adept at opening letters from or to 'people of interest', copying the contents, resealing them and sending them to their destinations. For 'special operation forces' he relied on the Consular then Imperial Guard's Gendarmes d'Elite. General Jean Savary headed this unit from September 1801 to June 1810 followed by General Antoine Durosnel until April 1814.

In recruiting spies, Bonaparte sought men with 'big ears and small tongues'.[4] He wanted to plant among the counterrevolutionary Chouans 'an agent who perfectly knows' them and who would be equally at home operating in Paris or their own territory to uncover all their conspirators.[5] He instructed Eugène, his viceroy in Italy and stepson, to organize a spy network for the larger cities and 'put at the head . . . an intelligent and adroit man who constantly follows all leads, accompanies you everywhere and recruits spies everywhere'.[6] On the eve of his 1809 campaign against Austria, he asked Fouché to find 'a man fluent in German and a bit aloof to head my espionage system in Germany. I want an honest man who can be entrusted with large sums of money without being tempted and who knows Austria and Bohemia.'[7] In France he recruited dozens of the social elite, including vocal critics, to spy for him.

Then, as always, most information was drawn via the 'three B's', bribery, burglary and blackmail, with cash reaping the most. He offered huge rewards for information leading to the arrests of counterrevolutionary kingpins. Publicizing swift and stern justice against enemy agents helped intimidate or deter others. He had the arrest of émigrés 'who behave badly or have the impertinence of declaring that they are acting against their country' be publicly justified by 'the pretext that they are English or Austrian agents'.[8]

A critical dimension of espionage is understanding how and why the practice varies from one culture to the next and then adapting one's strategy to those differences. For instance, he recognized that Hamburg, a city filled with spies and related intrigues, was dominated by a mercenary type of espionage: 'In a city like Hamburg, the police must have not one spy but ten. These spies are not government agents, not public officials, not even diplomatic agents; they are men who . . . seek pay from any source.' If most spies there were for sale, then France must outbid its rivals to purchase their services.[9]

A sense of proper timing is also vital. He issued orders for enemy spies and subversives to be arrested after he reckoned that his own agents had gathered as much possible information from them and their networks by observing them and could reap further windfalls by interrogating them. For instance, in November 1803, he issued these instructions to Foreign Minister Talleyrand: 'As for M. [Joseph] Vernegue, who at Rome is the well-known agent of comte de Lille [the future Louis XVIII], it is necessary to arrest him . . . He is implicated in intrigues against us and the court of Rome cannot refuse to arrest him.' Talleyrand should ensure that the cardinal legate and French ambassador worked together to extradite him to France.[10]

Renditions were among his repertoire of espionage operations. He had his ambassadors in Hamburg, Bremen, Lübeck and Frankfurt arrest and render to France as many royalist agents as possible. Of course, doing so violated the laws of the sovereign states to which the ambassadors were accredited but he put his anti-royalist campaign above such legal and diplomatic niceties.[11] In Hamburg, his most notorious rendition was that of George Rumbold, a British diplomat and spymaster. French troops seized him and his papers on the night of 24 October 1804; he was released without his papers on 11 November. That blatant violation of Hamburg's sovereignty provoked the latest round of condemnations from most European courts.

He spurned one technique for extracting information except under the most extraordinary circumstances. Torture was illegal in France and he wanted to keep it that way. Both 'reason and humanitarianism' motivated him. He recognized that 'torture produces nothing good' because 'the victims say anything that comes into their heads and whatever they believe they should say' to stop the pain.[12] Wielding psychology rather than agony was not just the best, but the only reliable and thus justifiable means of getting a suspect to talk. He issued these procedures: 'Individuals arrested each day who the police prefect cannot interrogate, will be conducted by subordinates only if the interrogations are legal and made by men who have my confidence and with the necessary diligence to avoid all harm or unjust detentions.'[13]

Interrogation techniques certainly included talking with the suspect hour after hour until he yielded. It often also involved threatening spies or traitors with execution or lesser conspirators with long prison terms, especially at Guyana's 'dry guillotine'. However, he insisted that physical brutality was practically, legally and morally wrong except under extraordinary circumstances. People will say anything to stop excruciating pain and in doing so more often utter lies rather than truths.

Being a good interrogator was a vital art of' governance. It involved the ability critically to listen, apply reason, extract information and then act on it. Those skills were innate in some gifted people but could be learned by most people. To develop these skills in his officials, he issued these instructions: 'My secret goal is to have enthusiastic men who learn police techniques and immerse themselves in details . . . That they be sent to different places of the empire to study the localities, individuals and march of affairs and reveal the scabrous affairs . . . Finally they should apply this knowledge, not theoretically, but practically to govern.'[14] Above he emphasized training and hands-on experience. He explained to Eugène: 'You are mistaken if you believe that you drew everything possible from the interrogation. The art of interrogating prisoners is one derived from the experience of war and tactics.'[15] He coached key officials on lines of questioning that might best yield intelligence. For instance, Justice Minister Regnier should 'have the two individuals most compromised by the reports brought in secret to Bicetre prison. Have them interrogated on the groups where they gather . . . the different ways to know who composes those groups . . . and how they pick those who agitate . . . Have all the information on these individuals compiled from the secret police bureaus.'[16]

He carefully read interrogation transcripts and often criticized the proceedings. For instance, he was upset that police had mishandled two suspected members of Georges Cadoudal's group who were arrested in 1803. He pointed out that one suspect was badly questioned and the other too lightly questioned. As for the latter, 'the instant he was allowed to realize that he had nothing to fear . . . he filled with confidence'. Minor conspirators should be spared the hangman's noose if they identified higher-ranking conspirators.[17] Yet he could be heartless toward spies that had been wrung dry of information. He instructed General Louis Davout how and why to dispose of a spy his troops had caught and interrogated: 'Name a five-officer commission to judge and have him shot as a spy. This example is necessary; our coasts are inundated with these miscreants.'[18] Napoleon himself was a skilled interrogator. His best-known breakthrough was with Louis-Alexandre de Launay, Count d'Antraigues, a royalist agent who, after an all-night session, Napoleon talked into revealing an ongoing plot to overthrow the Directorate. He cut a deal whereby d'Antraigues could 'escape' after the information led to the arrests of all the conspirators.[19]

Napoleon's agents planted spies among the exiled royalists. One well-placed agent intercepted and copied letters between the would-be Louis XVIII and various recipients. Yet rebel and spy rings mushroomed no matter how many the government uncovered and crushed. Interrogations revealed that most led back to London, albeit via some intriguing detours along the way. For instance, Francis Drake, a British diplomat in Munich, the capital of Bavaria, was the kingpin for a network of agents and subversives in France and elsewhere. Yet Drake was not omnipotent. French agents succeeded in secretly intercepting, copying, then releasing many letters between Drake and his spies. Bonaparte conceived ensnaring Drake with two double agents. Jean Méhée de la Touche would claim to be part of a rebel Jacobin group committed to overthrowing the First Consul and would convey secret documents, some contrived by Bonaparte, that proved his group's access to the French government's inner sanctums. Captain François Rosey would defect from Strasbourg's garrison with an appeal for aid in a pending royalist revolt that would spread across France. Ideally, Drake would introduce both men to actual Jacobin and royalist agents conspiring against France. Meanwhile, Talleyrand would pressure Bavaria's government to suppress the anti-Bonaparte newspapers the *Gazette General* and *Mercure Universal*, published at Regensburg and subsidized by England. Ambassador Louis Guillaume Otto would oversee both operations. Drake fell for it. He gave Rosey 75,000 francs then hurried to London to ask for more money and men to fund the conspiracy. Rosey returned to Strasbourg. Bonaparte had published on 5 April 1804, a report on Drake and his network. In doing so, he hoped at once to expose British intelligence to ridicule and paranoia.[20]

The art of propaganda is critical not just for ruling people but also for undermining other rulers. Propaganda wars accompany hot and cold wars alike. For instance, in 1804 Bonaparte worried that the 'Dutch army is discontented and most people are the same'. He blamed English agents for embroiling that discontent. Countering that forced him 'to interfere in this country's affairs'. Yet he was uncertain how to proceed. He asked Talleyrand to gather as much information as possible on all leading citizens and solicit the opinion of Roger Schimmelpennick, the Dutch ambassador to France, who Bonaparte greatly respected.[21]

Bonaparte continually had favourable essays and stories planted in newspapers to counter negative stories. For instance, in November 1803, he instructed then Second Consul Cambacérès 'to have placed in small newspapers articles that throw scorn on the carriers of false news'.[22] In July 1801, he had Fouché force French newspapers to censor themselves with the following logic: a key goal of English agents was to upset French commerce and strew worries among the French public. French newspapers were inadvertently contributing to that gloom by printing British propaganda stories. Henceforth, each newspaper must ensure that it published nothing like that. When a newspaper persisted in publishing politically incorrect stories, he had his authorities either force the editor to resign or outright shutter the press. He also barred from France a lengthening list of newspapers published abroad.[23]

He launched a propaganda war against anti-French publications in Hamburg in December 1803. He sought to uncover who was behind articles published by *Le Journal des Debats* 'that had alarmed the country and echoed propaganda that the English want to spread . . . The English have at Hamburg a deposit of reports to alarm Europe.' He called for countering British propaganda by subsidizing newspapers that 'unmasked, in a suitable manner, false rumours'.[24] He had Talleyrand issue a diplomatic note to Hamburg, deploring the libels against the First Consul and France published by newspapers and journals that were often underwritten with British gold. He wanted not merely to pressure Hamburg's government into censoring those anti-French publications, but closing the port to British trade.

Napoleon Bonaparte's most acidic critic was a woman. Madame Germaine de Staël personified for him the worst kind of woman – loud, bossy, opinionated and mannish-looking.[25] She stalked him like a fanatical groupie, fantasizing that she, the world's reigning female genius, would bag him, the world's reigning male genius. At a crowded reception she cornered him to demand that he reveal who was the greatest woman, living or dead, expecting to be crowned with that laurel. Instead he quipped: 'The woman who has the most children.' That briefly rendered her speechless until she blurted if it was true that he did not like women. 'Forgive me, Madame', he replied, but I greatly love mine.' He then turned on his heel and strode away.[26]

De Staël avenged herself by wielding her poisonous tongue and pen against him and his policies. In 1803, Bonaparte finally got fed up and had Fouché exile her and her companion, Benjamin Constant, from Paris.[27] They holed up at Coppet, her family's chateau near Geneva, where they muted their published criticisms in hopes of being invited back to the capital. She soon dashed his hopes that he had heard the last of her. As he was launching his 1805 campaign against Austria, she irritated him. Once again he had Fouché to remove the irritation: 'Madame de Staël pretends that I gave her permission to come to Paris and she wants to stay there. She must be returned to Coppet. You know that I am not imbecilic enough to want her at Paris . . . She has mixed herself in French affairs . . . Let her friends know that she will be arrested within forty leagues of Paris.'[28] He finally relented and let de Staël visit Paris in 1807. Politics rather than sympathy motivated him. His loathing for the woman was undiluted. He hoped to use her as bait. He had Fouché ensure that she and her coterie were constantly watched. Undoubtedly to Napoleon's regret, de Staël was clever enough not to commit any grievous indiscretion let alone act of treason during her sojourn.[29]

* * *

A royalist plot nearly killed Bonaparte on the evening of 24 December 1800 as he journeyed by coach from the Tuileries Palace to the Opera to hear Joseph Haydn's oratorio 'The Creation of the World'.[30] An 'infernal machine' exploded seconds after his driver whipped his horses into a canter around a suspicious cart partly blocking the Rue Saint-Nicaise. The bomb killed eight people and wounded twenty-eight; among the dead was the girl the terrorist paid to hold the cart's horse after he ignited the fuse and hurried away. Bonaparte went on to attend the concert; the audience gave him an adoring standing ovation after learning what he had just survived so fearlessly.

Bonaparte was convinced that Jacobins were behind the plot. Fouché begged to differ, explaining that what little evidence his agents had gathered pointed to royalists. On 5 January 1801, the Senate approved the First Consul's request to compile a list of 130 Jacobin suspects to be arrested, tried and, if guilty, sentenced to the 'dry guillotine' of Guyana; 94 met that fate. The police eventually arrested the two actual cart-bomb terrorists on 18 January; an interrogation indeed revealed royalist rather than Jacobin links.[31]

A far more extensive plot developed a few years later.[32] George Cadoudal and six others disembarked from a British cutter on 21 August 1803, journeyed to Paris and seeped into the counterrevolutionary underground. Jean Pichegru and seven others stepped ashore and hurried to Paris on 16 January 1804. The plan was to murder Bonaparte en route between Paris and Malmaison followed by a coup ideally led by General Jean Moreau, France's second most prestigious general. Pichegru sidled up to Moreau and made his pitch on 28 January. Moreau declined that offer and two more jointly by Pichegru and Cadoudal on 1 and 6 February. Yet he also did not inform the police about the conspiracy, apparently hoping that the plotters would do the dirty work of murdering Bonaparte, clearing the way for him to take power unsullied by directly being a co-conspirator.

That might well have happened had not on 8 and 9 February police arrested three conspirators who under interrogation revealed the plot. The most shocking revelation was Moreau's complicity. Bonaparte had him watched 'until the time was right to arrest him', while the postmaster general ensured that all letters addressed to him, especially those that crossed the Channel, were intercepted and read.[33] Moreau's time came on 15 February, when Bonaparte had him and all his papers seized as General Jean Bessières encircled Paris with troops and barricaded its emanating roads. People wanting to enter or leave required a pass, obtained only after a police interview. The authorities steadily unravelled the web as fruitful interrogations led to new arrests, searches, interrogations and incriminating evidence. Police nabbed Pichegru on 28 February and

Cadoudal on 9 March. The lockdown lasted six weeks until Bonaparte believed that the police had arrested nearly all the conspirators.

Bonaparte then took these additional measures: 'First, have placed in all the newspapers an article that reveals the English, the moment they sent Georges to our shores, gathered money from all the émigrés who could be found in Germany; second, dispatch two agents, one to Munich, the other to Fribourg, to record the names of all the émigrés that can be found there . . . so that we can arrest them if they match our list of émigré suspects.'[34] All along he tried to impress on his subordinates that deterring future plots was the ultimate goal of their efforts: 'Europe must know that they should conspire no more against me.'[35] He extended the security crackdown to the English Channel coast, especially the stretch along which his Army of England was deployed. He issued elaborate instructions to Generals Nicolas Soult, Louis Davout and Auguste Marmont at their respective headquarters. They should distinguish smugglers from agents:

> Have arrested on site the sailors and fishermen who communicate with the English. I blame myself for neglecting before now to have them arrested. Make them talk. I authorize you . . . to promise them a pardon if they make revelations. If you see any [hesitations], you can even, following the usage for previous men suspected of espionage, use thumb-screws on them . . . Confer secretly with the mayor and . . . all those who, deep in their consciences, know that they have conspired with the English; have them arrested.[36]

As for spies, after extracting as much intelligence as possible, send them 'before a military commission then have them shot; you must have your share of these miserable English who inundate us'.[37] He wanted to inspire greater vigilance, not provoke panic, so he downplayed the conspiracy's danger: 'One must not worry too much about this affair in Paris by giving it more importance than it merits.'[38]

Moreau admitted that he had met Pichegru twice and Cadoudal once, yet, rather than immediately inform the authorities, kept secret their plot to murder Bonaparte and overthrown the government. This enraged Bonaparte, who called Moreau 'an ingrate and traitor who the French people could not punish enough'.[39] But he eventually reflected that Moreau was 'a good man easily led astray which explained his irregularities'.[40] For that, he merely had Moreau sentenced to two years in prison, then released after a few months, stripped of his citizenship and deported. His decision to spare Moreau was a political rather than a legal choice. Moreau was highly popular among the Jacobins and his former army's officers and soldiers. If he approved Moreau's execution for treason he would at once make him a martyr while his enemies would accuse him of using the conspiracy as an excuse to eliminate his worst rival. He had Justice Minister Cambacérès privately pressure the judges to render a light penalty. Napoleon later admitted that 'I was not yet sufficiently firm in my position to come to an open rupture with a man who had numerous partisans in the army and who only lacked the energy to attempt to put himself in my place. It was necessary to negotiate with him as a separate person, as indeed at that time, he really was.'[41] On 24 June, Bonaparte issued a decree exiling Moreau from France for life.

As for Pichegru, he was found hanged in his cell on 6 April. Bonaparte was enraged by rumours that he had Pichegru killed: 'What would I have gained? A man of my character does not act without grand motives.'[42] Indeed, for those hard practical reasons Pichegru almost certainly died at his own hand than that of another. In doing so he cheated the hangman since he would have been executed along with Cadoudal and other conspirators with overwhelming evidence that they were traitors. The trial opened on 28 May and the verdicts were announced on 10 June. Cadoudal and nineteen others received death sentences, Moreau and four others prison terms and twenty-one other acquittals.

The large number of conspirators topped by Moreau's treason shook Bonaparte profoundly: 'Nothing equals the utter stupidity of this entire tragedy except its nastiness.' He just could not comprehend how national heroes like Moreau and Pichegru could betray their country: 'The human heart is an abyss that trumps all understanding; the most penetrating search cannot reach its depths.'[43] Indeed, he was so enraged and stunned that he cancelled ongoing talks for a prisoner exchange with the British. What was the connection? He saw the talks as a cynical British pretence for conducting espionage and subversion in France: 'English envoys are nothing but spies.' After all, 'the English king had never wanted to establish a single exchange' in the previous war, despite his efforts. So now Bonaparte ordered Marine Minister Decrès to ensure that no English envoy stepped ashore at Toulon or elsewhere on French soil.[44]

Unfortunately, Bonaparte did not stop with these measures. Consumed with fear and anger, he committed an act that horrified people across Europe and gave his enemies a propaganda windfall to wield against him. He ordered the rendition of a key counterrevolutionary suspect, but had him summarily tried and executed rather than interrogated and prosecuted if there was a viable case against him. Louis de Bourbon, duc d'Enghien, was Prince Louis Bourbon de Conde's then 32-year-old son who lived in a palace at Ettenheim, Baden, near the Rhine River and not far from Strasbourg on the west side. Interrogations revealed that a young Bourbon prince was an agent but did not reveal his name. Enghien appeared to fit that profile.

Bonaparte planned the operation minutely.[45] Under a pseudonym, General Michel Ordener journeyed by stagecoach to Strasbourg. There he privately met the region's commander, General Jean Leval and explained that his mission was to lead 300 dragoons by boat across the Rhine to Ettenheim, surround the town, seize d'Enghien and all his papers and return to France. Quite likely the traitor and former French general Charles Dumouriez could be nabbed with d'Enghien. Meanwhile, General Armand Caulaincourt would lead 200 dragoons across the Rhine to Offenbach, surrounded the town and seize Baroness Marie Reich and her papers along with possibly Spencer Smith and other English agents at her residence. Finally, Leval himself would lead 300 dragoons to a strategic crossroads between those towns to assist either effort and thwart any rescue forces. Officers would enforce the strictest discipline over their troops. The dragoons would take their muskets, full cartridge boxes and four days' rations. Each general would carry 12,000 francs to pay off any Baden officials who demanded bribes or Baden subjects who suffered damages. Meanwhile, Talleyrand would provide diplomatic cover by pressuring Duke Charles Frederick of Baden to accept the rendition, while readying French agents in Hamburg, Frankfurt and other cities with royalist agents to prepare to seize and render to France any agents revealed by interrogating d'Enghien and his coterie.

Bonaparte learned early on 20 March that his men had flawlessly pulled off their mission and would soon arrive with the prisoner at Vincennes castle outside Paris. But no other suspects were found nor was any smoking gun of d'Enghien's link with any specific plot discovered among his papers; his letters with would-be Louis XVIII and other royalist exiles were mostly polite exchanges. Bonaparte issued a list of eleven questions with which to interrogate d'Enghien, including whether he had ever fought against his country, received money from England or served England. He would then be asked about his ties to various conspiracies and conspirators. But those questions were mere formalities. He had already judged d'Enghien guilty and 'had little doubt' that General Pierre Hulin and his seven-man military commission would reach the same verdict, 'issue a death sentence and have him executed and buried on the grounds'.[46] The commission fulfilled Bonaparte's expectations. D'Enghien was found guilty of treason and executed by a firing squad after midnight on 21 March. Although often attributed to Talleyrand, it was Fouché who declared that the trial and execution of the duc d'Enghien on trumped up charges 'was worse than a crime, it was a blunder'.[47] The act diluted or destroyed the genuine sympathy aroused by revelation of the Cadoudal conspiracy to assassinate him.

Bonaparte tried to finesse any foreign condemnation of d'Enghien's execution on 26 March by having Talleyrand issue the foreign ambassadors a letter accusing Britain's government of trying to murder him. On 20 April, Home Secretary Robert, Lord Hawkesbury sent those same governments a letter denying that allegation. On 30 May, Napoleon had Talleyrand condemn the British cabinet for its 'plots, crimes and subversions'.[48]

The international reaction to the news of d'Enghien's rendition and execution was mixed. That from Vienna, Madrid, Stuttgart and Munich was muted. Beyond Britain the most vociferous protest came from Russia. Tsar Alexander called for a day of mourning for d'Enghien, had a formal note condemning d'Enghien's execution presented to French Ambassador Gabriel Hedouville and issued a similar protest to the Imperial Diet at Regensburg. That infuriated Bonaparte, who quipped that 'it was bad enough to have to swallow English snubs at sea without also having to swallow Russian impertinence'. He had Talleyrand explain 'in firm, proud language' to Russian Ambassador Peter Oubril that 'my intention is not to suffer the haughty tone of the court of St Petersburg ... or its interfering in France's domestic affairs'. He was then to condemn Russia for harbouring the would-be Louis XVIII and his court and aiding their counterrevolutionary agents. Finally, he was to explain that 'I do not at all want war, but I fear no one and my accession to emperor is as illustrious as the Republic's birth'.[49] Bonaparte recalled Hedouville, who left St Petersburg on 7 June.

Relations worsened. On 21 July 1804, Oubril issued a demand from Alexander that Bonaparte renounce any designs on the Middle East and withdraw his troops from southern Italy. Bonaparte had Talleyrand condemn Russia for wanting 'to see with pleasure the rekindling of war on the continent', justify all the measures taken for French security and declare that France would never submit to his demands.[50] Alexander responded by recalling Oubril. The two countries were poised for war but for now each hesitated to take that fatal step.

Chapter 10

The Emperor

'I did not at all usurp the crown. I retrieved it from the gutter. The people put it on my head.'

'I implore you to come and give me, in the most eminent degree, the religious character for the sacred act of coronation for the first French emperor.'

'The Revolution is over.'

Napoleon Bonaparte justified his transformation of France's government from a consulate into an empire and himself from a first consul into an emperor with these words: 'I did not at all usurp the crown. I retrieved it from the gutter. The people put it on my head.'[1] Like countless of his other assertions, this was disingenuous. Becoming Emperor Napoleon I was definitely his idea and he carefully managed each stage of that revolution from above, although key allies and countless people backed it either enthusiastically or warily.

It was the chronic struggle against counterrevolutionary forces, culminating with the crushing of Cadoudal's conspiracy and d'Enghien's execution in early 1804 that tipped him toward assuming imperial powers. Of his many rationales for doing so, the most important was 'to end Bourbon hopes' that one day they would retake France's throne. Indeed Cadoudal recognized that irony, quipping on his way to the guillotine that: 'We have achieved more than we intended. We came to give France a king. We have given her an emperor.'[2]

For Bonaparte to become emperor, however, would enrage millions of people devoted to a French Republic. He discreetly solicited the views of trusted civil and military leaders over whether he should take that step. For instance, he asked General Nicolas Soult 'to instruct me in detail the army's opinion on a measure of this nature'. He assured Soult that he would do so 'for the sole goal of the Nation's interests'.³ With his inner circle's support, the next step was secretly to forge a Senate consensus to name him emperor, not a tough challenge since he had handpicked them, followed by an open, hopefully nearly unanimous popular vote in favour.

The Senate presented him with an extraordinary message on 27 March 1804. First, the senators thanked him for leading the efforts to thwart the counterrevolutionary plot and, more importantly, championing and personifying the French Revolution itself:

> You founded a new era; but you must eternalize it . . . You are pressured by time, by events, by conspirators, by the ambitious . . . You can arrest time, master events, break the conspirators, disarm the ambitious, calm all of France by creating new institutions to bolster your edifice . . . Great man, realize your work and give immortality to your glory. You have thrown chaos into the past; you confer blessings on the present; you guarantee our future . . . The Senate and people are one with you.⁴

Bonaparte replied that

> you have judged the supreme magistrate's heredity necessary for protecting the French people against the plots of our enemies . . . and assuring . . . the triumph of public equality and liberty . . . We have been constantly guided by this grand truth: that sovereignty resides in the French people, in every sense, without exception and must be for their interest, for their happiness and for their glory.

Having said that, he asked the Senate 'to let me know your entire thoughts'.⁵

The Senate overwhelmingly declared Napoleon Bonaparte France's emperor on 18 May 1804; there were only three nays and two abstentions. The constitution was rewritten to incorporate this revolutionary change and all the necessary details. A plebiscite approved the constitution by 3,572,329 to 2,579, with four of ten eligible voters turning out. The result was publicized on 30 November 1804. As with other plebiscites, the numbers were cooked by doubling the yes votes and throwing out nearly all the no votes.⁶

Emperor Napoleon I did not immediately launch a flurry of economic, military and political initiatives. He had already implemented his most important reforms during his four previous years as First Consul. His imperial regime's most immediately apparent change was in style rather than substance. He took the first steps toward establishing an imperial court and nobility on 19 May 1804, the day after the Senate declared him emperor.[7] He made Christophe Duroc the Grand Marshal of the Palace, Charles Talleyrand-Perigord the Grand Chamberlain, Armand Caulaincourt the Grand Master of Horse, Cardinal Joseph Fesch the Grand Confessor and Louis Ségur the Grand Master of Ceremonies, each with a dozen or so staff. He awarded eighteen generals with a marshal's baton, hoping to sooth any among them seething with jealousy or republican outrage. He carefully chose the list to include tight loyalists like Berthier, Murat, Lannes, Bessières, Soult, Davout and Moncey; distant loyalists like Brune, Mortier and Ney; republican critics and adversaries like Bernadotte, Masséna, Augereau, Jourdan and Lefebvre; and revolutionary-era but now inactive heroes like Sérurier, Kellermann and Perignon. He would appoint eight others: Victor in 1807; Macdonald, Marmont and Oudinot in 1809; Suchet in 1811; Gouvion St Cyr in 1812; Poniatowski in 1813; and Grouchy in 1815. The Consular Guard became the Imperial Guard.

Court etiquette was explained in decrees issued on 19 May and 13 July 1804. Napoleon named his court's ninety-four members on 14 July 1804. A strict hierarchy prevailed, presided over by himself and Josephine as the emperor and empress, then his mother and siblings as princes and princesses, with the rest boasting specific titles. *'Vous'* and *'monsieur'* replaced *'tu'* and *'citoyen'*, respectively, as proper forms of address. His court was just the apex of his aristocracy. Eventually he granted 3,263 titles, creating 7 princes, 21 dukes, 452 counts, 1,550 barons and 1,474 knights.[8]

The etiquette evolved with the titles. On the eve of the marriage of his brother Jérôme and Catherine of Württemberg in August 1807, Napoleon issued instructions on protocol for the guests:

> The great number of princes who find themselves in Paris at this moment renders necessary the regulation of ranks between them and the princes of my family . . . All the princes of my family will only take rank around me in order of their rank among themselves . . . Consuls of state, ministers, senators, grand officers of the empire and grand dignitaries take their respective places in order of seniority . . . My brothers outrank, not just in my palace but everywhere, grand dukes and . . . princes. They do not even bow in my palace to emperors or kings . . . France's grand dignitaries are treated like princes. They pass constantly in

my palace before all the princes of the Confederation and foreign empires and kingdoms.[9]

Those rules must have rankled with many a foreign highborn with a venerable pedigree as he was forced literally to bow before the Bonaparte clan's nouveau royals, especially if the new was just as haughty as the old.[10]

Although fine dining had never gone of style, it became opulent during the Empire. Napoleon himself ate quickly and simply, but now struggled to sit through elaborate court banquets with multiple dishes and wines. The Empire's leading gourmets were Cambacérès and Talleyrand, who competed to host the most extravagant, creative dining experiences. Talleyrand enjoyed a decisive edge by employing Antoine Carême, that age's most brilliant chef.

As for executive power, not much changed between the Consulate and the Empire. Since the constitution already granted the First Consul near-dictatorial powers, the biggest adjustment was changing the wording to read imperial or emperor. A section was added on the imperial succession. Only male, legitimate heirs were eligible, although the son could be either natural or adopted. The emperor and empress each enjoyed a civil list or budget of 912,999 francs and 432,000 francs, respectively that they could spend as they wished. He retained the Consulate's political system with its four mostly rubber-stamp bodies, the State Council, Senate, Tribunate and Legislative Corps. He added an Imperial High Court composed of sixty senators, twenty state consuls and twenty cassation court judges. The Imperial High Court investigated and ruled on accusations by individuals and groups that their civil rights had been violated. Winning a case was tough but not impossible. From 1804 to 1814, the Imperial High Court ruled in favour of only 44 of 585 plaintiffs.[11] He kept nearly all his ministers at their posts, Talleyrand at Foreign Affairs, Gaudin at Finance, Barbé-Marbois at the Treasury, Regnier at Justice, Decrès at Marine, Berthier at War and Dejean at War Administration. He brought back Joseph Fouché as police minister on 9 July 1804, having fired him on 1 August 1802 for opposing his being named Consul for Life. He would live to regret his magnanimity. He replaced an exhausted but still willing Antoine Chaptal with Jean Champagny as Interior Minister on 8 August 1804; much later Chaptal avenged himself against Napoleon in his biting memoirs.

With more power came more repression. As for French newspapers, in April 1805, Napoleon decided that 'I will reduce them from fourteen to seven and conserve none that flatter me; I have no need for their praise; but [will keep] those that have a virile French heart, that show a true attachment to me and my people'.[12] Fouché was his hatchet man for those to be terminated. On 22 April 1805, he received the Emperor's orders

> to suppress a bit more the newspapers; make them print favourable articles. Warn them that if they do not conform, I will suppress all of them . . . The Revolution is over . . . I will never suffer newspapers saying anything contrary to my interests. They can make a few little articles where they can display a little venom but anything more and I will shut their mouths.

The reason for the severity was that, with war against Russia and Austria likely and 'English agents . . . circulating on the continent', any negative articles strengthened the enemy and weakened France.[13] The emperor had Fouché 'suppress all news that was disagreeable or disadvantageous for France because one can only suspect that they are dictated by the English'.[14]

Napoleon was eager to garner international recognition of his imperial regime. On 14 June, he wrote every European government then at peace with France, addressing each fellow royal sovereign as 'brother' and expressing his desire for close relations.[15] Every country sent him congratulations except Russia and Sweden, along with his ongoing enemy Britain. Bitter debates usually preceded each government's decision to officially recognize Napoleon as France's emperor. Nearly all the noble ruling families viewed him as a vulgar, belligerent upstart but varying blends of fear and courtesy kept them from openly saying so.

In August 1804 Napoleon launched a diplomatic offensive designed to browbeat and entice Russia away from Britain and toward France. He had Talleyrand warn Ambassador Peter Oubril that 'if Russia embroils itself with France, its impotence will be such that Europe would cease to have the consideration and esteem for it that it would have with France. If it unites with Austria, it will be beaten and the power of France will be colossal.' He scorned Russian meddling in Europe as being as absurd as French meddling in Persia. He offered the Tsar a face-saving way to reverse course by identifying at his court a nefarious faction bought by English gold to champion English over Russian interests.[16] He scapegoated former ambassador Arkadi Markov as 'the source of all types of intrigues . . . against public tranquillity' by backing 'French emigrants and other agents on the

English payroll'. He insisted that 'France wants peace on the continent, has done everything to advance it with Russia and will spare nothing to maintain it'.[17] He pointed out the contradiction whereby the Tsar at once recognized would-be Louis XVIII as France's legitimate sovereign while signing legally binding treaties with Napoleon's France. Finally, he played the emotionally most wounding diplomatic card of all against the tsar by publicly questioning 'the morality of the court of St Petersburg, where the Emperor extends favours . . . to those who murdered his own father'.[18] None of these tactics worked. Indeed, the last one at once deepened Alexander's anguish and his animosity toward France and Napoleon.

Napoleon studiously ignored his rival with the best claim to his crown. The would-be Louis XVIII, then living with his entourage in Warsaw, issued a declaration on 6 June that Napoleon had usurped his rightful throne. Frederick William recognized Napoleon as emperor and forced the pretender to leave Prussian territory. Alexander welcomed Louis and his followers to take refuge in a palace at Mittau in the Russian empire.

* * *

Napoleon's most important diplomacy regarding his imperial rule's legitimacy was with Rome. He wanted to be universally viewed as a modern Charlemagne who had unified and justly reigned over a swath of Europe like his predecessor had a thousand years before. To spotlight that image, he visited Charlemagne's tomb at Aix-la-Chapelle (Aachen) from 2 to 10 September 1804. But wishful thinking was surely not enough. Only the pope's blessing could fulfil his longing.

Napoleon one-upped Charlemagne's coronation on Christmas Day 800. Rather than travel to Rome to receive the pope's blessing like Charlemagne, Napoleon got the pope to journey to Paris to bless him. On 15 September, he wrote to Pius VII with a request to

> give me new proof of the interest that you take in my destiny and that of this great nation, in one of the most important events offered in world history. I implore you to come and give me, in the most eminent degree, the religious character for the sacred act of coronation for the first French emperor. This ceremony will acquire a new lustre if Your Holiness makes it yourself. You will draw on my family and my people the benediction of God.[19]

Although he had no intention of actually doing so, his key enticement to Pius was hinting that he might restore the Catholic Church as France's state religion. He ensured that the pope's journey to Paris was accompanied by honour guards and at each stop officials rendered him homage. He genuinely liked Pius and wrote him courteous, warm and encouraging letters as he approached Paris and showered him with such sentiments after his arrival.[20]

Pius chalked up only two minor victories during five and a half months of efforts from November 25 when Napoleon met him at Fontainebleau until he departed Paris on 4 April 1805. One was in alliance with the empress against the emperor. Josephine and Napoleon had only a civil, not a religious marriage. Josephine implored Pius to sanctify their marriage. Napoleon reluctantly agreed after Pius informed him that otherwise he would not attend the coronation. Pius married them on the eve of the coronation. Beyond that, Napoleon promised to discard the ridiculous Revolutionary calendar and revert to the Gregorian calendar, including Sundays as days of rest, starting on 10 January 1806.

The coronation took place in Notre-Dame Cathedral on 2 December 1804.[21] Nearly a thousand select people packed the cathedral, including the court, government, military, diplomatic, social, business and religious elites. The ceremony vividly displayed France's separation of church and state. Pius led the mass. He then sat before the altar watching as Napoleon pointedly crowned himself and then Josephine followed by his oath to uphold the constitution. After the emperor and empress sat on their thrones, Pius rose to lead the Te Deum. Jacques Louis David's huge, stunning painting of the coronation is accurate in nearly all its detail. He captured the moment after Napoleon had crowned himself and lowered the empress's crown toward a kneeling Josephine. All his regime's major players are shown smiling approvingly, including his mother who was actually in Rome. Although the pope's hand is raised in blessing, he did not do so until later in the ceremony. What the painting glosses over are the jealousies, regrets and misgivings that afflicted many who attended. The three-hour ceremony exhausted everyone, especially Napoleon and Josephine, weighed down with their heavy robes. That burden was soon lifted but far worse ones appeared over the next decade. The pope's presence at Napoleon's coronation was a devastating blow to the royalists who prayed for a Bourbon restoration. The would-be Louis XVIII, however, obstinately clung to his claim.

The coronation was the centrepiece for weeks of balls, banquets and military parades. On 5 December, the regiments massed on the Champs de Mars as Napoleon awarded each an imperial flag topped by a bronze eagle. None of this came cheap. The coronation and its attendant ceremonies cost France's government about 3.2 million francs but may have stimulated 20 million francs of economic activity.[22]

* * *

Napoleon opened 1805 with a diplomatic offensive. He sent pleas for peace to George III and Francis II on 1 January and to Ferdinand IV and Maria Carolina the following day.[23] His longest and bluntest letter was with the Neapolitan queen; he warned her that French troops would overrun her realm and depose her and her husband if she dared ally with Britain and Russia. He asserted that 'I want peace with Naples, with all of Europe, even with England; but I fear war with no one'.[24] Neither the Austrian nor British monarch stooped to reply directly, while the Neapolitan monarchs responded with civility and conciliation.[25] He continually insisted that 'my efforts for peace and the repose of the world are constant and demand nothing as long as they are compatible with the honour of my crown and the happiness of my people'.[26]

* * *

One crown was not enough for Napoleon. He just as deftly contrived the receipt of a second as he had the first. On 28 May 1804, just a couple of weeks after the French Senate named him emperor, the Italian Republic's Consulate proposed transforming itself into a monarchy and thus Napoleon from its president into its king. There were strings attached: Catholicism would remain the state's religion; the territory could never be reduced, only enhanced; and any king after Napoleon had to reside permanently in Italy. Napoleon coyly replied on 23 June that 'I have read and meditated with all suitable attention to the Consulate's different proposals . . . The Italian Republic will remain independent . . . We will establish, as the Consulate wishes, an order of things that conform to the spirit of the century.'[27] For now he would continue to mull the Consulate's offer and give them a specific response at an appropriate time. He feared that Austria might declare war against him if he accepted the Italian crown. He wanted France prepared for the possibility. It was not until 17 March 1805 that he arranged for Italy's Senate to formally turn the republic into a kingdom.[28]

That same day Napoleon wrote to Francis of his desire for peace to prevail between their realms. He issued a litany of reasons why Britain rather than France had caused the ongoing war between them. From this war, he sought no new territory for France, only the independence of Malta from Britain and Corfu from Russia. He promised to separate the French and Italian crowns just like Francis separated his Imperial and Austrian crowns.[29] He then bolstered his gentle message with a tough one. He had Talleyrand tell Austrian Foreign Minister Louis Cobenzl that 'I don't want war but if I must have it, I want it sooner than later'.[30]

When Austria did not declare war, Napoleon confidently embarked on what became a three-and-a-half-month sojourn in Italy with his coronation the centrepiece. He left his palace of Saint-Cloud near Paris on 31 March and did not return until 18 July. During that time he inspected his kingdom's cities, palaces, roads, bridges, factories, warehouses, schools, regiments and fortresses and issued streams of orders to appropriate officials for their improvement. He lingered in Milan, his Italian monarchy's capital, a solid month from 9 May to 10 June. He crowned himself with Lombardy's Iron Crown at Milan's cathedral on 26 May 1805. There was one small wrinkle. This time he was unable to entice the pope to preside and had to make do with Cardinal Gian Caprara. Yet he was exultant that his coronation was conducted 'with pomp', the church 'was really beautiful and the ceremony was as nice as that in Paris while the weather was superb. In taking the crown of iron and placing it on my head, I added these words: "God gives me it, evil to those who touch it". I hope that will be a prophecy.'[31]

Chapter 11

The Sun of Austerlitz

'I am surrounded by 120,000 men and 3,000 boats who await a wind favourable to plant the imperial eagle atop the Tower of London. Only time and destiny know when that will be.'

'I want to attack Austria and be at Vienna before November and square off with the Russians if they are there.'

'Calm yourself young man! And remember this: there can be no shame in being conquered by Frenchmen.'

Although Napoleon genuinely wanted peace with Britain, he believed that only victory in war could make that happen. To defeat the world's greatest seapower, France needed naval allies, of which Spain was essential. Napoleon entangled Charles IV in treaties that obliged Spain to transfer ever more of its fleet and treasury to French control. These culminated when Charles declared war against Britain on 12 December 1804, then committed thirty-two ships-of-the-line to the French armada against England in a treaty signed on 4 January 1805. The king was quicker to ratify than to fulfil his treaties. In pressuring Madrid, Napoleon was gentle with Charles but had his foreign minister and ambassador get tough with their counterparts. The emperor assured the king that they would prevail against Britain 'if Your Majesty keeps his promise' on sharing his treasure and fleet with France.[1] He was pleased to receive Prime Minister Manuel Godoy's written pledge to cooperate. He sent his aide, Andoche Junot, to work with Godoy 'against our common enemies'.[2] He instructed Junot to

> tell the king that I count on all his energy to help me restore the power balance on the seas . . . that I have my eyes on Spain's conduct as does the rest of Europe to know if it will act decisively

for the honour and dignity of its crown . . . Meet several times with [Godoy] and tell him I have confidence in him . . . and that all that is missing is money.

The spoils of victory would let Spain recoup that investment, especially from Portugal: 'If Portugal refuses to close its ports to England, to embargo English vessels and to confiscate English merchandise, the two ambassadors must simultaneously leave; war will be declared immediately against Portugal and its property . . . will be immediately confiscated in the two states . . . and we will take over Portugal.'[3]

As for other naval allies, one clear success was Francophile Roger Schimmelpennick's elevation to be the Batavian Republic's ruler or Grand Pensioner. French operatives worked with key Dutch officials and politicians to engineer his election. In his congratulatory letter, Napoleon foresaw that he would at once advance the good of his people and their alliance with France. He asserted that 'to search for prosperity for Holland beyond our friendship and our zone of peace would be an illusion'. He then asked Schimmelpennick to supply five ships-of-the-line to the combined fleet of France and Spain, while suppressing all smuggling with Britain. He pledged that once the allies defeated Britain, the Netherlands would regain its lost trade, colonies and wealth.[4]

* * *

The Army of England was deployed in a cluster of camps either along the Channel coast or nearby from Etaples to Ostend, with most around Boulogne. During one of his visits, Napoleon boasted that 'I am surrounded by 120,000 men and 3,000 boats who await a favourable wind to plant the imperial eagle atop the Tower of London. Only time and destiny know when that will be.'[5] Most men adjusted to the tedium of camp life even as they longed for action. Without foreigners to fight, some squared off with each other, common soldiers in sometimes murderous brawls, officers in often murderous duels. These became so frequent that Napoleon finally had this proclamation issued: 'No French soldier has the right to expose his life for futilities and that blood spilled without honouring the flag and the country is a crime.'[6]

Of course, the French army could only invade England if the French and Spanish navies somehow dominated the English Channel long enough for the troops to row themselves across. Napoleon initiated that mission on 3 September 1804, when he summoned Marine Minister Denis Decrès and Admirals Pierre Villeneuve and Edouard Missiessy to explain the broad outlines of his strategy. Although the plan's details changed considerably over the next year, its essence was for his fleet commanders to break free of their respective blockades, race westward across the Atlantic, deposit troops and supplies, then race back by different routes.[7] Ideally, the enemy would give chase westward, get confused over the whereabouts and intentions of the French squadrons and search the Caribbean in vain. Meanwhile, the French squadrons would mass with Spain's fleet at Ferrol. The final stage involved sailing toward Ireland, then veering sharply eastward into the English Channel until its narrowest stretch where 'we will be before Boulogne absolute masters of the sea'.[8] He gave his admirals the leeway they needed to reach that end. Unanticipated opportunities and challenges would arise along each commander's journey. For instance, he told Villeneuve that 'the direction that you must take immediately after your junction at Ferrol will depend on so many circumstances', like how many enemy warships were drawn to the Caribbean, the strength of enemy warships at Ferrol, any losses of men, supplies and warships along the way and how much time was needed to replenish those losses. On 14 April 1805, he designated Villeneuve the commander of the combined fleet that would sail to the English Channel, but soon regretted that choice. On 9 June, he expressed this fear to Decrès: 'I estimate that Villeneuve does not have the necessary character.'[9] Tragically, that assessment would prove to be all too true.[10]

* * *

Napoleon's obsession with invading England blinded and deafened him to a threat swelling eastward. Despite the enormous resources at his disposal, he could not outbid the British in buying allies. In 1805, Whitehall forged the Third Coalition against France with £1,250,000 for every 100,000 troops a country fielded for a year. Britain's first secret treaty was with Sweden on 1 March, then Russia on 11 April and finally Austria on 9 August. The campaign lasted only several months so Sweden eventually received £132,000 for 12,000 troops, Russia £350,000 for 180,000 troops and Austria £1,000,000 for 250,000 troops.[11]

Despite all the hard evidence of the powerful and expanding coalition massing against him, Napoleon clung to the hope that somehow Russia and Austria were bluffing. Russia, and especially its Tsar, mystified him. He found Alexander's character 'too uncertain and too weak to the point that, reasonably, one cannot hope for a general peace'. He warned that 'Russia must not misunderstand my character and that of my peoples'.[12] Yet he dismissed as British propaganda the news that Russia had allied with Britain. He was just as dismissive of Austria. On 6 June, he told Talleyrand his astonishing hope to alleviate tensions with Vienna by having each sovereign bestow medals on distinguished leaders of the other side. The exchange never took place and would have had no effect on Austria's march to war if it had. But the notion's very naiveté reveals how incredulous Napoleon was that Austria would want to launch yet another war against France. In mid-July he shrugged off hard intelligence that two Russian armies were marching west to join forces with Austria against France.[13]

* * *

Napoleon reached Boulogne on 3 August 1805 and set up his headquarters at the chateau of Pont-de-Briques outside that city. His Army of England numbered 167,500 men and 1,730 transport vessels.[14] He wrote his wife that 'I will stay here twenty days. I have here lovely armies, lovely fleets and all that lets me pass the time agreeably. I just lack my good Josephine, but it is not necessary to tell her that.'[15]

He was excited to learn of a sea battle on 9 August: 'My warships at Ferrol fought, prevailed and mastered the sea after having fulfilled their mission . . . This day is among the French navy's most beautiful.'[16] But he waited in vain to learn that Villeneuve followed up his attack by sailing north toward the Channel. He soon learned that the initial report was wrong and Britain rather than France could cheer victory in that battle. He condemned Villeneuve as a poor leader with double vision of the enemy's actual numbers. On 13 August, he instructed Decrès to inform Villeneuve that the emperor was displeased that he was wasting precious time and that he should sail with the first favourable winds to join Allemand's squadron at Rochefort. Now the plan was for them jointly to attack rather than evade any enemy fleet in their way to the Channel. That same day, Napoleon wrote to Villeneuve, spurring him 'to sail boldly against the enemy' in a campaign in which 'my soldiers of land and sea have never shed their blood for a more noble result'.[17]

Napoleon increasingly interrupted his gaze on the Channel with glances south-east toward Austria. On 3 August, he had Foreign Minister Talleyrand send the latest plea to Vienna for peace along with a warning: 'The emperor believes in peace with Austria; however, if its troops continue to mass and its magazines fill, the emperor will conclude that Austria wants war . . . and he will march into Germany to entirely pacify Austria.'[18] On 6 August he received a letter from Austria's foreign ministry justifying its military build-up and offering to mediate peace between France and England. Napoleon wrote to Talleyrand that 'Austria must learn by my response that this declaration is not sufficient, that action is necessary; that the route of preparation is the route to war'.[19] Four days later he had Talleyrand again warn Austria to honour its peace treaty with France.[20]

Napoleon's loved ones were rarely far from his mind. On 12 August he was delighted to receive, a letter from his stepdaughter Hortense and he swiftly replied: 'My dear little girl, your letter is amiable like all that comes from you.' He arranged for Hortense and his nephew Napoleon Charles to visit him for five or six days to 'put a little gaiety in our camp life'.[21] That same day he had Talleyrand send Cobenzl his latest peace plea.[22] He longed just as achingly as for his wife. He scribbled these words to her:

> I seldom hear from you. You forget your friend. That's not good. I did not know that the waters of Plombières were truly the River Lethe. It seems that drinking the waters of Plombières made you say: 'Ah, Bonaparte, if I die who will you love?' . . . All done, beauty, spirit, feelings, the sun itself? But that will never happen. It is you who I want, the happiness that I enjoy from Josephine's goodness.[23]

Napoleon had no sooner sealed his letter to Josephine than he received two messages, Vienna's latest denials that it was preparing for war and a report from Ambassador François Rochefoucauld, revealing that Austria's government was lying; indeed, Austrian troops were massing in the Tyrol, Venetia and on the Bavarian frontier. That finally spurred Napoleon to action: 'I want to attack Austria and be at Vienna before November and square off with the Russians if they are there . . . I want the Austrians to surrender in Bohemia and Hungary. That will give me the leisure to war against England.' Yet he still regretted embarking on a war against Austria: 'I prefer above all that Austria places itself in a truly pacific state.' He had Talleyrand fire off a last appeal to Francis, at once detailing French grievances and reasons why peace should prevail, then send copies to all the courts of Europe.[24] That same day, he renamed the Army of England the Grand Army. He was willing to make huge concessions in return for peace. On 23 August, he had Talleyrand assure Berlin and St Petersburg that he would evacuate Holland, Switzerland, southern Italy and Hanover if the British evacuated Malta and the rest of the Mediterranean.[25]

Meanwhile, Napoleon launched a whirlwind diplomatic campaign to entice seeming fence-sitters into an alliance. His most important success was solidifying France's budding alliances with Baden, Württemberg and, especially, front-line Bavaria. He promised each ruler more territory and a higher rank of nobility. He would be good to his word. He tried but failed to get Hesse-Darmstadt to ally with France and contribute 4,000 troops to the campaign. He had a diplomatic message sent to the Imperial Diet at Regensburg, justifying his campaign against Austrian and Russian aggression.[26]

Napoleon thought he had won over the Kingdom of Naples but that proved to be an illusion. That realm played an important role in his strategic calculations. If Naples remained neutral, France's army in northern Italy would face only Austrian forces attacking from the east and north. He was confident that his army there would not just hold the line but eventually counter-attack and drive the Austrians from northern Italy. That, however, would be impossible if a Neapolitan army marched against the French army's southern flank.

Napoleon was well aware of Queen Maria Carolina's burning animosity against him and France, having received copies of intercepted letters of hers in which she vented her feelings. In February 1805, he humiliated and intimidated her by revealing what he knew. She apologized for her vehemence. His reply was at once blunt and encouraging: 'You do not conceal the hatred you carry for France . . . I am not surprised at your outlook . . . Having said that . . . I hope . . . that one day . . . Your Majesty will view us differently . . . I have no other goal than tranquillity for you, your family and your people.' He ended his letter with this veiled threat: 'What interest could I have in overthrowing states and their thrones? The only thing that matters is whether the government is directed toward the people's true interests.'[27] Yet Maria Carolina's contrition was feigned. She was soon badmouthing Napoleon and France again. That prompted Napoleon to have a diplomatic note circulated to all friendly governments denouncing 'the indecent remarks that the queen of Naples makes publicly against the French'. The ambassadors would then share copies of the queen's intercepted letters with their scathing remarks about not just France but many other countries and personalities.[28]

That publically silenced the queen for a while. Yet she was confident that eventually France would be defeated. She and her milquetoast husband were playing a double game. On 10 September, the king secretly agreed to host a joint British and Russian army that would march with the Neapolitan army against the French in northern Italy, then on 21 September, he ratified a treaty signed in Paris whereby his realm would remain neutral if French troops left his kingdom.

Napoleon was confident that he would defeat Austria and Russia but victory would take far more time, blood and treasure if Prussia joined them. Keeping Prussia neutral was critical to his strategy; enticing Prussia into an alliance would have been ideal. He thought he knew just what could seal the first and entice the second. In July 1803, he had General Adolphe Mortier march his division into Hanover and take it over, then offered it to Frederick William if he allied Prussia with France against Britain. The Prussian king politely declined that and periodic reoffers for the next two and a half years. Napoleon repeatedly assured him of 'my desire to overcome all difficulties to maintain peace on the continent', and in March 1805 conferred the Legion of Honour on him.[29] Although Frederick William may have read Napoleon's words with scepticism and worn the Legion of Honour with discomfort, the new emperor's ambitions did not currently appear to threaten Prussian interests. He assured Napoleon that Prussia would stay on the sidelines. In August, as Napoleon devised his campaign plan, he sought a formal peace treaty with Prussia. He wrote to Frederick William that he and 'Europe bear witness that I have been attacked since I am menaced on all my frontiers . . . I have been too lenient toward Austria, which is too powerful to leave Europe in peace and respect German liberties'.[30] The following day, he dispatched his trusted aide Christophe Duroc to Berlin to secure a deal whereby Prussia took Hanover in return for staying neutral and backing the territorial integrity of France's German allies.[31] Without that, Napoleon would have had to keep an army of observation on Prussia's frontier and keep glancing over his left shoulder as he marched against Austria. Frederick William agreed in principle but would not commit himself formally. That was good enough for Napoleon who explained to Talleyrand that 'the position of my forces does not permit a single transaction of weakness. In giving Hanover to Prussia, I gave a gift that . . . augmented my forces by 40,000 men and . . . with Prussia's firm and vigorous cooperation I leave with 200,000 men for the Rhine.'[32]

Turkey was an obvious potential ally against Britain. In March 1804, Napoleon sent his trusted aide and friend, General Guillaume Brune, to Constantinople to talk Selim III into allying against Britain.[33] When Selim demurred, Napoleon warned that he did so at his peril: 'the Porte will defeat himself through weakness . . . England, in concert with Austria, will invade European Turkey; and the Porte is so opaque that he lets troops pass that are directed against him'.[34] As evidence mounted in 1805 that Russia had joined the coalition, allying not just with Turkey but even Persia rose in importance. He sent letters to Selim and Shah Feth Ali, asking both to join France in warring against Russia and Britain. He crafted his letter to Selim to provoke his pride:

> You, descendant of the great Ottomans and emperor of one of the world's greatest empires . . . how can you endure suffering under rules imposed by Russia? . . . As for me, I want to be your friend . . . If you want to remain servilely beneath your enemies, I will be against you . . . Roust yourself, Selim! . . . Join your true friends, France and Prussia or you will lose your country.[35]

His letter to Feth Ali at once praised and disparaged Persia, 'a noble country . . . inhabited by spiritual and intrepid men . . . Men of the East have courage and genius but are ignorant of certain skills and negligent of certain disciplines.' Napoleon promised to send advisors to remedy those deficiencies.[36]

* * *

Austria had three front-line armies, each commanded by a grand duke who was Francis's younger brother, Ferdinand's 72,000 troops in the Danube valley, John's 23,000 troops in the Tyrol and Charles's 50,000 troops in Venetia. Tens of thousands more Austrian troops would reinforce those armies. More importantly, three Russian armies were slowly marching westward, Mikhail Kutuzov's 38,000 troops, Friedrich von Buxhowden's 40,000 troops, including Tsar Alexander and his 8,000 Imperial Guard troops led by his younger brother Constantine and Levin von Bennigsen's 20,000 troops. The Austrian plan was for Ferdinand and Charles to invade Bavaria and Italy, respectively, while John joined his troops to the army that most needed him. The plan had two potentially fatal flaws. The worst was that the Austrians would attack before the Russians joined them, thus giving Napoleon the chance to destroy them separately in succession. The second was the failure for Vienna and St Petersburg to note the difference between their respective Gregorian and Julian calendars; the Austrians could not understand why the Russians were usually at least ten days behind their promised timetable.

Napoleon was unaware of the second flaw but would gleefully exploit the first. He planned to quickmarch his army to cut off and destroy Ferdinand's army before reinforcements and that succession of Russian armies joined him. Meanwhile, Eugène would blunt Charles's offensive then launch a counteroffensive. Both French armies would march toward and join forces at Vienna, where the allies most likely would fight a decisive battle.

Napoleon's army numbered 210,500 troops, including 29,500 cavalry and 396 guns split unequally among corps led by Jean Bernadotte, Auguste Marmont, Louis Davout, Nicolas Soult, troops, Jean Lannes, Michel Ney and Charles Augereau, while Joachim Murat and Jean-Baptiste Bessières commanded the 15,600-man cavalry reserve and 6,000-man Imperial Guard, respectively. General Guillaume Brune stayed behind with 25,000 troops to guard the coast. All the corps were posted along the English Channel except Bernadotte's which was in Hanover. Then there were the allied contingents waiting nervously in their realms, Bavaria's 25,000 troops, Württemberg's 10,000 troops and Baden's 5,000 troops. The French would join the Bavarians while the Württembergers and Badeners guarded communication and supply lines back to France.

Meanwhile, in Italy, Eugène nominally commanded the Italian army, with Marshal Jean-Baptiste Jourdan his advisor until André Masséna arrived to take actual command. Napoleon was sensitive to Jourdan's feelings at being replaced by Masséna, assuring him that although his leadership pleased him, his fragile health concerned him, so he wanted the younger and more robust Masséna to lead the campaign.[37] In southern Italy, General Laurent Gouvion St Cyr would unite his 20,000 troops, then march north to join Eugène.[38]

Napoleon issued intricate marching orders to the Grand Army and Army of Italy between 26 and 31 August. Having set his army in motion, he left his headquarters on 2 September and two days later reached Malmaison Palace seven miles west of Paris. He spent the next three weeks mostly at Saint-Cloud Palace, where he put the finishing touches on his land campaign, launched a new naval campaign and addressed an array of other pressing issues.[39]

* * *

The decision to wage war against Austria and Russia meant postponing indefinitely the invasion of England and thus the necessity for the combined French and Spanish fleet to sail to Boulogne and protect that passage. Yet for nearly a month Napoleon sought a decisive battle against the British fleet. Then he was stunned to learn that Villeneuve had violated orders and sailed south to Cadiz.[40] That forced a radical change of plans. On 14 September, he ordered Villeneuve to sail into the Mediterranean, first to join forces with Spain's fleet at Cartagena, then on to Naples to unload supplies for Gouvion St Cyr's army and finally to Toulon for provisions and repairs. He ended his letter stating that 'the success of these operations essentially depends on the promptness of your departure from Cadiz'.[41] The next day, he ordered Marine Minister Decrès to dispatch Admiral François Rosily-Mesros to replace Villeneuve as the fleet's commander.[42]

* * *

The Austrians played perfectly into Napoleon's hands.[43] General Karl Mack was Ferdinand's field commander and the grand duke largely followed his advice. The Austrians invaded Bavaria on 8 September. The Bavarian army did not stand and fight but withdrew north of the Danube River. The Austrian army secured the Danube valley's south side, with an advanced corps around Reidlingen, three corps around Ulm and a corps around Neuberg by late September.

In mid-September, Murat's cavalry corps crossed the Rhine at Strasbourg and advanced into the Black Forest to distract the Austrian army marching westward, while an arc of five French corps crossed the middle Rhine River and quick-marched on parallel roads toward a stretch of the Danube east of Ulm and Bernadotte's corps marched south from Hanover. After brushing aside the forward Austrian positions, Murat abruptly veered north and then east to spearhead the advancing French corps.

Napoleon left Saint-Cloud on 23 September and three days later was in Strasbourg, where he stayed until 1 October, before moving his headquarters to Ludwigsburg on 3 October. His first strategic challenge was more diplomatic than military. Berlin protested after Bernadotte marched through Prussia's province of Ansbach. Napoleon wanted to give the Prussians no excuse to join the coalition. He had Duroc and Otto smooth over any ruffled feathers for Frederick William and personally wrote the king an apology.[44]

Bernadotte was not the only troublesome marshal. All along, Napoleon tried to manage Murat like an especially spirited stallion, either urging him on or reining him in as was most effective. In early October he cautioned Murat 'to spare nothing to nourish your horses; slow down your march to six hours a day so you do not fatigue them'. He then explained that 'you are going to flank my march, which is a delicate manoeuvre involving an oblique march to the Danube. It is necessary, therefore, if the enemy wants to take the offensive that I am warned in time.'[45]

The campaign's first phase was virtually bloodless. Shoe-leather and horseshoes rather than musket balls and bayonets determined the

French victory. The French corps reached the Danube's north bank below Ulm from Münster to Ingolstadt, then crossed to sever the Austrian army's supply lines as far south as Augsburg before turning west for the kill. French troops trounced Austrian detachments in a series of small battles, Wertingen on 8 October, Gunzburg on 9 October, Haslach on 11 October, Memmingen on 13 October, Elchingen on 14 October and Ulm on 15 October, each yielding thousands of prisoners. The largest haul came on 21 October, when Mack surrendered 23,000 soldiers at Ulm. Ferdinand managed to escape with 6,000 cavalry. Napoleon assigned his German allies the task of disarming and guarding the prisoners, while his French corps advanced down the Danube valley. His message to Murat was similar to those to his other marshals: 'I congratulate you on your success. But do not rest. Pursue the enemy, sword in your reins and cut his communication routes.'[46]

In all, the French captured at least 60,000 men and 120 guns during the campaign's three-week Ulm phase. Napoleon triumphantly wrote to Talleyrand that 'my plan has been executed as I conceived it. I perfectly trumped the enemy and half of their 100,000-man army is taken, dead, wounded or deserted.'[47] He informed the Senate that: 'The war's first object is already fulfilled. The Bavarian elector is re-established on his throne. The unjust aggressors have been struck as with lightning and with God's help, I hope in a short time to triumph over my other enemies.'[48] To Josephine, he explained: 'I realized my design. I destroyed the Austrian army by simple marches.'[49]

After reaching Munich on 26 October, Napoleon tarried for several days in which he squeezed in a pheasant hunt with King Maximilien Joseph and had a concert given for the Bavarian court's ladies between studying intelligence reports and issuing orders to his commanders.[50] He wrote to Josephine that the Bavarians had 'a very beautiful court . . . and everyone is very friendly, even the Electrice, who is very nice even though she is the English king's daughter'.[51] He even found time to glance back at Paris and complain to Police Minister Fouché that 'the newspapers did not at all animate the public spirit. Our newspapers are read everywhere, even in Hungary. Have articles placed revealing that Germany and Hungary are the dupes of English intrigue; that the German emperor sells the blood of his people for gold; that Germany is rising against the English.'[52]

Kutuzov and his 35,000 Russian troops reached Braunau on the Inn River on 23 October, but withdrew soon after learning that Napoleon had destroyed the Austrian army that he was supposed to join. The French pursued, mopping up scattered fleeing Austrian detachments and nipping at the heels of Kutuzov's Russians. The largest clash came on 11 November, when Kutuzov turned and attacked Mortier at Durrenstein, with each side suffering 4,000 or more casualties.

Napoleon's worst fear was that Prussia might soon march against him. He urged Duroc to redouble his efforts to console Prussia's leaders, while he fired off his latest letter to Frederick William, detailing his easy victories, pointing to the peace treaties binding their countries, encouraging him to take over Hanover and lauding his honest character.[53]

Napoleon had good reason to worry. Alexander joined Frederick William and his wife Louise at Berlin on 25 October. They travelled together a dozen miles to Potsdam, where in torchlight before the tomb of Frederick the Great at his palace of Sans Souci, they pledged to destroy Napoleon. Frederick William ordered the Prussian army to mobilize on 1 November. All that remained was for the king and his government to find a pretext for warring against France. The most immediate effect of the Prussia army's mobilization actually weakened the coalition. Sweden's King Gustav IV feared the Prussians more than the French and promptly withdrew from the coalition into neutrality.

On 3 November Napoleon urged Murat to surge across the Danube and inundate the countryside with his cavalry. Murat led his men off at a gallop but soon came to an abrupt stop when he agreed to an armistice with the Austrians. Napoleon was infuriated when he found out and fired off his latest blistering letter to his wayward cavalry commander: 'It is impossible to find words with which to express to you my discontent. You only command my advanced guard and you do not at all have the authority to make an armistice without my order. You cost me the fruit of my campaign. Break immediately the armistice and march against the enemy.'[54] Yet, rather than fulfil his orders to cross the Danube and harass the enemy, Murat instead cantered his cavalry toward undefended Vienna. This provoked yet another angry letter from Napoleon: 'I cannot approve your manner of marching; you go like a scatterbrain and you do not weigh at all the orders that I give you . . . You have received the order . . . to follow the Russians, sword in your reins . . . in forced marches.'[55]

The corps of Murat and Lannes paraded into Vienna on 12 November. Vienna is on the Danube's west bank and the enemy was on the east bank. Four bridges crossed the river at or near Vienna. Murat and Lannes seized the Tabor Bridge by a bold ruse that might have ended disastrously. As French troops deployed on the bank behind them, the two marshals rode nonchalantly across the bridge to inform the Austrian commander that a truce was in effect and that he should withdraw his troops from the river. Astonishingly, the commander did not await confirmation, let alone orders from his superiors, but promptly departed with his men. Murat and Lannes gleefully brought their troops across the Danube to secure the far bank.

The French advanced so swiftly that their supply wagons fell further behind. They requisitioned food and other essentials from the cities and towns they marched through and distributed spoils from captured Austrian depots. The biggest hauls came at Vienna and Braunau whose warehouses were packed with provisions, munitions, shoes, coats and blankets critical for a winter campaign. While the troops were footsore and ragged, their victories kept their morale high. For weeks the biggest challenge was keeping warm and dry through bouts of frigid temperatures, rain and snow. The emperor shared those rigours with his men: 'Although I bivouacked the last eight days in the open air, my health is good. This evening I will sleep in a bed in a beautiful chateau ... and I changed my shirt for the first time in eight days.'[56]

Meanwhile the French campaign opened in Italy. Masséna led his 45,000 troops across the Adige River on 18 October, and caught up to Charles's 49,000 troops at Caldiero on 29 October. For three days, Masséna launched a series of attacks that Charles skilfully countered. In all the French and Austrians suffered 8,700 and 5,700 casualties, respectively. Charles then withdrew north-east toward Austria as Masséna awaited St Cyr to join him. Meanwhile, 7,800 British and 14,000 Russian troops disembarked in Naples where they joined forces with the 22,000-man Neapolitan army and prepared to march north to attack the Kingdom of Italy.

Word of a financial crisis in Paris darkened Napoleon's military triumphs. Normally good news calms financial markets. But as the Grand Army was routing the Austrian and Russian armies, wild rumours that the nation's vaults were empty provoked a run on the banks. Treasury Minister François Barbé-Marbois pleaded with Napoleon to hurry back to the capital as soon as possible to restore confidence and to convene the Legislative Corps to raise taxes to pay off the largest institutions. Not surprisingly that news and plea infuriated Napoleon. He rejected that notion and instead ordered him to work with other public financial institutions to scrape up money in various accounts and prop up any company 'too big to fail' that genuinely teetered on the brink of bankruptcy. He did promise to return to Paris as soon as he won the war.[57] He received far more disastrous news that rattled him as well as financial markets. On 21 October, Admiral Lord Nelson's fleet of twenty-seven ships-of-the-line had destroyed or captured twenty-two of Villeneuve's combined fleet of thirty-three ships-of-the-line, eighteen French and fifteen Spanish, off Cape Trafalgar.

* * *

Napoleon set up his headquarters at Schönbrunn Palace half a dozen miles outside of Vienna on 14 November and began planning his campaign's next phase which, ideally, would not take place.[58] He preferred to end the war with diplomacy rather than bloodshed. He sent Francis several letters criticizing all the aggressive acts he took culminating with war, citing his army's devastating defeats and urging him to break with the Russians and begin peace negotiations. He sent his trusted aide, General Jean Savary, to Alexander with a conciliatory message calling for peace.[59] Savary and Alexander talked for many hours but the Tsar remained committed to Austria. Napoleon considered Alexander 'a truly brave and dignified man but . . . surrounded by those who sold out to the English'.[60]

The delicate diplomacy with Prussia was ongoing. Among his advisors, Frederick William was the rope in a tug-of-war between softliners who upheld neutrality and hardliners who wanted to war against France. Francis and Alexander asserted enormous pressure on him to join his army with theirs. On 3 November, the king partly submitted by signing a treaty whereby Prussia joined 100,000 troops to the coalition as soon as it received £1,250,000 in British subsidies. Meanwhile, Frederick William sent a trusted advisor, Christian Haugwitz, to Napoleon's headquarters to look for an excuse for war. Napoleon had Talleyrand 'try every way to determine just what Haugwitz wants . . . Make him understand that, if he really wants peace, Prussia must stand down' its army.[61]

* * *

The remnants of the Austrian army joined with the armies of Kutuzov and Buxhowden around Olmütz, a hundred miles north of Vienna. Alexander named Kutuzov the Russian army's commander. The Allied army numbered about 82,000, including 69,000 Russians and 13,000 Austrians. The two emperors and their generals debated their options throughout November.[62]

Napoleon left the Schönbrunn Palace on 16 November to establish his headquarters at Znaim on 17 November, then at Brünn (Brno) on 22 November. Nearby were the corps of Bernadotte, Lannes, Soult, Davout, Murat and the Imperial Guard or about 74,000 troops.[63] His other corps were widely dispersed. Mortier guarded Vienna. Marmont was at Graz, blocking an advance by Charles from that direction. Ney and Augereau occupied Austria's western provinces of Tyrol and Voralberg, respectively. Kellermann and Lefebvre were in central Germany guarding against a Prussian attack toward Napoleon's rear. Masséna was marching through Styria after Charles.

A mere 20 miles separated the opposing headquarters at Olmütz and Brünn. The road led east from Brünn half a dozen miles before angling north to Olmütz. Napoleon deployed his corps several miles east of Brünn and posted 1,400 troops at Wischau about halfway to Olmütz. His strategy was to entice the Allies to come to him for a battle on ground that he had carefully chosen.

With Peter Bagration's 12,000-man corps leading the way, the Allied army began a gingerly advance in five parallel columns on 26 November. Two days later, Bagration's troops routed the French at Wischau then scattered them again at Rausnitz a few miles west. Napoleon reacted by galloping couriers off with orders to Davout and Mortier to quickmarch their troops to the pending battle and sending his aide Jean Savary to the Allied headquarters to propose a 24-hour armistice.

The ease with which the Russians chased off the French followed by Napoleon's armistice request swelled the Allied belief that the enemy was overextended, starving and demoralized. Alexander and Francis agreed to a truce, then dispatched Prince Peter Dolgorouski to present their peace terms to Napoleon. When he met Napoleon on the night of 30 November, Dolgorouski haughtily demanded that the French withdraw from all their conquests since 1792, including Italy and Belgium. Napoleon explained how he tricked Dolgorouski and thus the Allied leaders:

> The Russian emperor is surrounded by twenty or so rascals who led him astray . . . He sent me Prince Dolgorouski and in our talks he spoke to me as if he were speaking to some inferior that he wanted to send to Siberia . . . In his excessive arrogance, he interpreted my extreme moderation as a mark of fear. This was what I intended. From a military view this was realized at the battle of Austerlitz where the enemy conducted themselves with inconceivable ignorance and presumption.[64]

Yet Napoleon was disappointed that the Allied leaders had made such non-negotiable demands. He informed Talleyrand that 'I want promptly to make peace . . . Tomorrow there will probably be a serious battle with the Russians that I very much want to avoid because it will needlessly spill blood.'[65]

Among his nearly fifty battles, Austerlitz was Napoleon's masterpiece in how he tactically conceived and executed it. But it was also an enormous gamble. He abandoned the Pratzen Heights, a broad high plateau east of the Goldbach stream, and deployed his army along the west side of those easily-forded waters. The Pratzen faced the centre of his line. His right flank was anchored by three small villages just above the juncture of the Goldbach with the Littawa that meandered from east to west. He deliberately deployed relatively few troops there, hoping to entice the Allies forward to occupy the heights and then ascend to attack his right flank. If so, then his centre would march forward to retake the Pratzen and thus split the Allied army asunder, while his left attacked the Allied right and reinforcements bolstered his own right. The front line consisted of Soult on the right, Bernadotte in the centre and Lannes and Murat on the left, with Davout and the Imperial Guard in reserve.

Rather than mass their artillery on the heights and pound the French army before massively attacking, the Allies did what Napoleon hoped they would. During the night preceding the battle, Alexander and Francis could see the clusters of campfires in the valley below. The French right was sparsely illuminated. They reasoned that by shattering that flank then marching forward half a dozen miles they would sever Napoleon's army from the road to Vienna. The Allied leaders were confident of victory. Their army was not only more numerous but they believed that the enemy suffered from low morale and was short of supplies. The plan made sense except for one critical lapse. Russia's Imperial Guard infantry, cavalry and artillery along with other reserve forces should have occupied and remained on the Pratzen Heights at least until there was no chance that the French could retake them.

Napoleon enjoyed an unexpected but critical ally on the morning of 2 December. Fog covered much of the valley until the sun slowly dispersed it by late morning. For hours Russian and Austrian gunners lacked clear targets. The Allied infantry marched blindly forward to blunder into French infantry and cannons firing short-range canister shot. Alexander and Francis could hear but not see the fighting that raged for several miles up and down the Goldbach valley. They would only surmise that French reinforcements had bolstered the right flank when the firing there intensified and surged back and forth. When Soult's forces fell back, Napoleon ordered Davout's corps forward to retake the lost ground. In late morning, Alexander made the critical decision to send his reserves down from the Pratzen plateau to break the stalemate on the lower Goldbach.

This was the moment that Napoleon had eagerly awaited. He sent two infantry divisions, horse artillery batteries and the Guard cavalry across the Goldbach and up the Pratzen's long steep slope. Alexander ordered the Russian Imperial Guard forward to secure the heights. The French infantry poured volleys into the Russians then charged with lowered bayonets while the horse artillery fired canister and the French Guard cavalry smashed into their flanks. Russia's Imperial Guard broke and ran. The French deployed across the Pratzen and repelled several counter-attacks. Napoleon ordered the rest of Bernadotte's corps and the Imperial Guard to march atop the Pratzen. Meanwhile, Davout smashed through the Allied left and Lannes and Murat crushed the enemy's right. Alexander ordered the remnants of the Allied army to retreat.

The French suffered 1,305 dead, 8,350 wounded and 573 prisoners for a total of 10,220 casualties or 16 per cent of their total forces, while the Russians lost 21,000 men, including 9,000 prisoners and 143 guns and the Austrians 5,912 men, including 1,686 prisoners and 37 guns or 33 per cent of the Allied army.[66] When a distraught Russian Imperial Guard officer was brought before him, Napoleon tried to console him: 'Calm yourself young man! And remember this: there can be no shame in being conquered by Frenchmen.'[67]

The following day, Napoleon ordered his troops to pursue the shattered Allied army. The French rounded up thousands of demoralized Allied troops and scores of abandoned supply wagons and guns. He rejected a request for an armistice by Austrian Prince Johann Liechtenstein when he appeared before him under a white flag that day, but agreed to meet a contrite and humiliated Francis on 4 December. Napoleon informed Talleyrand that 'the German emperor . . . would have concluded peace on the spot . . . He asked me for an armistice which I granted him . . . He asked me for an armistice with the Russians. I granted it on condition that . . . the Russians evacuate Germany in stages and return to their homes.' The French victory at Austerlitz was crushing. Now the Austrians must accept the reality that 'they risked everything and lost. They must accept the toughest conditions' for peace.[68]

* * *

Having won the war, Napoleon was now determined to win a just and lasting peace. For months he had mulled how to do that. France was the victim of Austrian aggression in 1792, 1798 and now 1805. Napoleon had decisively defeated the Austrians in 1797 and 1800, then appeased Vienna with peace treaties that cost the Austrians little money or land. Appeasement clearly encouraged rather than deterred Austrian belligerence. This time Napoleon was determined to punish Austria harshly for its latest aggression, while rewarding his allies.

The rewards came first to show the Austrians the benefits of being France's ally rather than her enemy. The treaties between France and Bavaria on 10 and 16 December, Württemberg on 11 December and Baden on 12 December committed them to perpetual bilateral peace and alliance; the promotion of the Bavarian elector and Württemberg grand duke to king and the duke of Baden to grand duke; and territorial gains for each German state at Austria's expense. Under the Treaty of Schönbrunn signed on 15 December 1805, Prussia renounced its alliances with Russia, Austria and Britain; allied with France; severed trade with Britain; recognized the territorial aggrandizement of France's German allies; and agreed to the terms of any future treaty between France and Austria, all in return for taking Hanover.

Only then did Napoleon turn to Austria. Under the Treaty of Pressburg signed on 26 December 1805, the Austrians ceded Dalmatia and Istria to the Kingdom of Italy; the Tyrol, Brixen, Trent, Augsburg and Voralberg to Bavaria which was made a kingdom; and isolated territories in southwest Germany to Württemberg and Baden, which became a kingdom and grand duchy, respectively; paid France 40 million francs in reparations; and recognized Napoleon as France's emperor and Italy's king. In return, Napoleon pledged independence to the Batavian and Helvetian Republics and got Bavaria to grant Würzburg to Tuscany's former grand duke Ferdinand, Francis's brother.

Napoleon sincerely believed that with this web of treaties he had forged a lasting peace, at least on the Continent. Yet within ten months he would be back at war again. And once again he would do so against his will.

Chapter 12

The Ghost of Frederick

'France's defence costs half its revenues . . . Europe will change, hatreds will recede. New empires must be established and consolidated over time. I will reduce my army by half. I will even withdraw my army from Italy.'

'I am forced to take up arms to defend myself and it will be with the greatest regret if I have to employ them against Your Majesty's troops. I will consider this war a civil war since the interests of our states are linked. I want nothing from you; I have asked nothing from you.'

'Sire, you have been vanquished.'

'I want to conquer the sea by land power.'

Napoleon strode into the Tuileries in Paris on 26 January 1806. Awaiting him was an array of daunting problems that had proliferated without his decisive leadership during his nearly four month's absence. He immediately got to work in fourteen-hour days.

With the peace treaties ratified, all that seemingly remained was for French troops and their allies to pack up and head for their respective homes, while freeing tens of thousands of Austrian prisoners of war. That was easier ordered than implemented. For instance, he had most French cavalry stay in their foreign camps where the horses devoured local forage until spring greened the grasslands and they could munch their way back to France; otherwise thousands would have starved to death during a winter journey. And some troops did not return but were dispatched to occupy newly-won realms like Dalmatia, Istria,

Venetia, Berg and Cleves or to a brief war that conquered southern Italy.[1]

Money was the bottom line of France's problems.[2] On 1 February, Napoleon informed Finance Minister Martin Gaudin that he needed 60 million francs just to cover critical immediate expenses. France's debt had skyrocketed from war costs, financial panic and economic plunge. Corruption exacerbated France's money woes. Fiscal incompetence and blatant theft lurked nearly everywhere Napoleon peered. Much of that he blamed on Treasury Minister François Barbé-Marbois: 'I am busier than you can imagine. Marbois has left everything in the worst imaginable disorder.'[3] Fortunately the emperor himself was a first-rate accountant and steadily restored fiscal sanity to his realm.

The 40 million francs in reparations from Austria certainly helped alleviate France's money woes. Atop that, Napoleon embarked on a financial reform campaign as vigorous, sweeping and swift as any of his military campaigns.[4] He cut spending, raised an array of taxes and started a new lottery. He worked closely with Gaudin to ensure that all available revenues flowed into state coffers within France and Italy and then out to fund vital needs. The French Revolution had taken a progressive step in ending tax privileges for the aristocracy and the Church. Now everyone owed taxes. Collection, however, remained an elusive pursuit. The government received revenues from an array of property taxes; sales taxes on salt, alcohol and tobacco; licences; customs; lotteries; seizures and sales of property; and 'contributions' from allies. Atop that he raked in money from his empire, 19,200,000 francs from Italy, 1,000,000 francs from Genoa, 2,000,000 francs from Parma, 180,000 francs from Etruria and 25,000 from Piombino. The bill imposed on the new acquisitions in Venetia was exorbitant: 400,000 francs from Verona, 1,000,000 francs each from Vicenza and Udine, 1,500,000 francs each from Treviso and Padua and 2,000,000 from Trieste.[5] Indeed he sought as wide an array of sources of money as possible to avoid becoming too dependent on any individual one. He explained: 'My financial system should consist of establishing a great number of indirect contributions of which the very modest tariff would be susceptible to being augmented according to need.'[6]

In promoting fiscal austerity, Napoleon did not spare his beloved army but sought a peace dividend for his realm. In April 1806, he wrote: 'France's defence costs half its revenues ... Europe will change, hatreds will recede. New empires must be established and consolidated over time. I will reduce my army by half. I will even withdraw my army from Italy.'[7] And he began to take steps to those ends. He cut the draft quota and amalgamated newer regiments with veteran ones to bring the latter up to strength. He had the supply system rationalized to improve efficiency and cut waste. He invested some savings to meet pressing needs. For instance, he had annual musket production increased to 200,000 with the goal of a million muskets stockpiled in five years.[8]

All that was the easy part. Much more challenging was shifting mindsets from the prevailing corruption, waste and speculation to honesty, efficiency and investment. For that Napoleon focused his attack on newspapers that peddled the greed and fear that roiled markets and inspired stealing. 'It is time to restrain the journalists who are perpetually alarming commerce and the nation', Napoleon informed Police Minister Fouché in March.[9]

In some places, Napoleon had to assert hard power to get things done. Exacerbating France's financial woes were those of Italy which were worse. Viceroy Eugène had racked up 1,500,000 francs in debt for his household expenses alone, while the royal budget was 2,700,000 francs in debt. Napoleon ordered Eugène to cut expenses and raise revenues, while replenishing the Italian army's ranks thinned by the campaign.[10] All those measures offended countless persons and groups. When a revolt erupted in Parma, Napoleon ordered his commander in Italy, General Andoche Junot, 'to have five or six villages burned and sixty or so people shot. Make extremely severe examples because the consequences of what has happened in Parma for a month are incalculable for Italy's security . . . Nothing is more salutary than terrible examples appropriate given.'[11] When Junot hesitated to do so, he rebuked him for 'your extreme indulgence. Without a severe example the Italian people will always be ready to revolt. You always tell me about their complaints but in a vague manner and never who is complaining . . . It is essential that you repress the existing disorder.'[12] Junot eventually cracked down. Those rebels who evaded death or capture returned to their livelihoods. But the hatred they and their compatriots held for French rule smouldered beneath the tranquil surface.

* * *

Unfinished geopolitical business was inevitable. The most immediate was what to do with the kingdom of Naples. On 10 September 1805, Ferdinand and Maria Carolina had secretly agreed to host a joint British and Russian army that would march with the Neapolitan army against the French in northern Italy, then, on 21 September, promised Napoleon that they would remain neutral if French troops left southern Italy. On 14 October, General Laurent Gouvion St Cyr began marching French troops north from their garrisons. On 19 November, an armada disgorged 14,000 Russian and 7,800 British troops in Naples, where they joined the 22,000-man Neapolitan army. The allies spent the next month organizing and planning an offensive northward. Then came word of the Austerlitz disaster and the peace and armistice deals. The British and Russians hastily withdrew their troops from Naples.[13]

The fate of Ferdinand and Maria Carolina now rested in Napoleon's hands. For Napoleon, justice demanded only one result for such a blatant and cynical violation of an international treaty: 'I would be weak if I pardoned her incendiary excesses toward my people. It is necessary for her to cease to reign.'[14] He ordered Generals Masséna and St Cyr to conquer that realm and on 12 January 1806 hurried Joseph after them to run the country. On 19 January, he informed his brother that, after 'the Bourbons cease to reign at Naples, I want to place on the throne a prince of my house, you first of all, if that suits you'. On 27 January, he expressed the hope 'that you will be happy with Masséna; if not, send him back . . . I am counting on you entering Naples by February's first week'. He worried that the French would start their occupation on the wrong foot: 'Do not tolerate any robbers . . . The queen of Naples sent money here to try to corrupt us. Do not divert yourself for anything . . . Do not at all let [Commissioner Antoine] Saliceti steal.' That admonition was ironic given Napoleon's ambitions: 'My intention is to put the kingdom of Naples in my family . . . as well as those of Italy, Switzerland, Holland and the three German kingdoms.'[15] He asked his uncle, Cardinal Joseph Fesch, 'to take possession of all the palaces of the king of Naples in Rome and the Roman states in the name of France'.[16] On 31 January, he sent word to Joseph that ambassador Marzio Gallo had defected from the Bourbons to the Bonapartes; Napoleon was confident that Gallo was just the first of ever more Neapolitans who would swear allegiance to the new rulers: 'I want my blood to reign in Naples as long as it reigns in France.'[17] He would get his wish.

The 41,000-man French army crossed the frontier on 8 February 1806. The Neapolitan troops mostly fled or surrendered after little or no resistance. Ferdinand and his entourage had sailed to Palermo on 23 January; Maria Carolina, made of sterner stuff, stayed until 11 February. French troops secured Naples on 14 February, while contingents marched to seize the key ports of Reggio, Otranto, Taranto and Brindisi. Neapolitan troops held the fortress of Gaeta before surrendering on 18 July.

Napoleon declared Joseph the King of the Two Sicilies on 30 March 1806 and his older brother gingerly settled himself onto the throne. The Neapolitans paid a hefty price for their 'liberation'. Napoleon had

Joseph levy 30 million francs from his new kingdom, hardly the best way to introduce himself to his subjects' hearts and minds. Anticipating that, Napoleon warned him to disarm the mob and promptly crush any revolts. He criticized Joseph for being too slow and indecisive and urged him to confiscate the property of the former monarch and his supporters, catch and shoot any English secret agents, and invade and conquer Sicily.[18]

Napoleon hated leaving any job half-done. He had conquered the mainland parts of the kingdoms of Piedmont and Naples, but their monarchs escaped to their respective island strongholds of Sardinia and Sicily and there defied his demands that they completely submit to him. British seapower deterred him from trying to invade either island. A worsening problem elsewhere diverted him from those elusive prizes.

* * *

The Prussian King Frederick William III was a well-intentioned but weak-willed man who presided over a bitterly divided government. Christian Haugwitz and Karl von Hardenberg respectively led the moderate and hardline factions that debated whether Prussia should go to war against France. Although the king instinctively favoured peace, his wife, Queen Louise, was an outspoken hardliner. The hardliners pressured Frederick William into rejecting the bilateral treaty with France signed on 15 December 1805.

Napoleon was furious when Haugwitz arrived to renegotiate the treaty in Paris on 1 February 1806. He was determined that the next version would give less to and take more from Prussia.[19] Under the treaty signed on 15 February, Prussia retained Hanover, accepted all the territorial aggrandizements of France and its German allies under existing treaties along with any treaty that followed France's war with Naples, allied with France and ended trade with Britain.

This time Frederick William ratified the treaty then marched his troops into Hanover and ordered Prussia's ports closed to British shipping on 26 March. Britain replied by blockading Prussian ports and seizing any Prussian merchant vessels at sea or in British ports. When Prussia remained defiant, Britain declared war on 11 May.

Napoleon had enlisted an important ally against Britain. Yet he initiated a series of provocative policies that steadily transformed that ally into an enemy. The ink was barely dry on the treaty when he sought to rewrite it. He intended to name Joachim and Caroline Murat the Duke and Duchess of Berg and Cleve, which France had taken by treaty from Bavaria and Prussia, respectively. He sought to 'round off' their realm by including the tiny enclaves of Essen, Werden, Mark and Wittgenstein. Prussia had acquired the abbeys of Essen and Werden in 1803 and wanted to keep them. Hesse-Cassel and Nassau, the respective owners of Mark and Wittgenstein, were open to generous offers. On 15 March, Napoleon ordered Murat to takeover Berg and Cleve and announce that he was their duke by 25 March. Ansbach was another bone of contention between Paris and Berlin. Hardliners had urged Frederick William to war against France after Bernadotte's corps passed through that isolated Prussian territory in September 1805. In the February 1806 treaty, Napoleon secured Ansbach for Bavaria in return for Prussia taking Hanover. Napoleon ordered Bernadotte and his troops to occupy Ansbach even though Frederick William had not yet ratified the treaty. Hardliners vehemently denounced the treaty and called either for war with France or a treaty that retained Ansbach along with Hanover. Frederick William had Haugwitz send a letter of protest to Paris. On 30 March, Napoleon dictated a long reply to Frederick William, listing his grievances and asserting ways to resolve them.[20]

Frederick William wrote to Alexander on June 23, declaring Napoleon an enemy and calling for an alliance between Prussia and Russia. The Tsar promised to back the king against Napoleon. Their diplomats got to work crafting a secret alliance treaty. Meanwhile, Alexander played a double-game against Napoleon. He sent Peter Oubril to Paris to negotiate a peace treaty that he had no intention of fulfilling.

* * *

Napoleon was largely responsible for the series of convulsive revolutionary political acts that transformed Germany. The 1801 Treaty of Lunéville between France and Austria did not just affect those two countries. Like Austria, Prussia, Baden, Württemberg and Hesse-Darmstadt lost territory west of the Rhine to France. Unlike Austria, those four states were entitled to be compensated with even more territory east of the river. Then there was Ferdinand, the Duke of Tuscany, who received Salzburg as compensation for losing his Italian realm. The Holy Roman Empire had to approve all these exchanges. That institution had experienced extraordinary changes in recent years and now teetered on the brink of extinction.

Never before in the Imperial Diet's thousand-year history had its 360 members faced such an ominous agenda as when they had gathered at Regensburg in August 1802. Most of them would no longer exist if the reason for convening were achieved. Under the Diet's 'mediatisation' principle, the major states were going to eliminate and divide the smaller states among themselves. It took half a year of haggling and payoffs to do so. On 25 February 1803, the Diet announced that henceforth the Holy Roman Empire would consist of three electorates, twenty bishoprics, forty-four abbeys, forty-five free cities and a dozen secular states; three million people found themselves with new sovereigns. The biggest winners were Prussia, Bavaria, Württemberg and Baden which respectively got five, one and a half, four and seven times more subjects east of the Rhine than they ceded to France west of the river. Better that or nothing. Around 150 tiny states disappeared from the map altogether. The Diet now consisted of ten upper house and 130 lower house members. With 77 of the 130 members of the lower house Protestant, the Holy Roman Empire's religious and thus political balance appeared to have shifted from Vienna to Berlin. For now, the Austrian king Francis remained the Holy Roman Emperor.[21]

Then there was Napoleon. He sought to displace Austrian and Prussian influence over the southern and northern German states by transforming the Holy Roman Empire into the Confederation of the Rhine dominated by France and its junior allies, Bavaria, Württemberg and Baden. That meant eliminating a hundred more mini-states and joining them into a couple of score larger states. He presented this justification for doing so: 'It is genuinely in French interests that the German Empire reorganizes itself into a powerful position . . . Current circumstances demand the destruction of the small German principalities. United with our three sovereign allies, they will give a regiment or more and form a distinct spirit in the German empire.'[22]

On 12 July Foreign Minister Talleyrand convened a conference with the German states before which he unveiled a treaty whereby the Holy Roman Empire transformed itself into the Confederation of the Rhine. That happened on 25 July, when sixteen states signed the treaty. On 1 August, the Diet voted to dissolve the Holy Roman Empire. On 4 August, Francis renounced his title as the Holy Roman Emperor and announced that henceforth he would be solely Austria's emperor. At Frankfurt, the Confederation of the Rhine established a bicameral Diet with an upper College of Kings and a lower College of Princes; the Diet elected Charles Dalberg the Confederation of the Rhine's prince primate or sovereign leader. Eventually the Confederation expanded to thirty-six members.

The Confederation of the Rhine was allied by treaty with France and each member was committed to providing a specific number of troops in wartime which together totalled 117,920 men. The ten largest contingents were Bavaria's 30,000, Westphalia's 25,000, Saxony's 20,000, Württemberg's 12,000, Baden's 8,000, Berg's 5,000, Hesse-Darmstadt's 4,000, Würzburg's 2,000, Mechlinbourg-Strelitz's 1,900 and Saxe-Gotha's 1,100. The minor contingents were Anhalt-Bernburg's 240, Anhalt-Dessau's 350, Anhalt-Kothen's 210, Arenberg's 379, Frankfurt's 968, Hohezollern-Hechingen's 93, Hollenzollern-Sigmaringen's 197, Isemberg's 291, Leyen's 29, Lichtenstein's 40, Lippe-Detmold's 500, Lippe-Schaubourg's 150, Mecklenburg-Schwerin's 400, Nassau-Usingen and Nassau-Weilburg's 840, Oldenburg's 800, Reuss-Ebersdorf's 90, Reuss-Greiz's 90, Reuss-Lobenstein's 90, Reuss-Schleiz's 90, Salm-Salm's 108, Salm-Kryburg's 215, Saxe-Coburg's 400, Saxe-Hilburghausen's 200, Saxe-Meningen's 300, Saxe-Weimar's 800, Schwarzbourg-Rudolstadt's 325, Schwarbourg-Sondershausen's 325 and Waldeck's 400.[23] During campaigns Napoleon mostly used the ten largest contingents as for front-line troops and the rest to guard lines of communication.

* * *

As for the war with Britain, a flicker of light for a possible diplomatic resolution unexpectedly appeared. France's nemesis Prime Minister William Pitt died on 23 January 1806. George III formed a coalition government led by William Grenville and including the liberal Charles James Fox as the Foreign Secretary. 'The new English cabinet appears to have principles more reasonable than the former', Napoleon concluded in March.[24] Fox and Talleyrand exchanged letters in early April over possibly holding talks. Napoleon initially rejected the British government's insistence that Russian diplomats join them but finally agreed on 2 June. Armed with the power to negotiate a peace treaty, Francis Seymour, Lord Yarmouth, arrived in Paris on 14 June. After six weeks of haggling between Talleyrand and Yarmouth, Napoleon happily noted that 'the English appear to be softening'.[25] Sicily was the biggest problem: the British wanted Ferdinand to retain it; Napoleon wanted it to remain part of the Kingdom of the Two Sicilies ruled by Joseph, while compensating Ferdinand with the Balearic Islands.

Meanwhile, Russian ambassador Peter Oubril joined the talks. Napoleon assigned Henri Clarke to cut a bilateral deal with Oubril. Under a treaty signed on 20 July, Russia accepted France's treaties with Austria and the German states, ceded Cattaro to France, recognized a Ragusa Republic under Turkish sovereignty; retained sovereignty over the Republic of Seven Islands, and agreed that Ferdinand be given the Balearic Islands while Joseph took his entire kingdom. Napoleon's delight turned to rage on 3 September when he learned that Alexander refused to ratify the treaty.

Peace with Britain proved to be just as elusive. On 5 August, James Maitland, Lord Lauderdale, joined Yarmouth and strongly insisted on retaining all the French and Dutch colonies that Britain had taken along with Malta and getting back Hanover, while Napoleon had to grant independence to the Netherlands. When Yarmouth and Lauderdale threatened to break off talks on 11 August, Napoleon yielded to all their demands except the Netherlands which he had transformed into a kingdom with his brother Louis as king. Yarmouth walked out. The talks with Lauderdale sputtered on. Then came word that Fox had died on 14 September. Napoleon recognized that any chance of peace had died with him.[26] He later described Fox's death 'as one of my career's fatalities; had he lived affairs would have taken a completely different turn . . . and we would have cemented a new order in Europe'.[27]

* * *

Meanwhile, the naval war continued. On 31 January 1806, Napoleon informed Marine Minister Decrès that 'I have not yet definitively devised a war plan for the fleet; that depends entirely on the moment when my army will be completely available'.[28] Within a month, he had devised his latest elaborate naval strategy and sent it to the appropriate admirals to implement. At Brest, Admiral Zacharie Allemand's five ships-of-the-line, five frigates and four smaller warships should sail to the Baltic and scour the seas of enemy vessels, capturing those with valuable cargos and burning the rest. After returning and reprovisioning, Allemand should escort a convoy to the West Indies to drop troops and supplies at Martinique and Guadeloupe. He should head back via America's east coast and then to the Irish coast, capturing or burning enemy vessels along the way before finally dropping anchor at Brest.[29]

Napoleon sought to make the Adriatic a French sea. His empire had engulfed Venetia, Dalmatia, the Papal States and southern Italy with his brother as the King of Naples. Three other great powers, however, prevented Napoleon from realising his dream. Austria retained the coast from Trieste to Fiume. Ottoman governors ruled Greece and Albania. Russia occupied the enclave of Cattaro midway on the Adriatic's east coast and the Seven Islands stretching between the Adriatic and Ionian seas. Napoleon sought to squeeze those rivals from their lands. His success with Austria would have to await another war between them and he never tried to take the Ottoman provinces, but he soon made progress with Russia. He received word in May 1806 that the Russians would soon cede Cattaro to France. He ordered Generals August Marmont and Jacques Lauriston to occupy Cattaro.[30]

Napoleon wrote his latest letter to Turkish Sultan Selim III in March 1806, trying to nurture ties between them. As usual his words were at once practical and condescending. He lauded their relationship for epitomizing 'principles of mutual moderation, conservatism and reciprocity'. He then gave the sultan unsolicited advice on how to handle his rebellious, mostly Christian province of Serbia. Ironically, given the revolts that plagued his own empire, he criticized Serbia's governor for provoking the uprising by his tyrannical rule. He called on Selim to reconcile the people with their government with judicious compromises sensitive to their needs.[31] How easy it is for anyone, including Napoleon, to say what is right yet do what is wrong. Nonetheless, Selim admired him, accepted French ambassador Horace Sebastiani as a close advisor and embarked on an array of military, economic and education reforms designed to modernize his empire. Napoleon's most vital interest with Constantinople was hardly good government: 'The goal of all negotiations is to close the Bosporus to the Russians.'[32] He wanted the Turks to bottle up the Russians in the Black Sea and contain them far beyond the Danube by defending Moldavia and Wallachia. Eventually Selim agreed to do so.[33] Selim's reforms eventually provoked his downfall. He offended an array of conservative military, religious and economic leaders who murdered him on 28 July 1808 and put his reactionary cousin on the throne as Mustafa IV.[34]

* * *

Prussia's government secretly decided to go to war against France on 7 August 1806. Two days later Frederick William quietly ordered his army to mobilize. Within two months the Prussians hoped to have their armies massed and supplied for an offensive that drove the French west of the Rhine.[35]

Napoleon was oblivious to the fateful decision taken in Berlin. For another month he believed that the Prussians remained deadlocked between the hardliners and moderates and urged Ambassador Antoine Laforest to redouble his efforts to work with the peace faction against the war faction. For five years now a chronic irritant had clouded Napoleon's view of Berlin. Girolamo di Lucchesini, Prussia's ambassador, got under Napoleon's skin. The emperor despised Frederick the Great's former librarian for being a mélange of pendant, meddler and shyster.

He had been stuck with Lucchesini even though he had repeatedly signalled Berlin that he preferred an alternative. He criticized Foreign Minister Talleyrand for letting the ambassador trick him and instructed him 'to say nothing to Mr. Lucchesini; if he comes to speak to you, reproach him for his personal conduct for sharing intelligence with agitators and that he writes his court absurd and stupid things that cause follies'.[36] Although Prussia would have still declared war against France even with an ambassador congenial to Napoleon, Lucchesini's abrasive personality definitely exacerbated the rotting relationship.[37] Berlin finally recalled Lucchesini in August. Whatever diplomatic merits the new ambassador, Wilhelm von Knobelsdorf, bore within him, he presented an ultimatum along with his credentials on 12 September. Frederick William demanded that Napoleon withdraw his army west of the Rhine.

Napoleon hoped to avert war by appealing directly to Frederick William that same day. He lamented that 'I am forced to take up arms to defend myself and it will be with the greatest regret if I must employ them against Your Majesty's troops. I will consider this war a civil war since the interests of our states are linked. I want nothing from you; I have asked nothing from you.'[38] He promised to demobilize his army if Frederick William did likewise. He had Talleyrand offer that same face-saving proposal to his counterpart Haugwitz.[39]

The emperor's words and promises were sincere. To Talleyrand, he explained that 'I have absolutely no interest in disturbing the continent's peace'. Tragically, Berlin appeared to want war even though 'the idea that Prussia can engage alone against me seems so ridiculous that it does not merit discussion'. He reckoned that an alliance with Russia had emboldened Prussia. He fumed at the paradox that trapped him. To prevent war,

> I have to do two things, first reassure Prussia and find the means of returning to the former tranquillity . . . secondly, to reinforce my army in Germany . . . But these two measures are contradictory. If they fear the troops that I have [in Germany], they will consequently fear the reinforcements that I send there. Thus I must give both reassurance and fear to get Prussia to demobilize . . . Instead of saying, 'Disarm or war!' which would be too frightening to the Prussians, I will say, 'Disarm if you want me not to arm more'.[40]

Napoleon did exactly that but Prussia's hawks straitjacketed Frederick William and neither appeasement nor brinkmanship could have prevented the war they zealously sought. In a letter of 26 September, the king repeated his ultimatum, this time with a deadline of 8 October for the French army's withdrawal west across the Rhine. Napoleon also failed to convince Saxon King Frederick Augustus III not to ally with Prussia as Berlin's militarists intimidated him into joining their rush to war.[41]

Prussia's determination to go to war against France baffled Napoleon:

> We search their motives without the power to penetrate them. The letters that His Prussian Majesty writes are friendly. His foreign minister has notified our diplomat that he recognizes the Confederation of the Rhine and that he does not object to arrangements made in central Germany. Is Prussia's build-up the result of its coalition with Russia or only the intrigues of different parties that exist in Berlin and the cabinet's rashness?

He cited various realms that the Prussians might use war as an excuse to conquer: 'Among all these motifs, what is the truth?'[42] He held out hope that the Prussians would come to their senses and step firmly back from the brink of war just before the cannons began roaring. Meanwhile, he received and believed Vienna's reassurances that Austria would stay firmly on the sidelines in any war between France and Prussia.[43]

Just in case, Napoleon had begun readying his army for war in August.[44] He massed provisions and munitions in a chain of depots leading to the front. He brought regiments up to strength. He ensured that the infantry had enough shoes and the cavalry enough shod horses. He had his Confederation of the Rhine allies mobilize their troops. He ordered Dutch King Louis, his brother, to mobilize his army and navy mostly to guard his frontiers against British threats, but send a 12,000-man corps to demonstrate against Wesel on the Rhine and so distract Berlin. He left Paris on 26 September and established his Grand Army's headquarters at Mainz on the 28th. He spent nearly a week there issuing streams of orders then moved to Würzburg on 2 October. He received Prussia's declaration of war on 7 October.

The 146,000 Prussian troops in central Germany were split between three armies, Frederick, Duke of Brunswick's 75,300 troops, Prince Frederick Hohenlohe's 42,000 troops and General Ernst von Ruchel's 29,000; another 25,000 troops were deployed in East Prussia. St Petersburg had committed two 30,000-man armies but they were then still marching through western Russia. Like the Allied plan in 1805, that of 1806 had a fatal flaw. The Prussians would fight Napoleon before the Russians joined them. Waiting would have delayed the war until the spring of

1807 and Prussia's war hawks contemptuously rejected that notion. Prussia had one other ally, Sweden, which had declared war against France on 31 October 1805. But Frederick William and Gustavus IV did not coordinate strategy and the Swedes ended up playing no significant role in the campaign.

Napoleon had only about 100,000 troops in six corps led by Soult, Davout, Lannes, Ney, Augereau and Bernadotte, while Murat headed the cavalry reserve and Lefebvre and Bessières the Imperial Guard infantry and cavalry, respectively. As usual he was confident that superior strategy would compensate for inferior numbers. His plan was to race his corps in three parallel lines north through the Thuringer Forest into Saxony and down the Saale and Elster river valleys then angle north-west against the Prussian army's rear.[45]

As his army marched into Saxony on 8 October, Napoleon had a proclamation distributed that began: 'Saxons, the Prussians have invaded your territory. I have arrived to liberate you.'[46] The first battle came at Saalfeld on 10 October, when Lannes's corps routed Prince Louis Ferdinand of Prussia's corps; Louis was killed in the fighting. Napoleon confidently informed Talleyrand that: 'The affairs are going completely according to what I calculated.'[47] Nonetheless, he was still willing to accept peace even without a decisive victory. On 12 October, he implored Frederick William: 'Why shed so much blood? To what end? . . . I have been your friend for six years. I do not want to profit from this type of frenzy that animates your advisors, that made you commit political errors that have astonished all of Europe and enormous military errors that cannot be reversed . . . Sire, you have been vanquished.'[48]

Jena is on the west bank of Saale River with steep wooded slopes on either side of the valley. Hohenlohe had deployed 38,000 troops several miles north-west of the town, while Ruchel's 15,000 troops were half a day's march beyond. Napoleon and the corps of Lannes, Ney and Augereau along with his Imperial Guard, reached Jena on 13 October. That night the French ascended the slopes by different routes to the rolling farmland beyond.

The French and Prussian fought two decisive battles on 14 October. Near Jena, the Prussians attacked the French as they appeared. After the French repelled those attacks, Napoleon ordered a counter-attack that routed Hohenlohe's army. Meanwhile, 13 miles north at Auerstadt, Davout's 27,000-man corps repelled a series of attacks by Brunswick's 60,500-man army; although nearby, Bernadotte failed to march his corps to support Davout. Napoleon lauded Davout for his brilliant victory and later made him the Duke of Auerstadt.[49] He ordered his corps commanders to pursue the Prussian army's remnants relentlessly. His 1806 campaign was truly brilliant. In a few weeks, the French killed or wounded 25,000 Prussians, captured 140,000 along with 2,000 guns and overran nearly the entire kingdom. Frederick William fled with around 20,000 troops all the way to Königsberg, where he awaited rescue by the Russians.

Napoleon simultaneously played good and bad cop with Frederick William. He sent the king his latest plea for peace on 19 October, hoping that the devastation of his army five days earlier would finally bring him to reason. His choice was either immediately to surrender unconditionally or witness French troops destroy the rest of his army and overrun the rest of his realm. He refused to grant an armistice that would give the Russian army time to arrive.[50] Tragically, once again, Prussia's hawks prevailed. Typically, Napoleon then upped the ante. He announced on 23 October, that France would annex all Prussian territory between the Rhine and Elbe rivers including Brunswick, Hanover and Osnabrück, while Holland would take East Frisia. For now France would administer Prussia's allies, Saxony and Hesse-Cassel, before later deciding their respective fates.

A couple of clouds darkened the campaign. Once again Bernadotte was a gross liability for France. Napoleon castigated him: 'I am not at all in the habit of recriminating against what happened in the past since it cannot be remedied. But your corps did not find itself to the battlefield and that was disastrous.' He then cited a litany of Bernadotte's blunders that tragically cost French lives by prolonging the campaign. Typically, after tearing down a miscreant, he ended by trying to rebuild him: 'All that is certainly awful but since then you have offered proofs of your zeal . . . and you can give further proofs of your talents and your devotion to me.'[51] Indeed, five weeks later Bernadotte redeemed himself in the emperor's eyes when he sent him captured Prussian regimental flags: 'I have seen with pleasure the activity and talents that you have deployed in these circumstances and the distinguished courage of your troops. I bear you my satisfaction.'[52] His brother, the Dutch King Louis, was just as inept, prompting this condemnation: 'Your kingdom has not rendered me a single service . . . You must furnish me no less than 20,000 troops. You govern your kingdom with too much softness . . . Everything is poorly administered. A kingdom can only be administered with vigour and energy.'[53]

Napoleon established his headquarters at Frederick the Great's palace of Sans Souci in Potsdam outside Berlin on 24 October. He stood in long, contemplative silence before his hero's tomb. Then he committed an act of shameless pillage by stealing Frederick's sword, saying it was worth more to him than millions of francs.[54] He triumphantly entered Berlin on 27 October and installed himself in the Charlottenburg palace. Among the countless decisions he made during a month at Berlin, one saved a prominent man's life and another adversely affected the lives of tens of millions of Europeans and would be a major reason for his eventual downfall.

French authorities caught Franz von Hatzfeld, Berlin's governor, committing espionage. A military commission found him guilty and sentenced him to be shot. Yet when Hatzfeld's pretty, pregnant wife begged Napoleon for clemency, he burned the evidence before her eyes. He later explained that 'I am convinced that her husband was guilty as charged and that the laws of war condemn him for a capital crime. I always avoid interfering in disputes over judgments.' Yet 'Madame Hatzfeld's profound sweetness and sorrow forced me' to pardon her husband.[55] A political motive also might have moved him. Executing the nobleman Hatzfeld might have provoked as much rage and condemnation among Europe's nobility as d'Enghien's execution had three years earlier. A vital means and end of Napoleon's power was trying to win over more hearts and minds than he repelled.

With Prussia's army mostly destroyed and its territory mostly overrun, Napoleon shifted his thoughts to his other major enemy. He reasoned that if he could not defeat Britain with naval power, he just might be able to do so with trade power. With his Berlin Decree of 21 November 1806, he established the Continental System to attempt to completely sever all trade between Britain and Europe under his control. Within France, the Marine, Treasury and Interior ministries had overlapping duties to enforce the blockade. He charged General Edouard Mortier with asserting the embargo along the German coast and navigable river mouths like the Elbe and Oder and free cities like Hamburg, Bremen and Lübeck. His decrees of Fontainebleau on 13 October 1807 and Milan on 23 November 1807 bolstered the embargo.[56]

The Continental System was a logical strategy to employ against Britain with its naval and mercantile superiority. Europe bought 40 per cent of British exports. Napoleon reasoned that the loss of those profits would certainly harm and ideally cripple Britain: 'I want to conquer the sea by land power.'[57] Angry manufacturers would pressure the government to make peace. What he failed to anticipate was how self-destructive the Continental System would be. Not only would the blockade actually hurt France and Europe worse than Britain, his attempts to sever all of Europe from Britain would ultimately destroy his own power.[58]

* * *

Napoleon made another critical decision at Berlin that would have enormous consequences. He issued orders on 3 November 1806 for his advance corps to march into Prussia's Polish provinces and secure Warsaw before the Russians did.[59] He explained that 'the Russians are far enough away but we may possibly meet them ... within a month. Thus there is no time to lose. Everything will be decided by that battle.'[60]

Murat led the Grand Army's advance guard into Warsaw on 28 November. Napoleon had each corps march through the city, cross the Vistula River, then deploy for winter quarters in a defensive arc a dozen or so miles from the city. He warned his marshals to withdraw and concentrate if a larger Russian force appeared before them. As always, he wielded the power of the press to enhance his military and diplomatic victories. He ordered General Henri Clarke, Berlin's governor general, to ensure that all newspapers heralded the Grand Army's triumphant march into Warsaw. Clarke should ensure that the newspapers published only good news to counter all the bad news spread by France's enemies. Rumours forced Napoleon to peer even further west beyond Germany to Paris itself. He issued the same complaint that Parisian newspapers printed too many negative stories and not enough positive ones. He had Fouché rectify that.[61]

His decision to march further east all the way to Warsaw and beyond was a strategic trade-off.[62] He sought to position his army deep in Poland, reconstitute a Polish realm and ally, extend the Continental System, pressure the Prussians to capitulate and await the Russian onslaught in the spring. But in doing so he stretched his own supply lines and shortened his enemy's. That would have been a serious self-imposed handicap even in the best conditions, let alone in winter when snow and ice buried the wretched Polish roads. In doing so he took an enormous risk. Had the Austrians joined the coalition and marched north against Napoleon's rear while the Russians and Prussians advanced against his front, the Polish campaign would have ended catastrophically for France and its emperor.

Despite the captured magazines, each corps was faltering from fatigue and attrition. The soldiers still on their feet needed shoes and winter coats. The wounded and sick needed doctors and medicine. To fill his regiments' depleted ranks, he ordered 48,200 infantry and 10,000 cavalry drawn from regiments deployed in France, Italy, Holland and Germany, along with 80,000 conscripts from the class of 1807. A huge problem was guarding and feeding over 140,000 prisoners.

His hope that his advance into Poland would force the Prussians to open peace negotiations proved illusory. He complained that 'the

Prussian king has declared that he is no longer the master of ratifying the suspension of arms because he is entirely in the arms of the Russians'.[63] On 6 December, he wrote the king criticizing him for 'breaking all negotiations and disavowing the negotiators', acts that are already in 'the domain of history'.[64]

If one people ever genuinely greeted invading French troops as liberators, it was the Poles. That is hardly surprising. In three stages during 1772, 1793 and 1795, Russia, Prussia and Austria devoured swaths of that ancient kingdom until nothing remained, then repressed and exploited their respective shares. The burning desire of most Poles to free themselves was compounded by word of and, for some adventurers, participation in the exhilarating liberalism and nationalism of the American and French revolutions.

Napoleon was stunned to witness that: 'All of Poland has risen. Priests, nobles, bourgeois, everyone is a soldier. It is not in my power to prevent this national eruption.'[65] He expected that 'Poland will soon have 60,000 men under arms'.[66] He had Davout help General Henri Dombrowski organize Polish regiments at Posen equipped from supplies captured with the fortress, then together march to Warsaw. He had King Joseph hurry to him the Polish Legion along with any Polish officers under his command. He wanted a Polish corps ready for action by early 1807.[67]

Polish delegations arrived at Napoleon's headquarters at Posen and implored him to liberate their country. The mood was intoxicating as Poles celebrated their liberation. Napoleon was looking forward to 'going tomorrow to a ball where they will make me a noble of the city. The women will be presented to me . . . It is the first time since Poland's destruction that they will show themselves. Everyone easily speaks French and . . . loves France.'[68] The emperor would find himself smitten with one beguiling young women he met at one of these soirees.

Napoleon struggled not to get carried away in the excitement. Diplomatically he had to tread lightly. Although the Austrians remained on the sidelines, periodically he nervously glanced over his shoulder to see if they were still there. Vienna would go to war against him if he tried to return Poland to its pre-1772 frontiers. At most he would reconstitute a Poland composed of the Russian and Prussian regions, but could do so only after crushing the Russian and Prussian armies, an event that was most likely sometime late next spring or early summer. He instructed Antoine Andreossy, his ambassador in Vienna, to reassure his hosts that: 'I want peace with Austria . . . While I favour the insurrection of Prussian and Russian Poles, I will never get involved with Austrian Poles.'[69] The best deterrent against the Austrians marching against his rear were his armies in north-eastern Italy and Dalmatia, led respectively by Viceroy Eugène and Marshal Marmont, marching against their rear. He instructed those commanders to reinforce their forces and keep them at a high state of readiness. Meanwhile, Eugène should ensure that Italy's newspapers be filled with praise for Austria and relations between Vienna and Paris.[70]

A major obstacle to Poland's recreation was the Poles themselves. They were splintered into countless factions that jostled with each other for power. The cacophony of pleas for Napoleon's support was deafening. He recognized that he did not understand Polish politics well enough to impose a government. Instead he insisted that they first create a workable representative government that he could endorse.[71]

Just who could best lead a reconstituted Polish kingdom? The safe choice was Saxon elector Frederick Augustus III who had once also held the title of King of Poland until the Russians, Prussians and Austrians deprived him of it. Napoleon thought him a well-meaning but weak man who had meekly acquiesced in Prussia's takeover of his country and army. Could such a man be entrusted with running Poland? Frederick Augustus was already allying his country to France and paying 25 million francs in reparations to fulfil a treaty to be signed on 11 December and was in Berlin awaiting what he hoped would be a summons to Warsaw. Yet, the emperor discouraged him from making the journey. The excuse was that the roads were too wretched and the fighting was still going on. The real reason was that Napoleon was mulling three other possibilities.[72]

Josef Poniatowski was a prominent nobleman and general but Napoleon found him 'light and inconsequent . . . He has little support in Warsaw.'[73] Then there was Prince Adam Czartoryski, who Napoleon respected but was too close to Tsar Alexander. Finally, there was Thaddeus Kosciusko who struggled to be Poland's George Washington.[74] Indeed, he knew Washington, having fought bravely for several years in America's war of independence against Britain. He led a valiant but doomed resistance against Russia in 1792 and 1794. Napoleon instructed Fouché to 'send Kosciusko . . . to join me but secretly and under another name . . . Give him money for his expenses. Also send all the Poles with him.'[75] When he learned that the Pole balked at the invitation, Napoleon reasoned that 'If Kosciusko wants to come, fine; if not things will proceed without him. Yet it would be better if he came.'[76] By February 1807, he 'attached no importance to Kosciuszko whose . . . behaviour proves that he is nothing more than a fool'.[77]

In mid-December, Levin Bennigsen's 50,000-man Russian army marched westward to rescue the retreating Prussians under Anton Lestocq, then withdrew as French forces converged. Napoleon won a victory with a night attack of 8,000 troops of Davout's corps against 15,000 Russians under Alexander Osterman-Tolstoy 20 miles north of Warsaw at Czarnowo on 23 December; the Russians lost around 1,850 men as they withdrew across the Bug River; around 850 French were killed and wounded. Advanced French forces clashed with withdrawing Prussians at Biezun on 23 December and Soldau two days later. The biggest battle came in a snowstorm at Pultusk around 30 miles north of Warsaw on 25 December, when Bennigsen's 40,000 Russian troops fought off Lannes and Ney whose combined forces numbered 26,000; the French and Russians each suffered around 3,500 casualties. Bennigsen withdrew that night eventually to winter quarters at Bialystok. The following day, elements of the corps of Augereau, Davout and Murat numbering 16,000 men attacked 9,000 Russians under André Galitzin at Golymin; the Russians stood their ground before retreating that night to join Bennigsen.[78]

The emperor did not order a pursuit but instead dispersed his corps to their winter quarters. He then hurried to Warsaw and immersed himself in the maze of Polish politics. To his delight, he found his geopolitical schemes increasingly coloured by romance.

* * *

Napoleon still passionately loved Josephine despite their many years as a couple and mutual infidelities. He greatly missed her and in mid-November encouraged her to journey to Berlin to be with him. After attending a ball in Posen celebrating the anniversary of his coronation and Austerlitz on 2 December, he wrote her just to express that 'I love you and I desire you'.[79] He received a letter from her the next morning and replied with two letters. Josephine apparently loved him just as deeply. She related dreams where he was unfaithful, but claimed that she was not jealous. In his first letter he related that her dreams deepened his lust for her since obviously she would not have had them without being jealous. In his second letter, he wrote that 'to desire a women is a fire that devours oneself', that he 'hoped to summon you in a few days', and that her letter's passion inflamed him.[80] But he not only did not summon her, citing the worsening roads, weather and Russian threat, but told her to return to Paris. He laughed away her fears that he was being seduced by Polish beauties. He imagined that Adelaide

La Rochefoucauld, her malicious maid of honour, was cruelly making her jealous.[81] Actually Josephine's fears were justified. A beautiful Polish women had indeed intoxicated Napoleon with her charms.

Marie Walewska was 21 years old and married to a 66-year-old count who was incapable of consummating their marriage.[82] She poured her passions into the cause of Polish independence. Just how Marie and Napoleon met will forever remain obscure. Versions have Murat, Talleyrand or Polish nobles involved in the matchmaking.[83] Regardless, Napoleon fell madly in love with Marie: 'I see nothing but you. I esteem nothing but you. I desire nothing but you. Promptly reply to calm my impatient ardour.'[84] Her reply was prompt but agitated rather than calmed him. 'Did I displease you?' he fired back. 'I had reason to hope for the opposite. Have I been mistaken? Your eagerness has slowed while mine has increased. You take away my repose! . . . Give a little joy and happiness to an impoverished heart ready to adore you.'[85] Was Marie having serious second thoughts or simply playing hard to get? Regardless, her cool distance tormented him: 'How can a smitten heart be satisfied that longs to throw itself at your feet . . . that paralyzes me with the fiercest desires . . . Only you can remove the obstacles that separate us. Come! . . . All your desires will be fulfilled.' He then played the patriotism card: 'Your country will be dear to me when you take pity on my impoverished heart.'[86] She came and surrendered completely. He was overjoyed and could not wait to see his 'beautiful, perfect, ravishing, angel' again.[87] He sent her flowers and invited her to romantic dinners and sought to weave 'a mysterious link between us, a secret rapport amidst the surrounding crowd'.[88]

Alas, such a secret was impossible to keep from a prying, salacious crowd. Rumours of Napoleon's mistress swiftly reached Josephine. Although she did not directly confront him, she expressed all her sorrow and tears. He sent her words lauding her virtues and longing to spend his nights with her but duty prevented from doing so. She should never doubt his love for her but should be cheerful and dignified as befitting an empress. Rather than return to Paris, Josephine established a court at Mainz, where she fretfully awaited a summons from her husband to join him in Warsaw, a summons that never came. Instead he sent her a letter every week or so acknowledging hers, commenting on recent events and asking her to dismiss any disturbing rumours originating in Warsaw.

Throughout the early months of 1807, memories and fantasies about Maria diverted Napoleon from the campaign's endless duties and nasty weather, capped by the bloodbath at Eylau. In mid-March, he wrote her that 'I have not been a day without desiring you . . . I long to see you . . . That depends on you. Do not doubt, Marie, my feelings . . . A thousand kisses on your hands and your charming mouth.'[89]

* * *

Napoleon was determined to launch a naval blow at Britain even if it was only symbolic. He had Marine Minister Decrès order the French squadron at Cadiz to break through the blockade and sail to the Cape of Good Hope, Isle de France in the Indian Ocean, Manila in the western Pacific Ocean and finally back to France, thus circumnavigating the world. If that was not possible then the Cadiz squadron should sail to Toulon. Meanwhile, the Lorient squadron of two ships-of-the-line and two frigates should sail along Africa's west coast; the Rochefort squadron should sail for the Baltic Sea; and two frigates at Bordeaux should sail for Isle de France. The point of these expeditions was 'to worry the English and force them to reinforce their colonies'.[90]

Word from his admirals that trying to break through the British blockades with their superior gunnery, seamanship and numbers of warships would be suicidal pushed Napoleon into a deep funk. He admitted that 'Spain and France . . . must renounce embarking on sea adventures where we are the weakest and instead follow our advantages on land. If Spain deployed the same energy that I show, we would realize all our projects.'[91] He cancelled his elaborate plan for a flurry of expeditions. Instead, he had Decrès accelerate the warship building programme designed to catch up to Britain's Royal Navy.[92] He eyed Sicily as a key target. French troops had overrun the Italian mainland half of the Kingdom of Two Sicilies and installed Joseph as king, but Ferdinand and Maria Carolina had fled to their palace at Palermo. Napoleon instructed both Decrès and Joseph to build up their forces and plan for invading Sicily.[93]

* * *

Napoleon's attempts to entice the Ottoman and Persian rulers to go to war against Russia during this time were diplomatic sideshows. Just the journey from Paris or Warsaw to Istanbul took a month or so of riding and sailing and Tehran was a month or so beyond that. Even if the Sultan and Shah agreed, it would take months for them to mobilize armies and march them to the frontier. By that time, Napoleon should have ended his campaign, ideally with a knockout blow to Russia's army and Prussian auxiliaries.

Nonetheless, Napoleon exerted considerable time and effort to doing so. As for Selim III, he authorized Ambassador Sebastiani to sign a secret alliance treaty with him. He had the Grand Army's 'glorious victory' bulletins translated into Turkish and sent to Selim. He wrote Selim periodic updates of his victories and eastward march. On 1 December, he fired off this missive designed to challenge the Sultan's manhood: 'Prussia, Russia's ally, has disappeared. I have destroyed its armies and I am the master of its fortresses. My armies are on the Vistula and Warsaw is in my power. The Prussian and Russian Poles have revolted and formed armies to reconquer their independence. It is the moment for you to reconquer yours.'[94] On New Year's Day 1807, he actually urged Selim to launch a jihad: 'The moment has come to restore the Ottoman Empire to its ancient glory . . . Your frontiers are invaded. Call your faithful subjects to the defence of all that you hold dear. These are your cities, your mosques, it is the very name Muslim that the Russians want to destroy . . . I pray to God that He blesses your armies.'[95]

Selim declared war against Russia on 27 December, but the second front that the Turks opened in spring 1807 had no discernible effect on Napoleon's campaign. Napoleon had General Marmont in Dalmatia send military aid to Turkish governors in neighbouring provinces and had Talleyrand offer Selim to send a squadron into the Black Sea to aid Turkey's operations against the Russians.[96]

* * *

The Grand Army was strategically well deployed but logistically isolated at the end of a seemingly endless and fraying umbilical cord. Napoleon lamented that: 'My position would be beautiful if I had provisions. The lack of provisions renders it mediocre.'[97] Each corps had a magazine – Warsaw for Lannes, Pultusk for Davout, Plock for Soult, Thorn for Ney, Wyszogrod for Augereau, Bromberg for Bernadotte, Posen for Jérôme – but the warehouses were nearly empty. Those forward depots depended on depots in Stettin, Berlin and Magdeburg. Along the hundreds of miles between them supply wagons bogged down either in snow or mud depending on wildly fluctuating temperatures. Soldiers subsisted on half rations of provisions and ammunition. Looting worsened as soldiers preyed on civilians for what their army could not provide. And they were the lucky ones. Disease and frostbite killed or crippled thousands of their comrades. Thousands of horses starved to death;

the famished men devoured their carcasses, even cracking the bones and digging out the marrow. Only a fraction of artisans and spare parts were available to repair muskets, cannon wheels, uniforms, shoes and anything else that broke down. As always, hard power's bottom line was how to pay for it. Napoleon sent this blunt message to François La Bouillerie, who collected requisitions from conquered peoples: 'I need money.'[98]

As if the trickle of supplies getting to the front were not troubling enough, Napoleon increasingly worried about the security of the subjected or intimidated realms between the front line and France. A revolt erupted in Hesse-Cassel. Napoleon issued these instructions to General Joseph Lagrange, the governor: 'Burn the principal village where the insurrection was born and execute the thirty ringleaders. A striking example is necessary to repress the hatred of the peasants and militants . . . for the rest of Germany, where it would be disastrous if revolts erupted with impunity.'[99] Meanwhile he sought to mend any unravelling ties with his allies. He wrote to heads of powerful and powerless states alike – Charles IV of Spain, Francis I of Austria, John I of Portugal, Frederick Augustus III of Saxony, Charles Augustus of Saxe-Weimar and Frederick of Saxe-Hildburghausen – calling for closer ties and assuring them that all was well on the Polish front and that he would crush the enemy in the spring.[100]

And then there were the Russians, whose Cossacks probed and raided the French encampments. Napoleon ordered his marshals to send out strong patrols to locate the Russian forces but avoid getting drawn into any serious fighting on the enemy's turf. He was relieved to get word that on 8 January 1807, Generals Jérôme Bonaparte and Dominique Vandamme received the surrender of Breslau (Wroclaw), after a month's siege. Napoleon sought to secure the Baltic coast. He sent Generals Mortier and Lefebvre to besiege Stralsund and Danzig, respectively.

Napoleon left Warsaw for the front on 30 January. His decision to resume operations in the dead of winter would grind his army down and culminate with the bloodbath at Eylau.[101] Yet it seemed like a good choice when he made it. In late January he received intelligence reports that Bennigsen's 67,000-man army of mostly Russian troops was vulnerable to being encircled. Napoleon hooked Ney and Bernadotte north and then east to sever the link between the Russians and the Prussians on the coast. With the main army, Napoleon caught up to Bennigsen at Eylau on 6 February. The enemy outnumbered him by 58,000 to 48,000 and outgunned him by 336 guns to 200. The opposing armies were equal in two ways: both sides lacked food and shelter and had spent the long freezing night huddled together, hunger gnawing their stomachs. With Napoleon around Eylau were the corps of Soult, Murat, Augereau and the Guard. Three other corps were within a day's march. Bernadotte and Ney were respectively 15 and 12 miles west; Davout was ten miles south-east. Napoleon tried to pull off a double envelopment of the enemy. He sent orders to Ney and Bernadotte to hook around the Russian right and Davout around the Russian left.

The battle began on the morning of 7 February, when Napoleon ordered Murat's cavalry forward followed by Soult then Augereau with the intention of provoking the Russians into attacking. The Russians did attack and nearly captured Eylau before the Imperial Guard infantry drove them back. Napoleon launched Augereau against the Russian left but a swirling snowfall disoriented his troops. The French shuffled slowly through the deepening snow before massed Russian artillery which opened fire, killing or wounding over 5,000 men within half an hour. The Russians counter-attacked and were about to punch through. Napoleon ordered Murat to charge with the Reserve of Cavalry which drove them back. Davout and Ney did not arrive until 8 February. Bennigsen ordered his army to withdraw as they approached his flanks.

Technically Napoleon could claim a victory since he stood his ground and the enemy eventually retreated. But there was little to rejoice in that Pyrrhic battle other than most of his men survived. He privately admitted as much: 'There was a very bloody battle yesterday at Preussisch-Eylau. The battlefield is ours but I lost heavily which is all the more disturbing given my isolation.'[102] The official published bulletin trumpeted Eylau as a victory that drove the enemy 100 miles from the Vistula, killing 7,000 and capturing 15,000 Russians, while suffering 1,900 dead and 5,700 wounded.[103] In reality, each side suffered as many as 25,000 casualties. As Napoleon withdrew his army back into winter quarters, he sent his aide General Henri Bertrand to present peace terms to Frederick William. The initiative died when the Prussian king refused to make peace separate from his Russian ally.[104]

*   *   *

Rebuilding his shattered army would take Napoleon months.[105] He was short of thousands of cavalry horses and hundreds of artillerymen and sent orders for France to forward as many of each as were available. He called up 80,000 conscripts from the class of 1808. The army administration itself was buckling under stress, exhaustion and lethargy. Napoleon complained that 'I have never had more need for . . . all the elements that serve to let me understand the situation of my forces. The bureaus of war are asleep . . . They must regularly send me reports on the situation. I am angry to have to repeat this so often.'[106] Although Davout was perhaps the best marshal overall, the endless, miserable campaign was eating away at him. The emperor admonished him for his silence: 'I would like to know how you have been if during the last few days you have lost or won as well as all the intelligence that can let me better understand the real situation of your corps. Respond with the greatest detail on all these objects.'[107]

Napoleon and his soldiers endured a horrendous Polish winter of deep freezes and snows broken by thaws that drowned the land in mud and frigid water, a harbinger of what lay five years ahead on the Russian steppes. Cossacks attacked small, isolated bodies of his troops, killing, wounding or capturing hundreds and looting and burning supply wagons. Napoleon lamented that 'I have lost a hundred or so wagons, part destroyed by Cossacks, part broken by the bad roads'.[108] His cavalry either could not catch the Cossacks or galloped into ambushes. Again this was just a taste of the future. He intended to deploy the Polish corps to screen the French army from the Cossacks, but the equipping and training of those troops was weeks behind schedule. He attributed the delay mostly to its commander, Joseph Poniatowski, who 'puts lightness in all affairs' while provoking animosities with other commanders like Generals Dombrowski and Joseph Zayonchek. Poniatowski did not lead his corps into the field until 1 March.[109]

A bit of Napoleon's winter gloom lightened when he learned that Jérôme and Vandamme received Schweidnitz's surrender on 23 February. He relaxed further after talking with a captured Russian general and learning that the enemy army was too depleted and exhausted to launch an offensive until spring at the earliest. Lefebvre opened the siege of Danzig on 19 March.[110] Napoleon asked Lefebvre 'to dream that your glory is attached to the important prize of Danzig and that all Europe has eyes on you'.[111] The garrison would hold out for more than two months.

Napoleon learned that Frederick William had brought the moderate Friedrich Zastrow into his exiled government to offset the hardliner Karl Hardenberg. Once again, he reached out to the king for peace. Frederick William sent General Friedrich von Kleist to Osterode. Napoleon presented Kleist a choice of negotiating peace bilaterally or in a European congress. When Kleist embraced the latter, Napoleon wrote to Frederick William that he was happy to agree to a peace congress where all the belligerents could sit down to end the war.[112] He sketched the outlines of a settlement for Talleyrand to negotiate: The restoration of Prussia's king to his throne and over his state, the Ottoman Empire's integrity and a Poland whose final expanse was open to compromise. An alliance between France and another powerful European state would best preserve the subsequent peace: 'The tranquillity of Europe depends on either France and Austria or France and Russia marching together. I proposed that several times to Austria. I will do so again . . . The end will be a system between France and Austria or between France and Russia; because there will be no repose for peoples, who all need it, without this union.'[113] Prussian and Russian hardliners once against spiked any peace talks. That left Napoleon with no choice but to impose a peace with a decisive victory. Yet he did not give up on a negotiated rather than a forced peace. Two months later on 29 April, hoping to forestall another round of carnage, he made his latest appeal to Frederick William just before launching his campaign.[114] And once again, the Prussian king politely rejected the offer. The war would go on.

At least one situation noticeably improved. Gloom pervaded his headquarters in the cramped mansion at Osterode from the day he moved in on 22 February until he left on 1 April. His new residence at Finkenstein was filled literally and figuratively with fresh air: 'I just brought my headquarters to a very beautiful chateau.'[115] It was at Finkenstein that Napoleon scored a diplomatic success, however minor. His efforts to entice Shah Feth Ali against Russia and Britain actually bore fruit. He was astounded and charmed when a Persian delegation appeared at Berlin in February. He had Talleyrand invite the Turkish ambassador to Berlin to negotiate an alliance among the three empires. When Turkish squeamishness forestalled an alliance, the Persians journeyed to Napoleon's headquarters, appearing on 26 April. A week later, on 4 May, diplomats signed a treaty whereby the Shah would boycott trade with Britain in return for French military advisors, artillery and other modern weapons: a defensive bilateral alliance would activate in the future if Russia and Britain warred simultaneously against either of them.[116]

* * *

By late May 1807, Napoleon had completely rebuilt his army since the devastation of Eylau. He now commanded about 123,000 infantry, 30,000 cavalry and 5,000 artillerymen manning 300 gun. On the eve of his campaign, he proudly observed: 'My army is superb . . . I have never seen the cavalry so beautiful.'[117] Danzig's surrender on 26 May with terms dictated by Napoleon removed a huge strategic thorn in his side and would soon free most of Lefebvre's corps for the campaign.[118]

Napoleon then launched his offensive.[119] Bennigsen concentrated his army at Heilsberg. The corps of Soult, Lannes and Murat attacked there on 10 June. As at Eylau, the French won the field at an enormous cost, around 12,500 casualties to the Russians' 8,000. Four days later Napoleon won the decisive victory that had eluded him. The Alle River horseshoes around Friedland on the left bank. On 14 June, the anniversary of Marengo, Lannes' corps was deployed on the slopes west of town. Bennigsen sought to crush Lannes before the other corps came to his rescue. To do so, his 48,000 troops crossed the four bridges over the Alle River then fanned out. Lannes brilliantly countered each piecemeal attack while Napoleon and most other corps hurried up. As the French army swelled before him, Bennigsen desperately ordered more attacks to break through. The French parried each thrust, then Napoleon ordered Mortier, Victor and Ney to counter-attack. The French routed the Russians, inflicting 20,000 casualties and capturing 20 guns while suffering 11,500 dead and wounded.

Over the next ten days the French pursuit captured thousands more Russians as Bennigsen desperately hurried his army eastward and did not halt until he was beyond the Niemen River.[120] Meanwhile Prussian General Anton von Lestocq abandoned Königsberg to avoid being cut off. On 24 June, Napoleon informed Talleyrand that:

> The Russians say they want to negotiate peace . . . The Russian emperor approached within a league and assured me that he desired a meeting . . . Their tone is very changed today. The army and the government reveal a great thirst to end things. Their horizon is painted black and they foresee a great storm is ready to strike their empire if they do not conjure up peace.[121]

Napoleon and Alexander agreed to conduct negotiations at the town of Tilsit on the Niemen River.[122]

The emperors met on a barge anchored midstream in the Niemen on 25 June. A huge tent was erected atop the barge. The agreed-upon protocol was for the imperial boats to begin from opposite banks and each reach the barge simultaneously. Napoleon had his rowers double the pace so that he could step atop the barge and stride across it to welcome the Tsar aboard. It was bromance at first sight. Napoleon excitedly wrote Josephine that 'I just saw Emperor Alexander. I am very happy with him. He is a very handsome and good young emperor. He has more spirit than one might imagine.'[123] He lauded the Tsar for 'his spirit, grace and education' and for being 'easily seduced'.[124] Alexander in turn was enthralled with Napoleon, a Tilsit syndrome that over the years would gradually but steadily dissipate as bitter resentment re-emerged. The emperors hosted and toasted each other at elaborate banquets; rode horseback for hours in the surrounding countryside; exchanged medals, the Legion of Honour for the Grand Order of Saint Andrew; and talked incessantly of their mutual imperial dreams.

And then there was the Prussian king. The day after Napoleon and Alexander first met, the Tsar introduced the emperor to him. Napoleon found Frederick William in his 'private life a good, honest and loyal man, but in his political capacity he was a naturally pliable man; one could master him merely by the power of raising one's hand against him'.[125] Nonetheless, Napoleon embraced Frederick William as well in a diplomatic ménage a trois that lasted several weeks: 'They spend every evening with me and we pass a grand part of the day together. Everything makes me think that peace will soon be concluded.'[126]

A femme fatale complicated relations among the three after she joined them on 6 July. Like most men who saw her, Napoleon was smitten with Queen Louise, a beguiling and conniving belle. He invited her to dine with the three monarchs, then presented her a long-stemmed red rose when she arrived. After thanking him, she suggested that Magdeburg would best accompany such a lovely gift.[127] He demurred. She was seated between the two emperors, who competed with flattery to win her smiles and compliments. She in turn 'proved herself to be the master of the conversation, always dominating it, returning ceaselessly to her goal, perhaps too much so'.[128] Napoleon informed Josephine that 'the beautiful Prussian queen dined with me yesterday. I had to defend myself from several concessions to her husband that she wanted me to make. I was gallant but guarded my policy. She is very friendly . . . When you read this, peace with Prussia and Russia will have been concluded and Jérôme will be recognized as Westphalia's king with 3 million people.'[129] He tried to reassure his wife with these words 'The Prussian queen is truly charming; she is full of coquetry toward me; but do not be jealous. I am an oilcloth upon which everything slides off. It would cost me too much to be the gallant.'[130] He later admitted that if Louise had 'arrived when negotiations began, she could have greatly influenced the results'. Her effect would have been to strengthen Alexander's will rather than weaken his 'but fortunately she came when things were too advanced'.[131]

Napoleon was a canny diplomat who knew when to be subtle and flexible and when to be harsh and unyielding. His strategy at Tilsit was to punish Prussia harshly and Russia lightly. He sought at once to make an example of Prussia, whose aggression started the war, by imposing a humiliating, debilitating peace; destroy the alliance between Prussia,

Russia and Britain; and forge an alliance between France and Russia against Britain. He embedded these goals in the treaties of Tilsit signed with Russia on 7 July and Prussia on 9 July.

The treaty with Russia had public and secret versions. Openly Russia recognized the expansion of France's territory, Napoleon as king of Italy, Louis as king of Holland, Joseph as king of Naples and Jérôme as the king of a future Westphalia, along with the Confederation of the Rhine and the Grand Duchy of Warsaw. Russia would offer to mediate peace between France and Britain. Russia would withdraw from Walachia and Moldova before negotiating a peace treaty with Turkey. Secretly Russia ceded Cattaro and the Seven Islands, thus leaving France the Adriatic Sea's master. Russia would mediate between France and Britain, with Hanover exchanged for French colonies, but if peace was not concluded by 1 November, would a month later declare military and economic war against Britain. Russia recognized Joseph's kingdom to include southern Italy and Sicily; Ferdinand IV would be compensated with the Balearic Islands. Russia agreed to join France in pressuring Sweden, Denmark and Portugal to sever trade with Britain. France agreed to mediate peace between Russia and Turkey for three months then war against Turkey if the sultan remained obdurate. Napoleon accompanied the treaty with a letter that elaborated key elements:

> An alliance is solid between two states when it is founded on political rapports that derive from commercial and geographical interests . . . Emperor Napoleon's policy is that his immediate influence does not surpass the Elbe . . . and that the country between the Niemen and Elbe will be the barrier that separates the great empires . . . Prussian territory will extend to the Elbe. Poland will be restored . . . The navigation of the Vistula will be free . . . Saxony will cede the Elbe's right bank to Memel.[132]

With exchanges of letters, Napoleon got Alexander to agree to his interpretation of the treaty and future relations between their empires.[133]

With its Treaty of Tilsit, Prussia's territory and population was halved and its army limited to 42,000 troops. Frederick William ceded all territory between the Rhine and Elbe rivers, Danzig and its share of Poland; the latter cession became the Grand Duchy of Warsaw. Prussia also had to recognize the expansion of France's territory, Napoleon as king of Italy, Louis as king of Holland, Joseph as king of Naples, Jérôme as the king of a future Westphalia, along with the Confederation of the Rhine and the Grand Duchy of Warsaw. Prussia had to war with

France against Britain. Prussia had to pay France an indemnity that Napoleon would determine.

The harsh peace inflicted upon Prussia atop that inflicted upon Austria in 1805 infuriated Foreign Minister Talleyrand, who later recalled: 'I was indignant for all that I saw and all that I heard, but I was obliged to hide my indignation.'[134] All along Talleyrand had argued that French expansion should end at its natural frontiers. He warned Napoleon that his attempts to control ever more of Europe would inevitably provoke a coalition that overwhelmed him and France. Talleyrand proved to be prescient. After returning to Paris he resigned in protest on 9 August 1807, although he retained his court positions. Napoleon replaced him with Jean-Baptiste de Nompère de Champagny, duc de Cadore, a skilled diplomat who would implement rather than challenge the emperor's policies.

Napoleon headed back on the long road from Tilsit to Paris on 10 July, but tarried for several days each in Königsberg and Dresden to forge treaties. The Treaty of Königsberg, signed between French and Prussian diplomats on 12 July, provided a timetable for the withdrawal of French forces from Prussian territory as soon as Prussia paid its indemnity; until then, French forces would garrison Prussian fortresses and march freely across Prussian territory. Under the Treaty of Dresden signed on 22 July, the Saxon king Frederick Augustus would become the Grand Duke of Warsaw and both of his realms would be allied with France. The French would retain 30,000 troops in the Grand Duchy of Warsaw.[135]

Napoleon finally reached Saint-Cloud, his palace outside Paris, on 29 July 1807. He had been away ten months since 26 September 1806, when he departed to fight Prussia and Russia. Awaiting him were a mountain of bills to pay for his war and empire along with an array of other problems.[136] As he immersed himself in the endless details of governance, his mind frequently flitted eastward far beyond the horizon where Marie Walewska still besotted him. Writing to her was among the first things he did after reaching his palace: 'My sweet and dear Marie, You who love your country so much can understand my joy in returning to France after nearly a year's absence. This joy would be complete if you were with me but I have you in my heart . . . You will join me . . . soon when affairs leave me the liberty to call you.'[137] He never did summon Marie to Paris. The thoroughly entangled affairs of his empire and family took precedence.

Chapter 13

The Kingmaker

'My family is a political family.'

'My brothers do not back me up. Their only princely quality is their foolish vanity; they lack talent and energy. I have to govern for them.'

'If I name you the king of Spain, would you agree?'

Napoleon made and broke kingdoms and marriages alike, often for related reasons. He justified such acts by insisting that the interests of the Bonaparte clan and French national interests were one. To those conflated ends he committed history's most blatant acts of nepotism. As emperor he named all his siblings princes or princesses except his estranged brother Lucien. He crowned Joseph first the King of Naples then the King of Spain; Louis and his stepdaughter Hortense the King and Queen of Holland; Jérôme the King of Westphalia; Caroline and his stepbrother Joachim Murat first the Grand Duchess and Duke of Berg and Cleve then the Queen and King of Naples; Elisa and his stepbrother Felix Baciocchi first the Duchess and Governor of Piombino and Lucca then Tuscany's Grand Duchess and Governor; Pauline and his stepbrother Camille Borghese the Duchess and Duke of Guastalla; and his stepson Eugène the viceroy of his Italian kingdom. Foreign Minister Talleyrand partly explained why: 'Dupe of his imagination which dominated his judgment, he said emphatically that he had to raise around France a rampart of thrones to replace the line of fortresses created by Louis XIV.'[1]

As for matchmaking, Napoleon arranged the marriage of his stepdaughter Hortense to his brother Louis, his stepson Eugène to the Bavarian Princess Augusta and his stepniece Stephanie to Baden's Prince Louis. He forced Jérôme to divorce his American wife Elizabeth with whom he had a son, then later marry Princess Catherine of Württemberg.

The penalty for those who defied his will was harsh. He severed his relationship with Lucien and exiled him from France when he refused to divorce the mother of his children. Napoleon's marriages may have advanced his political goals but mostly inflicted unhappiness on the couples themselves.

Napoleon wanted his relationships with the brothers and sisters that he had enthroned to be that between a master and his marionettes. He tried to micromanage his family as tightly as he did his empire. He made it clear that those realms and their rulers were subordinate to his will. In a letter to Elisa, he laid down the rules governing the political relationship among his siblings' realms and the French emperor:

> You have the right to ask me about the decisions of my ministers; but you do not have the right to stop them from executing their orders. The ministers speak in my name; no one has the right to paralyze . . . the execution of orders that they transmit . . . There is in France no authority superior to that of a minister. Thus I do not want to enter into a question's foundation since, even when my minister is wrong, only I am the judge.[2]

He could be as spiteful as he was generous. He deposed a defiant Louis and converted the Kingdom of Holland into French departments.

The constitution and subsequent laws and decrees sided with Napoleon. Of course, that legal world was self-serving since Napoleon devised it. The Senate's declaration of him as emperor on 18 May 1804, which he orchestrated, subordinated the imperial family to his will. He elaborated his powers and their duties in a decree of 30 March 1806, whereby the imperial family was subordinate to the French nation which was subordinate to him: 'Their births, their marriages, their deaths, the adoptions that they might make interest the entire nation and influence, more or less, its destiny.' The imperial family was literally a police state run by Napoleon: 'The emperor is the common leader and father of his family. As for their titles, he exercises on those he confers paternal power during their minorities and always preserves over them the power of surveillance, police and discipline.'[3]

In practice, the 'marionettes' proved to have their own very independent minds and behaviours that often infuriated 'the master'. His efforts to force his family to conform to his vision was about as effective as herding a bunch of cats. They grabbed his carrots and dodged his sticks without changing their ways. In varying degrees and ways, each of his loved ones reacted with passive-aggression to his orders. In doing so they acted like any dictator's subjects. He intimidated any dissent with long written and spoken diatribes that mixed reason and anger. At times he blasted each of them for being incapable of doing anything right. All the victim could do was meekly weather the storm until it passed. Consciously or subconsciously his victims may have actually enjoyed provoking his rants since that was the only power they had. And if each was as incapable as he insisted, then why bother trying harder to meet his impossible demands? Talleyrand explained their psychology: 'Napoleon enjoyed worrying, humiliating and tormenting those whom he had elevated; and they, placed in a perpetual state of suspicion and irritation, worked sordidly to damage the power that created them and they regarded him as their principal enemy.'[4]

Being part of the French empire both conferred benefits and demanded duties, but the emperor took far more than he gave.[5] And that was where the worsening problems arose. He granted each realm a French-style constitution and legal code, abolished feudalism and nationalized most Catholic Church property. He extracted ever more troops and taxes and forbad their trade with Britain and even with neutral countries like the United States. In doing so, his millions of subjects received mostly political abstractions and platitudes while losing the flower of their manhood and their wealth. And naturally that enraged them. His siblings were trapped between his soaring demands and their subjects' soaring discontent. But Napoleon harboured his own complaints against them: 'My brothers do not back me up. Their only princely quality is their foolish vanity; they lack talent and energy. I have to govern for them.'[6]

Nonetheless Napoleon genuinely loved his family. He tried to find time to write his wife and other family members even amid his military campaigns. He frequently ended his letters asking the recipient to share his kisses and hugs with other loved ones. In assessing his family, he summed up the essence and, more importantly, his deep feelings for each member:

> Joseph in any country would be an ornament of society, Lucien that of any political assembly. Jérôme, in maturing, would have properly governed. Louis would have whined and made a scene everywhere. My sister Elisa had a male mind, a strong soul; she would have shown much philosophy in adversity. Caroline is powerfully clever and capable. Pauline the most beautiful woman of her time, perhaps, has been and would be until the end the best living creature. As for my mother, she is worthy of all types of veneration. What family so numerous could present a lovelier ensemble! Add to that beyond our political torments that

we love each other. For myself, I never ceased an instant to sense the heart of my brothers. I loved all of them and I believe that they felt the same for me.[7]

He became his family's psychologist and marriage counsellor in chief. He gave plenty of good advice that he failed to follow himself. He may have been a workaholic, but he knew when to take a break for other pleasures. He shared this revealing advice to Eugène, likely after an appeal from his spouse:

My son, you work too hard; your life is too monotonous. That may be good for you because work for you is a way to relax. But you have a young wife, who is pregnant. I think that you should arrange to pass an evening with her and a little party. Why not go to the theatre once a week? I think you should also . . . go hunting once a week . . . You should have gaiety in your home . . . I lead the same life you do but I have an old wife who does not need me to amuse her and I also have much more business to attend. Yet, truth be told, I have more fun and diversions than you do . . . You formerly loved pleasure; you should revive your tastes.[8]

The family tensions were not just between them and him, but also between the Bonaparte and Beauharnais clans. His own family disliked Josephine from the beginning and lost no opportunity to snub her even after she became empress. In April 1807, he had to insist that his mother follow imperial protocol and do something that she scorned: 'It is suitable that you dine each Sunday at the empress's home and site of the family dinner. My family is a political family. When I am absent the empress is always the head . . . It is an honour that I make to the members of my family. That does not prevent me, when I find myself in Paris . . . from dining with you.'[9]

Napoleon did make one mostly happy match. He found a beautiful, vivacious fiancée for Eugène, in Augusta Amelie, the Bavarian king's daughter. Louis Constant, his valet, gushed that 'never had two people been better made to love each other'.[10] Napoleon sent his aide Christophe Duroc with a request to Maximilien Joseph on 21 December 1805, after his victory over Austria. The king promptly agreed.[11] All that remained was to inform the unsuspecting groom. On New Year's Eve, Napoleon had a courier gallop off across the snowy Alps to Milan with these words to Eugène: 'I arrived in Munich where I arranged your marriage with

Princess Augusta. It has been publicized. This morning the princess visited me and I interviewed her a long time. She is very pretty. You will find her portrait on a cup but she is much better.'[12] Four days later he summoned Eugène to come 'promptly and secretly' to Munich to marry his bride.[13] Actually Napoleon was himself smitten with Augusta. He gushed to his sister Elisa that 'Augusta is one of the most beautiful and perfect persons of her sex'.[14] 'Believe me', he wrote Augusta, 'that I will love you like a father and that you will hold for me all a daughter's tenderness.'[15]

* * *

Of all the family members that Napoleon entrusted with political power, the least unreliable was Eugène, the viceroy of Italy.[16] Eugène dutifully struggled to take Napoleon's advice which was pretty much incessant. For instance, Napoleon offered these guidelines for governing Italians:

> You are still at an age when you do not know the perversity of the human heart. Those who do know cannot recommend enough that you be circumspect and prudent . . . Our Italian subjects are naturally more deceitful than French citizens. You have only one means of conserving their esteem and being useful for their happiness, it is not to entirely trust anyone, to not tell anyone what you really think of the ministers and grand officials surrounding you.[17]

He channelled Machiavelli with this line: 'They will only esteem you if they fear you and they will only fear you as far as they perceive that you understand their duplicitous and false character.'[18]

He also issued more general advice:

> Speak as little as possible. You are not skilled enough and your education is not refined enough for you freely to deliver lectures. Know how to listen and rest assured that silence often produces the same effect . . . Do not be ashamed to ask questions . . . Do not at all imitate my conduct . . . Preside little over the State Council. You lack enough knowledge to preside with success. It would be better for you to attend under a chairman . . . who presides in your place . . . The army is the great object with which to occupy yourself and use your own knowledge. Work twice weekly with your ministers, once with each of them . . . In public ceremonies

and festivals . . . know well the place you must occupy and what you must do . . . Surround yourself with young people of the country, the old are good for nothing.'[19]

Napoleon was determined to transform Italian political culture.[20] He had Eugène organize a Royal Guard whose officers came from elite families. He organized military schools at Milan, Bologna and Pavia: 'My goal, in appealing to young men from the principal families, is to revolutionize morals. We should have masters teaching these youths. Soldiers of the Guard would have the privilege of entering after two years of service.'[21] He sponsored public education, although students had to pay for the privilege.

* * *

Napoleon's second most unhappy forced marriage was between Louis and Hortense.[22] Louis was then 24, moody, introverted, insecure, in fragile health and easily roused to jealously. Hortense was then 18, pretty, vivacious and flirtatious. He had a crush on her cousin Stephanie Beauharnais. She had a crush on Christophe Duroc. Much against their respective wills, Louis and Hortense succumbed to that of Bonaparte and married on 3 January 1802, in a double ceremony with Caroline Bonaparte and Joachim Murat. Despite that inauspicious beginning, Hortense subsequently gave birth to three sons, Napoleon Charles on 11 October 1802, Napoleon Louis on 18 December 1804 and Louis Napoleon on 20 April 1808. Napoleon was ecstatic when Hortense brought Napoleon Charles into the world and adored him as if it were his own flesh and blood. Some whispered that he was.[23]

Napoleon loved Hortense deeply. He wrote: 'My dear girl, I would like you to write me and I beg you to give me news because for a month I have not heard from you, while your health and your state of pregnancy greatly concerns me . . . Nothing can alter the paternal love that I have for you.'[24] In the icy depths of his 1807 campaign in Poland, he 'received your letter and that of M. Napoleon. I suspect that he did not know too much what he wrote and that the hand had been directed by his little mama. Regardless hug him for me. I would be so relieved to see him but must set aside that pleasure until my return to France which I hope will not be long.'[25] He was not just eager to see his namesake: 'As soon as I return to Paris, I will write Louis to let you come. You do not doubt the pleasure that I will have to see you and share with you the tender attachment that I have for you.'[26]

Napoleon adopted Napoleon Charles as the heir to his throne. For that reason, Louis was the first brother that Napoleon made a king. In a series of steps, Napoleon transformed the Batavian Republic into the Dutch kingdom. In early 1805, he insisted that the Dutch scrap their political system and adopt a French style-government blueprint, first to be refined by a constitutional committee whose members he essentially picked, then approved by a plebiscite. The Dutch leaders followed his script, including stuffing ballot boxes so that the plebiscite overwhelmingly embraced the proposed constitution by 14,096 to 136 voters, although 300,000 eligible voters refused to join the political charade. The pro-French Rutger Jan Schimmelpennick became the Grand Pensioner or executive on 29 April 1805.[27] He then had the puppet government vote first to become a kingdom then to invite Louis to be its king. The Kingdom of Holland became official with a treaty signed between France and the Batavian Republic on 24 May 1806. The emperor informed his king-to-be that 'It is necessary to make your coronation the inauguration of a new, powerful epoch'.[28]

Unfortunately, Louis was incapable of fulfilling the role that Napoleon intended for him. Louis personified a passive-aggressive psyche. He reacted to his older brother's domination and orders by doing the opposite. Of course, nothing could have been more self-defeating. Napoleon mercilessly blistered him for his failings: Louis never took his advice and instead did ridiculous things; he marched his troops too fast or too slow; he wasted money on frivolities while failing to invest in his realm's vital infrastructure, he acted without thinking. He got everything backwards:

> You are too paternal and feminine in running your government and too stern in running your family. You treat a young woman like you were leading a regiment. Mistrust the people who surround you . . . The opinion of those men is the inverse of public opinion . . . You have the best and most virtuous woman and you make her unhappy. Let her dance as much as she wants; it is natural at her age . . . She sees her life passing . . . Make the mother of your children happy.[29]

A month later Napoleon piggybacked on his reply to a cheerful letter from Hortense by giving her some marital advice:

> You know better than me that your first duty is to please your husband. I know that he was wrong to display his jealousy,

although in doing so he let you see how much he loves you. You must stay constantly with him and be agreeable to all his ways. Louis is a just man, even if he has some unusual ideas. You will find complete happiness when you sacrifice everything.[30]

Actually Napoleon was afraid that Hortense would take a lover and wreck her marriage and prestige as the Dutch queen. He enlisted Josephine in his attempt to head that off: 'Advise Hortense to stay close to her husband . . . She must enjoy being agreeable to the father of her children.'[31] The animosities between Louis and Hortense worsened. Napoleon tried to reassure her that 'the king fundamentally loves you', while 'you have the right to be happy' and 'each of you should be given what is due you'.[32]

As Napoleon readied the Grand Army for his spring 1807 campaign, he received heart-breaking news. His first step-grandson, namesake and heir Napoleon Charles died of croup on 5 May. The news plunged him into deep sorrow:

> I am very affected by the loss of little Napoleon. I would want his father and mother to take from nature as much courage as me to know how to handle all of life's evils. But they are young and less reflective of the fragility of things on this earthly plane . . . When will we be wise? When we will be animated by true Christian charity and when will our actions be guided by not causing sorrow and not humiliating anyone?[33]

As he crawled his way out, he extended his hand to Hortense. He worried that her grief, however understandable, had rendered her insensible and threatened her own life and he urged her accept the harsh reality that 'life is strewn with so . . . much evil'.[34] He diluted his own mourning with fatalism and work. 'It was his destiny' was his reply to a condolence letter over the death of his nephew.[35] 'For evil without remedy', Napoleon wrote Josephine, 'one must find other consolations', most importantly one's loved ones who still lived.[36]

* * *

Caroline was the most politically treacherous of his siblings.[37] Talleyrand said she had the mind of Cromwell in the guise of a pretty woman. Napoleon lamented that his rise to supreme power and his generosity to his family had warped her.[38] He granted the Duchies of Berg and

Cleves to Murat and Caroline on 15 March 1806, then fused those realms into the Grand Duchy of Berg, with its capital at Dusseldorf, on 12 July 1806. Caroline responded with indignation rather than gratitude. Hortense explained that Caroline was 'upset that her husband was named the grand duke of Cleve and Berg, which she found too small a thing for him and herself. She never wanted to go there.'[39]

Murat and Caroline pressured Napoleon to raise the status of their children to equal those of Louis and Hortense.[40] The emperor impatiently explained that a king's children far outranked those of a grand duke. Murat retorted that as the sovereign of a foreign duchy, he and his wife were technically foreigners and so should be free to determine their own children's status. The thought that his brother-in-law and sister would have any true loyalty other than France disgusted Napoleon: 'As for the guarantee for your children, I must shrug my shoulders with pity; I am embarrassed for you. You are French. I hope your children will be; all other sentiment would be so dishonourable that I beg you to never tell me about it.'[41] Little more than a year later, Napoleon was again forced to literally and figuratively put in his grasping marshal his proper place when Murat, undoubtedly prodded by Caroline, tried to jump the queue:

> Your rank in my palace is fixed by the rank that you have in my family and your rank in my family is fixed by my sister's rank... As for the variations you have tried with your etiquette... you should know better than... placing yourself before persons who should be before you. You are a man who should be the happiest on earth, but you spoil your happiness by not knowing when enough is enough... You should ask for only what is due you.[42]

* * *

Joseph was Napoleon's most reliable sibling.[43] Although Napoleon was younger, he dominated Joseph from an early age. He provided insights into how he did so in this critique of a speech Joseph made as the president of Ajaccio's directory in April 1791:

> I read your address. It has its good points but those are drowned among jumbles of useless pedantic flowers. My friend, you still have much to do. Your style is too diffuse, too lax. There is neither energy nor nerve. It makes worldly men yawn. Another problem is that they see that you are going to flood them with

extraordinary promises that are inappropriate to common sense. If, instead of four pages your address had been half a page, it would have been excellent. The few ideas would have been sufficient for the purpose.

He then recommended several essays for Joseph to model his own speeches on.[44] Joseph accepted rather than resented that and countless other impositions. Napoleon later recalled: 'Joseph hardly helped me but is a good, strong man; his wife, Queen Julie, is the best creature who exists. Joseph and I always strongly loved each other and worked together; he sincerely loved me. I do not doubt that he would do anything for me. He did what he could for me. His intentions were good.'[45]

Napoleon rewarded Joseph with the thrones of first Naples and then Spain. After Napoleon Charles died, Napoleon designated Joseph his successor with this justification: 'I think that the experience of governing combined with your good spirit and naturally happy outlook, will strengthen your character and render you proper to lead this immense machine, if ever destiny should make you live longer than me.'[46]

* * *

Jérôme was the most spoiled of the Bonaparte boys, being surrounded as a child by his sisters then living with Napoleon after he took power and got rich.[47] He was handsome and personable, but vain and irresponsible. Napoleon sent Jérôme to sea as much to sever him from temptations and instil discipline as to launch his naval career. Jérôme embarrassed and enraged Napoleon by deserting his ship in the Caribbean and journeying to Baltimore, where he fell passionately in love with and wed Elizabeth Patterson on 25 December 1803. Napoleon had his ambassador in America warn Jérôme that 'I will not recognize a marriage of a young man of nineteen years contracted against the laws of his country'.[48] On 2 March 1805, he decreed their marriage void. After learning that the couple had reached Lisbon, he ordered that Jérôme be arrested and brought to him while Elizabeth, who was pregnant, would be shipped back to America. Jérôme finally succumbed. During a meeting with Napoleon in Alexandria, Italy on 6 May 1805, he apologized and promised to divorce Elizabeth. His wife meanwhile had sailed to England where, on 7 July 1805, she gave birth to a son she named Jérôme. She eventually accepted Napoleon's offer of a annual alimony of 600,000 francs.[49]

Napoleon promoted Jérôme to captain and put him in nominal command of a frigate and two smaller warships at Genoa. He wrote

Twenty-seven-year-old General Bonaparte would, in less than eight years' time, become Emperor of the French and the most powerful man in Europe.

Bianchi's lithograph of a young Captain Bonaparte explaining to senior officers how the Siege of Toulon could be won. The strength of his argument won over his superiors and his policy was adopted – and the siege was successful.

Pont de Lodi, 10 Mai 1796 by Charles Etienne Pierre Motte. It was after the Battle of Lodi that Napoleon reputedly said: 'I never before bore the belief that I was a superior man. It was only at Lodi that I came to believe that I could become . . . a decisive actor on the political scene. And there was born the first spark of the highest ambition.'

Thomas Charles Naudet's drawing of Napoleon leading his troops across the bridge at Arcole in November 1796. The successful storming of the Austrian positions across the bridge showed that men would follow him even in the most difficult and dangerous situations.

General Bonaparte at Lanato in 1796. This lithograph by Lordereau is intended to demonstrate Napoleon's forthright character.

Bonaparte in Egypt. Child of the Revolution, the idealistic Bonaparte took science and culture to Africa. A more pragmatic Napoleon abandoned his troops and returned to France when it suited his political objectives.

Bonaparte reviewing his Consular Guard. The forerunners of his Imperial Guard, these men were devoutly loyal to Napoleon and were treated with similar respect by him.

A typically 'heroic' scene of the day with Bonaparte leading his troops, in this instance at the Battle of Marengo.

Bonaparte in his full Consular regalia, already displaying his propensity for elaborate display.

Continuing the above theme, Napoleon was well aware of how pomp and ceremony could move people's hearts, and this is exemplified in this aquatint and line engraving which commemorates the displays erected to celebrate the coronation of Napoleon and Josephine as Imperial majesties.

Even Napoleon's divorce from Josephine was an elaborate affair full of poignancy and high drama.

A portrait of Napoleon drawn just before he embarked on his disastrous Russian campaign which ultimately led to his downfall.

J. Baillie's *Napoleon and Son*. Napoleon dreamed of establishing a Bonaparte dynasty, but none of his heirs possessed his powers of leadership.

A scene depicting Napoleon's triumphant return to Paris in March 1815. So powerful was Napoleon's charisma that despite the long years of war the French people had endured, he was welcomed back by the joyful Parisians.

Napoleon retreating after the Battle of Waterloo. Such was Napoleon's influence upon world affairs, the word Waterloo has become part of the English lexicon to mean a final, crushing defeat.

The end of a dream. A sorrowful Napoleon on the deck of HMS *Bellerophon* in Plymouth Sound awaiting his banishment to St Helena.

Jérôme that he did so to convey 'proof of his confidence that you will conduct an illustrious career and justify the great hopes that the nation holds for you'.[50] It is hard to imagine anyone in 'the nation' who held such hopes beyond the Bonaparte clan. Certainly the officer corps, and especially those charged with babysitting him, deeply resented that the emperor had not merely forgiven his spoiled kid brother's capital offence of desertion but rewarded him by promoting him over scores of others on the seniority list.[51] Then, in 1806, Napoleon brought him ashore and began promoting him until he became a brigadier general in the 1807 campaign.

Napoleon's nation-building peaked with his creation of the Kingdom of Westphalia, which was just a geographic expression before he got his hands on its pieces. He established that realm from the top down. Embedded in the two Treaties of Tilsit of July 1807 were clauses that justified his takeover and amalgamation of several small states along with Prussian territory between the Rhine and Elbe into one, with its capital at Cassel. He then made Jérôme its king; found a suitable bride to be his queen; handpicked a four-man regency to advise him; wrote a constitution through which to govern; presented a version of the Code Napoleon for justice; and issued detailed instructions on how to organize the army.[52]

Napoleon matched Jérôme with Catherine, the daughter of King Frederick of Württemberg.[53] To his pending sister-in-law, he wrote: 'Although the moment when I will have the satisfaction of receiving you is approaching, I cede to eagerness in expressing to you my feelings of tender friendship . . . I am sure that you will bring happiness to my brother and that I will only applaud all the days of your union.'[54] Jérôme and Catherine married in a religious ceremony at Stuttgart on 22 July 1807, then in a civil ceremony at Paris on 22 August. The marriage was troubled from its beginning. Although Catherine was beautiful and loving, Jérôme cheated on her shamelessly.[55]

Jérôme and Catherine officially began their reign on 1 September, but did not actually settle into their palace in Cassel until 8 December 1807. To Jérôme, Napoleon issued these words along with the constitution:

> Your people must enjoy a liberty, equality and well-being unknown to the peoples of Germany and this liberal government will, in one way or another, produce the most salutary changes for the Confederation . . . What people would want to return to arbitrary Prussian rule after tasting the benefits of a wise and liberal administration? The peoples of Germany along with those of France, Italy and Spain, desire equality and liberal

ideals . . . Be a constitutional king. When the century's reason and enlightenment are threatened, wield your power to issue wise policies. You will find that your acts will be a powerful force in influencing your neighbouring absolute kings to follow.[56]

Those were the ideals. He then instructed him to divide Westphalia into departments, appoint a qualified prefect to each and implement the constitution and the Code Napoleon by 1 January 1808. And above all: 'Never forget that you are French.'[57]

Tensions soon soared between the emperor and his newly-minted king. Jérôme ignored all of Napoleon's advice, advisors, laws and institutions. Instead he engaged in an orgy of spending that brought his realm to the brink of bankruptcy. Napoleon blistered him for being a spendthrift: 'Do not make stupid expenses that make you Europe's laughing stock and end up provoking your people's indignation. Sell your furniture, your clothes, your jewels and pay your debt. Honour passes before all. You have had the bad grace to not pay your debts . . . especially in a time where your people suffer from the war.'[58] Jérôme ignored those dictates.

* * *

Of his sisters, Napoleon was the least close to Elisa, who lacked Pauline's power to turn heads and Caroline's power to control them.[59] Although he recognized the intelligence and resolve behind Elisa's reserve, he fumed that politically she could have done much better than the man she married, Felix Bacciochi, an undistinguished captain and minor Corsican noble. Nonetheless, that couple was the first to benefit from his empire's spoils. He named them the sovereigns of the city-states of Piombino and Lucca respectively on 18 March and 26 June 1805. Like her siblings with thrones, Elisa was expected to follow Napoleon's commands. Unlike her siblings, she largely did so promptly and efficiently without excuses and with few complaints. In return, he promised her a generous present in March 1808: 'As soon as I have the state of the domains in Tuscany my intention is to give you a beautiful property in that country, rendering you 200,000 to 500,000 francs revenue net. This will be a nice supplement to your civil list. It is suitable to keep this secret . . . I just ordered for your daughter properties worth 150,000 francs.'[60]

Under the treaties between France and Spain of San Ildefonso on 1 October 1800 and Aranjuez on 21 March 1801, the Grand Duchy of Tuscany was transformed into the Kingdom of Etruria and given to Louis de Bourbon, the husband of Charles IV's daughter Marie Louise. Louis died on 23 May 1803, before he could possess his new realm. Queen Marie Louise and her infant son did not move into their palace in Florence until August 1803. Although Napoleon's letters to Marie Louise were supportive, he naturally suspected her of playing a double game since she was a Bourbon and was as emotionally tied to Naples and Madrid as she was fearful of Paris.[61] But he did what he could to assuage any trepidation she might have harboured even as he nibbled away at her realm's sovereignty before devouring it. For instance, in September 1807, he assured her that the troops that he had recently sent into Livorno would stay only as long as it took to rid that strategic port of British commerce and spies. He called on her 'to consecrate resources for public service in the most just, pious way. The interests of agriculture, industry and human leisure lead to the adoption of a paternal system. That is the view of all wise and farsighted governments. It will be that of Your Majesty's government.'[62]

Nonetheless, the queen had good reason to worry about the future of her throne. It bothered Napoleon that 'a branch of the house of Spain continues to be established in the centre of Italy'.[63] He hoped to give Marie Louise a generous slice of Portugal to call her home and then mesh Etruria either with his Italian kingdom or France. Under the Treaty of Fontainebleau signed on 27 October 1807, Spain ceded Etruria to France in return for taking title to two-thirds of Portugal, to be realized by a joint French and Spanish conquest of that country. Napoleon broke the news to her on 5 December 1807: 'Your Majesty must be pressed to take yourself to Spain or, at least leave the country with as much dignity that reflects your rank.'[64] On 10 December 1807, as French troops marched into Florence, she left with her son and court and within a month was reunited with her parents. On 24 May 1808, he annexed Tuscany to France and divided it into departments. Finally, on 2 March 1809, he designated those departments the Grand Duchy of Tuscany and named Elisa its grand duchess and Felix its governor general.

* * *

Pauline was renowned for being one of the era's most beautiful women.[65] She and Napoleon shared a quasi-incestuous passion for each other. He adored her for her beauty, charm and sweetness and she hero-worshipped him. Not surprisingly her first husband, General Henri Leclerc, looked and behaved like her big brother. In January 1803, Napoleon informed Pauline than her husband had died gloriously at his post although actually he had died a miserable death from yellow fever in Saint Domingue.⁶⁶ Romance soon cut short whatever mourning Pauline was feeling. Camille Borghese, a dashing Roman nobleman, swept her off her feet. They secretly married on August 31, 1803, just eight months after her first husband's death. She soon tired of him for refusing to match in military deeds his heroic bluster and style.

After learning of her marriage in November, Napoleon called on the family to support Pauline and form good relations with the Borghese clan.⁶⁷ He named Borghese the governor-general of all French departments in the Italian peninsula. He offered these encouraging words to Pauline:

> Distinguish yourself by your sweetness, your kindness to everyone . . . Conform yourself to the customs of the country; scorn nothing; find everything beautiful and never say, 'Things are better in Paris than here'. . . . The only nationality you must never receive is the English . . . Finally, love your husband, make your home happy and especially don't be . . . capricious. You are 24, you must be mature and sensible.⁶⁸

Five months later, Bonaparte expressed his disappointment over Pauline's behaviour: 'I learned with sorrow that you lacked the good spirit to conform to Roman values; that you showed scorn for the inhabitants and ceaselessly fixed your eyes on Paris.'⁶⁹ He was worried that Pauline's behaviour was adversely affecting his policy of trying to draw Roman high society ever closer to France. He had their uncle and the French ambassador to Rome, Cardinal Fesch, deliver the letter to Pauline, while explaining that although she was steadily losing her beauty, she could choose always to be kind-hearted and sensitive to others. Their mother would soon arrive in Rome to guide her most whimsical daughter.

* * *

Napoleon's worst matchmaking was between his stepdaughter Stephanie Beauharnais and Charles, heir to the Grand Duchy of Baden. The wedding took place at the Tuileries on 8 April 1806. At first gaze, Charles was smitten with his pretty French princess. Alas, Stephanie was disgusted by her fat, loutish groom and cried throughout the ceremony.⁷⁰ Three months later, Napoleon offered her this advice: 'Love your husband, who merits all the attachment for him that he has for you. Be agreeable to the Elector, who is your first duty as he is your father . . . Treat your people well because sovereigns are made only for their happiness . . . They will love and esteem you if you love and esteem their country.'[71]

Charles swiftly tired of his disdainful wife and thereafter took a sadistic pleasure in tormenting her. Word reached the emperor. Napoleon fired off these angry words:

> The princess, your spouse, has been deathly ill for six weeks and not only have you not seen her but you have abandoned her to several intriguers . . . You have so little heart as to leave your wife without care . . . If you want to continue your conduct then send home my daughter . . . As for you, God will treat you as you deserve . . . I see that the bad that people say about you . . . is true . . . Behave yourself so that I do not have to intervene in these affairs.[72]

He then issued an equally blunt message to Grand Duke Charles Frederick: 'You have ignored the bad treatment toward my daughter . . . They are of such a nature that the tenderness I have for this child and my honour force me to intervene. Every day I repent the marriage that I made.' He threatened to recall his daughter and 'interfere in the interior affairs of your court' if Stephanie was not well treated by all, especially her husband.[73] He sent a trusted aide, Augustin de Talleyrand-Perigord, to investigate the situation and sternly warn Charles to change his ways. But respect can no more be commanded than love. Despite being shadowed by the emperor's wrath, Charles and his court continued to bully Stephanie. And, beset by an array of other more pressing problems, Napoleon could only fume. After Charles Frederick died on 10 June 1811, Charles became Baden's Grand Duke and made Stephanie's life worse than ever.[74]

* * *

Lucien was possibly the most talented Bonaparte sibling after Napoleon. Like his older brother he was highly intelligent and decisive.[75] Indeed, it was Lucien's quick thinking during the November 1799 coup when Napoleon was muddled that led him to the Tuileries rather than the guillotine. For that Napoleon was at once grateful and resentful. He made Lucien his Interior Minister, then angrily fired him after Police Minister Fouché presented a thick file of evidence that his brother was blatantly corrupt and had permitted the publication of a pamphlet comparing the First Consul to Oliver Cromwell. He sent Lucien to Madrid to negotiate treaties with the Spanish and Portuguese monarchs, then angrily recalled him when he did not get everything on the First Consul's wish list.

Atop Lucien's failings, Napoleon hated his wife Alexandrine, whom he married on 26 October 1803: 'Lucien prefers a dishonoured woman, who gave him a child before he married her, who was his mistress while her husband was in Saint Domingue . . . I can only groan at such wild behaviour of a man born with such talents and of an egoism without example yanking him from a beautiful future . . . and the route of duty and honour.'[76] He was furious when he learned of the marriage because he wanted Lucien to wed Marie Louise, the Etrurian king's recent widow. With probably tormented mixed feelings, Lucien refused. Napoleon's bullying finally led to a final break between them on 10 April 1804; two days later Lucien and his family left Paris for exile at Rome. After becoming emperor, Napoleon offered Lucien titles and positions but only if he divorced his wife and married a foreign princess who could advance French and thus Bonaparte's power. Lucien spurned the temptation.

The emperor's latest offer came three years later. By 1807, Lucien may have been long out of sight but remained embedded in Napoleon's mind. They met in Mantua during his inspection of his Italian kingdom from 23 November to 24 December. Napoleon wrote Joseph that

> I chatted with him for several hours . . . His thoughts and language are so far from mine that I had trouble understanding what he meant . . . Lucien seems to be struggling with different feelings and lacks the strength of character to take a side. Anyway I should tell you that I am ready to make him a French prince and recognize his daughters as my nieces if first he annuls his marriage. If he does that I will set her up in a corner of Italy but under the name of Madame Jouberthon, not that of Lucien and . . . put her in the first rank of society . . . You see that I have exhausted all my means of recalling Lucien who is still young and can employ his talents for his country.[77]

Although tempted, Lucien ultimately sent word that he would remain faithful to his wife. The cruel choice imposed by his brother must have eaten away at him. In March 1808, Napoleon reported to Joseph that 'Lucien has behaved badly in Rome by insulting Roman officers who took my side and he showed himself to be more Roman than the pope.

I want you to write him to leave Rome and retire to Florence or Pisa . . . He declared himself the enemy of me and of France. If he persists in these sentiments there will be a refuge for him in America.'[78]

Napoleon learned in January 1810, that Lucien and his family had reached Turin on their way to Paris. He instructed Camille Borghese, Pauline's husband and Italy's governor-general, secretly to inform Lucien that not only did Napoleon forbid him from returning to Paris without his permission but he had to stay south of the Alps. That ban would be lifted only if Lucian succumbed to 'the arrangement'.[79] Lucien never did.

* * *

Napoleon believed that the conquest of Portugal would seriously damage Britain.[80] He explained to Charles IV of Spain that:

> For sixteen years Portugal has displayed the scandalous conduct of a government that sold out to England. The port of Lisbon has been for them an inexhaustible treasure mine . . . It is time to shut Oporto and Lisbon . . . We cannot achieve peace without isolating England from the continent . . . I count on Your Majesty's energy in this circumstance because it is indispensable in forcing England to the peace that will bring tranquillity to the world.[81]

He emphasized that 'the interest of Your Majesty's people and mine demand that we vigorously war against Portugal'.[82]

On 19 July he had Foreign Minister Champagny issue an ultimatum to Portugal's ambassador that his government either had to close its ports to British trade or else suffer the consequences. He organized at Bayonne a 20,000-man corps led by General Andoche Junot. He coordinated with Madrid the massing of supplies at key cities to sustain Junot's corps on the long march across northern Spain to Lisbon.

Napoleon impatiently waited three months for Portugal to comply. When the Portuguese remained defiant, on 12 October he galloped off a courier to Junot ordering him to march to Lisbon. He gave Junot a to-do list after he conquered Portugal: disarm and dismiss the Portuguese army; seize the Portuguese fleet; close the ports to British vessels; confiscate any British vessels and merchandise and arrest any Britons in Portugal; occupy the fortresses; take over the treasury and all sources of revenue; send Prince Regent John to Paris; run the country with the help of all knowledgeable Portuguese willing to collaborate; and decisively crush any revolts. French and Spanish diplomats signed the Treaty of

Fontainebleau on 27 October which detailed how the allies would conquer and divide up Portugal.

Junot led his army's vanguard into Lisbon on 30 November. He met no resistance. Prince Regent John and his court had packed into several vessels and with a British naval escort had sailed away to Rio de Janeiro the previous day. Junot's troops held only Lisbon along with Santarem and Abrantes up the Tagus River valley leading back to Spain, while Spanish troops occupied the frontier fortress towns of Elvas and Almeida. Junot took possession of five Portuguese ships-of-the-line and five frigates anchored at Lisbon but had no reliable sailors to man them. The Russian Admiral Dmitri Siniavin commanded a fleet of nine decrepit warships that had been anchored in Lisbon Bay since 30 October, but dared not sail home in the face of overwhelming British naval power. Portuguese officials and soldiers still controlled most of their country, especially Oporto, the second-largest city. Junot dutifully tried to fulfil Napoleon's to-do list but that provoked riots in Lisbon and elsewhere. Napoleon ordered Junot to 'make severe examples' of the rebels 'and maintain yourself by making them fear you'.[83] But Napoleon's attention on Portugal's problems was distracted by a worsening crisis next door.

The Bourbons who ruled over Spain were not a happy family. King Charles IV was well-meaning, slow-witted, weak-willed, indolent and not highly sexed. A frustrated Queen Maria Louisa had a prolonged affair with a dashing minor noble in the Guard Corps named Manuel Godoy, then talked her husband into rapidly promoting him up through the military and political ranks until he became prime minister. Crown Prince Ferdinand bore varying hatreds for his mother, father and Godoy and conspired to overthrow them and become king. On 11 October 1807, he wrote Napoleon a letter lauding his greatness and requesting marriage with a French princess.[84]

As Napoleon contemplated this extraordinary request, he received alarming news from Spain. Charles had learned of Ferdinand's plot and on 29 October 1807 ordered him placed under house arrest. In a tearful meeting, the father granted the forgiveness that his prodigal son begged. With the scandal still fresh, Charles took an astonishing step in November 1807. He wrote Napoleon of his hope to bolster their alliance by a marriage between Ferdinand and one of the emperor's princesses.

Napoleon did not reply for two months as he mulled various possibilities. His worst worry was that Ferdinand's repentance was feigned and that he would rebel against his father once more. The result could be violence that imperilled a loved one. Yet a union between the French and Spanish crowns certainly beckoned. For that political marriage to advance

French interests, he needed a strong woman who could be the power behind the throne after Ferdinand became king. But who among his unmarried nieces was capable of that? He toyed with the idea of wedding Lucien's daughter Charlotte to Ferdinand but dropped the notion when his brother still refused to annul his marriage and succumb to his choice of a bride for him. He finally wrote to Charles that, while he wanted to strengthen their alliance, he hoped that 'Your Majesty will understand that not a single man of honour would ally with a son dishonoured by his declaration without the assurance that he had reacquired all the good graces'.[85]

Fearing that Spain was about to implode into anarchy and civil war, Napoleon took advantage of the alliance to position as many troops as possible across the country to shore up the crumbling Spanish throne or seize it if need be.[86] In early December 1807, he sent a corps into Spain to occupy key cities on the road between Bayonne and Lisbon including San Sebastian, Pamplona, Vitoria, Burgos, Leon and Salamanca. On 20 February, he appointed Murat to command his swelling army there and instructed him to take over Spain in two phases. During the first phase, Murat would make his headquarters at Vitoria to secure a line from Pamplona to Burgos, before marching to occupy Madrid; meanwhile another corps would march from Perpignan to Barcelona. Murat led 10,000 troops into Madrid on 23 March. During the second phase, two corps would cross Spain to secure the naval bases at Cadiz and Cartagena. He informed Murat that 'I hope war will not take place . . . but my habit is to leave nothing to hazard. If war happens you will be beautifully positioned . . . But I want to stay friends with Spain and fulfil my political goal without hostilities.'[87]

That goal of peaceful relations with the Spanish people was increasingly problematic. Sporadic violence broke out against the French and worsened. Lone soldiers were assaulted in the cities. Couriers cantering along the roads linking French forces were stopped, murdered and robbed. Napoleon feared not just riots in the cities but guerrillas in the countryside. He warned Murat that 'the movements in Spain resemble those we encountered in Egypt so keep your troops united and guard the convoys with large forces'.[88]

Murat was to treat the king, crown prince and entire Spanish court with the utmost courtesy and respect as their protector. That too was increasingly problematic as a crisis erupted over just who was Spain's rightful king. Napoleon's suspicions about Ferdinand were correct. He had curried favour with the many government and military leaders who shared his scorn for Godoy and his parents. The coup came on

17 March at Aranjuez Palace, 27 miles south of Madrid. Ferdinand and his cabal arrested Godoy and forced his father to abdicate. His coterie then declared him King Ferdinand VII. Charles had a letter pleading for help smuggled to Napoleon.

That plea and the whole sordid conflict disgusted Napoleon. In late March he reached a critical decision: 'I have resolved to put a French prince on the throne of Spain.' Of all people he first asked his brother Louis, who he mercilessly criticized for mismanaging Holland: 'If I name you the king of Spain, would you agree?'[89] Louis wisely declined the offer. Napoleon then asked Joseph to join him at Bayonne, where he would be made the king; Joseph reluctantly agreed.[90] But first he had to take the throne from both its current and would-be occupants.

Napoleon reached Bayonne on 15 April and installed himself in the nearby Chateau de Marracq. There he issued orders and promises while waiting, spider-like, as his troops entangled Spain and its royal family in an increasingly elaborate military, political and psychological web. He instructed Murat to invite the king, queen, crown prince, other royal princes and Godoy to Bayonne. In doing so, Murat should assure them of his

> intention to conserve the . . . country's independence as well as all class privileges . . . Those who want a liberal government and Spain's regeneration will find that in my system. Those who fear that the queen and prince of peace [Godoy] will return [to power] can be assured that those two individuals will be without influence and credibility . . . The good Spaniards who want tranquillity and good administration will find the advantages in a system that maintains the Spanish monarchy's integrity and independence.[91]

Murat should 'act vigorously: governors, intendants and bishops must react against the disorders that are taking place . . . You can declare that I recognize Charles IV, that I guarantee Spain's integrity, that the prince of peace will be exiled and that I have dedicated myself to helping King Charles with my imperial advice and power to reorganize his kingdom.'[92]

Murat was to print proclamations and get newspapers to publish and priests to preach the message that a conference at Bayonne between Napoleon, Charles and Ferdinand would decide who should best govern Spain and the Cortes or national assembly would ratify that choice. The articles should hint strongly that the House of Bonaparte might replace the House of Bourbon on the Spanish throne. He was to spread the word to the country's most influential people that Spain's destiny depended on their conduct. He was to round up all remaining Bourbon relatives, including the Etrurian queen and her family, and send them to Bayonne. Finally, he should quietly deploy his troops to be able to swiftly and decisively crush any rebellions in Madrid and other occupied cities.[93]

Meanwhile, Napoleon masterfully lassoed Ferdinand into coming to Bayonne in a long letter sent on 16 April. Ostensibly, he replied to Ferdinand's appeal to side with him against Godoy and his father and wed him to a French princess. With flattering words, he seemed to back both requests. He agreed that deposing Godoy 'appeared necessary for the happiness of himself and his subjects', and 'I will offer him refuge in France'. However, he expressed his concern for 'the events of Aranjuez' because of

> the danger of kings accustoming their peoples to shed blood for justice on their behalf . . . How can one prosecute the prince of peace without doing the same to the queen and your father? This prosecution feeds factious hatreds and passions. The result will be disastrous for your crown. You do not have the right to judge the prince of peace: his crimes . . . are lost in the rights of the throne.

As for his father's abdication, 'that took place as my armies spread across Spain and, in the eyes of Europe and posterity, I appeared to have . . . precipitated the overthrow of my friend and ally'." before this then criticized Ferdinand's attempted coup the previous October which 'deeply saddened me'. In sum, Ferdinand had committed many wrongs. Yet Napoleon was not only willing to forgive all that for the good of Spain and France but possibly even play matchmaker.[94]

So, not surprisingly, Ferdinand hurried to Bayonne where he believed that Napoleon would settle everything in his favour. He and his entourage, including his younger brothers Carlos and Antonio, reached Bayonne on 20 April. To his shock, Napoleon received him not as the king but as the crown prince. The following day, Napoleon had Foreign Minister Champagny begin pressuring Ferdinand to renounce his claim to the throne. Godoy arrived on 26 April and the king and queen on 30 April.

Napoleon had enticed Spain's ruling family into a gilded cage.[95] He ensured that his guests were housed, wined, dined and flattered as luxuriously as possible. He also had any couriers to or from them intercepted and the messages decoded. He triumphantly wrote to

Talleyrand that: 'This tragedy, if I am not mistaken, is in the fifth act. The denouement is about to appear.'[96] Napoleon was mistaken. The tragedy was actually in the first act and would unfold horrifically over the next six years with its denouement at Fontainebleau in April 1814.

Of all the bitter diplomatic gatherings that Napoleon convened over the decades, few matched that of 30 April. And that was the point. Charles and Maria Louisa on one side and Ferdinand, Carlos and Antonio on the other glared hatefully at each other while begging Napoleon to take their side. He later recalled that 'when I had them at my feet and could judge for myself their utter incapacity, I took . . . advantage of this unique situation . . . to regenerate Spain, to undermine England and . . . form the foundation for European peace and security'.[97] After that harsh reminder of why they had ended up in Bayonne, Napoleon kept them mostly apart to talk Charles and Ferdinand into granting him the throne in return for opulent retirements at separate French chateaus with huge annual stipends. He dismissed the son as 'very stupid, very vicious and very anti-French', but respected the father 'who was a brave man' with 'the air of a frank and good patriarch'.[98] Charles was fatalistic; Ferdinand was defiant.

Shocking news arrived from Madrid of a mass uprising against French troops on 2 May. Murat ruthlessly crushed the revolt but not before over 200 French and 1,000 Spaniards died in the fighting. A furious Napoleon marched into Ferdinand's room and accused his agents of fomenting the riots and threatened to have him executed as a rebel. That threat along with a 1 million franc bribe did the trick with Ferdinand. Charles and Maria Louisa eagerly grabbed offers of 7.5 million and 400,000 francs, respectively, with which to enjoy their golden years. The younger sons Antonio, Carlos and Francisco pocketed 400,000 francs each.

The father and son signed their abdication treaties on 5 and 10 May, respectively. The parents and their daughter, the deposed Etrurian queen and her children and Godoy, would reside at Compiègne and enjoy income from Chambord. The sons would board at Talleyrand's chateau of Valencay, where they were under constant surveillance to ensure that they did not escape. Napoleon had Murat issue to the Spanish people a proclamation to justify what he had done and inspire their loyalty to him: 'Spaniards, after a long agony, your nation perished. I saw your evils. I came to end them. Your grandeur, your power will be part of mine. Your princes have ceded to me all their rights to the Spanish crown.'[99]

Although Talleyrand was forced to be silent at the time, he was absolutely appalled by what Napoleon did and why he did it:

> The emperor, having for a long time lost sight of France's true interests, was ardently carried away . . . with the ambition of placing a member of his family on one of Europe's premier thrones and to achieve that attacked Spain with impunity . . . For that he can never be forgiven. When one studies all the actions . . . of Napoleon during this time so important for his destiny, one comes nearly to believe that he was carried away by a sort of fatalism that blinded his high intelligence.[100]

For an awkward month Spain's throne and assembly sat empty as Napoleon's invitees pondered the conflicting merits of staying put or heading for Bayonne. By 6 June, 91 of the 150 members of the Cortes had straggled into Bayonne, enough for Napoleon to declare a quorum. In separate votes the Cortes dutifully ratified the abdication treaties and declared Joseph Spain's new king. Two days later, Joseph and his entourage reached Bayonne. Naturally Napoleon coached Joseph on his acceptance speech: 'You must speak of the sorrow that troubles you for what has taken place in Spain which obliges you to use force to suppress it . . . and reveal the desire to soon be among your new subjects to conciliate all interests and begin your reign with acts of clemency.'[101] That same day, Joseph and his new court set forth for Madrid. Napoleon had couriers gallop ahead the joyful news for Murat to spread via newspapers, proclamations and sermons that the Cortes had proclaimed Joseph to be Spain's lawful monarch.[102] Despite Napoleon's meticulous stage-managing of the political theatre, an enraged audience would soon spook Joseph into fleeing from his perch on the Spanish stage.

Chapter 14

The Sisyphus of the Peninsula

'I will find in Spain the Pillars of Hercules but I will not find the limits of my power.'

'I will need a long war to win the throne of Spain.'

With Spain's throne, Napoleon had two empires, two fleets, two armies and two treasuries, at least on paper. He informed King Joseph that his new realm included '11 million inhabitants plus 150 million in annual revenues not counting immense revenues and possession of the Americas'.[1] To realize all that he had to secure Spain's fleets at Cartagena and Cadiz, the loyalty of Spain's army from the highest generals to the lowest privates and the loyalty of Spain's officials in Iberia, North and South America, the West Indies and the Philippines.

Napoleon utterly failed to do any of this. A classic hydra dilemma explains why. The more he and his minions tried to assert French power, the more they provoked violent resistance to that power. The murders of stray French soldiers along the roads of rural Spain and the Madrid riots in March and May 1808 were mere harbingers of the horrors to come. Yet Napoleon had no illusions over what lay ahead: 'I will need a long war to win the throne of Spain.'[2] What he could not foresee is that he would lose that long war.[3]

He also knew that his long war would be incredibly expensive. Ideally this war, like all wars, should pay for itself. He ordered Marshal Murat to empty the palaces of Aranjuez and Escorial of all their treasures, including the crown jewels, to help underwrite the conquest of Spain. That was just the beginning of what became Spain's systematic looting. And, of course, that policy was self-destructive – the more the French looted, the more enemies they made, so they looted more to help pay the cost of trying to repress their hydra-like enemies.[4]

Napoleon provoked the same dilemma in Portugal. In mid-May 1808, he ordered General Junot to draw another six million francs from Portugal atop the two million that he had already extracted. And that was just the down payment on 50 million that the emperor intended to realize from his latest conquest. Ideally, many of the revenues squeezed from Portugal would eventually come from the conquest of Brazil, the jewel in its colonial crown. Junot was to gather and send to Paris any information on Brazil's economy, population, ports and defences. Finally, Junot was to organize a legion of Portuguese troops. In return for all these impositions, Junot was to publish the Code Napoleon, presumably to assuage any hard Portuguese feelings that French rule was all about taking and not giving.[5] The hard-pinched Portuguese can be forgiven for dreaming of the day they might make the French literally eat the words of Napoleon's supposedly enlightened law code. That day was fast approaching.

Another chronic problem was the lack of unified or vigorous command over French forces in the Iberian Peninsula, briefly alleviated only when Napoleon was in Spain from November 1808 to January 1809.[6] The emperor upset Murat by naming his brother rather than him King of Spain and instead having him take Joseph's former throne in Naples. For a week in late May, Murat lay in bed with an illness probably as much emotional as physical. Napoleon sent General Jean Savary to Madrid to replace Murat as the French commander, then got second thoughts. In mid-July, he asked Marshal Jean-Baptiste Jourdan to journey from Naples to Madrid and resume his role of advising Joseph. He explained to Joseph that 'Savary is a very good man for secondary operations but is not experienced and calculating enough to head such a grand machine. He understands nothing of this unfolding war. I want Jourdan to reach him soon. His experience as a commander in chief, with all the calculations and combinations, is unsurpassed.'[7]

In mid-May 1808, Napoleon launched the second phase of his campaign to conquer Spain.[8] The divisions of Generals Philibert Duhesme and Jean Verdier would take Barcelona and Saragossa, respectively, while Generals Pierre Dupont, Adrien Moncey and Jean-Baptiste Bessières would quick-march their corps to capture Cadiz, Cartagena and Ferrol, respectively and thus seize the three largest Spanish fleets along with the local treasuries. He spurred his generals with these words: 'I must not lose any time. I need those vessels because I want to strike a grand coup before the season's end.'[9] What he intended was to unite the French and Spanish fleets along with scores of transports and pack them with 25,000 troops; although he had not yet picked their destination, he dreamed of somehow asserting control over Spain's American empire and milking it for all it was worth.[10] The field commanders dutifully set forth on the hot dusty roads to their distant objectives. None would fulfil his mission and one would suffer a catastrophe.

The widely-dispersed Spanish army numbered over 100,000 troops, of which the largest forces were the 30,000 split between Generals Gregorio Cuesta and Joaquin Blake in Galicia, 30,000 under General Francisco Castanos in Andalusia and 17,000 under General Felipe Cervellon around Valencia. Bessières routed Blake and Cuesta at Medina del Rio Seco and eventually captured Leon, Benavente and Zamora, but lacked enough troops to march safely on to Ferrol. Duhesme took Barcelona but only after bypassing the Spanish-held fortresses of Gerona and Figueras on the road back to Perpignan, the jump-off French city for eastern Spain. General Jose Palafox mobilized 10,000 men in Saragossa to repel an attack by Verdier and his 8,000 troops. Likewise, Cervellon repulsed the attack by Moncey's 10,000 troops to capture Valencia. The worst fate befell Dupont. After detaching contingents to guard his communications, he had only 13,000 troops when he reached Cordoba then hastily withdrew before Castanos's army with nearly three times more men. He got as far as Bailen when Castanos caught up, cut him off, trounced him in battle and convinced him to surrender his now 18,000 troops with the Convention of Andujar on 20 July.

Meanwhile, that same day King Joseph, his advisors and an entourage of Spanish liberals triumphantly entered Madrid. They did not stay long. On 31 July, they beat a hasty and humiliating retreat after learning of Bailen and did not stop running until they reached Vitoria. Napoleon did not learn until 5 August 'of the horrible catastrophe of General Dupont' who committed 'one of the most extraordinary acts of incompetence and stupidity'. Thus, 'my army will be obliged to evacuate Madrid to concentrate'.[11]

That was not the only evacuation of a conquered capital. The news from Portugal was just as dismal. In early August, General Sir Arthur Wellesley landed a 20,000-man British army at Mondego Bay, Portugal, then marched south toward Lisbon. Napoleon reacted with triumph to word of the expedition: 'I want to strike great coups and I hope to have a general peace before next January since the English are imprudent enough to engage in a land war.'[12] Events soon eviscerated that vision. Wellesley defeated small French detachments at Obidos and Roliça, then 13,000 troops under Junot at Vimeiro. Junot was a wilier diplomat than general. He talked Generals Hew Dalrymple and Harry Burrand, who had superseded Wellesley in command, to sign on 22 August the

Convention of Cintra, whereby the British fleet sailed Junot, his 26,000 troops and their loot back to France. Compared to Andujar, the blow of Cintra was glancing rather than crushing. Napoleon wrote Junot these consoling words: 'You have done nothing dishonourable. You brought back my soldiers, eagles and cannons. However, I would have hoped that you would have done better.'[13]

Within a month the emperor had lost all of Portugal and most of Spain.[14] His vision of seizing Spain's overseas empire literally went up in gunsmoke. General Cuesta had not just rejected Napoleon's offer to be his viceroy in Mexico, but marched his army against the French invaders.[15] By July 1808, Napoleon admitted to Marine Minister Decrès that 'the affairs of Spain have taken such a serious turn over the last month that maybe we should not hazard my projects of sending so many troops overseas... In any event... several expeditions are needed but... must be postponed for now.'[16]

French defeats in the Peninsula tarnished Napoleon's prestige and image of infallibility that he incessantly nurtured. He launched a public relations campaign to justify his intervention in Spain and dismiss the setbacks. For instance, to Tsar Alexander 'I send . . . the constitution that the Spanish Junta just adopted. The country's disorders reached such an inconceivably dismal degree that I was obliged to interfere in its affairs. I have, by the irresistible force of events, created a system to ensure Spain's happiness . . . In this new situation Spain will always be independent of me.' He assured the Tsar that the new king would follow France's enlightened policies of ridding Spain of feudalism and the Inquisition and imposing a modern political system to better the lives of the Spanish people.[17]

As if Napoleon did not have enough worries, he had to buoy Joseph's sagging morale at the worsening maelstrom that trapped him: 'Keep up your spirits . . . and doubt not that things will end better and swifter that you think.'[18] Perhaps as much to encourage himself as his brother, he boasted that: 'I will find in Spain the Pillars of Hercules but I will not find the limits of my power.'[19] He similarly tried to inspire the troops that he was rushing toward Spain with these words:

> Soldiers, you have triumphed on the banks of the Danube and the Vistula, you have crossed Germany in forced marches. Today I am making you cross France without a moment of rest. Soldiers I need you . . . The hideous presence of [Britain] sullies the soil of Spain and Portugal . . . We will carry our eagles triumphantly to the Pillars of Hercules where we have outrages

to avenge . . . A long enduring peace will be the prize for your work.[20]

The chronic parade of dismal news soon smothered his spasms of bluster.

* * *

As if France's worsening quagmire in Spain was not disheartening enough, Vienna provoked a war scare in late August 1808 by mobilizing its reserves. Napoleon responded by mobilizing the Confederation of the Rhine contingents and reinforcing the French army in Germany and Poland. To Württemberg's King Frederick I, he offered these consoling words: 'I had hoped to spare the evils of war from the Confederation by carrying the war to foreign territory because the worst evil that can afflict a nation is to become the theatre of war.' After assessing the geopolitical situation in Central and Eastern Europe, he assured Frederick that Vienna would most likely soon stand down before the combined French and Confederation armies.[21] He was just as confident in a letter to Marshal Soult who commanded French troops in Central Europe: 'Austria was far from wanting war. All its militia movements are inspired by excessive fear . . . Austria promised me to be as of September 1, on the same footing as before summer. I await the effect of this promise so I can dismiss the Confederation troops.'

And Vienna soon did stand down as reason supplanted zeal among Francis I's advisors; they did not want a campaign in late 1808 to mirror the catastrophic campaigns of 1797, 1800 and 1805 at Napoleon's hands. The mood, however, shifted sharply back toward belligerence after the Austrians learned that Napoleon had departed to command his army in Spain. They thrilled at the notion of capitalizing on his absence with a blitzkrieg that overran southern Germany all the way to the Rhine. Their autumn 1808 mobilization acted as an insightful dress rehearsal for the spring 1809 campaign.

* * *

Napoleon invited nearly all of Europe's heads of state and their entourages to meet at Erfurt for several weeks in late September and early October 1808.[22] He announced the conference's official reason: 'I am going to Erfurt to bring peace to Europe.'[23] The actual purpose was to unify Europe behind him against his enemies. The bottom line for those he charged with organizing the conference was this: 'I want to astonish

Germany with my splendour.'²⁴ They realized his vision. After arriving on 27 September, he mostly conducted diplomacy informally through nearly nonstop hobnobbing with his fellow sovereigns at banquets, balls, plays, concerts and hunts. He also squeezed in notable meetings with German literary giants Johann von Goethe and Christophe Wieland.

Napoleon wielded Erfurt's glittering diplomatic bulk against the two great powers that he had not invited in hopes of keeping peace with Austria and forging peace with Britain. He wrote these tough words to the Austrian Emperor Francis:

> I have been the master of dismembering Your Majesty's empire . . . I did not want to do so . . . Now our accounts are closed and I want nothing more from you . . . I am always ready to guarantee your monarchy's integrity . . . With the right conduct, Your Majesty . . . can make his people happy . . . The best policy today is simplicity and truth.²⁵

Francis soon replied with soothing words that he shared Napoleon's desire for peace while his government steadily strengthened the army for a future war. Napoleon launched his latest plea for peace to British King George III:

> Sire, currently Europe is united at Erfurt. Our first thought is to cede to the vow and need of all peoples to search for a prompt peace with Your Majesty . . . The long, bloody war that tore apart the continent had ended . . . Many changes have taken place in Europe. Many states have been overthrown . . . We are united to beg Your Majesty to listen to the voice of humanity . . . to conciliate all interests and with that, to guarantee the existing powers and assure the happiness of Europe.²⁶

The emperor's bottom line for peace was *uti possidetis* or each side keeping what it had taken. As usual, the king and his cabinet disdainfully snubbed Napoleon and his peace plea. Foreign Minister George Canning did write Russian Foreign Minister Nicolas Romanzov that Britain rejected *uti possidetis* and would only consider attending a European peace congress if returning Portugal and Spain to their former rulers were part of the settlement.²⁷ Napoleon had Foreign Minister Jean Champagny inform Canning that Britain's position was a deal breaker because Joseph was Spain's rightful king by international treaties ratified by the Cortes; he said nothing of Portugal, leaving open the possibility of accepted the Braganza dynasty's return. He called again on the British to accept *uti possidetis* for peace.[28] This time he did not receive even an indirect response.

All along, Napoleon tried to rekindle his bromance with Alexander. Although the emperor still gushed over the Tsar, the mutual magic of Tilsit was long past: 'I am pleased with Alexander . . . If he were a woman, I believe I would make him my lover.'[29] To that the Tsar feigned to reciprocate such feelings while trying to extract hefty concessions. After one critical session, Napoleon wrote him of his desire 'to give convincing proof of my friendship for you and how much I cherish being with you'. He then granted Alexander's request to reduce Prussia's reparations by 20 million francs.[30] He was struck by how much the Tsar had changed since they parted 15 months before: 'He came to Erfurt quite a different man from what he appeared to be at Tilsit. I noticed at Erfurt that he was defiant and unspeakably obstinate. He wanted to treat with me as between equals. As a matter of fact, circumstances were in his favour and he took advantage of them.'[31]

Napoleon secretly informed Alexander that he intended to divorce the barren Josephine and marry a royal princess with whom to produce an heir for his imperial throne. He asked the Tsar to consider having his sister Ann become France's empress. Alexander replied that Ann was only 14 years old and, anyway, their formidable mother, the Empress Dowager, would have the last word on who her youngest daughter married. Napoleon did not press his suit.[32]

In the end, Alexander made only token concessions. A treaty between Russia and France signed on 12 October 1808 renewed their alliance against Britain; formed a defensive alliance against Austria and committed them to peace with Britain founded on *uti possidetis*, the recognition of Joseph as Spain's king, the cession of the Ottoman Empire's provinces of Wallachia and Moldavia to Russia and the integrity of the Ottoman Empire's other territory.

The Tsar had an unexpected but key ally in blunting Napoleon's advances. Talleyrand was the serpent in Napoleon's diplomatic garden. He sidled up to Alexander to urge: 'It is up to you to save Europe and the only way to do that is to resist Napoleon. The French are a civilized people; their emperor is not.'[33] Although for years he had bristled at Napoleon's imperialism, he still revelled at being at centre stage of his glittering power. For him the conference's most memorable event came the last morning when everyone gathered: 'He was surrounded by princes whose armies he had destroyed, whose states he had reduced or obliterated. Not one of them dared to request anything from him.'[34]

As Napoleon wrapped up the conference, he dashed off this promise to Joseph: 'I have settled all my business with the Russian emperor. I leave tomorrow for Paris and will be at Bayonne before November 1 . . . The war could be ended with a single blow by a clever combined manoeuvre and for that it is necessary that I be there.'[35]

* * *

By October 1808, France had a foothold in Spain from Bayonne to Vitoria and a toehold in Barcelona. In all, the French had around 75,000 troops before reinforcements in November and December swelled the number to 150,000. The 125,000 Spanish troops were split among widely dispersed armies with mutually jealous commanders, making communications testy and coordination impossible. The largest Spanish armies were Blake's 43,000 troops in Asturias, mostly around Astorga and Reynosa; General Fernando Belveder's 13,000 near Burgos; Castanos's 34,000 around Logrono; and Palafox's 25,000 around Saragossa; General Juan Vives's 25,000 besieging Barcelona; and General Teodoro Reding's 15,000 in Tarragona. British forces included General Sir John Moore's 25,000 troops at Ciudad Rodrigo and General Sir David Baird's 12,000 at Corunna. In Madrid, a Supreme Junta of 35 members convened to serve as Spain's provisional government. On 25 September 1808, the Junta declared Ferdinand VII their lawful king. For now, the Spanish and British commanders sat tight, waiting for the French to move. They would not wait long.

Brimming with confidence, Napoleon left Paris on 29 October and reached Vitoria, his first headquarters in Spain, on 6 November. From there, he raced off couriers with orders to his corps commanders. Those of François Lefebvre and Claude Victor were to move against Blake; Nicolas Soult and Jean Bessières against Belveder; Jean Lannes and Michel Ney against Castanos's front and rear, respectively; Adrien Moncey against Palafox; and Laurent Gouvion St Cyr against Vives.[36] His commanders were to wield this tactic: 'No matter how many Spaniards there are, you should march straight toward them. They are incapable of holding. Feinting and manoeuvring are unnecessary.'[37]

And that was what happened. The French routed the Spanish in every battle and asserted control over swaths of northern Spain. Napoleon marched with the central army into Madrid on 4 December. There he elatedly wrote to Police Minister Fouché that:

> You are wrong to worry about me. The Spaniards are no more vicious than any other nation. The weather here is as beautiful as

May in France. We have . . . defeated the enemy and established ourselves in Madrid. Send me good police chiefs for Madrid and Lisbon. I need not big talkers but impartial and honest men who will not profit from the circumstances by dishonourable stealing.[38]

He had Armand Caulaincourt, his ambassador to Russia, inform Alexander that he had nearly won the war in Spain. He had destroyed the Spanish army and his 200,000 troops were spreading steadily over the country; too much mud explained why the entire country was not completely conquered, but that was just a matter of time.[39]

Meanwhile, a threat and opportunity arose far westward over the horizon. British commander Sir John Moore's original plan was for him and Baird to join forces at Astorga to support any Spanish army east of that city. After learning that the French corps had fanned out across northern Spain, he ordered Baird to meet him at Valladolid from which to strike the westernmost corps, Soult's, before withdrawing to Astorga.

Upon getting wind of the British advance, Napoleon ordered the corps of Soult, Lefebvre, Bessières and his Imperial Guard to converge against them. Moore hastily withdrew when he learned of the French advance. What then transpired was one of the most famous races in military history as the British ever more desperately tried to reach a port where a fleet might rescue them, while the French tried to catch them before they did.

The further Napoleon marched across Spain the more often he craned his neck to peer back over 1,500 or so miles of Europe to Vienna. On the eve of 1809, he wrote to War Minister Clarke that: 'It is indispensable that we hold ourselves ready for the month of March if Austria moves; it seems like that power is actively working with England.'[40] He issued orders to Clarke in Paris, Marshal Davout in Germany, Prince Eugène in Italy, Marshal Marmont in Dalmatia and other key generals in France and across the empire to prepare for war by recruiting regiments to full strength; stockpiling munitions, provisions, blankets, shoes, saddles and forage; massing draft animals and wagons; and planning a rapid offensive against the closest Austrian forces. He withdrew his Imperial Guard from Spain and refurbished it for the likely campaign ahead. He urged France's allies, the Confederation of the Rhine and Russia, to ready themselves for war. Finally, he tasked his police chiefs, diplomats and allied governments to gather as much intelligence as possible about Austrian forces and intentions, while getting friendly newspaper editors to counter Austrian propaganda.

Meanwhile, a message stopped Napoleon in his tracks at Astorga on 2 January 1809. A conspiracy was possibly budding against him in

Paris. How true was that report? The best place to find out was in Paris. The next day he turned the advance over to Soult and headed eastward, stopping two days at Benavente then ten days at Valladolid. Additional messages confirmed the seriousness of the initial warning. He left Valladolid on 15 January and, by travelling 600 miles nearly nonstop by coach with brief stops just to change horses and a day's rest at Tartas, strode into the Tuileries in Paris late on 24 January.

Meanwhile, Soult pushed his exhausted, hunger-pinched men on. Along the way, they captured thousands of even more exhausted and starving redcoats. On 15 January, Soult caught up with Moore at Corunna and attacked the next day, but the British repulsed the French; Moore was killed in the fighting. Over the next few days, a British fleet evacuated 26,000 troops; those men would form the core of the army that General Wellesley would command in Portugal later that year. Meanwhile, Joseph reappeared in Madrid on 22 January 1809. The French had retaken Spain's political capital and many big cities. The British army was gone and the Spanish armies were scattered and depleted. For now, the French conquest of the rest of the Iberian Peninsula appeared to be only a matter of time.

Chapter 15

The Gatekeeper of Vienna

'This menace goes directly to my heart . . . to think that blood and tears will flow again. The day that Austria will give the signal for war will be for me a day of mourning.'

'It seems that Austria wants war. She will have it.'

Napoleon was seething when he summoned his key advisors to meet at the Tuileries on 28 January 1809, four days after his return.[1] He was unable to find any hard information about the conspiracy that had been hatched while he was campaigning in Spain. Indeed, what the 'conspiracy' amounted to was nothing more than speculation between Police Minister Fouché and Grand Marshal of the Palace Talleyrand over who should replace Napoleon if he died; the consensus was that Joachim Murat should take power and they sent the Neapolitan king a letter to ready himself should the worst happen. Such musings profoundly disturbed Napoleon as wishful thinking, especially by uniting long-standing political foes Talleyrand and Fouché. Although Cambacérès was his government's most loyal and competent member, the emperor privately vented some of his frustration against him: 'How could you ignore their reconciliation after such a long enmity? Do you not know the ambitions of these two characters and can you doubt that their rapprochement would not be prejudiced against me?'[2] He also privately castigated Fouché the day before the meeting:

> You do nothing at all with the Paris police and you leave a free field for running all sorts of spiteful rumours . . . A police minister must be responsible for rumours made to mislead the population. If you occupy yourself a bit more in this aspect of public administration, you will find the threads of the intrigues of agents who provoke this spiteful system in Paris.[3]

During the meeting, the emperor sought to intimidate his underlings so thoroughly that none of them would ever again dare to discuss, let alone plan, his replacement. He fixed his rage on Talleyrand: 'You are a thief, a coward, a man without faith. All your life you have avoided your duties. You have betrayed, tricked everyone. For you nothing is sacred. You would sell out your own father. I plied you with riches yet you are . . . against me . . . You are shit in a silk stocking.'[4] His rage spent, he strode from the room. Talleyrand typically had the last word. 'What a pity such a great man is so ill-bred . . . That is something that I will never forgive.'[5]

Napoleon stripped Talleyrand of his title as the palace's Grand Marshal but let him remain the Empire's Grand Elector. Why did he single out Talleyrand for a tongue-lashing and punishment? He was using divide and rule tactics by making an example of Talleyrand and sparing Fouché, hoping to drive them apart. He also vented his anger against the man he feared less. He was aware of how potentially dangerous his police chief was but regarded Talleyrand and his crowd as pesky gadflies to humble rather than dangerous conspirators to jail or exile. He dismissed Talleyrand as 'still abandoning himself to the free spirits and bad morality of the coterie who surrounds him, which generates all sorts of nasty gossip against me'.[6] Actually, Talleyrand was pocketing bribes from a widening array of governments, including then or later Austria, Prussia, Russia and Britain. Perhaps no man sold out his country to more foreign countries. Yet, to his last breath Talleyrand insisted that he did so to save France and Europe from Napoleon.[7]

* * *

Having dealt with this immediate threat, Napoleon turned to a more distant one.[8] Fortunately his preparation orders over the previous month had advanced so far that he could boast that 'I am ready for everything'.[9] His unexpected return to his capital further galvanized his administration and stunned Austrian ambassador Clemens von Metternich. Napoleon gleefully noted that: 'My sudden arrival in Paris has already changed the Austrian tone and fear has replaced arrogance and extreme confidence.'[10]

That may have been true for Metternich and his entourage, but had an opposite effect in Vienna. For months, Austria's Aulic Council or inner government was split between war and peace factions led by Chancellor Johann Philip Stadion and Archduke Charles, respectively. On 8 February, Francis presided over his government's now-united decision to make war against France with the bizarre 'logic' that there was no choice since

Napoleon was preparing for war against them. Of course that would not have happened had the Austrians not initiated the vicious circle of belligerent build-up and rhetoric.

Reports from spies of Vienna's decision soon filtered back to the Tuileries. That hardly fazed Napoleon. In mid-February, he declared: 'It seems that Austria wants war. She will have it.'[11] For now, however, two important reasons kept the emperor from ordering large numbers of troops to march to allied frontiers on the way to Vienna. First, he wanted to avoid giving the Austrians an excuse for launching a war that he did not want. Second, he wanted to shield his troops from the bitter winter cold: 'It is unnecessary to hurry in forming the camps; that serves nothing and March is a season too unfavourable for sending my troops from their winter quarters.'[12] Although Italian winters were milder, they were not necessarily healthier. He informed Viceroy Eugène that 'there is no reason to greatly fear the Austrians who are afflicted with sickness. If the seasonal rains render the camps unhealthy then quarter the troops in the villages.'[13]

He still hoped to avoid war altogether but with this caveat: 'I want peace with Austria, but a solid peace and I have the right to demand it after having saved three times that power's independence.' He referred to the relatively mild treaties that he had negotiated with Vienna in 1797, 1801 and 1805 to end wars that the Austrians had started. Peace now depended on 'Austria completely demobilizing and contenting itself with reciprocal guarantees'. Should war result, 'as for provinces from the vanquished monarchy . . . I want nothing for myself'. However, Vienna's three crowns – Austrian, Hungarian and Bohemian – 'might be divided which could be mutually beneficial for France and Russia'. The more he thought about it, the more he reasoned that: 'I should dismember Austria. I believed the emperor's promises . . . The experience of three years proves that I was tricked.'[14]

Of the array of preparations that Napoleon made ideally to deter or, if that failed, fight Austria, a critical element was at best ambiguous. Surely the Austrians would not be foolish enough to war against the French Empire to the west and the Russian Empire to the east. That catastrophic two-front scenario should have inhibited all but Austria's most zealous hawks. The more clearly united and prepared Paris, St Petersburg and their minor allies were for war, the more likely that Vienna would be deterred. He explained: 'Austria would fall before our knees if we make a firm, concerted demand that they stand down.'[15] In early March, he instructed Ambassador Armand Caulaincourt to inform the Tsar that, if Austria attacked, 'I count on Emperor Alexander to keep his promise to march his armies'.[16] Coordination between the French and Russian armies hundreds of miles apart would be impossible, but Napoleon sought Alexander's plans and pledge to threaten and, if need be, attack Austria: 'I cannot plan an attack without knowing Your Majesty's deployments . . . There is not a moment to lose for Your Majesty to camp your troops on our common enemy's frontier.'[17] The trouble was that, despite repeated entreaties, Alexander made wishy-washy rather than decisive statements over his commitment to the alliance. Napoleon deeply lamented that had Alexander 'wanted to speak firmly at Erfurt' against the Austrians in October 1808, none of this would have been necessary. He 'foresaw that war is inevitable if' Alexander 'and I do not jointly issue tough, decisive language to Austria'.[18]

Austria's latest aggression perplexed him: 'I can conceive nothing from the dizzying madness that has seized that country's heads.'[19] He could only reason that they 'imagine that to fight against them I must bring with me my army from Spain'.[20] He constantly tasked his diplomatic and military chiefs to 'find good intelligence on the march of Austrian troops . . . and the rumours of war that spread among the merchants'.[21] On 23 March, he ordered Fouché to arrest all Austrian couriers journeying between Paris and Vienna, decode their messages and send them to him.[22] He was confident that Prussia would not join Austria, but just in case, he left Marshal François Kellermann and his corps at Mainz and Jérôme in Westphalia to deter a Prussian attack on Napoleon's left flank.[23]

* * *

So what does explain Austria's decision for war? Hatred and hubris are a volatile mix. Most Austrian leaders festered to avenge their previous disastrous, humiliating defeats at Napoleon's hands and not just retake all the productive lands and peoples that had been lost, but conquer even more at France's expense. Austrian hubris swelled with the successful military reforms that Charles initiated after the previous catastrophic war. The army was now organized into French-style corps whose troops were trained in French-style light infantry tactics as well as regular tactics. Then there were the numbers, over 290,000 regular troops, including 36,000 cavalry, 13,000 gunners and 760 field guns, backed by 180,000 *landwehr* or militia. Austria could not have expanded its army to such levels let alone launched it in a prolonged war had not Britain underwritten most of the costs. On 24 April 1809, envoys signed the latest bilateral subsidy treaty, this one whereby London paid Vienna an initial £2,000,000 then £400,000 monthly for the duration of the war.[24]

Alas for the Austrians, soft power had not kept up with hard power, at least among the army's leaders. Nepotism still determined senior command positions. Of Francis's four younger archduke brothers, Charles was an excellent commander while John, Louis and Ferdinand were mediocrities at best. Nor did the Austrian corps commanders match their French counterparts in skill and drive. Yet, if the French had the qualitative edge in officers, man for man the average Austrian soldier was likely superior to the average French soldier in physical strength and training. The quality of the French army's rank and file probably peaked in 1805 then steadily eroded through the campaigns in Germany, Poland and Spain. By 1809, raw, reluctant conscripts outnumbered hardened veterans in the French army.

Napoleon sent the thirty-eight members of the Confederation of the Rhine and the Duchy of Warsaw word to begin preparing for war on 15 February and begin massing their forces on 4 March. The Confederation eventually mobilized about 70,000 troops; most guarded supply lines and deterred Prussia.[25] He was sensitive to rulers who worried about entrusting their troops to French generals. For instance, he assured Württemberg's King Frederick that although General Dominique Vandamme would command his troops, he would be the sole French officer and he was an experienced general.[26] He was severe toward states that refused to supply troops or funds; he later sent troops into those states to confiscate and sell any Austrian property.[27]

Napoleon submitted a million-franc bill to Treasury Minister Mollien on 25 March. That was just a preliminary cost. The bills would soar as the campaign unfolded. As always, he intended partly to pay his war debts by extracting as much money and other requisitions as possible from his enemies and allies alike, while minimizing tax increases and loans for his beleaguered French subjects.[28]

* * *

Napoleon had armies on four fronts.[29] His army in Bavaria numbered 165,000 troops split among the corps of François Lefebvre's Bavarians on Austria's frontier, backed by Nicolas Oudinot and André Masséna and behind them Jean Lannes and Jean-Baptiste Bessières's cavalry reserve. Louis Davout's corps was deployed near Nuremburg. The Imperial Guard was marching from Paris and would not catch up to the army until it reached Vienna. Elsewhere, Eugène Beauharnais's army numbered 68,000 troops in north-eastern Italy; Auguste Marmont's corps numbered 10,500 troops in Dalmatia; and Polish General Josef Poniatowski's corps numbered 18,000 troops in the Duchy of Warsaw.

Napoleon's initial strategy in 1809 differed from his 1800, 1805, 1806, 1807 and 1808 campaigns when he marched rapidly attempting to encircle and destroy the enemy. This time he would let the Austrians come to him. That would at once expose Austrian aggression for what it was while ideally fighting the enemy on ground of his own choosing. He identified Regensburg (Ratisbonne) as the focal point of the campaign's first phase. He would converge his corps there to crush the Austrian advance, then pursue the remnants to Vienna and beyond. Elsewhere each commander would march against the nearest Austrian forces.

Austria's strategy involved simultaneous invasions by Charles and 209,000 troops up the Danube valley into Bavaria; General Jean Chasteler de Courcelles and 10,000 troops into the Tyrol to rally its former Austrian subjects against Bavarian rule; John and 50,000 troops into the Kingdom of Italy; and Ferdinand and 40,000 troops into the Duchy of Warsaw. Charles split his seven corps into three groups: Heinrich Bellegarde and Karl Kollowrat-Krakowsky would attack Davout north of the Danube; Friedrich Hohenzollern-Hechigen, Franz Rosenberg and Johann Lichtenstein would advance along the south bank of the Danube; and Johann von Hiller, Michael von Kienmayer and Archduke Louis would advance further south and then veer north to cut off the enemy attack by the centre group. Without declaring war, Austria's onslaught into Bavaria began on 9 April. The attacks south of the Danube initially succeeded in driving back the French and Bavarian forces, but Davout checked then drove back Bellegarde and Kollowrat.

Napoleon did not leave Paris until 13 April and within days was in the Danube valley, moving rapidly to keep up with the fast-paced campaign.[30] He issued his first round of orders on 17 April. His plan was a huge pincer movement whereby his corps converged at Regensburg. The result was four rapid-fire victories in four days at Abensberg, Landshut, Eckmühl and Regensburg between 20 and 23 April. The decisive battle came at Eckmühl on 21 and 22 April; a spent ball bruised Napoleon's Achilles tendon on the second day. In all, the Austrians and French suffered about 30,000 and 20,000 casualties, respectively, during this phase of the campaign.

Inexplicably, Napoleon marched on Vienna rather than after the battered but still intact Austrian army that escaped north of the Danube. In doing so he violated his own principle that any military campaign's primary objective is the enemy army's destruction after which any political objectives fall like ripe fruit. He wrote to Saxon King Frederick

Augustus that 'I will be in Vienna in a few days. God has accorded us striking protection for the justice of our cause and punished the Austrian court's ingratitude, dishonesty and bad faith.'[31] As he marched down the Danube valley, he received disturbing reports about setbacks far beyond the southern horizon.

* * *

Inspired by popular uprisings against the French in Spain, Austrian and other German leaders tried to provoke similar revolts against the French and their allies in central Europe. Three revolts broke out in Westphalia. Although Jérôme's army crushed the rebels, the guerrillas succeeded in diverting that army from the main campaign around Vienna. In Saxony, Prussian renegade Major Ferdinand von Schill led the Black Legion of 5,000 assorted German-speaking volunteers who chased King Frederick Augustus from his capital of Dresden on 10 May. The Saxon army defeated the Black Legion and killed Schill at Stralsund on 30 May.

The bloodiest and most prolonged rebellion erupted in the Tyrol that straddles the Alps with a succession of high passes leading to deep valleys opening north and south. General Johann Gabriel Chasteler de Courcelles combined his regular forces with rebels led by Andreas Hofer around Innsbruck. Chasteler was among the era's most ruthless generals. He captured a column of 700 unarmed French conscripts and massacred them. He also had 1,800 Bavarian prisoners massacred. Napoleon ordered Lefebvre to crush the Tyrolean uprising and destroy Chasteler. Lefebvre routed Chasteler at Worgel on 13 May. The Tyrolean revolt, however, sputtered on until Italian troops captured Hofer on 19 January 1810. Napoleon wrote Eugène that: 'I would have had you send him to Paris but since he is at Mantua send a military commission there to judge him and then have him shot.'[32] Hofer was executed on 20 February 1810.

Meanwhile, hoping to deter Chasteler and others from committing more massacres, Napoleon ordered the arrest in Vienna of three prominent princes, including Metternich's father, and their rendition as hostages to Paris. That did not inhibit Chasteler but it did outrage Emperor Francis, who retaliated by holding two French generals hostage. The hostages were exchanged in July. On 30 July, Napoleon instructed Lefebvre

> to take 130 hostages from each canton, pillage and burn at least six big villages in all of Tyrol along with the houses of the leaders

and that you declare that I will submit the country to fire and blood if the rebels do not surrender with their arms . . . Make a law that any house in which a firearm is found will be razed, that any Tyrolean found with arms will be executed . . . You have power in your hands. Be terrible and act in a way so that we can partly withdraw our troops from Tyrol.[33]

As in Bavaria, Austria's invasion of Italy initially succeeded.[34] Archduke John's army routed Eugène's at the Battle of Sacile on 16 April, inflicting 6,000 casualties while suffering 4,000. Eugène retreated behind the Adige River. Napoleon blistered him for losing his battle then taking days to inform him:

> I see with sorrow that you have neither the habit nor notion of war . . . War is a serious game in which one can compromise ones reputation and country . . . I made a mistake in giving you the army's command; I should have sent Masséna and made you the cavalry commander under his orders . . . If circumstances are too pressing, you must write the king of Naples to come to the army . . . You will hand over command and serve under his orders.[35]

His worst fear was that 'my affairs are lost in Italy and you do not dare to tell me and . . . I will soon find the enemy army in Italy on my right flank'.[36]

Eugène reorganized and replenished his army, then led it forward to victory over John at the Battle of the Piave River on 8 and 9 May, inflicting 5,000 casualties while suffering 2,000. He marched his army through Udine, caught up to the enemy's rearguard at Spilembergo on 11 May and smashed it in a double envelopment that killed, wounded or captured 2,100 Austrians. Having lost over half his army since the campaign began, John retreated into Austria in hope of uniting with Charles. Napoleon sent Marshal Étienne Macdonald to assist Eugène. Together they doggedly pursued John and captured Laibach on 23 May.

Meanwhile, the Austrian attack into Dalmatia that began on 10 April was also initially successful. Marmont withdrew all the way to Zara before massing his forces and taking the offensive. He defeated the Austrians in three separate battles then marched to capture Fiume on 28 May and joined forces with Eugène at Laibach on 3 June. Eugène's combined forces nipped at John's heels then attacked and routed his army at Raab on 24 June. John withdrew to Pressburg north of the Danube as

Eugène began a siege of Raab's citadel. Eugène left behind troops at Raab and marched north to join Napoleon on 5 July.

Ferdinand invaded the Duchy of Warsaw on 17 April and defeated Poniatowski's army at the Battle of Raszyn outside Warsaw on the 19th. The Austrians laid siege to Warsaw which Poniatowski abandoned on 23 April. Ferdinand pursued but Poniatowski turned and defeated him at Grodchno on 26 April and Gora Kalwaria on 2 and 3 May, then recaptured Warsaw on 2 June. A Russian army led by General Dmitri Galitzin invaded Galicia on 12 June, but avoided combat as he and Ferdinand reached a secret understanding that they would pantomime rather than actually fight each other. Poniatowski and Gallitzin did join and march unopposed into Cracow on 15 July, which effectively ended fighting on that front.

* * *

Meanwhile, Napoleon's victorious army marched down the south side of the Danube valley, mopping up scattered Austrian detachments.[37] Typically the French troops outmarched their own supply wagons but feasted off provisions packed in enemy supply wagons and depots that they overran. The army suffered a worsening shortage of horses, with thousands of cavalrymen on foot and hundreds of guns and wagons left stranded. To alleviate those shortages, Napoleon made Passau the principal depot. Passau was an excellent strategic position as the junction for three rivers and with a citadel high above the town. He had contingents collect as many boats as possible along the Danube for eventually crossing that river. He massed his pontooneers, engineers and sappers.

Napoleon established his headquarters at Schönbrunn Palace half a dozen miles west of Vienna on 11 May. Vienna capitulated the next day. He had Foreign Minister Champagny spread word of his triumph to Europe's major capitals and summon Metternich to Vienna for peace talks. Metternich never showed. Although Napoleon had defeated Austria's army and captured its capital, the main enemy army still numbered over 150,000 troops just miles beyond the four blown-up bridges that once crossed the Danube. He needed to inflict a knockout blow to the Austrians to force them into a peace treaty on his terms.

Napoleon had General Henri Bertrand, his chief engineer, select an appropriate place to construct pontoon bridges across the Danube. Bertrand chose Lobau Island as a staging area for moving the army to the north bank. The island was large enough for several corps to camp there. Although the river on Lobau's south side was 825 yards across, it was only 125 yards across on the north side. Pontooneers completed a bridge linking the south bank and Lobau by 19 May. The corps of Lannes, Masséna and Oudinot along with the cavalry reserve and Imperial Guard crossed to deploy on the island. As pontooneers constructed the north bridge, the Austrians demonstrated the vulnerability of Napoleon's strategy. Upstream they launched into the Danube's swift spring current a debris-packed barge that smashed through the bridges on the south side. As repairs were swiftly made, Napoleon deployed contingents on boats upstream to intercept a steady flow of barges, but one barge got through to smash a new hole in the bridge.

Nonplussed, Napoleon ordered Masséna and Lannes to lead their corps across and fan out to occupy the villages of Aspern and Essling, respectively, a mile from the bridgehead early on the morning of 21 May; Oudinot and the cavalry reserve followed later that day. Charles launched a massive attack by the corps of Hiller and Heinrich Reuss on the French army's left flank, Bellegarde and Hohenzollern on the centre and Rosenberg on the right flank. In all, the 83,996 Austrian infantry and 14,253 cavalry outnumbered the 50,000 French infantry and cavalry by three to two, while the 292 Austrian guns were twice as numerous as the 144 French ones.

The French repelled a series of attacks throughout the day and retook the villages after the Austrians overran them. Napoleon ordered the Imperial Guard across and had Davout quickmarch his corps from Vienna. Davout and his men got no further than Lobau Island. The Danube rose by three feet and the current flowed faster, forcing the pontooneers to extend the shaky bridges. A barge smashed through the north bridge. The pontooneers worked desperately through the night but could not complete the damaged bridge and two parallel bridges.

The Austrians resumed their attacks early the next morning. The French drove back the Austrians then counter-attacked but a lack of ammunition and troops forced them to withdraw to their starting positions. The bridge was finally repaired. That night Napoleon withdrew his army to Lobau. In all, each side suffered around 25,000 casualties. Among those mortally wounded was Marshal Lannes whose legs were torn off by a cannon ball. Napoleon wept bitterly as he watched him die an excruciating death. To his widow, he wrote: 'My pain is equal to yours. I lost the most distinguished general of my armies, my companion in arms for sixteen years, who I consider my best friend.'[38]

* * *

Napoleon spent the next six weeks building up his troops and supplies for what he hoped would be a decisive surge against the Austrians.[39] He tried to provoke a revolt in Hungary by promising them independence and alliance like the Duchy of Warsaw but nothing happened. He learned from his earlier debacle in crossing the Danube. This time he had sixteen bridges erected across the river, with two at the former crossing on Lobau's north-west side and nine on Lobau's north-east, east and south-east sides and the other five on the south side leading to Vienna. On 30 June, he sent a small force across the north-west bridges to draw the Austrians' attention, while he crossed 180,000 troops and 488 guns over the other bridges.

Charles chose not to attack the French when they were most vulnerable, but instead kept his 142,000 troops on a carefully prepared position half a dozen miles from the Danube. His right was anchored on a large hill overlooking the Danube then extended eastward through a series of villages to his centre. His left was atop a broad plateau with the Russbach River below. Napoleon not only faced that formidable Austrian line but kept nervously glancing south-eastward for any sign of John leading 12,500 troops from Pressburg against his rear. He had no good attack option. If he assaulted the Austrian centre or right, the Austrian left could descend and attack his right in hope of severing the French from most of their bridges. If he tried to swing around the Austrian left, the Austrians would simply extend that flank along the plateau's heights while the centre and left attacked the French flank and rear.

Napoleon finally chose to launch a massive attack on the Austrian centre and left, with the corps of Masséna, Bernadotte, Eugène, Oudinot and Davout extending from west to east or 110,000 men altogether. In reserve to exploit any breakthrough were the 8,000 men of Bessières' cavalry reserve, the 11,000-man Imperial Guard, the 10,000 men of Marmont's corps and 7,000 men of Karl von Wrede's Bavarian division. The Austrians repelled all those attacks on 5 July, inflicting heavy losses. Napoleon resumed his attacks the morning of 6 July, this time sending Macdonald's corps against the Austrian right as the other corps fought their way over the same corpse-strewn ground. On the French right, Davout's men fought their way up the plateau for a tenuous position at the top, but the Austrian right routed the French attacks then charged after them; Napoleon finally rallied his battered left flank at Essling and the nearby bridges. He then launched Marmont, Wrede, the Guard and the cavalry reserve to smash through the Austrian centre. With his army split asunder, Charles ordered a retreat.

No battle before Wagram counted more combatants and casualties. The French and Austrian suffered 37,568 and 41,750 dead, wounded and prisoners, respectively.[40] Napoleon triumphantly wrote Josephine that: 'My enemies are defeated, battered, completely routed . . . I crushed them.'[41] That was a gross exaggeration. Charles still had 100,000 men in his army. He fanned out Davout, Marmont and Masséna in pursuit on 8 July. Marmont caught up to the Austrians at Znaim and attacked on 10 July. Masséna marched to the sound of the guns and turned the Austrian flank on 11 July. Each side suffered around 6,000 casualties. As Charles withdrew his army to Brünn, he sent General Liechtenstein with a request for an armistice to Napoleon. On 12 July, Napoleon granted an armistice after explaining that in principle he would accept peace only on the basis of *uti possidetis* but in practice would be generous in returning territory to Austria.[42] He then turned over the talks to Foreign Minister Champagny and his counterpart, Clemens von Metternich.

* * *

A 39,000-man British expedition led by General John Pitt, Earl of Chatham, began landing on Walcheren Island in the Netherlands on 30 July 1809.[43] Napoleon's first reaction to news of the British invasion was a shrug: 'I do not see what the English can do. They cannot take Flushing since the dams can be cut. They cannot take the fleet since they cannot sail to Antwerp.'[44] He ordered Marshal François Kellermann to Walcheren to command the army there. On 8 August, after learning that the British had taken Flushing, he issued a flurry of orders to build up French forces on that front and a strategy for eventually ejecting the British and had Bernadotte replace Kellermann. He remained optimistic that as long as everyone did his duty and followed his orders: 'The English expedition will have only one result, it will perish by fevers and inaction.'[45] In this Napoleon was prescient. Although the British lost little more than 100 casualties in battle, Walcheren Fever or malaria afflicted over 11,500 men, of whom 4,006 died before the British finally withdrew and sailed away on 9 December.

During the campaign two of Napoleon's subordinates committed troubling gaffs. Bernadotte proved to be as inept in this campaign as he was in his preceding roles. The final straw for Napoleon was when, with a proclamation, Bernadotte 'betrayed the secret of his position by an excess of vanity'. Atop that he 'never ceased corresponding with conspirators in Paris'. In mid-September, Napoleon replaced Bernadotte with Bessières.[46] Even worse was when Police Minister Fouché called out the National Guard across north-eastern France ostensibly to counter the British invasion. Napoleon chastised Fouché for acting illegally, wasting money and causing a panic, then ordered him to dismiss the National Guard.[47] What really disturbed Napoleon was fearing that while he was on campaign an opponent could take power and call out the National Guard against him. That nearly happened three years later.

* * *

The peace talks with the Austrians lasted three months, from the Armistice of Znaim on 12 July 1809 to the Treaty of Vienna on 14 October. Although Napoleon had others conduct the daily talks, he directed diplomatic strategy through them.[48] He asserted his framework for a settlement on 22 July. First, he wrote to Francis that he hoped 'this fourth peace treaty that will succeed those of Campo Formio, Lunéville and Pressburg, will be the last, re-establish a durable tranquillity on the continent and serve as a shelter from English intrigues. I regard this as a very happy moment because of the four wars that Your Majesty has waged against France, the last three were . . . useful only to England.'[49] Then he had Foreign Minister Champagny issue a declaration to guide the conference. The declaration's first section presented a history lesson of Austrian aggression and French victories in four wars. Napoleon had been generous and forgiving of Vienna following the first three wars: 'France never wanted any Austrian possessions. In three successive wars she restored immense territories without any compensation. She had hoped that in exchange for this moderation, the Austrian emperor would have valued friendship and recognition with her.' Instead, Vienna started a fourth war. Nonetheless, Napoleon was willing once again to grant Austria generosity and forgiveness as long as the Austrians agreed to three preliminary conditions and a principle: They would dismiss the *landwehr* or militia, cut their army's size in half and expel any French in Austrian service; *uti possidetis* or each keeping what one had would be the principle guiding the peace talks. With *uti possidetis* Austria faced potentially huge losses of land, people and revenue in any peace treaty since French troops now occupied most of Austria including Vienna. Obviously, Napoleon would only consider evacuating those lands if the Austrians promised to fulfil those three specific steps and the broader principle.[50]

What followed were weeks of talks about the preliminaries. The Austrians stonewalled on making any concessions and tried to provoke revolts in French occupied territory. Although Napoleon readied his army for another campaign, he hoped to avoid any more loss of life. The Znaim armistice expired on 12 August, but Napoleon kept his troops in camp and redoubled his diplomatic efforts. He had Champagny explain to Metternich that he was ready to return any lands that his army occupied as long as the Austrians agreed in writing that he did not have to do so and asked specifically for what they wanted back: 'If they want Salzburg, I will return it; if they want Trieste, I will return it; if they want Galicia, I will return it.' But Napoleon was losing patience. If the Austrians refused to concede, he 'would plant his eagles' atop his conquests, 'destroy feudal rights', and embed the Code Napoleon in the ruins. The choice was up to the Austrians.[51]

The Austrians lost heavily by their foot-dragging. By early September, they would not get back everything that they requested. Napoleon would split the Tyrol and Voralberg between Bavaria and Italy to eliminate Austria's strategic wedge along the spine of the Alps. That was certain. But he was also thinking of deposing Francis and splitting his empire into three smaller states, Austria, Bohemia and Hungary.

In mid-September Napoleon tried to end the impasse with his latest appeal to Francis, this time by making two huge concessions. He renounced *uti possidetis* and breaking up the Austrian empire into three states. He was prepared to settle if Austria split Tyrol and Voralberg between Bavaria and Italy and Galicia between Poland and Russia. As to the future, 'once peace is re-established between us, it only depends on Your Majesty to reassert relations between our states. This result could have already been obtained after the peace of Lunéville, which would have avoided the events inflicted on our peoples and you, Monsieur, my brother, many bad moments', but instead Francis let English gold corrupt his court.[52]

Francis replied by sending his aide, General Ferdinand Bubna, to meet privately with Napoleon. On 23 September, Napoleon passed Bubna a long letter for Francis detailing and justifying his terms, criticizing him for threatening to renew the war and hoping that he would understand that his latest concessions proved 'my repugnance to spill blood and my desire to re-establish peace on the continent'.[53] He elaborated his terms and views in another letter three days later, with the most important new point a call for a European peace conference that would include Britain. And once again he expressed his sorrow that Francis had issued his latest threat to resume the war: 'This menace goes directly to my heart . . . to think that blood and tears will flow again. The day that Austria will give the signal for war will be for me a day of mourning.'[54] Francis sent Liechtenstein to join Bubna at the talks but the Austrians remained intransigent.

Napoleon finally lost all patience. On 6 October, he had Champagny issue an ultimatum that the Austrians either accept his terms or resume the war. That did the trick. Under the Treaty of Schönbrunn signed on 14 October 1809, Austria ceded Illyria, Istria and Carinthia to France; Salzburg, Berchtesgaden and much of upper Austria to Bavaria; and four-fifths of Galicia to the Duchy of Warsaw and the rest to Russia. In addition Austria would sever all diplomatic and trade relations with Britain, reduce its army to 150,000 troops and pay reparations of 85,000,000 francs to be split among France and its allies. In his congratulatory letter to Francis, he expressed his hope 'that all our differences are reconciled, that the peace will be perpetual between us'.[55] Tragically, the bilateral peace lasted merely three years and Austria once again broke it.

Chapter 16

The Antichrist

'I am Charlemagne, the Church's sword and emperor.'

'We can only attribute our so prompt and striking success to the special protection that divine Providence has given us so many proofs.'

'They want to denounce me as a Christian! This ridiculous thought can only appear from those who are profoundly ignorant of the century in which we live . . . The pope who would carry such a belief would cease to be a pope in my eyes. I would consider him to be the Anti-Christ sent to overthrow the world and inflict evil on mankind.'

'I am angry that they have arrested the pope; that's a great folly . . . But there is no remedy. What is done is done.'

Napoleon was hardly a regular churchgoer. Indeed after his boyhood only rare reasons of state detoured him to Mass. His absence was only partly attributable to the near-impossibility of such a hyperactive soul staying seated for minutes, let alone hours.

How did Napoleon view religion? He was a profound existentialist and psychologist: 'Man thrown into life wonders: Where did I come from? Who am I? Where am I going? These are the mysterious questions that propel us toward religion.' What happens then is that religion imposes a faith so powerful that most adherents stop questioning: 'One believes in God because everyone else around one does . . . One knows only to think of the doctrine that one has been taught.' Thus does the power of conformity trump the combined powers of imagination and reason for most people. Only a few individuals keep questioning the nature of reality. Napoleon was just such an irrepressible soul: 'That had been my march. I believed but my belief found itself troubled, uncertain . . . when I was around thirteen years old.' The result was that he abandoned Catholic dogma.[1]

When asked just what he did believe, he replied: 'I am far from being an atheist, but I cannot believe all that I have been taught in the face of my reason without being false and hypocritical.'[2] He scorned 'the absurd words and iniquitous acts of those who preach to us'.[3] In comparing religions, he observed: 'All proclaim the existence of a God; that is undeniable. But all our religions are clearly conceived by men.' He questioned Christianity's universalist pretentions: 'Why has ours not always existed? Why is it exclusive? . . . .Why has it not always been everywhere? It is that men are always men. It is that priests are always slipping everywhere into fraud and lies.'[4]

Yet he deeply admired many teachings of Moses, Jesus and Mohammad, the respective founders of Judaism, Christianity and Islam. He found not just moral but spiritual truths in every religion. He believed in not the Biblical God, but the mysterious, powerful spiritual force of Providence that for reasons beyond human understanding at times interfered in worldly affairs to help or harm nations, groups and individuals. He believed that Providence favoured him. What else could explain his stunning rise from an obscure, penniless captain to become Europe's master: 'We can only attribute our so prompt and striking success to the special protection that divine Providence has given us so many proofs.'[5] He mostly believed this statement to France's bishops following the Battle of Austerlitz in 1805: 'The striking victory that our army won over the combined Austrian and Russian armies, commanded personally by the Russian and Austrian emperors, is visible proof of God's protection which extends solemn acts and grace throughout our empire.'[6]

Overall Napoleon reckoned that religion did more good than harm, especially in the hands of progressive leaders. He enthusiastically backed the religious orders that fed the hungry, nursed the sick, sheltered the homeless, raised orphans and schooled children. He sought to protect those charitable institutions while ensuring that they lived up to their missions. But religion's most vital role was stability rather than charity: 'In religion, I do not see the mystery of the incarnation, but the mystery of the social order. It associates with Heaven an idea of equality that keeps rich men from being massacred by the poor . . . Society is impossible without inequality; inequality intolerable without a moral code and a moral code unacceptable without religion.'[7]

So, after taking power, Napoleon was eager 'to re-establish religion . . . for its . . . true principles . . . and alleviate with marvels human worries . . .

Religious sentiments are so consoling that it is a benefit of heaven to possess them.' As a ruler, he used religion's institutions and dogmas as one of many political tools to control the masses:

> How would that be a resource for us? What power would I have over men and their things? . . . No doubt my type of scepticism . . . as an emperor benefited the people; otherwise how could I have exercised a true tolerance? How could I have equally favoured all sects . . . if I had been dominated by one? How would I have preserved my independence and my movements under the advice of a confessor who governed me with the fear of hell?[8]

He insisted that humanitarianism as much as cynicism motivated him: 'It was in making myself Catholic that I ended the war in Vendée; in making myself a Muslim that I established myself in Egypt; in making myself an ultramontane that I won over . . . Italy. If I governed a nation of Jews, I would re-establish Solomon's temple.'[9] His primary concern was that the leaders and followers of any religion practised in France, not just the Catholic majority but also the small pockets of Protestants and Jews, were loyal citizens who paid their taxes and, when called, became soldiers. To that end, he had to undo much of the damage to the Catholic Church and other religions inflicted by the Revolution: 'My first duty is to prevent any poisoning of my people's morality because atheism is the destroyer of all morality not only in individuals but in nations.'[10]

* * *

Naturally Napoleon's most important and contentious relations were with the Catholic Church, given its inseparable history from France itself, its national hierarchy of power and its number of followers. As someone who studied and thought deeply about the Bible, he understood that politics rather than spirituality determined most Catholic Church dogma. For nearly seventeen centuries, Rome's obsession with suppressing and exploiting humanity often grossly violated Jesus's actual moral acts and teachings. He did not mince his words when the Papacy offended him. He saw most Vatican grandees as worldly, hypocritical men bloated with hubris and greed. He relished debating with priests, bishops and even the pope himself over theological questions. The inability of his jousting opponents to defend themselves with anything other than platitudes let alone score with stinging rational attacks solidified his view that his version of theology was superior and that he had to save the Church from itself.

He oversaw the negotiations that led to the concordats of France and Italy with Rome in 1802 and 1803, respectively. In both countries, the government supervised the Church and appointed its bishops. Catholicism was rationalized with only one bishop per department, the consolidation of parishes, the nationalization of most monasteries and convents and the state's administrative and legal supremacy over the Church. In France, he abolished the Revolutionary calendar and re-established the Gregorian calendar, Sunday as a weekly holiday and the four Church holidays of Christmas, Easter, Assumption and All Saints starting on 1 January 1806. The concordats differed in one significant way. In France there was no official religion while Catholicism was Italy's official religion. After the concordat, the Church made a rapid comeback in France. By 1810, there were six cardinals, 11 archbishops, 50 bishops, 212 vicars, 490 canons, 3,348 priests and 24,000 lay assistants. The number of parishes was around 27,000, down from 36,000 before the Revolution but still considerable.[11]

The Catholic Church had either discriminated against or outright persecuted Protestants and Jews for as long as each faith had adherents in France. Of 30 million French people in 1800, Protestants numbered around 200,000 and Jews around 55,000. By 1810, as annexations expanded France to include 44 million people, Protestants now numbered around 900,000 and Jews around 170,000. Napoleon initiated concordats with those faiths. As with Catholicism, two ministries, Cults and Interior, had overlapping jurisdiction over policy toward Protestants and Jews. Months of talks between the government and Protestant groups resulted in a concordant on 8 April 1802. Protestants agreed to bear allegiance to the state and organize into parishes of at least 6,000 adherents in return for enjoying the freedom to worship in designated churches.

Jews intrigued and inspired Napoleon.[12] He was the first European leader to champion rights and opportunities for Jews. In his conquests he unlocked the gates of ghettos and stripped Jews of the yellow stars they were forced to wear. Among his most revolutionary acts was to usher Judaism into the modern world. He understood that because historically Jews 'were prosecuted or hid from prosecution, diverse doctrines and practices appeared'.[13] On 22 July 1806, he called for Jewish leaders to unite in a Grand Sanhedrin or council that had not met since the Romans crushed a Jewish revolt in AD 66. The Grand Sanhedrin would have 111 members dedicated to reconciling Jewish laws and customs with French laws and customs. To guide them, he presented a list of questions that forced them to debate and forge a consensus on their history, theology, institutions, practices and perceptions. Perhaps the most plaintive question was 'in Jewish eyes, were the French brothers or strangers?'[14] To Interior Minister Jean-Baptiste Champagny, he wrote:

> As for the project of organizing a Jewish nation, the Sanhedrin must be reasonable. Convoke it for a period such that I can send away those who are disruptive. It is necessary to separate from the laws of Moses all that is intolerant, to declare a portion of these laws civil and political and to permit religious believers all that is related to morality and the duties of French citizenship.[15]

The Grand Sanhedrin met from 9 February to 9 March 1807. The president was David Sintzheim, Strasbourg's grand rabbi. They achieved a broad consensus on the questions that Napoleon posed to them, but then took another year to hammer out specifics. The government published the results as four decrees between 17 March and 20 July 1808. As with Catholics and Protestants, Jews received full rights to worship within their synagogues in return for pledging loyalty to France's government.[16]

* * *

Napoleon modelled his relationship with Rome to that established by Charlemagne a millennium earlier: 'For the Pope I am Charlemagne because, like Charlemagne, I united the crowns of France and Lombardy . . . I reduced the pope to be the bishop of Rome.'[17] He insisted that Pius and the Church hierarchy recognize that 'I am Charlemagne, the Church's sword and emperor'.[18] He asserted a strict wall of separation between state and church. Citing Jesus's teaching about rendering onto Caesar that due Caesar and rendering to God that due God, he forbad any church interference in civil affairs. Ultimately the state was superior to the church and could do whatever was necessary to maintain public order and tranquillity. He instructed Police Minister Fouché to let the religious orders know that they were under constant surveillance and any adherents that conspired against the Empire would be imprisoned and their property seized. He lumped Jesuits with other radical groups and was determined that they would never return to France.[19] He forced his siblings to confiscate and sell the property of religious orders. When Elisa complained that the priests were preaching sermons against her while Rome was issuing diplomatic protests, he told her to ignore them.[20] He offered this advice to Joseph on how to justify repressing the monasteries: 'The language must be in the spirit of religion rather than philosophy. The grand art of governing is not that of a man of letters or a writer . . . The art is that each edict has the style and character of the affected profession.'[21]

These measures prompted a protest by Pius VII in August 1805 that Napoleon was violating the concordat. Napoleon replied that actually he had acted decisively to save the French Church from 'the philosophical spirit of the century that would have degraded and eventually ruined all religious establishments'. For instance,

> most convents are disorganized and all are under the threat of imminent suppression. I reorganized them, wanting them to continue to exist. In doing so I disputed the philosophical spirit of the age and instead consecrated the principle of the utility of religious institutions . . . As for the parishes, my goal is to render them wealthier . . . Thus I find myself disagreeably affected that . . . after having done all that to the satisfaction of the clergy, Your Holiness is discontented with me.[22]

A crisis erupted in October 1805, when Napoleon ordered General Gouvion St Cyr to occupy Ancona to prevent a potential takeover by a combined British, Russian and Neapolitan fleet. Pius protested that incursion. Napoleon fired back, justifying his occupation and condemning the pope for tolerating the presence of English, Russian, Sardinian and Swedish agents in Rome and their merchants in Papal State ports. He ordered his uncle and ambassador to Rome, Cardinal Joseph Fesch, to oversee the arrests of those agents and merchants and the confiscation of their property. Fesch was also to pressure Cardinal Ercole Consalvi into resigning; Napoleon pegged Consalvi as being most responsible for turning the pope against him.[23] In December 1805, he instructed Fesch to go to Bologna and there 'get tough with Cardinal Consalvi; I want you to straighten him out'.[24]

When Pius issued another protest, the emperor sternly insisted that the pope know his place in a letter of 14 February 1806:

> Your Holiness is the sovereign of Rome. Your relations with me are the same as those of your predecessor with Charlemagne. You are the sovereign of Rome but I am the emperor. My enemies must be yours . . . I will always have filial deference for Your Holiness as our religious head but I am accountable only to

God . . . I know that you want to do well but you are surrounded by men who do not want that, who have bad principles and who, instead of working against evil, work for it.

He tried to reassure Pius that although 'all Italy will submit to my law, I will not touch the Church's independence'.[25] Two months later he warned Pius that he would recall his ambassador if the Vatican remained obdurate. On 14 May 1806, he ordered Fesch to abruptly and publicly leave Rome and turn over affairs to his deputy Charles Alquier.[26] Two reasons motivated the switch. Alquier was far tougher than Fesch and was not a priest and thus beholden to Rome.

The intimidation worked for now. Napoleon ordered French troops to secure key cities and fortresses across the Papal States. These orders to General Jean Lemarois, one of his occupation generals, were typical: 'Seize all military authority without tolerating any interference from the pope's agents and put the port, its surroundings and the forts in a good state of defence.'[27] He insisted that all cardinals, bishops and priests were subject to the sovereign of the country in which they resided. As for Pius VII, 'he will be the bishop of Rome like his predecessors in the eight centuries since Charlemagne'.[28] Although he finally got Consalvi to resign on 17 June 1806, the bitterness among the pope and the church hierarchy swelled. He complained that: 'The court of Rome is behaving badly . . . My intention is to keep Ancona and Civitavecchia' as bases for controlling the central stretches of Italy's west and east coasts.[29] Of course, Rome's alleged 'bad behaviour' might well be attributable to Napoleon's in stripping the pope of his worldly political power and territory.

The attempts by Joseph, Eugène and Elisa to assert the Code Napoleon and confiscatory policies in their respective realms across Italy provoked resistance by prominent and obscure Catholic leaders alike. That in turn enraged Napoleon who vented an extraordinary storm of pent-up venom against the Papacy in a letter to Pius on 22 July 1807:

Do you believe that the rights of the throne are less sacred in the eyes of God than the rights of the tiara? There were kings before there were popes . . . I have benefited religion more than the pope, who has done wrong, not by intention but by following the advice of several irascible men who surround him . . . They want to denounce me as a Christian! This ridiculous thought can only appear from those who are profoundly ignorant of the century in which we live. It is an error a thousand years old. The pope who would carry such a belief would cease to be a pope in my eyes. I would consider him to be the Anti-Christ sent to overthrow the world and inflict evil on mankind . . . The court of Rome has preached rebellion for two years in Lucca and Italy . . . I will cease to recognize the current pope the day I am persuaded that these problems come from him . . . The pope is too powerful. The priests are not made for governing . . . Jesus Christ said his kingdom is not of his world. Why does the pope not want to render to Caesar that which is Caesar's? . . . Is religion founded on anarchy, on civil war and on disobedience? Is that what Jesus taught? The pope menaces me by appealing to my people . . . I hold my crown from God and the will of my people. I am responsible only to God and my people. I will always be Charlemagne for the court of Rome.[30]

A crisis between Paris and Rome erupted in January 1808.[31] Alquier informed Napoleon that a coterie of Ferdinand IV's supporters and British agents were embedded in the Vatican and turning Pius against him, his Italian kingdom and Joseph's Neapolitan kingdom. Napoleon ordered General Alexandre Miollis to march his division into Rome to occupy Castel Sant'Angelo, which protected the Vatican, and arrest the foreign agents and their papal allies, while doing nothing to dishonour the pope. Miollis and his men entered Rome on 2 February. Of his mission, Miollis fully accomplished the first part and partly the second part, but in doing so violated the last part. The emperor had the Papal States split in two along the spine of the Apennine Mountains, with Generals Miollis and Lemarois, respectively, controlling the territory westward and eastward.

The next crisis came in spring 1809. To fight Austria, Napoleon stripped Italy, including Rome, of all but token numbers of troops. In early April, anti-French agents capitalized on that weakness by provoking riots in Rome. Napoleon ordered Miollis to ruthlessly crush the insurrection. He offered these rather chilling instructions to Eugène: 'It is said that Udine's bishop is behaving badly. If so, you must have him shot; it is finally time to make examples of these priests.'[32] The bishop escaped execution.

Napoleon decreed on 17 May, that the Papal States were henceforth annexed to France and would be divided into departments. He had a hand-picked consulate govern, gendarmes assume police functions, his Civil Code replace existing laws and military commissions judge and execute any rebels, all under the shadow of Miollis and his troops. He issued these instructions: 'The military commissions must assert justice against the monks and other agents who carry themselves to excess. One of the consulate's first measures is to suppress the inquisition.'[33] He wrote to Miollis: 'I have entrusted you to maintain Rome's tranquillity. You must not suffer any obstacle. You must judge before a military commission all individuals who act contrary to the army's security; you must have arrested, even in the pope's palace, all those who plot against public tranquillity and the security of my soldiers.'[34]

Miollis lowered the papal flag and raised the French atop Castel Sant'Angelo on 10 June 1809. Two days later, on 12 June, Pius VII issued this statement: 'We declare that Napoleon I, Emperor of the French and all his adherents, troublemakers and advisors have incurred the excommunication that had previously been threatened.'[35] Meanwhile, Napoleon authorized Neapolitan King Joachim Murat to govern the Papal States and, on 17 June ordered him to have Cardinal Bartolomeo Pacca arrested and sent to France. 'As for the pope, if he resists, one need not pay more attention to him than to an ordinary bishop.'[36] Two days later he added: 'If the pope, contrary to the spirit of his state and the evangels, preaches revolt and violates his palace's immunity to print proclamations and seed trouble, you must arrest him.'[37] Napoleon was furious when he got word of his excommunication on 20 June. He wrote these fatal words to Murat: 'I learned that the pope excommunicated us. That is a great folly . . . He is a madman that must be locked up . . . Have arrested Cardinal Pacca and all his adherents.'[38]

The snatch came on the night of 5 July, when General Étienne Radet with 240 gendarmes barged into the Quirinale Palace, shoved aside several cardinals shielding Pius and hauled him away. After learning the results of Radet's operation, Napoleon claimed that: 'I am angry that they have arrested the pope; that is a great folly. They should arrest Pacca and leave the pope tranquilly at Rome. But there is no remedy. What is done is done.' He again called for arresting Pacca and warning him that 'if a single Frenchman is assassinated by the effect of his instigations, he will be the first who pays with his head'.[39]

As for Pius, Napoleon wanted him brought neither to France nor returned to Rome. He ordered him taken to Savona, 24 miles west of Genoa, and kept in the bishop's palace, where he could wander freely but would be cut off from all outside communication. He deemed 400 infantry and 50 cavalry sufficient to guard Pius. He believed that 'the pope is a good man but ignorant and fanatical'.[40] He had those in charge 'take care that the pope lacks nothing'.[41] He wrote to Miollis that although, 'I am angry that the pope was taken from Rome . . . I am satisfied with your zeal. The pope will never again enter Rome.'[42] The pope's arrest should not have surprised him. At best his instructions to Murat and Miollis were ambiguous. His subordinates could be forgiven for believing that their emperor was giving them the wink, nod and nudge equivalent of Henry II's cry, 'who will rid me of this turbulent priest!'[43]

As elsewhere, a huge bill followed closely on the heels of French 'liberation' of the Papal States from despotism and feudalism. Although Napoleon insisted that 'the annexation of Rome is not an affair of finance but of high politics', he still imposed a contribution of four million francs on his new subjects.[44] At the same time he had missionary orders in France dissolved. His excuse was that 'I want religion in my realm, but do not want to convert anyone'.[45] The real reason was that the orders sided with Pius against him. On 26 September, he ordered all the monasteries and convents closed across his Italian realm.

Pius held a trump card in the face of his imprisonment and Napoleon's annexation of the Papal States. Everything that the emperor did made the pope's excommunication of him appear more reasonable in the eyes of Catholics and countless Protestants and that damaged his legitimacy. Napoleon's only chance of getting Pius to revoke the excommunication would be to return Rome and the Papal States to the situation in January 1809 and he had no intention of doing that. So he was stuck. His conquest of the Papal States had at once enhanced his hard power and diminished his soft power.

Napoleon's next act against Pius came in May 1812 after he learned that two British warships were off Savona. Fearing that the British might try to rescue Pius, he had him transferred to Fontainebleau Palace for safekeeping. Worried about the disastrous public relations results if Pius died while in his custody, he ordered an excellent doctor and surgeon to attend Pius. He provided Pius with a court of five cardinals and four priests.[46]

Napoleon's Russian catastrophe in 1812 forced him to rethink several long-standing policies of which one was toward the Papacy. Eleven days after returning to Paris, he displayed toward Pius newfound flexibility if not outright humility: 'I have always conserved the same friendship for yourself. Perhaps we can arrive at the goal of wanting to end all differences that divide the state and church. As for me, I am strongly disposed, but that depends entirely on Your Holiness.'[47] Three weeks later, on 19 January 1813, Napoleon, Marie Louise and their son paid Pius an unexpected visit and embraced him with affection. Pius was touched and eagerly agreed when Napoleon suggested that they forge a new concordat. On 25 January 1813, Napoleon and Pius signed the Treaty of Fontainebleau whereby France's emperor and Italy's king acknowledged the Papacy's spiritual authority in those realms, the Papacy could resume its international diplomatic relations, Napoleon would forgive and release any cardinals, archbishops, bishops and priests that he had incarcerated and the pope alone could fill the Church's hierarchy in the Papal States.[48] The emperor's pardon backfired when some of the more bitter cardinals like Pacca and Consalvi urged Pius to repudiate the treaty, which he did on 24 March 1813. Napoleon was livid but could do nothing more than keep Pius at Fontainebleau for safekeeping.

Napoleon changed his policy toward the pope if not the Papacy after his German catastrophe in 1813 and in the shadow of the pending Allied invasion of France. On 23 January 1814, just days before he hurried to the front, he had Pius VII released and returned to Rome. It was a conciliatory gesture to an old man whom he respected and liked. Pius's nearly five-year exile ended after he reached Rome on 24 May, a few weeks after Napoleon began his exile on Elba.

Chapter 17

The Titan

'The glory of my regime consists in changing the face of my empire's territory.'

'I had plenty of ships but no sailors. I was struggling with England to force it to make peace. For that all I had was the Continental System.'

'Despite the resources that I draw from conquered countries . . . according to my ministers' budgets, I eat all my revenues.'

'The future generation must not suffer from the hatreds and petty passions of the present generation.'

Napoleon's empire consisted of four parts.[1] He directly governed France that he expanded far beyond its natural frontiers from 83 departments and 29 million people in 1790 to 102 departments and 34 million people after his Treaty of Campo Formio with Austria in 1797, then with additional conquests, 134 departments and 44 million people in 1812. The biggest expansion of French territory came in 1809 and 1810 to engulf Illyria, composed of Dalmatia and large parts of Croatia, Carinthia, Carniola and Tyrol; north-west and western Italy except for the Grand Duchy of Tuscany was divided into fifteen departments; Spain's provinces of Catalonia, Aragon, Navarre and Biscay stretching broadly from the Mediterranean to the Atlantic; and all of Holland. He was also the King of Italy whose territory engulfed most of northern and eastern Italy and included five million people; his stepson Eugène governed Italy on his behalf. Then there were the kingdoms and principalities that he made and distributed to his siblings like Holland for Louis until the annexation, Naples and then Spain for Joseph, Berg and Cleves then Naples for Caroline, Westphalia for Jérôme and Piombino and Lucca then Tuscany for Elisa. Finally, there was the puppet Confederation of the Rhine with its 39 member states and 14 million people and quasi-puppet Grand Duchy of Warsaw with 3.8 million people. The empire's formal seat of government was the Tuileries in Paris but was really wherever the emperor happened to be. Napoleon spent many long days administering his realm from the palaces of the Grand Trianon at Versailles, Saint-Cloud, Malmaison, Fontainebleau and Compiègne in the countryside within a day or two of Paris and from each headquarters when he was on campaign.

* * *

Napoleon envisioned Paris as the new Rome of a great empire. Not all roads may have led to Paris, but twenty-seven converged there. Indeed he even mulled installing the papal seat in Paris but never pulled it off. For the emperor, the circulation of information was as critical as commerce on that network. He had a system of couriers and relay stations established that conveyed dispatches from Paris to his empire's far reaches in days and, even more astonishing, a semaphore system deployed that in clear weather transmitted a message from Paris to Strasbourg in six hours, to Brest in eight hours and to Milan in twenty-four hours.

Paris's population swelled during his brief era, from 546,586 in 1801 to 622,631 in 1811, much smaller than London's 1,000,000 inhabitants but much larger than Naples's 430,000, Moscow's 300,000, Vienna's 250,000, St Petersburg's 220,000, Amsterdam's 217,000, Dublin's 195,000, Berlin's 172,000, Madrid's 168,000 and Rome's 153,000.[2] Paris then had twelve *arrondissements* or districts, each with its own mayor appointed by Napoleon. Paris also had its own police prefect, Louis Dubois until 1810 then Étienne Pasquier. The emperor may have loved his capital but he was not terribly fond of Parisians whom he found 'ungrateful and cold'.[3]

Throughout Napoleon's 15 years in power, transforming Paris into a capital worthy of his imperial dreams was among his most cherished obsessions. Half a century before Baron Georges Haussmann, he began bringing fresh air, water, elbow-room and elegance to a cramped, fetid, medieval city via long boulevards, arcades, squares, fountains, pavement, bridges, street lights, sewers and monuments. He worked carefully with architects and engineers to ensure that each project was an affordable mix of beauty, function and harmony with its surroundings. He expressed his approach with these lines: 'What architectural style should be followed? Architects would want adopted a single style . . . Opinions vary considerably over questions of economy, common sense and good taste. It is necessary to let each existing section whose character reflects its century, be adapted by new work in the most economical genre. At the same time it is important to align the styles.'[4] Two ancient civilizations dominated his empire's style, Rome for the buildings and Egypt for the furniture.

Napoleon's architectural legacy is impressive.[5] With the Arch of Titus in Rome as the model, he had constructed the magnificent Arc du Carousel at the Louvre Palace's west end. From there the Champs-Élysées slopes gently upward for a mile and a half to a low ridge upon which he had built the even more stunning Arc de Triomph as a monument to the army with the names of the greatest generals and victories chiselled in stone. The Arc du Carousel was inaugurated on his birthday in 1810, but he saw only the foundations laid for his Arc de Triomph which would not be finished until 1836. He had the bronze cannons captured during his Austerlitz campaign transformed into curved sheets with scenes commemorating the Grand Army and attached to a huge column in the Place Vendôme, capped by a stature of himself. He expanded the Louvre Palace with a section built around a square. He had nearly the north side of a kilometre of the Rue de Rivoli covered and lined with an arcade. He had high quays erected to tame the Seine River in central Paris. He celebrated commerce with two new buildings, a rectangular Roman-style edifice for the Bank of France and a circular building for the Stock Exchange. He ordered the completion of the Madeleine Church, designed like a giant Greek temple, which was begun during the Revolution. He had erected fifteen stately fountains whose waters gushed day and night for thirsty Parisians. He had eight markets created so that Parisians were never far from haggling for food, clothing, fuel and other goods from hordes of vendors. He had six huge warehouses erected to store provisions if the harvests failed. He had three new bridges added to the existing twelve. He had the Canal d'Orouq dug to connect the Seine and Marne Rivers. To ensure that his new works were as beautiful as they were functional, he hired such outstanding architects as Charles Percier, Jean Chalgrin, Pierre Fontaine and Alexandre Brogniart. Beyond Paris he ordered triumphal arches erected at the entrances to Metz and Nancy in eastern France to hearten his troops as they marched to or from their latest campaign. He intended that his grand building projects would stimulate a renaissance of arts and crafts or as he put it: 'I want the triumphant arches to nourish for ten years French sculpture.'[6]

Napoleon revelled in all these projects: 'The glory of my regime consists in changing the face of my empire's territory.'[7] He intended the changes he brought to Paris to serve as the model for the rest of his realm. For that, in March 1805, he had each prefect conduct a three-month study of his department 'to furnish all information . . . that could interest the government' on questions of the effectiveness of administration, justice and taxation; conditions of roads, canals and bridges; attitudes toward conscription, taxation and religion; the quality of education in the schools; the state of agriculture, industry and commerce; and individuals with outstanding merits who should be recognized and nurtured. Each report should conclude with practical recommendations for improving all these dimensions of the nation.[8]

Napoleon promoted measures to reward innovation and invention. For instance, amid the stresses of his 1807 campaign, he found time to consider then instruct Interior Minister Champagny to place 'in the Institute the statue of [Jean] d'Alembert, who among French mathematicians of the last century, contributed the most to this first among the sciences'. Champagny was formally to present the statue before the Institute's assembled members 'to reveal proof of our esteem and constant will to accord funds and encouragement to the work of this community, which is so important for the prosperity of our people'.[9] In June 1807, he initiated an annual 12,000-franc prize for the individual or group that through theory or practice contributed the most to fighting diseases.[10] His patronage of innovation transcended nationality. For instance, he enthusiastically supported the attempts of American Robert Fulton to develop a steamboat 'that could change the face of the world'. He had a commission formed to examine the ideas and inventions of Fulton and other visionaries: 'A grand truth, a concrete, palpable truth, is before our eyes. It will be for these gentlemen to see and seize it.'[11]

He tried to modernize every realm that he conquered. He took enormous pride in the law code whose writing he had overseen and sought to impose it throughout his empire. Amid his 1806 campaign in Prussia and Poland, he wrote to Louis that: 'I am sending you the decrees whereby I have organized the mail, customs and gendarmerie of the Hanseatic cities. I want you to do the same in East Frisia . . . I hope that you have taken the same steps for Amsterdam and Rotterdam.'[12] He also encouraged the promotion of the arts and sciences. He granted his Italian kingdom a priceless gift in May 1808, when he had Eugène establish Italian Institutes in Milan, Pavia, Bologna, Padua and Venice, modelled on the French Institute in Paris. In each, the region's leading savants met for enlightened discussion, research and publication.[13]

French was obviously the language of the Empire. Most nobles and many merchants were already proficient in that tongue, a skill that Napoleon intended to imbue in all his subjects. For instance, he had Archchancellor Cambacérès 'demand of Genoa that all marriage contracts are made in French'. Ideally, Genoans would be able to express themselves in Italian or French so that they never have to sign or obey documents that they did not understand.[14]

* * *

Napoleon's power was never quite absolute. He recognized the importance of keeping at least a semblance of republican institutions to mask his dictatorship. His constitution gave the various legislatures mostly the power to say or vote contrary to what he wanted although he was free to ignore what they did. Police Minister Fouché's advice that he take away even that measly power angered him. He complained to Archchancellor Cambacérès: 'Does he think I must decimate the Senate? Does he not understand the Constitution? Does he not know that I have no complaints against anyone in that body which does not cease to give me proofs of its loyalty?' He wondered if Fouché's advice had some ulterior motive, that in curbing the Senate's power in the name of state security he actually hoped to undermine it by creating resentment and dissent among the senators that currently did not exist.[15] He sharply reprimanded him: 'Have you lost your head? . . . Repress the confusion rather than make it. Calm public opinion instead of agitating it. Be the superior and not the rival of your subordinates . . . Imitate your colleagues who help me instead of fatigue me and who make the government work, while curtailing their private passions.'[16]

The paradox of running a police state is figuring out how to police the police. Napoleon tried to finesse that perennial problem with multiple, overlapping authorities. Each morning he studied intelligence, crime and political reports from the Police, Interior, Justice and War Ministries which competed to be as accurate, in-depth and comprehensive as possible. Paris had its own police chief who reported directly to Napoleon rather than the Police Minister. Then there was the Gendarmerie, an elite mobile military force formally under the War Ministry but always at Napoleon's command for 'special operations'. To head these institutions, he tapped mostly men that he trusted like René Savary, Étienne Pasquier and Pierre Real, who in turn eyed Joseph Fouché, a man who was impossible to trust completely but was brilliant at his profession. Yet, despite all this, the emperor's authority was not impregnable. The worst security breach was the coup attempt led by Claude Malet and a small cabal on 22 and 23 October 1812, while Napoleon was just withdrawing from Moscow. Wielding forged documents, the conspirators briefly took over the police ministry and city hall and seized Savary and Pasquier before other authorities overpowered and arrested them.

For Napoleon the previous monarchy offered many lessons on how not to rule a country. If that regime's decadence ultimately doomed it, then Napoleon insisted on a no-nonsense imperial court of stately ceremonies designed to mould 'a new man' of integrity, loyalty and courage, free from the extremes of both the Bourbons and the Revolutionaries. The result was a boring court drained of wit and fun. It was especially tedious for young people who wanted to gossip, dance and flirt. At one point Napoleon actually denounced Hortense and her friends for being too animated: 'In another time all that might have been charming. At present that is inappropriate. A princess must give the example of marching with her century. We are not in the time of amiable and frivolous things. One must only be grave and serious.'[17] That killjoy attitude actually undermined his power by alienating those who would have adored him had he been light-hearted and open-minded.

Two districts or *faubourgs* in Paris symbolized very different but potential sources of dissent and outright rebellion, the Jacobin-leaning Saint Antoine and the royalist-leaning Saint Germain. The Faubourg Saint Antoine was a largely working-class area on the right bank near the Bastille's ruins. During the Revolution mobs from Saint Antoine, swelled with radicals from other districts, had attacked and destroyed the Bastille as a symbol of oppression, marched to Versailles and forced the king, queen and their court to return to Paris, massacred the Swiss guards at the Tuileries and committed other atrocities. For now they were bitter and sharp-tongued but cowed amidst their grinding poverty and suppression. On the left bank the Faubourg Saint Germain was a rich, stylish neighbourhood whose salons were animated by acerbic wits who found plenty to ridicule in the emperor and his regime. Napoleon ensured that spies infiltrated both worlds.

Not surprisingly, censorship under Emperor Napoleon exceeded that under First Consul Bonaparte. All along he was Janus-faced, at once acclaiming and crushing freedom of the press. He insisted to Fouché that: 'I wish that censorship did not exist . . . I do not want to censor.'[18] Although he repeatedly had Fouché tighten the screws, he was genuinely perplexed over how far to restrict press freedoms. He complained that 'the newspapers are generally badly managed. It may be difficult to remedy that.' He then went down a list of newspapers and pointed out the flaws of each. He insisted that 'I do not want to re-establish the law of lese-majesty . . . However, I do not want to let a newspaper speak for the Bourbons.'[19] He offered this Orwellian justification for suppressing and manipulating the press: 'Newspaper reform will soon take place because it is too monstrous to have newspapers that only enjoy freedom of the press without any responsibility and that from malevolence or incompetence hawk all the rumours that alarm commerce and always favour English interests . . . Today it is no more a question of being not bad, but of being completely good.'[20]

He preferred self-censorship to censorship. He usually had Fouché warn newspaper owners not to print anything that they would regret. For instance, in July 1809, he was angry to read alarming articles in the *Gazette de France* that Prussia was about to declare war, that Russia was against France and that Italy was revolting: 'Let the editor-in-chief of this newspaper know that I will suppress it if it continues to print such articles . . . In general our newspapers are always ready to seize upon anything that damages the public tranquillity and gives false ideas of our position.'[21] If self-censorship failed, then he would embed in that newspaper 'two or three' editors 'to read the articles and extract all that would not be good to print . . . I will suppress newspapers whose editor is the dupe of rumours and prints harmful articles.'[22] Eventually he had official 'editors' examine each word of each article before it was published, then 'suggest' changes to the publication's own editor. An imperial decree of 2 August 1810 reorganized special-interest publications into strict divisions among literature, art, science and agriculture and forbad them any political commentary. As if all this were not enough, he also dictated and planted his own essays in the newspapers. He offered this justification for doing so: 'It is with official articles that wise, truly talented men write history. These articles are full of me and they are what I solicited and invoked.'[23] Here the emperor mistakes propaganda for history. Defying Napoleon could even be deadly. In August 1806, he had a Nuremburg publisher named Johann Palm tried and executed for refusing to reveal the author of an anti-French book that he had printed.

The number of daily newspapers dwindled to six, *Le Moniteur*, *Le Journal des Débats*, *Le Journal de Paris*, *La Gazette de France*, *Le Journal de l'Empire* and *Le Publiciste*, along with the weekly *Mercure de France*, then to five in 1810 when *La Gazette de France* and *Le Publiciste* merged. Of the survivors, the most prominent were *Le Moniteur*, which was essentially the government's mouthpiece, and *Le Journal des Débats*, which published lively, provocative pieces that skirted the edge of what the emperor considered acceptable. From 1799 to 1813, the former's readership rose from 3,500 to 9,400, while the latter's soared from 800 to 20,000.[24] Those figures are hardly surprising since Napoleon had shut down scores of other newspapers leaving readers with little choice but what was left.

Napoleon also censored books that he feared threatened his regime and shut down shops that sold them. He decreed on 5 February 1810 that from 1 January 1811, licences would be renewed for only twenty publishers in Paris and sixty across the departments. That drastically accelerated the decline of Parisian publishers that had numbered 221 in 1799. He even had plays censored either by having offending passages rewritten with politically-correct messages or preventing them from being staged. Censorship was the overlapping duty of the rival Interior and Police Ministries. In their zeal they slammed publishers with a double whammy of intrusions and inhibitions. The censors rejected 81 and corrected 168 of 697 proposed works in 1811; rejected 30 and corrected 43 of 720 in 1812; and rejected 14 and corrected 2 of 585 in 1813. As for plays, of more than 3,000 submitted from 1800 to 1815, around 7 per cent had to be rewritten.[25] His efforts to stamp out any possible dissent extended far beyond France. For instance, in March 1809, he complained to Joseph about the publication in Madrid of a literary review in a newspaper that, in debating the novel *Don Quixote*, appeared unfavourably to compare the policies of France and former king Charles III in progressively governing Spain. He feared that such debates, if allowed to persist under the guise of literature, could erode the legitimacy of Joseph's monarchy. So the emperor ordered the king to suppress the newspaper.[26] Not surprisingly, his 15 years in power were not a high point for French literature. Perhaps the most enduring works of fiction are René Chateaubriand's *l'Atala* (1801), and *René* (1802) and Germaine de Staël's *Delphine* (1802) and in non-fiction Destrutt de Tracy's *Les Elements d'Ideologie* (1801), Maine de Biran's *l'Influence de l'habitude sur la faculté de penser* (1802) and de Vilers' *l'Exposition de la Philosophe du Kant* (1801). All these works appeared when he was First Consul.

Paris had a vibrant theatre culture with three grand venues – the Theatre Française, Opera and Opera Comique – and twenty-five secondary theatres. Napoleon loved the theatre and as emperor attended 682 performances of 374 plays, of which 177 were tragedies and the rest comedies, operas or ballets.[27] As with everything that interested him, he got involved even to the point of intervening in a squabble among rival showbusiness egos. He gripped to Fouché that 'I am discontented with the opera leaders. Make it known to director Bone that his intrigues will not succeed with me. I do not see why Boutron wants to prevent the others from earning their bread and is so exclusive. I beg you to put an end to all this.'[28] More nefariously, from February 1810, he reviewed any proposed productions of plays and operas to ensure that no works that he deemed subversive were produced. The staging of *Mort d'Abel* prompted this policy. He let the production continue but thereafter rejected any works with allegorical themes that imaginative viewers might interpret as criticizing his rule.[29] And most infamously, Napoleon ended up alienating the greatest musical genius of that age or any other. Ludwig van Beethoven deeply admired his fellow genius Bonaparte for his military, economic and legal triumphs as a general and First Consul. He dedicated his third symphony to Bonaparte only to burn the dedication page after learning that he had become Emperor Napoleon I. Nonetheless, Beethoven's music provides the soundtrack for the Age of Napoleon.

Napoleon believed in art for power's stake, not in art for art's sake.[30] For him the propaganda value of a painting, sculpture, musical score or monument exceeded its aesthetic value. In August 1805, he explained to advisor Pierre Daru that: 'My intention is to turn the arts toward subjects that perpetuate memories of what has taken place over the past fifteen years.'[31] And to that end he was happy to be generous. The Imperial Library alone yearly distributed 200,000 francs to commission various artworks. His refurbishing of what would become his imperial chateaux like Versailles, Compiègne, Fontainebleau and others provided steady work for furniture makers like François Jacob-Desmalter and Pierre Levasseur, goldsmiths and silversmiths like Martine Biennais and jewellers like Étienne Nitot along with the porcelain production at Sèvres and tapestry production at Gobelins and La Savonnerie. One positive element of French rule was when Napoleon's satellite rulers emulated their master by opening their own public art museums like what became Milan's Brera Museum begun by Eugène, Naples's Capodimonte by Joachim and Amsterdam's Rijksmuseum by Louis.

Two paintings of Napoleon crossing the Saint Bernard pass during his 1800 campaign illustrate the stark contrast between propaganda and history paintings. Louis David's stunning official vision depicted Napoleon on a rearing white horse with the snow-capped Alps in the background; his red cape is flowing and he fiercely glares at the viewer as he points toward a rock upon which his name is chiselled above those of Hannibal and Charlemagne. The version by Paul Delaroche depicted a freezing Bonaparte mounted on a mule amidst deep snow. Delaroche's painting revealed what actually happened, David's painting revealed what Napoleon wanted the world to believe had happened. Delaroche's version was not possible during Napoleon's time and was actually painted in 1849.

After becoming emperor, he continued his education reforms that he began as First Consul.[32] On 15 December 1805, he declared that he was adopting the children of all the fathers that died at Austerlitz and would educate them at imperial lycées. Not surprisingly, he paid the closest attention to l'École Spéciale Militaire, which he installed at Fontainebleau in 1802, then moved to St Cyr in 1808. On 11 March 1806, he first proposed founding an imperial university but did not issue decrees for doing so until 17 March and 17 September 1808. He inaugurated the *baccalaureate* or university entrance examination system in 1809.

Meanwhile, he opened a lycée for girls at Ecouen, outside of Paris, in 1807. However he sought to educate them with traditional rather than modern values. His justification for doing so revealed his own very traditional values:

> What will be taught to the girls that will be students at Ecouen?... The weakness of women's brains, the mobility of their ideas, their destination in the social order, the necessity of constant and perpetual resignation and a sort of indulgent and easy charity, all that can only be obtained by religion, by a religion charitable and sweet... I want girls to graduate who are not just very agreeable but virtuous... Students must also learn to calculate, write, know the principles of their language and finally learn orthography. They should learn a little geography and history but... not Latin or another foreign language... Dance is necessary for the health of the students... and also music but only vocal training... Of all the educations, the best is that from mothers... My intention is principally to come to the aide of girls who lost their mothers or whose parents are poor... I am assured that the establishment will arrive at the most solid, highest reputation.[33]

These reforms significantly advanced the structure if not the achievements of education in France. By 1808, there were about 900,000 students enrolled in 31,000 primary schools, 50,000 students in 750 secondary schools and 15,000 students in 35 lycées, along with about 25,000 students in private secular schools and 18,000 students in Catholic schools. Schools for the arts also flourished; the Conservatory of Arts counted 300 students by 1810. The literacy rate, however, improved only modestly from 1789 to 1815, with boys rising from 47 per cent to 54 per cent and girls from 27 per cent to 34 per cent.[34]

For Napoleon a critical element of schooling was promoting patriotism. He wrote to Fouché that:

> I am informed that émigré families withhold their children from conscription... It is a fact that the ancient, rich families that are

not in the system are obviously against it. I want you to make a list of the ten principal families from each department and the fifty for Paris and include each member's age, fortune and physical condition. I intend to decree that all the young men aged at least sixteen years who belong to these families attend St. Cyr military school . . . The future generation must not suffer from the hatreds and petty passions of the present generation.[35]

* * *

Napoleon hoped eventually to develop his empire's economy with the same policies that he wielded in France. The trouble was that his military needs continually clouded his economic vision. He drained his empire of troops and treasure rather than stimulated its economy by investing in its infrastructure and industries. Yet he did launch some development projects, most notably in his Italian kingdom. He genuinely believed that his conquests brought enlightenment to the conquered. Surely his subjects would recognize that replacing feudalism with modern administration and law was worth the extraction of the taxes that paid for it and the troops that protected it. Alas, most of his subjects failed to make that connection. Instead, they bitterly resented the French for depleting their wealth and young men. Napoleon faced a chronic problem of subversion across his empire. Plotters mushroomed no matter how many arrests, interrogations and executions his swelling police state made.

The worst source of discontent was Napoleon's Continental System or severance of trade with Britain that he established and strengthened with the Berlin Decree of 21 November 1806, the Fontainebleau Decree of 13 October 1807 and the Milan Decree of 17 December 1807, then expanded across most of the rest of Europe by treaties with Russia, Prussia, Austria, the Confederation of the Rhine, the Duchy of Warsaw, Italy, Naples and Spain. His justification for doing so was simple but tough to refute: 'I had plenty of ships but no sailors. I was struggling with England to force it to make peace. For that all I had was the Continental System.'[36]

The Continental System had schizophrenic results.[37] Ports withered economically to ghosts of their former selves as ships rotted at anchor, warehouses and shops emptied and knots of jobless angry sailors, artisans, carpenters and makers of sails, ropes and other products loitered in the streets and taverns. Smuggling provided only very limited relief to those few who conveyed or could afford to buy the goods at sky-high prices. Inland, however, existing factories ramped up production and entrepreneurs started new businesses to serve the demand for goods that once emanated from Britain. In France, industrial production steadily surpassed that of the 1780s which revolutionary excesses had diminished during the 1790s. Less successful were efforts to grow crops or substitutes for products that once came from tropical colonies. In France, Napoleon allocated public funds to help underwrite the production of cotton and indigo, chicory for coffee and sugar beets for sugar. Although cotton production quintupled from 1795 to 1815, it never matched demand so prices soared. As for trade, the Continental System eventually tipped the balance in 1811 from chronic deficits into surpluses that lasted until 1816. Customs revenues, however, plummeted from 60 million francs in 1807 to 11 million in 1809.[38]

Then there were the political effects, of which all undermined the empire. The blockade magnified latent royalism in French ports like Bordeaux, Nantes, La Rochelle, Le Havre and Toulon that especially depended on the colonial and slave trade. The higher prices for goods and crackdown on smuggling provoked widespread resentment among all rulers including those that Napoleon placed on thrones. Indeed, Napoleon eventually deposed his own brother Louis for turning a blind eye to smuggling.

The emperor could not even prevent violations under his very nose. He was annoyed to learn that Josephine had wielded her charms to sweet-talk a key official into violating the Continental System on her behalf. He wrote to the Finance Minister that: 'I learned that the customs director allowed the entrance of merchandise prohibited as contraband under the pretext that the empress ordered them . . . All that concerns the empress and my family must especially be brought to my attention . . . When laws weigh heavily on society everyone must give an example of following them.'[39]

And eventually Napoleon himself succumbed. He issued a decree on 3 July 1810 that contradicted his Continental System's law and spirit. Henceforth, entrepreneurs could purchase licences to trade an ever-longer list of products with Britain. He did so to ease the worsening economic situation across ever more of his empire. The ports suffered from chronic depression. Natural disasters like planting season frosts and deluges sharply reduced harvests from 1810 to 1813 and caused food costs to soar. Less trade meant fewer revenues. The licences would at once raise revenues, profits, employment and supplies of goods. Ironically, Napoleon's policy may have rescued Britain's economy and thus its government's political will to keep fighting when both were on the ropes.

* * *

Napoleon could only fume that his domination of Europe would be incomplete as long as Britain stayed in the fight. The Royal Navy was as invincible at sea as the emperor was on land. Indeed, it was hard enough before Trafalgar and virtually impossible afterwards for the French navy regularly to deliver troops and supplies to its dwindling number of West and East Indian colonies, let alone square off with British squadrons in the surrounding waters. The Royal Navy's blockade of French ports was overwhelming and nearly seamless. Frigates and privateering vessels might slip through on dark nights with favourable winds to raid enemy shipping but large squadrons faced destruction if they sailed forth. Napoleon would have Marine Minister Decrès draw up plans for large-scale naval expeditions only to scrap them as Decrès explained the near-impossible odds against their success.

Napoleon hoped that after Russia declared war against Britain in December 1807, the Royal Navy would have to stretch its deployment of warships thinner to extend its blockade to Russia.[40] He had Decrès issue standing orders for his fleet commanders to prepare to exploit any opportunities to sail on long-standing missions. But the blockade remained as formidable as ever. Only a small expedition to supply Corfu was able to slip through. He then had 'twenty frigates depart, two by two, to cruise to the world's far corners' and ravage British shipping along the way.[41] Meanwhile, he had new warships built with the long-term vision that one not so distant year the French navy would be strong enough to defeat the British navy.

French naval operations in 1809 got off with a big bang in January when Napoleon ordered French warships in each port to fire thirty shots to celebrate the British expulsion from Spain; the gesture's only likely effect was to puzzle those manning the blockading British warships. Although an expedition did succeed in landing 500 reinforcements at Guadeloupe in March, more colonial strongholds fell, Guyana on 12 January and Santo Domingo on 7 July. In late September, Napoleon authorized Decrès to organize three expeditions. One would sail from Rochefort with 5,000 troops and supplies to reinforce Guadeloupe and then retake Isle des Saints. Another would sail from Lorient with 1,200 troops to retake Guyana. The third would sail from Cherbourg to retake Senegal then head on to resupply Isle de France in the Indian Ocean.[42] The stifling blockade ensured that none of these expeditions sailed.

* * *

Bitterly Napoleon recognized that his empire trapped him in a vicious circle. He needed troops to keep order, but troops cost money which was raised with taxes, which caused more disorder, which demanded more troops to suppress and taxes to pay for that suppression and so on. The Continental System compounded that vicious circle by economically devastating ports and their adjacent regions and embittering millions of people against him. It also deprived him of tariff revenues which he made up for with higher taxes.

He admitted in January 1808, that 'I have a great need for troops and money. My armies are in Portugal, Spain, Naples, Dalmatia and Germany and to my 800,000 men under arms, I just drafted another 80,000. Despite the resources that I draw from conquered countries . . . according my ministers' budgets, I eat all my revenues.'[43] That dilemma metastasized during the 1809 war against Austria. After returning to Paris on 15 November, after an absence of seven months, he was dismayed to find 'my financial affairs badly in disarray, the English expedition cost me 30 million francs. The new levies and the immense armaments that I made for Spain continue to ruin me . . . I cannot reduce at all the burden of my Italian kingdom.'[44] He complained to War Minister Clarke in December 1809 that: 'My expenses are enormous. Today we must think seriously of reforms. My army in its present form consumes three times the revenues of France.'[45]

French Budgets (Millions of Francs)[46]

	1805	1806	1807	1808	1809	1810	1811	1812	1813	1814
Civil	266	294	286	286	275	271	334	343	250	110
Military	438	582	459	492	506	480	663	722	723	546
Total	704	876	745	778	781	751	997	1,065	973	656

Year after year revenues fell further behind spending.[47] Napoleon took some preliminary steps in 1810 to trim if not cut expenses. He had Clark 'spread the word that all budgets must be made on the hypothesis of . . . peace in Germany and . . . war in Spain'.[48] He put his army in Italy on a peace footing and his army in Illyria on a half-peace footing. He ordered 'a report on all the possible savings concerning security, the peace with Vienna, our position in Germany and our continuing war in Spain. Significant savings should be made by the administration's employees.'[49]

Budget cutbacks posed their own dilemma. Although wars are destructive, military spending does stimulate the economy as soldiers shell out money in taverns and brothels, while the war and navy ministries pay for armaments, provisions, uniforms, construction and countless of other needs. Much of the civilian budget was invested in developing infrastructure that bolstered economic growth and thus revenues. From 1804 to 1814, the infrastructure budget was 799,599,055 francs, of which 30,605,000 was invested in bridges, 122,588,000 in canals, 62,055 in palaces, 102,421,000 in Parisian construction projects, 277,485,000 on roads, 117,329,000 in ports and 149,000,000 in diverse other works.[50] But all that infrastructure spending could at best only partly fill the economic chasm caused by the Continental System.

* * *

Somewhere well into a decade of marriage, Napoleon and Josephine settled into a relationship of mutual affection and understanding.[51] She mitigated his rages with tenderness and reason. He still passionately loved her and she knew how to fulfil his passion. He sent this sweet message to her when she was taking the waters at Plombières: 'I love you as much as our first day because you are good and amiable above all.'[52] He reassured her that

> your happiness is inseparable from mine. The feelings that you have inspired in me so long ago cannot be changed except by you . . . My life is composed of many sorrows, but only your sweet, amiable and uninhibited nature makes it bearable . . . My destiny is to always love you . . . My intention is to console you, my desire is to please you, my will is to love you.[53]

Relations between them certainly benefited when Josephine stopped cheating on Napoleon after he returned from Egypt and seized power. Their marriage became traditional; she sublimated her sexuality with extravagant shopping trips while he released his with a series of flings and mistresses. She half-heartedly tried but failed to accept the double standard with Gallic resignation. Although he was discreet, she had spies in his camp. Rumours inevitably seeped back to her from wherever he was, even the wilds of Poland. She made her displeasure known as she pestered him if they were true. He replied with affection, flattery and humour: 'I love only my little Josephine, good, sulky and capricious, who knows how to quarrel with grace along with all else she does, except when she is jealous and she becomes a complete demoness.'[54]

A critical point in their relationship came in 1809, during his weeks at the Schönbrunn palace as peace talks dragged on between France and Austria. Napoleon was increasingly antsy. He was torn between wanting to wrap up a treaty then hurry back to Paris and lingering at the Schönbrunn where Marie Walewska had journeyed all the way from Warsaw to share his nights. Josephine's jealousy flared when the gossip reached Paris, especially after Napoleon summoned his doctor, Jean Corvisart, to examine Marie for a possible pregnancy. He tried to reassure Josephine with letters complaining that Vienna bored him and that he longed to rejoin her in Paris as soon as he concluded peace with the Austrians.[55] Then he was exhilarated to learn that Marie was indeed pregnant.

Designating a proper heir to his throne had been among his obsessions. The natural progression would have been a son of his older brother Joseph, but he had only daughters. The next in line, Lucien, ruled himself out with his refusal to divorce his wife and marry into the nobility. Napoleon eagerly adopted Napoleon Charles, the first son of Louis and Hortense, but croup killed that child when he was four and a half years old. When a peace treaty finally freed Napoleon to depart for Paris on 16 October, he was determined to divorce Josephine and wed a princess from a key European state and from a family known for its fecundity; from her womb he would seed a dynasty.

Pauline was as politically adept as any of the Bonaparte siblings, but her specialty was sexual rather than international or national intrigues. She performed her most useful political service to Napoleon shortly after he arrived at Fontainebleau Palace. Pauline fixed her big brother up with her friend, Christine de Mathis, and acted as their go-between to pass love letters and arrange trysts first at Fontainebleau then at the Grand Trianon at Versailles.[56]

Leaving a bed with Marie at Schönbrunn and leaping into a bed with Christine at Fontainebleau diluted some of the anguish of what he had to do. Josephine immediately knew that something was terribly wrong when he greeted her coldly rather than affectionately. For weeks he rarely saw her only to treat her harshly when he did. He was trying to harden them both but instead only worsened their torments. It was at the Tuileries on 30 November 1809 that he finally informed her that he intended to divorce her. He tried to be stern but as she burst into deep sobs he did too.[57]

Napoleon gathered his extended family and key advisors to process the divorce at the Tuileries on 14 December 1809. He began calmly reading a statement until his voice choked with these words: 'She has embellished my life for fifteen years.'[58] Under the settlement Josephine would retain her titles of empress and queen, areceive three million francs annually, have her two million franc debt paid off; and own the Élysée Palace in Paris. The deal contained legal as well as moral and philosophical contradictions. The Catholic Church sanctified both French coronations and marriages, yet, under French law, a marriage could be and a coronation could not be dissolved. They signed the documents then tearfully parted, Josephine for Malmaison, Napoleon for the Grand Trianon. He did what he could to ease her sorrow. He visited her at Malmaison on Christmas Eve and had her dine with him at the Grand Trianon on Christmas Day. Thereafter they exchanged bittersweet letters, gifts and visits. He often ended his letters by reassuring her how much he would always love her and he truly meant that.[59]

Meanwhile, Napoleon remained obsessed with Catherine, summoning her whenever he could snatch some precious time away from pressing affairs of state and family. And then hovering in his mind was Marie Walewska, swelling with the first child that he was confident of having fathered. She wrote to him shortly after returning to Warsaw. He replied that he cherished her letters, she was in his thoughts and he wanted her always to be happy. He eventually would be ecstatic to learn that she had given birth to a son and both were in excellent health.[60]

The political priority was finding an appropriate empress.[61] For that, he established a council among his closest advisors. During meetings throughout January 1810, the council split over whether Russia or Austria was the best political choice from which to extract a fertile royal womb. Obviously, a marriage between France and Russia would strengthen the bonds between Europe's greatest land powers and intimidate all other states squeezed between them; that in turn would better deter Vienna and Berlin singly or even jointly from challenging either of them. Austria was France's worst continental threat, having launched wars against France in 1792, 1798, 1800 and 1809. And for that very reason some, including Talleyrand, argued that Francis would be unlikely to approve another war against France if his daughter were France's empress. Perhaps an Austrian bride would best preserve the uneasy peace. Napoleon leaned toward Russia. Indeed, nearly a year and a half earlier during the Erfurt conference of October 1808, he first raised the possibility with Alexander of wedding one of his sisters. The notion profoundly disturbed Alexander on emotional and religious levels. He shuddered to imagine one of his beloved sisters wed to a man that he increasingly feared as a Minotaur and, in doing so, force her conversion from Russian Orthodoxy to Catholicism. He sidestepped the request by noting that Catherine was about to marry the Duke of Oldenburg's son while Anne was only 14; regardless, the decision was ultimately up to their indomitable Tsarina dowager mother. That left an Austrian bride, which the council approved on 29 January.

The next step was formally to get Francis's approval to marry his 18-year-old daughter, Marie Louise.[62] Rather insensitively, Napoleon sent Eugène to ask Austrian ambassador Karl von Schwarzenberg to convey the request to the potential father-in-law. When he received Francis's acceptance, he sent Marshal Louis Berthier to Vienna to conclude the deal. The 42-year-old groom assured the bride's mother, Empress Maria Theresa, that his desire to marry Marie Louise came from his awareness of 'the excellent virtues and qualities of which this princess is endowed', and that 'I will devote myself to rendering her days happy'.[63] The parents agreed with very mixed feelings. Meanwhile Napoleon worried that a marriage and alliance with Austria would worsen the already remote chance of peace with the British, agitated by what they would interpret as France's latest aggrandizement. He had his diplomats in the various capitals spin his choice of an Austrian bride as designed to strengthen peace in Europe.[64]

The marriage contract and subsequent protocol was modelled on that between Louis XVI and Marie Antoinette. The contract was signed by proxy at Vienna on 8 March. He sent Caroline and an entourage in carriages with a cavalry escort to meet the bride and her entourage at Braunau, on the Austrian-Bavarian frontier, then return with her to France.

Napoleon sought to assuage any fear and loathing that Marie Louise might harbour for him as a man 22 years her senior who had inflicted devastating defeats on her country in four wars. He lauded her wonderful qualities as the reason why he asked her father for her hand in marriage and promised to cultivate her happiness with as much care as possible in hope that one day he would be agreeable to her. He expressed his deep gratitude and joy that she had consented to marry him. His excitement swelled as he anticipated his pretty virgin bride. He was so eager to please her that he even got his stepdaughters Hortense and Stephanie to give him dancing lessons, especially for the waltz. Finally he could not constrain himself and hurried from Paris. Breaking protocol, he met her on the road near Compiègne Palace, nervously introduced himself and then whisked her away to the imperial bedchamber. The night was blissful for him and she seemed eager to please and be pleased.[65]

Napoleon was so besotted that he delegated his work to his subordinates for the next several months and spent as much time as possible with his new wife.⁶⁶ He was generous with more than his time – he gave her an annual allowance of 500,000 francs. He soon discovered that he had married a very young woman, who was pretty and passionate but also spoiled and childlike. She was shy, which many people mistook for haughtiness. Tears came easily to her and he was generally defenceless against them. She was jealous of Josephine and cried whenever anyone, especially he, mentioned her. Nonetheless, he genuinely loved and esteemed her: 'If the French understood the merits of this woman, they would prostrate themselves before her.'⁶⁷

The marriage's primary purpose was soon fulfilled. Marie Louise went into labour around midday on 20 March 1811. The prolonged birth process was inflicting excruciating pain on her. The baby appeared to be stuck. If the cruel choice was between the life of the mother or the child, Napoleon grimly told the doctors to save his beloved wife. Fortunately, Marie Louise's body finally yielded her baby. The emperor was ecstatic that not only were both safe, but that he finally had a male heir. To celebrate, he ordered 101-gun salutes fired in Paris and elsewhere across his empire.⁶⁸

Napoleon adored his son, who was christened Napoléon François Joseph Charles.⁶⁹ Naturally, he carefully planned the education of him and other royal princes:

> Destined to occupy diverse thrones and rule diverse nations, these children would have to draw from common principles . . . To better facilitate the fusion and uniformity of the federal parties of the empire, each . . . prince would be raised . . . with ten or so children, more or less his same age, from that country's first families . . . And what advantage that would have for the well-being of the peoples who compose the European association! . . . The education of these princes would be founded on general knowledge, grand visions, . . . and the application of details rather than the study of theories.⁷⁰

Napoleon's concern with educating princes from an early age was spurred by his inability to get his own siblings to follow his orders for the realms he made and gave them.

* * *

The Continental System was an utter disaster for Holland, whose exports plummeted from 150 million to 10 million florins and merchant fleet from 2,400 to 300 ships between 1805 and 1809.[71] Meanwhile, Napoleon had ordered Dutch King Louis to raise a 25,000-man army. Louis was trapped between the emperor's increasingly onerous demands and his subjects' swelling misery and bitterness. He tried to alleviate the later by turning a blind eye to smuggling but that provoked storms of invective and threats from Napoleon when he found out: 'If Holland separates from the continent's cause, I will separate from it . . . If Holland does not return to the same footing with France and does not re-enter the system, it must be declared that peace cannot be guaranteed.'[72] He was merciless in criticizing his brother: 'I have repeated to you a hundred times. You are not the king and you do not know how to be one . . . I always regret that I have given you a throne where you . . . are so useful to our enemies and make as much evil as possible to the empire and France.'[73]

Napoleon first broached to Louis the notion of France's annexation of Holland on 21 December 1809. He did so in a long letter in which he made a typical lawyer-like argument against Louis and for his policy: 'When Your Majesty mounted the throne part of the Dutch nation wanted to be united with France. The esteem that I have for this brave nation brings me to want to preserve its name and its independence. I myself designed its constitution which is the foundation for Your Majesty's throne and I placed you there.' He had hoped that Louis would act on the understanding that he was subordinate to Napoleon and that Dutch interests were subordinate to French interests. But 'I finally realized that I bore a vain illusion . . . Your Majesty, in mounting the throne, forgot that he was French . . . Those Dutch who incline toward France have been neglected and persecuted. Those who serve England have been put above all.' He then issued an ultimatum. Louis must sever all commerce and communication with Britain, ready the Dutch fleet for war, increase the army to 25,000 troops, revoke the titles of marshals that he had awarded and end any privileges for the aristocracy that violated the constitution. He then ended his letter by asserted that, even if Louis did all that, the union of Holland with France might be in the best interests of both nations.[74]

Napoleon then devoured Holland in a series of very big gulps. In January 1810, he massed 20,000 troops at Antwerp under the command of Marshal Nicolas Oudinot and ordered other regiments to places in northern France within a few days march of Holland. On 11 January 1810, he had Oudinot march to occupy Bergen-op-zoom and Breda. Meanwhile, he had Louis informed that he should keep all Dutch troops in their barracks and he would be responsible should any blood be shed. He issued orders on 27 January for Oudinot take over all key military positions between the Rhine and Scheldt rivers and on 1 February, to take over all civil positions in that region; he could requisition all needed provisions from the local authorities. With that territory in his hands, Napoleon then demanded on 12 February that Louis cede it to him.

The final straw was Napoleon's discovery of a secret effort by Louis, Fouché and the financier Gabriel Ouvrand to seek a back channel for peace talks with Britain.[75] It so happened that Napoleon was trying to develop his own channel and those maverick efforts undermined his ego and authority. He vented his rage against Fouché during a council of ministers meeting on 2 June 1810, then accepted his resignation the next day. He then turned his guns against Louis, who, reduced to being a puppet king of a rump territory, finally abdicated on 2 July 1810. Napoleon annexed Holland to France on 9 July and divided it into nine departments on 27 October.[76]

Napoleon was nearly as critical of Jérôme's handling of Westphalia. If Louis's sin was caring too much about his subjects, Jérôme's was caring too little. Amidst the opening phase of his 1809 campaign, Napoleon excoriated Jérôme: 'Your kingdom is without police, finance and organization. Monarchies are not founded upon festivals and disorderly luxury.'[77] He was just as contemptuous of Jérôme as a general, blistering him for 'waging war like a satrap'. He insisted that his younger brother 'Cease being ridiculous. Return your diplomatic corps to Cassel. Have no baggage train. Have no table other than yours. Make war like a young soldier who needs glory and reputation. Try to merit the rank that you have received. Have enough character to write and speak suitably.' If he did all this he could earn 'the esteem of France and Europe'.[78] Jérôme's failure to reform triggered this tirade:

> I am angry with you because you have shown in the war such little talent and even good sense. You are closer to the profession of a courtier than a soldier. At your age I conquered Italy and defeated the Austrian army three times more numerous than mine. But I never had flatterers or the diplomatic corps following me. I made war as a soldier ... As for the future, I do not want you to dishonour yourself by abandoning your command, but I want even less any more condescending idiots from my family reflecting badly on my military glory ... You are a spoiled young man although full of beautiful natural qualities.[79]

Although Jérôme did not suffer Louis's fate, Napoleon legally, militarily and financially subordinated Westphalia to France in a treaty signed on 14 January 1810.

As for their royal styles, the reigns of Joseph and Murat could not have differed more when they were the kings of Naples. Joseph was a lawyer by training and temperament. Murat was a flamboyant cavalry commander who even as a marshal led charges against the enemy. As for substance, both enriched themselves from their subjects, but Murat was far more tolerant of the native corruption.

Napoleon's shadow darkened the Kingdom of Naples as it did his other puppet realms. Caroline and Murat not only had to underwrite the costs of French troops stationed on their territory, but endure the constant presence of French 'advisors' who reported anything contrary to the emperor's interests. Napoleon was increasingly enraged by Murat's incompetence and extravagance:

> I am extremely wounded by your perpetual proclamations... that blame your predecessor, who had endured all the spines while you enjoy the fruits and to which you owe eternal appreciation. I am angry that you feel so little for what you owe me... As for the individuals that are at the court of Sicily and war against me, but whose property you do not confiscate, I will take for myself that indemnity from your kingdom... If the Constitution is activated, the Code Napoleon is executed without modification and part of the public debt is paid, I will guarantee the rest of the debt.[80]

He called on Murat to embark on cost-cutting measures, starting with the army: 'Your Majesty must restrain his expenses and diminish his recruitment because the power of states consists in having good and faithful troops rather than just lots of troops.'[81] He summed up Murat's misrule with these words: 'You sacrifice for a false popularity... In truth, you have lost your head.'[82]

Napoleon had excused Murat from his 1809 campaign so that the king could crush lingering resistance within the southern peninsula then conquer Sicily. Murat's sole significant military coup during his reign was capturing Capri, 20 miles from Naples, on 18 October 1809 after an eleven-day siege. He failed to destroy the mélange of brigands and rebels that infested Calabria and other parts of his realm. His most humiliating failure was the invasion of Sicily on 17 September 1810. Part of him appears to have actually welcomed that debacle. Atop all of Napoleon's demands and criticisms, he bristled at the emperor's instructions to General Paul Grenier, who commanded 8,000 French troops in the kingdom, not to do anything, including supporting the invasion of Sicily, without a direct imperial order. So despite or more likely because of that, Murat ordered General François Caivagnac to land his 3,500 troops near Messina. General James Campbell immediately attacked and captured 843 French troops while the rest managed to escape. If Murat thought that the disaster would force Napoleon to cede control of Grenier, he had learned nothing of substance about him during their now eighteen-year-old relationship.[83]

As if Murat's failings as a ruler were not aggravating enough, Napoleon also had to contend with the royal couple's worsening political and personal estrangement. Each formed a political faction of officials, officers and merchants. They had separate bedrooms and increasingly blatant affairs with others. The nadir came in August 1811 when Murat published love letters between Caroline and Jean Daure, the war minister. In doing so, he exposed himself to ridicule as a cuckold as much as he reinforced the salacious gossip about his wife. But he did bolster his political power as Daure fled and the king named one of his faction to be war minister.

This provoked Napoleon's latest searing letter to Murat: 'Recall that I made you king only to serve my system's interests. Do not be mistaken. If you cease to be French, you will be nothing for me.'[84] First Caroline and then Murat hurried to Paris to plead their respective cases before the emperor. Much to his later chagrin, Napoleon negotiated a truce between them by wielding a trump card – they would both lose their thrones if they failed to do so.

Inspired by that classic axiom, the enemy of my enemy is my friend, Caroline and Murat did reunite. Like virtually everyone under his thumb, they increasingly saw Napoleon as their foe and oppressor rather than ally and benefactor. In May 1810, Caroline predicted a future catastrophe: 'I see nothing but shame preceding inevitable destruction in this abominable alliance.'[85] That was not just extraordinarily prescient. In trying to sidestep that nightmare, she and Murat would exceed her brother in brutal, unsentimental Machiavellian politics.

Napoleon would not learn of the extent of their betrayal until it was far too late to counter it. He was, however, well aware that his puppets wanted to cut their strings. The result was a tug-of-war over hearts, minds and fortunes in the Neapolitan kingdom. Napoleon tried to yank back his slipping influence by decreeing on 6 July 1811, that any French citizens in that realm were loyal to their emperor and not to the reigning king.

Napoleon faced a protest from his hitherto most obedient brother in the spring of 1811. For nearly three years now, Joseph had sat upon the throne of a country torn apart by a vicious war. As if that were not debilitating enough, he had to endure Napoleon's demands for revenues to finance his war across the Iberian Peninsula. As if Joseph's reign was not unstable and tenuous enough, Napoleon made it more so. In 1810 Napoleon had annexed Spain's provinces of Catalonia, Aragon, Navarre, Biscay, Burgos and Valladolid. Spain's worsening war and economy along with Napoleon's incessant demands for more contributions caused Spain's national debt to skyrocket from 9,600,000 francs to 87,200,000 francs in 1813 and Spain's debt to France to quintuple from 28,533,333 francs to 165,000,000 between 1808 and 1813. During the same years the cost for France to war in Spain quintupled from 141,866,666 francs to 864,533,000 francs.[86]

Fed up, Joseph disobeyed a longstanding order to stay in Spain and instead journeyed to confront Napoleon. They had a tumultuous encounter at Rambouillet Palace on 16 May. Joseph threatened to abdicate if Napoleon did not stop making impossible demands upon him. The emperor finally agreed to grant the king a commanding general for the French armies in Spain and more money to underwrite the war and other expenses. Yet after Joseph returned to Madrid, Napoleon reneged on both promises. He did not increase the subsidy for Spain and he sent Marshal Jean-Baptiste Jourdan to serve as Joseph's advisor rather than as a commander-in-chief for all French troops in the peninsula.

* * *

Napoleon also faced growing resistance from the great powers he had defeated and diminished. The afterglow of warm feelings lingered in Paris and Vienna following the marriage of Napoleon and Marie Louise. However, with time issues re-emerged to give monarchs things to worry about and diplomats things to haggle over. Chancellor Clemens von Metternich led Austria's efforts to revise the bilateral relationship. Francis rejected Napoleon's call for a free trade treaty. Napoleon rejected Francis's request to return Illyria to Austria.

The 1807 Treaty of Tilsit and follow-up impositions devastated Prussia's territorial, economic and military power. This locked the country into a vicious circle of too few revenues from households and businesses to underwrite both the state's budgets and indemnity payments to France, which had to be covered by borrowing more money, which increased interest payments and dampened the economy, thus further cutting revenues. Tilsit's forced reduction of the army to 42,000 troops at once slashed expenses and pride. The Prussians fumed, longed and prepared for vengeance.

The initial indemnity bill presented at Tilsit in July 1807 was 170 million francs, but Napoleon acceded to Alexander's request at the Erfurt Conference in October 1808 to cut the bill to 120 million francs. By early 1810, Berlin owed Paris 100 million francs and pleaded near bankruptcy for not paying up. Napoleon had little leverage to extract that money. Under the treaty, his troops could march across Prussia and garrison its key fortresses, including Magdeburg. He toyed with the idea of marching 60,000 troops to Magdeburg as a show of strength, but finally dismissed it. That might provoke Berlin either to war or a blunt refusal ever to pay, neither of which was in French interests. Instead he proposed to cede Glogau and a portion of Silesia but Berlin still claimed an inability to pay. So for now the emperor put that dilemma on a political back burner.[87]

The anti-French faction in Frederick William's court was as virulent as ever although more publicly muted. That faction lost two key members. Napoleon forced Heinrich von Stein, who led Prussia's military and economic reforms, to flee into exile in January 1809. Then Queen Louise died in July 1810. However, former first minister Karl von Hardenburg returned from retirement to his old post and there carried on Stein's reforms and Louise's hatreds.

Then there was Sweden whose government literally adopted a Frenchman into its royal family. That new member would eventually war against rather than with Napoleon. Russia's conquest of Finland led to a coup in Stockholm that overthrew and exiled Gustavus IV and enthroned Duke Sudermanie as Charles XIII. But Charles was childless and doddering and his ministers and Diet sought a vigorous heir. A consensus emerged to offer French Marshal Jean-Baptiste Bernadotte, who had shown compassion to Swedish prisoners during the 1806 campaign, to be the heir to the Swedish throne.

That presented Napoleon with a dilemma. Bernadotte's hatred and jealousy against him went back nearly two decades. Napoleon was as brilliant a general as Bernadotte was third-rate at best. Indeed among Napoleon's generals, none was more inept and backstabbing than Bernadotte. His failures to obey orders during the 1805, 1806, 1807 and 1809 campaigns made French victories costlier and lost at least one battle, Eylau. After his 1809 campaign, Napoleon disparaged him as 'a worn out man who wants money, pleasures and grandeur, but does not want to achieve them through war's dangers and fatigues'.[88] He found plenty of fault with Bernadotte: 'He has mediocre talents. I do not trust him at all. He always has an ear open to the conspirators who inundate this great capital. In war, he is the same. His absence nearly lost me the battle of

Jena. He was humdrum at Wagram. He could not be found at Eylau . . . and did nothing special at Austerlitz.'[89]

Yet, rather than cashier Bernadotte, Napoleon plied him with unmerited promotions, titles and riches. What explains such indulgences? Sentiment trumped justice. Bernadotte had wooed and married Napoleon's first love, Désirée Clary, the younger sister of his brother Joseph's wife Julie. That inspired in Napoleon not jealousy but a wish that Désirée be happy. He admitted to Joseph that 'the reason I gave the title of duke and prince to Bernadotte was in consideration for your wife', and naturally much more so for Désirée, although that was unsaid.[90] Napoleon's generosity provoked resentment rather than inspired gratitude in Bernadotte.

And now Napoleon had the power to thwart Bernadotte's chance to become Sweden's crown prince. He had severe misgivings: 'I suffered a presentiment that . . . Bernadotte . . . a serpent nourished at our breast . . . to our detriment was leaving us to join our enemies and we had to watch and fear him.'[91] Nonetheless, he gave the nod to Stockholm. The Diet elected Bernadotte the crown prince on 2 August 1810. He arrived in Stockholm on 2 November 1810 and soon disillusioned Napoleon of any hopes that he would serve French rather than Swedish interests. His first decisive act came on 17 November 1810, when he talked the king and his council out of a pending declaration of war against Britain. Eventually he would lead Sweden's army against France. But he would only do so after Napoleon suffered his devastating defeat in Russia.

As for Russia, Napoleon sought to rekindle the spirit of Tilsit with Alexander. He fired off in February 1808 what became his most astonishing, wide-ranging letter to the Tsar. Oriental dreams of emulating Alexander the Great still animated Napoleon. He tried to excite Alexander in a joint military campaign through Constantinople and the Ottoman Empire all the way to the Euphrates River mouth on the Persian Gulf, with the ultimate goal of 'making England tremble and bringing the continent to its knees'. He observed that

> the mutual interests of our two states is to be combined and balanced . . . Your Majesty and I would have preferred the sweetness of peace and passing our lives amidst our vast empires, occupied with enlivening and being enlivened by the arts . . . but the enemies of the world do not want that . . . Wisdom, politics and destiny forces us to go where the irresistible march of events leads us. This swarm of pigmies . . . bend and

follow the movements that Your Majesty and I order and the Russian people will be happy from the glory, riches and fortune that result from these great events . . . The work of Tilsit will determine the destiny of the world.[92]

Four years later Napoleon invaded Russia with more than half a million troops.

Chapter 18

The Lord of the Kremlin

'I am far from having lost hope for peace but since he has embarked on the disastrous process of negotiating at the head of a powerful and numerous army, my honour demands that I also negotiate at the head of a powerful and numerous army. I do not at all want to start hostilities, but I want to position myself to repulse them. I do not at all want to violate Russian territory, but I want to be ready to retaliate should they violate the Confederation's territory.'

'I think it will be over within three months.'

'In the existing state of affairs, I can only hold my grip on Europe from the Tuileries.'

Why did Napoleon invade Russia in June 1812?[1] Years later on St Helena, he explained his reasoning:

> I was able to march against Russia at the head of the rest of Europe. The enterprise was popular. The cause was European. This was the last effort that remained for France to do; its destiny and that of the new European system were the goal of this struggle. Russia was England's last resource. World peace was in Russia and the success could not be doubted.[2]

That answer is at once disingenuous and truthful. It certainly conveys the mingled hubris and delusions that drove him onward through each stage of the invasion to the point of literal no return for half a million of his own troops. If Spain was Napoleon's 'ulcer', Russia became his holocaust. Yet, like Spain, neither his war against Russia nor its catastrophic results were inevitable. He and Tsar Alexander could have avoided war with face-saving concessions on critical issues. Essentially the emperor and the Tsar got locked into a game of chicken that each was determined to win no matter what. Neither wanted war but, far more, neither wanted to lose face by yielding to the other. Ostensibly the war was provoked by deadlocks over the Grand Duchy of Warsaw, the Duchy of Oldenburg and the Continental System.

As early as January 1810, Alexander asked Napoleon to sign a treaty whereby he pledged never to convert the Duchy of Warsaw into the Kingdom of Poland. Two reasons compelled Napoleon to reject that request. First, he always wanted to keep his options open for unforeseen opportunities. Second, his influence over the Duchy of Warsaw would sharply diminish if he crushed Polish hopes that their 'liberator' would eventually restore their kingdom. Not wanting to completely disappoint Alexander, Napoleon sent him a draft treaty with ambiguous language over Poland's future.[3] Alexander rejected that version and in doing so deprived them both of a face-saving way to resolve the issue. Alexander's rigidity on Poland would be a major reason why Russia and France went to war in June 1812.

Then Napoleon committed a blatant act of imperialism that deeply offended Alexander. The Duchy of Oldenburg numbered 160,000 people and stretched alongside the North Sea between Holland and Hamburg. It was a new state, having been established in 1773. Its current duke, Peter of Holstein-Gottorp, took power in 1783. The Romanov and Holstein-Gottorp families had been linked since Peter the Great's daughter, Anne, married a member in 1721 and later gave birth to the future Tsar Peter III. Those familial ties were renewed on 9 August 1808, when Alexander's sister Catherine married George, Peter's son. Alexander considered Oldenburg among the Russian empire's fiefs. Yet Oldenburg was in the Confederation of the Rhine whose members were treaty-bound to provide troops to Napoleon if he requested them. Peter refused to supply a contingent during the 1809 war against Austria. Napoleon used this treaty violation as an excuse to annex Oldenburg on 13 December 1810. When Alexander protested, Napoleon replied that Oldenburg's fate was in the sphere of French rather than Russian influence. That may have been true had the duke's son not been married to the Tsar's sister. Alexander demanded that Napoleon compensate Peter and his dynasty with Danzig. Napoleon first refused then compounded Alexander's anger by offering tiny, landlocked Erfurt instead.

Alexander retaliated by taking Russia out of the Continental System. On 31 December 1810, he decreed that henceforth, taxes on imported luxury goods arriving by land would be raised and those arriving by sea would be lowered. That was deliberately designed to diminish trade with France and encourage trade via third parties with Britain. Napoleon condemned Alexander's trade policy as 'advantageous to England and contrary to the Tilsit treaty'.[4] But Napoleon was as helpless to reverse Alexander's Continental System decision as Alexander was helpless to reverse Napoleon's Oldenburg decision.

Napoleon reasoned that if diplomacy alone could not get Alexander to accept his positions on the Continental System, Oldenburg and Poland, the threat of war might. Starting in 1811, he began assembling an army that eventually numbered over 600,000 troops, half French, half foreign. Poland would be the army's staging area and would supply the largest foreign continent, 50,000 troops. In January 1812, he explained his brinksmanship strategy in the game of chicken between them:

> I had to assemble my army . . . These preparations have taken a year. Now 500,000 men are going to cross Germany . . . not with hostile sentiments but for my armies to find themselves on the Vistula before the Russians . . . I am far from having lost hope for peace but since he has embarked on the disastrous process of negotiating at the head of a powerful and numerous army, my honour demands that I also negotiate at the head of a powerful and numerous army. I do not at all want to start hostilities, but I want to position myself to repulse them . . . I do not at all want to violate Russian territory, but I want to be ready to retaliate should they violate the Confederation's territory.[5]

Napoleon threw himself into a typical whirlwind of preparations for war against Russia.[6] He called up 80,000 men from the class of 1812. He withdrew 50,000 troops from Spain to march across Europe and join his invasion army. He had parallel chains of depots filled to capacity from France and other rear-echelon supply countries across Europe to the Niemen with the largest at Wesel, Mainz, Hamburg, Magdeburg, Stralsund, Elbing, Berlin, Stettin, Glogau, Warsaw, Thorn, Danzig and Königsberg. Each depot usually also had an adjacent hospital. He revamped his artillery and engineer corps, eliminating redundancies and imposing efficiencies. He tried to ensure that all his troops were regularly and fully paid and fed, received four pairs of shoes and carried the standard 1777 model musket. Each regiment would start the campaign with wagons carrying 1,500 uniforms, 1,500 vests, 3,000 trousers, 1,000 coats and 300 shakos. Each month thereafter each regiment would receive two wagons filled with 200 uniforms, 400 vests, 800 trousers,

100 coats, 200 shakos and 800 pairs of shoes. He organized pontoon trains and special units for repairing and building bridges. He had tens of thousands of draft animals and riding horses herded from across his empire and allies to his swelling forces, 15,000 from Prussia alone. He typically sought to anticipate special needs that his army might encounter. For instance, he asked for an analysis of what type of wagon was best suited to Russian roads and how many draft animals were needed to pull it. After examining various wagon designs, he ordered one implemented that cut the weight by a quarter while maintaining the same load. This would considerably ease the burden and thus attrition of draft animals. To further lighten their burden, he ordered his officers to rid themselves of all unnecessary baggage. He asserted a propaganda war to precede, accompany and follow his military campaign.

As always, spies worked double-time in the months before a probable war. And, as always, other spies worked double-time to counter their work. Napoleon was especially concerned about the espionage of Colonel Alexander Ivanovich Tchernitchev, one of the Tsar's aides de camp, who ran agents out of the Russian embassy in Paris and eventually fled with an intelligence treasure trove on the eve of the invasion.[7]

Napoleon launched no significant naval operations in 1812. Nearly two decades of a nearly nonstop British blockade had literally and figuratively rotted away his navy. Few vessels were ready for sea and fewer crews retained the sailing and gunnery skills to stand much of a chance in a battle against British warships. The best that he could do was authorize a few frigates to run the blockade for the open sea to raid British shipping. The British captured one frigate that ventured forth.[8]

As if having arm-twisted virtually all European states into militarily and financially backing him against Russia was not heady enough, the ongoing war between Russia and Turkey since 1806 further encouraged Napoleon's aggression. He sought to nurture Turkey as an ally to keep a large portion of Russia's army tied down on that distant front.[9] That was to no avail as the Russians defeated the Turks in a series of battles in early 1812, leading to the peace treaty of Bucharest on 28 May, just a month before Napoleon's invasion. Most Russian troops on that front soon received orders to march north to fight the invaders.

Then, unexpectedly, Napoleon got another ostensible ally on 18 June 1812, when the United States declared war against Britain. He did not learn about that war until he was deep in Russia and thereafter never did anything to support the Americans against his chronic enemy. Although that war had no immediate effect on his own, indirectly the more military, industrial and financial power that London diverted to North America, the less it could send to St Petersburg.

Napoleon's false pride not only stymied a chance to enlist an ally but eventually converted that country into an enemy. Angry that Crown Prince Bernadotte served Swedish rather than French interests, he rejected his overtures for an alliance against Russia in February 1811 with these words: 'France does not need Sweden . . . desires nothing from her and asked nothing from her.'[10] From then until early 1812, he might have enticed Sweden as an ally by promising to help Stockholm recover Finland which Russia had conquered in 1808. Indeed he might have won his Russian campaign if a Swedish army had invaded Finland and threatened St Petersburg, thus stretching Russia's army possibly to breaking point. Instead Sweden and Russia signed a succession of treaties: Stockholm recognized its loss of Finland on 24 March 1812; they pledged neutrality on 18 August 1812; and they allied against France on 7 January 1813. In March 1813, Bernadotte would lead Sweden's army against Napoleon.

* * *

Napoleon hoped for a diplomatic solution through the years, months, weeks and days preceding his crossing of the Nieman River and for months thereafter. In the first half of 1812, he wrote Alexander several times but tried to sway him with flattery rather than compromises. On 24 February, he assured the Tsar of his continued esteem, but raised no issues. On 25 April, he insisted that although he remained committed to peace, if war was necessary it would not change his warm feelings for the Tsar. He sent General Louis Narbonne to directly express these sentiments and the Tsar responded with his own polite platitudes.[11]

Whatever their misgivings, most of Napoleon's advisors fatalistically accepted his decision to war against Russia. Only one Cassandra begged the emperor to reconsider. Armand Caulaincourt was the ambassador to Russia from November 1807 to February 1811. During that time he had numerous deep, prolonged talks with Alexander. Caulaincourt warned that Alexander would never surrender no matter how many defeats his army suffered, having repeatedly insisted that 'I shall not be the first to draw my sword, but I shall be the last to sheathe it'.[12]

Napoleon and Marie Louise left Paris on 9 May and reached Dresden on 17 May, where he had summoned his allied sovereign leaders. The theme of his diplomacy there and beyond was this message: 'I want nothing from Alexander. I am not at all making war against Russia any more than I am making war against Spain. I have only one enemy and that is England. That is what I am going after in Russia and everywhere.'[13] He spent most of his time at Dresden trying to awe his fellow rulers, their wives and their entourages. Fully displaying their glittering splendour, France's emperor and empress presided over a succession of carefully choreographed ceremonies, balls, banquets, hunts, concerts and plays. Marie Louise was distraught when Napoleon bid farewell at Dresden. He hoped that she would feel better after she stayed with her family in Prague for a while before returning to Paris. Thereafter he tried to write her at least once daily to assure her of his abiding love, safety and eventual return. He asked her to send him details of her daily activities. On 1 June, he wrote: 'I think it will be over within three months.'[14]

* * *

By June 1812, Napoleon had mobilized 615,000 troops split among three armies numbering altogether 450,000 troops massed on the Russian frontier with another 165,000 troops in reserve in Poland and Germany. No unified group of armies before or since was more diverse. Half of his troops were French and the other half a composite of Poles, Austrians, Prussians, Westphalians, Bavarians, Saxons, Badeners, Swiss, Dutch, Hessians, Italians, Neapolitans, Illyrians, Dalmatians, Croats, Spanish and Portuguese, to name the most prominent. The largest foreign contingents included 50,000 Poles, 30,000 Austrians, 30,000 Bavarians, 27,000 Italians 25,000 Westphalians, 20,000 Prussians, 20,000 Saxons, 8,000 Badeners and 20,000 troops from other Confederation of the Rhine states. The infantry was 48 per cent French and 52 per cent foreign and the cavalry was 64 per cent French and 36 per cent foreign.[15]

As for the frontier armies, Napoleon commanded the central and largest with 250,000 troops split among the corps of Nicolas Oudinot, Michel Ney and Louis Davout along with Joachim Murat commanding the cavalry reserve, Jean Lariboisière the artillery reserve, Adolphe Mortier the Imperial Guard infantry Corps of one Old Guard division and two Young Guard divisions and Jean-Baptiste Bessières the Imperial Guard cavalry. One of the two adjacent armies was commanded by Viceroy Eugène Beauharnais which included his own mostly Italian corps and Laurent Gouvion St Cyr's Bavarians. Inexplicably, he assigned Jérôme Bonaparte to command an army composed of the corps of Joseph Poniatowski's Poles, Jean Reynier's Saxons and Dominique Vandamme's Westphalians. Finally, two small armies guarded the left and right flanks.

General Julius Grawert's 20,000 Prussians comprised two-thirds of Marshal Étienne Macdonald's army assigned to capture Riga. General Karl von Schwartzenberg's 30,000 Austrians were far to the south near the Pripet Marshes with the mission of blocking Russian armies coming from that direction. Reserve forces included the corps of Claude Victor and Charles Augereau along with many smaller contingents.[16]

On paper, Russia had more than twice as many armed men as the invaders; the 1,318,324 enrolled included 815,045 regulars, 330,000 militia and several hundred thousand auxiliaries. The real numbers, however, were only about half that because of desertion, disease, corruption, fraud and bad bookkeeping. On the western front Russia fielded only 241,000 troops split among three armies. Mikhail Barclay de Tolly wore three hats as war minister, commanding general and general of the largest army with 136,000 troops and 558 guns deployed around Vilna. General Peter Bagration led the second-largest army of 57,000 troops and 216 guns deployed a hundred or so miles south around Volkovysk. A third army of 48,000 troops and 164 guns led by General Alexander Tormazov was strung out along dusty roads hundreds of miles further south, marching north after defeating the Turks. The rest were scattered elsewhere across Russia's vast empire, although many would eventually join the war against the invaders, while tens of thousands more men would be recruited to fill the army's ever depleting ranks. The Russian empire's expanse was reflected in the array of backgrounds for its leading generals: Barclay de Tolly was Livonian, Bagration was Armenian, Levin Bennigsen was Hanoverian, Peter Wittgenstein was Austrian and only Mikhail Kutuzov and Tormazov were actually Russian.[17]

Russia enjoyed plenty of strengths besides sheer numbers of soldiers. Thanks largely to Barclay's reforms, Russia's army of 1812 was superior to that of 1807 in organization, training, logistics and tactics. He reorganized the army into French-style corps, instructed Russian jägers in French light infantry tactics, replaced hickory ramrods with steel ones for muskets and revamped the supply system. The Russians also would benefit greatly from fighting on their own turf with supply lines a fraction the length of the invaders'. Then, of course, there were the vast distances that Napoleon's troops would have to trudge between the frontier and the capitals of Moscow and St Petersburg. Finally and perhaps most decisively, they were acclimated and prepared for the Russian winter.

On the eve of his campaign, Napoleon faced two seemingly irresolvable dilemmas, one moral and the other practical. Technically France and Russia were still at peace. He would be the aggressor the moment his troops crossed the Niemen River and marched into Russia.

That troubled him. In his previous wars against other Great Powers he could argue that France was the victim of foreign aggression. This time was different and he could not mask that reality no matter how much propaganda he planted in newspapers or published as bulletins across his empire. Yet a far more troubling practical problem loomed over all. Despite his Herculean efforts at logistics, as a harbinger of the devastation that lay ahead, Napoleon's army was already short of food. He desperately wrote his supply commander at Königsberg that 'I am in great need of provisions'.[18]

As Napoleon made his plans, he left almost nothing to chance strategically.[19] He anticipated various ways that the Russians could attack then positioned his corps and instructed each commander how to react in various scenarios. His strategy leading up to the invasion 'was to advance on my left and refuse my right', hoping to entice the enemy against his recessed right while sweeping around the enemy's flank and into the Russian rear. That was a potentially risky manoeuvre since the enemy might rapidly advance and destroy his right while his left was still marching. That could be avoided if 'the right does not commit itself against superior forces and manoeuvred from position to position while the grand part of the Russian army finds itself hit in its flank'.[20]

Napoleon's strategy failed as soon as his army began crossing the Niemen on 24 June.[21] Barclay rejected the bait and instead, screened by cavalry and Cossacks, withdrew his army a day or so ahead of the advanced invading forces. That meant that Jérôme's army had to march even faster and further to outflank the Russians. He carefully detailed what Jérôme had to do, emphasizing that 'you must attack when I attack'.[22] All his commanders carefully followed his instructions except Jérôme who he blistered for 'never joining a battle and being ignorant of all the customs and usages of war'.[23]

After reaching Vilna on 28 June, Napoleon made that city his operational centre. He setup a huge supply depot. He left Foreign Minister Hugues Maret, the Duke of Bassano, and the diplomatic corps there to await anxiously the latest news from the front. One problem disappeared on 14 July, when Jérôme quit in a huff and rode with his entourage back to Westphalia. Most importantly, Vilna became the capital for a provisional Lithuanian government headed by Governor General Thierry Hogendorp that Napoleon formed on 24 August. He had Hogendorp raise nine regiments as the core of a Lithuanian army and urged him to forge good relations with the Duchy of Warsaw. Napoleon intended his latest government to be a model for the Lithuanian people; it did but not as he intended. Incompetence and conflicting interests soon deadlocked the new government. None of Napoleon's letters urging Hogendorp and his colleagues to work together had any noticeable effect. He had Maret work with the leaders but he was just as incapable of forging unity.[24]

Napoleon hoped that the shock of invasion capped by a victory or two would convince Alexander to open talks between them. The trouble was that the Russian army did not stand and fight so he could not boast any victories. The only fighting involved daily skirmishes and occasional limited battles between Napoleon's advanced forces and the enemy's rearguards. The letter he received from the Tsar on 1 July should have destroyed any hope for negotiations under all but one situation. Alexander pledged to keep fighting as long as a single French soldier remained on Russian soil. In his long reply, Napoleon justified his invasion and called for peace but never offered any concrete concessions that might entice Alexander into talks.[25]

The further the invaders marched, the hungrier most got as they emptied their supply wagons and quickly devoured the meagre pickings looted from peasants. Alexander approved a scorched-earth strategy whereby his troops destroyed whatever supplies they could not carry away. Meanwhile, Cossacks attacked foraging parties, forcing regiments to send out more men and slowing their advance. Tens of thousands of horses died from eating green grain and rotten straw or being ridden to death in Murat's fruitless attempts to catch up to the enemy. Even the Imperial Guard was increasingly short of horses. The troops needed more of everything, including French muskets. The Russian muskets that they captured had a larger calibre and were badly made. As disease, desertion and violence steadily thinned the ranks of his regiments at the front, Napoleon called forward a steady stream of regiments stationed across Poland, Germany and even France itself.

So far, the only significant battle occurred when Davout staved off an attack by Bagration at Mogilev on 23 July, but the Russian defeat merely spurred the pace of their withdrawal. Napoleon attempted a wide flanking movement to trap Barclay at Vitebsk, but again the Russians quick-marched to safety after relatively light losses. Having failed twice to cut off and destroy Barclay, once at Vilna and now at Vitebsk, he resolved to launch a third enveloping movement to engulf Barclay, recently joined by Bagration, at the walled city of Smolensk. But before he could do so, he had to rest and succour his badly depleted, disorganized and starving troops. Russia's high command played into Napoleon's hands by deciding to fight for Smolensk. Napoleon was naturally afraid that the Russians would again swiftly withdraw so this time he attacked directly rather than manoeuvre to cut off the Russian army and force it to attack him. The result was a two-day battle on 17 and 18 August, whereby Napoleon's troops captured Smolensk at a cost of 9,000 casualties, while inflicting 6,000 dead, wounded and captured on the enemy. That limited victory might have been decisive had Junot obeyed orders to attack the Russian flank. Napoleon caught up to the retreating Russians at Valutino-Gora on 19 August and fought another inconclusive battle, holding the field with 8,768 casualties to Russian losses of 5,000.

Napoleon then made a critical decision that later haunted him. He mulled over but rejected the notion of wintering at Smolensk and consolidating the territory that his troops had overrun behind him. A decisive victory had evaded him. The weather was hot but dry. Winter was months away. Smolensk was filled with captured supplies. His distant flanks were secure as Macdonald had advanced to Riga on the Baltic Sea, while Schwarzenberg staved off Tormazov far to the south. It made no sense to sit tight as the Russian army swelled in numbers beyond the eastern horizon. A swift march might finally trap and destroy Barclay, thus forcing Alexander to sue for peace. So he ordered his men forward on the road to Moscow.

Meanwhile, Mikhail Kutuzov replaced Barclay as Russia's army commander on 29 August. Kutuzov chose to stand and fight near the village of Borodino 70 miles west of Moscow. His army numbered 111,000 troops, 7,000 Cossacks and 640 guns, backed by 10,000 or so militia. Napoleon's army approached on the afternoon of 6 September. He now had only 135,222 troops, including 90,507 infantry, 29,219 cavalry and 15,496 artillerymen manning 587 guns.[26] In a meeting with his corps commanders, Davout urged Napoleon to manoeuvre around rather than directly attack the Russian army. The emperor angrily rejected the idea. He was tired of long marches that exhausted his troops and horses but never trapped the Russians. He would mass his batteries to devastate the Russian army followed by overwhelming infantry then cavalry attacks.

The battle began early the morning of 7 September. Throughout the day, a stomach ailment tormented Napoleon, blurring his concentration. Despite horrendous losses, the Russians absorbed the barrages and attacks. The French eventually captured severed fortified positions called the fleches and then the Grand Redoubt in the Russian line's centre. The Russians fell back in good order and awaited the latest assault. Berthier and Murat implored Napoleon to order forward the Old Guard to administer the coup de grace. Napoleon refused, fearing the destruction of his finest troops 3,000 miles from Paris. Instead he ordered more bombardments and assaults. After twelve hours of combat, Kutuzov finally ordered a retreat. The French and Russians suffered 29,000 and 44,000 casualties, respectively.

Kutuzov withdrew the remnants of his army through Moscow, then angled south 45 miles to Tarutino beyond the Nara River. It was an excellent position. He at once threatened Napoleon in Moscow and his communication line westward, while protecting against a French offensive toward the agrarian city of Kaluga and the industrial city of Tula, respectively 100 miles south-west and 113 miles south of Moscow. St Petersburg was nearly 440 miles north-west of Moscow. If Napoleon was foolish enough to march that way, Kutuzov could retake Moscow then follow him. Meanwhile, Kutuzov replenished his army with provisions from Kaluga, munitions from Tula and more troops from an arc of cities.

Napoleon and his entourage triumphantly entered Moscow on 14 September. He established his headquarters in the Kremlin where he would remain until 19 October.[27] Moscow's beauty stunned him: 'It has 500 palaces as lovely as the Élysées, French style furniture of extraordinary luxury, several imperial palaces and magnificent barracks and hospitals.'[28] He had only a fleeting time to savour that beauty.

The night that Napoleon reached Moscow, arsonists organized by Governor Fyodor Rostopchin began destroying water pumps and kindling fires. Over four days the conflagration destroyed three-quarters of the city and left a hundred thousand or more people homeless. From Moscow's still smouldering ruins, Napoleon expressed to Alexander his sorrow and bewilderment:

> The beautiful and superb city of Moscow exists no more. Rostopchin had it burned. Four hundred incendiaries have been arrested in the act. All declared that the government and police director ordered them to set the fires . . . How could they destroy one of the world's most beautiful cities and the work of centuries to obtain such a meagre goal? That has been their conduct since Smolensk.[29]

The long, grinding campaign capped by the destruction of Moscow drained Napoleon of his usual decisiveness. He deployed his Old Guard in the Kremlin and at key places across the ruined city, his Young Guard on the outskirts and the remnants of his corps in an arc just beyond the horizon. He issued orders to organize a police force, repair the water pumps, feed the homeless, open hospitals and see what supplies could be salvaged. But mostly he vainly waited week after week for a message from Alexander asking for terms. He would have saved his army and empire had he withdrawn after two weeks rather than lingered for six.

The turning point came on 3 October, when Napoleon dispatched General Jacques Lauriston to Kutuzov's headquarters before going to St Petersburg to negotiate with Alexander.[30] Kutuzov refused to let Lauriston proceed until he received orders from the Tsar to do so. That refusal jolted Napoleon from his stupor. He reasoned that at the very least a message to and from the Tsar at St Petersburg would take several weeks. Then the Tsar might simply repeat his vow not to negotiate as long as a single enemy soldier remained on Russian soil. And, in the unlikely event that he agreed to talk, his intention might be to delay the French army in Moscow while the Russian army swelled in numbers and the snows deepened over the subsequent weeks and months.

Napoleon issued a stream of orders to prepare his army for the long withdrawal westward, the destination and route still undecided. Despite the devastation of Moscow, his troops discovered plenty of warehouses packed with provisions and munitions that had escaped the flames. Indeed they scrounged enough provisions to sustain the army to Smolensk or even Vilna if need be. The problem was getting them there. The army was critically short of draft animals for his guns and wagons. Hundreds of wagons were needed just to carry the 10,000 or so wounded and sick, who began to be evacuated with heavy escorts. Atop that Napoleon needed several thousand horses to mount all his cavalrymen. He overlooked a critical preparation; after the temperatures plummeted, without spiked horseshoes thousands of riding and draft animals would break their legs on the icy roads. He also desperately needed more troops. He ordered Claude Victor's corps and smaller forces, to advance. He had orders sent to Paris and Milan to conscript 140,000 and 30,000 troops, respectively, for 1813. He instructed the Confederation of the Rhine princes to replenish the ranks of their regiments in Russia. He worried that the worsening news seeping from Russia would dampen the zeal of his allies, especially Prussia and Austria.[31]

He initially intended to winter his corps in a defensive circle around Smolensk. The question was how best to get there. He ruled out the route his army had taken from there to Moscow since his troops had scavenged any food available from the cities and countryside along that way. He finally decided to march down the south-west road a hundred miles to capture Kaluga, with its food supplies, then perhaps send a corps 70 miles east to destroy Tula, with its arms industry, before angling west to Smolensk on a route that had not been looted or fought over and thus should reap provisions.[32]

When the long retreat westward began on 20 October, Napoleon's army numbered 95,000 troops and 500 guns to Kutuzov's 117,000 troops and 622 guns.[33] Mortier's 10,000-man corps was the last to leave Moscow; Mortier complied with Napoleon's orders to have the Kremlin's walls blown up behind them. Learning of Napoleon's advance, Kutuzov shifted his army westward to block the way at Maloyaroslavets on 22 October. Napoleon ordered an attack. The battle seesawed until the French finally bludgeoned the Russians off the field late that day, with each suffering around 7,000 casualties. The next morning Cossacks nearly captured Napoleon as he reconnoitred with a few followers. The merciless battle followed by his heart-pounding escape spooked him into a critical decision seemingly justified by that adage 'better the devil one knows than the devil one does not know'. He had no idea how many Russians lay beyond that south-west horizon on the road to Kaluga, but he feared overwhelming numbers who would fight fiercely. He reluctantly ordered his army to head north then west on the corpse-strewn devastated route they had taken from the Niemen to Moscow.

With Kutuzov hounding him, Napoleon's steadily dwindling army faced a gauntlet of converging Russian forces westward, with the largest Generals Peter Wittgenstein's 67,000 troops from the north and Vassilivich Chichagov's 36,000 troops and Tormazov's 30,000 troops from the south. On the northern front, Macdonald and St Cyr together had about 48,000 troops but would break off the siege of Riga and withdraw to Tilsit, Poland as Essen's army, now with 45,000 troops, pursued him. On the southern front, Schwarzenberg and Reynier had about 41,000 troops but would withdraw to Bialystok, Poland by early December.

When the retreat began, most days were sunny and cool, while temperatures dropped below freezing at night. The first snow fell then quickly melted on 25 October. Within a couple of weeks the snow not only lingered but deepened as temperatures plummeted. Day and night hundreds of men starved or froze to death. Day and night Cossacks roamed like wolves around the steadily diminishing mob that was once an army, murdering and robbing the stragglers. Advanced Russian troops battled and snipped off ever more of the rearguard, with the worst loss 7,000 killed or captured at Viazma on 3 November.

Napoleon received stunning news on 6 November. A group of conspirators had tried to take power in Paris.[34] The aborted coup's leader was General Claude Malet, who in 1809 was convicted with several others for plotting to assassinate him. He was imprisoned rather than shot because the plot appeared to involve more talk than action. Malet escaped and this time acted. On 22 October, he and several others briefly took over the Paris military command by wielding forged documents and claims that Napoleon was dead. Eventually authorities recognized the fraud and mustered loyal troops that arrested Malet and eighty-four other suspects. In the subsequent trial Malet and fourteen others were found guilty of treason and executed on 29 October. Napoleon was alarmed to discover that his carefully-constructed empire appeared to be nothing more than an elaborate house of cards. He longed to get back to Paris and reassert control as soon as he had extracted his army's remnants from Russia: 'In the existing state of affairs, I can only hold my grip on Europe from the Tuileries.'[35]

Napoleon reached Smolensk on 9 November and spent five days there trying to reorganize and reequip his army's survivors. He had long before given up any notion of wintering there. The city's warehouses were nearly bare while the converging Russian armies had overwhelming numbers of troops. He resumed the retreat on 15 November. Kutuzov became bolder, attacking and inflicting a series of defeats on the rearguard, with the worst loss 13,000 killed and 26,000 captured at Krasnoi from 14 to 18 November.

When the frigid, fast-flowing Berezina River barred the way on 21 November, Napoleon had about 15,000 effective troops trailed by 25,000 or so stragglers. Victor was to the west with 12,000 troops. Three Russian armies with 100,000 troops altogether approached, Wittgenstein from the north, Kutuzov from the east and Chichagov from the south. Napoleon deployed his engineers in the icy waters to construct two bridges which most of his troops crossed on 22 November as Victor's troops repelled an attack by Chichagov's army. Although Napoleon escaped with 20,000 troops, the Russians captured 30,000 regulars and stragglers at the Berezina.

Napoleon issued his 29th Bulletin on December 3. For once an imperial bulletin did not lie, but revealed that the army had suffered devastating losses. The bulletin countered rumours that he had died with these words: 'The emperor's health has never been better.' Tragically the same could not be said for the hundreds of thousands of soldiers and civilians who had perished during the campaign. Despite his army's critical position, he was about to turn his back on it: 'I believe my presence in Paris is necessary for France, for the empire and even for the army.'[36]

Napoleon handed over command of his army's remnants to Murat at Smorgoni on 5 December and headed with Caulaincourt and a few other aides to Paris. He fled an apocalypse. Just how many people died during the 1812 Russian campaign will never be known. Mostly likely 500,000 troops were killed, captured or deserted and 175,000 horses perished from

Napoleon's army; they abandoned 1,131 guns. Russia's nature rather than soldiers was the worst enemy. For every man killed in battle, ten died from disease, heatstroke, starvation or frostbite. Of the dead, 100,000 or so starved or froze to death, diseases killed 100,000 or so more; and violence killed the rest. The Russians may have suffered the deaths of 250,000 troops along with several hundred thousand civilians. Napoleon squeezed those horrors from his mind as he did whatever he could to rebuild his army and crumbling empire.

Chapter 19

The Dying Gaul

'Your Majesty should not worry. We will emerge triumphant from this struggle.'

'All of Europe marched with us a year ago. All of Europe marches against us today . . . Thus we will have to redouble our nation's efforts . . . Posterity will say that when the great and critical circumstance presented themselves, France and I rose to the occasion.'

'If the nation backs me the enemy marches at its peril. If fortune betrays me . . . I do not have a throne.'

Napoleon's return from the Niemen to Paris could not have contrasted more starkly with what he experienced along that route seven months earlier. In May and June 1812 he had paraded eastward literally and figuratively as Europe's head, with more than 600,000 troops, half French and half foreign, and scores of states behind him; with pomp and swagger he had nodded at the adoring or fearful sovereigns bowing before him or glanced through the windows of his gilded coach at the throngs lining the roads trying to glimpse him. Now he was a fugitive with the alias Count Gerard de Reneval and job title of Caulaincourt's aide, racing first by sleigh and then carriage 1,300 miles in thirteen days. He dared not tarry almost anywhere for fear of being recognized and perhaps mobbed, arrested or murdered.[1]

Along the way Napoleon conducted only two acts of diplomacy. He spent the night at the French ambassador's residence at Dresden, where he tried to downplay the catastrophe with Saxon Elector Frederick Augustus. But Saxony was a minor power. It was essential to keep Austria and Prussia from breaking their alliance or, far worse, switching sides. On 14 December, he wrote to Francis and Frederick William, admitting a setback, claiming that he still had 80,000 troops to thwart Russia's advance and promising eventually to vanquish Alexander.[2] He would soon receive alarming news from Berlin and Vienna. He was bearded and filthy when he tried to enter the Tuileries on the night of 18 December. Sceptical guards kept him at bay until someone reliable could vouch that the emperor had indeed returned.

For weeks thereafter, Napoleon performed zombie-like the essential steps of trying to rebuild his shattered military, political, financial and diplomatic power.[3] He was 'sombre, sad and faraway. He showed himself little in public and seemed to fear being badly received . . . He offered himself under a new light. He was no longer the always victorious leader. One saw for the first time someone misfortunate . . . condemned his faults and mourned the losses.'[4] With Eugène he admitted his 'despondency' over the catastrophe:

> It has taken me years to cultivate self-control to prevent my emotions from betraying themselves. Only a short time ago I was the conqueror of the world, commanding the largest and finest army of modern times. That is all gone now! . . . I have devoted myself to silencing that chord within me . . . Without this self-control, do you think I could have done all I've done.[5]

Meanwhile, Russia's high command split over what to do next. Commanding General Mikhail Kutuzov wanted to halt at the frontier. Having liberated Russia from Napoleon, Alexander was eager to liberate the rest of Europe but hesitated. A Prussian general decided the issue. General Johann Yorck von Wartenburg commanded the 17,000 Prussians attached to Marshal Étienne Macdonald's corps. On 30 December, Yorck signed at Tauroggen a neutrality pact with Russian envoys and withdrew into Prussia. That encouraged Alexander to order his armies to march west beyond the Niemen. Meanwhile Austrian General Karl von Schwarzenberg withdrew his army into Austrian Galicia with the unwritten understanding that the Russians would respect that frontier. Alexander wrote Francis a plea to break his alliance with France.

Eugène now commanded the remnants of the army in eastern Poland. Although Napoleon had given the command to Murat, he in turn passed that baton to Eugène then hurried back to Naples. Learning of the Russian advance, Eugène retreated to Posen on the Vistula River. His sojourn there was brief. Word of vast numbers of advancing Russian troops in several armies drove him back to Berlin.

When Eugène entered Berlin, Frederick William III was not there to greet him. On 2 January, the Prussian king, his family and his government had escaped to Breslau before eventually reaching the Russian army's headquarters. Under the Treaty of Kalisch signed on 28 February 1813, Alexander and Frederick William pledged 150,000 and 80,000 troops, respectively, to destroy Napoleon's empire, with no separate peace; Prussia did not formally declare war until 17 March. Russian and Prussian troops marched triumphantly into Berlin on 4 March. A large force of Russian and Prussian troops would besiege or blockade the 70,000 or so mostly second-rate French or allied soldiers garrisoning the fortress cities of Danzig, Glogau, Thorn, Kustrin, Stettin, Spandau, Torgau, Magdeburg and Wittenberg stranded behind Allied lines.

Napoleon might have forestalled Prussia's defection had he agreed in January to Frederick William's demands that his realm be restored to its pre-1806 borders and France pay hard cash for what it owed for requisitions. But hubris kept Napoleon from surrendering what he had previously taken. Over the next year that same hubris would torpedo half a dozen other chances to cut his losses and walk away with a peace treaty that kept him in power.

Napoleon's most urgent task was rebuilding the Grand Army.[6] To that end, he fired off letters daily to War Minister Henri Clarke, Chief of Staff Alexandre Berthier and Director of War Administration Jean Lacuée on a myriad of issues. As usual, he seemed to know the location of each regiment of this army, although the task was far simpler given the catastrophe in Russia. To refill depleted surviving regiments he drafted 100,000 men from years back to 1810, withdrew 30,000 troops from Spain and transferred 12,000 sailors, mostly gunners, into the army. He sought to rebuild his Imperial Guard to at least 20,000 infantry, 10,000 cavalry and 60 guns with 600 artillerymen. In two ways he made up for his poorly trained and inferior numbers of infantry. He brought more cannons and had his troops deploy in two rather than three lines facing the enemy. The worst shortage was horses; he had what few horses were available gathered from his shrinking empire. He had small mountains of munitions and provisions produced, sent and packed in fortresses near the front. Magdeburg was the central magazine for the Elbe army with rear magazines in Cassel, Frankfurt and Mainz. And somehow, he had to pay for it all. He had Treasury Minister Nicolas Mollien establish a central treasury at Magdeburg with branches in Hamburg, Mainz, Berlin, Stettin, Kustrin and Glogau. Mollien could only partly fulfil his order. Enemy armies soon besieged the last three sites and chased the French from Berlin.

With Prussia having switched sides and Austrian neutrality teetering, it was critical for Napoleon to shore up his remaining alliances and find new ones. Each ally had suffered its own horrendous losses in Russia and would baulk at contributing more troops. His upbeat words to Danish King Frederick VI were typical of what he fired off to other allies: 'I guarantee to Your Majesty Norway and the integrity of your state; nothing in the world can make you lose a single part . . . I will have . . . a 30,000 man corps for the security of Your Majesty's states . . . Your Majesty should not worry. We will emerge triumphant from this struggle.'[7]

Napoleon also had to patch up relations with Jérôme. Considering his humiliating treatment of Jérôme early in the Russian campaign, he probably felt a bit sheepish about now asking his brother for help. He finally got around to it on 18 January, writing: 'According to the usage that that I have always practised in important circumstances, I believe I must communicate to Your Majesty the situation of our affairs.' He began by falsely boasting that he had defeated the Russians in every battle. He then explained the devastating retreat, blaming overwhelming converging numbers of Russian troops, the wolf-like Cossacks, the snowstorms and the sub-zero temperatures, capped by the Prussian corps' defection. Finally, he called on Jérôme to rebuild Westphalia's contingent and join it with the Grand Army massing on the Elbe.[8]

Napoleon had to rebuild confidence and trust at home. On 14 February, he addressed the Legislative Corps during its opening session. He had a lot of explaining to do. He began by recounting French victories from the Niemen to Moscow and back, but: 'The winter's excessive vigour and premature arrival imposed on my army a terrible calamity. In a few nights I saw all change. I had great losses that would have broken my soul if . . . I' was not committed 'to the interests, glory and future of my people'. He then put a positive spin on the situation in Spain, Italy and the concordat with Rome. Finally, he hit them up for money: 'I have need of great resources to take care of all the expenses that the circumstances demand.'[9] By now many, perhaps most, of the legislators despised Napoleon's tyranny but dared not protest. They would not be so reticent ten months later after the latest series of catastrophes.

At this point Napoleon recognized that he fought on the edge of a political abyss. While the chance of being killed was a constant in combat, this time he faced the possibility of being not just defeated but also dethroned. And if so, his only fall-back was having his three-year-old son, 'the King of Rome', recognized as his successor. For that he established a regency council with Marie Louise presiding, assisted by a dozen key advisors including most prominently Cambacérès and Talleyrand, respectively his most competent supporter and secret enemy. The setup, however, violated the France's cultural and constitutional proscriptions against having female rulers. He called on the Legislative Corps to change that 'unjust, impolitic and immoral' policy. They complied.[10]

* * *

Napoleon left Paris on 15 April 1813 and two days later was at Mainz.[11] He spent a week there overseeing the training and organization of the troops and planning the campaign with his corps commanders. He commanded around 179,000 mostly raw conscripts split among corps led by Michel Ney, Auguste Marmont, Nicolas Oudinot, Laurent Gouvion St Cyr, Louis Davout and Henri Bertrand. His army of 1813 was a shadow of that of 1805, when it peaked as a fighting force. Most of the 20,000 cavalry lacked tactical skills.

After Kutuzov died on 29 April, Alexander replaced him with Ludwig von Wittgenstein. Although Wittgenstein was nominally the Allied commander-in-chief, Alexander cast a long shadow at his headquarters. The Allied army advanced in two wings and a reserve. Wittgenstein commanded the right wing composed of 19,000 Russians and 30,000 Prussians in two corps led by Gebhard von Blücher and Friedrich Bülow von Dennewitz.

Napoleon commenced his advance on 25 April and deployed his army around Erfurt, which became his new headquarters. On 1 May, he launched his corps eastward.[12] His plan was simply to retake the central Elbe River valley then march north to Berlin, defeating any enemy forces along the way. Fifty miles north, Eugène and his 50,000 troops marched in tandem to guard his left flank before joining him east of the Elbe. Napoleon assigned Davout's 35,000-man corps to retake and hold Hamburg. Although denying that port to the enemy was important, Davout's brilliance would have been far better wielded on the central front while a lesser luminary handled that sideshow.[13]

With so little cavalry, Napoleon was myopic if not outright blind to the enemy's positions and numbers. Huge clouds of cavalry and Cossacks guarded the Allied armies and charged any French cavalry that appeared. He sent Ney followed by Marmont and Bertrand toward Lützen on 1 May. He thought the Allied army was near Leipzig. Actually Wittgenstein's army was encamped on a broad plateau south of Lützen. Spotting the enemy, Ney marched his men south to attack while Marmont supported him and Bertrand hurried his corps toward the sound of the guns. Wittgenstein ordered his army to descend from the plateau with Blücher and Yorck on the right and left, respectively, backed by Berg, Winzingerode and the Prussian Guard. The battle seesawed until early afternoon when Napoleon arrived with the Imperial Guard and sent forward the Young Guard against the enemy's centre while Bertrand turned the enemy's left flank. That battle might have been decisive had the French matched the Allies in cavalry but the enemy infantry simply disappeared behind an impenetrable screen of horsemen. Wittgenstein withdrew his army to a plateau behind the Spree River with Bautzen on the east bank. Reinforcements swelled the Allied army to 96,000 troops, including Alexander and his Imperial Guard. Napoleon's limited victory came at a huge cost, 20,000 casualties compared to 11,000 for the Allies. Despite or perhaps because of that, he spun the victory as much as he could. In his proclamation to the army, he praised his troops for their conduct and promised that 'the battle of Lützen will be put above the battles of Austerlitz, Iena, Friedland and Borodino'.[14]

Napoleon established his headquarters at the Marcolini Palace in Dresden. He sent Eugène back to Italy to prepare the kingdom for possible war against Austria; Oudinot now commanded that northern army whose mission was to block an advance from Bülow's army that shielded Berlin.[15] Napoleon split his own army into two wings; down the Elbe at Torgau the left included 79,500 infantry and 4,800 cavalry led by Ney; at Dresden, the emperor himself commanded 110,000 infantry and 12,000 cavalry. This campaign's emotional toll on Napoleon was especially harsh after cannon balls shattered the lives of two close friends, Jean-Baptiste Bessières and Christophe Duroc.

Meanwhile, under Chancellor Clemens von Metternich's guidance, Austrian Emperor Francis was inching away from his alliance with his son-in-law into neutrality followed by, if he did not get all that he wanted, alliance with Russia, Prussia and Britain. He sent General Ferdinand von Bubna to Dresden with an offer to mediate peace based on these terms: restoration of Austria and Prussia to their respective pre-1805 and pre-1807 territory; France reduced to its natural frontiers of the Rhine, Alps and Pyrenees; Napoleon's repudiation of his Italian throne; independence for the Netherlands, Hamburg and Lübeck; and elimination of the Duchy of Warsaw and the Confederation of the Rhine. Napoleon angrily rejected all these terms except the Duchy of Warsaw's elimination and Illyria's transfer to Austria if it remained a French ally. He also agreed 'to opening negotiations for a general peace and convening a congress in an intermediary city from the diverse belligerent courts. As soon as

I learn that England, Russia, Prussia and their allies have accepted this proposition, I will hasten to send a plenipotentiary to the congress and I will engage my allies to do the same.'[16]

Napoleon counted on a knockout victory to let him dictate the terms of any peace congress. The Battle of Bautzen that raged on 20 and 21 May might have delivered that victory had Ney followed his orders. The plan was for the main army to attack the enemy's front while Ney encircled and crushed the enemy's right. Ney, however, advanced cautiously rather than decisively which let Wittgenstein redeploy his reserve to block his attack. Once again, like a Sumo wrestler, the French shoved the Allies off the field, but suffered far more casualties, 15,000 to 10,000, while failing to score a knockout. The Allies withdrew eastward. The French army was too battered to follow immediately but by 1 June advanced as far as Breslau on the Katzbach River. Elsewhere, Davout retook Hamburg on 27 May and Oudinot repelled Bülow's attack on 28 May but failed to pursue the enemy. These were pyrrhic victories as the French lost far more than the Allies. So far, the French had suffered 25,000 combat casualties while 50,000 troops were on the sick list, including hundreds mutilated not by the enemy but by themselves. Napoleon was shocked to learn that conscripts had shot or cut off their trigger fingers to evade combat.[17]

Napoleon sent Armand Caulaincourt to the Allies on 26 May to negotiate an armistice. He agreed on 2 June to a 36-hour truce, then, on 5 June, to extend it to 20 July as diplomats negotiated a peace treaty. He explained his gamble: 'This armistice will interrupt the course of my victories. Two considerations have made up my mind: my shortage of cavalry, which prevents us from striking great blows and Austria's hostile attitude . . . I will wait until September to strike great blows. I want to be in a position to crush my enemies.'[18] He gave no specific negotiating points or power to the two envoys that he dispatched to the talks, other than the attitude that 'the French army never had need of the armistice'.[19] He later admitted that the armistice was among his worst mistakes. At that point he had more troops immediately available than the Russians and Prussians. Over the next two months the Allies would build up their forces until they outnumbered Napoleon's by a ratio of five to three. That might not have mattered had Napoleon diplomatically cut his losses and signed a peace treaty that kept him in power over a France reduced to its 1792 frontiers, but he had no intention of doing that. Instead, he concentrated his efforts on rebuilding his army's ranks, munitions and provisions to resume the campaign. His diplomatic failure led to his military failure.

Napoleon and Metternich did not meet until 26 June. For nine and a half hours Napoleon vented a barrage of rants, boasts and promises. He chided Metternich for taking nearly a month before seeing him. He bragged about his two victories and assured him of more should the fighting resume. He warned that Austria would be crushed if it joined the coalition. He offered Illyria if Austria remained neutral but otherwise was determined to keep the existing French empire intact. He denounced his father-in-law for betraying him and thus his daughter. He emphasized various points by cursing and throwing his bicorne hat on the floor. He ended by demanding of Metternich 'how much has England given you to play this role against me'. Metternich reddened but said nothing. A long silence followed as each waited for the other to respond. Napoleon finally broke it by calling for a peace congress. He left Metternich with the hope that 'the cession of Illyria was not his last word'.[20]

Napoleon and Metternich held a shorter meeting on 30 June, when they agreed to extend the truce to 10 August, during which Austria would mediate peace impartially as a conciliator rather than an arbitrator.[21] That same day Napoleon wrote to Francis that:

> I want peace. If the Russians are as moderate as me, they will promptly make it. If to the contrary, they want me to give concession that attack my honour and the interests of my allies, they will succeed at nothing. Your Majesty knows the feelings I have for him. I hope that you will not let yourself be carried away into war.[22]

Amidst the negotiations news arrived that elated the Allies and deflated the French. Wellington's army had routed Joseph's army at Vitoria on 21 June. The French hold on Spain was now confined to two short coastal stretches leading from San Sebastian and Barcelona back to the border along with Pamplona.

During the eight-week truce, the Allied army soared in numbers while a small stream of raw conscripts joined the French. Typically Britain gilded the alliance. Under treaties signed at Reichenbach on 14 and 15 June, Berlin and St Petersburg would divvy up £2,000,000 in proportion to the number of soldiers they fielded. Under the Reichenbach Convention, signed on 27 July, Austria agreed to join the Allies if Napoleon rejected their terms. On 19 July, Napoleon did succeed in forging an agreement with Denmark to form a joint corps of 20,000 French and 12,000 Danes and the sale of 10,000 Danish horses to France.[23] The Allied offensive would kill those plans.

The Prague conference opened on 12 July, with Metternich representing Austria, Wilhelm Humboldt Prussia and Johann von Anstett Russia, but with no French envoy. Napoleon squandered two weeks before sending Caulaincourt to Prague on 26 July. Then the proceedings immediately stalled as Caulaincourt was forced to protest Anstett's presence as a former Frenchmen; Napoleon never negotiated with those that he considered traitors. Once a face-saving way was found to finesse Anstett's presence, Caulaincourt could merely report that Napoleon's only concession was agreeing to the Duchy of Warsaw's demise. On 7 August, Metternich issued an ultimatum: not only would the Duchy of Warsaw being split among Austria, Prussia and Russia, but Austria and Prussia would revert to their respective pre-1805 and pre-1807 borders; the Confederation of the Rhine would be dissolved; the Netherlands, Hamburg and Lübeck would become independent; and Prussia would get Danzig and Austria would get Illyria. Had Napoleon swiftly and simply signed the ultimatum he would have retained a France that embraced much of Belgium and Germany west of the Rhine. Instead he sent a counter-proposal that agreed on Warsaw and Illyria but rejected everything else. Austria declared war on 10 August.

Napoleon immediately sent marching orders to his commanders. He also sought to win a public relations war by issuing a refutation of Austria's behaviour and having Foreign Minister Maret expand those arguments via ambassadors.[24] He re-entered the ring looking for a chance to land a shattering blow against the enemy: 'It seems to me that the current campaign cannot lead us to a good result unless it is preceded by a great battle.'[25] Two months later he found his great battle at Leipzig but hardly the result he wanted.[26]

There were now four main Allied armies: General Bernadotte's 110,000 Prussians, Swedes and Russians near Berlin; Blücher's 95,000 Russians and Prussians near Breslau; Bennigsen's 60,000 Russians marching from Warsaw; and Schwartzenberg's 230,000 Austrians near Prague. In all, the Allies had mustered more than 495,000 troops or nearly twice the 295,000 French troops. Napoleon had about 150,000 under his immediate command. Elsewhere Oudinot's 110,000 troops threatened Berlin, while Davout's 35,000 troops were squandered guarding Hamburg. Davout's presence with Napoleon or Oudinot might have drastically changed the campaign's outcome. On paper the Allied advantage appeared less formidable in artillery, with 1,380 guns to the French army's 1,284; but without enough draft animals, hundreds of French guns were stranded at depots and fortresses. Hovering a hundred miles or so south-west of the central front was a potential fifth coalition army, General Karl von

Wrede's 30,000 Bavarians. Like Austria, Bavaria would soon violate its treaty of alliance with France.

The Allies had agreed on a simple but ultimately deadly strategy at Trachtenberg on 12 July. The armies would converge against Napoleon, attack his subordinates, but withdraw before him. That would steadily erode and drive back the French perimeter while sidestepping any lingering dregs of Napoleon's military genius. Eventually they would corner and assault Napoleon with overwhelming forces.

That strategy's wisdom was highlighted after Schwarzenberg advanced to Dresden, held by St Cyr. Napoleon quick-marched 120,000 troops there and routed the 170,000 Austrians in a two-day battle that ended on 21 August; the Austrians suffered 38,000 casualties to 10,000 for the French. Defeats elsewhere soon diluted that victory. Bülow's army routed Oudinot's at Grossbeeren on 23 August. Blücher's army devastated Macdonald's at Katzbach on 26 August. General Osterman-Tolstoy's army nearly wiped out Vandamme's at Kulm on 29 August. Bülow's army destroyed two-thirds of Ney's at Dennewitz on 8 September. During the month since the fighting resumed, the French had suffered 100,000 casualties with another 50,000 on the sick list. A lull descended over the front as each side struggled to replenish its ranks.

In early October, Napoleon withdrew most of his army to the region around Leipzig, pursued by Schwarzenberg from the south-east, Bennigsen from the east and Blücher and Bernadotte from the north-east.[27] He left behind St Cyr and 35,000 troops to defend Dresden; had Napoleon brought them to Leipzig he might well have won rather than lost that battle. Leipzig was on the Elster River's east bank with a single bridge across to the west bank and the long road to France. Initially he had not intended to fight a decisive battle there, only a delaying action to buy time to evacuate all the wounded and supplies. But on 15 October, he decided to concentrate his army there for a critical showdown. He arrived the next day and deployed his army in an arc north, east and south of the city.

No battle of the Napoleonic era involved more troops or lasted longer than Leipzig. The four-day struggle began early on 16 October and ended late on 19 October. The Battle of Leipzig was the largest in history in the numbers engaged and casualties before the First World War. Napoleon's army peaked at 225,000 men and the Allies at 380,000. Napoleon lost 81,000 men, 45,000 killed and wounded and 36,000 captured, while the Allies suffered 54,000 casualties. The terrain was broken with lots of villages, large fields, streams and marshes. Napoleon hoped to take advantage of that terrain to attack isolated segments of the swelling enemy army and devastate counter-attacks. Eventually the Allies overwhelmed the French with sheer weight of numbers. Then, after Napoleon ordered a retreat, he lost another 10,000 or so men captured after the bridge was prematurely blown up.

Napoleon retreated along his supply lines back toward France.[28] General Karl von Wrede with 43,000 Bavarian and Austrian troops blocked his way at Hanau on 30 October. Napoleon had only 20,000 troops immediately with him but in the two-day battle managed to rout the Allies, inflicting around 9,000 casualties while suffering half that. He reached Frankfurt and deployed his army around the city on 2 November. He galloped off couriers to Cambacérès and Clark with orders for them to orchestrate raising at least another 120,000 men and as much money as possible. The steady Allied march westward forced him to withdraw to Mainz and spread his 80,000 remaining troops along the west bank of the Rhine.

After returning to Paris on 10 November, he called on the Senate and Legislative Corps to somehow scrape up 150,000 more conscripts then, a month later, doubled that number to 300,000.[29] Only a fraction of that number was actually drafted. Anticipating an invasion by Wellington's army into south-western France, he ordered a reserve army massed behind the Pyrenees to support either Soult at Bayonne or Suchet at Barcelona. He tasked Clarke to find the troops for that army. That never happened. He had about 70,000 troops besieged in various fortresses in Germany and Poland. He had an officer pass through the lines with a proposal to Schwarzenberg that he would surrender those fortresses in return for the troops being allowed to march home with honours of war and their arms. That never happened. He ordered Eugène in northern Italy not to abandon the line of the Adige River without a big battle. That would happen early in 1814. He ordered the dikes broken in Holland when the Allies invaded. That too would happen early in 1814. He anticipated a 672 million franc war budget for 1814. He would receive and spend only a portion of that.

He was increasingly worried about the political impact in Paris of his latest catastrophe. He wrote Cambacérès 'to say a word to the pusillanimous councillors of state and senators. I am told . . . that they display fear and little character. Be persuaded that my infantry, cavalry and artillery have such a superiority over that of the enemy that there is nothing to doubt.'[30] To boost morale he had sixteen captured enemy flags paraded through Paris. Another problem magnified his political and strategic problems: 'There are in France 120,000 prisoners. Nearly everywhere the population is worried about these dangerous neighbours.' He sought to remedy that by ensuring on a ratio of one national guardsman for every ten prisoners.[31]

He received a sweet letter from his sister Pauline pledging her fortune to his needs. He replied:

> My expenses have been considerable this year and will be more the next year. I accept the gift you want to give me but the good will and resources of my people are such that I believe my means are assured to deal with the enormous expenses that will be demanded for the campaigns of 1814 and 1815. If this coalition of Europe against France prolonged itself beyond that and if I do not have the success that I have the right to hope from French bravery and patriotism, then I will make use of your gift and all those that my subjects want to give me.[32]

* * *

The Allied sovereigns met at Frankfurt in early November to hammer out their latest consensus on what they wanted to do and how best to do it. The key military questions were when and where to invade France. They agreed to keep Napoleon on the run to distract him from mobilizing France's manpower, munitions, provisions and other needs against them. That meant a winter campaign. As for where, they decided on the broadest possible front to force Napoleon to spread his forces as thin as possible. Schwarzenberg's 200,000 troops would outflank the Rhine River barrier by funnelling through Basel in Switzerland while Blücher's 100,000 troops would cross the central Rhine from Koblenz to Mainz; those armies would converge on the Langres plateau and source of several river valleys including the Marne, Aube and Seine meandering toward Paris. Meanwhile, Bülow would cross the lower Rhine with 35,000 Prussian troops to overrun the Low Countries, aided by General Thomas Graham with 8,000 British troops. The Allies feared leaving Davout's corps in Hamburg and the French garrison in Magdeburg in their rear. The 100,000 or so troops among Generals Bernadotte, Winzingerode and Bennigsen were detached to bottle up those enemy forces. In northern Italy, General Heinrich von Bellegarde marched with 74,000 troops against Eugène. From southern Italy, Murat would turn his coat and march north with 30,000 troops against Eugène. Finally, Wellington with 70,000 British and Portuguese troops would invade south-west France with Bayonne the first objective.

The key political questions involved the fate France: who should rule it and what penalties should it suffer? The Allied sovereigns knew that Napoleon would fight to the death if he knew they intended to depose him. Yet if they let him retain power, he might steadily rebuild his army to reconquer his empire. They shelved the question of who should rule France for now. In what became known as the Frankfurt Declaration, they agreed that any lasting peace must be grounded on a balance of power, the sovereign independence of all states and France confined to its 1792 'natural frontiers'. They sent that message to Napoleon via Louis Saint Aignan, a French diplomat captured during the Leipzig retreat. Napoleon sent back word that he agreed in principle with the declaration. Metternich replied that Napoleon should explicitly accept his entire checklist of demands. Napoleon dictated what became a fifty-page set of rebuttals and demands that Caulaincourt dutifully penned and sent to Metternich on 2 December. Tragically, that message came too late. The Allies had literally and figuratively marched forward giant steps during the three weeks from their dispatch of Aignan until they received a specific reply. After crossing the Rhine with little resistance, they forged a consensus on 1 December, that Napoleon must be deposed and that France should be reduced to its 1789 'historic frontiers', and if that meant a fight to the finish, they were confident that they would ultimately triumph.

Napoleon was prepared to fight to the death to defend his regime, although by now with far less confidence that he could survive, let alone prevail.[33] There was a shortage of nearly everything, men, muskets, guns, munitions, provisions and, especially, horses to mount cavalry and pull wagons, caissons and guns. Huge stockpiles of munitions and provisions had been abandoned in magazines that the enemy had captured. There was little left in France's own warehouses and what remained had to be transported to the front.

Napoleon turned to the Legislative Corps and Senate to approve the vast expenditures vital for rebuilding the army to resist the looming enemy invasion. The reception was chilly when he addressed the Legislative Corps' opening session on 19 December. Typically, he put the best possible spin on his latest disasters, essentially blaming his allies rather than himself:

> Striking victories lustred the French army during this campaign. Unprecedented defections rendered those victories futile. Everyone turned against us. France will be in danger without French energy and unity. In these great circumstances my first thought has been to call you near me. My heart needs your presence and the affection of my subjects . . . I have conceived and executed grand designs for the prosperity and happiness of all . . . It is with regret that I ask new sacrifices of my generous people.[34]

The applause was tepid. A committee led by Deputy Joseph Laine was tasked with examining Napoleon's policies and proposals. Laine read their report before the Legislative Corps on 28 December. The report first criticized Napoleon's policies that led to the series of catastrophes and then called for peace and civil liberties. The following day the Legislative Corps voted 223 to 51 to approve the report. Napoleon's reaction was scathing:

> You separate in your report the throne from the nation. Comprehend that the throne without the nation is nothing but four pieces of wood covered with a velvet strip. The nation is the throne, the throne is the nation . . . I am the people's only representative . . . I have a title. You do not. What are you in the Constitution? You are nothing.[35]

That same day Napoleon's hand-picked Senate presented him these gratifying words:

> The enemy has just invaded our territory . . . Empires, like men, have their days of mourning and prosperity. It is in great circumstances that one recognizes great nations. No, the enemy will not tear apart this beautiful and noble France . . . We will fight for our dear country between the tombs of our fathers and the cradles of our children. Sire, obtain the peace by a last effort dignified for you and for France.[36]

He tried to be as inspiring in his address to them: 'All of Europe marched with us a year ago. All of Europe marches against us today . . . Thus we will have to redouble our nation's efforts . . . Posterity will say that when the great and critical circumstance presented themselves, France and I rose to the occasion.[37]

Napoleon released two celebrity prisoners in January 1814. He sent Pope Pius back to Rome and Ferdinand VII back to Madrid. Each gesture was too little too late. He was deluded to believe that they would take their respective realms into neutrality. He revealed his thinking on the tangled diplomatic, military and political situation in a 4 January letter to Caulaincourt. As for diplomacy,

> it was doubtful that the allies were in good faith and that England wanted peace. Me, I want it, but solid, honourable . . . I accept the basis of Frankfurt but it is probable that the allies have other

ideas. Their propositions are only a mask. Once the negotiations are under the influence of military events, one can only speculate over the results.

He was right about all of this. Caulaincourt should

> listen to everything and observe everything . . . Do they want to reduce France to its ancient limits? That is degrading. They are mistaken if they believe the evils of war can make a nation desire such a peace. There is not a French heart that will not feel opprobrium within six months and reproach the government lax enough for signing it.

In this, he probably overestimated the value most French attached to an empire over peace. By now virtually all French were sullen and distrustful and some outright opposed to his regime. Whether an organized opposition arose against him depended on how well he took advantage of peace to restore their well-being. He was gambling that a decisive military victory could preserve his empire: 'If the nation backs me the enemy marches at its peril. If fortune betrays me . . . I do not have a throne.' As for a specific diplomatic strategy Caulaincourt should follow, 'I cannot prescribe anything. For now limit yourself to letting me know everything you learn.'[38] Having said that, he did issue Caulaincourt a list of what France should keep and could cede. By all means, he should insist that France retain its existing departments in Holland, the Rhine's left bank and Italy. But, if necessary, he could cede Holland and Italy as independent countries in return for keeping Antwerp, Mainz, Elba, Corsica and Lucca. If Italy was divided Joseph should get Tuscany and France should retain Piedmont. Any preliminary agreement 'should be as imprecise as possible to gain time'.[39]

He tried to exacerbate tensions among the Allies with a letter of 16 January to Metternich in which he wrote:

> Supposing that the future continues to favour the allies, it is important . . . that Austria considers carefully what would be the situation in Europe the day after France lost a battle in its heart. Such an event would counter the equilibrium that Austria aspires to establish as well as the family ties of Emperor Francis . . . All these considerations led me to think that in the current position of the armies . . . a suspension of arms would be reciprocally advantageous.[40]

He never received a reply.

* * *

Napoleon left Paris on 24 January 1814 and joined his 36,000 troops at Brienne on 28 January.[41] His strategic situation in eastern France was dire but not hopeless. The Allied strategy involved parallel advances toward Paris by Blücher and Schwarzenberg down the Marne and Seine River valleys, respectively. The Aube River flowed between the two and part of Blücher's army marched down that valley. With detachments, desertion and disease, the armies of Blücher and Schwarzenberg now numbered 60,000 and 100,000 troops, respectively.

Napoleon's strategy was simple. He would get between the Allied armies to attack and defeat each separately. The site of the campaign's first two battles must have tugged at his heartstrings. He had studied at the military school at Brienne for five years. His troops defeated Blücher's advance guard at Brienne on 29 January, then deployed a few miles south with the village of La Rothière at the centre of his line; his victory cost him about 3,000 killed and wounded while inflicting 4,000 casualties on the enemy. Blücher massed his army and attacked on 1 February; the sheer numbers overwhelmed the French. Each side suffered about 6,000 casualties, but Napoleon could not afford that loss along with about fifty guns. He withdrew 20 miles west to Troyes on the Seine River.

As Blücher and Schwarzenberg converging against him, Napoleon launched a series of attacks. He trounced Blücher at Champaubert on 10 February, Montmirail on 11 February, Château-Thierry on 13 February and Vauchamps on 14 February, then turned against Schwarzenberg, defeating Wittgenstein's corps at Nangis on 17 February and Montereau on 18 February. He then marched to Sezanne, a central position where he could rest his troops, mass supplies and attack the first enemy army that ventured his way or down the Marne or Seine valleys, each a dozen miles north or south. Blücher retreated north toward Lâon and Schwarzenberg east to Bar-sur-Aube. During a council of war at Bar-sur-Aube on 24 February. Alexander, Francis, Frederick William and Castlereagh. When Schwarzenberg advised a withdrawal to the Langres plateau, Alexander insisted that they stay and fight.

Napoleon was beset with his own worries. His army was increasingly short of munitions and provisions. Ever more soldiers marched and fought with empty cartridge boxes and stomachs. Snow and freezing rain impeded movement during many days and rendered miserable the nightly bivouacs. He learned on 13 February that Murat had declared war against him and was attacking Eugène in northern Italy. Murat had turned his coat on 1 January 1814, when he signed a treaty with Austria to war against Eugène in return for retaining his throne with the bonus of acquiring Ancona. With the destruction of Napoleon's regime just a matter of time, Murat sought only the survival of his own. As the invaders advanced, they inflicted a terrible vengeance on the French. Napoleon was enraged that: 'The enemy troops are acting horribly everywhere. All the inhabitants are refugees in the woods. One finds no more peasants in the villages. The enemy eats everything, takes all the horses, takes all the animals, takes all the clothing, take all the property of the peasants. They assault everyone, men and women, and commit a great many rapes.'[42]

Throughout the campaign, Napoleon's mind kept twisting back to Paris where Joseph presided over a volatile, divisive population and increasingly venomous political pit. He worried that his mild-mannered brother might lose control, especially given 'the evil spirit of Talleyrand and some men to put the nation to sleep and prevent me from carrying on the war'. He wanted to send his wife and son to a safe chateau south of the Loire but feared that might provoke panic and disruptions in Paris.[43] His worst fear was that the Allies would capture and carry away his wife and son to Vienna: 'I would prefer that they cut my son's throat than see him raised in Vienna as an Austrian prince.' He warned Joseph that if Talleyrand wants 'to leave the empress in Paris in case our forces must evacuate, then he is committing treason. I repeat to you, beware of this man. I practised it for sixteen years while at the same time I favoured him. But he is surely our family's worst enemy.' Here Napoleon was prescient. He then issued these terse instructions: 'If news arrives of a lost battle or my death . . . make the empress and the king of Rome leave for Rambouillet; order the Senate, State Council and all the troops to reunite on the Loire.' He was then to negotiate a regency of Marie Louise for her son.[44]

Meanwhile, the peace talks opened at Chatillon on 5 February. The Allies informed Caulaincourt that France would be reduced to its 1791 borders. Caulaincourt galloped off a courier with that message to Napoleon. Had Napoleon immediately agreed, he would have retained his throne. But, warped by anger and delusions, he rejected the demand. The Allies promptly ended negotiations.[45] Following his string of victories in late February, Napoleon sent Caulaincourt these conflicting instructions: 'I give you carte blanche to save Paris and avoid a battle that will be the nation's last hope.' Then, having said that, he essentially revoked it: 'Your attitude must be the same. You must do everything for peace but . . . sign nothing without my order because only I know my position . . . I desire only a solid and honourable peace and that can only be on the basis proposed at Frankfurt.'[46] That had not been an option since mid-December. He wrote Francis that 'I did all I could to avoid the battle that took place. Fortune smiles on me.' He then made a series of false claims that he had destroyed Blücher's army, was destroying Schwarzenberg's army and had as many troops as the Austrians. These were his terms:

> I ask Your Majesty to avoid the chances of a battle. I ask peace of you, a prompt peace founded on the proclamation made by Prince Schwarzenberg on December 1 . . . on the basis that has been offered by Prince Metternich. Count Nesselrode and Lord Aberdeen to Baron Saint Aignan . . . Your Majesty can in a word end the war, assure the happiness of the peoples of Europe and end the evils of a nation as prey.[47]

Diplomacy was unfolding within the Allied camp but it was not favourable to France. The Congress at Chaumont opened on 1 March. It took nine days of negotiations before they signed the Treaty of Chaumont on 9 March, but backdated it to 1 March to display unity and decisiveness. They agreed to maintain their alliance for 20 years with each committing 150,000 troops against France; Britain would underwrite the alliance with £5 million; France would be reduced to its 1791 borders; all members had to agree to any peace treaty and no member could conduct a separate peace.

With only 24,000 troops left, Napoleon marched north against Blücher in early March. He drove Blücher from Craone on 7 March, but was defeated at Lâon during a battle that raged on 9 and 10 March in which Blücher's army swelled to 100,000 men. He withdrew to Rheims where on 12 March, he routed a Russian corps. He sent a week at Rheims replenishing his ranks and supplies, then turned south with 28,000 troops against Schwarzenberg's 100,000 troops. The decisive battle came at Arcis-sur-Aube on 20 and 21 March. The strain of this latest campaign atop two years of catastrophes ate away at Napoleon and he may have sought the ultimate escape. When a sputtering shell landed in the damp earth nearby, he did not spur his horse away but instead walked his horse over it. The shell exploded, eviscerating the horse but leaving Napoleon untouched. Outnumbered nearly four to one, Napoleon had no choice but to withdraw. Yet, instead of heading west toward Paris, Napoleon made an enormous gamble – he marched east to cut the enemy's supply lines.

That strategy might have succeeded had Cossacks not captured a courier carrying a letter from Napoleon to Marie Louise explaining his intentions. Blücher and Schwarzenberg decided literally to turn their backs on Napoleon and converge their armies at Paris. The final Allied offensive began on 25 March. Blücher routed Mortier and Marmont at La-Fère-Champenoise on that day. The next day, far in the Allied rear, Napoleon won his last battle of that campaign by defeating an enemy force at Saint Dizier. After learning that Schwarzenberg and Blücher had joined forces before Paris on 28 March, Napoleon hurried his 20,000 troops westward. With overwhelming forces blocking the roads leading to Paris, Napoleon veered south-west to Fontainebleau, 43 miles south of the capital.

The end was just over the horizon. Paris had no fortifications, apart from two heights on the outskirts, Belleville to the north-east and Montmartre to the north. To defend the city, Marmont and Mortier had only about 30,000 regular troops and 12,000 National Guards. On 28 March, the Regency Council voted nineteen to three that Marie Louise remain in Paris as a symbol of resistance. Then Joseph read a letter from Napoleon calling for the regency council to abandon Paris for Blois on the Loire River if the Allies threatened to attack. So that is what they did on 29 March, reaching the Blois two days later. Meanwhile, Marshal Philibert Sérurier, the governor of the Invalides, ordered all 1,417 captured enemy battle flags burned. The Allies attacked Paris on 30 March. In what was the largest battle of the 1814 campaign, they captured the heights and routed the defenders, with each side suffering 9,000 casualties. Marmont and Mortier surrendered the city.

The coup that Napoleon had feared throughout his 14 years in power finally took place. Talleyrand's time had come. He had stayed behind when the government fled. For years he had been on the payrolls of various foreign states, exchanging secret information for cash. During this campaign he had sent agents through the lines to the Allied camp. He received a request from Alexander to stay at his mansion during his time in Paris. That played perfectly into Talleyrand's plans. Talleyrand welcomed the parade of victorious Allied sovereigns leading their armies into Paris on 1 April. The following day, Talleyrand engineered Senate votes that deposed Napoleon and imposed a provisional government with a five-man executive headed by himself.

From 30 March to 2 April, a succession of couriers bearing bad news galloped up to Napoleon's headquarters: the Allies had taken Paris; Augereau had abandoned Lyon; Soult had retreated to Toulouse; the

Senate had deposed him. The most important message was a letter to Napoleon from Alexander, in which the Tsar demanded that he surrender unconditionally to spare any more senseless bloodshed and destruction, but pledged that the Allies would generously underwrite his retirement and exile. Napoleon had only 20,000 troops immediately with him to fight 150,000 or more Allied troops deployed around Paris. Munitions and provisions were nearly exhausted. Yet, despite all that Napoleon was dead set to keep fighting until victory or the glorious deaths of himself and his men.

His generals were no longer willing to do that. On 4 April, Ney, Berthier, Macdonald, Savary, Oudinot, Moncey, Caulaincourt and Lefebvre confronted him with the inescapable reality that victory was impossible and any more resistance was futile. When Napoleon angrily rejected their advice and asserted that the army would follow him, Ney retorted: 'No! From now on it will only obey its commanders, us.'[48] Napoleon bitterly agreed to dispatch Ney, Caulaincourt and Macdonald to ask the Allies for terms.

As his envoys haggled with the Allied leaders in Paris, Napoleon received the stunning news that Marmont had surrendered his 11,000 troops on 4 April. The following day his envoys returned with the Allied promise to buy out Napoleon and his family with 'golden parachutes'. Negotiations over the details began and lasted six days. Napoleon was a canny haggler. Under the treaty signed on 11 April, the French government would grant Napoleon 2,500,000 francs annually, his mother 300,000 francs, Joseph 500,000 francs, Louis 200,000 francs, Hortense 400,000 francs, Jérôme 500,000 francs, Elisa 300,000 francs and Pauline 300,000 francs. Napoleon would retain his title and rule the island of Elba for his lifetime. Marie Louise would receive 1,000,000 francs annually and the duchies of Parma, Plaisance and Guastalla, to be inherited by their son. Eugène would receive a realm yet to be determined. Josephine's existing pension was reduced to 1,000,000 francs. A detachment of Old Guard grenadiers would accompany Napoleon to Elba. He would receive one warship, a brig. Any Frenchmen who followed him into exile would retain their citizenship. But he paid a heavy price for all this. The Allies stripped him permanently not merely of his French throne but, as it turned out, his wife and son.

After signing the treaty, Napoleon issued an abdication declaration:

> The allied powers having proclaimed that Emperor Napoleon was the sole obstacle to the reestablishment of peace in Europe, the Emperor Napoleon, faithful to his oath, declares that he

renounces, for himself and his heirs, the thrones of France and Italy and that there is not a single sacrifice, including that of his life, that he is ready to make for the interests of France.[49]

That evening Napoleon wrote these plaintive words to Marie Louise: 'I received your letter. I see there all your sorrows which add to mine . . . Carry yourself well, conserve your health . . . for your son who needs your care. I am going to leave for the island of Elba, where I will write you. Write me often . . . Adieu, my good Louise Marie.'[50] That night he tried to kill himself by ingesting a poison that he had carried with him since his Russian campaign, but it had lost its deadly potency and just made him violently sick. After recovering the next morning, he fatalistically prepared for his journey into exile.

Chapter 20

The Odysseus

'Soldiers, today is the anniversary of Marengo and Friedland, which twice decided Europe's fate . . . Soldiers, we have forced marches to make, battles to fight and perils to run, but with perseverance, victory will be ours: the rights, the honour and the happiness of the country will be reconquered.'

'Because you've been beaten by Wellington you consider him to be a good general. I say he is a bad general and that the English are bad troops.'

Referring to himself in the third person, Napoleon recalled the morning of his departure for Elba: 'The emperor left his apartment and descended the grand marble staircase. The Old Guard stood in ranks in the courtyard . . . The emperor embraced the Old Guard's eagles as they were presented to him. Tears ran down the soldiers' cheeks.'[1] In his farewell address, he tried to bolster their spirits: 'For twenty years I have found you constantly on the road of honour and glory. In this latest time, you have not ceased to be models of bravery and fidelity. With men like you, our cause was never lost.' He then explained that the war was ceaseless and could have become a civil war. For those reasons he agreed to abdicate. 'Do not feel sorry for me', he urged. 'If I agreed to give up, it is again to serve your glory. I want to write about the great things that we have done together.' He would have liked to embrace them all but they were too numerous so instead he embraced the flag that they had served.[2]

A commissioner from each of the four Allies would escort Napoleon across France to Fréjus, his embarkation port. Britain's envoy, Lieutenant Colonel Neil Campbell, would accompany him into exile. Campbell's first encounter with Napoleon was deflating, hardly the grand monarch that he had imagined:

I saw before me a short, active-looking man, who was rapidly pacing the length of his apartment like some wild animal in his cell. He was dressed in an old green uniform with gold epaulets, blue pantaloons and red topboots, unshaven, uncombed, with the fallen particles of snuff scattered profusely upon his upper lip and breast. Upon his becoming aware of my presence, he turned quickly toward me and saluted me with a courteous smile.[3]

Napoleon's journey to Elba was humiliating, mournful and at times fearful.[4] The cavalcade left Fontainebleau on 20 April 1814 and reached Fréjus a week later. Along the way, enraged men and women vented the pent-up hatred that his incessant wars, taxes, conscriptions, deprivations, maimings and death had aroused within them. When word reached the procession that a volatile crowd awaited him in a town or city ahead, he disguised himself in a uniform of one of his former enemies and rode on horseback rather than in the coach. Near Valence, he ran into Marshal Charles Augereau and they had a heated exchange. Napoleon reproached him for his slow operations and failing to defend Lyon despite commanding a fine army. Augereau condemned him for his megalomania that had lost them everything. Napoleon offered his hand but Augereau refused to take it. They parted in different directions and never saw each other again.[5]

Fréjus evoked bittersweet memories in Napoleon during his stay from 27 to 29 April. Nearly 15 years earlier he had stepped ashore there after sailing from Egypt, before hurrying on to Paris where a month later he took power. Since then he had experienced several lifetimes of epic triumphs and disasters. Fréjus was now where he embarked aboard HMS *Undaunted* for the voyage to his exile on Elba.

* * *

Napoleon stepped ashore at Porto Ferraio, Elba, on 4 May.[6] For several days he and his entourage resided at the city hall until more appropriate lodgings were found at the Villa Mulini on heights overlooking the port. The man who had once ruled 44 million people across a swath of Europe now ruled 11,400 people on a small island 16 miles long and from 3 to 10 miles wide. The man who had once commanded an army of over 600,000 troops and a navy of hundreds of warships, now commanded an 'army' of 700 Old Guard grenadiers, 100 Polish Lancers and 1,200 militiamen and a 'fleet' consisting of the 16-gun brig *Constant* and four gunboats.

Napoleon harboured an irrational fear of being assassinated or being abducted by Barbary pirates. He was guarded not just by his 2,000 troops and five vessels but by passing and sometimes patrolling British and Neapolitan warships. He lived largely unsupervised in his own cramped, dull world. Campbell was the sole Allied envoy on Elba; he had a vessel at his command that he used to reach the Italian mainland where he journeyed to Florence for prolonged sojourns with his mistress. Napoleon would take advantage of one of his absences. Boredom aside, he and his entourage ate and drank well on Elba, which was covered with orchards and vineyards, pastures where sheep and goats grazed and stone pens where pigs wallowed, while the surrounding seas yielded an array of fish, lobster, shrimp, octopus, squid and molluscs.

His government's annual revenue from Elba's included 360,000 francs from taxes on iron mine production, 20,000 francs from salt production and 28,000 francs from fishing. He soon exhausted that and began piling up debts in a flurry of road, port and palace improvement projects atop his military forces. In all his budget came to 652,000 francs. He counted on paying off that debt with the article of the Fontainebleau treaty requiring France annually to give him 2,500,000 francs, but Louis XVIII refused to honour that promise.[7]

With little to do but mull the results of his titanic blunders, he fell into a deep depression, worsened when he learned that diphtheria had killed Josephine at Malmaison on 29 May. His spirits lifted a bit when Pauline arrived on 1 June. She tarried for several days before sailing on to Naples to visit her sister Caroline and brother-in-law Joachim, still monarchs. Undoubtedly, she passed on potential plans for them to consider then returned with their response. Meanwhile, his mother Letizia arrived in August to keep him company until his own departure half a year later. Finally, Marie Walewska and their four-year-old son, Alexander, arrived for a secret two-day visit in early September.[8]

* * *

The notion that the French people were seething against Louis XVIII and his regime was a gross exaggeration.[9] The Allies let off France rather lightly considering the disasters that Napoleon's policies had deliberately or inadvertently inflicted on Europe. Under the Treaty of Paris signed on 30 May 1814, France was allowed to retain its 1792 frontiers and all its looted art without having to pay an indemnity or have foreign troops stationed on its soil. On 4 June, Louis XVIII granted a charter which re-established Catholicism as the state religion and set up a bicameral parliament with a hand-picked Chamber of Peers and an elected Chamber of Deputies whose members were determined by 90,000 eligible voters and 10,000 eligible office-holders out of 30 million French people; one's taxes determined one's degree of citizenship, with voters and office-holders confined to those annually paying over 300 francs and 1,000 francs, respectively. The new king essentially began his reign with a vast amnesty that was unannounced but understood; he neither persecuted those responsible for countless executions including that of his own brother, nor returned property confiscated during the Revolution. The French enjoyed a peace dividend when Louis cut the army from 500,000 to 200,000 troops. France's only significant disgruntlement was among those career officers suddenly deprived of their livelihood and prestige.

Meanwhile, all the states of Europe had representatives in Vienna for a Congress that officially opened on 1 November 1814 and closed after the Final Act or treaty settling Europe's affairs was signed on 9 June 1815.[10] Louis XVIII had named Talleyrand his Foreign Minister and sent him to represent France at Vienna. Talleyrand brilliantly pressured the four great powers, Britain, Austria, Russia and Prussia, to promote France into their inner circle from the secondary tier of Sweden, Spain and Portugal. Among his goals was to get the other great powers to depose Murat and restore Ferdinand IV to his throne in Naples and strip Napoleon of his realm of Elba and instead send him far away to the Azores.[11]

* * *

Napoleon was well informed about key debates and decisions in Paris and Vienna via messages from Joachim and Caroline Murat at Naples and from spies elsewhere on the Continent, along with letters, newspapers and gossip carried by visitors stepping ashore from vessels. He bristled at how Louis XVIII and his new regime were undoing many of his legal, administrative, economic, financial, educational and social reforms. He was angry enough not to receive the 2,500,000 franc annual pension from France as required by the Fontainebleau treaty and to learn that none of his family had received any payments owed them. Then he was incensed at word that on 18 December, Louis XVIII had confiscated all Bonaparte family property in France. He raged with jealousy to hear that Marie Louise and her dashing Austrian escort, Colonel Adam von Neipperg, were lovers. His stomach churned to hear that at the Congress of Vienna the great powers' list of problems to resolve included whether to exile him to a far more remote island. He was heartened by reports of growing discontent against the Bourbon regime and nostalgia for his own rule. The tipping point came on 12 February when former Prefect Édouard Fleury de Chaboulon secretly arrived with a message detailing all these points and hopes from a long list of officers and officials that he would return. Given all that atop excruciating boredom, Napoleon reasoned that he had nothing to lose and everything to regain by heading to Paris. So that is what he did.[12]

Napoleon and his 'army' embarked on 26 February.[13] Crammed aboard the brig *Constant* and six smaller vessels were 1,175 troops, including 607 Old Guard grenadiers, 118 Polish Lancers, 100 gunners with four guns and 26 draft horses, 300 Corsican light infantry, 50 gendarmes, 80 civilians and 8 horses for Napoleon and his officers; horses for the cavalry would have to be secured in France. His mother and Pauline wished him goodbye; the plan was for them to stay on Elba until Napoleon secured both France and peace with the rest of Europe. That night Napoleon ordered anchors hoisted and sails unfurled after the tiny flotilla received a favourable if weak wind toward France.

Napoleon was thinking tactically rather than strategically when he chose his departure date. Campbell was visiting his mistress in Florence, while a small British warship was not scheduled to reach Porto Ferraio until 28 February. So he did not have to seize Campbell or the warship before leaving and thus avoided committing overt acts of war. But he should have known that the Allies would march their armies against him if he somehow retook power. His attempt to do so grossly violated the Treaty of Fontainebleau. What he most needed was time. Had he waited a few more weeks he might have gained a month or more to prepare France for the inevitable onslaught.

The Congress of Vienna was about to break up. The great powers had resolved all the major issues. All that remained were the treaty's finishing touches and a signing ceremony for the participants. Then the weary diplomats and their entourages could return to their near or distant realms. And once that happened, it would take weeks of correspondence for the leaders of Britain, Prussia, Austria and Russia to forge a strategy against Napoleon, then weeks more to set their armies in motion. By that time Napoleon might have overrun the Low Countries and extended French rule eastward to the Rhine.

The flotilla dropped anchor east of Antibes and the expedition disembarked on 1 March. The campaign began inauspiciously when the infantry regiment guarding Antibes bloodlessly captured 100 grenadiers that Napoleon sent to secure the town. That may have been a blessing in disguise, at least for the emperor's ambitions. He was mulling a choice. He could march his men westward to the Rhône valley then up it or he could take the rugged road due north through the mountains. Lots of regiments like the one in Antibes awaited him along the Rhône valley or would swiftly converge there, overwhelming him. But he could outflank them by marching through the mountains. After securing supplies, horses and wagons in nearby undefended Cannes, he led his men northward. Meanwhile, the *Constant* sailed to Naples with word to Murat of what happened while the other vessels returned to Elba.

Along the route Napoleon had a proclamation distributed that justified his return and called on the people to support him. His gist of his argument was that he had reappeared to save the country from growing discontent against an illegitimate regime:

> For twenty-five years, France has had new interests, new institutions and a new glory which can only be guaranteed by a national government and a dynasty born in these new circumstance. The prince who reigns over you sits on his throne by the force of the same armies that ravaged our territory . . . French people, in my exile I heard your complaints and your voices . . . I crossed the sea amidst perils of all kinds. I arrive among you to retake my rights, which are yours.[14]

To the army and now Royal Guard he issued proclamations with similar appeals for them to rally to his side to depose an illegitimate regime and restore France to glory. He sent appeals for loyalty to towns and departments ahead on his path and one specifically to Marshal Ney, who he learned had vowed to Louis XVIII that he would bring Napoleon back in an iron cage.[15]

People along the way viewed Napoleon's passage with varying blends of enthusiasm, trepidation and loathing. Regardless, nearly all prudently exchanged their white cockades for tricolour one. A few small army detachments joined him. He faced no military opposition until he and his men reached a high plateau 20 miles south of Grenoble, on 7 March. There the 5th Regiment was deployed in line.

This was the most critical moment of Napoleon's return. He halted his column then trotted forward alone and reined in a score of yards before them. What happened next was an astonishing assertion of his art of power combined with an equal measure of luck:

> The battalion kept a profound silence. The commanding officer ordered them to aim their muskets; he was obeyed; if he had ordered Fire one cannot say what would have happened.

The Emperor did not give him time. He talked to the soldiers and asked them as usual: 'Well! How are you doing in the 5th?' The soldiers answered, 'Very well, Sire'. Then the Emperor said: 'I've come back to see you; do some of you want to kill me?' The soldiers answered, 'Oh! That, no!' Then the Emperor reviewed them as usual and thus took possession of the 5th Regiment. The head of the battalion looked unhappy.[16]

Finally the troops grounded their muskets and surged forward crying *'Vive l'Empereur!'* The Guard then came forward and the Frenchmen joyously embraced one another.[17]

From there Napoleon's march was a swelling triumphant parade as more regiments and commanders joined him, including Ney. Nearly as important, the prefects of ever more departments declared their loyalty to him. His army numbered 36,000 troops by the time he reached Fontainebleau, 43 miles south of Paris, on 20 March. That night Louis XVIII and his entourage piled into a caravan of gilded coaches and clattered north toward the Netherlands.

The progression from Elba to Paris was exhilarating and little short of miraculous. Looking back from St Helena, Napoleon recalled that 'I had crossed France . . . transported amidst the citizens' boisterous universal acclaim'. Yet after reoccupying the Tuileries, the disturbing realization struck him that he was no longer the man he once was: 'My previous confidence was no more . . . I felt that something was missing inside me . . . Gone was the fortune that had once shadowed my steps . . . A kind of magic had disappeared and I was engulfed by cold.'[18] Although Napoleon had always recognized the mingled roles of will and fate in determining each stage of his life, he was never more fatalistic than now. He certainly appears to have sleep-walked through much of his Hundred Days, especially his hundred-hour campaign that ended at Waterloo.[19]

Napoleon slept soundly in his old bed in the Tuileries on 21 March. Early the next day, he eagerly threw himself back into governing France. He established a barebones court with Henri Bertrand as Grand Marshal, Armand Caulaincourt as Grand Écuyer, Anatole Montesquieu as Grand Chamberlain and Philippe Ségur as Grand Master of Ceremonies; lacking an empress and money, any attempt to recreate his previous regime's opulence would have exposed him to withering ridicule. As for his government, he brought together familiar faces with many in their former posts, including Jean Cambacérès as Archchancellor and Justice Minister, Hugues Maret as Foreign Minister, François Mollien as Treasury

Minister, François Barbé-Marbois as Comptroller, Louis Davout as War Minister, Denis Decrès as Naval Minister, Lazare Carnot as Interior Minister and, most ominously, Joseph Fouché as Police Minister. With Talleyrand gone, Fouché would take his place as the most poisonous viper in Napoleon's garden.

Of his male family members, Joseph, Lucien and Jérôme managed to slip back; Napoleon made Joseph a political advisor, Lucien a state consul member and Jérôme an army division commander. Although tempted, Eugène and Louis could not get back from their respective exiles. As for female members, eventually his mother and Hortense joined him, but Allied authorities detained Elisa and Pauline, while Caroline remained uneasily in Naples. Napoleon's greatest regret was that the Austrian Emperor Francis ignored his plea that his wife and son join him.[20]

Napoleon's most dramatic steps shortly after retaking power were to declare freedom of the press, trial by jury and abolition of the slave trade. He promised to reign as a constitutional monarch. To that end, he summoned Benjamin Constant to the Tuileries several days after he retook power. Constant approached the emperor with no little trepidation. He had fiercely criticized Napoleon as a tyrant who had inflicted disasters on France. That was indeed why Napoleon wanted to see him. But rather than punish him, he asked Constant to chair a committee that would create a constitutional monarchy:

> Bring me your ideas. Free elections? Public discussions? Responsible ministers? Liberty? I want all that. Smothering the freedom of the press is especially absurd . . . I am a man of the people; if the people really want liberty, I owe it to them . . . I must lend an ear to their will, even to their whims . . . To revive France I will give it a suitable government.[21]

Then, less convincingly, he tried to justify his previous regime in a long harangue:

> The popular will responded to mine. I emerged from the people and my voice acted for them . . . They regarded me as their champion, their saviour against the nobles . . . I wanted a world empire and to achieve that, power without limits was necessary. To govern only France a constitution was better . . . The world invited me to act. Sovereigns and subjects rushed to be beneath my sceptre . . . I had grand designs . . . I was more than a conqueror . . . The work of fifteen years is destroyed and cannot be revived . . .

I want peace. I do not want to give you false hopes . . . I foresee a difficult struggle, a long war. To sustain it the nation reply on me, but in recompense she will demand liberty and she will have it.[22]

The subsequent constitution kept the existing structure of monarch (emperor rather than king), appointed Chamber of Peers and elected Chamber of Deputies, but expanded the number of eligible voters for the latter and explicitly listed civil rights entitled to all citizens. Napoleon announced on 1 June that the plebiscite approved the constitution by 1,532,357 to 4,802 votes, then the following day presented the constitution before a huge crowd on the Champs de Mars.[23] He announced to the legislatures on 7 June: 'Today was accomplished my heart's most pressing desire heart: I just began the constitutional monarchy.'[24] The scepticism with which his critics, left and right, viewed Napoleon's liberal measures was expressed by this assertion by a royalist: 'He forgot nothing and learned nothing.'[25]

As always, a critical problem was how to pay for everything. There was only 50 million francs in the treasury when Napoleon took power. Finance Minister Gaudin scraped together 150 million francs from various lenders and institutions atop a 40 million franc loan from the financier Gabriel Ouvrand. Treasury Minister Mollien devised a plan to raise 440 million francs through tax hikes and sales of government property.[26]

As for diplomacy, Napoleon asked Caulaincourt to initiate relations with all the states of Europe. He received no reply from foreign leaders to his pleas for peace. Hoping to sow discord, he sent the secret alliance treaty of 3 January 1815, that bound Britain, Austria and France against Russia and Prussia, to Alexander at Vienna; the Tsar summoned the respective representatives of those allies and burned the treaty before their eyes. Napoleon wrote to his brother-in-law Francis asking him to send him his beloved wife and son. He received no response.[27]

* * *

The Allied refusal to recognize Napoleon's return to power was inevitable.[28] Colonel Campbell was thunderstruck to step ashore at Porto Ferraio on 28 February and learn that his pigeon had flown the coop. He spread the alarm with letters to British officials in Vienna, Genoa and London. From there the word spread steadily across France and Europe. The news reached Vienna on the morning of 7 March, when a courier awakened Chancellor Clemens von Metternich. He convened the eight great power representatives to determine what to do. A consensus quickly jelled that for now the sensible reaction was to watch and wait. Surely even a military genius like Napoleon could not take over France with a mere thousand or so troops. On 13 March, the eight powers declared that in escaping from Elba 'Bonaparte destroyed the sole legal title to which his existence found itself attached. In reappearing in France with projects of troubles and upheavals, he deprived himself of the protection of the laws . . . Napoleon Bonaparte placed himself . . . as the enemy and disturber of world peace.'[29] On 25 March, after learning that Napoleon had returned to power, the great powers established the Seventh Coalition, although they did not formally declare war until 15 May. On 9 June, the Congress of Vienna formally ended with the signature of the Final Act or treaty whereby the great powers tried to restore as much of pre-1789 Europe as possible.

* * *

Then there was Europe's political wild card, Joachim Murat, Napoleon's brother-in-law whom he had made the King of Naples. A secret agent of Napoleon had sailed from Porto Ferraio on 6 February, bound for Naples. After arriving, he met alone with Murat to explain Napoleon's plan to return to Paris and ask Murat to join him in a coordinated diplomatic campaign to keep the peace or, if that failed, a coordinated military campaign that would not begin before July. Murat agreed but, before even learning whether Napoleon had regained power, jumped the gun, literally and figuratively. On 15 March, he declared war against Austria and marched north at the head of 85,000 troops. In doing so, as Napoleon disdainfully put it, 'he threw himself into the abyss' and worsened Napoleon's chances of survival by ruining 'all hopes of negotiations'.[30] Napoleon had Caulaincourt repudiate Murat's aggression along with his previous year's decision to join the Allies against France.[31]

Murat's army marched unopposed into Rome, Florence and Bologna as Austrian forces massed in the Po River valley then marched south against him. The Austrians routed the Neapolitans at the battle of Tolentino on May 2 and 3. Napoleon assessed Murat's campaign: 'He attacked the Austrians without a plan, without sufficient means and succumbed without resistance.'[32] Murat galloped away to Naples to join Caroline and their children, then they hurried north up the coast to Gaeta with its massive fortress protecting the port. There they parted, Caroline and the children for exile in Trieste, he for France. When Napoleon learned that he had disembarked at Toulon, he quipped: 'That makes two times that this man has betrayed my destiny.'[33] He refused Murat entry to France.

Meanwhile, the Austrian army marched into Naples on 22 May. Leading the advanced guard was none other than Lieutenant Colonel Adam von Neipperg, Marie Louise's lover and future husband. Soon Ferdinand IV was back on his throne in Naples after a decade-long exile in Palermo. Murat sheltered in Corsica during Napoleon's Hundred Days and beyond. Finally, rather than join his family in Trieste, he decided on a last quixotic gamble. He sailed with sixty-eight followers to retake his kingdom. They landed near the fishing village of Pizo, in Calabria and were quickly captured by Neapolitan troops on 28 September. A military commission found Murat guilty of treason and had him executed by firing squad on 13 October 1815.

* * *

Napoleon's most important task was to prepare for war.[34] That was complicated when most of his marshals either stayed home, fled or could not return from exile, most prominently Marmont, Macdonald, Masséna, St Cyr, Lefebvre, Mortier and Oudinot. Berthier either jumped or was pushed to his death from the top floor of his palace in Bamberg. Just a few marshals reported for duty – Davout, Soult, Grouchy and Suchet. The army's ranks were also split over the emperor's return, with many ecstatic and most enthusiastic, while some silently cursed and thousands deserted either from loyalty to the king or fear that Napoleon would lead them to their deaths. The number of deserters was so large that Napoleon issued a decree calling on them to return to their regiments with no questions asked.

Napoleon made poor use of his marshals that did show up. He relegated Louis Davout, his best all-round general, to head the War Ministry in Paris. He made Nicolas Soult, his third-best general, his chief of staff. They would have been far better choices than his actual wing commanders, Michel Ney and Emmanuel Grouchy, who struggled to lead three corps each. Ney and Grouchy were generally excellent at obeying Napoleon's commands but proved to be inept at comprehending a fast-paced, opaque strategic situation and acting decisively. However, his choice of Louis Suchet, his second-best general, to command in the Rhône valley was prudent; he had proven himself to be an outstanding independent commander in Spain.

Napoleon formed four armies (North, Moselle, Rhine and Alps) and three observation corps (Jura, Var and Pyrenees) on 30 April. Then the Vendée erupted in revolt. The 20,000 troops that he sent to crush those rebels might have brought him victory had they accompanied him to Belgium.[35] Nonetheless, the French army numbered 284,000 troops ready for duty on 1 June. That large number may seem impressive but around 80,000 of them were raw recruits still being equipped and trained at regimental headquarters scattered across France. Only 122,404 troops, including 21,652 cavalry and 358 guns, were in the Army of the North on the Belgian frontier. That army, however, was mostly composed of veterans or volunteers and was probably the best that Napoleon had commanded since 1805. He would make poor use of it. His four-day campaign that ended at Waterloo was his shortest and worst fought. Virtually anything that could go wrong did go wrong.[36]

Strategically, the immediate threat was in the Netherlands where two enemy armies were massing troops and supplies. Arthur Wellesley, the Duke of Wellington, commanded an Allied force of British, Dutch, Belgian and German troops that eventually numbered 92,309, including 68,829 infantry, 14,474 cavalry, 11,200 gunners and 255 guns. Only about a third of his troops were redcoats. Wellington established brigades that combined one British and two foreign regiments, hoping that the latter would be inspired to emulate the professionalism and courage of the former. His troops were deployed from the English Channel to Quatre Bras on the road leading from due south from Brussels to France. He split his army into three infantry corps, with William, Prince Orange's eastward, Rowland Hill's westward, the 10,000-man cavalry reserve led by Henry Paget, the Earl of Uxbridge, behind them and a reserve corps in Brussels under Wellington's command. Gebhard von Blücher commanded 130,246 Prussian troops including 85,000 infantry, 20,000 cavalry and 15,000 gunners and 288 guns, in four corps, with Hans Ziethen's just north of Charleroi, Georg Pirch's around Namur, Johann Thielemann's around Dinant and Friedrich von Bülow's around Liège.

The Allied war plan was simple. Wellington and Blücher were to stave off any invasion of the Low Countries and distract Napoleon while the other half a dozen Allied armies elsewhere steamrolled the small French forces before them. The other forces included Schwarzenberg's 225,000 Austrian troops which would march through Basle toward Paris; Barclay de Tolly's 200,000 Russian troops to the middle Rhine and on to Paris; Bachmann's 37,000 Austrian troops in Switzerland that would march toward the upper Rhône valley; Frimont's 50,000 Austrian and Piedmontese troops in north-western Italy that would march toward Lyon; and an army of 80,000 Spanish and Portuguese troops preparing to march against Bayonne. To counter those forces, General Rapp had 23,000 troops at Strasbourg, Lecourbe 8,400 at Besancon, Suchet 23,500 at Lyon, Brune 5,500 at Nice, Decean 7,600 at Perpignan, Clausel 6,800 at Bayonne, Lamarque 20,000 in the Vendée and Davout 20,000 at Paris.

Napoleon left Paris during the dark morning hours of 12 June and reached Charleroi the next day. His plan was simple but the best given his inferior number of troops. He would march his army in two wings on parallel roads straight at Wellington's left flank and Blücher's right flank, smash through and defeat each enemy in turn. Ney commanded the left wing with the corps of Reille, Lobau and d'Erlon; Grouchy the right wing with the corps of Vandamme and Gerard; Napoleon with the Guard and Reserve Cavalry followed Grouchy; D'Erlon's corps would march up a secondary road between the two wings and reinforce the wing that most needed it. That vague instruction would led to confusion and missed opportunities.

Napoleon chose 14 June as a very auspicious day on which to symbolically open his campaign with a proclamation to his army and a far wider audience: 'Soldiers, today is the anniversary of Marengo and Friedland, which twice decided Europe's fate . . . Soldiers, we have forced marches to make, battles to fight and perils to run, but with perseverance, victory will be ours: the rights, the honour and the happiness of the country will be reconquered.'[37] The campaign did not actually begin until early on the morning of 15 June, when his wings crossed the Sambre River at Charleroi, with Ney's marching north on the road toward Brussels and Grouchy's marching north-east toward Liège. Funnelling that many troops through Charleroi led to traffic jams and long delays. That night Ney's advanced guard camped a few miles short of that day's objective, the strategic crossroads of Quatre Bras. Grouchy's advanced guard halted a few miles south-west of Ligny on the road to Namur.

Wellington and Blücher were at their respective headquarters in Brussels and Namur, when couriers informed them of the French army's invasion. Each general sent flurries of orders to his corps commanders to rouse their troops and march toward the enemy. Wellington and Blücher met the next day to coordinate their movements and pledge to not let Napoleon split them apart.

Ney led his men cautiously up the Brussels road on the morning of 16 June. He halted his troops a half mile short of Quatre Bras where he saw enemy troops deployed. At that point Ney's 20,000 troops outnumbered the enemy's 8,000. Had Ney ordered an immediate attack his troops would have routed the enemy and captured the crossroads. That would have forced Wellington either to mass his forces and counter-attack or withdraw north. Instead, Ney, usually too impetuous, was now too cautious. He heartily respected and feared Wellington, having been trounced by him several times in the Peninsula. He knew that whenever possible Wellington hid his troops behind hills, villages or woods to mislead the enemy about their numbers and locations, as well as shelter them from enemy fire. He looked at the patches of woods and imagined British regiments massed behind them. So he waited until all his troops arrived, which took hours. Meanwhile, the British did the same more rapidly and with greater numbers. When Ney finally ordered an attack in early afternoon, the enemy's forces outnumbered his own. As the battle raged, Ney sent a courier galloping off to General d'Erlon whose corps was on the road running east-west between the French wings. D'Erlon was immediately to march against Wellington's left flank. D'Erlon dutifully followed his orders. The battle at Quatre Bras ended before d'Erlon's corps got there. The French finally pushed the Allies off the field, with their respective casualties 4,100 and 5,200 men.

Meanwhile, Napoleon deployed his army against the Prussian corps of Thielemann, Pirch and Ziethen at Ligny, half a dozen miles eastward. After massing his artillery and pounding the Prussian lines, Napoleon sent Vandamme and Gerard forward, much of the reserve cavalry around the enemy's left flank and ordered d'Erlon to attack the Prussian right flank. In mid-afternoon as the fighting seesawed along the line, d'Erlon's troops actually came into sight before withdrawing. Napoleon had to send in the Imperial Guard to tip the balance and bludgeon the Prussians from the field. The Prussians suffered 18,772 casualties to 13,721 for the French. The Prussian army was battered but not broken. Blücher was determined to keep his promise to Wellington. He sent Thielemann's corps north-eastward to protect his supply depot at Liège, while he headed north with the corps of Bülow, Pirch and Ziethen parallel to Wellington's withdrawal.

Napoleon sent 33,000 troops under Grouchy to pursue Blücher. Grouchy mistook Thielemann's force for the main army and followed him. Had he instead closely followed Blücher, the Prussians would have had to turn and fight, thus keeping them from reaching Waterloo on that decisive day. Without the Prussians attacking his right flank, Napoleon could have concentrated his forces for an overwhelming attack on Wellington before him. After reaching Quatre Bras in the early afternoon on 17 June, Napoleon was enraged to find Ney's wing resting rather than marching after the British. He had Ney rouse his troops and send them northward. Later that afternoon and into the night a storm raged, soaking the roads and slowing the French advance.

Wellington meanwhile had concentrated his army in a typically excellent position. He deployed most of his troops for a mile or so along a low ridge topped by an often sunken road. He anchored his right flank at the village of Braine l'Alleud with a stream running from south to north just beyond it. He anchored his left flank on woods called the Bois de Paris but deployed few troops there since he expected the Prussians to appear any hour from that direction. He then took advantage of two excellent positions south of the ridge. He placed a regiment inside the walled chateau of Hougoumont several hundred yards before his centre-right and the King's German Legion in the walled farm of La Haye Sainte a hundred yards in front of his centre. Two roads ran from the south to converge at the village of Mont St Jean a few hundred yards behind his centre; one ran past Hougoumont and the other past La Haye Sainte, giving their defenders clear fields of fire against any nearby advancing enemy troops. His position's only potential danger was the woods that stretched across his rear a couple of miles away. Should he have to retreat, his troops would either have to squeeze through the main road or become disordered as they struggled through the woods.

During the morning of 18 June, Napoleon watched his regiments and batteries parade past and mass along on a low ridge half a mile south and parallel to Wellington's; by noon 74,500 troops were in position. His headquarters was in a farmhouse called Le Caillou about a third of a mile behind his front line. He explained his plan to Ney and his corps commanders. Jérôme's division would attack Hougoumont on the Allied right to draw attention as massed batteries bombarded the rest of the enemy line, concentrating on the centre. D'Erlon's corps would then march straight at the enemy line east of the main road. The cavalry would exploit the breakthrough. When Ney and other Peninsula veterans worried that Wellington's tactics would stave off a frontal assault, Napoleon angrily replied: 'Because you've been beaten by Wellington you consider him to be a good general. I say he is a bad general and that the English are bad troops.'[38] That said, he then turned over the battle to Ney. Poor health was the most likely reason. An upset stomach and haemorrhoids kept him tight-lipped most of the day. He retired twice to rest inside his headquarters and once dozed in an armchair just outside.

Ney was renowned for his bravery, not his tactics. Throughout that decisive day he committed several blunders that lost what little chance of victory the French might have had. The battle began with an artillery duel of 246 French guns against 157 Allied guns. Wellington typically withdrew his troops to relative safety behind the low ridge. Ney failed to do the same. Ney launched d'Erlon's corps against the British centre-left, while Jérôme's division attacked Hougoumont. The Allied troops repelled both attacks. Wellington then ordered his cavalry to ride down d'Erlon's fleeing men. Ney sent his cavalry forward to repel the British cavalry. As each side regained its position, Ney ordered the bombardment resumed. Once again Wellington withdrew his troops beyond the ridge. Believing that the enemy was retreating, Ney ordered the cavalry reserve to charge. Wellington had his regiments form squares as he and his staff sheltered in one. The squares repelled the French cavalry. The French finally took La Haye Sainte and skirmishers crept forward to snipe at the enemy regiments on the low ridge.

Meanwhile, the Prussian army's advance corps under Bülow approached the village of La Haie Frischermont on the French right flank. Word of their advance roused Napoleon from his stupor. He dispatched part of Lobau's corps to counter them. The Prussians broke through and advanced toward the village of Plancenoit behind the French left flank. Napoleon sent the Young Guard to defend the village which changed hands several times in vicious fighting. With the Prussian army poised to crush his right, Napoleon ordered not a retreat but an attack, this time with the Old Guard directly against the British centre. At the last moment Wellington ordered his troops to rise and pour volleys into the enemy. The Old Guard broke and ran. The rout of the French army's most fabled regiments caused the rest of the troops to flee. Napoleon joined their flight.

Napoleon's last battle was his most ineptly fought. Each decision was poorly conceived, timed and executed. He failed to coordinate his infantry, cavalry and artillery attacks to devastate the enemy, but instead had each attack separately, thus letting Wellington counter each. His infantry attacks were piecemeal, a corps at a time, rather than an onslaught of all at once. The Old Guard might have broken through had it accompanied d'Erlon's attack in the early afternoon. Instead Napoleon sent the Old Guard into battle alone and the British decimated it. Wellington was as brilliant in managing the battle as Napoleon was inept. The timing of his troop movements and attacks were mostly exquisite. The French lost 25,000 dead and wounded and 8,000 prisoners along with 250 guns; perhaps another 13,500 deserted or were captured as the army's remnant retreated into France. The armies of Wellington and Blücher suffered 15,000 and 7,000 casualties, respectively. During the four day campaign the casualties were equal, 67,420 for the French, 40,250 for the Prussians and 21,850 for the Anglo-allied troops.[39]

Ironically, French generals elsewhere were triumphant. Rapp's division blunted Schwarzenberg's army advance at La Souffel near the Rhine. Lecourbe's division battered Colleredo's Austrian corps in four battles. Suchet's corps routed Frimont's army. Brune's division trounced Onasco's Spanish army at the frontier. Lamarque crushed the rebellion in the

Vendée. Had Napoleon decisively beaten Wellington and Blücher, the Allied sovereigns might have reconsidered fighting a war to the finish against him, especially if Napoleon had marched against Schwarzenberg. Instead, Grouchy and Soult rallied the army's remnants at Lâon. The armies of Wellington and Blücher were too depleted and exhausted to immediately pursue. When they did, they advanced cautiously. Grouchy skilfully withdrew before them and evaded their attempts to encircle him. Meanwhile, Schwarzenberg resumed his advance. With three times more men, the Allied victory was only a matter of time. Mercifully the war would end with a decisive diplomatic rather than military victory.

* * *

After Waterloo Napoleon raced back to Paris. His greatest immediate fear was being overthrown by the National Assembly. His fear would be realized. On 21 June, he reached the Élysée Palace and summoned his ministers to an emergency meeting. His ministers discouraged him from going directly to the Palais Bourbon to address the Chamber of Deputies. They feared for his safety from enraged legislators at the latest catastrophe that he had inflicted on France. Instead he sent them a message justifying his actions:

> After the battles of Ligny and Mont Saint Jean . . . I rendered myself to Paris to concert with my ministers the national defence measures and to hear from the Chambers all that was demanded for the country's safety. I formed a committee . . . to renew . . . negotiations with the foreign powers and end the war, if it accords with the country's independence and honour.[40]

The following day, both chambers voted overwhelmingly to depose Napoleon, then sent a bicameral delegation, led by Joseph, Marquis de Lafayette, to demand his abdication. Napoleon bitterly complied, issuing this proclamation:

> In beginning the war to sustain national independence, I counted on the union of all efforts, of all wills . . . as grounds for . . . success . . . The circumstances appear to have changed. I offer myself in sacrifice to the hatreds of France's enemies . . . My political life is terminated and I proclaim my son, under the title Napoleon II, Emperor of France.[41]

The chambers then formed a provisional government headed by Joseph Fouché. The next day, the government sent a delegation to the Allies to request an armistice.

The night of his abdication, Napoleon took poison, panicked and then induced himself to vomit it out before it killed him. The next morning he took a carriage to Malmaison. Josephine had died there the previous year, but Hortense was still living there and Marie Walewska visited him on 26 June. He spent three poignant days at Malmaison recalling the mostly happy times he had passed there with his loved ones, especially Josephine. His reverie was broken by word that the Allied armies were steadily advancing toward Paris. Fouché sent him advice to flee to Rochefort and try to escape France on a vessel bound for America.

* * *

Napoleon, Joseph and a few followers reached Rochefort on 3 July. Two French frigates and a brig were anchored there, the last warships of a once-powerful fleet. Napoleon sent their captains a request to be sailed to America. The captains pointed to HMS *Bellerophon*, the 74-gun flagship of half a dozen warships anchored across the bay and insisted that escape was impossible. That was the excuse. Apparently, they had received a message from Fouché ordering them to deny him any aid.[42] Napoleon turned down an offer from a Danish captain to smuggle him past the blockade to the United States. Joseph would later take the offer and begin a new life in America. They learned that the Allies had marched into Paris on 7 July and Louis XVIII and his entourage the following day. It was imperative to escape as soon as possible. Napoleon would likely face a firing squad if royalist or foreign troops captured him. For protection Napoleon and his followers moved to the Isle d'Aix in the bay on 12 July. Two days later the fugitives watched in alarm as tricolour flags were hauled down on the mainland and replaced by flags with golden fleur-de-lis against a white field. That left just one last option.

Napoleon had himself rowed to the *Bellerophon* and surrendered to its captain, Frederick Maitland, on 15 July. The *Bellerophon* sailed for England the next morning. The first port of call was Torbay, where on 24 July, Napoleon sent George, the Prince Regent, this message:

> In the face of all the factions that divide my country and the enmity of Europe's great powers, I have ended my political career. I come . . . to place myself in the threshold of the British people. I put myself under the protection of their laws that I may claim

from Your Royal Highness, the most powerful, the most constant and the most generous of my enemies.[43]

Napoleon received a reply on 31 July, three days after the *Bellerophon* dropped anchor at Plymouth. Addressing him as General Bonaparte, Admiral Lord George Keith Elphinstone, the Channel Fleet commander, and Henry Bunbury, the Undersecretary of State for War, came aboard to explain that he would spend the rest of life at Britain's colony of St Helena, an island in the South Atlantic roughly equidistant between Brazil and Angola. That decision was confirmed by a treaty signed by Britain, Austria, Prussia and Russia at Paris on 2 August 1815.

Napoleon vainly protested that decision then and till the end of his life.[44] He issued his first official plea on 4 August:

> I protest . . . against the violation of my most sacred rights, in disposing by force, my person and my liberty. I came freely aboard the *Bellerophon*. I am not a prisoner. I am the guest of England . . . I appeal to history; she will say that an enemy, who made twenty years of war against the British people, came freely, in his misfortune, to look for exile under its laws.[45]

Chapter 21

The Prometheus

'Men are only as great as the monuments that they leave behind.'

'We build success on chimeras and shrug at those who reason.'

After his first abdication, Napoleon wrote to Josephine that, 'in my retirement, I will substitute the pen for the sword'.[1] That pledge turned out to be premature as he escaped from Elba for the hundred-day Odyssey that climaxed at Waterloo. But his internment on St Helena gave him plenty of time to make good on his intention. Upon arriving on 16 October 1815, he plaintively asked his secretary Emmanuel de Las Cases, 'What shall we do in this lost land?' 'Sire', Las Cases replied, 'we will live in the past.'[2] And so they did for the next five and a half years until complications of stomach cancer killed him on 5 May 1821, when he was 51 years old.

Napoleon was allowed to take half a dozen assistants into captivity. Three were generals: Henri Bertrand, Grand Master of the Palace; Charles Tristan de Montholon-Semonville, one of Marshal Berthier's aides-de-camp; and Gaspard Gourgaud, an artillery commander. Las Cases was a naval officer who had fled to Britain during the Revolution then returned to France after Napoleon issued his pardon; he eventually worked his way up the administration into the emperor's confidence. Louis Marchand was Napoleon's head valet. Then there was the outsider who became an insider; Dr Barry O'Meara was HMS *Bellerophon*'s surgeon who volunteered to care for Napoleon and his entourage. Finally, Bertrand's wife and Las Cases's son shared their exile.

Napoleon tried to be philosophical about his fall from power:

> At this age I have had all my conquests. I governed the world. I calmed the tempest, founded a party, rallied a nation and created a government and an empire. All that remained was the title of emperor. I have been spoiled . . . From my entry into life

> I found myself provided with power and the circumstances of my power have been such that I had command. I recognized neither masters nor laws.³

Las Cases mourned that 'Emperor Napoleon, who had possessed so much power and had disposed so many crowns, found himself reduced to a miserable little shack of several square feet perched on a sterile rock'.⁴ That was only a slight exaggeration.

Life at the rambling farmhouse called Longwood, which he and his followers inhabited from 10 December 1815, was mostly dull, often dreary and at times downright miserable.⁵ Mildew and rats infested and fog engulfed Longwood. Even worse, emotionally Longwood was a claustrophobic hothouse of seething passions, resentments and jealousies, an artificial community that, as Las Cases explained, 'was an ensemble made purely by chance and not by affinities'.⁶ The only glue that bound the members was their devotion to Napoleon, who they mostly hero-worshipped, not just hanging on but often recording his every word and act. Like his colleagues, Las Cases remained star-struck by being with the emperor day after day, an experience that carried him to heights of exhilaration and depths of melancholy: 'I regarded those hands that had held so many sceptres . . . that had issued so many decisions for posterity.'⁷ Yet they also had to endure his whims and rages. Unable to confront the emperor for his faults, they vented their spleen all the more spitefully against each other, mostly beyond his hearing. In turn, Napoleon struggled to smooth over their spats.

Despite its remote location, Longwood was a fishbowl for its inhabitants. There was little privacy for so many people crammed in such a modest house. Even worse, British sentries were posted around the grounds and a British officer not only always accompanied Napoleon on any excursion but even had a seat at the table. The official British explanation was that the ceaseless redcoat presence was for Napoleon's protection, but obviously the soldiers were there to deter any escape plot. This so enraged Napoleon that for long periods he refused to go out and ate alone in his room. Compounding these miseries was Hudson Lowe, who arrived to become St Helena's governor on 14 April 1816. Lowe took sadistic pleasure in tightening the already onerous restrictions on Napoleon and his community.

Napoleon was in poor and declining health. He was increasingly corpulent and easily fatigued. He ate and slept irregularly. He was locked into a vicious circle of too little mental or physical exercise. His addiction to snorting snuff further fouled his life. He staved off chronic depression by dictating his memoirs or just reflecting aloud to his followers. A glass of madeira or champagne each evening briefly lightened the dark emotional cloud that engulfed him. His moods might abruptly seesaw. He could be chatty and affectionate one minute and grumpy and insensitive the next. At times he lost his temper and unfairly blistered a scapegoat. Yet sooner or later he made some reassuring gesture that restored amiability between them. Although he rarely admitted that he was wrong, he never forgot those who had given him exemplary service along the way.

For diversions, the tiny community read and discussed notable books, recited inspiring acts from favourite plays or mulled the political meaning of events in Europe or elsewhere culled from the latest packet of letters and newspapers. For a while Las Cases gave Napoleon English lessons but the emperor was a poor student and never became proficient. Most importantly, to the eternal gratitude of historians and their readers, Napoleon recited his memoirs and each aide wrote his own account of life in exile with the emperor, which included recording nearly every anecdote and maxim that he uttered.[8]

For his own memoirs, Napoleon dictated in the morning, his aides rewrote a legible copy of the text that afternoon and he corrected it that evening. It was exhausting work for the scribes to keep up with his rapid-fire words. Montholon recalled that 'when the emperor dictated, he continuously walked back and forth, with his head lowered and his hands behind his back . . . He walked or dictated more or less quickly, but always sticking to the interest that occupied him.'[9] He was determined to present, if not the last word, at least such powerful interpretations that he would overwhelm any alternate versions. He claimed that 'I worry little about all the libels launched against me. My acts and events reply better than the cleverest arguments for the defence.'[10]

Napoleon was hardly a reliable witness of his life. Not surprisingly, his version of his own history at once blends fact and fiction, provides insights and distortions, sets the record straight and askew, mostly takes credit for what went right and mostly targets scapegoats for what went wrong. He often wallows in self-pity and denies responsibility for the catastrophes that he had inflicted on France and Europe. Yet there is ample truth in Napoleon's boast: 'My monuments and institutions will celebrate me to the most distant posterity.'[11]

Power, Foresight and Hubris

Making sense of anyone's place in history is challenging enough, especially for someone who has an era named after him. One's power is equal to the range and impact, intended and unintended, of one's decisions on oneself and others. By that measure, Napoleon was among history's most powerful individuals. His decisions directly and indirectly affected the lives of not just a hundred million or so Europeans and other peoples around the world during his lifetime, but countless others beyond his grave since then. Indeed, the very notion of an 'Age of Napoleon' implies that he was powerful enough to change his world into something distinctly different from what preceded and followed it.

A critical element of power is the ability to foresee the actions and their consequences of those of oneself and others with whom one is involved. The better one can literally and figuratively look beyond distant horizons, the better one can determine the array of choices and their respective benefits and costs. Napoleon rightfully prided himself on being able to see multiple combinations of moves ahead on multiple military, diplomatic and political chessboards. Another strength was his ability to respond swiftly and decisively to changing challenges and opportunities, overcoming the former and seizing the latter. One key element of his political power was his ability at once to be independent of all factions and make all factions dependent on him, to transcend political differences and personify France.

Hubris was Napoleon's fatal flaw. Hubris is a form of tunnel vision that, for Napoleon, swelled with his power. His astonishing series of military and political victories that carried him to the heights of power convinced him that he was omniscient and omnipotent, God-like. Armand Caulaincourt, one of his foreign ministers, explained: 'Once he had an idea implanted in his head, the Emperor was carried away by his own illusion. He . . . became obsessed with it . . . Never have a man's reason and judgment been more misguided, more led astray, more the victim of his imagination and passion than the reason and judgment of the Emperor on certain questions.'[12] Warped by egomania and megalomania, he made numerous bad choices that eventually destroyed nearly everything that he created. His false, overweening pride blinded him to alternatives, especially if someone else suggested them. Caulaincourt offered his succinct explanation: 'Alas, the Emperor deluded himself; and our ruin followed on his misfortune.'[13]

Power and Autocracy

Napoleon seized national power twice, in November 1799 and March 1815, both times at bayonet point but without bloodshed. Like most of his other accomplishments, those nonviolent coups reflected inseparable measures of skill, audacity and luck. The 1799 coup was nearly a sure thing complicated and nearly lost by Bonaparte's bouts of indecision and erratic behaviour. The 1815 coup was truly epic, a stunning feat whereby Napoleon overcame overwhelming military and political forces arrayed against him.

Napoleon's critics then and since have denounced him as a tyrant who amassed and abused supreme powers. The charge that he headed a military dictatorship is baseless. Although he took power in military coups, his consulate and imperial governments were civilian rather than military dictatorships. Indeed a chronic worry of the First Consul and Emperor was being overthrown in a coup. Interior Minister Chaptal recalled that

> Napoleon was incessantly on guard against ambitious generals and discontented people; he was constantly occupied with smothering one or preventing the other. One always saw him observing a grand reserve toward the generals; he always held them at a great distance . . . If they distinguished themselves, he limited himself to saying that they had done their duty and he mentioned them honourably in his bulletins.[14]

Army officers and soldiers were his largest, although not unanimous, source of support. Countless grumbled and some outright plotted against him, most notoriously Generals Jean Moreau, Claude Malet and Joachim Murat.

Napoleon's power was never absolute. Indeed he had opponents literally beneath his very nose as they bowed before him. Within the government were two men who were brilliant at what they did but who Napoleon retained long after he had evidence that they worked against him. Charles Maurice Talleyrand-Perigord was Foreign Minister from November 1799 until August 1807, when he resigned, but he remained an advisor until March 1814; Joseph Fouché was the police minister almost continuously from November 1799 until June 1810, when Napoleon fired him for unauthorized negotiations with the British. Both were ruthless, skilled and lucky enough to have entered the Revolution's black hole in 1789 and emerged a decade later into the Consulate. Two venerable political axioms apparently kept Napoleon saddling himself with them: keep your friends close and your enemies closer; it is better to have enemies inside the tent pissing out than outside pissing in. Yet each eventually led a coup that overthrew Napoleon, Talleyrand in 1814 and Fouché in 1815.

Only Talleyrand had the savior-faire and sangfroid persistently to challenge Napoleon's views and choices. Napoleon's relationship with him was complex. He deeply respected Talleyrand's mind and diplomatic arts, if not his morality. In December 1812, he offered this assessment: 'He is a born intriguer and quite immoral, but he's very witty and certainly the most capable of all my ministers. We were on very cool terms for a long time, but I am no longer angry with him. He would still be minister if he had wished to be.'[15] Their initial meeting of minds in 1797 over how best to realize French security frayed and eventually split, with Talleyrand calling for France's expansion no further than its 'natural frontiers', while Napoleon was determined that France would engulf ever more of Europe. Talleyrand resigned as foreign minister a month after protesting the Tilsit treaties. Yet Talleyrand began betraying Napoleon virtually from the time that he joined his government. He was on the payroll of nearly all the great powers and several minor states to pass them critical intelligence and influence affairs in their favour. During the Erfurt conference in September 1808, he urged Tsar Alexander to save Europe by opposing Napoleon. In early April 1814, he engineered the Senate coup that made him head of the provisional government, deposed Napoleon and welcomed Louis XVIII as the French king. Although Napoleonphiles deplore Talleyrand as a traitor, he should instead be understood as a Cassandra. Over the years he repeatedly warned Napoleon that his imperialism and tyranny would inevitably unite Europe to war relentlessly against him until France was crushed and he was overthrown. As for the criticism of his perfidy against the emperor, Talleyrand always insisted that he had only betrayed Napoleon to save France and Europe.[16] He further argued that: 'The only dangerous conspirator against Napoleon was himself.'[17] He explained that:

> I loved Napoleon. I was even attached to his personality despite his faults. At first I was carried away by the irresistible allure of the great genius that he exuded . . . I basked in his glory and the reflection flowing on me for aiding him in his noble cause . . . During the time when he listened to the truth, I clearly stated it to him.[18]

Napoleon was especially leery of Fouché, who as police minister figuratively and literally knew where all the bodies were buried, including embarrassing and incriminating files on many of his family members and even himself. He greatly valued Fouché's sharp intellect, candour and ruthlessness. When he rebuked Fouché for having voted for executing Louis XVI, Fouché quipped: 'That was the first service that I was able to render your majesty.' When he asked him what he would do if his emperor were killed, Fouché replied: 'I would assume as much power as I possibly could in order to avoid being overtaken by events.'[19] Such a man could be a critical prop of his power as long as he remained loyal. And therein lay the risk, especially with his portfolio as police chief. Napoleon tongue-lashed and fired Fouché in June 1810 for communicating and negotiating with Britain without his authorization, but gave him a golden parachute by naming him governor of first Rome then Illyria. He recalled him as his Police Minister in March 1815. After Waterloo, Fouché led the effort to pressure Napoleon's abdication, head an interim government and invite Louis XVIII back to the throne.

Then there was Napoleon's brother-in-law and cavalry commander who he made the King of Naples. Joachim Murat was a loose cannon as a commander. No one exceeded and few matched Murat in raw courage, but he needed constant supervision to ensure that he kept to the script and did not sally off on often quixotic improvisations. He was too thick-skulled to be a good general: his tactics consisted of leading mass cavalry charges at already battered enemy troops; figuratively, he was myopic beyond a battlefield. Of the betrayals Napoleon suffered in 1814, he condemned Murat's as the worst. Had Murat joined forces with Eugène in northern Italy then marched toward Vienna, the Austrians would have had to divert their thrust toward Lyon to that front. That would have freed General Charles Augereau to march north from the Lyon front and join Napoleon in eastern France. And those reinforcements might have given Napoleon enough troops to win decisive rather than fleeting victories. Instead, Murat joined the Austrians in attacking and overwhelming Eugène, while the Allied armies in France eventually did the same to Napoleon. Then, after Napoleon returned to power in 1815, Murat tried to compensate for his previous year's betrayal but made a mess of things. He prematurely declared war against Austria, only to be routed and dethroned within weeks. With Murat eliminated, the Allies could concentrate on massing their armies against Napoleon and reject any of his pleas for negotiations. Napoleon attributed Murat's betrayal in 1814 and blunder in 1815 more to denseness than malevolence: 'He was not bright and his extreme shifts between vacillation and recklessness made him the dupe of conspirators.'[20]

Napoleon's dictatorship was indeed a police state, with powers both inherited, instituted and decreed. The French 'Republic' accumulated its own share of powers, including a suspect law in September 1793 and censorship laws in March 1793, April 1795 and September 1799 that enabled the government to arrest, censor and execute pretty much as it willed. Napoleon fine-tuned those already ample powers with his own censorship decree of January 1800. His 1800 constitution essentially gave him dictatorial powers as First Consul which he enhanced by having his system declare him First Consul for life in 1802 and Emperor in 1804. Yet the characterization of Napoleon's empire as a police state is overblown. His regime's secret police, censorship, political prisoners and political executions is typical rather than extraordinary for that era. Napoleon's regime was a mostly benevolent dictatorship rather than an absolute tyranny.

France was undoubtedly a far safer and less violent realm under Napoleon's rule than during the decade of revolution that preceded him. During his 15 years in power around 2,500 people were convicted and imprisoned for committing political crimes and perhaps 4,000 others were exiled from Paris, with Germaine de Staël the most notorious example. Those numbers, however, are from a population of 30 million in France with its 1792 borders and the 44 million people of Imperial France; they are also fractions of the 500,000 people incarcerated or exiled during the Revolution. As for politically-motivated murders, the 30,000 or so victims of the Revolution dwarf the handful under Napoleon's regime.[21] The duc d'Enghien's execution after a kangaroo-court conviction was the exception rather than the rule of Napoleonic justice.

Napoleon asserted that 'the French, during my tenure, were the freest in all Europe, except perhaps for the English'.[22] Indeed, in some ways, France may have been less repressive than Britain. The numbers of political prisoners and executions under Napoleon are much less than those in Britain during that era; the British slaughtered as many as 30,000 Irish to crush the revolt of 1798. Even though France had twice as many people, the execution rate for criminals was much lower than in Britain both as a portion of the population and for those who received the death sentence. For instance in 1813, 5,343 people were condemned but only 307 or 5.7 per cent were actually executed in France compared to 4,422 condemned and 713 or 16.1 per cent executed in Britain. Louis XVIII's courts proved to be more bloodthirsty than Napoleon's although still less than Britain's. In 1816, 6,897 people were condemned to death of whom 414 or 6.1 per cent were executed compared to 5,797 condemned and 890 or 15.3 per cent in Britain.[23]

As for torture, Napoleon argued that it was practically, legally and morally wrong. People will say anything to stop excruciating pain and in doing so more often utter lies than truths. Nonetheless, he would reserve torture as a measure of last resort, that era's equivalent of the ticking time bomb scenario. Here again, Napoleon may have been more moderate than most of his fellow rulers whose regimes practised torture to varying degrees.

Power and Modernization

Did Napoleon save or end the French Revolution? He insisted that he had rescued and personified rather than betrayed it: 'I sealed off the abyss of anarchy and unravelled the chaos. I sobered up the Revolution, ennobled the people and strengthened kings. I excited all emulations, rewarded merits and extended the limits of glory!'[24] He had a mixed record toward the Revolutionary ideals of 'liberty, equality and fraternity'. His Institute and Legion of Honour promoted fraternity. His revised law codes advanced equality with 'blind justice for all'. As for liberty, his policy of 'careers open to all talents' certainly championed economic freedom. However, he violated the liberal concepts of political representation and rights. He transformed a freely-elected legislature into an institution that rubber-stamped his decrees; he smothered a flourishing free press; and he locked up anyone who protested against his authoritarianism.

Napoleon sought a modern rather than republican France. He accelerated the elimination of the medieval world's feudal vestiges that the French Revolution initiated. A decree confiscated the property of the Catholic Church on 2 November 1789, that of the nobles who fled France on 27 July 1792 and abolished and confiscated all remaining feudal properties on 17 July 1793. Napoleon's law code drove the final legal nails into feudalism's casket.

The concept of the 'general will', popularized by Jean Jacques Rousseau, was a vital part of the legitimacy claimed by the Revolutionary, Consulate and Imperial governments. Just how was that determined? Plebiscites were the most obvious way. All three governments went through the motions of letting the people determine the fate of proposed constitutional changes. The catch was that each government shamelessly manipulated the vote by stuffing ballot boxes with yes votes and purging them of no votes.[25]

Overall Napoleon accelerated the development of French nationalism that had been slowly expanding for several centuries.[26] His legal reforms eliminated countless regional and class discrepancies and established a national system of equality before the law. His education

Question	Electorate	Abstentions	Yes	No
1793 Constitution	7,000,000	73%	1,866,000	12,766
1795 Constitution	7,200,000	74%	957,0009	15,000
1800 Constitution	7,900,000	62%	3,011,000	1,562
1802 Consul for Life	7,900,000	55%	3,568,885	8,374
1804 Hereditary Emperor	8,900,000	60%	3,524,000	2,579

reforms established the foundations of a national system that promoted patriotism along with knowledge. His continual celebration of French glory certainly promoted pride in a common identity as long as he kept winning victories. He also affected how the French expressed themselves. Caulaincourt observed that 'The Emperor had changed the national character. The French had become serious; their bearing was grave; the great questions of the day preoccupied all minds; petty interests were subordinated; the general sentiment was, one may say, patriotic; one would have blushed to show any other.'[27] Yet he diluted French identity by expanding the nation's territory to include ten million or so non-French speaking peoples.

Was the average French citizen better off, worse off or the same by July 1815 than he or she was in November 1799? That, of course is impossible to say confidently given the paucity and unreliability of socioeconomic statistics not just from those years but from those that preceded them. What is clear is that Napoleon's economic legacy was mixed. His investments in infrastructure, industry and innovation stimulated France's economic development while his ruinous wars sapped France's prosperity and devastated the lives of countless people. His Continental System wrecked maritime industries while promoting the manufacturing of products that could not be imported.

Overall, Napoleon's economic policies boosted the standard of living and quality of life for many and perhaps most French people. His investments in infrastructure like roads, canals, bridges and ports and his nurturing of manufacturers with subsidies, tax breaks and procurements undoubtedly spurred France's economic development although just how much can never be known. His public health measures that provided fresh water, clean streets and smallpox inoculations for Paris and other cities prolonged and bettered countless lives and can be roughly measured.

The population grew slowly from 28,615,000 to 30,271,000 or a mere 3.3 per cent between 1790 and 1816 compared to a 13.3 per cent increase for

Britain's population. That was despite the fact that marriages increased both because the Code Napoleon made them easier to contract and a married man with children could not be conscripted. Nearly every year of Napoleon's rule more than 900,000 children were born with the number peaking at 994,000 in 1814, presumably because the previous year so many men tried to make babies to dodge the draft. Meanwhile, infant mortality dropped by half during the quarter-century following 1789, largely the result of Napoleon's public health policies. Death in war was the key reason for France's slow population growth during this era. The exact figure will never be known but anywhere from 600,000 to 1,300,000 French men died from 1792 to 1815, with 400,000 to 1,000,000 dying during the imperial years from 1805 to 1815.[28]

Napoleon was a fiscal conservative who abhorred the very notion of himself or France being in debt to others. So he opposed borrowing money to finance France's government. His pay as you go policy kept France's national debt and thus its interest payments and interest rates relatively low. When the empire ended, France's debt equalled just 44 francs per person compared to Britain's debt of 1,140 francs per person! That was truly a remarkable achievement.[29]

A vital reason for Napoleon's success in slowing the rise of France's national debt was his policy of trying to make war pay for itself. He racked in 1.8 billion francs in contributions from allies and reparations from defeated enemies from 1800 to 1814. The trouble was that war expenses were three billion francs or 40 per cent more than that income. He had to fill that 1.2 billion franc gap with higher taxes on French citizens. Yet, despite his utterly disastrous war from June 1812 to April 1814, when he first abdicated, France's national debt was a mere 60 million francs. Had he sidestepped invading Russia and thus the resulting catastrophes, while instead paring his military expenses, his empire could have actually made a profit for France. If so, he could have generated a virtuous economic dynamic by cutting taxes and thus generating greater growth and revenues.[30]

Napoleon was justly proud of the results of his related legal and economic reforms:

> The degree of prosperity is due to the liberal laws regulating the grand empire like the suppression of feudalism, tithes and monastic orders . . . that created or freed a grand number of proprietors, especially today . . . for a multitude of formerly landless families. It is due to the equality of these shares, to the clarity and simplification of the property laws . . . and the

promptness with which they are judged that the number of trials diminish daily.[31]

Yet Napoleon undermined all those achievements with his Continental System which was an utter economic, strategic and political failure. Through his 15 years in power, Britain was Napoleon's nemesis, his obsession, his great white whale that he would eventually destroy his own regime in trying to destroy. He inaugurated the Continental System in November 1806 in hopes of bringing Britain to its knees by severing its trade with Europe. Instead the blockade empowered Britain and devastated France. Peoples across the French Empire and in France itself hated the blockade for the vicious economic circle it imposed of higher prices and joblessness and lower wealth and revenues, especially in seaports but often far inland. Governments raised taxes to compensate for lost tariff revenues and the worsening extractions at once diminished people's incomes and exacerbated hatreds. Although the blockade's losers vastly outnumbered its winners, some domestic industries like textiles did flourish when they did not have to compete with lower priced, better-made British products.

Then there was the system's self-inflicted military devastation. The 'logic' of extending or enforcing the blockade led Napoleon to the increasingly disastrous steps of trying to conquer first Portugal, then Spain and finally Russia. Ironically, Napoleon's attempts to conquer Portugal and Spain to deprive Britain of their trade actually gave Britain the opportunity to open a military front on the Continent that drained French power for six years. Meanwhile, the unending war with Britain and the Royal Navy's blockade locked the French navy into a vicious circle.[32] The blockade deprived the French navy of vital supplies and experience in sailing and gunnery skills; French warships and their crews atrophied in harbour compounded by the Marine Ministry's factionalism, corruption and incompetence.

For the first few years, the Continental System did hurt Britain's economy as income from trade with Europe plummeted. Yet ironically, Napoleon saved Britain when the Continental System most threatened to destroy it. The crisis climaxed in 1811 when disastrous harvests pushed Britain to the brink of mass starvation. Napoleon hoped to drain Britain's gold reserves and enrich his own by selling licences to export grain to Britain. In the long term, however, the Continental System actually accelerated Britain's economic development by forcing merchants, manufacturers, financiers, farmers and inventors to be more efficient and innovative. British trade diversified. Eventually the British muscled their way into profitable markets in Latin America, Asia, Africa and the Middle East. Beginning in 1810, exports actually surpassed imports, which meant more money was flowing into than out of Britain for the first time since 1780.

Overall, Napoleon's greatest political, economic, social and cultural achievements came as First Consul from November 1799 to May 1804. Thereafter war was central to his array of preoccupations and ultimately devastated most of what he had established.

Power and War

Is Napoleon's reputation for being a military genius overblown? In his book *Blundering to Glory*, Owen Connelly argued that 'Bonaparte regularly made strategic or tactical blunders which made scrambling necessary to win'.[33] That is true but misleading. No general can boast a spotless strategic or tactical record. Each must react or 'scramble' to blunt shifting threats and seize fleeting opportunities within war's thick fog. Sensitive war leaders from corporals to commanders-in-chief are haunted by the mistakes they made that unnecessarily lost lives and opportunities. The bottom line for evaluating any war leader is whether his decisions result in victory or defeat and at what military, economic, political and moral costs.

Overall Napoleon is history's greatest military leader. No other general won more battles and decisive campaigns than him. As for campaigns, he won those of Italy (1796–7), Egypt (1798–9), Austria (1805), Prussia (1806), Poland (1807), Spain (1808–09) and Austria (1809) and lost those of Palestine (1799), Russia (1812), Germany (1813), France (1814) and Waterloo (1815). As for battles, of forty-three where he commanded an army, he won thirty-five and lost eight (Bassano, Acre, Aspern-Essling, Leipzig, La Rothière, Lâon, Arcis-sur-Aube and Waterloo).

How does Napoleon compare to his era's other generals? Only Arthur Wellesley, the Duke of Wellington, surpassed him in the victory to campaign and battle ratios; he won every campaign and battle in which he led an army and lost only one siege, although he fought far fewer campaigns and battles. Wellington was a much more hands-on and successful tactician, but was methodical and prudent rather than decisive and relentless as a strategist. None of Wellington's campaigns match the brilliance of Napoleon's Italian campaign of 1796–7, Ulm and Austerlitz campaign of 1805, Jena-Auerstadt campaign of 1806 and eastern France campaign of 1814. All other generals of that era have much more mixed or questionable records. The Russian general Alexander Suvorov, for instance, may have been undefeated but racked up most of his victories against the Turks.

None of Napoleon's campaigns lasted longer or was more complex than his Italian campaign that began in April 1796 and ended eleven months later in March 1797. Strategically, the campaign's six phases fall into two types. He was on the offensive during his initial phase in Piedmont and final phase in Austria and on the defensive during the four intervening phases. Nonetheless, in each phase he was almost constantly advancing and attacking the most threatening or vulnerable enemy forces. During that campaign, Mantua was a grand distraction for both sides, although it burdened the Austrians far more. The Austrians sought to relieve and the French to capture that city.[34]

As for his greatest battles, Napoleon warned against trying to 'judge' any battle 'in isolation' from the context of 'place, action and intention'. Each battle 'was just a part of very vast combinations'.[35] Having said that, he considered Eckmühl the battle where he 'made the most beautiful manoeuvre that I ever made'.[36] Austerlitz was perhaps his most carefully planned and managed battle. He anticipated what the enemy would most likely do, deployed his corps to best defeat that effort and then decisively reacted to the subsequent threats and opportunities with flurries of orders to appropriate commanders.

Napoleon did more than merely synthesize the practices of the great generals who preceded him. No leader before him waged war as swiftly and relentlessly. He adapted promptly and decisively to shifting circumstances, realizing his maxim: 'The art of being sometimes audacious and sometimes prudent is the art of success.'[37] His brilliance at mathematics and study of Isaac Newton prompted this formula: 'The force of an army, like the quantity of movements in mechanics, is evaluated by its mass multiplied by its speed. Such marches, far from weakening an army, augment its strength and morale and accumulate the means of victory.'[38] The key was 'in every movement to aim for wining a good position' that ideally forced the enemy to attack you at a great disadvantage.[39] A soldier put it more prosaically: 'The emperor has found a new way of making war; he makes use only of our legs and our bayonets.'[40]

Napoleon's most important military innovation was the corps system which he initiated in March 1800. He devised corps as mini-armies with infantry, cavalry, artillery, engineers and supply trains that ideally marched within twelve hours of each other in echelon on parallel roads so that they could quickly mass on a battlefield or shift direction as opportunities or threats arose. He also introduced strategic reserves of artillery and cavalry that could rush to any battlefield. To lighten his army's load and quicken its pace, he forbad tents on campaign. Sooner or later all his enemies emulated his innovations to reduce the likelihood that he would again defeat them.

He initiated an unprecedented increase in the number of combatants and casualties, peaking with his Russian campaign when he mustered more than 600,000 troops, half French and the rest from several dozen other realms, for the invasion, then lost around 500,000 of them over the next half-year to combat, disease, starvation, desertion and freezing, while probably as many Russian soldiers and civilians died. The Peninsula campaign lasted six years and annually devoured around 50,000 French troops and probably as many enemy troops. The Napoleonic era's three bloodiest days were Borodino, Waterloo and Eylau. The epic three-day battle of Leipzig was the largest in the number of troops engaged and killed, followed by the two-day battle of Wagram.

So what went wrong? Historian David Chandler explains why Napoleon's string of victories turned to defeats:

> Every quality has its perversion and the dividing line between genius and madness is notoriously slender. As time passed, delusion began to cloud his powers of judgment at critical moments; he began to believe what he wanted to believe, not just the facts, objectively analysed . . . He began to gamble for increasingly high stakes . . . He refused to recognize what was feasible and what was not, relying on miracles to come to his rescue . . . His passion for orderliness, efficiency and centralization of power degenerated into selfish egotism and grinding tyranny.[41]

Napoleon made critical errors during his 1809 campaign. His initial mistake was putting Berthier rather than Davout in charge of the army in Germany. Berthier was an outstanding chief of staff but had never before held a significant independent command. The Austrian offensive rattled him into decisions that disorganized the French army which Napoleon had to untangle after his arrival. Far worse was his decision to march to Vienna rather than after the retreating Austrian army following the battles culminating with Regensburg. A rigorous pursuit snapping at the heels of the Austrians would have eventually forced Charles to turn and fight. His worst mistake was crossing the Danube with half his army while his other corps were distant. The Austrians nearly overwhelmed the French during the subsequent battle of Aspern-Essling on 21 and 22

May. For that Chandler condemned 'Napoleon's conduct' that 'bordered on madness, in challenging fate . . . by venturing on a battle without knowledge of the Austrian positions, without securing his passage of the river and without assembling his whole strength on the island of Lobau'. He also blasted Charles for letting Napoleon escape with his army's remnants to Lobau.[42]

Countless critics then and since consider Napoleon's cynical seizure of the Spanish throne and the subsequent horrendous war among his worst acts. Napoleon agreed: 'All my disasters came from entangling myself in this fatal knot. It destroyed my morality in Europe, complicated my difficulties and opened a front for the English army. Events have proven that I made a great mistake.'[43] He famously called the Peninsular War his ulcer but cancer would have been a more apt metaphor. There he fell into a psychologically nearly-inescapable trap of his own making. He envisioned Portugal and Spain as treasure mines to be looted for their gold, fleets and colonies. Instead, his empire blundered into a quagmire in the Peninsula as soon as Marshal Junot led his corps across the frontier in October 1807. Over the next four years, as his empire sank deeper, Napoleon reacted to the swelling British, Portuguese and Spanish resistance simply by committing more troops, hoping eventually to crush the enemy alliance with the sheer weight of men and guns. In doing so he committed so much prestige as well as hard power to conquering Portugal and Spain that he felt compelled to keep doubling down after each defeat. He 'reasoned' that if an array of enemy troops and guerrillas chased him from Spain's throne, similar forces elsewhere would be heartened to do the same, eventually destroying his empire. Yet, to counter that, he drained his empire's vitality by sinking ever more treasure and troops into that bottomless pit.

Then, from early 1812, Napoleon's mind was riveted to Europe's other end and he withdrew 50,000 troops from the Peninsula for his Russian campaign, leaving only 290,000 behind. The Russian apocalypse and the shift of the fighting to central Germany forced him to withdraw another 65,000 troops from Spain in 1813, leaving only 224,000 behind. In doing so, he trapped himself with a foot on two weakening stools that eventually collapsed beneath him.

Napoleon compounded his Peninsula problems by refusing to appoint a commander-in-chief for his scattered corps and instead trying to micromanage each general's strategy mostly from Paris but at times at an array of headquarters that stretched as far east as the Kremlin. He issued orders that straightjacketed his generals from creatively responding to shifting threats and opportunities. His orders were usually either irrelevant or harmful when they reached his field commanders weeks later. He often gave his commanders conflicting advice. He told them to conduct themselves according to circumstances while ordering them not to retreat and to hold each mountain pass to the last man. His commanders rarely did anything right in his eyes: 'All that happens in Spain is truly deplorable. The army appears commanded not by generals who wage war but by postal inspectors.'[44] He might have crushed resistance had he remained in Spain a year rather than a mere two months before racing off to war against Austria.

On St Helena, Napoleon wistfully remarked that had he 'died at Moscow his military glory and political career would have been matchless in world history'.[45] Russia was Napoleon's self-inflicted holocaust where he failed catastrophically at the related arts of diplomatic, political and military power compounded by bad luck. Politically he failed to play the Polish, Lithuanian and serf cards that were in his hands. He never warned Alexander that if the Tsar's intransigence forced him to defeat Russia once again, reconstituting not just a Polish kingdom but a Lithuanian kingdom, both allied with France and liberating the serfs would be included in any peace treaty. Evoking those existential Russian dreads might well have led to a summit and a face-saving accord. And if not, then Napoleon should have realized in succession all three threats. Just reconstituting the Kingdom of Poland would likely have drawn Alexander west against him. And if that happened, Napoleon would have encircled and crushed the Russian army with his superior forces. If Alexander refused to take that bait, Napoleon could have stayed in Vilna, where he actually did pause, to organize a Lithuanian government rather than head eastward, again hoping to entice Alexander westward. Historically, the Russians withdrew because the French pursued them. But had Napoleon sat tight to consolidate a Lithuanian kingdom and replenish his army's depleted men, horses and supplies, sooner or later the Russian armies would have come to him. And if not, Napoleon could have slowly marched eastward to Smolensk at a pace whereby his supply wagons kept up with his troops, all the while issuing emancipation proclamations to the serfs and recruiting volunteers into regiments. With that strategy, Napoleon would have saved his army and his throne rather than lose the former in 1812 and the latter in 1814.[46]

The Russian campaign was a classic case of an invader winning virtually all the battles yet losing the war. Napoleon's initial huge numbers of troops were actually a liability rather than asset. The result, at least until Smolensk, was a contest between a sumo wrestler and a judo master. Knowing the odds against them, the Russians nimbly sidestepped

Napoleon's sweeping pincer manoeuvres at Vilna, Vitebsk, Drissa and Smolensk. Meanwhile, Napoleon's army melted away from starvation, disease and desertion. By the time, Napoleon reached Borodino, the Russians actually outgunned him. Despite that, at Borodino, Napoleon tactically continued to practise sumo rather than judo. He rejected Davout's plea to encircle rather than directly attack the Russian army. He did so because he assumed that the Russians would simply withdraw again. That most certainly would have happened, but eventually Kutuzov would have had to stand and fight a decisive battle somewhere before Moscow a mere 70 miles away.

Then Napoleon lingered seven weeks in Moscow. Had he spent two weeks refurbishing his army then withdrawn to winter at Smolensk, he would have saved it. He certainly had a face-saving reason to do so. The Russians had torched Moscow, rendering much of it uninhabitable. But Napoleon clung to the delusion that Alexander would plead for peace even though he had repeatedly sworn that he would not negotiate as long as a single enemy soldier remained on Russian soil. Meanwhile, Alexander's armies swelled with reinforcements.

Napoleon might have saved his army had he pushed down the road to Kaluga after capturing Maloyaroslavets after a vicious battle. He could have replenished his provisions at Kaluga and his munitions 70 miles east at Tula, then burned both cities before marching west to Smolensk. But here fears over the unknown route and enemy before him got the better of him. He withdrew north then west on the devastated route that he had taken from the Niemen to Moscow.

During the 1813 campaign, Napoleon committed an array of strategic and diplomatic mistakes. In June he committed a grave folly by accepting a two-month armistice that he had no intention of using for diplomacy; the allies benefited from that long breather by building up their forces until they outnumbered the French by a ratio of five to three. He then violated a critical military maxim that may have cost him the campaign. He had always emphasized the importance of concentrating one's forces to destroy enemy armies instead of dispersing them to defend or take cities. Yet he did just that. Not once but twice he sent armies north to take Berlin, but more numerous Allied forces routed first Oudinot then Ney. Berlin was a distraction rather than an asset. Ideally, he would have screened that front while adding most soldiers there to his own army. The 35,000 troops under Davout that defended Hamburg and the 35,000 troops under St Cyr that he left behind at Dresden in October could have won him victory at Leipzig in October 1813 or a score of battles in 1814; St Cyr surrendered on 11 November; Davout held out until after learning of Napoleon's abdication. Napoleon also had nearly 70,000 troops garrisoning a dozen or so citadels far behind the enemy lines. However, those troops were mostly second-rate and tied down an equal or greater number of enemy troops that screened or besieged them. His decision to fight at Leipzig was among his worst mistakes. An elementary principle of warfare is to avoid fighting with one's back to an unfordable body of water against a more numerous enemy. That is exactly what Napoleon did. Behind his army was the Elster River over which one bridge linked Leipzig to the western bank. He fanned out his corps a few miles from Leipzig. In that epic four-day battle from 16 to 19 October 1813, he lost 81,000 troops, half captured, and 328 guns. And he might have avoided that disaster had he simply accepted the Allied terms that would have broken up his empire and confined France to its 1792 borders.

The Waterloo campaign was Napoleon's shortest and worst fought. He mostly blamed others for his defeat.[47] He reflected that: 'In less than a week I saw an assured victory for the destiny of France three times escape from my hands. Without the desertion of a traitor I would have annihilated the enemy in opening the campaign. I would have crushed them at Ligny if my left had done its duty. I would crushed them at Waterloo if my right had appeared.'[48] Essentially 'the Belgian campaign was lost by marshals who did not execute the emperor's orders'.[49] He did reproach himself for wasting valuable time tinkering with a new constitution and other political issues when he should have devoted himself to mobilizing France for war. He did heap praise on his troops: 'Never had the French soldier shown more courage, good will and enthusiasm; he was filled with feelings of superiority over all other European troops. His confidence in the emperor was total . . . but shadowing him was his mistrust of the other commanders. The betrayals of 1814 were always present in his spirit.'[50]

As usual, Napoleon mingles interesting points with fantasies. He might well have won had Davout and Soult commanded his wings rather than Ney and Grouchy. The campaign was actually decided on 16 June rather than 18 June. The campaign might have been victorious had Ney been aggressive rather than cautious at Quatre Bras, swiftly seized that crossroads and then marched up to Waterloo that day. That would have driven a huge wedge between Wellington and Blücher. He might have also won had Ney not recalled d'Erlon when that corps was about to attack Blücher at Ligny. That flank attack would have shattered Blücher's army and pushed it north-east. Napoleon then could have sent Grouchy in pursuit while sending d'Erlon north to Wavre and then west to outflank Wellington before Waterloo, while Napoleon led Ney's wing north up the main road. His defeat at Waterloo was inevitable when Blücher retreated north to Wavre then headed west to attack the French right flank. He would not have won had Grouchy followed Blücher since Blücher could have simply turned his last corps against Grouchy while continuing to attack at Waterloo with his other two corps. A secondary event contributed to his defeat. Without the storm on 17 June, his army could have deployed that night before Wellington's army at Waterloo and attacked early the next morning rather than in early afternoon.

* * *

Napoleon's critics condemn him as an insatiable warmonger. That charge infuriated Napoleon, who insisted that 'I am accused of loving war too much but actually I was always the one who was attacked'.[51] That statement would have been true had he dropped the word 'always' and inserted 'usually' before 'attacked'. The Austrians initiated war in 1798 that Napoleon, after taking power as First Consul, ended in 1800. The British initiated war in 1803. The Austrians along with the Russians and Neapolitans initiated war in 1805. The Prussians and Russians initiated war in 1806. The Austrians initiated war in 1809. The Prussians. Austrians and Swedes joined the Russians to war against him in 1813. The Austrians, Russians, Prussians, Dutch and British initiated war in 1815. That is a lot of wars. In contrast, Napoleon initiated three wars, against Portugal in 1807, Spain 1808 and Russia in 1812; with his recommendation, the Directorate ordered him to invade Egypt and thus provoke a war with the Ottoman Empire in 1798.

Another reality that confounds the black legend of Napoleon is the nature of most of the peace treaties that came from the wars. Although the Austrians started five of six wars against France between 1792 and 1815, Napoleon was actually restrained rather than rapacious in his demands. He let the Austrians off lightly in the first two peace treaties, Campo Formio in 1797 and Lunéville in 1801. He got tough after having to defeat Austria again in 1805 and tougher in 1809, with the respective treaties of Pressburg and Schönbrunn. Yet, he later regretted being too lenient in 1809 after Austria launched its latest war against France in 1813. Rather than break up the Austrian empire into its Austrian, Bohemian and Hungarian components, each with a different dynasty, he let Francis remain the emperor of a slightly smaller realm. As for treaties with other great powers, he agreed to conciliatory terms with Britain at Amiens in 1802 and with Russia at Tilsit in 1807, but harshly punished the aggressor

Prussia at Tilsit in 1807. Yet elsewhere he was hardly restrained in his ambition to topple existing dynasties or create new kingdoms and put his siblings on the thrones. His ambitions swelled with his power and then exceeded it, which brought his downfall.

The turning point in Napoleon's foreign policy came during the war against Prussia and Russia from October 1806 to July 1807. Before then back to when he took command of the army of Italy in March 1796, he followed the republic's policies of asserting France's 'natural frontiers' and developing 'sister republics' as allies. But the combination of the ongoing war against Britain since March 1803, devastating defeat at Trafalgar in October 1805, Austrian and Russian aggression in 1805 and Prussian aggression in 1806 provoked Napoleon to shift his foreign policy. After crushing Prussia's army and overrunning most of Prussia, he inaugurated his Continental System in November 1806 and thereafter sought to unite as much of Europe as possible under his rule or the rule of his sibling monarchs and reduce as many other states as possible to satellites. He envisioned himself as a new Charlemagne who would spread enlightened government, law, prosperity and peace across Europe. Napoleon's power peaked during the five years from the Treaty of Tilsit in June 1807 to the invasion of Russian in June 1812.

Napoleon did not invent imperialism. People have been conquering and colonizing others since the beginning of time. Yet he did excel as an imperialist, at least for a decade. He understood the dilemmas of conquering foreign peoples. Imperialism has related strategic, economic and psychological goals. Ideally, conquests paid for themselves by extracting profits and revenues from subject populations, denying one's rivals those same benefits and bolstering one's own national cohesion. Naturally the native peoples hate being ruled and exploited by foreigners. The more rapacious the exploitation, the greater the chance that people will revolt. Destroying the lives and property of rebels can swell the enemy ranks as fence-sitters believe they have nothing to lose and seek vengeance, a phenomena known as the hearts, minds and hydra dilemma.[52] He recognized the dilemma of colonization: 'such is the nature of any conquered people, they disguise their feelings and their values and prostrate themselves with respect before those who hold their lives and property in their hands.'[53] Meanwhile, they bided their time and awaited the chance to fight for independence.

Despite understanding the dilemmas of imperialism, Napoleon repeatedly entangled himself in it. His conquests provoked revolts in Lombardy in 1796, Calabria in 1806, Tyrol in 1809 and Spain from 1808 to 1814. In addition, after taking power in November 1799, he inherited an ongoing revolt in Saint Domingue. His 'solution' was crushing the revolt so swiftly and brutally that the survivors thereafter fatalistically accepted and obeyed the dictates of foreign rule. In all, he had thousands, perhaps tens of thousands, of rebels slaughtered with arms in their hands or summarily tried and executed after they surrendered. That worked everywhere except Saint Domingue and Spain whose rebels had invincible allies, yellow fever and Britain, respectively. He never understood the nature of the guerrilla war in Spain and clung to his idealistic justifications for trying to conquer that realm: 'Their hatred will wear out when they see that we bring them only wiser laws, a code more liberal; and better suited to the times in which we live, that the ancient customs and the Inquisition by which the country used to be governed. At present the Spaniards are fighting because they still believe that we want to make Frenchmen of them.'[54]

The most dazzling of Napoleon's imperial dreams inspired him to emulate Alexander the Great by conquering first Egypt then the Middle East before finally marching to India. That dream died at the siege of Acre in May 1799. He also dreamed of carving out a Caribbean empire but that New World dream died with around 20,000 or so of his soldiers who perished from yellow fever. He seemingly buried those two dreams by cutting his overseas losses, shrugging off Britain's takeover of Egypt and Saint Domingue's independence and selling Louisiana to the United States in 1803. The disastrous Battle of Trafalgar in October 1805 appeared to be the final nail in the coffin of those dreams. Yet they revived briefly after he took title to the throne of Spain and its overseas empire in May 1808. The resistance of Spain's army and guerrillas, soon joined by a British army led by General Arthur Wellesley, disillusioned him of his hope to reap vast revenues from Spain's colonies in the New World and elsewhere.

* * *

Napoleon faces serious war crime charges. By the late eighteenth century, an international law of war did exist, defined much more by principles and practices than legally-binding treaties. The key values included respecting private property and non-combatants, treating prisoners of war humanely and forbidding massacres and assassinations.

The worst war crime charge against him was his order to execute 2,000 to 4,000 Turkish prisoners of war on a beach outside Jaffa during his 1799 Palestine campaign. He legally justified that act by arguing that many of them had violated the parole not to fight that they had earlier given when they surrendered. But that legal defence obviously cannot be applied to those who had never given their parole. His fallback position was that European standards did not apply to non-Europeans who regularly massacred and enslaved those they defeated: 'The rights of man that softens the evils of war does not extend protection to monsters who dishonour human nature.'[55] Finally, he insisted that by waging war as ruthlessly as Muslims and Arabs, he would ultimately lessen its victims by ending the war sooner than if he let European standards prevail. However specious such arguments may be, he apparently lost no sleep over what happened at Jaffa.

During that same campaign Napoleon committed another controversial act. Is mercy killing justified? Should someone end someone else's unbearable suffering by ending his life? That is what Napoleon had done to a score or so wounded men at Jaffa that could not be transported back to Egypt. He ordered his doctors to kill them with overdoses of opium to prevent them from suffering a crueller fate at the hands of the Arabs. Yet Napoleon had an alternative. He could have surrendered his men into the care of Captain Sidney Smith, who commanded British forces at Acre. But pride kept him from doing so.[56]

All along Napoleon insisted that he waged war according to the laws and morality that prevailed where he waged it. Indeed, he condemned the British for committing war crimes, specifically for repeatedly trying to assassinate him and for their cruelty to their prisoners of war. For both practical and humanitarian reasons, he persisted in trying to negotiate prisoner exchanges with Britain. In all, from 1803 to 1814, the British held nearly twice as many French prisoners, 130,000, as the French held British prisoners, 72,000. During the Peninsular War, Napoleon offered a swap of two Spanish and one British for three French. That was a bad deal for London since the quality of French and British soldiers were equal while Spanish soldiers were inferior. The British rejected that offer as they had his previous ones.[57]

How do alleged British war crimes during the era compare to Napoleon's? British redcoats may have slaughtered as many as 30,000 Irish during the 1798 rebellion. Wellington let his soldiers sack or commit mass robbery, rape and murder against the citizens of Ciudad Rodrigo and Badajoz after capturing those cities. The British Empire expanded to engulf the Cape Colony, Malta and much of India. Not once but twice, the British attacked Copenhagen and destroyed its fleet even though Denmark was neutral both times; around 2,500 people died during the British bombardment in 1807.

The British tried murdering Napoleon at least once and probably more times via foreign agents that they trained, equipped and financed. The Royal Navy and privateers captured and mostly kept thousands of neutral merchant ships along with their cargos and impressed or forced at least 10,000 foreign sailors to serve on British warships. The British treated their prisoners far worse than French-held prisoners; disease and starvation killed tens of thousands of men in British prison dungeons and hulks.

So were British statesmen, generals, admirals and sea captains collectively as or guiltier than Napoleon of committing war crimes? Were Napoleon's crimes justified because other leaders committed similar crimes? Was Napoleon's imperialism justified because imperialism is as old as humanity?

To explain is not necessarily to justify. Saying that other leaders and countries committed as bad or worse crimes does not let Napoleon off the moral hook. Each government faced moral dilemmas and strategic imperatives. For excellent related strategic, economic and political reasons, Britain remained at war nearly nonstop against France from 1793 to 1815, with a mere fourteen-month breather from March 1802 to May 1803. In contrast, Austria's justifications for launching wars against France in 1798, 1805, 1809 and 1813 were flimsy at best.

For more than two centuries, the 'black legend' that depicts Napoleon as an insatiable warmonger and war criminal has distorted understanding of the era. In reality, Napoleon had more wars launched against him than he launched against others, while both Britain and France, along with other countries, can be accused of committing an array of war crimes. Britain's are largely unknown for two reasons. The alleged crimes were initiated by a variety of political and military leaders over two decades thus obscuring them compared to those ordered by one man, Napoleon. Britain was among the coalition of victors whose nationalistic writers imposed their version of history for generations after Napoleon was exiled to St Helena. Napoleon's propaganda ended with his fall; British and other anti-Napoleon propaganda persisted long thereafter. In France, 'black legend' writers had a head start of decades before 'golden legend' writers sympathetic to Napoleon began producing antidotes. Both the 'black' and 'golden' legends distort history. The elements of truth in each must be extracted and combined to form a balanced, realistic portrayal of Napoleon.

Power and Unintended Consequences

The assertion of power often unleashes forces that are not just unintended but unwanted. Napoleon certainly sought to modernize the realms his soldiers overran from Lisbon to Warsaw and Naples to Berlin but only under either French rule or hegemony.[58] Once the genies of nationalism and liberalism escaped from their ideological bottles, they could not be stuffed back inside no matter how hard Napoleon and subsequent conservative regimes tried doing so with mass repression and exploitation. That was true both in Europe and in Europe's overseas colonies. Liberalism and nationalism eventually rendered one's colonies far more expensive than they were worth. A people's revolution under those banners was nearly impossible to destroy; indeed trying to do so merely accelerated the revolution's inevitable triumph. The better strategy was to co-opt rather than crush those forces, as Napoleon recognized: 'The colonial system . . . is finished for us as it is for the European continent: we must renounce it and hereafter fight for freedom of the seas and universal free trade.'[59] The challenge was managing decolonization so that prosperity was enhanced rather than crimped for as many people as possible: 'We must imagine a type of emancipation from these colonies . . . over time . . . that can profit from the new connections and more advantageous relationships.'[60]

Those forces first manifested themselves with the revolutions that erupted in Spain's New World empire in 1810 and destroyed most of it by 1821, as half a dozen independent countries emerged from the ruins. In Europe, 1848 was the great year of revolution; although reactionary forces managed to crush most of them, they would repeatedly re-emerge until the final triumph in 1992. Napoleon's 1798 conquest of Egypt unleashed a war between modern and traditional forces not just for that country but eventually across the Middle East that have battled each other incessantly and mercilessly.

Napoleon was the grandfather if not the father of Italy and Germany. Before he conquered and reorganized those regions, Italy and Germany were little more than geographical expressions, with the former split among a dozen states, the latter among several hundred. Italian and German were more language groups than languages with countless dialects that made clear communication among them difficult or outright incomprehensible. When Napoleon established the Confederation of the Rhine as a French ally and bulwark against Prussia, Austria and Russia, he did not care about the political systems of the thirty-nine members as long as they were loyal to him. Yet he had a different vision for Italy and might eventually have fulfilled it: 'Italy, isolated by natural limits, separated by the sea and very high mountains from the rest of Europe, seems to be called to form a great and powerful nation . . . Italy is a single nation. The unity of language, of customs, of literature must, in a future more or less distant, finally unite the inhabitants in a single government.'[61] Regardless, the ultimate goal of Napoleon's efforts to unify swathes of Italy and Germany, as well as impose a modernist revolution from the top down in Spain, was to enhance French power. Yet, in doing so, he unleashed forces of liberalism and nationalism that eventually turned against him. On St Helena, Napoleon reflected that: 'Today political circumstances are no longer the same; the times have greatly changed ... French principles are in everyone's head and reproduce themselves everywhere. It is a disorderly torrent that one can vainly hope will be arrested by the dams of patience, moderation and flexibility.'[62]

Finally, Napoleon provoked a different sort of European unity than he envisioned, but one far more successful. During the Congress of Vienna the great powers – Austria, Russia, Britain, Prussia and France – forged principles and behaviours for a 'concert of Europe' that prevented a general war from engulfing the Continent for another century.

Another extraordinary long-term result was the transformation of the United States from a third-rate power into a superpower. By selling the Louisiana Territory to the United States in 1803, Napoleon intended to strengthen America against Britain. Nonetheless, he would have been astonished to observe how rapidly Americans capitalized on that acquisition. Through subsequent acts of diplomacy, sometimes preceded by war, the United States expanded across the rest of the continent and then acquired a small overseas colonial empire. Along the way, America experienced its own related, agrarian, industrial, financial and mercantile revolutions that made it the world's largest and most dynamic economy by the late nineteenth century. Washington capitalized on America's economic superpower to led alliances to victory in three global struggles during the twentieth century, the First World War, the Second World War and the Cold War and become the leader of the global economy. The chances of any of that happening would have diminished sharply without the initial Louisiana Purchase.

Power and Legacy

Ultimately Napoleon failed spectacularly and repeatedly at the art of power until he destroyed his regime, twice! Numerous related reasons explain why but boil down to this – his ambitions exceeded his abilities. The art of power has multiple dimensions but perhaps the most critical is knowing one's limits. Bloated by hubris, Napoleon grossly exceeded his. He let his military and diplomatic victories warp him. He rejected advice contrary to his prejudices, denigrated his enemies as his inferiors and even believed himself superior to the destructive power of Russia's winter.

Overall Napoleon's policies were disastrous for France and Europe. He left France with less people, territory and wealth than when he took power. Under the Treaty of Paris, signed on 20 November 1815, France was reduced to its 1789 frontiers, had to pay 700,000,000 francs in reparations to the Allies and had to underwrite an army of occupation that would remain until the reparation were paid off, which turned out to be three years. During the wars that Napoleon fought when he ruled France at least a million people across Europe and beyond died, directly or indirectly, while millions more were grievously wounded or had their property devastated. Not once but twice during his rule, enemy troops marched into Paris in 1814 and 1815, a shame that France also suffered in 1420, 1871 and 1940. And the political wheel turned full circle. From 1789 through 1815, France experienced an absolute monarchy, a constitutional monarchy, various forms of a republic culminating with the consulate, an empire, a constitutional monarchy, a constitutional imperium and finally an absolute monarchy once again. Napoleon's legacy contrasts sharply with that of Louis XIV. The 'Sun King' has also been condemned for plunging France into a series of wars, but at least he succeeded in expanding French territory while his regime became a model for Europe's monarchs and survived him for another 77 years.

The art of power ultimately depends on results. One is powerful only so far as one gets what one wants. That becomes more challenging as one's ambitions rise. As his power grew, Napoleon increasingly failed to practise what he preached. As a student of Machiavelli, he knew well that power was inseparable from matching appropriate ends with available means. Indeed, he brilliantly followed that principle during his first decade or so as a general and statesman. But those ever more soaring victories eventually warped him as his ambitions exceeded his abilities.

His power peaked at Tilsit in 1807 then he began squandering it the next year with his attempts to subject Spain to his empire from 1808 capped by the war to force Russia back into the Continental System in 1812. Napoleon trapped himself in a security dilemma. The more he enhanced French power, the more he threatened and enraged the other great powers, which eventually succeeded in unifying and destroying him. He recognized that 'each new addition for France alarmed everyone else. They made loud cries and put aside peace.'[63] When Napoleon failed, he failed spectacularly. His empire might have endured for generations had he not embarked on his Peninsula and Russian campaigns. The chronic 'Spanish ulcer', as he called it, ate away at his empire for six years, while the Russian campaign destroyed half a million of his troops within six months.

* * *

Napoleon's last campaign was his most ambitious of all – he sought to conquer history itself. In that he won a resounding victory. For that he had critical allies, first among the handful of devotees who followed him into exile, then ever since among hundreds of historians who celebrated his achievements much more than they deplored his catastrophes.

Then there is outright mythology. Napoleon is the ultimate romantic hero. His most enduring image is that of the young, lean, fierce-faced general with oversized bicorn and flowing cape on a rearing white stallion with the Alps behind him, pointing to a rock inscribed with his name above those of Charlemagne and Hannibal. This is the Napoleon who championed rather than violated the French Revolution's ideals; who liberated subjected and exploited peoples rather than subjected and exploited them; who personified not despotism but liberalism, nationalism, transnationalism and cosmopolitanism. Enchained on the rock of St Helena, he was a martyr rather than a traitor to those great causes. That mythical hero has inspired countless people to struggle to do better and even achieve greatness and will continue to do so until the end of time. As such perhaps only religious leaders like Moses, Buddha, Jesus or Muhammad have more powerfully affected how swaths of humanity perceive and act in the world than Napoleon.

Napoleon once said: 'Men are only as great as the monuments that they leave behind.'[64] He also once said: 'We build success on chimeras and shrug at those who reason.'[65] Both are enduring and inseparable epitaphs for Napoleon's life and art of power.

Endnotes

Unless otherwise indicated, campaign statistics and treaty details come from the following respective sources: Digby Smith, *The Greenhill Napoleonic Wars Data Book* (London: Greenhill Press, 1998); Michel Kerauret, ed., *Les Grand Traites de l'Empire*, 3 vols (Paris: Nouveau Monde Editions/Fondation Napoleon, 2002, 2004).

Abbreviations

Correspondance de Napoleon	Napoleon Bonaparte, *Correspondance de Napoleon Ier, publiée par ordere de l'empereur Napoleon III*, 16 vols, (Paris: Claude Tchou, 2002).
Napoleon Correspondance	Thierry Lentz et al., eds, *Napoleon Bonaparte Correspondance Generale*, vols 1–12 (Paris: Fayard, 2004–15).
Talleyrand Mémoires	Emmanuel Waresquiel, ed., *Mémoires et Correspondances de Talleyrand* (Paris: Robert Laffont, 2007).

Introduction: Napoleon and the Art of Power

1. Napoleon to Captain Leduc, 19 February 1806, *Napoleon Correspondance* no. 11507, 6:144; Napoleon to Joseph, 10 November 1808, ibid. no. 19233, 8:1209.
2. Rather than hard and soft he used 'earthly' and 'terrestrial'. Bruno Colson, *Napoléon: De la Guerre* (Paris: Perrin, 2011), 53.
3. For literature reviews of the debate, see: Pieter Geyl, *Napoleon For and Against* (New Haven: Yale University Press, 1949); Charles J. Esdaile, 'The Napoleonic Period: Some Thoughts on Recent Historiography', *European History Quarterly*, vol. 23 (1993), 415–32; Leigh Ann Whaley, *The Impact of Napoleon, 1800-1815* (Lanham, Maryland: Scarecrow

Press, 1997). For 'golden legend' Napoleonphiles, see: Michel Franceschi and Ben Weider, *The Wars Against Napoleon: Debunking the Myth of the Napoleonic Wars* (New York: Savas Beattie, 2008); Sylvain Page, *Le Mythe Napoléonien: De Las Cases à Victor Hugo* (Paris: CNRS Editions, 2013); For 'black legend' Napoleonphobes, see: Roger Caratini, *Napoléon: Une Imposture* (Paris: Archipoche, 2002); Serge Cosseron, *Les Mensonges de Napoléon* (Paris: Perrin, 2002); Charles Esdaile, *Napoleon's Wars: An International History* (New York: Viking, 2007).

Hundreds of books have been written on Napoleon. Among the more prominent recent biographies and other studies that I have used for his study are: Jean Tulard, *Napoléon, ou, le Mythe du Sauveur* (Paris: Fayard, 1987); Alan Schom, *Napoleon Bonaparte* (New York: Harper Collins, 1997); Robert Asprey, *The Rise of Napoleon Bonaparte* (New York: Basic Books, 2000); Robert Asprey, *The Reign of Napoleon Bonaparte* (New York: Basic Books, 2001); Steven Englund, *Napoleon: A Political Life* (Cambridge, Mass.: Harvard University Press, 2004); Philip Dwyer, *Napoleon: The Path to Power* (New Haven, Conn.: Yale University Press, 2007); Philip Dwyer, *Citizen Emperor: Napoleon in Power* (New Haven, Conn.: Yale University Press, 2013); Andrew Roberts, *Napoleon: A Life* (New York: Viking, 2014). By far the most up-to-date analysis of Napoleon as a ruler is the four-volume modern classic by Thierry Lentz: *Le Grand Consulat, 1799-1804* (Paris: Fayard, 1999); *Nouvelle Histoire du Premier Empire: Napoléon et la Conquête de l'Europe 1804-1810* (Paris: Fayard, 2002): *Nouvelle Histoire du Premier Empire: L'Effondrement du Système Napoléonien, 1810-1814* (Paris: Fayard, 2004); *Les Cent-Jours (1815)* (Paris: Fayard, 2007).

4. Buonaparte to Désirée, 14 June 1795, *Napoleon Correspondance* no. 303, 1:228–9.
5. Philip Henry, Earl Stanhope, *Notes of Conversations with the Duke of Wellington* (London: Prion, 1998), 59–60.
6. Sylvain Page, *Le Mythe Napoléonien: De Las Cases à Victor Hugo* (Paris: CNRS Editions, 2014).
7. Louis Chardigny, *L'Homme Napoléon* (Paris: Perrin, 2010), 183.
8. Louis Constant *Mémoires Intimes de Napoleon Ier par Constant son valet de chamber*, 2 vols (Paris: Mercure de France, 1967), 1:556–7.
9. Jean-Antoine Chaptal, *Mes Souvenirs sur Napoléon* (Paris: Mercure de France, 2009), 86–7.
10 Napoleon to Clarke, 2 March 1809, *Napoleon Correspondance* no. 20198, 9:144.

11. Napoleon to Clarke, 7 July 1808, *Napoleon Correspondance* no. 18494, 8:839.
12. Chaptal, *Souvenirs*, 81.
13. Richard von Metternich, ed., *The Memoirs of Prince Metternich, 1774-1815*, vols 1–2 (London: Richard Bentley, 1880), 1:271.
14. Emmanuel de Las Cases, *Mémorial de Sainte-Helene*, 2 vols (Paris: Seuil, 1968), 2:1309.
15. Ibid., 2:1290.
16. Bonaparte to Augusta, 3 June 1806, *Napoleon Correspondance* no. 12219, 6:482.
17. Constant, *Mémoires*, 1:468–69, 2:29; Hortense Bonaparte, *Mémoires de la Reine Hortense* (Paris: Mercure de France, 2006), 70.
18. Clemens von Metternich, *Mémoires, Documents, et Ecrits Diverse laisses part le Prince de Metternich*, 8 vols (Paris: Plon, 1880–4), 1:290.
19. Napoleon Bonaparte, *Mémoires de Napoléon, la Campagne d'Italie* (Paris: Talladier, 2010), 127.
20. Bonaparte to Clarke, 16 April 1803, *Napoleon Correspondance* no. 7580, 4:103.
21. Bonaparte to Madame Brueys, 19 August 1798, *Napoleon Correspondance* no. 2869, 2:297.
22. Bonaparte to Josephine, 5 April 1796, *Napoleon Correspondance* no. 461, 1:323.
23. Napoleon to Josephine, 14 February 1807, *Napoleon Correspondance* no. 14312, 7:191.
24. Las Cases, *Mémorial*, 1:276–7.
25. Napoleon to Fouché, 24 May 1807, *Napoleon Correspondance* no. 15707, 7:823–4.
26. Napoleon to Frederick William III, 9 May 1805, *Napoleon Correspondance* no. 10009, 5:287.
27. Armand Caulaincourt, *With Napoleon in Russia* (New York: Dover Publications, 2005), 340.
28. Chaptal, *Souvenirs*, 145, 147.
29. Louis Bourrienne, *Mémoires de M de Bourrienne sur Napoléon*, 5 vols (Paris: Garnier, 1899–1900), 4:359.
30. Constant, *Mémoires*, 1:223, 60.
31. Buonaparte to Joseph, 24 June 1795, *Napoleon Correspondance* no. 308, 1:232.
32. Napoleon to Junot, 8 May 1806, *Napoleon Correspondance* no. 12077, 6:412.
33. Napoleon to Hortense, 16 June 1807, *Napoleon Correspondance* no. 15867, 7:894.

34. Las Cases, *Mémorial*, 1:283.
35. Bonaparte to Pauline, 1 July 1802, *Napoleon Correspondance* no. 6979, 3:1012.
36. Napoleon to Josephine, 3 August 1805, *Napoleon Correspondance* no. 10491, 5:529.
37. Napoleon to Josephine, 6 November 1806, *Napoleon Correspondance* no. 13482, 6:1106.
38. Las Cases, *Mémorial*, 1:313.
39. Ibid., 1:674–5.
40. Ibid., 1:273–4.
41. Buonaparte to Joseph, 24 June 1795, *Napoleon Correspondance* no. 308, 1:232.
42. Bonaparte to Lauriston, 12 December 1804, *Napoleon Correspondance* no. 9439, 4:968–9.
43. Bonaparte to Thevenard, 4 September 1798, *Napoleon Correspondance* no. 3088, 2:390.
44. Las Cases, *Mémorial*, 1:846.
45. Bonaparte to Talleyrand, 7 October 1797, *Napoleon Correspondance* no. 2149, 1:1245.
46. Las Cases, *Mémorial*, 2:1309–10.
47. Ibid., 2:1211–12.
48. Ibid., 2:1461–2.
49. Ibid., 1:494.
50. Bonaparte to Talleyrand, 7 October 1797, *Napoleon Correspondance* no. 2149, 1:1244–6.
51. Colson, *Napoléon*, 89.
52. Chaptal, *Souvenirs*, 81, 102.
53. Napoleon to Eugène, 14 April 1806, *Napoleon Correspondance* no. 11896, 6:324.
54. Napoleon to Fouché, 7 October 1804, *Napoleon Correspondance* no. 9328, 4:924.
55. Bonaparte to Talleyrand, 7 October 1797, *Napoleon Correspondance* no. 2149, 1:1245.
56. Napoleon to Joseph, 4 May 1807, *Napoleon Correspondance* no. 15528, 7:743.
57. Las Cases, *Mémorial*, 1:541.
58. Napoleon to Fouché, 15 January 15, 1806, *Napoleon Correspondance* no. 11286, 6:41.
59. Agathon Fain, *Memoirs* (Paris: Arlea, 2001), 115.
60. Las Cases, *Mémorial*, 2:1458–9.

61. Napoleon to Joseph, 11 February 1808, *Napoleon Correspondance* no. 17181, 8:149.
62. Napoleon to Fouché, 14 May 1805, *Napoleon Correspondance* no. 10056, 5:309.
63. Napoleon to Murat, 19 May 1808, *Napoleon Correspondance* no. 17995, 8:581.
64. Napoleon to Joseph, 3 June 1806, *Napoleon Correspondance* no. 12223, 6:484.
65. Napoleon to Marescalchi, 19 June 1805, *Napoleon Correspondance* no. 10301, 5:432.
66. Las Cases, *Mémorial*, 1:769.
67. Bonaparte to Brignole, Genoan president, 6 October 1797, *Napoleon Correspondance* no. 2147, 1:1243–4.
68. Las Cases, *Mémorial*, 2:952.
69. Ibid., 1:313.
70. Germaine de Stäel, *Considérations sur les Principaux Événements de la Révolution Française* (Ann Arbor: University of Michigan Library, 2009), 400.
71. Las Cases, *Mémorial*, 1:254.
72. Bonaparte to Melzi, 25 November 1803, *Napoleon Correspondance* no. 8334, 4:472.
73. Bonaparte to Melzi, 20 February 1804, *Napoleon Correspondance* no. 8681, 4:615.
74. Bonaparte to Fouché, 28 April 1805, *Napoleon Correspondance* no. 9926, 5:245.
75. Napoleon to Fouché, 6 May 1806, *Napoleon Correspondance* no. 12068, 6:407.
76. Napoleon to Champagny, 7 March 1807, *Napoleon Correspondance* no. 14523, 7:288.
77. Napoleon to Fouché, 17 January 1806, *Napoleon Correspondance* no. 11286, 6:41.
78. Napoleon to Fouché, May 4, 1805, *Napoleon Correspondance* no. 9976, 5:268–9,
79. Las Cases, *Mémorial*, 2:1214.
80. Ibid.
81. Ibid., 1:182.
82. Ibid., 1:351.
83. Ibid., 1:767.
84. Napoleon to Joseph, 31 May 1806, *Napoleon Correspondance* no. 12206, 6:475.

85. For key documents on Napoleon's economic perspectives and policies, see: Las Cases, *Mémorial*, 1:867–70; Chaptal, *Souvenirs*, 116–26; Napoleon to Champagny, 7 March, 22 June 1807, *Napoleon Correspondance* nos. 14522, 15898, 7:286–7, 906–7. For secondary books, see: Pierre Branda, *Le Prix de la Gloire: Napoléon et l'Argent* (Paris: Fayard, 2007); Robert Morrissey, *The Economy of Glory: From Ancien Regime to the Fall of Napoleon* (Chicago: University of Chicago Press, 2013). For articles, see: Emile James, 'Napoléon et la Pensée économique de son temps', *Revue de l'Institut Napoléon* no. 100 (July 1966), 113–23; André Thepot, 'Une Nouvelle Colbertisme', *Napoléon et l'Empire*, ed. Jean Mistler, 2 vols (Paris: Hachette, 1968); Jacques Wolff, 'Jean-Baptiste Say et Napoléon: La Heurt des Conceptions Liberales et authoriairies', *Revue de l'Institut Napoléon*, vol. 1, no. 190 (2005), 53–67.
86. Las Cases, *Mémorial*, 2:1441.
87. Chaptal, *Souvenirs*, 116.
88. Kenneth Morgan, *The Birth of Industrial Britain: Social Change, 1750-1859* (New York: Pearson, 2004); Joel Mokyr, *The Enlightened Economy: Britain and the Industrial Revolution, 1700-1850* (New York: Penguin, 2011); Barrie Trinder, *Britain's Industrial Revolution: The Making of a Manufacturing People* (New York: Carnegie Publishing, 2014).
89. Napoleon to Cambacérès, 4 January 1807, *Napoleon Correspondance* no. 13941, 7:29.
90. Napoleon to Champagny, 27 March 1807, *Napoleon Correspondance* no. 14924, 7:470.
91. Las Cases, *Mémorial*, 1:688.
92. Napoleon to Murat, 21 May 1808, *Napoleon Correspondance* no. 18028, 8:602.
93. Las Cases, *Mémorial*, 2:1441–2.
94. Napoleon to Champagny, 22 February 1810, *Napoleon Correspondance* no. 23170, 9:1741.
95. William Nester, *Titan: The Art of British Power in the Age of Revolution and Napoleon* (Norman: University of Oklahoma Press, 2016).
96. Bonaparte to Directory, 10 October 1797, *Napoleon Correspondance* no. 2153, 1:1249.
97. Chaptal, *Souvenirs*, 119.
98. Bonaparte to Directory, 21 June 1796, *Napoleon Correspondance* no. 710, 1:463.
99. William R. Nester, *Napoleon and the Art of Diplomacy: How War and Hubris Determined the Rise and Fall of the French Empire* (New York: Savas Beattie, 2012).

100. Napoleon to Talleyrand, 28 February 1806, *Napoleon Correspondance* no. 11575, 6:175.
101. Napoleon to Joseph, 18 April 1807, *Napoleon Correspondance* no. 15309, 7:639.
102. Bonaparte to Lannes, 16 April 1804, *Napoleon Correspondance* no. 8807, 4:675.
103. Bonaparte to Joseph, 13 February 1801, *Napoleon Correspondance* no. 6017, 3:562.
104. Bonaparte to Lannes, 14 May 1803, *Napoleon Correspondance* no. 7640, 4:133.
105. Caulaincourt, *With Napoleon in Russia*, 26–7.
106. Las Cases, *Mémorial*, 1:799.
107. Napoleon to Murat, 30 September 1809, *Napoleon Correspondance* no. 22234, 9:1287.
108. Napoleon to Fouché, 9 April 1809, *Napoleon Correspondance* no. 20783, 9:466.
109. Napoleon to Champagny, 13 January 1809, *Napoleon Correspondance* no. 19805, 8:1470; Napoleon to Champagny, 13 January 1809, ibid. no. 19812, 8:19805.
110. Napoleon to Joseph, 8 March 1806, *Napoleon Correspondance* no. 11624, 6:199.
111. *Talleyrand Mémoires*, 261.
112. For books on strategy and tactics by participants, see: Baron Henri de Jomini, *The Art of War* (Westport, Conn.: Greenwood Press, 1862); Carl von Clausewitz, *On War* (New York: Wadsworth Classic, 1999). For leading secondary sources, see: David Chandler, *The Campaigns of Napoleon: The Mind and Method of History's Greatest Soldier* (New York: Macmillan, 1966); Gunther Rothenberg, *The Art of War in the Age of Napoleon* (Bloomington: Indiana University Press, 1981); David Chandler, *On the Napoleonic Wars* (London: Greenhill Books, 1991); David Gates, *The Napoleonic Wars, 1803-1815* (New York: Arnold Press, 1997); Vincent Esposito and John Etling, *A Military History and Atlas of the Napoleonic Wars* (London: Greenhill Books, 1999); Owen Connelly, *Blundering to Victory: Napoleon's Military Campaigns* (New York: Rowan and Littlefield, 2006); Robert Harvey, *War of Wars: The Great European Conflict, 1793-1815* (New York: Carol and Graf, 2006); Jonathan Riley, *Napoleon as a General* (London: Hambledon Continuum, 2007); Charles Esdaile, *Napoleon's Wars: An International History, 1803-1815* (New York: Viking, 2007); David Bell, *The First Total War: Napoleon's Europe and the Birth of Warfare as We Know It* (New York: Houghton Mifflin, 2007); Christy

Pichichero, *The Military Enlightenment: War and Culture in the French Empire, From Louis XIV to Napoleon* (Ithaca, N.Y.: Cornell University Press, 2017).

113. Napoleon to Joseph, 13 December 1805, *Napoleon Correspondance* no. 11175, 5:887.
114. Antoine Thibaudeau, *Mémoires sur le Consulat, 1799 à 1804* (Paris: Ponthieu, 1827), 390.
115. Las Cases, *Mémorial*, 2:1461.
116. Bonaparte to Hedouville, 29 December 1799, *Napoleon Correspondance* no. 4825, 2:1121.
117. For the best book on Napoleon's concept of war, Colson, *Napoléon: De la Guerre*. See also: Jay Luvaas, *Napoleon on the Art of War* (New York: Touchstone, 1999).
118. Napoleon to Joseph, 21 July 1808, *Napoleon Correspondance* no. 18639, 8:917.
119. Las Cases, *Mémorial*, 2:1498.
120. Chaptal, *Souvenirs*, 128.
121. Las Cases, *Mémorial*, 1:279.
122. Napoleon to Joseph, 8 August 1806, *Napoleon Correspondance* no. 12687, 6:704
123. Napoleon to Mortier, 23 October 1806, *Napoleon Correspondance* no. 13319, 6:1028.
124. Napoleon to Joseph, 15 November 1805, *Napoleon Correspondance* no. 11101, 5:850.
125. Bonaparte to Directorate, 20 January 1797, *Napoleon Correspondance* no. 1306, 1:798.
126. Las Cases, *Mémorial*, 2:1498–9.
127. Napoleon to Clarke, 29 August 1809, *Napoleon Correspondance* no. 21926, 9:1092.
128. Napoleon to Clarke, 14 September 1809, *Napoleon Correspondance* no. 22078, 9:1182–4.
129. Colson, *Napoléon*, 239.
130. Las Cases, *Mémorial*, 1:350.
131. Napoleon to Ganteaume, 23 June 1804, *Napoleon Correspondance* no. 8951, 4:743.
132. Las Cases, *Mémorial*: 1:147.
133. Ibid., 1:127.
134. Napoleon to Lauriston, 12 December 1804, *Napoleon Correspondance* no. 9439, 4:968.
135. Napoleon to Ganteaume, 22 August 1805, *Napoleon Correspondance* no. 10626, 5:598.

136. Las Cases, *Mémorial*, 1:350.
137. Bonaparte, *Mémoires: la Campagne d'Italie*, 75.
138. Napoleon to Berthier, 6 May 1805, *Napoleon Correspondance* no. 8879, 5:271.
139. Bonaparte to Marmont, 12 March 1804, *Napoleon Correspondance* no. 8731, 4:637–8.
140. Napoleon to Reinhard, 18 May 1807, *Napoleon Correspondance* no. 15655, 7:800.
141. Chaptal, *Souvenirs*, 128–9.
142. Louis François Lejeune, *Mémoires du General Lejeune*, 2 vols (Paris: Editions de Grenadier, 2001), 22–3.
143. Napoleon to Dejean, 21 February 1809, *Napoleon Correspondance* no. 20094, 9:91.
144. Napoleon to Eugène, 13 March 1806, *Napoleon Correspondance* no. 11674, 6:223.
145. Bonaparte to Murat, 8 August 1803, *Napoleon Correspondance* no. 7917, 4:260.
146. Napoleon to Eugène, 21 February 1809, *Napoleon Correspondance* no. 20096, 9:92.
147. Las Cases, *Mémorial*, 2:901–02.
148. Napoleon to Eugène, 16 March 1809, *Napoleon Correspondance* no. 20401, 9:263.
149. Bonaparte, *Mémoires de Napoléon, la Campagne d'Italie*, 102.
150. Napoleon to Savary, 8 March 1809, *Napoleon Correspondance* no. 20300, 9:204.
151. Napoleon to Joseph, 21 April 1806, *Napoleon Correspondance* no. 11938, 6:346.
152. Napoleon to Murat, 16 May 1805, *Napoleon Correspondance* no. 10065, 5:313.
153. Napoleon to Joseph, 21 July 1808, *Napoleon Correspondance* no. 18639, 8:917.
154. Napoleon to Clarke, 10 October 1809, *Napoleon Correspondance* no. 22314, 9:1336–7.
155. Las Cases, *Mémorial*, 2:957.
156. Ibid., 1:316.
157. Ibid., 2:1531.

Chapter 1: The Rebel

1. For the best book on Napoleon's childhood, see: Dorothy Carrington, *Napoleon and his Parents* (New York: Viking, 1988).

2. Pierre de Passano, *Histoire de l'Annexion de la Corse* (Paris; Horvath, 1990).
3. Peter Thrasher, *Pasquale Paoli: An Enlightened Hero* (New York: Archon Books, 1970); Michel Verge-Franceschi, *Pasquale Paoli: Un Corse de Lumières* (Paris: Fayard, 2005).
4. Carrington, *Napoleon and his Parents*, 192.
5. Las Cases, *Mémorial*, 1:775.
6. Buonaparte to Archidiacre Lucian Bonaparte, 28 March 1785, *Napoleon Correspondance* no. 4, 1:47.
7. Theodore Iung, *Bonaparte et son Temps, 1769-1799*, 3 vols (Paris: Charpentier, 1880–91), 1:168.
8. Ibid., 1:125.
9. Buonaparte to Désirée, 10 August 1795, *Napoleon Correspondance* no. 321, 1:247.
10. Napoleon to Josephine, 24 July 1804, *Napoleon Correspondance* no. 9015, 4:775.
11. Buonaparte to Joseph Fesch, 29 August 1788, *Napoleon Correspondance* no. 21, 1:65.
12. For the most comprehensive books on the French Revolution, see: Will and Ariel Durant, *Rousseau and Revolution* (New York: Simon and Schuster, 1967); William Doyle, *The Oxford Book of the French Revolution* (New York: Oxford University Press, 1989); Simon Schama, *Citizens: A Chronicle of the French Revolution* (New York: Vintage, 1990); Ian Davidson, *The French Revolution: From Enlightenment to Tyranny* (New York: Pegasus, 2017).
13. For his observations on the unfolding French Revolution in 1789, see: Napoleon to Letizia Bonaparte, 12 January, 15 April 1789, *Napoleon Correspondance* no. 22, 1:67–8; no. 25,1:72; Napoleon to Archidiacre Lucian Bonaparte, 28 March, [n.d.] July, 1789, *Napoleon Correspondance* no. 23, 1:68–71; no. 32, 1:79–80; Napoleon to Joseph Bonaparte, [n.d.] May 1789, *Napoleon Correspondance* no. 26, 1:73.
14. Buonaparte to Joseph, 22 June 1792, *Napoleon Correspondance* no. 65, 1:113.
15. Las Cases, *Mémorial*, 2:1198–9.
16. Buonaparte to Giubega, [n.d.] June 1789, *Napoleon Correspondance* no. 28, 1:74–6.
17. Buonaparte to Paoli, 12 June 1789, *Napoleon Correspondance* no. 29, 1:76.
18. Napoleon to Matteo Buttafuoco, 23 January 1791, *Napoleon Correspondance* no. 44, 1:91–6.

19. Napoleon to Pascal Paoli, 2 March 1793, *Napoleon Correspondance* no. 77, 1:122–3.
20. For the Terror, see: R.R. Palmer, *Twelve Who Ruled: The Year of Terror in the French Revolution* (Princeton, N.J.: Princeton University Press, 1941); David Andress, *The Terror: The Merciless War for Freedom in Revolutionary France* (New York: Farrar, Straus, and Giroux, 2006); Timothy Tackett, *The Coming of the French Revolution* (Cambridge, Mass.: Harvard University Press, 2017).
21. Buonaparte to National Convention, 18 April 1793, *Napoleon Correspondance* no. 79, 1:124–5.
22. For the Allied takeover and siege, see: Robert Forczyk, *Toulon 1793: Napoleon's First Great Victory* (London: Osprey Books, 2005); Bernard Ireland, *The Fall of Toulon: The Last Opportunity to Defeat the French Revolution* (London: Cassell Military Books, 2005); Charles James Fox, *Napoleon Bonaparte and the Siege of Toulon: The First Victory of a Future Emperor of France, 1793* (London: Leonaur, 2010).
23. For key documents on Buonaparte's Toulon campaign, see: Buonaparte to Vaucluse Department's administrators, 15 September 1793, *Napoleon Correspondance* no. 85, 1:128; Buonaparte to Brigade Gasendi's commander, 15 September 1793, *Napoleon Correspondance* no. 87, 1:129; Buonaparte to la Seyne's municipal officers, 21 September 1793, *Napoleon Correspondance* no. 88, 1:129; Buonaparte to Beausset's municipal officers, 14 October 1793 (2 letters) *Napoleon Correspondance* no. 92 and 93, 1:131; Buonaparte to the People's Representatives on Mission, 16 October 1793, *Napoleon Correspondance* no. 96, 1:133–4; Buonaparte to Saint-Nazaire's municipal officers, 17 October 1793 *Napoleon Correspondance*, no. 98, 1:135; Buonaparte to Bandol's municipal officers, 17 October 1793, *Napoleon Correspondance* no. 99, 1:135; Buonaparte to Brigade Gasendi's commander, 18 October 1793, *Napoleon Correspondance* no. 101, 1:136; Buonaparte to the People's Representatives on Mission, 22 October 1793, *Napoleon Correspondance* no. 102, 1:137.
24. Buonaparte to Felix Joseph Antoine Chauvet ordnance commander, mid-October 1793, *Napoleon Correspondance* no. 95, 1:133.
25. Buonaparte to the People's Representatives on Mission, 22 October 1793, *Napoleon Correspondance* no. 102, 1:137.
26. Buonaparte to the Committee of Public Safety, 25 October 1793, *Napoleon Correspondance* no. 105, 1:139.
27. Buonaparte to War Minister Bouchotte, 14 November 1793, *Napoleon Correspondance* no. 111, 1:143.

28. Martin Boycott-Brown, *The Road to Rivoli: Napoleon's First Campaign* (London: Cassell, 2001), 98.
29. Buonaparte to the Representatives of the People, 12 August 1794, *Napoleon Correspondance* no. 236, 1:197–8.
30. Christopher Hibbert, *Napoleon: His Wives and Women* (New York: W.W. Norton, 2002).
31. Marie Célestine Amélie d'Armalié, *Une Fiancée de Napoléon: Désirée Clary, Reine de Suède, 1777-1860* (Paris: Adamant Media Corporation, 2001).
32. Buonaparte to Désirée, 10 September 1794, *Napoleon Correspondance* no. 244, 1:201–02.
33. Buonaparte to Désirée, 11 April 1795, *Napoleon Correspondance* no. 290, 1:221.
34. Buonaparte to Désirée, 14 June 1795, *Napoleon Correspondance* no. 303, 1:228–9.
35. Buonaparte to Joseph, 24 June 1795, *Napoleon Correspondance* no. 308, 1:232.
36. Buonaparte to Joseph, 9 August 1795, *Napoleon Correspondance* no. 320, 1:246.
37. Buonaparte to Désirée, 10 August 1795, *Napoleon Correspondance* no. 321, 1:247.
38. Buonaparte to Joseph, 30 July 1795, *Napoleon Correspondance* no. 317, 1:242–3.
39. For conflicting accounts of this critical day, see: Las Cases, *Mémorial*, 1:372–84; Paul Barras, Paul, Mémoires de Barras (Paris: Mercure de France, 2010), 217–30, 249–51.
40. Bonaparte to Joseph, 6 October 1795, *Napoleon Correspondance* no. 346, 1:269.
41. For the first that survives, see: Bonaparte to Drez, 20 October 1795, *Napoleon Correspondance* no. 350, 1:271.
42. For a good biography, see: Eric Le Nabour, *Barras: Le Vicomte Rouge* (Paris: Lattes, 1982).
43. Las Cases, *Mémorial*, 1:787.
44. Barras, *Mémoires*, 276. For Barras's venomous views of Bonaparte, see ibid., 94, 137–43, 149–50, 159, 162, 213–30, 235, 249–84.
45. For the development of the relationship between Bonaparte and Josephine, see: Las Cases, *Mémorial*, 1:383, 665–73. For their first meetings, see: Hortense, *Mémoires*, 49–50. For the best books, see: Evangeline Bruce, *Napoleon and Josephine: An Improbable Marriage* (New York: Citadel, 2001); Eleanor Delorme, *Josephine: Napoleon's Incomparable Empress* (New York: Henry Abrams, 2002); Andrea

Stuart, *The Rose of Martinique: A Life of Josephine Bonaparte* (New York: Grove Press, 2005); Kate Williams, *Ambition and Desire: The Life of Josephine Bonaparte* (New York: Ballantine Books, 2014).
46. For Barra's venomous views of Josephine, see: Barras, *Mémoires*, 249–70, 390.
47. Hortense, *Mémoires*, 49.
48. Las Cases, *Mémorial*, 1:666.
49. Bonaparte to Josephine, [n.d.] December 1795, *Napoleon Correspondance* no. 387, 1:285.
50. Bonaparte to Josephine, 14 March 1796, *Napoleon Correspondance* no. 313, 1:298.

Chapter 2: The Master of Italy

1. Las Cases, *Mémorial*, 2:948.
2. Boycott-Brown, *The Road to Rivoli*, 131.
3. Bonaparte to Masséna, 27 March 1796, *Napoleon Correspondance* no. 427, 1:305.
4. Philippe Paul Ségur, *Histoire et Mémoires*, 7 vols (Paris: Firmon-Didot, 1877), 1:194.
5. Bonaparte to Carnot, 28 March 1796, *Napoleon Correspondance* no. 424, 1:303.
6. Bonaparte, *Mémoires: la Campagne d'Italie*, 140.
7. Bonaparte to Directory, 8 April 1796, *Napoleon Correspondance* no. 471, 1:328.
8. Bonaparte to Josephine, 30 March 1796, *Napoleon Correspondance* no. 439, 1:310.
9. Bonaparte to Josephine, 7 April 1796, *Napoleon Correspondance* no. 467, 1:326.
10. Bonaparte to Colli, 8 April 1796, *Napoleon Correspondance* no. 470, 1:328.
11. Bonaparte, *Mémoires: la Campagne d'Italie*, 75–6.
12. For the best book on the campaign (from which the statistics for this section are drawn unless otherwise noted), see: Boycott-Brown, *Road to Rivoli*. See also: Carl von Clausewitz, *Napoleon's 1796 Campaign* (Lawrence: University Press of Kansas, 2018). For Bonaparte's account, see: Bonaparte, *Mémoires: la Campagne d'Italie*.
13. Bonaparte, *Mémoires: la Campagne d'Italie*, 79.
14. Ibid., 81.
15. Las Cases, *Mémorial*, 1:395.

16. Bonaparte to Directory, 24 April 1796, *Napoleon Correspondance* no. 524, 1:358.
17. Las Cases, *Mémorial*, 1:397.
18. Bonaparte to Directory, 24 April 1796, *Napoleon Correspondance* no. 522, 1:357.
19. Bonaparte to Directory, 2 April 1796, *Napoleon Correspondance* no. 530, 1:361.
20. Bonaparte to Colli, 25 April 1796, *Napoleon Correspondance* no. 520, 1:356.
21. Bonaparte to Directory, 27 April 1796, *Napoleon Correspondance* no. 539, 1:367.
22. Bonaparte to Barras, [n.d.] April 1796, *Napoleon Correspondance* no. 553, 1:375.
23. Bonaparte to Directory, 29 April 1796, *Napoleon Correspondance* no. 546, 1:370–1.
24. Bonaparte to Josephine, 8 June 1796, *Napoleon Correspondance* no. 662, 1:435–6.
25. Bonaparte to Josephine, 24 April 1796, *Napoleon Correspondance* no. 526, 1:359.
26. Bonaparte to Barras, 11 June 1796, *Napoleon Correspondance* no. 672, 1:441.
27. Bonaparte to Joseph, 15 June 1796, *Napoleon Correspondance* no. 694, 1:453.
28. Bonaparte to Josephine, 15 May 1796, *Napoleon Correspondance* no. 595, 1:396–7.
29. For official accounts of the campaign's second phase, see: Bonaparte to Directory, 1, 7 June 1796, *Napoleon Correspondance* nos. 640, 656, 1:422–4, 431–2.
30. Las Cases, *Mémorial*, 1:137.
31. Bonaparte to Directory, 6 May 1796, *Napoleon Correspondance* no. 574, 1:385.
32. Bonaparte to Directory, 6 May 1796, *Napoleon Correspondance* no. 575, 1:386.
33. Bonaparte to Barras, 14 May 1796, *Napoleon Correspondance* no. 596, 1:397–8.
34. Bonaparte to Carnot, 14 May 1796, *Napoleon Correspondance* no. 597, 1:398.
35. Bonaparte to Directory, 14 May 1796, *Napoleon Correspondance* no. 599, 1:400.
36. Henri Gratien Bertrand, *Cahiers de Sainte Hélène: Journal, 1816-1817*, 3 vols (Paris: Sulliver Albin Michel, 1951), 3:78.

37. Bonaparte to Directory, 6 May 1796, *Napoleon Correspondance* no. 573, 1:385.
38. Bonaparte to Directory, 1 June 1796, *Napoleon Correspondance* no. 639, 1:421–2.
39. Bonaparte to Berthier, 25 May 1796, *Napoleon Correspondance* no. 629, 1:416.
40. Bonaparte to Despinoy, 31 May 1796, *Napoleon Correspondance* no. 638, 1:421.
41. Bonaparte to Directory, 1 June 1796, *Napoleon Correspondance* no. 639, 1:421–2.
42. Bonaparte, *Mémoires: la Campagne d'Italie*, 210.
43. Bonaparte to Genoa's Senate, 15 June 1796, *Napoleon Correspondance* no. 697, 1:454–5.
44. Bonaparte to Novi governor, 16 June 1796, *Napoleon Correspondance* no. 700, 1:457.
45. Bonaparte to la Tour, 25 May 1796, *Napoleon Correspondance* no. 632, 1:417.
46. For key letters on how Bonaparte made war pay for war, see: Bonaparte to Directorate, 18, 22 May, 4, 26 June, 2 July 1796, *Napoleon Correspondance* nos. 610, 623, 653, 725, 744, 1:407, 413, 429–30, 471–2, 484; Bonaparte to Faipoult, 21 May 1796, ibid. no. 620, 1:411–12.
47. Bonaparte to Oriani, 24 May 1796, *Napoleon Correspondance* no. 627, 1:415.
48. For an excellent account of the subsequent siege of Mantua along with the wider context of the campaign, see: Phillip Cuccia, *Napoleon in Italy: The Sieges of 1796-1799* (Norman: University of Oklahoma Press, 2014).
49. Bonaparte to Directory, 21 June 1796, *Napoleon Correspondance* no. 710, 1:463.
50. Bonaparte, *Mémoires: la Campagne d'Italie*, 125.
51. Ibid., 150.
52. For key documents on this phase and the results, see: Bonaparte to Directory, 1, 2, 8 October 1796, *Napoleon Correspondance* nos. 958, 961, 980, 1:607–09, 612–13, 620–1.
53. Bonaparte to Francis, 2 October 1796, *Napoleon Correspondance* no. 962, 1:614.
54. Bonaparte to Garrau, 3 November 1796, *Napoleon Correspondance* no. 1044, 1:657.
55. Bonaparte to Directory, 13 November 1796, *Napoleon Correspondance* no. 1058, 1:664.

56. For key documents on this phase, see: Bonaparte to Baraguey d'Hilliers, 3 November 1796, *Napoleon Correspondance* no. 1043, 1:656; Bonaparte to Berthier, 4, 5, 22 November, 6, 9 December 1796, ibid. nos. 1045, 1050, 1069, 1094, 1121, 1180, 1:658, 661, 675, 685–6, 701–02, 729–30; Bonaparte to Directory, 13, 19, 24 November, 6 (2 letters), 28 December 1796, ibid. nos. 1059, 1062, 1077, 1100, 1101, 1210, 1:664–6, 668–9, 678, 688–90, 690–1, 747–9; Bonaparte to Lespinasse, 4 November, 25 December 1796, ibid. nos. 1047, 1197, 1:659–60, 740–1; Bonaparte to Carnot, 19 November 1796, ibid. no. 1060, 1:666–7; Bonaparte to Clarke, 29 November 1796, ibid,. no. 1086, 1:681–2.
57. Bonaparte to Directory, 19 November 1796, *Napoleon Correspondance* no. 1062, 1:668.
58. Bonaparte to Josephine, 23 November 1796, *Napoleon Correspondance* no. 1074, 1:675–6.
59. Bonaparte to Battaglia, 8 December 1796, *Napoleon Correspondance* no. 1112, 1:696–7.
60. For Bonaparte's key letters on this phase of the campaign, see: Napoleon to Directory, 17, 18 January 1797, *Napoleon Correspondance* nos. 1294, 1300, 1330, 1:790, 793–6, 812–13; Bonaparte to Lespinasse, 24 January 1797, ibid. no. 1323, 1:806–10; Bonaparte to Carnot, January 28, 1797, ibid. no. 1331, 1:813–14.
61. Bonaparte to Directory, 17 March 1797, *Napoleon Correspondance* no. 1455, 1:877–8. For key documents on this phase, see: Bonaparte to Joubert, 11, 15 (2 letters) March 1797, *Napoleon Correspondance* nos. 1451, 1452, 1453, 1:874–5; Bonaparte to Directory, 17 (2 letters), 20, 22, 25 March, 1, 5 (2 letters), 8, 16 April 1797, ibid. nos. 1454, 1455, 1460, 1466, 1476, 1486, 1489, 1490, 1495, 1512, 1:876–8, 880–1, 883–4, 889–90, 895–6, 898, 898–9, 901–02, 913; Bonaparte to Manin, 9 April 1797, ibid. no. 1497, 1:905; Bonaparte to Lallement, 9 April 1797, ibid. no. 1499, 1:906–07.
62. For the best book on Archduke Charles and his campaigns, see: Gunther Rothenberg, *Napoleon's Great Adversary: Archduke Charles and the Austrian Army, 1792-1814* (New York: Sarpedon, 1995).
63. Bonaparte to Charles, 31 March 1797, *Napoleon Correspondance* no. 1484, 1:894.
64. Bonaparte, *Mémoires: la Campagne d'Italie*, 225.
65. For Bonaparte's account of the negotiations, see: Bonaparte to Directory, 16, 19, 22, 30 (4 letters) April 1797, *Napoleon Correspondance* nos. 1514, 1516, 1517, 1518, 1519, 1520, 1:914–16, 917–19, 919–20, 920–1, 921–2, 922–3, 923–4.
66. For the background to the Venetian revolt, see: Bonaparte, *Mémoires: la Campagne d'Italie*, 239–54; Bonaparte to Directory, 24 March, 8

April 1797, *Napoleon Correspondance* no. 1472, 1495, 1:887–8, 901–02; Bonaparte to Carnot, 25 March 1797, ibid. no. 1475, 1:889; Bonaparte to Pesaro, 5 April 1797, ibid. no. 1491, 1:900. Bonaparte to Lallemand, 9 April 1797, ibid. no. 1499, 1:906–07; Bonaparte to Kilmaine, 9 April 1797, ibid. no. 1500, 1:907–08; Bonaparte to Joubert, 13 April 1797, ibid. no. 1505, 1:910.

For the military and diplomatic campaign to crush Venice, see: Bonaparte to Donato and Giustinian, 30 April 1797, *Napoleon Correspondance* no. 1522, 1:924; Bonaparte to Lallement, 30 April 1797, ibid. no. 1523, 1:924–5; Bonaparte to Bernadotte, 30 April 1797, ibid. no. 1524, 1:925; Bonaparte to Berthier, 2 May 1797, ibid. no. 1516, 1:926–8; Bonaparte to Directory, 3 May 1797, ibid. no. 1527, 1:928–9.

67. Bonaparte to Manin, 9 April 1797, *Napoleon Correspondance* no. 1497, 1:905.
68. For the best book on Napoleon's relations with Venice, see: Amable de Fournoux, *Napoléon et Venise, 1796-1814* (Paris: Editions de Fallois, 2002).
69. Bonaparte to Haller, 30 May 1797, *Napoleon Correspondance* no. 1601, 1:970.
70. Bonaparte to Brueys, 4 August 1797, *Napoleon Correspondance* no. 1864, 1:1100–01.
71. Bonaparte to Brueys, 17 September 1797, *Napoleon Correspondance* no. 2035, 1:1180.
72. Bonaparte to Directory, 11 October 1796, 8, 14, 19 May 1797, *Napoleon Correspondance* nos. 988, 1538, 1549, 1561, 1: 624–5, 934, 941–2, 948–50; Bonaparte to Garrau, 9 October 1796, ibid. no. 983, 1:622; Bonaparte to Lombardy Congress, 10 December 1796, ibid. no. 1125, 1:703–04; Bonaparte to Lombardy, 27 May 1797, ibid. no. 1590, 1:965–6; Bonaparte to Facci, President of Cispadane Congress, 1 January 1797, ibid. no. 1243, 1:767; Bonaparte to Berthier, 23 July 1797, ibid. no. 1809, 1:1069–70. For a good overview, see: Lucy Riall, *Risorgimento: The History of Italy from Napoleon to Nation-State* (New York: Palgrave Macmillan, 2008).
73. Bonaparte to Lombardy Congress, 10 December 1796, *Napoleon Correspondance* no. 1125, 1:703–04.
74. Bonaparte, *Mémoires: la Campagne d'Italie*, 298.
75. Bonaparte to Directory, 30 May 1797, *Napoleon Correspondance* no. 1600, 1:969–70; Bonaparte to Brignole, 7 June 1797, ibid. no. 1642, 1:989; Bonaparte to Brueys, 13 June 1797, ibid. no. 1667, 1:1001; Bonaparte to Genoan government, 16 June 1797, ibid. no. 1691, 1:1014.
76. Bonaparte to Foreign Relations Committee of the Ligurian Republic, 26 September 1797, *Napoleon Correspondance* no. 2100, 1:1218.

77. Bonaparte to Genoan provisional government, 11 November 1797, *Napoleon Correspondance* no. 2214, 1:1278–81.
78. Bonaparte to Directory, 12 November 1797, *Napoleon Correspondance* no. 2234, 1:1294.
79. Bonaparte to Talleyrand, 7 October 1797, *Napoleon Correspondance* no. 2149, 1:1244–5.
80. Bonaparte to Mattei, 21 October 1796, *Napoleon Correspondance* no. 1007, 1:639.
81. Bonaparte to Mattei, 22 January 1797, *Napoleon Correspondance* no. 1315, 1:802–03.
82. For key documents the war with Rome, see: Bonaparte to Directory, 1, 3, 7, 10 (2 letters), 19 February, 6 March 1797, *Napoleon Correspondance* nos. 1338, 1352, 1359, 1366, 1367, 1381, 1440, 1:817–18, 823–4, 828–9, 832, 833, 846–7, 868–9; Bonaparte to Berthier, 4 February 1797, ibid. no. 1355, 1:826; Bonaparte to Joubert, 17 February 1797, ibid. no. 1383, 1:842–3.
83. For Bonaparte's accounts of the negotiations, see: Bonaparte, *Mémoires: la Campagne d'Italie*, 287–301; Las Cases, *Mémorial*, 2:1331–6. For key Bonaparte's letters on negotiations, see: Bonaparte to Directorate, 27 May, 22 June, 2, 23 July, 19 September, 10 October 1797, *Napoleon Correspondance* nos. 1587, 1714, 1745, 1811, 2045, 1:962–3, 1025–6, 1038–9, 1071–2, 1185–6, 1248–9; Bonaparte to Clarke, 23, 26 July 1797, ibid. nos. 1810, 1815, 1:1070–1, 1074–6; Bonaparte to Talleyrand, 3, 6, 12 September 1797, ibid. nos. 1965, 1973, 2009, 1:1116, 1142–3, 1147–8.
84. Bonaparte to Clarke, 26 July 1797, *Napoleon Correspondance* no. 1815, 1:1074–6.
85. Bonaparte to Clarke, 17 July 1797, *Napoleon Correspondance* no. 1790, 1:1060–1.
86. Bonaparte to Francis II, 22 July 1797, *Napoleon Correspondance* no. 1812, 1:1072–3. Bonaparte to Austrian envoys, 28 (2 letters), 29 July 1797, ibid. nos. 1818, 1819, 1832, 1:1077–9, 1079–80, 1086.
87. For key documents on Antraigues, see: Bonaparte, *Mémoires: la Campagne d'Italie*, 256–7, 278, 297; Bonaparte to Berthier, 30 May 1797, *Napoleon Correspondance* no. 1598, 1:969; Bonaparte to Directory, 3 June 1797, ibid. no. 1618, 1:979–80; Bonaparte to Berthier, 4 June 1797, ibid. no. 1620, 1:980; Bonaparte to Berthier, 7 June 1797, ibid. no. 1638, 1:988; Bonaparte to Berthier, 26 June 1797, ibid. no. 1731, 1:1032–3; Las Cases, *Mémorial*, 2:1336–8. See also: Jacques Godechot, *Le Comte d'Antraigues: Un Espion du l'Europe des Émigrés* (Paris: Fayard, 1986).

88. For key documents on Bonaparte's actions to defend the government against the conspirators, see: Bonaparte to Directory, 15, 27 July 1797, *Napoleon Correspondance* nos. 1785, 1823, 1:1203–04, 1082; Bonaparte, *Mémoires: la Campagne d'Italie*, 280–3.
89. Le Nabour, *Barras*, 186–91.
90. Bonaparte to Directory, 18 September 1797, *Napoleon Correspondance* no. 2039, 1:1182; Bonaparte to Barras, 19 September 1797, ibid. no. 2040, 1:1182–3.
91. Bonaparte to Directory, 25 September 1797, *Napoleon Correspondance* no. 2092, 1:1213.
92. Bonaparte to Barras, 25 September 1797, *Napoleon Correspondance* no. 2084, 1:1209.
93. Bonaparte to Francis's envoys, 28 September (2 letters) 1797, *Napoleon Correspondance* no. 2102, 203, 1:1219–20; 1220–2.
94. Bonaparte to Talleyrand, 28 September 1797, *Napoleon Correspondance* no. 2101, 1:1218–19.
95. Bonaparte to Directory, 10 October 1797, *Napoleon Correspondance* no. 2153, 1:1248–9.
96. Bonaparte to Talleyrand, 18 October 1797, *Napoleon Correspondance* no. 2170, 1:1256–7.
97. Napoleon Bonaparte, *Mémoires de Napoleon: la Campagne d'Egypt* (Paris: Talladier, 2011), 53.
98. Bonaparte to Directorate, 10 October 1797, *Napoleon Correspondance* no. 2152, 1:1247–8.
99. For key documents on his return to Paris and activities, see: Las Cases, *Mémorial*, 1:750–61; Barras, *Mémoires*, 341–3.
100. For the best biographies, see: Duff Cooper, *Talleyrand* (New York: Grove Press, 1932); Rosalynd Pflund, *Talleyrand and His World* (Afton, Minn.: Afton Press, 2010); Georges Morlott et Jean Happart, *Talleyrand: Une Mystification Historique* (Paris: Veyrier, 1992); Emmanuel de Waresquiel, *Talleyrand: Le Prince Immobile* (Paris: Fayard, 2003).
101. Bonaparte to Camus, president of the National Institute, *Napoleon Correspondance* no. 2280, 1:1316–17.
102. Thierry Lentz, *Le 18 Brumaire: Les Coups d'État de Napoléon Bonaparte* (Paris: Perrin, 2010), 140.

Chapter 3: The Pharoah

1. Las Cases, *Mémorial*, 1:866, 2:970. For the best books on the Egyptian campaign, see: Christopher Herold, *Bonaparte in Egypt* (New York:

Harper and Row, 1962); Juan Cole, *Napoleon's Egypt: Invading the Middle East* (New York: Palgrave Macmillan, 2008); Nina Burleigh, *Mirage: Napoleon's Scientists and the Unveiling of Egypt* (New York: Harper, 2008); Paul Strathern, *Napoleon in Egypt* (New York: Bantam, 2009).
2. Bonaparte to Directory, 16 August 1797, *Napoleon Correspondance* no. 1908, 1:1118.
3. Bonaparte to Talleyrand, 13 September 1797, *Napoleon Correspondance* no. 2019, 1:1171.
4. Bonaparte to Directory, 12 November 1797, *Napoleon Correspondance* no. 2234, 1:1294.
5. Bonaparte to Directory, 23 February 1798, *Napoleon Correspondance* no. 2315, 2:36–7.
6. Bonaparte to Directory, 5 March 1798, *Napoleon Correspondance* no. 2322, 2:42–5. For the Directory's approval of the Egyptian campaign, see: Barras, *Mémoires*, 343–5.
7. Bonaparte to Ibrahim, 16 August 1797, *Napoleon Correspondance* no. 1909, 1:1118–19.
8. For documents on Bonaparte's preparations for his expedition, see: Bonaparte to Berthier, 8 March 1798, *Napoleon Correspondance* no. 2326, 2:46–7; Bonaparte to Army of the Orient Ordnance commissioner, 30 March 1798, ibid. no. 2352, 2:61–2; Bonaparte to Directory, 13 April 1798, ibid. no. 2390, 2:80–1; Bonaparte to Brueys, 17, 22 April 1798, ibid. nos. 2398, 2325, 2:84–5, 99–100.
9. Bonaparte to Directory, 13 April 1798, *Napoleon Correspondance* no. 2390, 2:80–1.
10. Bonaparte to Brueys, 22 April 1798, *Napoleon Correspondance* no. 2425, 2:99–100.
11. Bonaparte to Najac, 17 April 1798, *Napoleon Correspondance* no. 2401, 2:87.
12. Bonaparte to Louis Cobenzl, 25 April 1798, *Napoleon Correspondance* no. 2431, 2:102–03.
13. Bonaparte to Brueys, 28 April 1798, *Napoleon Correspondance* no. 2433, 2:103.
14. Bonaparte to Caffarelli, 28 April 1798, *Napoleon Correspondance* no. 2454, 2:104.
15. Bonaparte to Caffarelli, 2 May 1798, *Napoleon Correspondance* no. 2441, 2:108.
16. Bonaparte to Monge, 19 April 1798, *Napoleon Correspondance* no. 2415, 2:94.
17. Bonaparte, *Mémoires: la Campagne d'Egypt*, 56.

18. Ibid., 55–7; Bonaparte to Letourneux, Interior Minister, 26 March 1798, *Napoleon Correspondance* no. 2343, 2:55; Bonaparte to Monge, 2 April 1798, ibid. no. 2361, 2:67; Bonaparte to Monge, 5 April 1798, ibid. no. 2368, 2:70.
19. Bonaparte to Directory, 19 May 1798, *Napoleon Correspondance* no. 2496, 2:129.
20. Bonaparte, *Mémoires: la Campagne d'Egypt*, 55.
21. Bonaparte to Directory, 16 June 1798, *Napoleon Correspondance* no. 2536, 2:150–1; Bonaparte to Berthier, 17 June, 1798, ibid. no 2544, 2:154; Bonaparte, *Mémoires: la Campagne d'Egypt*, 64–8.
22. Bonaparte to Directory, 17 June 1798, *Napoleon Correspondance* no. 2547, 2:155.
23. Bonaparte to Directory, 13 June 1798, *Napoleon Correspondance* no. 2524, 2:144–5.
24. Herold, *Bonaparte in Egypt*, 47.
25. Bonaparte to Berthier, 9 June 1798, *Napoleon Correspondance* no. 2514, 2:140.
26. Bonaparte to Gabini, bishop of Malta, 12 June 1798, *Napoleon Correspondance* no. 2517, 2:141–2.
27. Bonaparte to Berthier, 14 June 1798, *Napoleon Correspondance* no. 2525, 2:146.
28. Bonaparte to Chabot, 15 June 1798, *Napoleon Correspondance* no. 2531, 2:148–9; Bonaparte to French consuls at Tunis, Tripoli and Algiers, 15 June 1798, ibid. no. 2532, 2:149; Bonaparte to Ali de Teplen, Pasha of Janina, 17 June 1798, ibid. no. 2539, 2:152; Bonaparte to Lavalette, 17 June 1798, ibid. no. 2549, 2:156.
29. Proclamation to Army, 22 June 1798, *Correspondance de Napoleon* no. 2710.
30. Bonaparte, *Mémoires: la Campagne d'Egypt*, 118.
31. Bonaparte to Directory, 19 August 1798, *Napoleon Correspondance* no. 2870, 2:298.
32. Bonaparte to Abou Bekr, Cairo pasha, 30 June 1798, *Napoleon Correspondance* no. 2560, 2:160.
33. Bonaparte to Ruffin, 1 July 1798, *Napoleon Correspondance* no. 2562, 2:161.
34. Bonaparte to Kléber, 7 July 1798, *Napoleon Correspondance* no. 2601, 2:180–1.
35. Bonaparte to Menou, 7 July 1798, *Napoleon Correspondance* no. 2601, 2:181–2.
36. Bonaparte to Directory, 17 October 1798, *Napoleon Correspondance* no. 3476, 2:543.

37. Bonaparte to Directory, 7 October 1798, *Napoleon Correspondance* no. 3404, 2:513–14.
38. Bonaparte to Directory, 19 August 1798, *Napoleon Correspondance* no. 2869, 2:298.
39. Bonaparte to Directory, 17 October 1798, *Napoleon Correspondance* no. 3476, 2:543.
40. Bonaparte, *Mémoires: la Campagne d'Egypt*, 195–6.
41. Las Cases, *Mémorial*, 1:170.
42. Bonaparte, *Mémoires: la Campagne d'Egypt*, 135.
43. Bonaparte to Cairo's Sheiks and notables, 22 July 1798, *Napoleon Correspondance* no. 2616, 2:188.
44. Bonaparte to Caffarelli, 5 August 1798, *Napoleon Correspondance* no. 2776, 2:254.
45. Bonaparte to Dommartin, 20 September (2 letters), 1798, *Napoleon Correspondance* nos. 3267, 3268, 2:459.
46. Bonaparte to the administrative commission, 28 July (3 letters) 1798, *Napoleon Correspondance* nos. 2669, 2670, 2671, 2:214–15; Bonaparte to Sucy, 30 July 1798, ibid. no. 2689, 2:221.
47. Bonaparte to Rosetti, 1 August (2 letters) 1798, *Napoleon Correspondance* no. 2717, 2718, 2:232; Bonaparte to Ibrahim Bey, 12 August 1798, *Napoleon Correspondance* no. 2814, 2:270.
48. Bonaparte to Joseph, 25 July 1798, *Napoleon Correspondance* no. 2635, 2:199–200.
49. Bonaparte to Directory, 19 August 1798, *Napoleon Correspondance* no. 2870, 2:298–9.
50. Bonaparte to Brueys, 27 July 1798, *Napoleon Correspondance* no. 2654, 2:207.
51. Bonaparte to Brueys, 30 July 1798, *Napoleon Correspondance* no. 2676, 2:216.
52. Nicolas Harris Nicolas, ed., *The Dispatches and Letters of Vice Admiral Lord Viscount Nelson*, 7 vols (London: Cambridge University Press, 2011), 3:49–52; Brian Lavery, *Nelson and the Nile: The Naval War against Bonaparte, 1798* (London: Caxton, 2003).
53. Bonaparte to Directory, 19 August 1798, *Napoleon Correspondance* no. 2870, 2:299.
54. Bonaparte to Ganteaume, 15 August (2 letters) 1798, *Napoleon Correspondance* nos. 2832, 2833, 2:277–8.
55. Bonaparte to Directory, 17 December 1798, *Napoleon Correspondance* no. 3948, 2:728.
56. Bonaparte, *Mémoires: la Campagne d'Egypt*, 141.

57. Bonaparte to Monge and Berthollet, 18 October 1798, *Napoleon Correspondance* no. 3488, 2:548–9.
58. Bonaparte to Directory, 24 July 1798, *Napoleon Correspondance* no. 2625, 2:194–5.
59. Bonaparte to central administration, 3 August 1798, *Napoleon Correspondance* no. 2733, 2:238.
60. 'Finances of Egypt,' *Napoleon Correspondance*, 1147–51.
61. Bonaparte to Diwan of Cairo, 2 January 1798, *Napoleon Correspondance* no. 3996, 2:751; Bonaparte to Najac, 3 July 1798, *Napoleon Correspondance* no. 2571, 2:165.
62. Claire de Rémusat, *Mémoires de Madame de Rémusat, 1802-1808*, ed. P. de Rémusat (New York: Appleton, 1924), 100.
63. Bonaparte to Directory, 24 July 1798, *Napoleon Correspondance* no. 2625, 2:194–5.
64. Bonaparte to Reynier, 10 September 1798, *Napoleon Correspondance* no. 3130, 2:407.
65. Bonaparte to Girges-el-Gouhary, 7 December 1798, *Napoleon Correspondance* no. 3872, 2:699.
66. Bonaparte to Nassif Pasha, 22 August 1798, *Napoleon Correspondance* no. 2906, 2:317.
67. Bonaparte to Abdallah, Pasha of Syria, 31 October 1798, *Napoleon Correspondance* no. 3035, 2:369.
68. Bonaparte to Berthier, 25 July 1798, *Napoleon Correspondance* no. 2629, 2:197; Bonaparte to Alphonse Guys, ibid. no. 2860, 2:292–3.
69. Bonaparte to Ghalib-Ibn-Mussaid, Sharif of Mecca, 25 August 1798, *Napoleon Correspondance* no. 2941, 2:326–7; Bonaparte to Ghalib-Ibn-Mussaid, Sharif of Mecca, 6 September 1798, ibid. no. 3009, 2:394.
70. Bonaparte to Beauchamp, 11 December 1798, *Napoleon Correspondance* no. 3906, 2:712–13; Bonaparte to Yousef Pacha, Grand Vizir of the Ottoman Empire, 11 December 1798, ibid. no. 3920, 2:719; Bonaparte to Talleyrand, 11 December 1798, ibid. no. 3919, 2:718.
71. Bonaparte to Ahmed Djezzar, 22 August 1798, *Napoleon Correspondance* no. 2894, 2:311–12.
72. Bonaparte to French merchants of Jaffa, 27 August 1798, *Napoleon Correspondance* no. 2960, 2:338.
73. Bonaparte to Djezzar, 12 September 1798, *Napoleon Correspondance* no. 3148, 2:414
74. Bonaparte to Directory, 7 October 1798, *Napoleon Correspondance* no. 3404, 2:513–14.

75. Bonaparte to Directory, 8 September 1798, *Napoleon Correspondance* no. 3112, 2:399–400.
76. Bonaparte to Berthier, 10 December 1798, *Napoleon Correspondance* no. 3893, 2:707.
77. Bonaparte to Kléber, 30 July 1798, *Napoleon Correspondance* no. 2680, 2:218.
78. Bonaparte to Menou, 31 July 1798, *Napoleon Correspondance* no. 2699, 2:224–5.
79. Bonaparte to Berthier, 1 August 1798, *Napoleon Correspondance* no. 2707, 2:228–9.
80. Bonaparte to Zayonchek, 4 August 1798, *Napoleon Correspondance* no. 2771, 2:252.
81. Bonaparte to Murat, 12 September 1798, *Napoleon Correspondance* no. 3162, 2:419.
82. Bonaparte to General Dugua, 31 August 1798, *Napoleon Correspondance* no. 3033, 2:369.
83. Bonaparte to Berthier, 26 October 1798, *Napoleon Correspondance* no. 3539, 2:569.
84. Bonaparte to Berthier, 11 November 1798, *Napoleon Correspondance* no. 3656, 2:613.
85. Bonaparte, *Mémoires: la Campagne d'Egypt*, 185.
86. Ibid., 186.
87. Bonaparte to Mecca's sharif, 30 June 1799, *Napoleon Correspondance* no. 4489, 2:976.
88. Bonaparte to Djezzar, 19 November 1798, *Napoleon Correspondance* no. 3740, 2:647.
89. Bonaparte to Caffarelli, 10 December (2 letters) 1798, *Napoleon Correspondance* no. 3895, 3896, 2:708; Bonaparte to Reynier, 10 December 1798, ibid. no. 3905, 2:711. For other documents on Bonaparte's preparations for his Holy Land campaign, see: Bonaparte to Dommartin, 23 December 1798, ibid. no. 3982, 2:742–3; Bonaparte to Lagrange, 18 January 1798, ibid. no. 4106, 2:795–6; Bonaparte to Kléber, 21 January 1798, ibid. no. 4138, 2:806–07; Bonaparte to Berthier, 25 January 1798, ibid. no. 4159, 2:814; Bonaparte to Berthier, 29 January 1799, ibid. no. 4180, 2:823; Bonaparte to Berthier, 31 January 1799, ibid. no. 4191, 2:827–8; Bonaparte to Kléber, 31 January 1799, ibid. no. 4194, 2:829–30; Bonaparte to Dugua, 9 February 1799, ibid. no. 4230, 2:843–5; Bonaparte to Marmont, 9 February 1799, ibid. no. 4231, 2:845–6; Bonaparte to Desaix, 10 February 1799, ibid. no. 4234, 2:847–9; Bonaparte to Berthier, 26 February 1799, ibid. no. 4256, 2:860–1; Bonaparte to Caffarelli, 2 February 1799, ibid.

no. 4257, 2:862; Bonaparte to Daure, 26 February 1799, ibid. no. 4258, 2:863–4.
90. Bonaparte to Said ibn Sultan, 25 January 1798, *Napoleon Correspondance* no. 4164, 2:816; Bonaparte to Sultan of Mecca, 25 January 1798, ibid. no. 4166, 2;817.
91. Bonaparte to Tippoo-Sahib, 25 January 1798, *Napoleon Correspondance* no. 4167, 2:817.
92. For key documents on Bonaparte's Palestinian campaign, see: Bonaparte to Berthier, 26 February 1799, *Napoleon Correspondance* no. 4256, 2:86–91; Bonaparte to Daure, 26 February 1799, ibid. no . 4258, 2:863; Bonaparte to Berthier, 9 March 1799, ibid. no. 4271, 2:870; Bonaparte to Dugua, 9 March 1799, ibid. no. 4279, 2:873; Bonaparte to Directory, 13 March 1799, ibid. no. 4294, 2:881–3; Bonaparte to Marmont, 14 April 1799, ibid. no. 4321, 2:897–8; Bonaparte to Directory, 10 May 1799, ibid. no. 4346, 2:910–13.
93. Bonaparte to Marmont, 26 February 1799, *Napoleon Correspondance* no. 4281, 2:864–5; Bonaparte to Caffarelli, 26 February 1799, ibid. no. 4257, 2:862.
94. Bonaparte to Marmont, 26 February 1799, *Napoleon Correspondance* no. 4261, 2:863.
95. Bonaparte to the sheikhs of Gaza, Ramleh, and Jaffa, 9 March 1799, *Napoleon Correspondance* no. 4276, 2:4275.
96. Bonaparte to sheikhs of Jerusalem, 9 March 1799, *Napoleon Correspondance* no. 4277, 2:872–3.
97. Bonaparte to Directory, 13 March 1799, *Napoleon Correspondance* no. 4294, 2:882.
98. Bonaparte to Berthier, 9 March 1799, *Napoleon Correspondance* no. 4271, 2:870.
99. Bonaparte to Dugua, 9 March 1799, *Napoleon Correspondance* no. 4276, 2:873.
100. Bonaparte to Djezzar, 9 March 1799, *Napoleon Correspondance* no. 4280, 2:874.
101. Bonaparte to Grezieu, March 13, 1799, *Napoleon Correspondance* no. 4295, 2:883–4.
102. Napoleon to Fouché, 2 February 1807, *Napoleon Correspondance* no. 14256, 7:168.   For a good biography, see: Tom Pocock, *A Thirst for Glory: The Life of Admiral Sir Sidney Smith* (London: Thistle, 2013).
103. Bonaparte to Boyer, 17 April 1799, *Napoleon Correspondance* no. 4323, 2:900; Bonaparte, *Mémoires: la Campagne d'Egypt*, 255, 260, 266.
Bonaparte duel quote from Roberts, *Napoleon: A Life*, 196.
104. Bonaparte, *Mémoires: la Campagne d'Egypt*, 266.

105. Bonaparte to Directory, 10 May 1799, *Napoleon Correspondance* no. 4346, 2:912.
106. For key documents and perspectives on the campaign's casualties and Bonaparte's hand in the fate of many wounded, see: Bonaparte, *Mémoires: la Campagne d'Egypt*, 274–8; Las Cases, *Mémorial*, 1:165–7.
107. Gaspard Gourgaud, *Sâinte-Hèlene, Journal Inédit de 1815 à 1818* (Paris: Flammarion, 1899), 23 March 1816.
108. Pocock, *Thirst for Glory*, 123–4.
109. Bonaparte to Marmont, 26 June 1799, *Napoleon Correspondance* no. 4470, 2:968.
110. Bonaparte, *Mémoires: la Campagne d'Egypt*, 272.
111. For key documents on Bonaparte's last phase in Egypt, see: Bonaparte to Directory, 19 June 1799, *Napoleon Correspondance no.* 4405, 2:940–2; Bonaparte to Directory, 25 June 1799, ibid. no. 4440, 2:956–8; Bonaparte to Directory, 28 June 1799, ibid. no. 4479, 2:972–3; Bonaparte to Diwan of Cairo, 21 July 1799, ibid. no. 4633, 2:1032; Bonaparte to Directory, 28 June 1799, ibid. no. 4659, 2:1055–6.
112. Bonaparte to Diwan of Cairo, 27 June 1799, *Napoleon Correspondance* no. 4476, 2:971.
113. For one of numerous examples, see: Bonaparte to Mecca's sheriff, 30 June 1799, *Napoleon Correspondance* no. 4489, 2:976.
114. Bonaparte to Diwan of Cairo, 21 July 1799, *Napoleon Correspondance* no. 4633, 2:2043.
115. For his last Egyptian campaign, see: Bonaparte, *Mémoires: la Campagne d'Egypt*, 284–92.
116. These figures include mixed estimates from Smith, *Napoleon Wars Data Book*, 161, and Chandler, *Campaigns of Napoleon*, 244. For Bonaparte's conflicting but consistently exaggerated figures, along with accounts of the battle, see: Bonaparte to Desaix, 27 July 1799, *Napoleon Correspondance* no. 4654, 2:1042; Bonaparte to Marmont, 27 July 1799, ibid. no. 3656, 2:1043; Bonaparte to Directory, 28 June 1799, ibid. no. 4659, 2:1055–6; Bonaparte to Dugua, 2 August 1799, ibid. no. 4666, 2:1048; Bonaparte, *Mémoires: la Campagne d'Egypt*, 288–90.
117. Bonaparte to Youssef Pasha, 17 August 1799, *Napoleon Correspondance* no. 4743, 2:1077–9.For his accounts of his decision to return, see: Bonaparte, *Mémoires: la Campagne d'Egypt*, 272, 292, 293–306.
118. Bonaparte to Kléber, 22 August 1799, *Napoleon Correspondance* no. 4758, 2: 1088, 1086–8.
119. Bonaparte, *Mémoires: la Campagne d'Egypt*, 306.
120. Bonaparte to Directory, 10 October 1799, *Napoleon Correspondance* no. 4762, 2:1089.

Chapter 4: The Usurper

1. Jean Jacques Regis Cambacérès, *Cambacérès: Mémoires Inédits*, 2 vols (Paris: Perrin, 1999), 1:431.
2. For the relationship between Bonaparte and Josephine during his Egyptian campaign, see: Barras, *Mémoires*, 350–1, 355–9, 390, 392–5. For the best book on the coup, see: Lentz, *Le 18 Brumaire*. For firsthand versions, see: Las Cases, *Mémorial*, 1:786–97; Joseph Fouché, *Mémoires* (Paris: Arlea, 1993), 44–80; Cambacérès, *Mémoires*, 428–40; Barras, *Mémoires*, 391–474. For key documents on the relationship between Napoleon, Joseph and Lucien Bonaparte, see: Cambacérès, *Mémoires*, 1:435–47; Barras, *Mémoires*, 373–9, 394. For Josephine's role in the coup, see: Barras, *Mémoires*, 377–8, 410, 432–4.
3. Bonaparte to Talleyrand, 26 July 1797, *Napoleon Correspondance* no. 1822, 1:1081.
4. Bonaparte to Talleyrand, 21 September 1797, *Napoleon Correspondance* no. 2065, 1:1196–8. See also: Bonaparte to Talleyrand, 26 September (2 letters) 1797, *Napoleon Correspondance* nos. 2098, 2099, 1:1215–16, 1217.
5. George Lefebre, *The Thermidoreans and the Directory: Two Phases of the French Revolution* (New York: Random House, 1964); Denis Woronoff, *The Thermidorean Regime and the Directory, 1794-1799* (New York: Cambridge University Press, 1984).
6. Bonaparte, *Mémoires: la Campagne d'Italie*, 271.
7. For the best overview, see: William Doyle, *The Oxford History of the French Revolution* (New York: Oxford University Press, 1989).
8. Lentz, *Le 18 Brumaire*, 156.
9. *Talleyrand Mémoires*, 113.
10. Pasquale Pasquino, *Sieyès et l'Invention de la Constitution en France* (Paris: Jacob, 1998).
11. Lentz, *Le 18 Brumaire*, 183.
12. Fouché, *Mémories*, 65.
13. Lentz, *Le 18 Brumaire*, 247.
14. Bourrienne, *Mémoires*, 2:244.
15. For the best book on the coup see Lentz, *Le 18 Brumaire*.
16. Morlott and Happart, *Talleyrand*, 333–6.
17. Cambacérès, *Mémoires*, 1:438.
18. For the best book on Napoleon's Consulate, see: Thierry Lentz, *Le Grand Consulat, 1799-1804* (Paris: Fayard, 1999). See also: Martin Lyon, *Napoleon Bonaparte and the Legacy of the French Revolution* (New York: Palgrave, 1994); Isser Woloch, *Napoleon and His Collaborators: The Making of a Dictatorship* (New York: W.W. Norton, 2001); Frederick

Kagan, *The End of the Old Order: Napoleon and Europe, 1801-1805* (New York: Da Capo Press, 2006); Adolphe Thiers, *History of the Consulate and the Empire of France under Napoleon*, vol. 1 (New York: Palata Press, 2015).
19. Lentz, *Grand Consulat*, 355.
20. Ibid., 371.
21. Ibid., 162–4.
22. Las Cases, *Mémorial*, 212–16.
23. Chaptal, *Souvenirs*, 30.
24. Bonaparte to Fouché, 26 October 1800, *Napoleon Correspondance* no. 5722, 3:423.
25. Thierry Lentz, *Nouvelle Histoire du Premier Empire: La France et l'Europe de Napoleon, 1804-1814* (Paris: Fayard, 2007), 75.
26. Bourrienne, *Mémoires*, 4:304.
27. For related perspective and policies, see also: Bonaparte to Fouché, 3 July 1800, *Napoleon Correspondance* no. 5485, 3:324; Bonaparte to Bernadotte, 4, 18 July 1800, ibid. no. 5488, 5536, 3:324, 344.
28. Bonaparte to Saint Hilaire, 4 January 1800, *Napoleon Correspondance* no. 4844, 3:24.
29. Charles Tilly, *The Vendée* (Cambridge, Mass.: Harvard University Pres, 1964); Jean Gallet, *Les Paysans En Guerre: Gens de l'Ouest sous la Révolution* (Paris: Ouest France, 1988); Reynald Secher, *A French Genocide: The Vendée* (South Bend, Ind.: Notre-Dame University Press, 2003); George Hill, *The War in the Vendée and the Little Choanerie* (New York: Loreto, 2013).
30. Bonaparte to Berthier, 6 March 1800, *Napoleon Correspondance* no. 5050, 3:124.
31. Bonaparte to Faucheux, 2 July 1800, *Napoleon Correspondance* no. 5564, 3:355–6.
32. Bonaparte to inhabitants of the western departments, 28 December 1799, *Napoleon Correspondance* no. 4825, 2:1118–19; Bonaparte to Berthier, 29 December 1799, ibid. no. 3824, 2:1119–20; Bonaparte to Hedouville, 29 December 1799, ibid. no. 4825, 2:1121.
33. Bonaparte to Brune, 14 January 1800, *Napoleon Correspondance* no. 4872, 3:38–40.
34. Bonaparte to Brune, 8 February 1800, *Napoleon Correspondance* no. 4944, 3:73–4
35. Bonaparte to Brune, 5 March 1800, *Napoleon Correspondance* no. 5046, 3:121.
36. Bonaparte to Bernadotte, 1 May 1800, *Napoleon Correspondance* no. 5219, 3:201.

37. Philip Mansel, *Louis XVIII* (London: John Murray, 2005); Pierre de la Gorce, *Louis XVIII* (Paris: Frederique Patat, 2016).
38. Bonaparte to Provence, 7 September 1800, *Napoleon Correspondance* no. 5639, 3:386.

Chapter 5: The Peacemaker

1. For Bonaparte's key letters expressing his grand diplomatic strategy, see: Bonaparte to Talleyrand, 16 January, 30 November 1800, 27 January, 13 February 1801, *Napoleon Correspondance* no. 4881, 5810, 5975, 6018, 3:43–4, 463, 541–2, 562–3; Bonaparte to Joseph, 20 October 1800, 21 January 1801, ibid. no. 5700, 5950, 3:411–12, 531–2.
2. Bonaparte to Francis II, 25 December 1799, *Napoleon Correspondance* no. 4815, 2:1114–15.
3. Bonaparte to Talleyrand, 16 May 1800, *Napoleon Correspondance* no. 5526, 3:252.
4. Bonaparte to George III, 25 December 1799, *Napoleon Correspondance* no. 4817, 2:1115–16.
5. Jeremy Black, *George III: America's Last King* (New Haven, Conn.: Yale University Press, 2006); Chip Wagner, *Double Emperor: The Life and Times of Francis of Austria* (New York: Hamilton Books, 2018).
6. Bonaparte to Talleyrand, 16 January 1800, *Napoleon Correspondance* no. 4881, 3:43–4.
7. Bonaparte to Talleyrand, 10 March 1800, *Napoleon Correspondance* no. 5083, 3:136.
8. Bonaparte to Moreau, 21 December 1799, *Napoleon Correspondance* no. 4804, 2:1109.
9. For an outstanding account, see: John M. Sherwig, *Guineas and Gunpowder: British Aid in the Wars with France, 1793-94* (Cambridge, Mass.: Harvard University Press, 1969).
10. For an overview of all dimensions of the struggle, see: William Nester, *Titan: The Art of British Power in the Age of Revolution and Napoleon* (Norman: University of Oklahoma Press, 2016). For the naval struggle, see: Northcote Parkinson, *Britannia Rules: The Classic Age of Naval History, 1793-1815* (London: Royal Naval Museum, 1994); Roy Adkins and Lesley Adkins, *The War for all the Oceans: From Nelson at the Nile to Napoleon at Waterloo* (New York: Viking, 2006); Noel Mostert, *The Line Upon the Wind: The Great War at Sea, 1793-1815* (New York: W.W. Norton, 2017).
11. Bonaparte to Bruix, 14 January 1800, *Napoleon Correspondance* no. 4811, 3:21.

12. Bonaparte to Lacrosse, 4 January 1800, *Napoleon Correspondance* no. 4843, 3:22–4.
13. Bonaparte to Bruix, 22 February 1800, *Napoleon Correspondance* no. 5018, 3:106–07.
14. Bonaparte to Gravina, 22 February 1800, *Napoleon Correspondance* no. 5019, 3:107. See also, Bonaparte to Mazaredo, 17 March 1800, ibid. no. 5113, 3:149.
15. Bonaparte to Ganteaume, 24 February 1800, *Napoleon Correspondance* no. 5029, 3:111–12; Bonaparte to Bruix, 8 March 1800, ibid. no. 5068, 3:130–1.
16. For overviews of the French navy, see: Michel Verge-Franceshi, *La Marine Française au XVIII Siècle* (Paris: Sedes, 1996); Jean-Claude Gillet, *La Marine Imperiale: Le Grand Rêve de Napoléon* (Paris: Bernard Giovanangeli, 2010).
17. Bonaparte to Forfait, 24 July (2 letters) 1800, *Napoleon Correspondance* nos. 5559, 5560, 3:353–4.
18. James Arnold, *Marengo and Hohenlinden: Napoleon's Rise to Power* (London: Pen and Sword, 2008); Olivier Lapray, *The Battle of Marengo: The First Victory of the Century* (Paris: Histoire et Collections, 2014); Terry Crowdy, *Marengo: The Victory that Placed the Crown of France on Napoleon's Head* (London: Pen and Sword, 2018).
19. For Bonaparte's key letters on financing and reorganizing the army, see: Bonaparte to Gaudin, 8, 14 January 1800, *Napoleon Correspondance* nos. 4848, 4874, 3:26, 40–1; Bonaparte to Berthier, 12 January, 1, 6 March, 25 April 1800, ibid. nos. 4860, 4891, 5052, 5198, 3:31–2, 48–9, 113–14, 125, 189; Bonaparte to Augereau, 5 February 1800, ibid. no. 4934, 3:68. For the Guard's history, see: Henry Lachouque and Anne Brown, *The Anatomy of Glory: Napoleon and his Guard* (London: Greenhill Books, 1997).
20. Bonaparte to Clarke, 5 December 1799, *Napoleon Correspondance* no. 4786, 2:1102; Bonaparte to Berthier, 25 January, 2 April 1800, ibid. nos. 4905, 5158, 3:54, 170–1.
21. Bonaparte to Masséna, 5 March 1800, *Napoleon Correspondance* no. 5048, 3:122–3. For Bonaparte's other key letters on his grand strategy, see: Bonaparte to Moreau, 12 March 1800, *Napoleon Correspondance* no. 5095, 3:142; Bonaparte to Berthier, 27 April 1800, ibid. no. 5206, 3:195.

For Bonaparte's key letters organizing his own campaign, see: Bonaparte to Berthier, 25 January 1800, *Napoleon Correspondance* no. 4903, 3:54–6; Bonaparte to Berthier, 3 March 1800, ibid. no. 5040, 3:119; Bonaparte to Berthier, 23 April 1800, ibid. no. 5193, 3:185–6; Bonaparte to Carnot, 24 April 1800, ibid. no. 5195, 3:187–8; Bonaparte

to Berthier, 26 April 1800, ibid. no. 5202, 3:190–3; Bonaparte to Berthier, 28 April 1800, ibid. no. 5214, 3:199; Bonaparte to Berthier, 2 May 1800, ibid. no. 5223, 3:205–07; Bonaparte to Berthier, 14 May 1800, ibid. no. 5290, 3:236–7. For Bonaparte's key letters on his campaign, see: Bonaparte to Berthier, 19 May 1800, *Napoleon Correspondance* no. 5340, 3:25–58; Bonaparte to Moncey, 19 May 1800, ibid. no. 5346, 3:260–1; Bonaparte to Berthier, 20 May 1800, ibid. no. 5351, 3:262–3; Bonaparte to Berthier, 21 May 1800, ibid. no. 5352, 3:263–4; Bonaparte to Berthier, 24 May 1800, ibid. no. 5358, 3:268; Bonaparte to Brune, 24 May 1800, ibid. no. 5360, 3:269–70; Bonaparte to Carnot, 4 June 1800, ibid. no. 5398, 3:283–4; Bonaparte to Berthier, 8 June (3 letters) 1800, ibid. nos., 5423, 5424, 5425, 3:294, 295, 295–6; Bonaparte to Suchet, 8 June 1800, ibid. no. 5427, 3:297; Bonaparte to Berthier, 9 June 1800, ibid. no. 5429, 3:298–9.
22. Bonaparte to Masséna, 12 March 1800, *Napoleon Correspondance* no. 5094, 3:141.
23. Bonaparte to Moreau, 16 May 1800, *Napoleon Correspondance* no. 5323, 3:250–1.
24. Bonaparte to Moreau, 22 April 1800, *Napoleon Correspondance* no. 5190, 3:184.
25. Bonaparte to Moreau, 24 April 1800, *Napoleon Correspondance* no. 5197, 3:188.
26. Bonaparte to Josephine, 13 May 1800, *Napoleon Correspondance* no. 5289, 3:235.
27. Bonaparte to Berthier, 26 April 1800, *Napoleon Correspondance* no. 5202, 3:190–3; Bonaparte to Lannes, 27 April 1800, ibid. no. 5202, 3:194.
28. Bonaparte to Carnot, 4 June 1800, *Napoleon Correspondance* no. 5398, 3:283.
29. Bonaparte to the Cisalpine people, 5 June 1800, *Correspondance de Napoleon*, no. 4885.
30. Lentz, *Grand Consulat*, 235.
31. Bonaparte to Cambacérès and Lebrun, 15 June 1800, *Napoleon Correspondance* no. 5435, 3:301.
32. Bonaparte to Melas, 20 June 1800, *Napoleon Correspondance* no. 5459, 3:312.
33. Bonaparte to Francis II, 16 June 1800, *Napoleon Correspondance* no. 5440, 3:303–05.
34. Bonaparte to Francis II, 29 July 1800, *Napoleon Correspondance* no. 5578, 3:361.
35. Bonaparte to Carnot, 21 August, 13, 24 September1800, *Napoleon Correspondance* nos. 5614, 5643, 5651, 3:374, 388, 391–2; Bonaparte to

Brune, 9, 25 October 1800, 9 January 1801, *Napoleon Correspondance* nos. 5690, 5716, 5892, 3:407, 419, 503.

36. Hugh Ragsdale, ed., *Paul I: A Reassessment of his Life and Reign* (Pittsburgh: University of Pittsburgh Press, 1979); Roderick Macgrew, *Paul I of Russia, 1754-1801* (New York: Oxford University Press, 1992); Norman Saul, *Russia and the Mediterranean, 1797-1807* (Chicago: University of Chicago Press, 1970).
37. For key documents on Bonaparte's policy toward Paul, see: Bonaparte to Brune, 9 February 1800, *Napoleon Correspondance* no. 4946, 3:75–6; Bonaparte to Talleyrand, 4 June 1800, ibid. no. 5411, 3:288; Las Cases, *Mémorial*, 2:1033–5.
38. Bonaparte to Talleyrand, 4, 19 July 1800, *Napoleon Correspondance* nos. 5491, 5545, 3:326, 347.
39. Bonaparte to Frederic, Danish royal prince, 1 April 1801, *Napoleon Correspondance* no. 6176, 3:634.
40. Bonaparte to Paul I, 21 December 1800, *Napoleon Correspondance* no. 5853, 3:484. See also Bonaparte to Paul, 26 February, 12 March 1801, ibid. no. 6076, 6119, 3:587–8, 608.
41. Janet Hatley, *Alexander I* (London: Longmans, 1994); Michael Klimenko, *Alexander I: Portrait of an Autocrat* (New York: Hermitage Publishers, 2002); Marie-Pierre Ray, *Alexander I: The Tsar Who Defeated Napoleon* (Dekalb: Northern Illinois University Press, 2012).
42. Bonaparte to Talleyrand, 12 April 1801, *Napoleon Correspondance* no. 6206, 3:649. Bonaparte to Alexander I, 26 April 1801, *Napoleon Correspondance* no. 6239, 3;668; Bonaparte to Christian VII, 3 May 1801, ibid. no. 6250, 3:673; Bonaparte to Gustav IV, 3 May 1801, ibid. no. 6251, 3:673.
43. Bonaparte to Talleyrand, 16 April 1801, *Napoleon Correspondance* no. 6218, 3:657.
44. Bonaparte to Talleyrand, 24 April 1801, *Napoleon Correspondance* no. 6233, 3:664–5.
45. Piers Mackesy, *British Victory in Egypt: The End of Napoleon's Conquest* (London: Taurus Park, 2010).
46. For the best books on Napoleon's policy toward the Catholic Church, see: E.E.Y. Hales, *Napoleon and the Pope: The Story of Napoleon and Pius VII* (New York: Eyre and Spottiswoode, 1961); Robin Anderson, *Pope Pius VII* (London: Tan Books, 2000).
47. Bonaparte to Pius VII, 27 July 27 1801, *Napoleon Correspondance* no. 6384, 3:739.

48. Bonaparte to Pius VII, 14 May, 14 June, 8 July, 10 October 1802, *Napoleon Correspondance* nos. 6554, 6914, 6939, 7015, 3:807, 983–4, 994–5, 1028.
49. Bonaparte to Regnier, 27 March 1804, *Napoleon Correspondance* no. 8766, 4:655–6.
50. Chaptal, *Souvenirs*, 96.
51. John Ehrman, *The Younger Pitt* (Stanford, Calif.: Stanford University Press, 1969); Robin Reilly, *William Pitt the Younger* (New York: Putnam's Sons, 1978); Eric Evans, *William Pitt the Younger* (New York: Routledge, 1999); Charles Fedorak, *Henry Addington: Prime Minister, 1801-1804* (Akron: University of Akron Press, 2002).
52. For Bonaparte's key letters on the negotiations, see: Bonaparte to Talleyrand, 28 May 1801, *Napoleon Correspondance* no. 6305, 3:696; Bonaparte to Caillard, 3 July 1801, ibid. no. 6372, 3:731–2; Bonaparte to Talleyrand, September 17, 1801, ibid. no. 6494, 3:781–3.
53. Bonaparte to George III, 30 November 1801, *Napoleon Correspondance* no. 6665, 3:861.
54. Bonaparte to Decrès, 7 October 1801, 15 April 1802, *Napoleon Correspondance* nos. 6543, 6848, 6849, 3:801–02, 951–2; Bonaparte to Louis I, 10 October 1801, ibid. no. 6553, 3:807; Bonaparte to Pius VII, 10 October 1801, ibid. no. 6554, 3:807; Bonaparte to Talleyrand, 14 October 1801, ibid. no. 6579, 3:816–17; Bonaparte to Talleyrand, 15, 25 October 1801, ibid. nos. 6590, 6605, 3:820, 828; Bonaparte to Lacrosse, 19 April 1802, ibid. no. 6854, 3:953.
55. *Talleyrand Mémoires*, 243.

Chapter 6: The New World Dreamer

1. Antoine Metral, *Histoire de l'Expédition à Saint Domingue: Sous le Consulat de Napoleon Bonaparte, 1802-1803* (Paris: Editions Karthala, 1985); Martin Ros, *Night of Fire: The Black Napoleon and the Battle for Haiti* (New York: Da Capo, 1994); Pierre Branda and Thierry Lentz, *Napoleon, l'Esclavage, et les Colonies* (Paris: Fayard, 2006); Graham Nessler, *An Islandwide Struggle for Freedom: Revolution, Emancipation, and Reenslavement in Hispaniola, 1789-1809* (Chapel Hill: University of North Carolina Press, 2016).
2. Branda and Lentz, *L'Esclavage*, 28.
3. Michael Duffy, *Soldiers, Sugar, and Seapower: The British Expeditions to the West Indies and the War against Revolutionary France* (New York:

Oxford University Press, 1987); Martin Howard, *Death Before Glory: The British Soldier in the West Indies in the French Revolutionary and Napoleonic Wars, 1793-1815* (London: Pen and Sword, 2015).

4. Pierre Louis Roederer, *Oeuvres de comte P.-L. Roederer*, 8 vols (Paris: Firmin Didot Frères, 1854–9), 3:334.
5. Bonaparte to Lequoy-Mongiraud, 14 January 1801, *Napoleon Correspondance* no. 5923, 3:519.
6. Bonaparte to Forfait, 5 November 1800, *Napoleon Correspondance* no. 5745, 3:435.
7. Bonaparte to Toussaint Louverture, 4 March 1801, *Napoleon Correspondance* no. 6102, 3:600.
8. Bonaparte to Charles IV, 15 August (2 letters) 1800, *Napoleon Correspondance* no. 5605, 5606, 3:371–2.
9. Bonaparte to Talleyrand, 13 January 1800, *Napoleon Correspondance* no. 4870, 3:37–8.
10. Bonaparte to Talleyrand, 4 February 1801, *Napoleon Correspondance* no. 5996, 3:352–3.
11. Bonaparte to Talleyrand, 2 March 1801, *Napoleon Correspondance* no. 6094, 3:596–7.
12. Bonaparte to Lucien, 22 June 1801, *Napoleon Correspondance* no. 6339, 3:715. See also: Bonaparte to Lucien, 17 June 1801, ibid. no. 6335, 3:712–13.
13. Bonaparte to Berthier, 16 June 1801, *Napoleon Correspondance* no. 6331, 3:709–10; Bonaparte to Talleyrand, 10 July 1801, ibid. no. 6460, 3:726–7; Bonaparte to Talleyrand, 14, 15 August 1801, ibid. nos. 6418, 6419, 3:752–3; Bonaparte to Berthier, 8 October 1801, ibid. no. 6544, 3:802–03; Bonaparte to Gouvion St Cyr, 1 December 1801, ibid. no. 6666, 3:862–3.
14. Bonaparte to Prince Jean, 15 August 1802, 14 January, 10, 15 February 1803, *Napoleon Correspondance* nos. 7095, 7423, 7468, 7486, 3:1066–7, 4:29, 48, 50–1; Bonaparte to Talleyrand, 15 August 1802, 12 January 1803, ibid. nos. 7094, 7418, 3:1067–68, 4:26.
15. William R. Nester, *The Hamiltonian Vision: The Art of American Power in the Early Republic, 1789-1800* (Washington D.C.: Potomac Books, 2012), 138–43, 144–7. See also: Alexander de Conde, *The Quasi-War: The Politics and Diplomacy of the Undeclared War with France, 1797-1801* (New York: Charles Scribner's Sons, 1966); Howard Nash, *The Forgotten Wars: The U.S. Navy in the Quasi-War with France and the Barbary Pirates, 1789-1805* (New York: Barnes Company, 1968); William Stinchcombe, *The XYZ Affair* (New York: Praeger, 1980).

16. Napoleon to Champagny, 22 February 1810, *Napoleon Correspondance* no. 23170, 9:1741.
17. Order of the Day to the Republican armies, 7 February 1800, *Correspondance de Napoleon* no. 4573.
18. Andrew J. Montague, ed., *The American Secretaries of State and their Diplomats* (New York: Knopf, 1927), 2:254.
19. Nester, *Hamiltonian Vision*, 151–5.
20. For the most detailed plan, see: Bonaparte to Decrès, 31 October 1801, *Napoleon Correspondance* no. 6627, 3:837–43; For Bonaparte's other key letters on reasserting power over Saint Domingue and Louisiana, see: Bonaparte to Berthier, 21, 23 October 1801, ibid. nos. 6595, 6602, 6608, 3:822–3, 826, 829; Bonaparte to Barbé-Marbois, 23, 28 October 1801, ibid. nos. 6600, 6611, 3:825, 830; Bonaparte to Decrès, 23, 31 October 1801, ibid. nos. 6603, 6604, 6627, 3:827, 837; Bonaparte to Leclerc, 30 October 1801, ibid. no. 6621, 3:824; Bonaparte to Leclerc, 19 November 1801, ibid. no. 6648, 3:854–5.
21. Bonaparte to Decrès, 31 October 1801, *Napoleon Correspondance* no. 6627, 3:841.
22. Bonaparte to Toussaint Louverture, 18 November 1801, *Napoleon Correspondance* no. 6647, 3:853–4.
23. Bonaparte to Decrès, 31 October 1801, *Napoleon Correspondance* no. 6627, 3:840.
24. Bonaparte to Talleyrand, 13 November 1801, *Napoleon Correspondance* no. 6642, 3:851.
25. Bonaparte to Leclerc, 22 July 1802, *Napoleon Correspondance* no. 7038, 3:1040.
26. Bonaparte to Rochambeau, 4 February 1803, *Napoleon Correspondance* no. 7460, 4:44–5.
27. Las Cases, *Mémorial*, 1:806.
28. Branda and Lentz, *L'Esclavage*, 167.
29. Bonaparte to Talleyrand, 4 July 1802, *Napoleon Correspondance* no. 6992, 3:1017–18.
30. Bonaparte to Thomas Jefferson, 21 January 1803, *Napoleon Correspondance* no. 7438, 4:36.
31. Bonaparte to Decrès, 4 June 1802, *Napoleon Correspondance* no. 6927, 3:990.
32. Bonaparte to Forfait, 18 February 1801, *Napoleon Correspondance* no. 6048, 3:574.
33. Bonaparte to d'Hauterive, 25 July 1802, *Napoleon Correspondance* no. 7048, 3:1044; Bonaparte to Berthier, 10 February 1803, ibid. no. 7467, 4:47.

34. Charles A. Cerami, *Jefferson's Great Gamble* (Napier, Ill.: Sourcebooks, 2003); Jon Kurka, *A Wilderness So Immense: The Louisiana Purchase and the Destiny of America* (New York: Anchor, 2009); Robert Bush, *The Louisiana Purchase: A Global Context* (New York: Routledge, 2013).
35. William R. Nester, *The Jeffersonian Vision: The Art of American Power during the Early Republic, 1801-1815* (Washington D.C.: Potomac Books, 2013), 27.
36. Ibid., 38.
37. Ibid.

Chapter 7: The Great Reformer

1. 'Introduction,' *Napoleon Correspondance*, 3:13; Napoleon to Berthier, 5 March 1801, ibid. no. 6103, 3:601.
2. For key documents on Bonaparte's policies toward art and literature, see: Bonaparte to Lucien, 15, 16 July 1800, *Napoleon Correspondance* nos. 5527, 5531, 3:340, 342; Bonaparte to Chaptal, 9 August 1801, ibid. no. 6404, 3:746–7.
3. Bonaparte to Lucien, 10 September 1800, *Napoleon Correspondance* no. 5614, 3:387.
4. Bonaparte to Edward Livingstone, 10 April 1804, *Napoleon Correspondance* no. 8797, 4669.
5. Bonaparte to Chaptal, 17 March 1803, *Napoleon Correspondance* no. 7526, 4:76.
6. Bonaparte to Hauy, 8 February 1803, *Napoleon Correspondance* no. 7464, 4:46.
7. Bonaparte to Lucien, 3 March 1800, *Napoleon Correspondance* no. 5041, 3:120.
8. Napoleon to Frederick William III, 21 March 1805, *Napoleon Correspondance* no. 9719, 5:148.
9. Lentz, *France et l'Europe de Napoleon*, 224–30.
10. Napoleon to Decrès, 24 April 1805, *Napoleon Correspondance* no. 9897, 5:234.
11. Bonaparte to Rumford, 1 October 1803, *Napoleon Correspondance* no. 8096, 4:369.
12. Bernard Schwartz, ed., *The Code Napoleon and the Common Law World* (New York: Lawbook Exchange, 1998).
13. Bonaparte to Talleyrand, 13 January (2 letters) 1800, *Napoleon Correspondance* nos. 4867, 4868 3:35–6, 36.
14. Alain Plessis, *Histoires de la Banque de France* (Paris: Albin Michel, 1998), 163.

15. For key documents on Bonaparte's vision for financial reform, see: Bonaparte to Barbé-Marbois, 10 February, 18 March 1804, *Napoleon Correspondance* nos. 8656, 8744, 4:603, 644.
16. Bonaparte to Chaptal, 17 February 1801, *Napoleon Correspondance* no. 6034, 3:570.
17. Bonaparte to Berthier, 24 October 1803, *Napoleon Correspondance* no. 8182, 4:412.
18. Napoleon to Gaudin, 13 January 1808, *Napoleon Correspondance* no. 17010, 8:57.
19. Bonaparte to Chaptal, 15 May 1801, *Napoleon Correspondance* no. 6272, 3:683.

Chapter 8: The Reluctant Belligerent

1. For the best overview, see: Frederick Kagan, *The End of the Old Order: Napoleon and Europe, 1801-1805* (New York: Da Capo Press, 2006).
2. For key letters on Bonaparte's vision for Italy, see: Bonaparte to Melzi, 16 October 1802, 15 January, 21 February 1803, *Napoleon Correspondance* nos. 7216, 7426, 7489, 3:1125–6, 4:32, 56.
3. Bonaparte to Talleyrand, 27 June 1802, *Napoleon Correspondance* no. 6961, 3:1003.
4. Bonaparte to Berthier, 2 August (2 letters), 20 September 1802, *Napoleon Correspondance* nos. 7063, 7065, 7171, 3:1051–2, 1053–4, 1102–04; Bonaparte to de Saint Marsan, 29 August 1802, ibid. no. 7121, 3:1080–1; Bonaparte to Talleyrand, 2 November 1802, *Napoleon Correspondance* no. 7261, 3:1146–7.
5. For Bonaparte's key letters concerning the fate of Tuscany, now renamed Etruria, see: Bonaparte to Ferdinand I, duke of Parma, 20 June 1800, *Napoleon Correspondance* no. 5455, 3:311; Bonaparte to Louis I, 27 July 1801, ibid. no. 6382, 3:738; Bonaparte to Berthier, 25 September (2 letters) 1801, ibid. nos. 6516, 6520, 3:791–2, 793; Constant, *Mémoires*, 1:131–7; Hortense, *Mémoires*, 82.
6. Bonaparte to Talleyrand, 22 May 1802, *Napoleon Correspondance* no. 6905, 3:978–88.
7. Bonaparte to Charles IV, 23 May 1802, *Napoleon Correspondance* no. 6908, 3:980. Bonaparte to Louis I, 23 March, 29 August, 19 October 1802, ibid. nos. 6911, 7118, 7230, 3:981–2, 1079–80, 1133. For key letters on these events, see: Bonaparte to Charles IV, ibid. no. 7240, 3:1136–7; Bonaparte to Talleyrand, 2 November 1802, ibid. no. 7261, 3:1146–7; Bonaparte to Pius VII, 13 December 1802, ibid. no. 7362, 3:1189–90;

Bonaparte to Marie Louise of Spain, 18 June 1803, ibid. no. 7741, 4:177; Bonaparte to Louis II, 25 July 1803, ibid. no. 7860, 4:229.
8. Bonaparte to Berthier, 17 January 1801, *Napoleon Correspondance* no. 5938, 3:525.
9. Bonaparte to Talleyrand, 2 February 1801, *Napoleon Correspondance* no. 5982, 3:545.
10. Bonaparte to Talleyrand, 25 February 1801, *Napoleon Correspondance* no. 6073, 3:586; Bonaparte to Berthier, 19 February 1801, ibid. no. 6052, 3:576–7.
11. Bonaparte to Ferdinand IV, 28 July 1803, *Napoleon Correspondance* no. 7876, 4:238; Bonaparte to Maria Carolina, 28 July 1803, ibid. no. 7877, 4:238. Bonaparte to Talleyrand, 8 November 1803, ibid. no. 8231, 4:431.
12. Bonaparte to eighteen canton deputies, 10 December 1802, *Napoleon Correspondance* no. 7345, 3:1181–2; Bonaparte to Berthier, 23 February 1803, ibid. no. 7495, 4:59; Bonaparte to Talleyrand, 23, 30 September 1802, ibid. no. 7174, 7192, 3:1105–06, 1112–13; Bonaparte to Melzi, 16 October 1802, ibid. no. 7216, 3:1125–6.
13. Bonaparte to Mustapha Pasha, 18, 27 July 1802, *Napoleon Correspondance* nos. 7028, 7052, 3:1035, 1046; Bonaparte to Decrès, 18 July 1802, ibid. no. 7027, 3:1034; Bonaparte to Talleyrand, 18, 29 July, 29 August 1802, ibid. nos. 7029, 7058, 7125, 3:1036, 1049–50, 1082; Bonaparte to Sebastiani, 5 September 1802, ibid. no. 7142, 3:1089–90.
14. For Bonaparte's other key letters on foreign policy during this time, see: Bonaparte to Talleyrand, 19 February (2 letters), 12 March, 31 August 1802, *Napoleon Correspondance* nos. 6779, 6780, 6809, 7136, 3:913–16, 916–17, 931–2, 1086–7; Bonaparte to d'Hauterive, 25 July 1802, ibid. no. 7047, 3:1044; Bonaparte to Frederick William III, 6 September 1802, ibid. no. 7144, 3:2092; Bonaparte to Francis II, 19 October 1802, ibid. no. 7229, 3:1132–3; Bonaparte to Alexander, 28 August, 19 October 1802, ibid. nos. 7110, 7224, 3:1074, 1129–31; Bonaparte to Pius VIII, 28 August 1802, ibid. no. 7113, 3:1076–7.
15. Bonaparte to Pius VII, 4 August 1802, *Napoleon Correspondance* no. 7071, 3:1057.
16. Bonaparte to Talleyrand, 4 November 1802, *Napoleon Correspondance* no. 7265, 3:1148.
17. Bonaparte to Talleyrand, 28 December 1802, *Napoleon Correspondance* no. 7386, 3:1199.
18. Ibid.
19. Bonaparte to Decrès, 15 January 1803, *Napoleon Correspondance* no. 7245, 4:30–1.

20. Bonaparte to Melzi, 21 February 1803, *Napoleon Correspondance* no. 7489, 4:56.
21. Bonaparte to Frederick William III, 11 March 1803, *Napoleon Correspondance* no. 7517, 4:70.
22. Bonaparte to Alexander, 11 March 1803, *Napoleon Correspondance* no. 7543, 4:66; Bonaparte to Colbert, 11 March 1803, ibid. no. 7516, 4:69; Bonaparte to Talleyrand, 23 August (2 letters) 1803, ibid. no. 7956, 4:287–90.
23. For Napoleon's account of his exchanges with Whitworth from February to May 1803, see: Las Cases, *Mémorial*, 1:798–802.
24. Hortense, *Mémoires*, 112.
25. Bonaparte to Talleyrand, 1 May 1803, *Napoleon Correspondance* no. 7617, 4:122.
26. Bonaparte to Talleyrand, 10 May 1803, *Napoleon Correspondance* no. 7629, 4:127.
27. Napoleon to Talleyrand, 13 May 1803, *Napoleon Correspondance* no. 7638, 4:131–2; Napoleon to Berthier, 13 May 1803, ibid. no. 7637, 4:131.
28. Bonaparte to Louis d'Affry, 17 May 1803, *Napoleon Correspondance* no. 7644, 3:135.
29. Bonaparte to Jean of Portugal, 17 May 1803, *Napoleon Correspondance* no. 7647, 4:136.
30. Bonaparte to Pius VII, 17 May 1803, *Napoleon Correspondance* no. 7649, 4:137.
31. Bonaparte to Latouche-Treville, 2 July 1804, *Napoleon Correspondance* no. 8980, 4:758.
32. For key documents on France's policy toward Hanover, see: Bonaparte to Mortier, 11 July 1803, *Napoleon Correspondance* no. 7813, 4:209; Bonaparte to Berthier, 29 July (2 letters) 1803, ibid. nos. 7881, 7888, 4:240, 243–4; Bonaparte to Frederick William III, 29 July 1803, ibid. no. 7887, 4:242–3; Bonaparte to Mortier, 4 August 1803, ibid. no. 7908, 4:255.
33. Bonaparte to Berthier, 16 April, 21 November 1803, 13 January 1804, *Napoleon Correspondance* nos. 7579, 8298, 8585, 4:103, 457, 572; Bonaparte to Decrès, 8 August 1803, ibid. no. 7914, 4:258; Bonaparte to Regnier, 24 January 1804, ibid. no. 8614, 4:583–4.
34. For key documents on Bonaparte's initial war preparations, see: Bonaparte to Menou, 12 May 1803, *Napoleon Correspondance* no. 7654, 4:129–30; Bonaparte to Berthier, 13, 27 May, 6 June (2 letters), 17 July, 4, 8 August 1803, ibid. nos. 7657, 7676, 7697, 7833, 7904, 7972, 4:131, 147–8, 158–9, 217–18, 251–3, 298–307; Bonaparte to Talleyrand,

13 May, 19 June 1803, ibid. nos. 7638, 7752, 4:131–2, 181; Bonaparte to Lannes, 14, 17 May 1803, ibid. no. 7640, 7648, 4:133, 136; Bonaparte to Decrès, 21, 29 May, 3 June, 31 July, 22 August 1803, ibid. nos. 7661, 7683, 7691, 7890, 7950, 4:141–2, 151, 154–5, 244–5, 284–5; Bonaparte to Marescalchi, 22 May 1803, ibid. no. 7667, 4:144; Bonaparte to Barbé-Marbois, 24 May 1803, ibid. no. 7671, 4:146: Bonaparte to Melzi, 4 June 1803, ibid. no. 7694, 4:156; Bonaparte to Bourcier, 7 June 1803, ibid. no. 7704, 4:161; Bonaparte to Regnier, 3, 7 July 1803, ibid. nos. 7781, 7796, 4:194, 201; Bonaparte to Dejean, 26 July (2 letters), 8 August 1803, ibid. nos. 7864, 7865, 7915, 4:231–2, 259; Bonaparte to Murat, 2 August 1803, ibid. no. 7897, 4:248; Bonaparte to Bruix, 22 August (2 letters) 1803, ibid. no. 7948, 4:281–4; Bonaparte to Fleurieu, 9, 22 July 1803, ibid. nos. 7807, 7848, 4:206, 224.

35. Bonaparte to Decrès, 19 February 1802, *Napoleon Correspondance* no. 6777, 3:912. For a sampling on the debate over naval strategy during this time, see: Bonaparte to Decrès, 11 March, 21 May, 28 July 1803, ibid. nos. 7521, 7661, 4:74, 141–2, 237; Bonaparte to Ganteaume, 7 December 1803, ibid. no. 8388, 4:494; Bonaparte to Bruix, 28 December 1803, ibid. no. 8532, 4:551.

36. Bonaparte to Decrès, 15 January 1803, *Napoleon Correspondance* no. 7245, 4:31.

37. Bonaparte to Bruix, 4 October 1803, *Napoleon Correspondance* no. 8107, 4:376.

38. For key documents on the organization and expansion of the Consular Guard, see: Bonaparte to Berthier, 25 November 1803, 31 January 1804, *Napoleon Correspondance* no. 8328, 8624, 4:470, 590; Bonaparte to Lacuée, 1 December 1803, ibid. no. 8358, 4:482–3; Bonaparte to Decrès, 16, 30 January 1804, ibid. nos. 8597, 8622, 4:577, 589.

39. For other key documents on French relations with Spain during this time, see: Bonaparte to Talleyrand, 13, 16 August 1803, *Napoleon Correspondance* nos. 7930, 7946, 4:267–9, 272–3.

40. Bonaparte to Charles IV, 18 September 1803, *Napoleon Correspondance* no. 8051, 4:347.

41. Bonaparte to Talleyrand, 24 November 1803, 22 February 1804, *Napoleon Correspondance* nos. 8322, 8692, 4:467, 619; Bonaparte to Charles IV, 11 March 1803, ibid. no. 7515, 4:67–8.

42. Bonaparte to John of Portugal, 4 August 1803, *Napoleon Correspondance* no. 7907, 4:254–5; Bonaparte to Talleyrand, 4 August 1803, ibid. no. 7910, 4:256.

43. Bonaparte to President of the Batavian Directory, 9 April 1801, *Napoleon Correspondance* no. 6199, 3:646.

44. Bonaparte to Talleyrand, 9 April 1801, *Napoleon Correspondance* no. 6200, 3:646.
45. Bonaparte to Augereau, 25 July 1801, *Napoleon Correspondance* no. 6378, 3:735; Bonaparte to Batavian Directory, 25 July 1801, ibid. no. 6379, 3:735–6.
46. Bonaparte to Talleyrand, 15 April 1801, *Napoleon Correspondance* no. 6215, 3:655–6.

Chapter 9: The Spymaster

1. For documents giving glimpses into imperial espionage and counterespionage, see: Napoleon to Fouché, 7, 18 October, 17 December 1807, 24 February, 21 July 1808, *Napoleon Correspondance* nos. 16486, 16560, 16896, 17276, 18632, 7:1173, 1208, 1358, 8:201–02, 915; Napoleon to Champagny, 7 October 1807, ibid. no. 16484, 7:1172; Napoleon to Maret, 29 February 1812, ibid. no. 30094, 12:307.
2. Bonaparte to Fouché, 24 February 1802, *Napoleon Correspondance* no. 6788, 3:920–1.
3. Bonaparte to Regnier, 6 May 1804, *Napoleon Correspondance* no. 8865, 4:700.
4. Bonaparte to Jourdan, 20 April 1805, *Napoleon Correspondance* no. 9866, 5:219.
5. Bonaparte to Portalis, 29 January 1804, *Napoleon Correspondance* no. 8621, 4:588.
6. Napoleon to Eugène, 16 March 1809, *Napoleon Correspondance* no. 20401, 9:263.
7. Napoleon to Fouché, 5 April 1809, *Napoleon Correspondance* no. 20726, 9:437.
8. Bonaparte to Fouché, 24 February 1802, *Napoleon Correspondance* no. 6788, 3:920–1.
9. Bonaparte to Talleyrand, 26 December 1803, *Napoleon Correspondance* no. 8525, 4:548–9.
10. Bonaparte to Talleyrand, 12 November 1803, *Napoleon Correspondance* no. 8266, 4:445.
11. Napoleon to Talleyrand, 20 May 1805, *Napoleon Correspondance* no. 10096, 5:327.
12. Napoleon to Berthier, 11 November 1798, *Napoleon Correspondance* no 3656, 2:613.
13. Napoleon to Regnaud, 26 February 1809, *Napoleon Correspondance* no. 20152, 9:120.
14. Ibid.

15. Napoleon to Eugène, 20 June 1809, *Napoleon Correspondance* no. 21296, 9:749.
16. Bonaparte to Regnier, 15 October 1803, *Napoleon Correspondance* no. 8155, 4:402.
17. Ibid.
18. Bonaparte to Davout, 23 November 1803, *Napoleon Correspondance* no. 8310, 4:461–2.
19. Jacques Godechot, *Le Comte d'Antraigues: Un Espion du l'Europe des Émigrés* (Paris: Fayard, 1986).
20. For key documents on this and related operations, see: Bonaparte to Regnier, 1, 22 November 1803, 24 January 1804, *Napoleon Correspondance* nos. 8208, 8307, 4:422–3, 461, 583–4; Bonaparte to Talleyrand, 2 November (2 letters) 1803, ibid. nos. 8213, 8214, 4:424–5. See also: Jacques Godechot, *Les Contre-Révolutionaires* (Paris: Presses Universitaires de France, 1961); Elizabeth Sparrow, *Secret Service: British Agents in France, 1792-1815* (London: Boydell Press, 1999).
21. Bonaparte to Talleyrand, 27 April 1804, *Napoleon Correspondance* no. 8845, 4:692–3.
22. Bonaparte to Cambacérès, 10 November 1803, *Napoleon Correspondance* no. 8246, 4:437.
23. Bonaparte to Fouché, 21 July 1801, 16 August 1804, *Napoleon Correspondance* nos. 6371, 9112, 9157, 3:731, 4:824, 844–5.
24. Bonaparte to Regnier, 26 December 1803, *Napoleon Correspondance* no. 8522, 4:547–58.
25. For key documents on Napoleon's attitudes and actions against Madame de Staël beyond those cited below, see: Napoleon to Fouché, 19 April, 3 May 1807, 28 June 1808, *Napoleon Correspondance* nos. 15337, 15519, 7:650, 738–9; 18439, 8:810; Las Cases, *Mémorial*, 1:353–4. For the best biographies, see: Christopher Herold, *Mistress for an Age: A Life of Madame de Staël* (New York: Grove, 2002); Maria Fairweather, *Madame de Staël* (New York: Da Capo Press, 2005); Biancamaria Fontana, *Germaine de Staël: A Political Portrait* (Princeton, N.J.: Princeton University Press, 2006); Francine de Plessis Gray, *Madame de Staël: The First Modern Woman* (New York: Atlas, 2008).
26. Las Cases, *Mémorial*, 2:1089.
27. Biancamaria Fontana, *Benjamin Constant and the Post-Revolutionary Mind* (New Haven, Conn.: Yale University Press, 1991); Dennis Wood, *Benjamin Constant: A Biography* (New York: Routledge, 1993); Renee Winegarten, *Germaine de Staël and Benjamin Constant: A Dual Biography* (New Haven, Conn.: Yale University Press, 2008).

28. Napoleon to Fouché, 29 August 1805, *Napoleon Correspondance* no. 10702, 5:646–7.
29. Napoleon to Fouché, 26 May 1807, *Napoleon Correspondance* no. 15723, 7:829.
30. For the British role in both plots, see: Tim Clayton, *The Secret War against Napoleon: Britain's Assassination Plot on the French Emperor* (London: Pegasus, 2019).
31. For key documents on this plot, see: Bonaparte to Talleyrand, 12 April 1801, *Napoleon Correspondance* no. 6207, 3:649; Bonaparte to Fouché, 13 April 1801, ibid. no. 6209, 3:650. Fouché, *Mémoires*, 116–22.
32. For key documents on Bonaparte's counterespionage operations during the Cadoudal plot, see: Las Cases, *Mémorial*, 1:697–702, 2:1534–40; Bonaparte to Regnier, 15, 18, 20 October, 1 November, 26 December 1803, 3 January, 15, 16 February 1804, *Napoleon Correspondance* nos. 8155, 8163, 8168, 8208, 8522, 8548, 8670, 8674, 4:401–02, 404, 406, 422–3, 547–8, 558, 610, 612; Bonaparte to Berthier, 11 January 1804, ibid. no. 8574, 4:568; Bonaparte to Real, 8 February 1804, ibid. no. 8651, 4:610; Bonaparte to Soult, 13, 19 February, 1 March 1804, ibid. nos. 8665, 8679, 8702, 4:608, 614, 622–3; Bonaparte to Davout, 14, 19 February 1804, ibid. nos. 8666, 8677, 4:609, 613; Bonaparte to Marmont, 12 March 1804, ibid. no. 8731, 4:637–8.
33. Bonaparte to Lavalette, 15 February 1804, *Napoleon Correspondance* no. 8668, 4:610.
34. Bonaparte to Real, 19 March 1804, *Napoleon Correspondance* no. 8748, 4:647.
35. Fouché, *Mémoires*, 130.
36. Bonaparte to Soult, 14 February 1804, *Napoleon Correspondance* no. 8665, 4:608.
37. Bonaparte to Marmont, 12 March 1804, *Napoleon Correspondance* no. 8731, 4:637–8.
38. Bonaparte to Soult, 19 February 1804, *Napoleon Correspondance* no. 8679, 4:614.
39. Ibid.
40. Las Cases, *Mémorial*, 700.
41. Chandler, *Campaigns of Napoleon*, 269.
42. Las Cases, *Mémorial*, 2:1535.
43. Bonaparte to Dessolle, 8 March 1804, *Napoleon Correspondance* no. 8717, 4:629.
44. Bonaparte to Decrès, 2 March 1804, *Napoleon Correspondance* no. 8705, 4:624.

45. For key documents on the duc d'Enghien affair, see: Las Cases, *Mémorial*, 2:1540–4; Bonaparte to Berthier, 10 March 1804, *Napoleon Correspondance*, 8726, 4:633–4; Bonaparte to Real, 20 March 1804, ibid. no. 8749, 4:648; Bonaparte to Murat, 20 March 1804, ibid. no. 8751, 4:649; Bonaparte to Talleyrand, 18 March 1804, *Napoleon Correspondance* no. 8746, 4:645. For perspectives on the Cadoudal conspiracy and d'Enghien, see: Hortense, *Mémoires*, 117–24; Cambacérès, *Mémoires*, 1:705–16; Fouché, *Mémoires*, 165–70.
46. Bonaparte to Murat, 20 March 1804, *Napoleon Correspondance* no. 8751, 4:649. See also Bonaparte to Real, 20 March 1804, *Napoleon Correspondance* no. 8749, 4:648.
47. Fouché, *Mémoires*, 168.
48. Napoleon to Talleyrand, 30 May 1804, *Napoleon Correspondance* no. 8924, 4:730.
49. Bonaparte to Talleyrand, 13 May 1804, *Napoleon Correspondance* no. 8870, 4:704.
50. Napoleon to Talleyrand, 10 August 1804, *Napoleon Correspondance* no. 9078, 4:806–08.

Chapter 10: The Emperor

1. Las Cases, *Mémorial*, 1:157.
2. Roberts, *Napoleon: A Life*, 347.
3. Bonaparte to Soult, 14 April 1804, *Napoleon Correspondance* no. 8804, 4:672.
4. Senate to Bonaparte, 27 March 1804, *Napoleon Correspondance*, footnote 1, 4:688–9.
5. Bonaparte to Senate, 25 April 1804, *Napoleon Correspondance* no. 8834, 4:687–8.
6. Lentz, *Napoleon et la Conquête de l'Europe*, 57–8.
7. For the best overview, see: Philip Mansel, *The Eagle in Splendor: Inside the Court of Napoleon* (London: I.B. Tauris, 2015).
8. Lentz, *Napoleon et la Conquête de l'Europe*, 348.
9. Napoleon to Ségur, 22 August 1807, *Napoleon Correspondance* no. 16217, 7:1053–4.
10. For a fastidious array of rules of etiquette, see: Napoleon to Eugène, 20 December 1807, *Napoleon Correspondance* no. 16904, 7:1365–6.
11. Lentz, *Napoleon et la Conquête de l'Europe*, 31.
12. Bonaparte to Fouché, 24 April 1805, *Napoleon Correspondance* no. 9899, 5:235.

13. Napoleon to Fouché, 22 April 1805, *Napoleon Correspondance* no. 9875, 5:223.
14. Napoleon to Fouché, 20 May 1805, *Napoleon Correspondance* no. 10092, 5:325.
15. Napoleon to Charles IV, 14 June 1804, *Napoleon Correspondance* no. 8937, 4:738; Napoleon to Frederick William III, 14 June 1804, ibid. no. 8939, 4:739.
16. Napoleon to Talleyrand, 7 August 1804, *Napoleon Correspondance* no. 9067, 4:802.
17. Napoleon to Talleyrand, 24 August 1804, *Napoleon Correspondance* no. 9137, 4:835.
18. Napoleon to Talleyrand, 10 August 1804, *Napoleon Correspondance* no. 9078, 4:806.
19. Napoleon to Pius VII, 15 September 1804, *Napoleon Correspondance* no. 9223, 4:875.
20. For other key documents of Napoleon's relations with Pius surrounding the coronation, see: Napoleon to Melzi, 8 October 1804, *Napoleon Correspondance* no. 9340, 4:929; Napoleon to Pius VII, 1, 20 November 1804, ibid. nos. 9384, 9424, 4:946, 963.
21. For accounts of the coronation, see: Constant, *Mémoires*, 1:286–98; Hortense, *Mémoires*, 142.
22. Frederic Masson, *Le Sacre et la Coronnement de Napoleon* (Paris: Jacque Tallandier, 1978), 219–20.
23. Napoleon to Francis II, January 1, 1805, *Napoleon Correspondance* no. 9483, 5:20–1; Napoleon to George III, 1 January 1805, ibid. no. 9484, 5:21; Napoleon to Maria Carolina, 2 January 1805, ibid. no. 9485; Napoleon to Ferdinand IV, 2 January 1805, ibid no. 9487, 5:24.
24. Napoleon to Maria Carolina, 2 January 1805, *Napoleon Correspondance* no. 9485, 5:22.
25. Napoleon to Lacépède, 30 January 1805, *Napoleon Correspondance* no. 9535, 5:49–50.
26. Napoleon to Talleyrand, 10 May 1805, *Napoleon Correspondance* no. 10027, 5:294–5.
27. Napoleon to Melzi d'Eril, 23 June 1804, *Napoleon Correspondance* no. 8953, 4:743–4.
28. For key documents on the preparations for Napoleon's Italian coronation, see: Napoleon to Ségur, 28 March 1805, *Napoleon Correspondance* no. 9747, 5:161–2; Napoleon to Champagny, 20 April, 13 May 1805, ibid. nos. 9864, 10040, 5:218, 301; Napoleon to Jourdan, 20 April 1805, ibid. no. 9866, 5:219.

29. Napoleon to Francis II, 17 March 1805, *Napoleon Correspondance* no. 9700, 5:136–7.
30. Napoleon to Talleyrand, 16 April 1805, *Napoleon Correspondance* no. 9855, 5:213.
31. Napoleon to Cambacérès, 27 May 1805, *Napoleon Correspondance* no. 10137, 5:348.

Chapter 11: The Sun of Austerlitz

1. Napoleon to Charles IV, 22 February 1805, *Napoleon Correspondance* no. 9582, 5:72.
2. Napoleon to Godoy, 19 February 1805, *Napoleon Correspondance* no. 9573, 5:67.
3. Napoleon to Junot, 23 February 1805, *Napoleon Correspondance* no. 9591, 5:78–9.
4. Napoleon to Schimmelpennick, 12 May 1805, *Napoleon Correspondance* no. 10034, 5:298–9.
5. Napoleon to Brune, 27 July 1804, *Napoleon Correspondance* no. 9025, 4:780.
6. Napoleon to Soult, 27 October 1804, *Napoleon Correspondance* no. 9369, 4:941.
7. For key documents on the development of Napoleon's naval strategy that ended with Trafalgar, see: Napoleon to Decrès, 3, 29 September, 14 December 1804, 16 January (2 letters), 26 March, 4, 13, 23 (2 letters), 30 April, 4, 8, 24, 25, 29, 30 May, 8, 9 (2 letters), 14, 28 June 1805, *Napoleon Correspondance* nos. 9166, 9265, 9266, 9445, 9509, 9510, 9735, 9779, 9834, 9881, 9882, 9937, 9974, 9996, 10117, 10125, 10151, 10169, 10228, 10242, 10243, 10269, 10362, 4:849, 896–9, 900, 975–6, 5:34–7, 155–6, 177, 201–03, 225–7, 249–51, 266–8, 278–80, 337–8, 342–3, 353–4, 361–2, 390–1, 398–400, 415–16, 464–5; Napoleon to Villeneuve, 12 December 1804, 14 April, 8 May 1805, ibid. nos. 9441, 9623, 9842, 10006, 4:971–4, 5:96–7, 207–08, 283–6; Napoleon to Missiessy, 23 December 1804, ibid. no. 9465, 4:984–6; Napoleon to Ganteaume, 2 March (3 letters), 20, 26 July 1805, ibid. nos. 9619, 9620, 9623, 10429, 10468, 5:924, 96–7, 496–7, 515–16; Napoleon to Lauriston, 2 March (2 letters) 1805, ibid. nos. 9621, 9622, 5:94–6; Napoleon to Gourdon, 27 July 1805, ibid. no. 10472, 5:519; Napoleon to Lebrun, 11 August 1805, ibid. no. 10548, 5:556.
8. Napoleon to Villeneuve, 8 May 1805, *Napoleon Correspondance* no. 10006, 5:284.
9. Napoleon to Decrès, 9 June 1805, *Napoleon Correspondance* no. 10243, 5:400.

10. For the best overview of the naval campaign that ended at Trafalgar, see: Alan Schom, *Trafalgar: Countdown to Battle, 1803-1805* (New York: Oxford University Press, 1990). See also: Roy Adkins, *Nelson's Trafalgar: The Battle That Changed the World* (New York: Penguin, 2006); David Howarth, *Trafalgar: The Nelson Touch* (New York: Phoenix, 2005).
11. Sherwig, *Guineas and Gunpowder*, 143–65, 366.
12. Napoleon to Frederick William III, 9 May 1805, *Napoleon Correspondance* no. 10009, 5:287.
13. Napoleon to Cambacérès, 26 May 1805, *Napoleon Correspondance* no. 10128, 5:344; Napoleon to Decrès, 26 May 1805, ibid. no. 10129, 5:344; Napoleon to Murat, 26 May 1805, ibid. no. 10134, 5:347. Napoleon to Talleyrand, 6 June 1805, ibid. no. 10216, 5:382.
14. Schom, *Napoleon Bonapar*te, 366.
15. Napoleon to Josephine, 3 August 1805, *Napoleon Correspondance* no. 10491. 5:529.
16. Napoleon to Eugène, 13 August 1805, *Napoleon Correspondance* no. 10559, 5:564. See also: Napoleon to Fouché, 9 August 1805, *Napoleon Correspondance* no. 10559, 5:552.
17. Napoleon to Villeneuve, 13 August 1805, *Napoleon Correspondance* no. 10562, 5:568. See also: Napoleon to Decrès, 13 (2 letters) 14, 15 August 1805, *Napoleon Correspondance* nos. 10555, 10556, 10564, 10574, 5:561–3, 569–70, 574.
18. Napoleon to Talleyrand, 3 August 1805, *Napoleon Correspondance* no. 10495, 5:530.
19. Napoleon to Talleyrand, 7 August 1805, *Napoleon Correspondance* no. 10530, 5:548.
20. Napoleon to Talleyrand, 10 August 1805, *Napoleon Correspondance* no. 10543, 5:554.
21. Napoleon to Hortense, 12 August 1805, *Napoleon Correspondance* no. 10552, 5:558–60.
22. Napoleon to Talleyrand, 12 August 1805, *Napoleon Correspondance* no. 10553, 5:560.
23. Napoleon to Josephine, 13 August 1805, *Napoleon Correspondance* no. 10560, 5:564.
24. Napoleon to Talleyrand, 13 August 1805, *Napoleon Correspondance* no. 10561, 5:565–7.
25. Bonaparte to Talleyrand, 23 August 1805, *Napoleon Correspondance* no. 7957, 4:290.
26. For key documents on Napoleon's alliance strategy, see: Napoleon to Charles Frederick of Baden, 20 May 1805, *Napoleon Correspondance*

no. 10087, 5:323–4; Napoleon to Maximilien Joseph of Bavaria, 17 June 1805, ibid. no. 10284, 5:423; Napoleon to Talleyrand, 16, 18, 23 (2 letters), 25 (2 letters), 29 August, 5 September 1805, ibid. nos. 10586, 10594, 10645, 10646, 10664, 10665, 10705, 10751, 5:579, 583, 607–09, 622–3, 648, 670–1; Napoleon to Louis X of Hesse-Darmstadt, 17 September 1805, ibid. nos. 10828, 11288, 5:707, 6:42.

27. Napoleon to Maria Carolina, 21 February 1805, *Napoleon Correspondance* no. 9578, 5:69–71.
28. Napoleon to Talleyrand, 3 June 1805, *Napoleon Correspondance* no. 1022, 5:375–6.
29. Napoleon to Frederick William III, 24 March 1805, *Napoleon Correspondance* no. 9719, 5:148.
30. Napoleon to Frederick William III, 23 August 1805, *Napoleon Correspondance* no. 10643, 5:606.
31. Napoleon to Duroc, 24 August, 11 September 1805, *Napoleon Correspondance* nos. 10652, 10778, 5:614–15, 681–2; Napoleon to Talleyrand, 24 August, 12 September 1805, ibid. nos. 10656, 10787, 5:617, 685.
32. Napoleon to Talleyrand, 22 August 1805, *Napoleon Correspondance* no. 10629, 5:598–9.
33. Bonaparte to Brune, 16 March 1804, *Napoleon Correspondance* no. 8738, 4:641–2.
34. Napoleon to Brune, 27 July 1804, *Napoleon Correspondance* no. 9025, 4:779–80.
35. Napoleon to Selim III, 30 January 1805, *Napoleon Correspondance* no. 9536, 5:50–1.
36. Napoleon to Feth Ali, 16 February 1805, *Napoleon Correspondance* no. 9566, 5:63–4. See also: Napoleon to Feth Ali, 30 March 1805, ibid. no. 9753, 5:165.
37. Napoleon to Jourdan, 29 September 1805, *Napoleon Correspondance* no. 10892, 5:744–5.
38. Frederick Schneid, *Napoleon's Italian Campaigns, 1805-1815* (Westport, Conn.: Praeger, 2002).
39. For key documents on Napoleon's mobilization of his Grand Army and allies against Austria, see: Napoleon to Berthier, 24, 25 (3 letters), 26 (2 letters), 29 August, 5 (3 letters), 15, 19, 21, 22 September 1805, *Napoleon Correspondance* nos.10650, 10657, 10658, 10659, 10666, 10667, 10698, 10743, 10747, 10748, 10799, 10842, 10851, 10856, 5:614–15, 618–20, 624–7, 642–5, 666, 668–9, 691, 714–15, 718–20, 723–4; Napoleon to Dejean, 28 August 1805, ibid. no. 10686, 5:636;

Napoleon to Murat, 18 (2 letters), 20 September 1805, ibid. nos. 10838, 10849, 10855, 5:712–13, 722–3.

For key documents on mobilizing the Italian army, see: Napoleon to Eugène, 27 August, 1, 16, 22 September 1805, *Napoleon Correspondance* nos. 10672, 10673, 10731, 10814, 10859, 5:628–30, 660, 697–9, 725–6; Napoleon to Berthier, 5 September 1805, ibid. no. 10744, 5:666–7; Napoleon to Masséna, 18 September 1805, ibid. no. 10837, 5:711–12.

For key documents on the campaign's financing, see: Napoleon to Daru, 30 August 1805, *Napoleon Correspondance* no. 10708, 5:650–1; Napoleon to Barbé-Marbois, 31 August, 2 September 1805, ibid. nos. 10711, 10734, 5:652, 661–2.

40. Napoleon to Decrès, 29 August, 4 September 1805, *Napoleon Correspondance* nos. 10701, 10742, 5:646, 665.
41. Napoleon to Villeneuve, 14 September 1805, *Napoleon Correspondance* no. 10797, 5:690.
42. Napoleon to Decrès, 15 September 1805, *Napoleon Correspondance* no. 10803, 5:693; Napoleon to Rosily, 17 September 1805, ibid. no. 10829.
43. For key documents on the first phase of Napoleon's 1805 campaign until the capture of Vienna, see: Napoleon to Eugène, 29 September, 2 October 1805, *Napoleon Correspondance* no. 10890, 10921, 5:743–4, 760; Napoleon to Masséna, 29 September 1805, ibid. no. 10894, 5:745–6; Napoleon to Augereau, 30 September 1805, ibid. no. 10902, 5:750; Napoleon to Bernadotte, 2, 11 (2 letters), 19 (2 letters) October 1805, ibid. nos. 10917, 10987, 10988, 11015, 11016, 5:757–8, 791–2, 807–08; Napoleon to Davout, 3 October 1805, ibid. no. 10936, 5:767; Napoleon to Lannes, 3 October 1805, ibid. no. 10940, 5:769; Napoleon to Soult, 3, 12 (3 letters) October 1805, ibid. nos. 10945, 11003, 11004, 11005, 5:771–2, 800–02; Napoleon to Murat, 4, 5, 9, 12 (2 letters) October, 7, 17, 18, November 1805, ibid. nos. 10963, 10969, 10982, 11007, 11013, 11079, 5:779, 782, 788, 798–9, 799, 803, 806, 835–6; Napoleon to Otto, 11, 12 October 1805, ibid. nos. 10992, 11002, 5:794, 800; Napoleon to the Senate, 18 October 1805, ibid. no. 11010, 5:804–05. For the best book on the campaign, see: Robert Goetz, *1805 Austerlitz: Napoleon and the Destruction of the Third Coalition* (London: Greenhill Books, 2005). See also: Schneid, *Napoleon's Conquest of Europe*; R.G. Burton, *The Road to Austerlitz: Napoleon's Campaign of 1805* (London: Leonaur, 2008); F.N. Maude, *The Ulm Campaign 1805: Napoleon and the Defeat of the Austrian Army during the 'War of the Third Coalition'* (London: Leonaur, 2018). For an overview of the three years of war, see: Scott Bowden, *Napoleon and Austerlitz: The Glory Years, 1805-1807* (New York: Military History Press, 1992).

For key documents on Napoleon's coordination of his campaign with those of Eugène and Marmont, see: Napoleon to Marmont, 4 October 1805, *Napoleon Correspondance* no. 10962, 5:779.

For key documents on his diplomacy with his allies during the first phase, see: Napoleon to Frederick II of Württemberg, 29 September, 18 October, 2 November 1805, *Napoleon Correspondance* nos. 10901, 11012, 11066, 5:749, 805–06, 829; Napoleon to Charles Frederick of Baden, 2 October 1805, ibid. no. 10918, 5:758; Napoleon to Louis of Hesse-Darmstadt, 2 October 1805, ibid. no. 10925; Napoleon to Maximilien Joseph of Bavaria, 2 October 1805, ibid. no. 10926, 5:762–3; Napoleon to Berthier, 4 October 1805, ibid. no. 10932, 5:775.

44. Bonaparte to Duroc, 2 October 1805, *Napoleon Correspondance* no. 10920, 5:760; Napoleon to Otto, 3, 4 October 1805, ibid. nos. 10943, 10964, 5:770, 780; Napoleon to Frederick William III, 5 October 1805, ibid. no. 10966, 5:781.
45. Napoleon to Murat, 2 October 1805, *Napoleon Correspondance* no. 10927, 5:763.
46. Napoleon to Murat, 17 October 1805, *Napoleon Correspondance* no. 11007, 5:803.
47. Napoleon to Talleyrand, 17 October 1805, *Napoleon Correspondance* no. 11009, 5:804.
48. Napoleon to the Senate, 18 October 1805, *Napoleon Correspondance* no. 11010, 5:804–05.
49. Napoleon to Josephine, 19 October 1805, *Napoleon Correspondance* no. 11018, 5:808–09.
50. Napoleon to Josephine, 27 October 1805, *Napoleon Correspondance* no. 11056, 5:824.
51. Napoleon to Josephine, 4 October 1805, *Napoleon Correspondance* no. 10960, 5:778.
52. Napoleon to Fouché, 4 October 1805, *Napoleon Correspondance* no. 10958, 5:777.
53. Napoleon to Duroc, 24 October 1805, *Napoleon Correspondance* no. 11043, 5:817; Napoleon to Frederick William III, 27 October 1805, ibid. no. 11054, 5:822–3.
54. Bonaparte to Murat, 16 November 1805, *Napoleon Correspondance* no. 11112, 5:856.
55. Napoleon to Murat, 11 November 1805, *Napoleon Correspondance* no. 11086, 5:839. See also: Napoleon to Murat, 12 November 1805, ibid. no. 11087, 5:840.
56. Bonaparte to Joseph, 3 December 1805, *Napoleon Correspondance* no. 11143, 5:872.

57. Napoleon to Cambacérès, 15 November 1805, *Napoleon Correspondance* no. 11098, 5:848–9; Napoleon to Barbé-Marbois, 22 November 1805, ibid. no. 11125, 5:862–3.
58. For key documents on the campaign's final phase from Vienna to Austerlitz, see: Napoleon to Murat, 12, 14 November 1805, *Napoleon Correspondance* nos. 11087, 11096, 5:840, 846; Napoleon to Soult, 12 November 1805, ibid. no. 11088, 5:841–2; Napoleon to Berthier, 14 November 1805, ibid. no. 11091, 5:843–4; Napoleon to Lannes, 14 November 1805, ibid. no. 11093, 5:844–5.

    For key documents on coordinating the offensive of Eugène and Marmont with Napoleon's army, see: Napoleon to Marmont, 13, 14, 15 November 1805, ibid. nos. 11090, 11094, 11108, 5:842–3, 845, 854.

    For key documents on Napoleon's relations with his allies, see: Napoleon to Maximilien Joseph of Bavaria, 15 November, 5 December 1805, ibid. no. 11103, 11147, 5:851, 874; Napoleon to Frederick II of Württemberg, 16 November, 5, 13 December 1805, ibid. no. 11111, 11148, 11163, 5:855–6, 875, 881–2.
59. Napoleon to Francis II, 3, 8 November 1805, *Napoleon Correspondance* nos. 11069, 11082, 11117, 5:830–1, 836–7, 858–9; Napoleon to Alexander, 25 November 1805, ibid. no. 11133, 5:866–7.
60. Napoleon to Talleyrand, 30 November 1805, *Napoleon Correspondance* no. 11138, 5:869.
61. Bonaparte to Talleyrand, 22 November 1805, *Napoleon Correspondance* no. 11129, 5:864.
62. Goetz, *1805 Austerlitz*, 307–14, 345–54.
63. Ibid., 336–44.
64. Napoleon to Frederick II of Württemberg, 5 December 1805, *Napoleon Correspondance* no. 11148, 5:875.
65. Bonaparte to Talleyrand, 30 November 1805, *Napoleon Correspondance* no. 11138, 5:869.
66. Goetz, *1805 Austerlitz*, 278–81.
67. Philippe Paul Ségur, *An Aide-de-Camp of Napoleon: The Memoirs of General Count Ségur* (London: Worley Publications, 1995), 254.
68. Napoleon to Talleyrand, 4 December 1805, *Napoleon Correspondance* no. 11146, 5:8734.

Chapter 12: The Ghost of Frederick

1. Napoleon to Berthier, 27 December 1805, *Napoleon Correspondance* no. 11226, 5:911–14; Napoleon to Dejean, 15 March 1806, ibid.

no. 11691, 6:230–1; Napoleon to Talleyrand, 18 March 1806, ibid. no. 11725, 6:243–4.
2. For key documents on France's financial problems during this time, see: Napoleon to Joseph, 23 December 1805, *Napoleon Correspondance* no. 11214, 5:906; Napoleon to Gaudin, 4 February 1806, ibid. no. 11390, 6:84–6.
3. Napoleon to Berthier, 17 February 1806, *Napoleon Correspondance* no. 11480, 6:130.
4. For key documents on Napoleon's financial reforms, see: Napoleon to Gaudin, 23 February, 8, 9, 20 March, 9 April, 17 May 1805, *Napoleon Correspondance* nos. 9590, 9646, 9655, 9710, 10059, 10076, 5:76–7, 108–10, 113–14, 142–3, 188, 315, 318–19; Napoleon to Barbé-Marbois, 8 March, 2 June, 24 August 1805, ibid. nos. 9645, 10190, 10649, 5:107, 370–1, 610–12.
5. Napoleon to Eugène, 4, 16 February 1806, *Napoleon Correspondance* nos. 11386, 11476, 6:83, 129.
6. Napoleon to State Consul, 20 February 1806, Joseph Pelet de la Lozère, *Opinions de Napoleon sur divers sujets de politique et d'administration recuillies par un member de son Conseil d'État et récit de quelques événements de l'Époque* (Paris: Firmin Didot Freres, 1833), 236–7.
7. Napoleon to Eugène, 14 April 1806, *Napoleon Correspondance* no. 11896, 6:324.
8. Napoleon to Dejean, 14, 28 April 1806, *Napoleon Correspondance* no. 11894, 6:322–3, 372–5.
9. Napoleon to Fouché, 6 March 1806, *Napoleon Correspondance* no. 11608, 190.
10. For just a month's worth of imperial instructions and admonitions on Italy's finances, administration, and army, see: Napoleon to Eugène, 3, 5, 8, 11 (2 letters), 16, 18 (2 letters), 21, 25 (2 letters), 26, 27, 28 February, 2, 3, 12, 13 March 1806, *Napoleon Correspondance* nos. 11382, 11400, 11427, 11439, 11440, 11476, 11494, 11497, 11515, 11517, 11543, 11544, 11556, 11555, 11565, 11585, 11594, 11658, 11674, 6:81, 91, 103, 110, 129, 137, 138, 147, 148–9, 160–1, 164, 167–8, 171, 179, 184, 214, 222–4.
11. Napoleon to Junot, 4 February 1806, *Napoleon Correspondance* no. 11392, 6:66–7.
12. Napoleon to Junot, 18 February 1806, *Napoleon Correspondance* no. 11500, 6:139.
13. William H. Flayhart, *The Counterpart to Trafalgar: The Anglo-Russian Invasion of Naples, 1805-1806* (Columbia: University of South Carolina Press, 1992).

14. Napoleon to Talleyrand, 23 December 1805, *Napoleon Correspondance* no. 11213, 5:906.
15. Napoleon to Joseph, 12, 19 January 1806, *Napoleon Correspondance* nos. 11279, 11307, 11335, 6:36–7, 50–1, 63–4.
16. Napoleon to Fesch, 30 January 1806, *Napoleon Correspondance* no. 11346, 6:68.
17. Napoleon to Joseph, 31 January 1806, *Napoleon Correspondance* no. 11361, 6:75.
18. Napoleon to Joseph, 28 February, 2, 6, 12, 20 March 1806, *Napoleon Correspondance* nos. 11567, 11586, 11610, 11663, 11732, 6:172, 180–1, 191, 216–17, 246–7.
19. Napoleon to Talleyrand, 4 February 1806, *Napoleon Correspondance* no. 11395, 6:88.
20. Napoleon to Talleyrand, 14 March 1806, *Napoleon Correspondance* no. 11688, 6:229; Napoleon to Murat, 15 March 1806, ibid. nos. 11695, 11704, 6:232, 235–6; Napoleon to Bernadotte, 20 March 1806, ibid. no. 11727, 6:244–5; Napoleon to Frederick William III, 30 March 1806, ibid. no. 11797, 6:280–1.
21. Lentz, *Grand Consulat*, 458–60.
22. Napoleon to Talleyrand, 10 April 1806, *Napoleon Correspondance* no. 11869, 6:311–12.
23. Napoleon to Champagny, 14 February 1809, *Napoleon Correspondance* no. 20027, 9:56.
24. Napoleon to Joseph, 8 March 1806, *Napoleon Correspondance* no. 11624, 6:199.
25. Napoleon to Joseph, 5 August 1806, *Napoleon Correspondance* no. 12657, 6:690.
26. Napoleon to Joseph, 12 August, 13, 17 September 1806, *Napoleon Correspondance* nos. 12702, 12924, 12966, 6:711, 834, 854.
27. Las Cases, *Mémorial*, 2:1440–1.
28. Napoleon to Decrès, 31 January 1806, *Napoleon Correspondance* no. 11353, 6:71.
29. Napoleon to Allemand, 23 February 1806, *Napoleon Correspondance* no. 11336, 6:155–8.
30. For key documents on the conflicts between France and Russia over this region, see: Napoleon to Eugène, 6 May, 21, 28 July 1806, *Napoleon Correspondance* no. 12061, 12549, 12585, 6:403–04, 637–8, 652–4; Napoleon to Talleyrand, May 8, 1806, ibid. no. 12079, 6:413.
31. Napoleon to Selim, 12 March 1806, *Napoleon Correspondance* no. 11667, 6:218–19.

32. Napoleon to Talleyrand, 9 June 1806, *Napoleon Correspondance* no. 12263, 6:503.
33. For key documents on Napoleon's policy toward Turkey this year, see: Napoleon to Talleyrand, 9 June 1806, *Napoleon Correspondance* no. 12263, 6:503; Napoleon to Selim, 20 June 1806, ibid. no. 12337, 6:534.
34. Stanford Shaw, *Between Old and New: The Ottoman Empire under Selim III, 1789-1806* (Cambridge, Mass.: Harvard University Press, 1971).
35. F. Loraine Petre, *Napoleon's Conquest of Prussia, 1806* (London: Greenhill, 1993); F.N. Maude, *The Jena Campaign 1806: The Twin Battles of Jena and Auerstadt between Napoleon's French and the Prussian Army* (London: Leonaur, 2007); Peter Paret, *The Cognitive Challenge of War: Prussia 1806* (Princeton, N.J.: Princeton University Press, 2009); J.H. Anderson, *The Campaign of Jena 1806: Napoleon's Decisive Defeat of the Prussian King* (London: Leonaur, 2010).
36. Napoleon to Talleyrand, 22 August 1806, *Napoleon Correspondance* no. 12775, 6:744. See also: Napoleon to Talleyrand, 8 August 1806, *Napoleon Correspondance* no. 12684, 6:701–02.
37. For key documents on Napoleon's complaints against Lucchesini and the ambassador's deleterious effect on relations between France and Prussia, see: Napoleon to Talleyrand, 3 March, 23 May 1801, 12, 22, 25 August, 20 December 1805, *Napoleon Correspondance* nos. 6098, 6301, 10553, 10629, 10664, 11202, 3:598, 695, 5:560, 598–600, 622, 900–01.
38. Napoleon to Frederick William III, 12 September 1806, *Napoleon Correspondance* no. 12908. 6:823–4.
39. Napoleon to Talleyrand, 12 September 1806, *Napoleon Correspondance* no. 12915, 6:829–30.
40. Napoleon to Talleyrand, 12 September 1806, *Napoleon Correspondance* no. 12913, 6:826–7.
41. Napoleon to Talleyrand, 12 September 1806, *Napoleon Correspondance* no. 12914, 6:828.
42. Napoleon to Maximilien Joseph of Bavaria, 21 September 1806, *Napoleon Correspondance* no. 13051, 6:902–03.
43. Napoleon to Eugène, 15 September 1806, *Napoleon Correspondance* no. 12944, 6:843; Napoleon to Rochefoucauld, 3 October 1806, ibid. no. 13196, 6:969–70.
44. For key documents on organizing, mobilizing and moving the French army to the front, see: Napoleon to Dejean, 4, 5 (2 letters) September 1806, *Napoleon Correspondance* nos. 12858, 12872, 12873, 6:790–3, 800, 801; Napoleon to Berthier, 5 (2 letters), 9, 10 (2 letters), 15, 17, 19 (4 letters), 20 (2 letters), 22, 29 (3 letters) September, 5 October 1806, ibid.

nos. 12869, 12870, 12893, 12895, 12896, 12940, 12955, 12956, 12975, 12976, 12977, 12978, 13003, 13004, 1306, 13126, 13127, 13128, 13203, 6:798–9, 813–16, 840–1, 849–50, 861–6, 876–8, 906–07, 932–5, 973–4.

For key documents on Napoleon's mobilization of allied forces, see: Napoleon to Louis, 15 (2 letters), 19, 20, 22, 29 September 1806, *Napoleon Correspondance* nos. 12948, 12985, 12990, 13034, 13076, 13137, 6:845–6, 871–2, 893–4, 913–14, 939–40; Napoleon to Frederic I of Württemberg, 21 September 1806, ibid. no. 13049, 6:901–02; Napoleon to Maximilien Joseph I of Bavaria, 21 September 1806, ibid. no. 13051, 6:902–03; Napoleon to Ferdinand I of Würzburg, 29 September 1806, ibid. no. 13134, 6:937–8; Napoleon to Dalberg, Rhine Confederation prince primate, 1, 7 October 1806, ibid. nos. 13178, 13233, 6:961–2, 986–7.

45. For key documents on the campaign's Jena and Auerstadt phase, see: Napoleon to Louis, 30 September, 17, 20, 25 October, 5 November 1806, *Napoleon Correspondance* nos. 13162, 13283, 13297, 13339, 13464, 6:953–5, 1011–12, 1017, 1038–9, 1097; Napoleon to Soult, 5, 10 October 1806, ibid. nos. 13214, 13247, 6:978–9, 993–4; Napoleon to Lannes, 7, 8, 12 October, 5 November 1806, ibid. nos. 13230, 13241, 13253, 13468, 6:984–5, 990, 997, 1099; Napoleon to Murat, 10, 12, 13, 28 October, 2 November 1806, ibid. nos. 13246, 13254, 13265, 13368, 13420, 6:902–03, 997, 1003, 1052, 1072–3; Napoleon to Berthier, 23 October 23, 2 November 1806, ibid. nos. 13314, 13406, 6:1025–6, 1067–8; Napoleon to Davout, October 23, 1806, ibid. no. 13315, 6:1026–7; Napoleon to Mortier, 23 October 1806, ibid. no. 13319, 6:1028–30; Napoleon to Dejean, 25 October 1806, ibid. no. 13331, 6:1034–5; Napoleon to Songis, 26 October (1806, ibid. no. 13358, 6:1046–7; Napoleon to Bourcier, 4 November 1806, ibid. no. 13446, 6:1086; Napoleon to Lagrange, 5 November 1806, ibid. no. 13465, 6:1098.

46. Napoleon to the Saxon people, 10 October 1806, *Napoleon Correspondance* no. 13248, 6:994–5.

47. Napoleon to Talleyrand, 12 October 1806, *Napoleon Correspondance* no. 13257. 6:998.

48. Napoleon to Frederick William III, 12 October 1806, *Napoleon Correspondance* no.13259, 6:999–1000.

49. Among the litany of calumnies against Napoleon is that somehow he took credit for Davout's victory, when in reality he widely celebrated it. See: Napoleon to Davout, 16 October 1806, *Napoleon Correspondance* no. 13273, 61007; Napoleon to Talleyrand, 15 October 1806, ibid. no. 13272, 6:1007.

50. Napoleon to Frederick William III, 19 October 1806, *Napoleon Correspondance* no. 13288, 6:1014.

51. Napoleon to Bernadotte, 3 October 1806, *Napoleon Correspondance* no. 13312, 6:1023.
52. Napoleon to Bernadotte, 13 November 1806, *Napoleon Correspondance* no. 13561, 6:1141.
53. Napoleon to Louis, 6 November 1806, *Napoleon Correspondance* no. 13485, 6:1108.
54. Las Cases, *Mémorial*, 2:1158–9.
55. Napoleon to Princess Ferdinand, 28 October 1806, *Napoleon Correspondance* no. 13365, 6:1051.
56. For key documents on the implementation of Napoleon's Continental System, see: Napoleon to Talleyrand, 21 November 1806, *Napoleon Correspondance* no. 12618, 6:1164; Napoleon to Mortier, 16, 21 November, 2 December 1806, ibid. nos. 13599, 13619, 13717, 6:1156, 1164–6, 1211–12; Napoleon to Bourrienne, 7 January 1807, ibid. no. 13972, 7:44.
57. Napoleon to Louis, December 3, 1806, *Napoleon Correspondance* no. 13743, 6:1222.
58. Eli Heckscher, *The Continental System: An Economic Interpretation* (Oxford: Oxford University Press, 1922); François Crouzet, *L'Economie Britannique et le Blocus Continental, 1806-1813* (Paris: Presses Universitaires de France, 1958); Frank Melvin, *Napoleon's Navigation System: A Study of Trade Control during the Continental Blockade* (New York: Nabu Press, 2010); K. Aalestadl and J. Joos, *Revisiting Napoleon's Continental System: Local, Regional, and European Experiences* (New York: Palgrave Macmillan, 2014).
59. F. Loraine Petre, *Napoleon's Campaign, 1806-1807* (London: Greenhill, 2001).
60. Napoleon to Kellermann, 3 November 1806, *Napoleon Correspondance* no. 13435, 6:1079.
61. Napoleon to Clarke, 2, 5 December 1806, *Napoleon Correspondance* nos. 13709, 13754, 6:1207, 1228; Napoleon to Fouché, 14 January 1807, ibid. no. 14054, 7:81.
62. For key documents on the Polish campaign's first phase to Warsaw, see: Napoleon to Murat, 24, 28 November, 1, 5, 8, 9, 14, 29 December 1806, *Napoleon Correspondance* nos. 13643, 13655, 13700, 13757, 13788, 13795, 13847, 13901, 13988, 6:1176, 1182, 1203, 1230–1, 1245–6, 1248–9, 1272–3; Napoleon to Lannes, 5, 7 November, 29 December 1806, ibid. nos. 13436, 13498, 13900, 6:1080, 1114–15, 1297; Napoleon to Davout, 7 November (2 letters) 1806, ibid. nos. 13495, 13496. 6:111–13; Napoleon to Ney, 7, 10 November, 10, 14 December 1806, ibid. nos. 13502, 11532, 13807, 13549, 6:1117, 1128, 1254, 1273–4; Napoleon

to Berthier, 10 November 1806, ibid. no. 13533, 6:1129–30; Napoleon to Dejean, 12, 22 November 1806, ibid. nos. 13550, 13622, 6:1136, 1167; Napoleon to Cambacérès, 22 November 1806, ibid. no. 13621, 6:1166; Napoleon to Chasseloup, 15 December 1806, ibid. no. 13844, 6:1270–1; Napoleon to Lacuée, 15 December 1806, ibid. no. 13870, 6:1283–4; Napoleon to Soult, 15 December 1806, ibid. no. 13881, 6:1289; Napoleon to Daru, 21 December 1806, ibid. no. 13896, 6:1295.

For key documents on Napoleon's mopping-up campaign in and occupation of Prussia and northern Germany, see: Napoleon to Berthier, 4 November 1806, *Napoleon Correspondance* nos. 13442, 6:1083–5; Napoleon to Louis, 16 November 1806, ibid. no. 13597, 6:1155; Napoleon to Clarke, 27 November 1806, ibid. no. 13650, 6:1179–80.

63. Napoleon to Talleyrand, 27 November 1806, *Napoleon Correspondance* no. 13652, 6:1181.
64. Napoleon to Frederick William III, 6 December 1806, *Napoleon Correspondance* no. 13764, 6:1233.
65. Napoleon to Andreossy, 1 December 1806, *Napoleon Correspondance* no. 13684, 6:1197.
66. Napoleon to Cambacérès, 1 December 1806, *Napoleon Correspondance* no. 13691. 6:1199.
67. Napoleon to Davout, 13 November 1806, *Napoleon Correspondance* no. 13566, 6:1143; Napoleon to Joseph, 5 December 1806, ibid. no. 13756, 6;1229–30; Napoleon to Berthier, 2, 28 (2 letters) January 1807, ibid. nos. 13926, 14185, 14149, 7:20–1, 139–41.
68. Napoleon to Cambacérès, 1 December 1806, *Napoleon Correspondance* no. 13691, 6:1199.
69. Napoleon to Andreossy, 1 December 1806, *Napoleon Correspondance* no. 13684, 6:1197.
70. Napoleon to Eugène, 4 November, 5, 8 December 1806, *Napoleon Correspondance* nos. 13451, 13755, 13785, 6:1088–9, 1228–9, 1243–4; Napoleon to Marmont, 30 October 1806, ibid no. 13385, 6:1059.
71. Napoleon to Murat, 2 December 1806, *Napoleon Correspondance* no. 13719, 6:1213; Napoleon to Talleyrand, 28 March 1807, ibid. no. 14970, 7:488–9.
72. Treaty with Saxony, 11 December 1806, *Grands Traites de L'Empire*, 2:265–8; Napoleon to Frederick Augustus III, 18 November, 2, 12 December 1806, *Napoleon Correspondance* nos. 13609, 13714, 13837, 6:1160, 1210, 1267.
73. Napoleon to Murat, 2 December 1806, *Napoleon Correspondance* no. 13719, 6:1213.

74. Alex Storozynski, *The Peasant Prince: Thaddeus Kosciusko and the Age of Revolution* (New York: St. Martins Griffin, 2010).
75. Napoleon to Fouché, 3 November 1806, *Napoleon Correspondance* no.13233, 6:1078–9.
76. Napoleon to Fouché, 30 November 1806, *Napoleon Correspondance* no. 13680, 6:1195.
77. Napoleon to Fouché, 20 February 1807, *Napoleon Correspondance* no. 14342, 7:203.
78. For key documents on operations preceding Eylau, see: Napoleon to Daru, 3 January 1807, *Napoleon Correspondance* no. 13935, 7:24–6; Napoleon to Dejean, 3, 6, 8 January 1807, ibid. nos. 13936, 13962, 13984, 7:26, 39–40, 49–50; Napoleon to Berthier, 4, 13, 19 (2 letters), 21, 22, 23, 27 January 1807, ibid. nos. 13939, 14032, 14110, 14111, 14137, 14142, 14148, 14174, 7:27–8, 70–1, 105–07, 117–18, 120–1, 123–4, 134–5; Napoleon to Fouché, 8 January 1807, ibid. no. 13985, 7:51; Napoleon to Songis, 13 January 1807, ibid. no. 14049, 7:79; Napoleon to Davout, 15 January 1807, ibid. no. 14064, 7:85; Napoleon to Jérôme, 15, 19 January 1807, ibid. nos. 14069, 14121, 7:87–8, 111–12; Napoleon to Lacuée, 26 January 1807, ibid. no. 14172, 7:133.
79. Napoleon to Josephine, 2 December 1806, *Napoleon Correspondance* no. 13715, 6:1211.
80. Napoleon to Josephine, 3 December (2 letters) 1806, *Napoleon Correspondance* nos. 13739, 13740, 6:1220–1.
81. Napoleon to Josephine, 31 December 1806, *Napoleon Correspondance* no. 13916, 6:1302–03.
82. Christine Sutherland, *Marie Walewska: Napoleon's Great Love* (New York: Viking, 1979).
83. Lentz, *Napoleon et la Conquête de l'Europe*, 277–81. For documents on the development and diplomatic importance of Napoleon's relationship with Marie Walewska, see: Napoleon to Josephine, 16, 22 November 1806, 3, 7, 8, 16, 18, 23 (2 letters) January, 1 February, [n.d.], 15 March 1807, *Napoleon Correspondance* nos. 13595, 13624, 13938, 13978, 13988, 14088, 14106, 14155, 14156, 14238, 14242, 14659, 6:1154, 1168, 7:27, 46, 52, 97, 103, 126–7, 161, 162, 46; Constant, *Mémoires*, 1:408–15.
84. Napoleon to Marie Walewska, 18 January 1807, *Napoleon Correspondance* no. 14108, 7:105.
85. Napoleon to Marie Walewska, 18 January 1807, *Napoleon Correspondance* no. 14109, 7:105.
86. Napoleon to Marie Walewska, 17 January 1807, *Napoleon Correspondance* no. 14134, 7:116.

87. An amalgam from Napoleon to Marie Walewska, 23, 24, 29 (2 letters) January 1807, *Napoleon Correspondance* nos. 14157, 14166, 14221, 14222, 7:127, 129–30, 155–6.
88. Napoleon to Marie Walewska, 22 January 1807, *Napoleon Correspondance* no. 14139, 7:118–19.
89. Napoleon to Marie Walewska, 17 March 1807, *Napoleon Correspondance* no. 14715, 7:368.
90. Napoleon to Decrès, 10 December 1806, *Napoleon Correspondance* no. 13802, 6:1251–2.
91. Napoleon to Talleyrand, 15 December 1806, *Napoleon Correspondance* no. 13882, 6:1290.
92. Napoleon to Decrès, 4, 6, 13, 16, 26 January, 28 February, 26 March (2 letters), 22 April (2 letters) 1807, *Napoleon Correspondance* nos. 13946, 13960, 14043, 14080, 14170, 14436, 14914, 14915, 15391,15392, 7:31–2, 38, 76, 93, 131–2, 243, 463–4, 676–7.
93. Napoleon to Joseph, 19 May 1807, *Napoleon Correspondance* no. 15661, 7:803; Napoleon to Decrès, 21 May 1807, ibid. no. 15677, 7:809.
94. Napoleon to Selim III, 1 December 1806, *Napoleon Correspondance* no. 13704, 6:1205. See also: Napoleon to Selim III, 11 November 1806, 3, 7 April 1807, ibid. nos. 13545, 15079, 15163, 6:1135, 7:540–1, 575–6; Napoleon to Sebastiani, 1 December 1806, ibid. no. 13703, 6:1204–05; Napoleon to Cambacérès, 11 December 1806, ibid. no. 13811, 6:1256.
95. Napoleon to Selim III, 1 January 1807, *Napoleon Correspondance* no. 13924, 7:19–20.
96. Napoleon to Talleyrand, 29 January 1807, *Napoleon Correspondance* no. 14220, 7:155; Napoleon to Marmont, 30 January 1807, ibid. no. 14223, 7:156.
97. Napoleon to Talleyrand, 27 February 1807, *Napoleon Correspondance* no. 14431, 7:239–40.
98. Napoleon to Clarke, 2 January 1807, *Napoleon Correspondance* no. 13930, 7:22.
99. Napoleon to Lagrange, 8 January 1807, *Napoleon Correspondance* no. 13999, 7:53. See also Napoleon to Lagrange, 13 January 1807, ibid. no. 14047, 7:77–6.
100. Napoleon to Charles IV, 20 January 1807, *Napoleon Correspondance* no. 14128, 7:114; Napoleon to Francis I, 20 January 1807, ibid. no. 14131, 7:115; Napoleon to Jean I, 20 January 1807, ibid. no. 14135, 7:116; Napoleon to Frederick Augustus I, 25 January 1807, ibid. no. 14164, 7:129; Napoleon to Charles Augustus, 29 January 1807, ibid. no. 14216, 7:153; Napoleon to Frederick of Saxe-Hildburghausen, 29 January 1807, ibid. no. 14217, 7:154.

101. For key documents on the Eylau campaign, see: Napoleon to Clarke, 27, 28 January 1807, *Napoleon Correspondance* nos. 14180, 14189, 7:136–7, 142; Napoleon to Lefebvre, 28 January 1807, ibid. no. 14192, 7:143; Napoleon to Murat, 28 January, 2, 3 (2 letters) February 1807, ibid. nos. 14194, 14244, 14262, 14265, 7:144, 163–4, 170–1, 172; Napoleon to Berthier, 28 January (3 letters) 1807, ibid. nos. 14196, 14198, 14199, 7:145–7, Napoleon to Jérôme, 28 January 1807, ibid. no. 14202, 7:148–9; Napoleon to Mortier, 28 January 1807, ibid. no. 13203, 7:149; Napoleon to Soult, 3 February 1807, ibid. no. 14263, 7:171; Napoleon to Davout, 3 February 1807, ibid. no. 14264, 7:171–2.
102. Napoleon to Duroc, 9 February 1807, *Napoleon Correspondance* no. 14280, 7:177–8.
103. Fifty-eighth Bulletin, 9 February 1807, David Markham, *Imperial Glory: The Bulletins of Napoleon's Grand Armee, 1805-1814* (London: Greenhill Books, 2003), 143–4.
104. Napoleon to Bertrand, 13 February 1807, *Napoleon Correspondance* no. 14306, 7:188; Napoleon to Frederick William III, 13 February 1807. ibid. no. 14307, 7:189.
105. For key documents of the French army's rebuilding and battles after Eylau through May, see: Napoleon to Duroc, 19, 20, 25, 26 February 1807, *Napoleon Correspondance* nos. 14332, 14341, 14398, 14411, 14480, 7:198–9, 203, 223, 228–9, 263–4; Napoleon to Clarke, 20 February, 18, 26 March, 18 April, 4, 6 May 1807, ibid. nos. 14338, 14719, 14910, 15303, 15526, 15538, 7:201–02, 370, 461, 635–6, 741–2, 753; Napoleon to Mortier, 20 February 1807, ibid. no. 14347, 7:205–06; Napoleon to Jérôme, 23, 25 February, 13, 14, 19, 24 March, 6 May 1807, ibid. nos. 14380, 14599, 14608, 14624, 14745, 14860, 15552, 7:216–17, 224, 325, 332, 382, 434–44, 755–6; Napoleon to Berthier, 24 February, 23, 30, 31 March, 22 May 1807, ibid. nos. 14387, 14822, 14992, 15015, 15685, 7:291, 418–19, 498–9, 510–12, 814; Napoleon to Kellermann, 24 February, 20, 22 March, 21 April 1807, ibid. nos. 14392, 14774, 14811, 15379, 7:221, 397–8, 413–14, 668–70; Napoleon to Songis, 25 February 1807, ibid. no. 14405, 7:226; Napoleon to Rapp, 26 February 1807, ibid. no. 14417, 7:231; Napoleon to Soult, 26 (2 letters), 27 (2 letters), 28 February, 1, 5, 11, 18 (3 letters) March 1807, ibid. nos. 14418, 14429, 14430, 14445, 14455, 14488, 14569, 14729, 14730, 14731, 7:231–3, 237–9, 247–8, 252–3, 267, 307, 375–7; Napoleon to Bernadotte, 27, 28 February, 6 March 1807, ibid. nos. 14423, 14432, 14489, 7:234–5, 240–1, 268; Napoleon to Lefebvre, 27 February 1807, ibid. no. 14428, 7:237; Napoleon to Talleyrand, 27 February, 6 March 1807, ibid. nos. 14451, 14516, 7:239–40, 283–4;

Napoleon to Dejean, 28 February, 6, 15, 19, 20, 25 March, 22, 30 April, 19 May 1807, ibid. nos. 14437, 14501, 14649, 14741, 14767, 14886, 15275, 15393, 15659, 1572, 7:243–4, 274–5, 342–3, 381, 393–4, 444–6, 678–9, 718–20, 802; Napoleon to Daru, 6, 20, 22, 26 March, 29 May 1807, ibid. nos. 14497, 14764, 14801, 14911, 15768, 7:271–3, 391–2, 409, 461–2, 846–8; Napoleon to Ney, 6 March 1807, ibid. no. 14511, 7:280–1; Napoleon to Lacuée, 19, 20, 30 March 1807, ibid. nos. 14744, 14775, 15006, 7:382, 398, 505–07; Napoleon to Eugène, 19, 23, 25 (2 letters), 31 March, 6 May 1807, ibid. nos. 14749, 14833, 14891, 15021, 15550, 7:384, 423–4, 448–9, 514–16, 754–5; Napoleon to Cambacérès, 26 March, 1 April 1807, ibid. nos. 14909, 15035, 7:522–3; 7:457–60; Napoleon to Champagny, 27 March 1807, ibid. no. 14924, 7:469–70; Napoleon to Bertrand, 28 March, 5 May 1807, ibid. nos. 14938, 15539, 7:475–6, 749–50; Napoleon to Savary, 29 March 1807, ibid. no. 14985, 7:495; Napoleon to Gaudin, 29 April 1807, ibid. no. 15462, 7:709–15; Napoleon to Brune, 30 May 1807, ibid. no. 15786, 7:854–6.

106. Napoleon to Dejean, 29 April 1807, *Napoleon Correspondance* no. 15456, 7:706.

107. Napoleon to Davout, 20 March 1807, *Napoleon Correspondance* no. 14766, 7:393.

108. Napoleon to Dejean, 6 March, 1807, *Napoleon Correspondance* no. 14501, 7:274.

109. Napoleon to Duroc, 23 February 1807, *Napoleon Correspondance* no. 14375, 7:215; Napoleon to Dombrowski, 27 February 1807, ibid. no. 14426, 7:236; Napoleon to Berthier, 1 March 1807, ibid. no. 14446, 7:248.

110. For key documents on the siege of Danzig, see: Napoleon to Lefebvre, 6, 12, 28 March, 11, 14, 22, 29 May 1807, *Napoleon Correspondance* nos. 14508, 14589, 14957, 15205, 15604, 15622, 15691, 15777, 7:278–9, 316, 483, 591–2, 777, 784, 816, 850; Napoleon to Mollien, 28 March 1807, ibid. no. 14961, 7:485; Napoleon to Berthier, 29 April 1807, ibid. no. 15447, 7:702; Napoleon to Lannes, 14 May 1807, ibid. no. 15620, 7:783.

111. Napoleon to Lefebvre, 12 March 1807, *Napoleon Correspondance* no. 14589, 7:316.

112. Napoleon to Frederick William III, 26 February 1807, *Napoleon Correspondance* no. 14415, 7:230.

113. Napoleon to Talleyrand, 9 March 1807, *Napoleon Correspondance* no. 14540, 7:294–5. For other key documents concerning Napoleon's diplomatic and military ends and means, see: Napoleon to

Talleyrand, 14, 19, 26 March, 12, 16, 23 April 1807, ibid. nos. 14629, 14756, 14920, 15233, 15299, 15407, 7:334, 387–8, 466–7, 604–06, 684–5.
114. Napoleon to Frederick William III, 29 April 1807, *Napoleon Correspondance* no. 15461, 7:708.
115. Napoleon to Josephine, 2 April 1807, *Napoleon Correspondance* no. 15055, 7:531.
116. Napoleon to Feth Ali, 17 January, 2 February, 14 March, 3 April 1807, *Napoleon Correspondance* nos. 14094, 14257, 15069, 7:99, 168, 536; Napoleon to Talleyrand, 23 February, 3, 6, 13 March, 26, 27 April 1807, ibid. nos. 14385, 14458, 14516, 14615, 14621, 15436, 15443, 7:218, 254–5, 283–4, 320, 331, 697–8, 700; Napoleon to Abbas Mirza, 14 March 1807, ibid. no. 14616; Napoleon to Berthier, 4 April 1807, ibid. no. 15085, 7:544.
117. Napoleon to Kellermann, 8 May 1807, *Napoleon Correspondance* no. 15585, 7:769.
118. Napoleon to Lefebvre, 22, 26 May 1807, *Napoleon Correspondance* nos. 15691, 15726, 7:816, 830; Napoleon to Murat, May 26, 1807, ibid. no. 15729, 7:831; Napoleon to Berthier, 27 May 1807, ibid. no 15733, 7:832.
119. For key documents on the campaign that ended with Friedland, see: Napoleon to Clarke, 6 June 1807, *Napoleon Correspondance* no. 15845, 7:883; Napoleon to Davout, 6 June 1807, ibid. no. 15847, 7:884; Napoleon to Ney, 6 June 1807, ibid. no. 15851, 7:885–6; Napoleon to Rapp, 6 June 1807, ibid. no. 15852, 7:886–7; Napoleon to Victor, 6 June 1807, ibid. no. 15853, 7:887; Napoleon to Bernadotte, 7 June 1807, ibid. no. 15854, 7:887–8; Napoleon to Soult, 8, 13 (2 letters) June 1807, ibid. nos. 15856, 15863, 7:888, 892–3; Napoleon to Murat, 12, 13, 14 June 1807, ibid. nos. 15857, 15861, 15865, 7:889, 891, 893–4; Napoleon to Lannes, 13 (2 letters) June 1807, ibid. nos. 15859, 15860, 7:889–90.
120. For the pursuit after Friedland that ended with Tilsit, see: Napoleon to Soult, 16 June 1807, *Napoleon Correspondance* no. 15869, 7:895; Napoleon to Davout, 17 June 1807, ibid. no. 15870, 7:896; Napoleon to Murat, 17 June 1807, ibid. nos. 15871, 15873, 7:896, 897; Napoleon to Berthier, 18 June 1807, ibid. no. 15872, 7:897.
121. Napoleon to Talleyrand, 24 June 1807, *Napoleon Correspondance* no. 15923, 7:915–16.
122. For insights into Tilsit, see: Constant, *Mémoires*, 1:426–9.
123. Napoleon to Josephine, 25 June 1807, *Napoleon Correspondance* no. 15924, 7:916.
124. Las Cases, *Mémorial*, 1:455.
125. Ibid.

126. Napoleon to Joseph, 4 July 1807, *Napoleon Correspondance* no. 15953, 7:929.
127. Las Cases, *Mémorial*, 1:305, 830–3.
128. Ibid., 1:833.
129. Napoleon to Josephine, 7 July 1807, *Napoleon Correspondance* no. 15982, 7:939.
130. Las Cases, *Mémorial*, 1:305.
131. Ibid., 1:830–1.
132. Napoleon to Alexander I, 4 July 1807, *Napoleon Correspondance* no. 15946, 7:924–6.
133. Napoleon to Alexander I, 6 (2 letters), 9 July 1807, *Napoleon Correspondance* nos. 15995, 15996, 15993, 7:933–4, 944–5.
134. *Talleyrand Mémoires*, 257.
135. Jaroslaw Czubaty and Ursula Phillips, *The Duchy of Warsaw, 1807-1815: A Napoleonic Outpost in Central Europe* (New York: Bloomsbury Academic, 2016).
136. Napoleon to Mollien, 30 July, 27 August, 15 November 1807, *Napoleon Correspondance* nos. 16074, 16248, 16817, 7:988–9, 1006–7, 1323–5.
137. Napoleon to Marie Walewska, 29 July 1807, *Napoleon Correspondance* no. 16072, 7:987.

Chapter 13: The Kingmaker

1. *Talleyrand Mémoires*, 409.
2. Napoleon to Elisa, 17 August 1809, *Napoleon Correspondance* no. 21825, 9:1025.
3. Leon Lecestre, ed., *Lettres Inédite de Napoleon I*, 2 vols (Paris: Plon, 1897), 1:386, no. 558.
4. *Talleyrand Mémoires*, 345.
5. D.G. Wright, *Napoleon and Europe* (New York: Pearson, 1984); Michael Broers, *Europe Under Napoleon, 1799-1815* (New York; Arnold, 1996); Phillip Dwyer, *Napoleon and Europe* (New York: Routledge, 2001); Geoffrey Ellis, *The Napoleonic Empire* (New York: Palgrave Macmillan, 2007).
6. Caulaincourt, *With Napoleon in Russia*, 41.
7. Las Cases, *Mémorial*, 2:1429.
8. Napoleon to Eugène, 14 April 1806, *Napoleon Correspondance* no. 11898, 6:325.
9. Napoleon to Madame Mère, 18 April 1807, *Napoleon Correspondance* no. 15316, 7:642.

10. Constant, *Mémoires*, 1:359.
11. Napoleon to Maximilien of Bavaria, 21 December 1805, *Napoleon Correspondance* no. 11208, 5:903.
12. Napoleon to Eugène, 31 December 1805, *Napoleon Correspondance* no. 1124, 5:920.
13. Napoleon to Eugène, 3 January 1806, *Napoleon Correspondance* no. 11245, 6:21.
14. Napoleon to Elisa, 9 January 1806, *Napoleon Correspondance* no. 11273, 5:34.
15. Napoleon to Augusta, 19 January 1806, *Napoleon Correspondance* no. 11293, 6:45.
16. Carola Oman, *Napoleon's Viceroy: Eugène de Beauharnais* (London: Hodder and Stoughton, 1966).
17. Napoleon to Eugène, 7 June 1805, *Napoleon Correspondance* no. 10224, 5:386–8.
18. Napoleon to Eugène, 27 July 1805, *Napoleon Correspondance* no. 10471, 5:518.
19. Napoleon to Eugène, 7 June 1805, *Napoleon Correspondance* no. 10224, 5:386–8.
20. Juan Carlos Camignari, *Napoleon and Italy, 1805-1815* (New York: Histories and Collections, 2016).
21. Napoleon to Eugène, 14 June 1805, *Napoleon Correspondance* no. 10272, 5:418–19.
22. For insights on Louis and Hortense, see: Constant, *Mémoires*, 1:138–43. For Hortense's views on her relationship with Louis, see: Hortense, *Mémoires*, 78–9, 85–100, 105, 106–07, 108, 110, 114–16, 127–31, 138–9, 167–88, 213–14.
23. For the rumours, see: Las Cases, *Mémorial*, 1:670; Constant, *Mémoires*, 1:139–40; Sophie Henriette Cohendet, *Mémoires sur Napoleon et Marie Louise* (Paris: Mercure de France, 2014), 15–18; Fouché, *Mémoires*, 170–1, 205. For Napoleon's feelings and behaviour toward his nephew, namesake and heir, see: Hortense, *Mémoires*, 106, 111, 138, 194–5.
24. Napoleon to Hortense, 15 August 1804, *Napoleon Correspondance* no. 9103, 4:819.
25. Napoleon to Hortense, 8 January 1807, *Napoleon Correspondance* no. 13987, 7:51.
26. Napoleon to Hortense, 29 January 1807, *Napoleon Correspondance* no. 14210, 7:151.
27. Lentz, *Napoleon et la Conquête de l'Europe*, 111–12.
28. Napoleon to Louis, 7 January 1807, *Napoleon Correspondance* no. 13979, 7:47.

29. Napoleon to Louis, 4 April 1807, *Napoleon Correspondance* no. 15099, 7:551–2.
30. Napoleon to Hortense, 2 May 1807, *Napoleon Correspondance* no. 15498, 7:729.
31. Napoleon to Josephine, 2 May 1807, *Napoleon Correspondance* no. 15502, 7:731.
32. Napoleon to Hortense, 17 July 1808, *Napoleon Correspondance* no. 18602, 8:900.
33. Napoleon to Fouché, 20 May 1807, *Napoleon Correspondance* no. 15668, 7:806.
34. Napoleon to Hortense, 20 May 1807, *Napoleon Correspondance* no. 15669, 7:806.
35. Napoleon to Monge, 20 May 1807, *Napoleon Correspondance* no. 15673, 7:808.
36. Napoleon to Josephine, 24 May 1807, *Napoleon Correspondance* no. 15710, 7:825.
37. Cohendet, *Mémoires sur Napoleon et Marie Louise*, 25. Hubert Cole, *The Betrayers: Joachim and Caroline Murat* (New York: Saturday Evening Press, 1972).
38. Las Cases, *Mémorial*, 1:673.
39. Hortense, *Mémoires*, 175.
40. For insights into Murat and Caroline, see: Hortense, *Mémoires*, 57, 59, 61, 71, 91, 125–6, 136, 141, 164, 166–7, 211–12.
41. Napoleon to Murat, 30 July 1806, *Napoleon Correspondance* no. 12616, 6:671.
42. Napoleon to Murat, 21 August 1807, *Napoleon Correspondance* no. 16214, 7:1052.
43. Owen Connelly, *The Gentle Bonaparte: A Biography of Joseph, Napoleon's Elder Brother* (New York: Macmillan, 1968); Thierry Lentz, *Joseph Bonaparte* (Paris: Perrin, 2016).
44. Buonaparte to Joseph, 18 April 1791, *Napoleon Correspondance* no. 48, 1:99.
45. Las Cases, *Mémorial*, 1:672.
46. Napoleon to Joseph, 4 May 1807, *Napoleon Correspondance* no. 15528, 7:743.
47. Glenn Lamar, *Jérôme Bonaparte: The War Years, 1800-1815* (Westport, Conn.: Praeger, 2000).
48. Napoleon to Talleyrand, 30 July 1804, *Napoleon Correspondance* no. 9039, 4:786.
49. Napoleon to Jérôme, 6 May 1805, *Napoleon Correspondance* no. 9986, 5:274.

50. Napoleon to Jérôme, 2 June 1805, *Napoleon Correspondance* no. 10194, 5:372.
51. Napoleon to Berthier, 18 May 1805, *Napoleon Correspondance* no. 10072, 5:316–17; Napoleon to Decrès, 18 May 1805, ibid. no. 10073, 5:317.
52. For key documents on the establishment of the Kingdom of Westphalia, see: Napoleon to Berthier, 19 August 1807, *Napoleon Correspondance* no. 16199, 7:104; Napoleon to Jérôme, 19 August, 15 November (2 letters), 17 December 1807, ibid. nos. 16207, 16812, 16813, 7:1050, 1321–2, 1359–60.
53. For key documents on Napoleon's matchmaking between Jérôme and Catherine of Württemberg, see: Napoleon to Frederic I of Württemberg, 20 October 1806, 5, 22, 25 August 1807, ibid. nos. 13295, 16122, 16216, 16234, 6:13295, 16122, 16216, 16234, 7:1008–09, 1053, 1061; Napoleon to Catherine of Württemberg, 6 August 1807, ibid. no. 16126, 7:1011; Napoleon to Cambacérès, 21 August 1807, ibid. no. 16210, 7:1051.
54. Napoleon to Catherine, 6 August 1807, *Napoleon Correspondance* no. 16126, 7:1011.
55. Constant, *Mémoires*, 1:362, 436–8.
56. Napoleon to Jérôme, 15 November 1807, *Napoleon Correspondance* no. 16812, 7:1321.
57. Napoleon to Jérôme, 15 November 1807, *Napoleon Correspondance* no. 16813, 7:1322.
58. Napoleon to Jérôme, 16 July 1808, *Napoleon Correspondance* no. 18584, 8:892. For other key documents on the conflicts between Napoleon and Jérôme, see: Napoleon to Jérôme, 4, 30 January, 16 July 1808, 15 March, 26 September 1809, *Napoleon Correspondance* nos. 16955, 17116, 18584, 20385, 22202, 8:27, 115–16, 892; ibid. no. 20385, 9:252–3, 1270–1.
59. Margery Weiner, *The Parvenu Sisters: Elisa, Pauline, and Caroline Bonaparte* (London: Murray, 1964).
60. Napoleon to Elisa, 13 March 1808, *Napoleon Correspondance* no. 17396, 8:262.
61. Napoleon to Marie Louise de Bourbon, 6 January, 11, 28 April 1806, 8 January, 31 August, 16, 23 September 1807, *Napoleon Correspondance* nos. 11263, 11882, 12010, 13991, 16264, 16390, 16407, 6:28–9, 317, 380–1, 7:53–4, 1074, 1129, 1138.
62. Napoleon to Marie Louis of Tuscany, 23 September 1807, *Napoleon Correspondance* no. 16407, 7:1138.

63. Napoleon to Duroc, 25 September 1807, *Napoleon Correspondance* no. 16414, 7:1140.
64. Napoleon to Marie Louise of Etruria, 5 December 1807, *Napoleon Correspondance* no. 16854, 7:1339.
65. Flora Fraser, *Pauline Bonaparte: Venus of Europe* (New York: Anchor, 2010); Florence de Baudus, *Pauline Bonaparte* (Paris: Perrin, 2016).
66. Bonaparte to Pauline, 7 January 1803, *Napoleon Correspondance* no. 7408, 4:22.
67. Bonaparte to Joseph, 4 November 1803, *Napoleon Correspondance* no. 8216, 4:425.
68. Bonaparte to Pauline, 11 November 1803, *Napoleon Correspondance* no. 8252, 4:439.
69. Bonaparte to Pauline, 6 April 1804, *Napoleon Correspondance* no. 8789, 4:666.
70. Constant, *Mémoires*, 1:365–6.
71. For the quote, see: Napoleon to Stephanie, 13 July 1806, *Napoleon Correspondance* no. 12498, 6:613. See also: Napoleon to Charles of Baden, 4 January 1806, *Napoleon Correspondance* no. 11255, 6:25; Napoleon to Eugène, 3 March 1806, ibid. no. 11592, 6:184, Napoleon to Stephanie, 13 August 1806, ibid. no. 12709, 6:714.
72. Napoleon to Charles of Baden, 6 January 1809, *Napoleon Correspondance* no. 16958, 8:30.
73. Napoleon to Charles Frederick of Baden, 7 January 1808, *Napoleon Correspondance* no. 16959, 8:30.
74. For insights into Stephanie and her marriage, see: Hortense, *Mémoires*, 164–5.
75. For insights into the relationship between Napoleon and Lucien, see: Constant, *Mémoires*, 1:350–9.
76. Napoleon to Jérôme, 9 June 1805, *Napoleon Correspondance* no. 10244, 5:401.
77. Napoleon to Joseph, 20 December 1807, *Napoleon Correspondance* no. 16907, 7:1367.
78. Napoleon to Joseph, 11 March 1808, *Napoleon Correspondance* no. 17376, 8:251–2.
79. Napoleon to Borghese, 31 January 1810, *Napoleon Correspondance* no. 23007, 9:1664.
80. For key documents on the crisis with and takeover of Portugal, see: Napoleon to Charles IV, 8 September, 12 October, 13 November 1807, *Napoleon Correspondance* nos. 16336, 16508, 16776, 7:1106, 1181, 1306; Napoleon to Clarke, 12, 16 (2 letters), 28 October, 6, 23 (3 letters)

December 1807, ibid. nos. 16509, 16559, 16560, 16642, 16858, 16915, 16916, 16917, 7:1181, 1196–7, 1243, 1341, 1372–4; Napoleon to Junot, 31 October, 8, 12 November, 20, 23 December 1807, 7, 28 January, 4 March 1808, ibid. nos. 16673, 16739, 16772, 16908, 16825, 16963, 17094, 17327, 7:1256–8, 1288–9, 1303–05, 1369–70, 1376–8, 8:32, 102–03, 223–4; Napoleon to Decrès, 11 May 1808, ibid. no. 17843, 8:496–7.

81. Napoleon to Charles IV, 12 October 1807, *Napoleon Correspondance* no. 16508, 7:1181.
82. Napoleon to Charles IV, 13 November 1807, *Napoleon Correspondance* no. 16776, 7:1306.
83. Napoleon to Junot, 7 January 1808, *Napoleon Correspondance* no. 16963, 8:32.
84. Ferdinand Prince of Asturias to Napoleon, 11 October 1807, *Talleyrand Mémoires*, 272.
85. Napoleon to Charles IV, 10 January 1808, *Napoleon Correspondance* no. 16973, 8:36. See also, Napoleon to Charles IV, 25 February 1808, ibid. no. 17279, 8:202–03.
86. For key documents on the military buildup in Spain, see: Napoleon to Clarke, 19, 20 (2 letters), 26 February 1808, *Napoleon Correspondance* nos. 17239, 17242, 17246, 17285, 8:178–80, 181–2, 205–06; Napoleon to Murat, 20 February (2 letters), 6, 8, 9, 26, 27, 30 March, 1, 6 April 1808, ibid. nos. 17250, 17251, 17339, 17347, 17356, 17505, 17511, 17523, 17545, 17568, 8:185–8, 230–1, 235, 240–2, 314–15, 319–20, 326, 339–40, 352–3; Napoleon to Champagny, 9 March 1808, ibid. no. 17350, 8:236–7; Napoleon to Berthier, 19 March 1808, ibid. nos. 17424, 8:278–88; Napoleon to Bessières, 26, 30 March, 6, 16 April 1808, ibid. nos. 17486, 17522, 17559, 17622, 8:306–07, 325, 347–8, 381–3; Napoleon to Caulaincourt, 31 March 1808, ibid. no. 17524, 8:326–37.

    For key documents on Napoleon's moves to depose the Bourbons and take title to Spain, see: Napoleon to Louis, 27 March 1808, *Napoleon Correspondance* no. 17510, 8:318–19; Napoleon to Murat, 9, 10, 17, 21, 22, 24, 24, 25, 28, 29, 30 April, 1, 2 (2 letters), 5 (2 letters), 8, 12 May 1808, ibid. nos. 17581, 17592, 17641, 17673, 17678, 17686, 17698, 17715, 17723, 17734, 17743, 17750, 17758, 17759, 17778, 17779, 17815, 17881, 8:360, 366, 393–4, 411, 413, 417, 422, 430–1, 434–5, 440, 444–5, 447–8, 451–4, 463–4, 481–2, 517–18; Napoleon to Eugène, 18 April 1808, ibid. no. 17651, 8:400; Napoleon to Joseph, 18 April 1808, ibid. no. 17654, 8:402–03; Napoleon to Bessières, 25, 30 April, 2 May 1808, ibid. nos. 17687, 17738, 17754, 8:417–18, 442, 450; Napoleon to Marie Louis of Spain, 29 April 1808, ibid. no. 8:439; Napoleon to Duroc, 20 April 1808, ibid. no. 17741, 8:44; Napoleon to Talleyrand, 1,

9 May 1808, ibid. nos. 17751, 17826, 8:448–9, 487; Napoleon to Fouché, 9 May 1808, ibid. no. 17821, 8:484; Napoleon to Mollien, 9 May 1808, ibid. no. 17823, 8:485; Napoleon to Cambacérès, 15 May 1808, ibid. no. 17907, 8:535.
87. Napoleon to Murat, 14 March 1808, *Napoleon Correspondance* no. 17401, 8:264–5.
88. Napoleon to Murat, 15 April 1808, *Napoleon Correspondance* no. 17618, 8:380.
89. Napoleon to Louis, 27 March 1808, *Napoleon Correspondance* no. 17510, 319.
90. Napoleon to Joseph, 18 April 1808, *Napoleon Correspondance* no. 17654, 8:402–03.
91. Napoleon to Murat, 10 April 1808, *Napoleon Correspondance* no. 17592, 8:366. See also: Napoleon to Murat, 9 April 1808, ibid. no. 17581, 8:360.
92. Napoleon to Murat, 17 April 1808, *Napoleon Correspondance* no. 17641, 8:393–4.
93. Napoleon to Murat, 25, 26, 28, 29, 30 April 1808, *Napoleon Correspondance* nos. 17698, 17715, 17723, 1734, 17743, 8:422, 430–1, 434–5, 440, 444–5.
94. Napoleon to Ferdinand, 16 April 1808, *Napoleon Correspondance* no. 17624, 8:386–7.
95. For key documents on Napoleon's diplomacy at Bayonne, see: Constant, *Mémoires*, 1:476–88.
96. Napoleon to Talleyrand, 25 April 1808, *Napoleon Correspondance* no. 17699, 8:423.
97. Las Cases, *Mémorial*, 1:821.
98. Napoleon to Talleyrand, 1 May 1808, *Napoleon Correspondance* no. 17751, 8:448.
99. Napoleon to Murat, 25 May 1808 (with attached proclamation), *Napoleon Correspondance* no. 18092, 8:630–1.
100. *Talleyrand Mémoires*, 354.
101. Napoleon to Joseph, 16 June 1808, *Napoleon Correspondance* no. 18331, 8:766.
102. Napoleon to Murat, 2, 5, 6, 7 (with attached proclamation) June 1808, nos. 18214, 18238, 18240, 18248, 8:698, 712–14, 715, 718–21.

Chapter 14: The Sisyphus of the Peninsula

1. Napoleon to Joseph, 10 May 1808, *Napoleon Correspondance* no. 17829, 8:489.

2. Napoleon to Talleyrand, 1 May 1808, *Napoleon Correspondance* no. 17751, 8:448.
3. David Gates, *The Spanish Ulcer: A History of the Peninsular War* (New York: Da Capo Press, 1986); Charles Esdaile, *The Peninsular War: A New History* (New York: Palgrave Macmillan, 2003); Charles Esdaile, *Fighting Napoleon: Guerrillas, Bandits, and Adventurers in Spain, 1808-1814* (New Haven, Conn.: Yale University Press, 2004).
4. For key letters on Napoleon's attempts to make the war in Spain pay for itself, see: Napoleon to Murat, 2, 11, 13, 15 May 1808, *Napoleon Correspondance* nos. 17758, 17857, 17888, 17921, 8:451, 504–05, 522–3, 544–5; Napoleon to Azanza, 4 June 1808, ibid. no. 18230, 8:707–08; Napoleon to Joseph, 12 July 1808, ibid. no. 18539, 8:862–3.
5. Napoleon to Junot, 15, 18, 29 May 1808, *Napoleon Correspondance* nos. 17914, 17980, 18156, 8:539–40, 575, 668.
6. For command decisions during the summer of 1808, see: Napoleon to Murat, 2, 30 May, 13 June 1808, *Napoleon Correspondance* nos. 17759, 18168, 18291, 8:452, 677, 745–6; Napoleon to Jourdan, 17 July 1808, ibid. no. 18604, 8:901.
7. Napoleon to Joseph, 20 July 1808, *Napoleon Correspondance* no. 18625, 8:911.
8. For the best overviews of how Napoleon saw the strategic situation before Bailen, see: Napoleon to Savary, 13 July 1808, *Napoleon Correspondance* nos. 18553, 8:871–4; Napoleon to Joseph, 21 July, 2 August 1808, ibid. nos. 18639, 18683, 8:917–22, 942–4. For key documents on the campaign to crush Spanish resistance from May to July 1808, see: Napoleon to Murat, 6 (2 letters), 9, 15, 16, 19 (3 letters), 30 May, 4, 5, 8 June 1808, *Napoleon Correspondance* nos. 17787, 17788, 17824, 17921, 17947, 17995, 17996, 17997, 18236, 18238, 18249, 8:468–9, 485–6, 544–5, 558, 581–4, 677, 711, 712–14, 721; Napoleon to Bessières, 14 May (2 letters), 3 June (2 letters), 1 July 1808, ibid. nos. 17890, 17891, 18220, 18221, 18453, 8:524–56, 700–03, 820; Napoleon to Berthier, 30 May, 4, 15 June 1808, 2, 3, 7, 9, 14, 20, 30 July 1808, ibid. nos. 18164, 18232, 18304, 18463, 18466, 18490, 18510, 18854, 18625, 18676, 8:672–3, 709, 753–4, 824–5, 826–7, 836–7, 847–8, 874–6, 911–12, 937–9; Napoleon to Reille, 2, 8, 9 July 1808, ibid. nos. 18464, 18509, 18518, 8:825–6, 846–7, 851–2; Napoleon to Joseph, 12, 13, 19 July 1808, ibid. nos. 18540, 18552, 18619, 8:863, 870–1, 909; Napoleon to Savary, 3 August 1808, ibid. no. 18687, 8:947.
9. Napoleon to Murat, 19 May 1808, *Napoleon Correspondance* no. 17995, 8:581.

10. For key letters on Napoleon's attempts to organize expeditions to takeover Spanish colonies, see: Napoleon to Murat, 18, 19, 21 (2 letters), 26 May 1808, *Napoleon Correspondance* nos. 17989, 17995, 18026, 18028, 18107, 8:578, 581, 600–02, 639–40; Napoleon to Decrès, 21, 26 May, 7 July 1808, ibid. nos. 18018, 18100, 18496, 8:595–6, 634–7, 839–40; Napoleon to Gregorio de la Cuesta, 25 May 1808, ibid. no. 18089, 8:629.
11. Napoleon to Caulaincourt, 5 August 1808, *Napoleon Correspondance* no. 18688, 8:948.
12. Napoleon to Louis, 17 August 1808, *Napoleon Correspondance* no. 18712, 8:959.
13. Napoleon to Junot, 19 October 1808, *Napoleon Correspondance* no. 19075, 8:1142.
14. For key letters on Napoleon's war in Spain after Bailen and before his arrival, see: Napoleon to Clarke, 22 August 1808, *Napoleon Correspondance* no. 18736, 18865, 8:970–2, 1050–3; Napoleon to Dejean, 22 August 1808, ibid. no. 18738, 8:974–6; Napoleon to Lacuée, 10 September 1808, ibid. no. 18881, 8:1060,

    For the best overviews of how Napoleon saw the strategic situation after Bailen and before his arrival, see: Napoleon to Joseph, 30 August, 1, 14 September 1808, *Napoleon Correspondance* nos. 18797, 18805, 18915, 8:1004–07, 1011–19, 1074–7.
15. Napoleon to Gregorio Cuesta, 25 May 1808, ibid. no. 18089, 8:629; Napoleon to Murat, 26 May 1808, ibid. no. 18107, 8:639–40.
16. Napoleon to Decrès, 7 July 1808, *Napoleon Correspondance* no. 18496, 8:840.
17. Napoleon to Alexander, 8 July 1808, *Napoleon Correspondance* no. 18500, 8:841–2.
18. Napoleon to Joseph, 19 July 1808, *Napoleon Correspondance* no. 18619, 8:909.
19. Napoleon to Joseph, 31 July 1808, *Napoleon Correspondance* no. 18680, 8:940.
20. Napoleon to Berthier, 18 September 1808, *Napoleon Correspondance* no. 18931, 8:1090–1.
21. Napoleon to Frederick I, 7 September 1808, *Napoleon Correspondance* no. 18849, 8:1041–3.
22. For key accounts on the Erfurt conference, see: Constant, *Mémoires*, 1:498–507; *Talleyrand Mémoires*, 299–335.
23. Cambacérès, *Mémoires*, 232.
24. *Talleyrand Mémoires*, 304.

25. Napoleon to Francis I, 14 October 1808, *Napoleon Correspondance* no. 19060, 8:1135.
26. Napoleon to George III, 12 October 1808, *Napoleon Correspondance* no. 19033, 8:1131–2.
27. Napoleon to Romanzov, 18 November 1808, *Napoleon Correspondance* no. 19314, 8:1243; Napoleon to Champagny, [n.d.], ibid. no. 19323, 8:1246–7.
28. Napoleon to Champagny, 4 January 1809, *Napoleon Correspondance* no. 19684, 8:1407.
29. Napoleon to Josephine, 11–13 October, 1808, *Napoleon Correspondance* no. 19050, 8:1130.
30. Napoleon to Alexander I, 14 October 1808, *Napoleon Correspondance* no. 19058, 8:1134.
31. Caulaincourt, *With Napoleon in Russia*, 376.
32. For this and other details of their relationship at Erfurt, see: Las Cases, *Mémorial*, 1:834–7.
33. Richard von Metternich, ed., *The Memoirs of Prince Metternich*, 2:248.
34. *Talleyrand Mémoires*, 333.
35. Napoleon to Joseph, 13 October 1808, *Napoleon Correspondance* no. 19056, 8:1133.
36. For key documents on Napoleon's Spanish campaign, see: Napoleon to Dejean, 29 October, 5 November 1808, *Napoleon Correspondance* nos. 19164, 19196, 8:1177–8, 1191; Napoleon to Lery, 10 November 1808, ibid. no. 19251, 8:1208; Napoleon to Joseph, 10 November, 5, 22 December 1808, 10, 11, 16 January 1809, ibid. nos. 19233, 19443, 19623, 19770, 19788, 19873, 8:1209, 1299–1300, 1366–7, 1447–9, 1457–9, 1507–08; Napoleon to Berthier, 12 November, 9, 22 (2 letters), 23, 27, 31 December 1808, ibid. nos. 19238, 19465, 19616, 19617, 19626, 19628, 19649, 19695, 8:1212, 1308–09, 1318–19, 1376–80, 1387–8, 1413; Napoleon to Belliard, 5 December 1808, ibid. no. 19437, 8:1295–6; Napoleon to Clarke, 15 December 1808, 13 January 1809, ibid. nos. 19521, 1808, 8:1330, 1471; Napoleon to Kellermann, 21 December 1808, ibid. no. 19606, 8:1366–7; Napoleon to Bessières, 24 January 1809, ibid. no. 19882, 8:1514–15.

    For secondary sources, see: Chandler, *Campaigns of Napoleon*, 625–60.
37. Napoleon to Joseph, 16 January 1809, *Napoleon Correspondance* no. 19875, 8:1509.
38. Napoleon to Fouché, 7 December 1808, *Napoleon Correspondance* no. 19458, 8:1306.
39. Napoleon to Caulaincourt, 7 January 1809, *Napoleon Correspondance* no. 19706, 8:1317.

40. Napoleon to Clarke, 31 December 1809, *Napoleon Correspondance* no. 19657, 8:1384.

Chapter 15: The Gatekeeper of Vienna

1. For key accounts of Napoleon's confrontation with Talleyrand, see: Napoleon to Talleyrand, 27 January 1809, *Napoleon Correspondance* no 19945, 8:1544; Napoleon to Champagny, 28 January 1809, ibid. no. 19946, 8:1544–5; Hortense, *Mémoires*, 221–3.
2. Jean Cambacérès, *Mémoires Inedits*, 2 vols (Paris: Perrin, 1999), 2:250.
3. Napoleon to Fouché, 27 January 1809, *Napoleon Correspondance* no. 19937, 8:1541.
4. Étienne Pasquier, *Histoire de mon Temps: Mémoires de Chancellor Pasquier*, 6 vols (Paris: Plon, 1893–4), 1:358.
5. Richard von Metternich, ed., *The Memoirs of Prince Metternich*, 2:268–9.
6. Napoleon to Caulaincourt, 6 February 1809, *Napoleon Correspondance* no. 19976, 9:27.
7. For the best biography, see: Emmanuel de Waresquiel, *Talleyrand: Le Prince Immobile* (Paris: Fayard, 2003).
8. For Napoleon's most comprehensive explanation of the 1809 war with Austria, see: Las Cases, *Mémorial*, 2:1043–86. For secondary works, see: Chandler, *Campaigns of Napoleon*, 663–736; Robert M. Epstein, *Napoleon's Last Victory and the Emergence of Modern War* (Topeka: University Press of Kansas, 1994).

    For key documents on Napoleon's grand strategic outlook, see: Napoleon to Caulaincourt, 14 January, 23 February, 6, 21 March 1809, *Napoleon Correspondance* nos. 19824, 20105, 20238, 20472, 8:1479–81; 9:97–8, 165–7, 299–300, Napoleon to Frederick of Württemberg, 17 March 1809, ibid. no. 20435, 280–1.

    For key documents on Napoleon's military preparations for war with Austria, see: Napoleon to Eugène, 29 October 1808, 7, 12, 13, 14 January, 7, 13, 14 February, 14, 15 (2 letters), 16 (2 letters), 17, 18, 22, 28 March 1809, *Napoleon Correspondance* nos. 19168, 10799, 19811, 19833, 19887, 19888, 19987, 20024, 20037, 20366, 20379, 20381, 20382, 20400, 20401, 20431,20445, 20498, 20596, 8:1179–80, 1421–2, 1463–7, 1472–3, 1485–6, 1517–19, 9:33–4, 54, 60–2, 244–5, 250–2, 261–3, 277, 285, 313–14, 365–6; Napoleon to Clarke, 26 November, 21 December 1808, 1, 10, 11, 24 (2 letters) January, 13 (2 letters) February, 1, 12, 13, 23 (2 letters) March 1809, ibid. nos. 19393, 19951, 19766, 19780, 20015, 20016, 20166, 20339, 20343, 20344, 20514, 20515, 8:1274–5, 1358–9, 1393–4, 1444–5, 1454–5, 9:48–51, 126–8, 226–8, 230–6, 321–5; Napoleon to Lacuée, 5 December 1808, ibid. no. 19446, 8:1301; Napoleon to Borghese, 13 February 1809, ibid. no. 20014, 9:47; Napoleon to Berthier, 4, 6 (2 letters), 23 March 1809, ibid. nos. 20207, 20235, 20237, 20508,, 9:147–8, 162, 163–4, 318; Napoleon to Davout, 4, 17 March 1809, ibid. nos. 20219, 20424, 9:155, 273–4; Napoleon to Dejean, 16, 29 March 1809, ibid. nos. 20397, 20612, 9:260, 373–4; Napoleon to Daru, 25, 28 March 1809, ibid. nos. 20541, 20591, 9:336–8, 362–4.

For key documents on Napoleon's diplomatic preparations for war with Austria, see: Napoleon to Champagny, 7 (2 letters), 14, 24 (2 letters), 29 January, 8 February, 1 March (3 letters) 1809, *Napoleon Correspondance* nos. 19706, 19707, 19823, 19884, 19885, 19955, 19995, 20162, 20163, 20164, 8:1417–18, 1478–9, 1510, 1549, 9:39, 124–5; Napoleon to Alexander, 14 January 1809, ibid. no. 19818, 8:1476; Napoleon to Charles, Rhine Confederation Prince Primate, 15 January 1808, ibid. no. 19845, 8:1492; Napoleon to Charles Frederick of Baden, 15 January, 4 March 1809, ibid. nos. 19846, 20211, 8:1492–3, 9:150–1; Napoleon to Louis of Baden, 15 January 1809, ibid. no. 19847, 8:1493; Napoleon to Frederick Augustus, 15 January, 21 February 1809, ibid. nos. 19852, 20098, 8:1495, 9:93–4; Napoleon to Frederick of Württemberg, 15 January, 14 February 1809, ibid. nos. 19855, 20039, 8:1496, 9:63; Napoleon to Jérôme, 15 January 1809, ibid. no. 19854, 8:1496–7; Napoleon to Louis of Hesse-Darmstadt, 15 January 1809, ibid. no. 19859, 8:1500; Napoleon to Maximilien Joseph of Bavaria, 15 January 1809, ibid. no. 19860, 8:1501; Napoleon to Otto, 15 January 1809, ibid. no. 19861, 8:1501; Napoleon to Frederick William, 31 January 1809, ibid. no. 19959, 8:1551.

For key documents on Napoleon's propaganda and espionage preparations for war with Austria, see: Napoleon to Champagny, 13 January, 20, 21, 26 February, 14, 17 March 1809, *Napoleon Correspondance* nos. 19805, 20067, 20088, 20141, 20355, 20411, 8:1470, 9:76, 84, 115, 240, 267; Napoleon to Fouché, 13 January, 20, 23 February, 8, 28 March 1809, ibid. nos. 19812, 20080, 20119, 20297, 20599, 8:1473, 9:81, 105, 202–03, 367; Napoleon to Regnaud, 26 February 1809, ibid. no. 20152, 9:119–20; Napoleon to Savary, 8 March 1809, ibid. no. 2300, 9:203.

For key documents on the Imperial Guard, see: Napoleon to Bessières, 14 January, 11, 21 February 1809, *Napoleon Correspondance* nos. 19820, 20000, 20085, 8:1477, 9:83, 412; Napoleon to Clarke, 28 January, 24, 31 March 1809, ibid. nos. 19950, 20505, 20643, 8:1546–7, 9:330, 401; Napoleon to Fouché, 29 August 1809, ibid. no. 21950, 9:1094.

9. Napoleon to Joseph, 27 January 1809, *Napoleon Correspondance* no. 19942, 8:1542.

10. Ibid.
11. Napoleon to Eugène, 21 February 1809, *Napoleon Correspondance* no. 20096, 9:92.
12. Napoleon to Eugène, 27 February 1809, *Napoleon Correspondance* no. 20156, 9:121.
13. Napoleon to Eugène, 14 March 1809, *Napoleon Correspondance* no. 20366, 9:244.
14. Napoleon to Caulaincourt, 6 March 1809, *Napoleon Correspondance* no. 20238, 9:165–7.
15. Napoleon to Caulaincourt, 14 January 1809, *Napoleon Correspondance* no. 19823, 8:1478–9.
16. Napoleon to Caulaincourt, 6 March 1809, *Napoleon Correspondance* no. 20238, 9:165.
17. Napoleon to Alexander, 25 March 1809, *Napoleon Correspondance* no. 20521, 9:327.
18. Napoleon to Caulaincourt, 14 January 1809, *Napoleon Correspondance* no. 19824, 8:1480. For other key documents on Napoleon's attempts to get Alexander to commit an army and campaign plan to the war, see: Napoleon to Caulaincourt, 6, 24 March 1809, *Napoleon Correspondance* nos. 20238, 20523, 9:165–7, 328–9.
19. Napoleon to Frederick Augustus of Saxony, 21 February 1809, *Napoleon Correspondance* no. 20098, 9:94.
20. Napoleon to Frederick of Württemberg, 17 March 1809, *Napoleon Correspondance* no. 20435, 9:280.
21. Napoleon to Eugène, 1 March 1809, *Napoleon Correspondance* no. 20173, 9:131.
22. Napoleon to Fouché, 23 March 1809, *Napoleon Correspondance* no. 20519, 9:326.
23. Napoleon to Kellermann, 29 April, 17 May 1809, *Napoleon Correspondance* nos. 20934, 21033, 9:544, 597; Napoleon to Clarke, 19, 20 (2 letters) May 1809, ibid. nos. 21047, 21053, 21054, 9:603, 606–7; Napoleon to Jérôme, 28 May 1809, ibid. no. 21086, 9:624.
24. Sherwig, *Guineas and Gunpowder*, 209.
25. Napoleon to Rhine Confederation princes, 15 February 1809, *Napoleon Correspondance* no. 20044, 9:65–6; Napoleon to Champagny, 21 February 1809, ibid. no. 20090, 9:85–9; Napoleon to Charles Frederick of Baden, 4 March 1809, ibid. no. 20211, 9:150; Napoleon to Dalberg, 4 March 1809, ibid. no. 20218, 9:154; Napoleon to Frederick of Württemberg, 4, 6 March 1809, ibid. nos. 20220, 20260, 20535, 9:155, 181–2, 280–1; Napoleon to Louis of Hesse-Darmstadt, 4 March 1809, ibid. no. 20226, 9:157; Napoleon to Maximilien Joseph, 4, 14 March

1809, ibid. nos. 20227, 20370, 9:158, 246; Napoleon to Otto, 4 March 1809, ibid. no. 20228,, 9:158–9, Napoleon to Frederick Augustus of Saxony, 6 March 1809, 20261, 9:182–3; Napoleon to Jérôme, 6 March 1809, ibid. no. 20262, 9:183.

26. Napoleon to Frederick of Württemberg, 17, 31 March 1809, *Napoleon Correspondance* nos. 20435, 20654, 9:280, 406.
27. Napoleon to Daru, 14 May 1809, *Napoleon Correspondance* no. 21021, 9:590.
28. For key documents on Napoleon's preliminary financial steps to pay for the war, see: Napoleon to Mollien, 26 January, 12, 25, 29 March 1809, *Napoleon Correspondance* nos. 19922, 20341, 20547, 20618, 8:1533, 9:229, 340–1, 377–8.
29. Epstein, *Napoleon's Last Victory*; James Arnold, *Napoleon Conquers Austria: The 1809 Campaign for Vienna* (Westport, Conn.: Praeger, 1995); James Arnold, *Crisis on the Danube: Napoleon's Danube Campaign of 1809* (New York: Paragon, 1990); John Gill, *1809: Thunder on the Danube, Napoleon's Defeat of the Hapsburgs* (New York: Frontline Books, 2010).
30. For the key documents on Napoleon's strategic outlook and plans on the campaign's eve, see: Napoleon to Berthier, 30 March, 8 April 1809, *Napoleon Correspondance* nos. 20619, 20749, 9:378–90, 448–50. For the best book on the entire campaign, see: Epstein, *Napoleon's Last Victory*.

    For key documents on the campaign's first phase, see: Napoleon to Berthier, 2, 5, 8, 10 (2 letters), 12, 16, 22, 29 April 1809, *Napoleon Correspondance* nos. 20667, 20709, 20750, 20791, 20792, 20815, 20838, 20885, 20921, 9:412, 431–2, 450–1, 470–1, 481–2, 492–3, 518, 537–8; Napoleon to Clarke, 4 April 1809, ibid. no. 20698, 9:425; Napoleon to Oudinot, 4 April 1809, ibid. no. 20705, 9:429–10; Napoleon to Bertrand, 6, 10 April 1809, ibid. nos. 20733, 20793, 9:441, 471–2; Napoleon to Davout, 17 (2 letters), 21, 22 (2 letters), 26 April 1809, ibid. nos. 20847, 20848, 20881, 20887, 20888, 20908, 9:497–9, 516, 519–21, 530–1; Napoleon to Lefebvre, 17, 18 April 1809, ibid. nos. 20850, 20868, 9:500, 508–09; Napoleon to Masséna, 17 (2 letters), 18, 19 April 1809, ibid. nos. 20852, 20853, 20869, 20876, 9:501–02, 509–10, 513–14; Napoleon to Maximilien Joseph of Bavaria, 17 April 1809, ibid. no. 20855, 9:503; Napoleon to Wrede, 17 April 1809, ibid. no. 20859, 9:505; Napoleon to Bernadotte, 19 April 1809, ibid. no. 20871, 9:511; Napoleon to Lannes, 22 April 1809, ibid. no. 20889, 9:521; Napoleon to Josephine, 6 May 1809, ibid. no. 20975, 9:589.

For key documents on Napoleon's propaganda and espionage during the campaign's first phase, see: Napoleon to Champagny, 1 April 1809, *Napoleon Correspondance* no. 20663, 9:410; Napoleon to Fouché, 9 April 1809, ibid. no. 20785, 9:466; Napoleon to Frederick of Württemberg, 17 April 1809, ibid. no. 20849, 9:499; Napoleon to Maximilien Joseph of Bavaria, 17 April 1809, ibid. no. 20854, 9:502; Napoleon to Otto, 17 April (2 letters) 1809, ibid. nos. 20856, 20857, 9:503–04; Napoleon to Talleyrand, 25 April 1809, ibid. no. 20902, 9:528.

For key documents on the Imperial Guard, see: Napoleon to Lacuée, 11 (3 letters), 25 April 1809, *Napoleon Correspondance* nos. 20811, 20812, 20813, 20900, 9:479–81, 527; Napoleon to Clarke, 25 April 1809, ibid. no. 20895, 9:524–5.

31. Napoleon to Frederick Augustus of Saxony, 21 April 1809, *Napoleon Correspondance* no. 20882, 9:516.
32. Napoleon to Eugène, 12 February 1810, *Napoleon Correspondance* no. 23091, 9:1702.
33. Napoleon to Lefebvre, 30 July 1809, *Napoleon Correspondance* no. 21663, 9:933–4.
34. For key documents on the Italian campaign, see: Napoleon to Eugène, 2, 12, 26, 27, 30 April, 10, 28 May 1809, ibid. nos. 20676, 20826, 20911, 20917, 20941, 20999, 21083, 21084, 21141, 9:416, 487, 532–3, 535, 547–8, 580–1, 621–3.
35. Napoleon to Eugène, 30 April 1809, *Napoleon Correspondance* no. 20942, 9:548
36. Ibid.
37. For key letters on the campaign's second phase of pursuing the Austrians and capturing Vienna, see: Napoleon to Berthier, 1, 9, 13, 14 May 1809, *Napoleon Correspondance* nos. 20943, 20991, 21008, 21017, 9:550–2, 576, 584, 588–9; Napoleon to Davout, 1 (2 letters), 5, 7, 9 (2 letters), 13 May 1809, ibid. nos. 20946, 20947, 20964, 20977, 20995, 20996, 21013, 9:552–3, 563, 570, 577–8, 587; Napoleon to Lannes, 4, 6, 11 May 1809, ibid. nos. 20959, 20976, 21000, 9:560, 569, 581; Napoleon to Masséna, 7 May 1809, ibid. no. 20978, 9:570; Napoleon to Clarke, 13, 29 May 1809, ibid. nos. 21010, 21092, 9:585–6, 628–9; Napoleon to Bernadotte, 15 May 1809, ibid. no. 21025, 9:592. For Napoleon's propaganda and espionage during the campaign's second phase, see: Napoleon to Otto, 29 April 1809, *Napoleon Correspondance* no. 20937, 9:546, 569. For key documents on Napoleon's diplomacy during this phase, see: Napoleon to Champagny, 12, 13 May 1809, *Napoleon Correspondance* nos. 21001, 21009, 9:582, 585.

38. Napoleon to Marshal Lannes, 31 May 1809, *Napoleon Correspondance* no. 21106, 9:635.
39. For key documents on preparations for the Wagram phase, see: Napoleon to Davout, 5, 7, 9, 16, 18, 21, 23 June 1809, *Napoleon Correspondance* nos. 21138, 21154, 21172, 21239, 21265, 21317, 21340, 9:650, 659–60, 669, 717, 731–2, 760; Napoleon to Clarke, 10 June 1809, ibid. no. 21182, 9:674–88; Napoleon to Eugène, 5, 6, 7 (2 letters), 10, 15, 16, 18 (3 letters), 19 (2 letters), 20, 23, 29 June, 7 July 1809, ibid. no. 21150, 21157, 21158, 21185, 21232, 21240, 21254, 21266, 21267, 21268, 21279, 21280, 21298, 21342, 21443, 21465, 9:651–2, 656–7, 661–3, 689–90, 713, 718–19, 726, 732–6, 740–2, 750–1, 773–4, 818–20, 832; Napoleon to Bertrand, 15 June 1809, ibid. no. 21229, 9:711–12.
40. Epstein, *Napoleon's Last Victory*, 165.
41. Napoleon to Josephine, 7 July 1809, *Napoleon Correspondance* no. 21467, 9:933.
42. Napoleon to Maret, 22 September 1809, *Napoleon Correspondance* no. 22157, 9:1229.
43. For key documents on the Walcheren campaign, see: Napoleon to Clarke, 8 (2 letters), 9, 10, 13, 16, 18, 22 (2 letters) August, 5, 7 September, 21 October 1809, *Napoleon Correspondance* nos. 21732, 21733, 21739, 21755, 21786, 21813, 21833, 21871, 21981, 22003, 22382, 9:967–71, 975–7, 986, 1001–02, 1016–17, 1030–1, 1056–9, 1122–6, 1137–9, 1360–1; Napoleon to Louis, 12, 13 August, 21 September 1809, ibid. nos. 21778, 21788, 22133, 9:997, 1003, 1215–16; Napoleon to Fouché, 16 August 1809, ibid. no. 21816, 9:1019; Napoleon to Decrès, 18, 22 August 1809, ibid. nos. 21837, 21874, 1032–3, 1059–60.
44. Napoleon to Clarke, 6 August 1809, *Napoleon Correspondance* no. 21712, 9:356.
45. Napoleon to Fouché, 9 August 1809, *Napoleon Correspondance* no. 21741, 9:978.
46. Napoleon to Clarke, 11 September 1809, *Napoleon Correspondance* no. 22032, 9:1159.
47. For key documents on the Fouché controversy, see: Napoleon to Fouché, 18, 24, 26 (2 letters) September 1809, *Napoleon Correspondance* nos. 22105, 22170, 22199, 22200, 9:1201, 1239, 1268–70; Napoleon to Clarke, 18 September 1809, ibid. no. 22014, 9:1200–01; Fouché, *Mémoires*, 213–17.
48. For other key documents on the negotiations, see: Napoleon to Champagny, 24 August, 4, 10, 13, 15 (2 letters), 21 (2 letters), 22, 30 September, 1, 6 October 1809, *Napoleon Correspondance* nos. 21890, 21970, 22021, 22068, 22088, 22089, 22129, 22130, 22135, 22226, 22235,

22261, 9:1070–2, 1115–16, 1149–51, 1175, 1191–3, 1211–12, 1217–18, 1283, 1288, 1301; Napoleon to Francis, 23 September 1809, ibid. no. 22153, 9:1225; Napoleon to Maret, 23 September 1809, ibid. no. 22157, 9:1229–30.
49. Napoleon to Francis, 22 July 1809, *Napoleon Correspondance* no. 21603, 9:904.
50. Napoleon to Champagny, 24 July 1809, *Napoleon Correspondance* no. 21618, 9:910–11.
51. Napoleon to Champagny, 19 August 1809, *Napoleon Correspondance* no. 21847, 9:1037–9.
52. Napoleon to Francis, 15 September 1809, *Napoleon Correspondance* no. 22086, 9:1197.
53. Napoleon to Maret annex, 23 September 1809, *Napoleon Correspondance* no. 22157, 9:1229–31.
54. Napoleon to Champagny annex, 26 September 1809, *Napoleon Correspondance* no. 22184, 9:1256–9.
55. Napoleon to François, 15 October 1809, *Napoleon Correspondance* no. 22365, 9:1351.

Chapter 16: The Antichrist

1. For Napoleon's most in-depth explanations of his views and acts concerning religion and politics, see: Las Cases, *Mémorial*, 2:1093–5. For other key documents on Napoleon's policy toward religion in France, see: Napoleon to Portalis, 17 May 1805, *Napoleon Correspondance* no. 10071, 5:316; Napoleon to Bigot, 11 July 1808, ibid. no. 18525, 8:855, Napoleon to Maret, 17 February 1809, ibid. no. 20059, 9:73; Chaptal, *Souvenirs*, 96–102.
2. Las Cases, *Mémorial*, 1:784.
3. Ibid., 1:785.
4. Ibid., 1:784–5.
5. Napoleon to the bishops, 28 May 1807, *Napoleon Correspondance* no. 15755, 7:842.
6. Napoleon to the bishops, 3 December 1805, *Napoleon Correspondance* no. 11142, 5:871.
7. Roberts, *Napoleon: A Life*, 272.
8. Las Cases, *Mémorial*, 1:784–6.
9. Roederer, *Oeuvres*, 3:334.
10. Napoleon to Champagny, 13 December 1805, *Napoleon Correspondance* no. 11164, 5:882.
11. Lentz, *France et l'Europe de Napoléon*, 242, 247.

12. For key document on Napoleon's policy toward the Jews, see: Napoleon to Champagny, 22 July, 23 August, 29 November 1806, *Napoleon Correspondance* nos. 12557, 12776, 13666, 6:642–3, 746–7, 1185–8.
13. Napoleon to Champagny, 23 August 1806, *Napoleon Correspondance* no. 12776, 6:746.
14. Napoleon to Champagny, 22 July 1806, *Napoleon Correspondance* nos. 12557, 12776, 6:642.
15. Napoleon to Champagny, 29 November 1806, *Napoleon Correspondance* no. 13662, 6:1185.
16. For good books on the subject, see: Patrick Girard, *La Revolution Française et les Juifs* (Paris: Hachette, 1989); Jacques Olivier Boudon, *Napoleon et les Cultes* (Paris: Fayard, 2002); Pierre Birnbaum, *L'Aigle et la Synagogue: Napoleon, les Juifs, et l'État* (Paris: Robert Lafford, 2007).
17. Napoleon to Fesch, 7 January 1806, *Napoleon Correspondance* no. 11267, 6:31.
18. Napoleon to Fesch, 14 February 1806, *Napoleon Correspondance* no. 11450, 6:118.
19. Napoleon to Fouché, 7 October 1804, *Napoleon Correspondance* no. 9328, 4:924–5.
20. Napoleon to Elisa, 24 May 1806, *Napoleon Correspondance* no. 12163, 6:452–4.
21. Napoleon to Joseph, 14 April 1807, *Napoleon Correspondance* no. 15255, 7:614.
22. Napoleon to Pius VII, 19 August 1805, *Napoleon Correspondance* no. 10604, 5:588.
23. Napoleon to Pius VII, 7 January 1806, *Napoleon Correspondance* no. 11268, 6:31–2; Napoleon to Fesch, 14 February 1806, ibid. no. 11450, 6:118.
24. Napoleon to Fesch, 22 December 1805, *Napoleon Correspondance* no. 11210, 5:904.
25. Napoleon to Pius VII, 13 February 1806, *Napoleon Correspondance* no. 11445, 6:114.
26. Napoleon to Pius VII, 18 April 1806, *Napoleon Correspondance* no. 11921, 6:336–7; Napoleon to Fesch, 16 May 1806, ibid. no. 12125, 6:431.
27. Napoleon to Lemarois, 1 June 1806, *Napoleon Correspondance* no. 12218, 6:481.
28. Napoleon to Champagny, 1 April 1806, *Napoleon Correspondance* no. 17542, 6:37–8.

29. Napoleon to Joseph, 6 May 1806, *Napoleon Correspondance* no. 12071, 6:408–09.
30. Napoleon to Eugène, 22 July 1807, *Napoleon Correspondance* no. 16052, 7:973–7.
31. For key documents on this crisis, see: Napoleon to Eugène, 10, 23 January 1808, *Napoleon Correspondance* nos. 16975, 17059, 8:37–8, 80; Napoleon to Joseph, 10 January 1808, ibid. no. 16976, 8:38–9; Napoleon to Champagny, 22 January 1808, ibid. no. 17052, 8:75–7; Napoleon to Eugène, 18 February, 20 March 1808, ibid. nos. 17227, 17443, 8:172, 286–7.
32. Napoleon to Eugène, 10 May 1809, *Napoleon Correspondance* no. 20999, 9:580.
33. Napoleon to Murat, 17 June 1809, *Napoleon Correspondance* no. 21263, 9:730–1.
34. Napoleon to Miollis, 19 June 1809, *Napoleon Correspondance* no. 21288, 9:745.
35. Lentz, *Napoleon et la Conquête de l'Europe*, 488.
36. Napoleon to Murat, 17 June 1809, *Napoleon Correspondance* no. 21262, 9:730.
37. Napoleon to Murat, 19 June 1809, *Napoleon Correspondance* no. 21289, 9:745–6.
38. Napoleon to Murat, 20 June 1809, *Napoleon Correspondance* no. 21307, 9:755.
39. Napoleon to Fouché, 18 July 1809, *Napoleon Correspondance* no. 21562, 9:885.
40. Napoleon to Fouché, 6 August 1809, *Napoleon Correspondance* no. 21716, 9:959.
41. Napoleon to Borghese, 5 September 1809, *Napoleon Correspondance* no. 21979, 9:1121.
42. Napoleon to Miollis, 10 August 1809, *Napoleon Correspondance* no. 21760, 9:989.
43. For key documents on the excommunication by and imprisonment of Pius, see: Napoleon to Eugène, 17 February 1809, *Napoleon Correspondance* no. 20057, 9:72; Napoleon to Murat, 5 April 1809, ibid. no. 20728, 9:438; Napoleon to Gaudin, 17 May 1809, ibid. no. 21056, 9:599; Napoleon to Murat, 28 May, 20 June 1809, ibid. no. 21088, 9:625; Napoleon to Gaudin, 29 June, 22 August, 7, 26 September 1809, ibid. nos. 21445, 21877, 22010, 22201, 9:821, 1062–3, 1143, 1270; Napoleon to Berthier, 3 July 1809, ibid. no. 21460, 9:28–9; Napoleon to Fouché, 28 July, 6 August (2 letters) 1809, ibid. nos. 21640, 21716, 21717,

9:922, 958–9; Napoleon to Borghese, 13 August 1809, ibid. no. 21785, 9:1001; Napoleon to Bigot, 13 January 1810, ibid. no. 22863, 9:1602–4; Napoleon to Champagny, 14 January 1810, ibid. no. 22867, 9:1606–07; Las Cases, *Mémorial*, 2:1097–104.
44. Napoleon to Gaudin, 10 September 1809, *Napoleon Correspondance* no. 22030, 9:1157.
45. Napoleon to Fouché, 24 September 1809, *Napoleon Correspondance* no. 22171, 9:1239.
46. Napoleon to Borghese, 21 May 1812, *Napoleon Correspondance* no. 30651, 12:593–4; Napoleon to Cambacérès, 29 June 1812, ibid. no. 31058, 12:782; Napoleon to Duroc, 3 July 1812, ibid. no. 31097, 12:803.
47. Napoleon to Pius VII, 29 December 1812, *Napoleon Correspondance* no. 32169, 12:1322.
48. For the 1813 Concordat, see: Napoleon to Melzi, 25 January 1813, *Correspondance de Napoleon* no. 19510, 12:450–2.

Chapter 17: The Titan

1. For good books, see: Michael Broers, *Europe Under Napoleon, 1799-1815* (New York: Arnold, 1996); Thierry Lentz, *Napoleon et l'Europe* (Paris: Fayard, 2005).
2. Lentz, *France et l'Europe de Napoleon*, 525.
3. Roederer, *Oeuvres*, 3:495.
4. Napoleon to Champagny, 6 February 1805, *Napoleon Correspondance* no. 9559, 5:60.
5. For insightful documents on how he conceived and oversaw his architectural projects, see: Napoleon to Denon and Daru, 14 May 1806, *Napoleon Correspondance* no. 12115, 6:426–7; Napoleon to Champagny, 12 December 1806, ibid. nos. 13850, 15789, 6:1264, 7:857–8; Napoleon to Crétet, 12 March, 3 September 1808, ibid. nos. 17382, 8:254–5, 1024.

For key documents on Napoleon's economic infrastructure policies, see: Bonaparte to Chaptal, 14 April 1804, *Napoleon Correspondance* no. 8801, 4:670; Napoleon to Crétet, 7 March, 10 May, 12 July 1805, 10 April 1806, 14 November 1807, 16 December 1808, ibid. nos. 9643, 10016, 10386, 11854, 16796, 19544, 5:106, 289–9, 477, 6:305, 7:1314–16, 8:1339–40, Napoleon to Champagny, 22 May 1805, ibid. no. 10104, 5:330–1; Napoleon to Duroc, 4 October 1807, ibid. no. 16462, 7:1161–2; Napoleon to Montalivet, 5 July 1808, ibid. no. 18484, 8:833.

6. Napoleon to Denon and Daru, 14 May 1806, *Napoleon Correspondance* no. 12115, 6:426.
7. Napoleon to Crétet, 14 November 1807, *Napoleon Correspondance* no. 16796, 7:1315.
8. Napoleon to Roederer, 29 March 1805, *Napoleon Correspondance* no. 9750, 5:163–4.
9. Napoleon to Champagny, 17 March 1807, *Napoleon Correspondance* no. 14689, 7:359.
10. Napoleon to Champagny, 4 June 1807, *Napoleon Correspondance* no. 15823, 7:872.
11. Napoleon to Champagny, 21 July 1804, *Napoleon Correspondance* no. 9013, 4:774.
12. Napoleon to Louis, 3 December 1806, *Napoleon Correspondance* no. 13742, 6:1222.
13. Napoleon to Eugène, 18 May 1808, *Napoleon Correspondance* no. 17976, 8:573.
14. Napoleon to Cambacérès, 19 March 1807, *Napoleon Correspondance* no. 14735, 7:379.
15. Napoleon to Cambacérès, 13 July 1808, *Napoleon Correspondance* no. 18545, 8:865.
16. Napoleon to Fouché, 15 July 1808, *Napoleon Correspondance* no. 18551, 8:870.
17. Hortense, *Mémoires*, 282.
18. Napoleon to Fouché, 17 January 1806, *Napoleon Correspondance* no. 11286, 6:41.
19. Napoleon to Fouché, 4 April 1807, *Napoleon Correspondance* no. 15096, 7:549.
20. Napoleon to Fouché, 28 April 1805, *Napoleon Correspondance* no. 9926, 5:245.
21. Napoleon to Fouché, 24 July 1809, *Napoleon Correspondance* no. 21622, 9:912–13.
22. Napoleon to Fouché, 17 August 1809, *Napoleon Correspondance* no. 21826, 9:1024.
23. Las Cases, *Mémorial*, 1:816.
24. André Cabanis, *La Presse sous la Consulate et l'Empire* (Paris: Société des Études Robespierrites, 1975), 321–2.
25. Lentz, *France et l'Europe de Napoleon*, 356–7, 361–3.
26. Napoleon to Joseph, 27 March 1809, *Napoleon Correspondance* no. 20575, 9:355.
27. Lentz, *France et l'Europe de Napoleon*, 359. For a sampling of Napoleon as a literary and theatre critic, see: Napoleon to Fouché, 21 December

1806, *Napoleon Correspondance* no. 13915, 6:1301; Napoleon to Champagny, 16 January, 7 March 1807, ibid. nos. 14077, 14525, 7:90, 287–8.
28. Napoleon to Fouché, 2 May 1807, *Napoleon Correspondance* no. 15496, 7:728.
29. Napoleon to Rémusat, 13 February 1810, *Napoleon Correspondance* no. 23120, 9:1720.
30. For Napoleon's policies toward art, see: Napoleon to Cambacérès, 11 April 1805, *Napoleon Correspondance* no. 9814, 5:192; Napoleon to Lebrun, 15 April 1805, ibid. no. 9849, 5:211; Napoleon to Daru, 6 August 1805, ibid. no. 10517, 5:542–3; Napoleon to Champagny, 14 April 1806, 27 March 1808, 11 February 1809, ibid. nos. 11891, 17504, 23090, 6:320, 8:315, 9:1701; Napoleon to Crétet, 27 August 1807, ibid. no. 16247, 7:1066; Napoleon to Duroc, 15 February 1810, ibid. no. 23130, 9:1724.
31. Napoleon to Daru, 6 August 1805, *Napoleon Correspondance* no. 10517, 5:543.
32. For key documents on Napoleon's education policies, see: Napoleon to Lacuée, 23 March 1805, *Napoleon Correspondance* no. 9729, 5:152–3; Napoleon to Champagny, 17 April, 31 July 1805, ibid. no. 9857, 10480, 5:214, 523–4; Napoleon to Dejean, 25 October 1806, ibid. no. 13331, 6:1034–5; Napoleon to Lacépède, 22 October 1807, ibid. no. 16600, 7:1225–6; Napoleon to Crétet, 26 March 1808, ibid. no. 17495, 8:310–11; Napoleon to Clarke, 8 March 1809, 3, 14 April 1812, ibid. nos. 20288, 30455, 9:196–7, 12:462, 497–8; Napoleon to Fontanes, 7 February 1810, ibid. no. 23064, 9:1691.
33. Napoleon to Lacépède, 15 May 1807, *Napoleon Correspondance* no. 15632, 7:789–99.
34. Lentz, *La France et l'Europe de Napoleon*, 373–7, 390.
35. Napoleon to Fouché, 31 December 1808, *Napoleon Correspondance* no. 19647, 8:1387.
36. Las Cases, *Mémorial*, 2:1037. For Napoleon's rationale and vision for his Continental System, see: Las Cases, *Mémorial*, 2:1036–8. For key documents on how Napoleon tried to enforce it, see: Napoleon to Decrès, 11 May 1808, *Napoleon Correspondance* no. 17850, 8:500; Napoleon to Clarke, 15 May 1808, ibid. no. 17910, 8:536–8. For key documents on how the British evaded the Continental System, see: Napoleon to Gaudin, 29 March 1808, *Napoleon Correspondance* no. 17518, 8:323–4.For key documents on how Napoleon tried to promote French overseas trade, see: Napoleon to Crétet, 15 April 1808, *Napoleon Correspondance* no. 17613, 8:377–8; Napoleon to Decrès, 16 April 1808, ibid. no. 17623, 8:384–5.

37. Eli Heckscher, *The Continental System: An Economic Interpretation* (Oxford: Oxford University Press, 1922); François Crouzet, *L'Économie Britannique et le Blocus Continental, 1806-1813* (Paris: Presses Universitaires de France, 1958); Frank Melvin, *Napoleon's Navigation System: A Study of Trade Control during the Continental Blockade* (New York: Nabu Press, 2010); K. Aalestadl and J. Joos, *Revisiting Napoleon's Continental System: Local, Regional, and European Experiences* (New York: Palgrave Macmillan, 2014).
38. Lentz, *France et l'Empire de Napoleon*, 555.
39. Napoleon to Gaudin, 13 November 1807, *Napoleon Correspondance* no. 16785, 7:1310.
40. For some key documents on Napoleon's post-Tilsit naval strategy, see: Napoleon to Decrès, 15 August, 5 September, 12 December 1807, 25, 30 January, 6 February, 31 March, 13, 30 May, 10 June 1808, *Napoleon Correspondance* nos. 16172, 16292, 16880, 17067, 17113, 17145, 17530, 17885, 18167, 18268, 7:1030, 1086, 1351–2, 8:88–90, 1113–14, 131–2, 330, 519–20, 675–6, 730–5; Napoleon to Admiral Dordelin, 29 January 1808, ibid. no. 17103, 8:108; Napoleon to Captain Troude, 20 January 1808, ibid. no. 17140, 8:109; Napoleon to Joseph, 12 March 1808, ibid. no. 17388, 8:258; Napoleon to Ganteaume, 18 April 1808, ibid. no. 17653, 8:401.
41. Napoleon to Decrès, 19 August 1808, *Napoleon Correspondance* no. 18726, 8:966.
42. For key documents on Napoleon's naval operations for 1809, see: Napoleon to Decrès, 10, 29 January, 6, 9, 27 March, 12 April, 17 August, 7, 26, 30 September 1809, *Napoleon Correspondance* nos. 19768, 19956, 20257, 20318, 20569, 20823, 21824, 22007, 22193, 22230, 8:1445–7, 1548, 9:179–80, 215–16, 351–2, 485–6, 1023–4, 1141, 1264–5, 1284–6; Napoleon to Willaumez, 7 February 1809, ibid. no. 1993, 9:37–8.
43. Napoleon to Jérôme, 30 January 1808, *Napoleon Correspondance* no. 17116, 8:116.
44. Napoleon to Eugène, 22 November 1809, *Napoleon Correspondance* no. 22508, 9:1434.
45. Napoleon to Clarke, 18 December 1809, *Napoleon Correspondance* no. 22648, 9:1494.
46. Lentz, *France et l'Europe de Napoleon*, 395.
47. For key documents on the empire's finances, see: Napoleon to Gaudin, 10 September 1809, *Napoleon Correspondance* no. 22050, 9:1156–8; Napoleon to Daru, 29 December 1809, ibid. no. 22745, 9:1540–4; Napoleon to Maret, 18 January 1810, ibid. no. 22895, 9:1617–19.

48. Napoleon to Clarke, 18 December 1809, *Napoleon Correspondance* no. 22648, 9:1494.
49. Napoleon to Clarke, 18 December 1809, *Napoleon Correspondance* no. 22649, 9:1495–6. See also: Napoleon to Daru, 7 August, 1813, ibid. no. 20337.
50. Lentz, *France et l'Europe de Napoleon*, 423.
51. For insights into Josephine and their relationship, see: Constant, *Mémoires*, 1:317–33.
52. Bonaparte to Josephine, 19 June 1802, *Napoleon Correspondance* no. 6948, 3:998.
53. Bonaparte to Josephine, 11 November 1803, *Napoleon Correspondance* no. 8251, 4:439.
54. Napoleon to Josephine, 10 May 1807, *Napoleon Correspondance* no. 15594, 7:773.
55. Napoleon to Josephine, 26 August, 25 September 1809, *Napoleon Correspondance* nos. 21907, 22178, 9:1083, 2354.
56. For just those letters until the end of the year, see: Napoleon to Pauline, 9, 29 (2 letters), 30 November, 4, 6, 8 (2 letters), 9 (2 letters), 14, 15, 18, 22, 26 (2 letters), 31 December 1809, *Napoleon Correspondance* nos. 22640, 22543, 22544, 22545, 22552, 22517, 22575, 22576, 22597, 22607, 22616, 22651, 22705, 22725, 22726, 22765, 9:1411, 1448–9, 1451, 1459, 1460–1, 1471, 1475, 1480, 1497–8, 1522, 1555.
57. For how Napoleon handled his divorce with Josephine, see: Hortense, *Mémoires*, 216–19, 229–48; Cambacérès, *Mémoires*, 2:301–10.
58. Hortense, *Mémoires*, 240.
59. Napoleon to Cambacérès, 15. December 1809, *Napoleon Correspondance* no. 22609, 9:1476–7. Napoleon to Josephine, 16, 23, 26 (2 letters), 27 December 1809, 30 January 1810, ibid. nos. 22620, 22674, 22707, 22722, 22723, 22732, 9:1482, 1506, 1522, 1535, 1659.
60. Napoleon to Maria Walewska, 18 December 1809, 16 February 1810, *Napoleon Correspondance* nos. 22654, 23138, 9:1498, 1727.
61. For key documents on whom to marry, the marriage negotiations, wedding, and wedding night of Napoleon and Marie Louise, see: Las Cases, *Mémorial*, 1:233–5, 2:1227–8; Constant, *Mémoires*, 2:118–32; Hortense, *Mémoires*, 244–54; *Talleyrand Mémoires*, 339–41; Cambacérès, *Mémoires*, 2:324–8.
62. Alan Palmer, *Napoleon and Marie Louise: The Emperor's Second Wife* (New York: St. Martin's Press, 2001).
63. Napoleon to Marie Theresa, 15 February 1810, *Napoleon Correspondance* no. 23132. 9:1725.

64. Napoleon to Champagny, 26 February 1810, *Napoleon Correspondance* no. 23208, 9:1756–7.
65. Napoleon to Marie Louise, 23, 25, 26 February 1810, *Napoleon Correspondance* nos. 23188, 23205, 23215, 9:1748, 1753, 1760. Las Cases, *Mémorial*, 1:233; Constant, *Mémoires*, 2:122–6; Cambacérès, *Mémoires*, 2:331–3.
66. For the best first-hand account of their marriage, see: Cohendet, *Mémoires sur Napoleon et Marie Louise*. See also: Constant, *Mémoires*, 2:132–77, 195–9.
67. Chaptal, *Souvenirs*, 158.
68. Las Cases, *Mémorial*, 1:472–4; Cohendet, *Mémoires sur Napoleon et Marie Louise*, 59–63.
69. For Napoleon's relationship with his son, see: Constant, *Mémoires*, 2:199–204.
70. Las Cases, *Mémorial*, 1:236–7.
71. Lentz, *France et l'Europe de Napoleon*, 748.
72. Napoleon to Champagny, 17 July 1809, *Napoleon Correspondance* no. 21542, 9:874.
73. Napoleon to Louis, 21 September 1809, *Napoleon Correspondance* no. 22133, 9:1215.
74. Napoleon to Louis, 21 December 1809, *Napoleon Correspondance* no. 22686, 9:1510–12.
75. Fouché, *Mémoires*, 253–60.
76. For key documents on the crisis, see: Napoleon to Louis, 22 October, 21 December 1809, 6 January 1810, *Napoleon Correspondance* nos. 22395, 22686, 9:1366–70, 1510–13, 1570–1; Napoleon to Clarke, 5, 7, 11, 19, 27 (4 letters) January, 1, 2, 6, 7 February 1810, ibid. nos. 22795, 22805, 22851, 22901, 22970, 22972, 22973, 22974, 23013, 23024, 23051, 23062, 9:1572, 1568, 1598, 1621, 1646–50, 1667, 1671, 1685, 1690.
77. Napoleon to Jérôme, 29 April 1809, *Napoleon Correspondance* no. 20931, 9:542.
78. Napoleon to Jérôme, 17 July 1809, *Napoleon Correspondance* no. 21551, 9:878.
79. Napoleon to Jérôme, 25 July 1809, *Napoleon Correspondance* no. 21626, 9:914–15.
80. Napoleon to Murat, 15 December 1808, *Napoleon Correspondance* no. 19554, 8:1335.
81. Napoleon to Murat, 27 December 1809, *Napoleon Correspondance* no. 22734, 9:1536.
82. Napoleon to Murat, 12 November 1808, *Napoleon Correspondance* no. 19243, 8:1215.

83. Digby Smith, *Murat's Army: The Army of the Kingdom of Italy, 1806-1815* (London: Helion, 2018).
84. Napoleon to Murat, 30 August 1811, Lentz, *L'Effondrement du Systeme Napoleonien*, 46–7.
85. Caroline to Damas, 8 May 1810, Roger de Damas, *Mémoires de Roger de Damas*, 2 vols (Paris: Plon, 1914), 2:428.
86. Schom, *Napoleon Bonaparte*, 571.
87. Napoleon to Champagny, 6, 12 February 1810, *Napoleon Correspondance* nos. 23045, 23097, 9:1680, 1706–07.
88. Napoleon to Clarke, 29 July 1809, *Napoleon Correspondance* no. 21646, 9:925.
89. Napoleon to Fouché, 11 September 1809, *Napoleon Correspondance* no. 22035, 9:1161.
90. Napoleon to Joseph, 5 June 1806, *Napoleon Correspondance* no. 12228, 6:486.
91. Las Cases, *Mémorial*, 2:1032.
92. Napoleon to Alexander I, 2 February 1808, *Napoleon Correspondance* no. 17121, 8:120.

Chapter 18: The Lord of the Kremlin

1. For a summary, see: William R. Nester, 'Why Did Napoleon Do It?: The Matrix of Character, Circumstance, and Choice', *The Journal of International Diplomacy*, vol. 24, no. 3 (Fall 2013), 353–64.

    For overviews of French-Russian relations under Napoleon, see: Michael Adams, *Napoleon and Russia* (New York: Bloomsbury Academic, 2006); Dominic Lieven, *Russia against Napoleon* (New York: Penguin, 2009). For the 1812 campaign, see: Richard Riehn, *1812: Napoleon's Russian Campaign* (New York: John Wiley and Sons, 1991); Paul Austin, *1812: Napoleon's Invasion of Russia* (London: Greenhill, 2000); Adam Zamoyski, *Moscow 1812: Napoleon's Fatal March* (New York: Harper Collins, 2004); Theodore Dodge, *Napoleon's Invasion of Russia* (New York: Presidio Press, 2014).
2. Las Cases, *Mémorial*, 1:551. See also: Napoleon to Jérôme, 27 January 1812, *Napoleon Correspondance* no. 29845, 9:165–6.
3. Napoleon to Champagny, 6 February 1810, *Napoleon Correspondance* no. 23046, 9:1681–3.
4. Napoleon to Jérôme, 27 January 1812, *Napoleon Correspondance* no. 29845, 12:165.
5. Napoleon to Jérôme, 27 January 1812, *Napoleon Correspondance* no. 29845, 12:166.

6. For key documents on Napoleon's military buildup, see: Napoleon to Clarke, 2 (2 letters), 3, 5, 9 (2 letters), 16 (2 letters) January, 2 April (4 letters), 18 May 1812, *Napoleon Correspondance* nos. 29629, 29638, 29644, 29662, 29663, 29703, 29773, 29774, 30369, 30370, 30371, 30372, 30633, 12:33, 38–9, 46–8, 56, 75–80, 116–18, 439–58, 582–5; Napoleon to Lacuée, 2, 10, 13, 24 (2 letters), 29 January, 8 April 1812, ibid. nos. 29642, 29722, 29737, 29818, 29825, 29871, 30416, 12:416, 87–8, 95–6, 141–2, 145–8, 181, 477–9, 645–7; Napoleon to Berthier, 4, 8 (2 letters), 14, 20, 21, 25, 26 January, 8 February, 1, 3, 6, 16 March, 22 April, 23, 24 (2 letters), 28 May, 1 June 1812, ibid. nos. 29659, 29687, 29688, 29740, 29799, 29810, 29828, 29831, 29926, 30097, 30111, 30137, 30231, 30488, 30670, 30685, 30687, 30726, 30758, 12:52, 69, 97–9, 128–31, 136–8, 149–51, 152–7, 212, 308, 315, 326–7, 377–9, 513–16, 601–02, 610–13, 631; Napoleon to Collin de Sussy, 10 January, ibid. no. 29719, 12:86; Napoleon to Dumas, 14 January, 6 February 1812, ibid. nos. 29748, 29917, 12:103–04, 205–08; Napoleon to Duroc, 14 January 1812, ibid. no. 29749, 12:104–05,

Napoleon to Eugène, 8, 29 February, 26 May 1812, ibid. nos. 29948, 30090, 30702, 12:222, 302–05, 619–20; Napoleon to Davout, 26 May 1812, ibid. no. 30700, 12:618–19; Napoleon to Jérôme, 26 May 1812, ibid. no. 50704, 12:620–2; Napoleon to Oudinot, 26 May 1812, ibid. no. 30705, 12:622.

For key documents on how Napoleon financed his campaign, see: Napoleon to Davout, 7 January 1812, *Napoleon Correspondance* no. 29683, 12:66–7, Napoleon to Mollien, 29 February, 10 March (3 letters) 1812, ibid. nos. 30095, 30175, 30176, 30177, 12:307, 349–51.

For key documents on Napoleon's strategy should the Russians attack before all his forces were at the front, see: Napoleon to Berthier, 16, 25, 30 March, 18, 25 April 1812, *Napoleon Correspondance* nos. 30228, 30296, 30343, 30474, 30500, 12:376, 407–08, 429–30, 506–07, 520.

7. Napoleon to Maret, 2 March 1812, *Napoleon Correspondance* no. 30110, 12:314. Fouché, *Mémoires*, 278–80, 295–7.

8. For naval operations during 1812, see: Napoleon to Decrès, 8 February, 3 March 1812, *Napoleon Correspondance* nos. 29947, 30125, 12:220–1, 321; Napoleon to Missiessy, 18 February 1812, ibid. no. 30002, 12:254–7; Napoleon to Eugène, 3 March 1812, ibid. no. 30126, 12:322.

9. Napoleon to Mahmoud, 27 January, 4 April 1812, *Napoleon Correspondance* nos. 29847, 30396, 12:167, 469.

10. Napoleon to Champagny, 25 February 1811, *Napoleon Correspondance* no. 26002, 10:1235.

11. For letters between Napoleon and Alexander, see: Napoleon to Alexander, 24 February, 25 April 1812, *Napoleon Correspondance* nos. 30048, 30492, 12:278, 517; Napoleon to Cambacérès, 1 June 1812, ibid. no. 30772, 12:652–3.
12. Caulaincourt, *With Napoleon in Russia*, 6.
13. Constant, *Mémoires*, 2:220–1. For key documents on the Dresden conference, see: Napoleon to Frederick Augustus, 4 May 1812, *Napoleon Correspondance* no. 30586, 12:558; Napoleon to Clarke, 17 May 1812, ibid. no. 30628, 12:580–1.
14. Napoleon to Marie Louise, 1 June 1812, *Napoleon Correspondance* no. 30789, 12:661. For his initial burst of letters, see: Napoleon to Marie Louise, 29, 30 (2 letters), 31 May, 3, 4, 6 June 1812, ibid. nos. 30741, 30742, 30743, 30754, 30798, 30827, 30855, 12:638–9, 643, 665, 677, 690; Napoleon to Cambacérès, 1 June 1812, ibid. no. 30772, 12:652–3.
15. Riehn, *Napoleon's Russian Campaign*, 65–82.
16. Ibid., 50–2, 418–23, 426–43.
17. Ibid., 49–50, 83–92, 444–64.
18. Napoleon to Hogendorp, 23 June 1812, *Napoleon Correspondance* no. 31033, 12:770.
19. For key documents on Napoleon's plan of operations, see: Napoleon to Jérôme, 5, 15 June 1812, *Napoleon Correspondance* nos. 30846, 30936, 31020, 12:685–6, 728–9, 763–4; Napoleon to Berthier, 10, 11, 14, 16 June 1812, ibid. nos. 30890, 30895, 30913, 30941, 12:704, 707–08, 716, 731; Napoleon to Eugène, 10, 11, 15 June 1812, ibid. nos. 30895, 30988, 30935, 12:705–06, 709, 727–8, Napoleon to Davout, 15 June 1812, ibid. no. 30954, 12:726–7; Napoleon to Macdonald, 21 June 1812, ibid. no. 31023, 12:765–6.
20. Napoleon to Berthier, 11 June 1812, *Napoleon Correspondance* no. 30895, 12:708.
21. For key documents on the campaign from the Niemen to Smolensk, see: Napoleon to Berthier, 30 June, 3, 5, 6, 7, 8 (3 letters), 9 (2 letters), 11 (3 letters), 14, 16 July, 7, 10 August 1812, *Napoleon Correspondance* nos. 31062, 31094, 31115, 31121, 31132, 31139, 31140, 31141, 31174, 31175, 31187, 31188, 31199, 31223, 31236, 31429, 31457, 12:783–4, 801, 811, 814–15, 820–1, 823–6, 840–3, 849, 850, 856–7, 868–9, 875–6, 942–3, 968, 981–2; Napoleon to Jérôme, 4 July 1812, ibid. no. 31112, 12:810; Napoleon to Davout, 6, 9, 12, 31 July 1812, ibid. nos. 31119, 31180, 31215, 31374, 12:813, 845, 863–4; Napoleon to Eugène, 9 July 1812, ibid. no. 31181, 12:846; Napoleon to Maret, 22 July 1812, ibid.

no. 31315, 12:916–17; Napoleon to Clarke, 10 August 1812, ibid. no. 31466, 12:987–8.
22. Napoleon to Jérôme, 15 June 1812, *Napoleon Correspondance* no. 30936, 12:728.
23. Napoleon to Jérôme, 16 July 1812, *Napoleon Correspondance* no. 31243, 12:878–9.
24. Napoleon to Hogendorp, 24 August (2 letters) 1812, *Napoleon Correspondance* no. 31589, 31590, 12:1038; Napoleon to Maret, 24 August (3 letters), 1 September (2 letters) 1812, ibid. nos. 31591, 31592, 31593, 31649, 31651, 12:1038–9, 1066, 1067; Napoleon to Berthier, 1 September 1812, ibid. no. 31545, 12:1064; Constant, *Mémoires*, 2:220–30.
25. Napoleon to Alexander, 1 July 1812, *Napoleon Correspondance* no. 31068, 12:787–9.
26. Riehn, *Napoleon's Russian Campaign*, 239–41.
27. For key documents during Napoleon's Moscow sojourn, see: Napoleon to Berthier, 5 (2 letters), 6 (3 letters), 7, 9 October 1812, *Napoleon Correspondance* nos. 31808, 31811, 31828, 31835, 31836, 31865, 31881, 12:1133–4, 1135–6, 1145, 1148–50, 1162–6, 1174–5; Napoleon to Clarke, 5 October 1812, ibid. no. 31818, 31819, 12:1138–41; Napoleon to Eugène, 5 October 1812, ibid. no. 31826, 12:1143–4.
28. Napoleon to Marie Louise, 18 September 1812, *Napoleon Correspondance* no. 31732, 12:1101.
29. Napoleon to Alexander, 20 September 1812, *Napoleon Correspondance* no. 31736, 12:1103.
30. Napoleon to Kutuzov, 3 October 1812, *Napoleon Correspondance* no. 31792, 12:1126–7.
31. Napoleon to Maret, 23 September, 16 October 1812, *Napoleon Correspondance* nos. 31750, 31920, 12:1109–10.
32. For key documents on the debate over the route, see: Napoleon to Berthier, 10, 16, 18 October 1812, *Napoleon Correspondance* nos. 31885, 31907, 31933, 12:1177, 1185–6, 1198–9; Napoleon to Maret, 10 October 1812, ibid. no. 31922, 12:1192.
33. For key documents on Napoleon's retreat, see: Napoleon to Berthier, 19, 20, 21 (2 letters), 24, 26, 30 (2 letters) October, 3, 5, 6, 9, 11 (2 letters), 19, 21, 24 November, 5 December 1812, *Napoleon Correspondance* nos. 31944, 31951, 31958, 31959, 31967, 31971, 31977, 31978, 31996, 32014, 32019, 32031, 32033, 32036, 32061, 32065, 32069, 32103, 12:1204–05, 1208, 1211–12, 1217, 1218–19, 1222–3, 1229, 1236–8, 1239–40, 1244–7, 1260–1, 1265, 1267, 1294–6; Napoleon to Maret,

19 October, 29 November, 3 (2 letters), 4 (2 letters) December 1812, ibid. nos. 31948, 32085, 32094, 32095, 32098, 32099, 12:1206–07, 1279–84, 1290, 1292–3; Napoleon to Eugène, 22, 23 October 1812, ibid. nos. 31962, 31966, 12:1214, 1216; Napoleon to Lariboisière, 18 October 1812, ibid. no. 31938, 12:1201–02, Napoleon to Mortier, 18 October 1812, ibid. no. 31941, 12:1203.

34. For key documents on the attempted Malet coup, see: Napoleon to Cambacérès, 11 (2 letters), 14 November 1812, *Napoleon Correspondance* nos. 32038, 32039, 32052, 12:1247–9, 1254–5, Napoleon to Clarke, 11 (2 letters) November 1812, ibid. nos. 32040, 32041, 12:1249, Napoleon to Savary, 11 November (3 letters) 1812, ibid. nos. 32045, 32046, 32047, 32056, 12:1251–2, 1256; Caulaincourt, *With Napoleon in Russia*, 199–204; Fouché, *Mémoires*, 300–04. Cambacérès, *Mémoires*, 2:414–21.
35. Caulaincourt, *With Napoleon in Russia*, 261.
36. Napoleon to Maret, 29 November 1812, *Napoleon Correspondance* no. 32084, 12:1278.

Chapter 19: The Dying Gaul

1. Caulaincourt, *With Napoleon in Russia*, 271–323, 324–72, 373–400.
2. Napoleon to Maret, 11 December 1812, *Napoleon Correspondance* no. 32119, 12:1301–02; Napoleon to Francis I, 14 December 1812, ibid. no. 32121, 12:1303; Napoleon to Frederick William III, 14 December 1812, ibid. no. 32122, 12:1303–04.
3. For overviews of the 1813 and 1814 campaigns, see David Hamilton-Williams, *The Fall of Napoleon* (London: Brockhampton Press, 1994). For the 1813 campaign, see: Jonathan Riley, *Napoleon and the World War of 1813: Lessons in Coalition Warfighting* (London: Frank Cass, 2000); Michael Leggiere, *Napoleon and Berlin: The Franco-Prussian War in North Germany, 1813* (Norman: University of Oklahoma Press, 2002); Lorraine Petre, *Napoleon's Last Campaign in Germany, 1813* (New York: Forgotten Books, 2017); Jonathan Riley, *1813: Empire at Bay, The Sixth Coalition and the Downfall of Napoleon* (London: Pen and Sword, 2013); Michael Leggiere, *Napoleon and the Struggle for Germany: The Franco-Prussian War of 1813* (New York: Cambridge University Press, 2015).
4. Cohendet, *Mémoires sur Napoleon et Marie Louise*, 116.
5. Marquis de Noailles, ed., *The Life and Memoirs of Count Molé* (New York: George Duran Company, 1924).
6. For key documents on rebuilding the army in December 1812, see: Napoleon to Clarke, 25, 26, 29, 30 (3 letters) December 1812, *Napoleon*

Correspondance nos. 32151, 32153, 32158, 32171, 32172, 32173, 12:1314–15, 1316, 1318, 1323–5; Napoleon to Lacuée, 29, 30 December 1812, ibid. nos. 32165, 32174, 12:1321, 1325–6; Napoleon to Berthier, 30 December 1812, ibid. nos. 32170, 12:1323.

For key documents on rebuilding and deploying the army from January through April 1813, see: Napoleon to Clarke, 4, 6, 7, 12, 15, 18, 22, 25, 26, 27 January, 5, 6, 16 February, 11, 31 March, 2 April 1813, *Correspondance de Napoleon* nos. 19416, 19425, 19431, 19445, 19450, 19459, 19482, 19503, 19511, 19520, 19538, 15939, 19587, 19692, 19790, 19795; Napoleon to Berthier, 9, 20 January, 13 April 1813, ibid. nos. 19437, 19465, 19857; Napoleon to Lacuée, 18, 25 January 1813, ibid. nos. 19461, 19504; Napoleon to Lauriston, 20 January, 2, 6 March 1813, ibid. nos. 19468, 19640, 19467; Napoleon to Jérôme, 24 January, 2, 12 March 1813, ibid. nos. 19501, 19647, 19706; Napoleon to Eugène, 27 January (2 letters), 8, 13, 27 February, 5, 9, 15, 28 March 1813, ibid. nos. 19522, 19523, 19557, 19577, 19625, 19664, 19688, 19721, 19779; Napoleon to Davout, 2 March 1813, ibid. no. 19638; Decree on the Army's Organization, 12 March 1813, ibid. no. 19698; Napoleon to Ney, 13, 20 March, 10 April 1813, ibid. nos. 19714, 19746, 19839; Napoleon to Marmont, 7 April 1813, ibid. no. 19822.

For key documents on acquiring horses and rebuilding the cavalry, see: Napoleon to Lacuée, 18 January, 3, 8 February 1813, *Correspondance de Napoleon* nos. 19460, 19530, 19552; Napoleon to Eugène, 22, 24 January 1813, ibid. nos. 19480, 19500; Napoleon to Clarke, 8, 26 February, 1 March 1813, ibid. nos. 19550, 19612, 19628; Napoleon to Duroc, 23 February 1813, ibid. no. 19607.

For key documents on supplies, see: Napoleon to Eugène, 24 (2 letters), 26 January, 4 February 1813, *Correspondance de Napoleon* nos. 19497, 19498, 19518, 19535; Napoleon to Clarke, 13, 16 March 1813, ibid. nos. 19708, 19722; Napoleon to Duroc, 25 April 1813, ibid. no. 19903,

For key documents on finance, see: Napoleon to Mollien, 21 January, 27 February, 12 April 1813, *Correspondance de Napoleon* nos. 19473, 19621, 19847; Napoleon to Jérôme, 23 January 1813, ibid. no. 19493; Note Dictée en Conseil des Ministres, 24 January 1813, ibid. no. 19496.

7. Napoleon to Frederick VI, 5 January 1813, *Correspondance de Napoleon* no. 19424. For other key letters to allies, see: Napoleon to Frederick Augustus, 22 January, 2 March, 8 April 1813, *Correspondance de Napoleon* nos. 19481, 19649, 19831; Napoleon to Francis, 25 January 1813, ibid. no. 19511; Napoleon to King Frederick of Württemberg, 2 March, 8, 18, 24 April 1813, ibid. no. 19650, 19830, 19873, 19902;

Napoleon to Maximilien Joseph, 2 March 1813, ibid. no. 19651; Napoleon to Grand Duke Ferdinand Joseph of Würzburg, 2 March 1813, ibid. no. 19652.
8. Napoleon to Jérôme, 18 January 1813, *Correspondance de Napoleon* no. 19462.
9. Discours de l'emperor a l'ouverture de Corps Legislative, 14 February 1813, *Correspondance de Napoleon* no. 19581.
10. Cambacérès, *Mémoires*, 2:434.
11. For key documents on the 1813 campaign, see: Las Cases, *Mémorial*, 2:1174–95. For the best secondary accounts, see: Leggiere, *Napoleon and Berlin*; Munro Price, *Napoleon: The End of Glory* (New York: Oxford University Press, 2014).
12. For key documents on the first phase of the campaign, see: Napoleon to Berthier, 1, 4, 9, 13, 16, 18, 23, 24 (3 letters), 26 May 1813, *Correspondance de Napoleon* nos. 19835, 19959, 19987, 20001, 20015, 20020, 20034, 20036, 20037, 20038, 20048; Proclamation à l'Armée, 4 May 1813, ibid. no. 19952; Napoleon to Ney, 4, 13 May 1813, ibid. nos. 19956, 20006; Napoleon to Oudinot, 18 May 1813, ibid. no. 20023; Napoleon to Rogniat, 24 May 1813, ibid. no. 20041; Napoleon to Durosnel, 25 May 1813, ibid. no. 20043; Napoleon to Frederick Augustus, 25 May 1813, ibid. no. 20044. For a good overview of the first half of the 1813 campaign, see: George Nafziger, *Lützen and Bautzen: Napoleon's Spring Campaign of 1813* (London: Helion, 2017).
13. John Gallaher, *The Iron Marshal: A Biography of Louis N. Davout* (London: Greenhill, 2000).
14. Proclamation à l'Armée, 3 May 1813, *Correspondance de Napoleon* no. 19952.
15. Napoleon to Eugène, 18 May 1813 (2 letters), *Correspondance de Napoleon* nos. 20029, 20030.
16. Napoleon to Francis, 17 May 1813, *Correspondance de Napoleon* no. 20019.
17. Las Cases, *Mémorial*, 2: 1365–6.
18. Napoleon to Clark, 2 June 1813, *Correspondance de Napoleon* no. 20070.
19. Napoleon to Berthier with attached instructions for Moustier and de Flahault, July 19, 1813, *Correspondance de Napoleon* no. 20286.
20. Meeting of the emperor with Metternich, 23 June 1813, *Correspondance de Napoleon* no. 20175. Las Cases, *Mémorial*, 2:1230–2; Price, *Napoleon: The End of Glory*, 82–8.
21. Napoleon to Maret, 5 August 1813, *Correspondance de Napoleon* no. 20330.

22. Napoleon to Francis, 30 June 1813, *Correspondance de Napoleon* no. 20198.
23. Napoleon to Davout, 19 July 1813, *Correspondance de Napoleon* no. 20287.
24. Observations on Austria's declaration of war, 14 August 1813, *Correspondance de Napoleon* no. 20376; Napoleon to Maret, 17 August 1813, ibid. no. 20395.
25. Napoleon to Ney and Marmont, 12 August 1813, *Correspondance de Napoleon* no. 20360.
26. For key documents on the second phase of the 1813 campaign, see: Napoleon to Berthier, 12, 13 (2 letters), 16 (2 letters), 17, 18 (2 letters), 20, 23 (2 letters), 25, 27, 29 August, 3, 18 September, 1 October 1813, *Correspondance de Napoleon* nos. 20354, 20371, 20373, 20384, 20385, 20397, 20402, 20403, 20419, 20442, 20443, 20462, 20481, 20489, 20510, 20586, 20669; Orders for the Major General, 12 August 1813, ibid. no. 20356; Instructions, 12 August 1813, ibid. no. 20360; Napoleon to Oudinot, 12 August 1813, ibid. no. 20365; Napoleon to Davout, 13 August 1813, ibid. no. 20374; Napoleon to Ney, 16 August 1813, ibid. no. 20389; Napoleon to Macdonald, 16 August, 3, 24 September, 1 October 1813, ibid. nos. 20390, 20516, 20626, 20673; Napoleon to Poniatowski, 16 August 1813, ibid. no. 20392; Napoleon to Gouvion St Cyr, 17, 20, 25 August 1813, ibid. nos. 20398, 20413, 20461; Napoleon to Kellermann, 18 August 1813, ibid. no. 20404; Napoleon to Clarke, 18 August 1813, ibid. no. 20410; Napoleon to Vandamme, 20, 25 August 1813, ibid. nos. 20414, 20460; Napoleon to Maret, 22 August, 10 October 1813, ibid. no. 20437, 20746; On the general situation of my affairs, 30 August 1813, ibid. no. 20492; Napoleon to Mouton, 3, 13 September 1813, ibid. nos. 20518, 20555; Napoleon to Murat, 19 September, 13 October 1813, ibid. no. 20593, 20792; Napoleon to Daru, 23 September 1813, ibid. no. 20619; Napoleon to Poniatowski, 26 September 1813, ibid. no. 20642; Napoleon to Marmont, 27 September 1813, ibid. no. 20644; Napoleon to Arrighi, 10 October 1813, ibid. no. 20749; Notes on the reunion of the different corps, 12 October 1813, ibid. no. 20772; Bulletin 15, 24 October 1813, ibid. no. 20813, 20830; Napoleon to Cambacérès, 3 November 1813, ibid. no. 20650.
27. Digby Smith, *1813 Leipzig: Napoleon and the Battle of Nations* (London: Greenhill, 2006); George Nafziger, *Napoleon at Leipzig: The Battle of Nations, 1813* (London: Helion, 2018).
28. For key documents on the retreat to France, see: Napoleon to Cambacérès, 25 October (2 letters) 1813, *Correspondance de Napoleon*

no. 20832, 20833; Napoleon to Clarke, 25 October (2 letters), 2 November (2 letters) 1813, nos. 20834, 20835, 20854, 20856; Napoleon to Kellermann, 25 October 1813, ibid. nos. 20837, 20918; Napoleon to Berthier, 2 November 1813, ibid. no. 20874.

For key documents on the November preparations for the 1814 campaign, see: Napoleon to Clarke, 10, 11, 16 (2 letters), 18, 21, 28, November 1813, ibid. nos. 20898, 20900, 20912, 20931, 20948;

Napoleon to Berthier, 18 November 1813, ibid. no. 20848, Napoleon to Marmont, 12, 19 November 1813, ibid. nos. 20883, 20921; Napoleon to Mollien, 17 November 1813, ibid. no. 20902; Instructions for General d'Anthouard, 20 November 1813, ibid. no. 20928; Napoleon to Eugène, 20 November 1813, ibid. no. 20929; Napoleon to Mortier, 22 November 1813, ibid. no. 20934, Observations on the 1814 budget, 26 November 1813, ibid. no. 20947; Napoleon to d'Hastrel, 29 November 1813, ibid. no. 20951; Napoleon to Drouot, 30 November 1813, ibid. no. 20954.

29. For the 1814 campaign, see: F. Loraine Petre, *Napoleon at Bay 1814* (London: Greenhill, 1994); Michael Leggiere, *The Fall of Napoleon: The Allied Invasion of France, 1813-1814* (New York: Cambridge University Press, 2007); Andrew Uffindell, *Napoleon 1814: The Defence of France* (London: Pen and Sword, 2009); George Nafziger, *The End of Empire: Napoleon's 1814 Campaign* (London: Helion, 2015); Henry Houssaye, *Napoleon and the Campaign of 1814* (New York: Forgotten Books, 2018).
30. Napoleon to Cambacérès, 3 November 1813, *Correspondance de Napoleon* no. 20850.
31. Napoleon to Daru, 15 November 1813, *Correspondance de Napoleon* no. 20893.
32. Napoleon to Pauline, 25 October 1813, *Correspondance de Napoleon* no. 20831.
33. For key documents on the December preparations for the 1814 campaign, see: For the war administration director, 1 December 1813, *Correspondance de Napoleon* no. 20958; Napoleon to Daru, 6 December (2 letters) 1813, ibid. nos. 20975, 20976; Napoleon to Berthier, 7 December 1813, ibid. nos. 20977; Napoleon to Clarke, 7, 23, 24, 25 December 1813, ibid. nos. 20979, 21028, 21033, 21035; Napoleon to Decrès, 9 December 1813, ibid. no. 20993; Napoleon to Lebrun, 10 December 1813, ibid. no. 20996; Order, 21, 26 December 1813, ibid. nos. 21024, 21047; Decree, 26 December 1813, ibid. no. 21041.

For key documents on the January preparations for the 1814 campaign, see: Napoleon to Clarke, 2, 6, 11, 18 (2 letters), 20, 24 January 1814, *Correspondance de Napoleon* nos. 21057, 21065, 21084,

21109, 21111, 21118, 32233; Napoleon to Berthier, 10 January 1814, ibid. no. 21080; Orders for the Major General, 1, 15 January 1814, ibid. nos. 21055; 21100; Order, 2 January 1814, ibid. no. 21056; Decree on a Levee en Masse, 4 January 1814, ibid. no. 21061; Napoleon to Mollien, 7 January 1814, ibid. no. 21069; Napoleon to Kellermann, 8 January 1814, ibid. no. 21072; Instruction General, 13 January 1814, ibid. no. 21091; Napoleon to Nansouty, 13 January 1814, ibid. no. 21094; Notes, 18 (2 letters), 19 January 1814, ibid. no. 21113, 21114, 21116; Napoleon to Maison, 20 January 1814, ibid. no. 21120; Napoleon to Joseph, 20 January 1814, ibid. no. 21134.

34. Emperor's speech to the Legislative Corps, 19 December 1813, *Correspondance de Napoleon* no. 21020.
35. Jacques Olivier Boudon, *Histoire du Consulat et de l'Empire* (Paris: Perrin, 2000), 393.
36. Response Senate to Emperor, 29 December 1813, *Correspondance de Napoleon* no. 21054.
37. Cambacérès, *Mémoires*, 2:495.
38. Napoleon to Caulaincourt, 4 January 1814, *Correspondance de Napoleon* no. 21062.
39. Instructions for Caulaincourt, 4 January 1814, *Correspondance de Napoleon* no. 21063.
40. Napoleon to Metternich, 17 January 1814, *Correspondance de Napoleon* no. 21101.
41. For key documents on the campaign, see: Napoleon to Berthier, 26 January, 3, 5, 8, 9, 15, 18, 19, 27 February, 2, 12, 25 (2 letters) March, 1 April 1814, *Correspondance de Napoleon* nos. 21135, 21171, 21184, 21215, 21221, 21261, 21296, 21303. 21393, 2141, 21466, 21475, 21541; Orders, 26, 30 January 1814, ibid. nos. 21136, 21146; Napoleon to Victor, 26 January 1814, ibid. no. 21138; Napoleon to Mortier, 27 January, 6 February 1814, ibid. nos. 21140, 21192; Napoleon to Marmont, 29 January, 3 February 1814, ibid. nos. 21144, 21174; Napoleon to Clarke, 31 January (3 letters), 1 February, 1, 14 March 1814, ibid. nos. 21150, 21151, 21162, 21163, 21403, 21482; Napoleon to Joseph, 31 January, 6, 7 (2 letters), 9 (2 letters), 13, 14, 18, 21, 23, 24 February, 10, 17 March 1814, ibid. nos. 21160, 21190, 21193, 21195, 21226, 21236, 21253, 21293, 21328, 21356, 21360, 21460, 21508; Napoleon to Daru, 8 February 1814, ibid. no. 21214; Dispositions, 13 February 1814, ibid. no. 21244; Allocution to Old Guard, 3 April 1814, ibid. no. 21550; To the Army, 5 April 1814, ibid. no. 21557.

For Napoleon's assessment of his 1814 campaign, see: Las Cases, *Mémorial*, 2:1470–90. For the best book on the 1814 campaign, see:

Michael V. Leggiere, *The Fall of Napoleon: The Allied Invasion of France, 1813-1814* (New York: Cambridge University Press, 2007).
42. Napoleon to Caulaincourt, 2 February 1814, *Correspondance de Napoleon* no. 21168.
43. Napoleon to Joseph, 7 February 1814, *Correspondance de Napoleon* no. 21205.
44. Napoleon to Joseph, 8 February 1814, *Correspondance de Napoleon* no. 21210.
45. Napoleon to Caulaincourt, 2, 5, 13 February 1814, *Correspondance de Napoleon* nos. 21168, 21179, 21240.
46. Napoleon to Caulaincourt, 17 February 1814, *Correspondance de Napoleon* no. 21285.
47. Napoleon to Francis, 21 February 1814, *Correspondance de Napoleon* no. 21344.
48. Schom, *Napoleon Bonaparte*, 698.
49. Act of Abdication, 11 April 1814, *Correspondance de Napoleon* no. 21558.
50. Napoleon to Marie Louise, April 20, 1814, *Correspondance de Napoleon* no. 21561.

Chapter 20: The Odysseus

1. Napoleon Bonaparte, *Mémoires de Napoleon: L'Ile d'Elbe et Cent Jours* (Paris: Talladier, 2011), 54.
2. Adieux to the Guard, 20 April 1814, *Correspondance de Napoleon* no. 21561.
3. Sir Neil Campbell, *Napoleon at Fontainebleau and Elba, being a journal of occurrences, 1814 and 1815* (London: John Murray, 1869), 157–8.
4. For the journey to Elba, see: Bonaparte, *Mémoires: L'Ile d'Elbe et Cent Jours*, 54–61.
5. For two different versions of the encounter, see Cohendet, *Mémoires sur Napoleon et Marie Louise*, 168–9; Bonaparte, *Mémoires: L'Ile d'Elbe et Cent Jours*, 56.
6. For accounts of Napoleon's Elba exile, see: Bonaparte, *Mémoires: L'Ile d'Elbe et Cent Jours*, 63–79; Orders to General Drouet, 7 May, 3 July 1814, 2 January 1815, *Correspondance de Napoleon* nos. 21566, 21585, 21663; Orders, 10 May 1814, ibid. no. 21568; Napoleon to Drouet, 22 May 1814, ibid. no. 21570.
7. For key documents on Elba's finances, see: Napoleon to Bertrand, 24 June (2 letters), 3 July, 14 August 1815, *Correspondance de Napoleon* nos. 21581, 21582, 21586, 21609; Napoleon to Drouet, 6 September 1814, ibid. no. 21631.

8. For Pauline and Letizia, see: Napoleon to Bertrand, 24 July, 23 August, 11 September 1814, *Correspondance de Napoleon* nos. 21595, 21615, 21635; Decision, 29 September 1814, ibid. no. 21648; Budget for His Majesty, [n.d.] December 1814, ibid. no. 21662.
9. Philip Mansel, *Louis XVIII* (London: John Murray, 2005); Pierre de la Gorce, *Louis XVIII* (Paris: Frederique Patat, 2015).
10. Harold Nicolson, *The Congress of Vienna: A Study in Allied Unity, 1812-1822* (New York: Grove Press, 1946); Henry Kissinger, *A World Restored: Metternich, Castlereagh, and the Problems of Peace, 1812-1822* (London: Weidenfeld and Nicolson, 1999); Gregor Dallas, *The Final Act: The Roads to Waterloo* (New York: Henry Holt, 1996); Adam Zamoyski, *Rites of Peace: The Fall of Napoleon and the Congress of Vienna* (New York: Harper Press, 2007); David King, *Vienna 1814: How the Conquerors of Napoleon Made Love, War, and Peace at the Congress of Vienna* (New York: Broadway Books, 2009); Mark Jarret, *The Congress of Vienna and Its Legacy: War and Great Power Diplomacy after Napoleon* (London: I.B. Taurus, 2014).
11. Talleyrand to Louis XVIII, 15, 24 February 1815, *Talleyrand Mémoires*, 648–9, 651–2, 655; Talleyrand to Louis XVIII, *Talleyrand Mémoires*, 515.
12. For Napoleon's explanation, see: Bonaparte, *Mémoires: L'Ile d'Elbe et Cent Jours*, 81–4.
13. For his own accounts of his return to power, see: Las Cases, *Mémorial*, 2:1247–55; Bonaparte, *Mémoires: L'Ile d'Elbe et Cent Jours*, 84–126. See also Jonathan North, ed., *Napoleon on Elba: Diary of an Eyewitness to Exile* (London: Ravenhall Books, 2004), 188–9.
14. To the French people, 1 March 1815, *Correspondance de Napoleon* no. 21681.
15. To the Army, 1 March 1815, *Correspondance de Napoleon* no. 21682; To the Imperial Guard, 1 March 1815, ibid. no. 21683; Decree, 13 March 1814, ibid. no. 21686; Napoleon to Ney, [n.d.] March 1815, ibid. no. 21689.
16. Jean Savary, duc de Rovigo, *Mémoires de Duc de Rovigo*, 8 vols (Paris: Chez Colburn, 1828), 7:351–2.
17. Bonaparte, *Mémoires: L'Ile d'Elbe et Cent Jours*, 101.
18. Las Cases, *Mémorial*, 2:1468.
19. For Napoleon's Hundred Days culminating with Waterloo, see: Alan Schom, *One Hundred Days: Napoleon's Road to Waterloo* (New York: Oxford University Press, 1992); David Hamilton-Williams, *Waterloo: New Perspectives, The Great Battle Reappraised* (London: Brockhampton Press, 1993); Mark Adkin, *The Waterloo Companion: The Complete Guide to History's Most Famous Land Battle*

(Mechanicsburg, Penn.: Stackpole Books, 2001); Paul Dawson, *Waterloo, The Truth at Last: Why Napoleon Lost the Great Battle* (New York: Frontline Books, 2018).
20. Napoleon to Francis, 1 April 1815, *Correspondance de Napoleon* no. 21753.
21. Las Cases, *Mémorial*, 1:465. For key documents on the constitution, see: Act Additional of the Constitution, [n.d.], *Napoleon Correspondance* no. 21839; Decree, 30 April 1815, ibid. no. 21854
22. Las Cases, *Mémorial*, 1:464–5.
23. Emperor's discourse to Electoral College deputies, 1 June 1815, *Correspondance de Napoleon* no. 21997.
24. Emperor's discourse to the legislatures, 7 June 1815, *Correspondance de Napoleon* no. 22023.
25. Narcise-Achille de Salvandy, *Observations Critique sur le Champs de Mai* (Paris: Delaunay, 1815), 11.
26. For key documents on finance, see: Napoleon to Carnot, 25 March 1815, *Correspondence de Napoleon* no. 21710; Napoleon to Gaudin, 3 April (2 letters) 1815, ibid. nos. 21761, 21763; Napoleon to Mollien, 14 April 1815, ibid. no. 21803; Note Dictated in the Finance Council, 29 April 1815, ibid. no. 21853.
27. Napoleon to Caulaincourt, 3 April 1815, *Correspondance de Napoleon* no. 21759.
28. For accounts of how the great powers reacted to Napoleon's return, see: Talleyrand to Louis XVIII, 7, 12, 13, 14 March 1815, *Talleyrand Mémoires*, 664–6, 667–9, 669–71, 671–2.
29. Declaration, 13 March 1815, *Talleyrand Mémoires*, 670–1.
30. Bonaparte, *Mémoires: L'Ile d'Elbe et Cent Jours*, 162.
31. Napoleon to Caulaincourt, 15 April 1815, *Correspondance de Napoleon* no. 21809.
32. Las Cases, *Mémorial*, 1:410. For Napoleon's assessment of Murat's campaign, see: Bonaparte, *Mémoires: L'Ile d'Elbe et Cent Jours*161–6, 184–7.
33. Bonaparte, *Mémoires: L'Ile d'Elbe et Cent Jours*, 165.
34. For key documents on military preparations, see: Napoleon to Davout 21, 26, 27, 29, 30 (2 letters) March, 2, 3, 11, 15 (2 letters), 17, 18, 27 April, 1 (2 letters), 9, 12 (2 letters) 22 (2 letters), 23, 27, 28 May 1815, *Correspondance de Napoleon* nos. 21692, 21723, 21732, 21741, 21746, 21747, 21756, 21765, 21794, 21810, 21811, 21819, 21822, 21845, 21860, 21861, 21879, 21895, 21896, 21950, 21953, 21960, 21973, 21980; Napoleon to Decrès, 23 March 1815, ibid. no. 21698; Napoleon to Carnot, 27 March, 12 May, 1815, ibid. nos. 21728, 21898; Decree, 28

March 1815, ibid. no. 21737; Napoleon to Andreossy, 3 April 1815, ibid. no. 21767; Decree, 22, 30 April 1815, ibid. nos. 21831, 21855; Napoleon to Suchet, 20 May 1815, ibid. no. 21937; Napoleon to Rapp, 20 May 1815, ibid. no. 21938; Napoleon to Drouot, 30 May, 3 June 1815, ibid. nos. 21994, 22006.
35. For key documents on the Vendée revolt, see: Notes dictated in Council of Ministers, 21 May 1815, *Correspondance de Napoleon* no. 21945; Napoleon to Davout, 22 May 1815, ibid. no. 21948; Bonaparte, *Mémoires: L'Ile d'Elbe et Cent Jours*, 168.
36. For key documents on the campaign, see: Bonaparte, *Mémoires: L'Ile d'Elbe et Cent Jours*, 209–62; Order of the Day, 13 June 1815, *Correspondance de Napoleon* no. 22049; Order of Movement, 14 June 1815, ibid. no. 2053; Bulletin of the Army, 15, 20 June 1815, ibid. no. 22056, 22061; Napoleon to Ney, 16 June 1815, ibid. no. 22058; Napoleon to Grouchy, 16 June 1815, no. 22059; Order to each corps commander, 18 June 1815, ibid. no. 22060. For Napoleon's account of this grand strategy, see: Bonaparte, *Mémoires: L'Ile d'Elbe et Cent Jours*, 203–08.
37. To the Army, 14 June 1815, *Correspondance de Napoleon* no. 22052.
38. Roberts, *Napoleon*, 759.
39. Adkin, *Waterloo Companion*, 73–4.
40. Message to the Chamber of Representatives, 21 June 1815, *Correspondance de Napoleon* no. 22062.
41. Declaration to the French people, *Correspondance de Napoleon* no. 22063.
42. Las Cases, *Mémorial*, 1:69.
43. Ibid., 1:64.
44. Ibid., 1:83–4, 528–9.
45. Protestation, 4 August 1815, *Correspondance de Napoleon* no. 22067.

Chapter 21: The Prometheus

1. Napoleon to Josephine, 16 April 1814, Napoleon Bonaparte, *Lettres d'Amour à Josephine*, ed., Jean Tulard (Paris: Fayard, 1981), 400.
2. Las Cases, *Mémorial*, 1:82.
3. Ibid., 2:1391.
4. Ibid., 1:199.
5. For accounts of Napoleon's daily life on St Helena, see: ibid., 1:265–6, 296–7, 310–12, 336–7, 350–4, 365–6, 842, 2:953–4, 1572–87.
6. Ibid., 1:296.
7. Ibid., 1:243.

8. The most important works dictated by Napoleon to his inner circle on St Helena include: Napoleon Bonaparte, *Mémoires de Napoleon: la Campagne d'Italie*, vol. 1, *la Campagne d'Egypt*, vol. 2, and *L'Ile d'Elbe et Cent Jours* (Paris: Tallandier, 2010, 2011).

The most important works written by his inner circle on St Helena include: Las Cases, *Mémorial*; Henri Gourgaud, *Sâinte-Hèlene, Journal Inédit de 1815 à 1818* (Paris: Flammarion, 1899); Charles Montholon, *Recits de Captivité de l'Empereur Napoleon a Sainte Hélène, par le general de Montholon*, 2 vols (Paris: Paulin, 1847); Barry O'Meara, *Napoleon in Exile or a Voice from St Helena*, 2 vols (London: Simpkin and Marshall, 1822); Louis Marchand, *Mémoires du Marchand, premier valet et executeur testamentaire de l'empereur*, ed. Jean Bourguignon, 2 vols (Paris: Tallandier, 1991).
9. Montholon, *Recits de Captivité*, 15 March 1818.
10. Las Cases, *Mémorial*, 1:641.
11. Ibid., 1:327.
12. Caulaincourt, *With Napoleon in Russia*, 28.
13. Ibid., 209.
14. Chaptal, *Souvenirs*, 102.
15. Caulaincourt, *With Napoleon in Russia*, 318.
16. *Talleyrand Mémoires*, xxxiv.
17. Ibid., 412.
18. Ibid., 411.
19. Louis Madelin, *Fouché, 1759-1820*, 3 vols (Paris: Plon, 1903), 2:385, 1:413.
20. Bonaparte, *Mémoires: L'Ile d'Elbe et Cent Jours*, 163. For Napoleon's other views on Murat, see: ibid., 162–3, 183.
21. Lentz, *France et l'Europe de Napoleon*, 331. See also: Michael Sibalis, 'The Napoleonic Police State', in Philip Dwyer, ed., *Napoleon and Europe* (New York: Routledge, 2001); Peter de Polnay, *Napoleon's Police* (New York: W.H. Allen, 1970).
22. Las Cases, *Mémorial*, 2:968.
23. Lentz, *France et l'Europe de Napoleon*, 294.
24. Las Cases, *Mémorial*, 1:607.
25. Lentz, *France and Europe of Napoleon*, 95, 341.
26. David Bell, *The Cult of the Nation in France: Inventing Nationalism, 1680-1800* (Cambridge, Mass.: Harvard University Press, 2004).
27. Caulaincourt, *With Napoleon in Russia*, 71–2.
28. Lentz, *France et l'Europe de Napoleon*, 487–94.
29. Ibid., 406.
30. Roberts, *Napoleon: A Life*, 395–7.

31. Las Cases, *Mémorial*, 2:1423.
32. For Napoleon's explanation of this vicious circle, see: Las Cases, *Mémorial*, 2:942–6.
33. Owen Connelly, *Blundering to Glory: Napoleon's Military Campaigns* (New York: Rowman and Littlefield, 2006), ix.
34. Phillip R. Cuccia, *Napoleon in Italy: The Sieges of Mantua, 1796-1799* (Norman: University of Oklahoma Press, 2014).
35. Las Cases, *Mémorial*, 2:1159.
36. Bruno Colson, *Napoleon: De la Guerre* (Paris: Perrin, 2011), 78.
37. Napoleon to Joseph, 30 July 1806, *Napoleon Correspondance* no. 12612, 6:667.
38. Charles Montholon, *Memoirs of the History of France during the Reign of Napoleon*, 7 vols (London: Henry Colburn and Company, 1824), 4:316.
39. Montholon, *Recits de la Captivité*, 2:362.
40. Bulletin, 18 October 1805, Markham, *Imperial Glory*, 20.
41. Chandler, *The Campaigns of Napoleon*, xxxii, xxxviii, xl.
42. Ibid., 707.
43. Las Cases, *Mémorial*, 1:622.
44. Napoleon to Joseph, 16 August 1808, *Napoleon Correspondance* no. 18707, 8:957.
45. Las Cases, *Mémorial*, 2:1428.
46. For Napoleon's analysis of the results of restoring the kingdom of Poland, see: Las Cases, *Mémorial*, 2:1371–6.
47. For Napoleon's assessment of his comeback and final fall, see: Bonaparte, *Mémoires: L'Ile d'Elbe et Cent Jours*, 255–62; Las Cases, *Mémorial*, 2:1142–56, 1468–70, 1513–16, 1568–72.
48. Las Cases, *Mémorial*, 1:854.
49. Bonaparte, *Mémoires: L'Ile d'Elbe et Cent Jours*, 41.
50. Ibid., 257.
51. Las Cases, *Mémorial*, 1:608.
52. For the identification and elaboration of the hydra dilemma, see: William R. Nester, *Hearts, Minds, and Hydras: Fighting Terrorism in Afghanistan, Pakistan, America, and Beyond, Dilemmas and Lessons* (Washington D.C.: Potomac Books, 2012).
53. Bonaparte to Joseph, 24 May 1806, *Napoleon Correspondance* no. 12166, 6:455.
54. Caulaincourt, *With Napoleon in Russia*, 302–03.
55. Bonaparte to Talleyrand, April 12, 1801, *Correspondance de Napoleon* no. 5523.
56. Las Cases, *Mémorial*, 1:165–7.

57. Napoleon to Decrès, 6 March 1812, *Napoleon Correspondance* no. 30159, 12:328–9.
58. David Laven and Lucy Riall, eds., *Napoleon's Legacy: Problems of Government in Restoration Europe* (New York: Berg, 2000).
59. Las Cases, *Mémorial*, 1:807–08.
60. Ibid., 2:1206.
61. Bonaparte, *Mémoires: la Campagne d'Italie*, 65–6.
62. Las Cases, *Mémorial*, 1:726.
63. Ibid., 2:1284.
64. Napoleon to Chasseloup-Laubat, 23 June 1804, *Napoleon Correspondance* no. 8948, 4:742.
65. Napoleon to Caulaincourt, 24 March 1809, *Napoleon Correspondance* no. 20523, 9:329.

Bibliography

Primary

Ali, Mameluke, *Souvenirs sur l'empereur, presentes par Christophe Bourachot*, Paris: Arlea, 2000.
Barras, Paul, *Mémoires de Barras*, Paris: Mercure de France, 2010.
Beauharnais, Eugène, *Mémoires et Correspondances du Prince Eugène*, ed. Albert du Casse, Paris: Michel Levy, 1858.
Bertrand, Henri Gratien, *Cahiers de Sainte Hélène: Journal, 1816-1817*, 3 vols, Paris: Sulliver Albin Michel, 1951.
Bonaparte, Hortense, *Mémoires de la Reine Hortense*, Paris: Mercure de France, 2006.
Bonaparte, Jérôme, Mémoires *et Correspondances du Roi Jérôme et de la Reine Catherine*, ed. Albert du Casse, 7 vols, Paris: Dentu, 1861–6.
Bonaparte, Joseph, *Mémoires et Correspondances du Roi Joseph*, 10 vols, ed. Albert du Casse, Paris: Perrotin, 1854.
Bonaparte, Napoleon, *Correspondance de Napoleon Ier, publiée par ordere de l'empereur Napoleon III*, 16 vols, Paris: Claude Tchou, 2002.
Bonaparte, Napoleon, *Correspondance inédite officielle et confidentielle de Napoleon Bonaparte avec les cours étrangeres, en Italie, en Allemagne, et en Egypte*, 7 vols, ed. Charles Theodore Beauvais, Paris: Panchkoucke, 1909–20.
Bonaparte, Napoleon, *La Jeunesse de Napoleon*, 3 vols, ed. Arthur Chuquet, Paris: A. Colin, 1897–9.
Bonaparte, Napoleon, *Lettres inédites de Napoleon I à Marie Louise de 1810 à 1814*, ed. Louis Madelin, Paris: Editions des Bibliothèques nationales de France, 1933.
Bonaparte, Napoleon, *Lettres d'Amour à Josephine*, ed., Jean Tulard, Paris: Fayard, 1981.

Bonaparte, Napoleon, *Mémoires de Napoleon, la Campagne d'Italie*, Paris: Talladier, 2010.
Bonaparte, Napoleon, *Mémoires de Napoleon: la Campagne d'Egypt*, Paris: Talladier, 2011.
Bonaparte, Napoleon, *Mémoires de Napoleon: L'Ile d'Elbe et Cent Jours*, Paris: Talladier, 2011.
Bonaparte, Napoleon, *Napoleon Bonaparte Correspondance Générale*, 12 vols, ed. Thierry et al., Paris: Fayard, 2004–15.
Bonaparte, Napoleon, *Napoleon et Joseph Bonaparte, correspondance intégrale, 1784-1818*, Paris: Talladier, 2007.
Bonaparte, Napoleon, *Napoleon inconnu: papiers inédite, 1769-1793*, 2 vols, ed. Frederic Masson et Guido Biagi, Paris: Ollendorff, 1895.
Bourrienne, Louis, *Mémoires de M de Bourrienne sur Napoleon*, 5 vols, Paris: Garnier, 1899–1900.
Cambacérès, Jean Jacques Regis, *Cambacérès: Mémoires Inédits*, 2 vols, Paris: Perrin, 1999.
Campbell, Sir Neil, *Napoleon at Fontainebleau and Elba, being a journal of occurrences, 1814 and 1815*, London: John Murray, 1869.
Caulaincourt, Armand, *With Napoleon in Russia*, New York: Dover Publications, 2005.
Chaptal, Jean-Antoine, *Mes Souvenirs sur Napoleon*, Paris: Mercure de France, 2009.
Cohendet, Sophie Henriette, *Mémoires sur Napoleon et Marie Louise*, Paris: Mercure de France, 2014.
Constant, Louis, *Mémoires Intimes de Napoleon Ier par Constant son valet de chamber*, 2 vols, Paris: Mercure de France, 1967.
Damas, Roger de, *Mémoires de Roger de Damas*, 2 vols, Paris: Plon, 1914.
Fain, Agathon Jean Franôois, *Memoirs du Baron Fain*, Paris: Arlea, 2001.
Fleury de Charboulon, Edouard, *Les Cents Jours: Mémoires pour server à l'histoire de la vie privée, du retour et du regne du Napoleon en 1815*, (1820) Geneve: Slatkine, 1975.
Fouché, Joseph, *Mémoires*, Paris: Arlea, 1993.
Gourgaud, Gaspard, *Sâinte-Hèlene, Journal Inédit de 1815 à 1818*, Paris: Flammarion, 1899.
Jomini, Baron Henri de, *The Art of War*, Westport, Conn.: Greenwood Press, 1862.
Kerauret, Michel, ed., *Les Grand Traites de l'Empire*, 3 vols, Paris: Nouveau Monde Editions/Fondation Napoleon, 2002, 2004.
Las Cases, Emmanuel de, *Mémorial de Sainte-Helene*, 2 vols, Paris: Seuil, 1968.
Lecestre, Leon, ed., *Lettres Inédite de Napoleon I*, 2 vols, Paris: Plon, 1897.

Lejeune, Louis François, *Mémoires du General Lejeune*, 2 vols, Paris: Editions de Grenadier, 2001.
Marchand, Louis, *Mémoires du Marchand, premier valet et executeur testamentaire du l'empereur*, ed. Jean Bourguignon, 2 vols, Paris: Tallandier, 1991.
Markham, J. David, ed., *Imperial Glory: The Bulletins of Napoleon's Grand Armee, 1805-1814*, London: Greenhill Books, 2003.
Metternich, Richard Clemens Lothar, Fürst von, ed., *The Memoirs of Prince Metternich, 1774-1815*, vols 1–2, London: Richard Bentley, 1880.
Montague, Andrew J., ed., *The American Secretaries of State and their Diplomats*, New York: Knopf, 1927.
Montesquiou, Anatole de, *Souvenirs sur la Révolution, l'Empire, la Restauration, et la Regne de Louis-Philippe*, Paris: Plon, 1961.
Montholon, Charles, *Memoirs of the History of France during the Reign of Napoleon*, 7 vols, London: Henry Colburn and Company, 1824.
Montholon, Charles, *Récits de Captivité de l'Empereur Napoleon a Sainte Hélène, par le general de Montholon*, 2 vols, Paris: Paulin, 1847.
Napoleon (Prince) et Hanoteau, eds., *Lettres Personnelles des Souverains à l'Empereur Napoleon*, Paris: Plon, 1939.
Nicolas, Nicolas Harris, ed., *The Dispatches and Letters of Vice Admiral Lord Viscount Nelson*, 7 vols, London: Cambridge University Press, 2011.
Noailles, Marquis de, ed., *The Life and Memoirs of Count Molé*, New York: George Duran Company, 1924.
North, Jonathan, ed., *Napoleon on Elba: Diary of an Eyewitness to Exile*, London: Ravenhall Books, 2004.
O'Meara, Barry, *Napoleon in Exile or a Voice from St Helena*, 2 vols, London: Simpkin and Marshal, 1922.
Pasquier, Étienne-Denis, *Histoire de mon Temps: Mémoires de Chancellor Pasquier*, 6 vols, Paris: Plon, 1893–4.
Pelet de la Lozère, Joseph, *Opinions de Napoleon sur divers sujets de politique et d'administration recuillies par un member de son Conseil d'État et récit de quelques événements de l'Époque*, Paris: Firmin Didot Freres, 1833.
Remusat, Claire de, *Mémoires de Madame de Remusat, 1802-1808*, ed. P. de Remusat, New York: Appleton, 1924.
Roederer, Pierre Louis, *Oeuvres de comte P.-L. Roederer*, 8 vols, Paris: Firmin Didot Frères, 1854–9.
Rovigo, Jean Savary, duc de, *Mémoires de Duc de Rovigo*, 8 vols, Paris: Chez Colburn, 1828.
Salvandy, Narcise-Achille, *Observations Critique sur le Champs de Mai*, Paris: Delaunay, 1815.

Ségur, Philippe Paul, *Histoire et Mémoires*, 7 vols, Paris: Firmon-Didot Frères, 1877.
Staël, Germaine de, *Considerations sur les Principaux Evenements de la Révolution Française*, Ann Arbor: University of Michigan Library, 2009.
Stanhope, Philip Henry, Earl, *Notes of Conversations with the Duke of Wellington*, London: Prion, 1998.
Thibaudeau, Antoine, *Mémoires sur le Consulat, 1799 à 1804*, Paris: Ponthieu, 1827.
Waresquiel, Emmanuel ed., *Mémoires et Correspondance de Talleyrand*, Paris: Robert Laffont, 2007.

Secondary

Aalestadl, K. and J. Joos, *Revisiting Napoleon's Continental System: Local, Regional and European Experiences*, New York: Palgrave Macmillan, 2014.
Adams, Michael, *Napoleon and Russia*, New York: Bloomsbury Academic, 2006.
Adkin, Mark, *The Waterloo Companion*, Mechanicsburg, Penn.: Stackpole Books, 2001.
Adkins, Roy, *Nelson's Trafalgar: The Battle That Changed the World*, New York: Penguin, 2006.
Adkins, Roy and Lesley, *The War for all the Oceans: From Nelson at the Nile to Napoleon at Waterloo*, New York: Viking, 2006.
Anderson, J.H., *The Campaign of Jena 1806: Napoleon's Decisive Defeat of the Prussian King*, London: Leonaur, 2010.
Anderson, Robin, *Pope Pius VII*, London: Tan Books, 2000.
Andress, David, *The Terror: The Merciless War for Freedom in Revolutionary France*, New York: Farrar, Straus and Giroux, 2006.
Armalié, Marie Célestine Amélie de, *Une Fiancée de Napoleon: Désirée Clary, Reine de Suède, 1777-1860*, Paris: Adamant Media Corporation, 2001.
Arnold, James, *Crisis on the Danube: Napoleon's Danube Campaign of 1809*, New York: Paragon, 1990.
Arnold, James, *Napoleon Conquers Austria: The 1809 Campaign for Vienna*, Westport, Conn.: Praeger, 1995.
Arnold, James, *Marengo and Hohenlinden: Napoleon's Rise to Power*, London: Pen and Sword, 2008.
Asprey, Robert, *The Rise of Napoleon Bonaparte*, New York: Basic Books, 2000.
Asprey, Robert, *The Reign of Napoleon Bonaparte*, New York: Basic Books, 2001.

Austin, Paul Britten, *1812: Napoleon's Invasion of Russia*, London: Greenhill Books, 2000.

Baudus, Florence de, *Pauline Bonaparte*, Paris: Perrin, 2016.

Bell, David, *The Cult of the Nation in France: Inventing Nationalism, 1680–1800*, Cambridge, Mass.: Harvard University Press, 2004.

Bell, David, *The First Total War: Napoleon's Europe and the Birth of Warfare as We Know It*, New York: Houghton Mifflin, 2007.

Birnbaum, Pierre, *L'Aigle et la Synagogue: Napoleon, les Juifs, et l'État*, Paris: Robert Lafford, 2007.

Black, Jeremy, *George III: America's Last King*, New Haven, Conn.: Yale University Press, 2006.

Boudon, Jacques Olivier, *Histoire du Consulat et de l'Empire*, Paris: Perrin, 2000.

Boudon, Jacques Olivier, *Napoleon et les Cultes: Les Religions en Europe à l'aube du XIX siècle, 1800-1815*, Paris: Fayard, 2002.

Bowden, Scott, *Napoleon and Austerlitz: The Glory Years, 1805-1807*, New York: Military History Press, 1992.

Boycott-Brown, Martin, *The Road to Rivoli: Napoleon's First Campaign*, London: Cassell, 2001.

Branda, Pierre, *Le Prix de la Gloire: Napoleon et l'Argent*, Paris: Fayard, 2007.

Branda, Pierre and Thierry Lentz, *Napoleon, l'Esclavage, et les Colonies*, Paris: Fayard, 2006.

Broers, Michael, *Europe Under Napoleon, 1799-1815*, New York: Arnold, 1996.

Bruce, Evangeline, *Napoleon and Josephine: An Improbable Marriage*, New York: Citadel, 2001.

Bruley, Vyes and Thierry Lentz, eds., *Diplomaties au Temps de Napoleon*, Paris: CNSR Editions, 2014.

Burleigh, Nina, *Mirage: Napoleon's Scientists and the Unveiling of Egypt*, New York: Harper, 2008.

Burton, R.G., *The Road to Austerlitz: Napoleon's Campaign of 1805*, London: Leonaur, 2008.

Bush, Robert, *The Louisiana Purchase: A Global Context*, New York: Routledge, 2013.

Cabanis, Andres, *La Presse sous la Consulate et l'Empire*, Paris: Société des Études Robespierristes, 1975.

Camignari, Juan Carlos, *Napoleon and Italy, 1805-1815*, New York: Histories and Collections, 2016.

Caratini, Roger, *Napoleon une Imposture*, Paris: Archipoche, 2002.

Carrington, Dorothy, *Napoleon and his Parents*, New York: Viking, 1988.

Cerami, Charles A., *Jefferson's Great Gamble*, Napier, Ill.: Sourcebooks, 2003.

Chandler, David, *The Campaigns of Napoleon: The Mind and Method of History's Greatest Soldier*, New York: Macmillan, 1966.
Chandler, David, *On the Napoleonic Wars*, London: Greenhill Books, 1991.
Chardigny, Louis, *L'Homme Napoleon*, Paris: Perrin, 2010.
Clausewitz, Carl von, *On War*, New York: Wadsworth Classic, 1999.
Clausewitz, Carl von, *Napoleon's 1796 Italian Campaign*, Lawrence: University of Kansas Press, 2018.
Clayton, Tim, *The Secret War against Napoleon: Britain's Assassination Plot on the French Emperor*, London: Pegasus, 2019.
Cole, Hubert, *The Betrayers: Joachim and Caroline Murat*, New York: Saturday Evening Press, 1972.
Cole, Juan, *Napoleon's Egypt: Invading the Middle East*, New York: Palgrave Macmillan, 2008.
Colson, Bruno, *Napoleon: De la Guerre*, Paris: Perrin, 2011.
Connelly, Owen, *The Gentle Bonaparte: A Biography of Joseph Bonaparte, Napoleon's Elder Brother*, New York: Macmillan, 1968.
Connelly, Owen, *Blundering to Victory: Napoleon's Military Campaigns*, New York: Rowan and Littlefield, 2006.
Cooper, Duff, *Talleyrand*, New York: Grove Press, 1932.
Cosseron, Serge, *Les Mensonges de Napoleon*, Paris: Perrin, 2002.
Crowdy, Terry, *Marengo: The Victory that Placed the Crown of France on Napoleon's Head*, London: Pen and Sword, 2018.
Cuccia, Phillip R., *Napoleon in Italy: The Sieges of Mantua, 1796-1799*, Norman: University of Oklahoma Press, 2014.
Czubaty, Jaroslawy and Ursula Phillips, *The Duchy of Warsaw, 1807-1815: A Napoleonic Outpost in Central Europe*, New York: Bloomsbury Academic, 2016.
Dallas, Gregor, *The Final Act: The Roads to Waterloo*, New York: Henry Holt, 1996,
Davidson, Ian, *The French Revolution: From Enlightenment to Tyranny*, New York: Pegasus, 2017.
Dawson, Paul, *Waterloo, The Truth at Last: Why Napoleon Lost the Great Battle*, New York: Frontline Books, 2018.
De Conde, Alexander, *The Quasi-War: The Politics and Diplomacy of the Undeclared War with France, 1797-1801*, New York: Charles Scribner's Sons, 1966.
Delorme, Eleanor, *Josephine: Napoleon's Incomparable Empress*, New York: Henry Abrams, 2002.
Dodge, Theodore, *Napoleon's Invasion of Russia*, New York: Presidio Press, 2014.

Doyle, William, *The Oxford History of the French Revolution*, New York: Oxford University Press, 1989.
Duffy, Michael, *Soldiers, Sugar and Seapower: The British Expeditions to the West Indies and the War against Revolutionary France*, New York: Oxford University Press, 1987.
Durant, Will and Ariel, *Rousseau and Revolution*, New York: Simon and Schuster, 1967.
Dwyer, Phillip, *Napoleon and Europe*, New York: Routledge, 2001.
Dwyer, Philip, *Napoleon: The Path to Power*, New Haven, Conn.: Yale University Press, 2007.
Dwyer, Philip, *Citizen Emperor: Napoleon in Power*, New Haven, Conn.: Yale University Press, 2013.
Englund, Steven, *Napoleon: A Political Life*, Cambridge, Mass.: Harvard University Press, 2004.
Epstein, Robert M., *Napoleon's Last Victory and the Emergence of Modern War*, Topeka: University Press of Kansas, 1994.
Ehrman, John, *The Younger Pitt*, Stanford, Calif.: Stanford University Press, 1969.
Ellis, Geoffrey, *The Napoleonic Empire*, New York: Palgrave Macmillan, 2007.
Esdaile, Charles J., 'The Napoleonic Period: Some Thoughts on Recent Historiography', *European History Quarterly*, vol. 23 (1993), 415–32.
Esdaile, Charles J., *The Peninsular War: A New History*, New York: Palgrave Macmillan, 2003.
Esdaile, Charles J., *Fighting Napoleon: Guerrillas, Bandits and Adventurers in Spain, 1808-1814*, New Haven, Conn.: Yale University Press, 2004.
Esdaile, Charles J., *Napoleon's Wars: An International History*, New York: Viking, 2007.
Esposito, Vincent and John Etling, *A Military History and Atlas of the Napoleonic Wars*, London:
Greenhill Books, 1999.
Evans, Eric, *William Pitt the Younger*, New York: Routledge, 1999.
Fairweather, Maria, *Madame de Staël*, New York: Da Capo Press, 2005.
Fedorak, Charles, *Henry Addington: Prime Minister, 1801-1804*, Akron: University of Akron Press, 2002.
Flayhart, William H., *The Counterpart to Trafalgar: The Anglo-Russian Invasion of Naples, 1805-1806*, Columbia: University of South Carolina Press, 1992.
Fontana, Biancamaria, *Benjamin Constant and the Post-Revolutionary Mind*, New Haven, Conn.: Yale University Press, 1991.

Fontana, Biancamaria, *Germaine de Staël: A Political Portrait*, Princeton, N.J.: Princeton University Press, 2006.
Forczyk, Robert, *Toulon 1793: Napoleon's First Great Victory*, London: Osprey Books, 2005.
Fournoux, Amable de, *Napoleon et Venise, 1796-1814*, Paris: Editions de Fallois, 2002.
Fox, Charles James, *Napoleon Bonaparte and the Siege of Toulon: The First Victory of a Future Emperor of France, 1793*, London: Leonaur, 2010.
Fraser, Flora, *Pauline Bonaparte: Venus of Europe*, New York: Anchor, 2010.
Gallaher, John, *The Iron Marshal: A Biography of Louis N. Davout*, London: Greenhill, 2000.
Gallet, Jean, *Les Paysans En Guerre: Gens de l'Ouest sous la Révolution*, Paris: Ouest France, 1988.
Gates, David, *The Spanish Ulcer: A History of the Peninsular War*, New York: Da Capo Press, 1986.
Gates, David, *The Napoleonic Wars, 1803-1815*, New York: Arnold, 1997.
Geyl, Pietr, *Napoleon: For and Against*, New Haven: Yale University Press, 1949.
Gill, John, *1809: Thunder on the Danube, Napoleon's Defeat of the Hapsburgs*, New York: Frontline Books, 2010.
Gillet, Jean-Claude, *La Marine Impériale: Le Grand Rêve de Napoleon*, Paris: Bernard Giovanangeli, 2010.
Girard, Patrick, *La Révolution Française et les Juifs*, Paris: Hachette, 1989.
Godechot, Jacques, *Les Contre-Révolutionaires*, Paris: Presses Universitaire de France, 1961.
Godechot, Jacques, *Le Comte d'Antraigues: Un Espion du l'Europe des Émigrés*, Paris: Fayard, 1986.
Goetz, Robert, *1805 Austerlitz: Napoleon and the Destruction of the Third Coalition*, London: Greenhill Books, 2005.
Gorce, Pierre de la, *Louis XVIII*, Paris: Frederique Patat, 2016.
Gray, Francine de Plessis, *Madame de Staël: The First Modern Woman*, New York: Atlas, 2008.
Haegele, Vincent and Patricia Tyson Stroud, *Napoleon et Joseph Bonaparte: le pouvoir et l'ambition*, Paris: Talladier, 2010.
Hales, E.E.Y., *Napoleon and the Pope: The Story of Napoleon and Pius VII*, New York: Eyre and Spottiswoode, 1961.
Hamilton-Williams, David, *Waterloo: New Perspectives, The Great Battle Reappraised*, London: Brockhampton Press, 1993.
Hamilton-Williams, David, *The Fall of Napoleon: The Final Betrayal*, London: Brockhampton Press, 1994.

Harvey, Robert, *War of Wars: The Great European Conflict, 1793-1815*, New York: Carol and Graf, 2006.
Hatley, Janet, *Alexander I*, London: Longmans, 1994.
Heckscher, Eli, *The Continental System: An Economic Interpretation*, Oxford: Oxford University Press, 1922.
Herold, Christopher, *Bonaparte in Egypt*, New York: Harper and Row, 1962.
Herold, Christopher, *Mistress for an Age: A Life of Madame de Staël*, New York: Grove, 2002.
Hibbert, Christopher, *Napoleon: His Wives and Women*, New York: W.W. Norton, 2002.
Hill, George, *The War in La Vendée and the Little Chouannerie*, New York: Loreto, 2013.
Houssaye, Henry, *Napoleon and the Campaign of 1814*, New York: Forgotten Books, 2018.
Howard, Martin, *Death Before Glory: The British Soldier in the West Indies in the French Revolutionary and Napoleonic Wars, 1793-1815*, London: Pen and Sword, 2015.
Howarth, David, *Trafalgar: The Nelson Touch*, New York: Phoenix, 2005.
Ireland, Bernard, *The Fall of Toulon: The Last Opportunity to Defeat the French Revolution*, London: Cassell Military Books, 2005.
Iung, Theodore, *Bonaparte et son Temps*, 3 vols, Paris: Charpentier, 1880–1.
Jarret, Mark, *The Congress of Vienna and Its Legacy: War and Great Power Diplomacy after Napoleon*, London: I.B. Taurus, 2014.
Jouvenel, Bertrand de, *Napoleon et l'Économie Dirigée: Le Blocus Continental*, Paris: Toison d'Or, 1942.
Kagan, Frederick, *The End of the Old Order: Napoleon and Europe, 1801-1805*, New York: Da Capo Press, 2006.
King, David, *Vienna 1814: How the Conquerors of Napoleon Made Love, War and Peace at the Congress of Vienna*, New York: Broadway Books, 2009.
Kissinger, Henry, *A World Restored: Metternich, Castlereagh and the Problems of Peace, 1812-1822*, London: Weidenfeld and Nicolson, 1999.
Klimenko, Michael, *Alexander I: Portrait of an Autocrat*, New York: Hermitage Publishers, 2002.
Kurka, Jon, *A Wilderness So Immense: The Louisiana Purchase and the Destiny of America*, New York: Anchor, 2009.
Lachouque, Henry and Anne S.K. Brown, *The Anatomy of Glory: Napoleon and His Guard*, London: Greenhill Books, 1997.
Lamar, Glenn, *Jérôme Bonaparte: The War Years, 1800-1815*, Westport, Conn.: Praeger, 2000.
Lapray, Olivier, *The Battle of Marengo: The First Victory of the Century*, Paris: Histoire et Collections, 2014.

Laven, David and Lucy Riall, eds., *Napoleon's Legacy: Problems of Government in Restoration Europe*, New York: Berg, 2000.
Lavery, Brian, *Nelson and the Nile: The Naval War against Bonaparte, 1798*, London: Caxton, 2003.
Le Nabour, Eric, *Barras: Le Vicomte Rouge*, Paris: Lattes, 1982.
Lefebre, George, *The Thermidoreans and the Directory: Two Phases of the French Revolution*, New York: Random House, 1964.
Leggiere, Michael V., *Napoleon and Berlin: The Franco-Prussian War in North Germany, 1813*, Norman: University of Oklahoma Press, 2002.
Leggiere, Michael V., *The Fall of Napoleon: The Allied Invasion of France, 1813-1814*, New York: Cambridge University Press, 2007.
Leggiere, Michael, *Napoleon and the Struggle for Germany: The Franco-Prussian War of 1813*, New York: Cambridge University Press, 2015.
Lentz, Thierry, *Le 18-Brumaire: Les Coups d'État de Napoléon Bonaparte*, Paris: Perrin, 1997.
Lentz, Thierry, *Le Grand Consulat, 1799-1804*, Paris: Fayard, 1999.
Lentz, Thierry, *Nouvelle Histoire du Premier Empire: Napoleon et la Conquête de l'Europe, 1804-1810*, Paris: Fayard, 2002.
Lentz, Thierry, *Nouvelle Histoire du Premier Empire: L'Effondrement du Systeme Napoleonien, 1810-1814*, Paris: Fayard, 2004.
Lentz, Thierry, *Napoleon et l'Europe*, Paris: Fayard, 2005.
Lentz, Thierry, *Nouvelle Histoire du Premier Empire: La France et l'Europe de Napoleon, 1804-1814*, Paris: Fayard, 2007.
Lentz, Thierry, *Nouvelle Histoire du Premier Empire: Les Cent-Jours (1815)*, Paris: Fayard, 2007.
Lentz, Thierry, *Joseph Bonaparte*, Paris: Perrin, 2016.
Lieven, Dominic, *Russia against Napoleon*, New York: Penguin, 2009.
Luvaas, Jay, *Napoleon on the Art of War*, New York: Touchstone, 1999.
Lyon, Martin, *Napoleon Bonaparte and the Legacy of the French Revolution*, New York: Palgrave, 1994.
Macgrew, Roderick, *Paul I of Russia, 1754-1801*, New York: Oxford University Press, 1992.
Mackesy, Piers, *British Victory in Egypt: The End of Napoleon's Conquest*, London: Taurus Park, 2010.
Mansel, Philip, *Louis XVIII*, London: John Murray, 2005.
Mansel, Philip, *The Eagle in Splendour: Inside the Court of Napoleon*, London: I.B. Tauris, 2015.
Masson, Frédéric, *Le Sacre et la Couronnement de Napoleon*, Paris: Jacques Tallandier, 1978.
Maude, F.N., *The Jena Campaign 1806: The Twin Battles of Jena and Auerstadt between Napoleon's French and the Prussian Army*, London: Leonaur, 2007.

Maude, F.N., *The Ulm Campaign 1805: Napoleon and the Defeat of the Austrian Army during the 'War of the Third Coalition'*, London: Leonaur, 2018.

Melvin, Frank, *Napoleon's Navigation System: A Study of Trade Control during the Continental Blockade*, New York: Nabu Press, 2010.

Metral, Antoine, *Histoire de l'Expédition à Saint Domingue: Sous le Consulat de Napoleon Bonaparte, 1802-1803*, Paris: Editions Karthala, 1985.

Mokyr, Joel, *The Enlightened Economy: Britain and the Industrial Revolution, 1700-1850*, New York: Penguin, 2011.

Morgan, Kenneth, *The Birth of Industrial Britain: Social Change, 1750-1859*, New York: Pearson, 2004.

Morlott, Georges and Jean Happart, *Talleyrand: Une Mystification Historique*, Paris: Veyrier, 1992.

Morrissey, Robert, *The Economy of Glory: From Ancien Régime to the Fall of Napoleon*, Chicago: University of Chicago Press, 2013.

Mostert, Noel, *The Line Upon the Wind: The Great War at Sea, 1793-1815*, New York: W.W. Norton, 2017.

Nash, Howard, *The Forgotten Wars: The U.S. Navy in the Quasi-War with France and the Barbary Pirates, 1789-1805*, New York: Barnes Company, 1968.

Nafziger, George, *The End of Empire: Napoleon's 1814 Campaign*, London: Helion, 2015.

Nafziger, George, *Lützen and Bautzen: Napoleon's Spring Campaign of 1813*, London: Helion, 2017.

Nafziger, George, *Napoleon at Leipzig: The Battle of Nations, 1813*, London: Helion, 2018.

Nessler, Graham, *An Island-wide Struggle for Freedom: Revolution, Emancipation and Reenslavement in Hispaniola, 1789-1809*, Chapel Hill: University of North Carolina Press, 2016.

Nester, William R., *Napoleon and the Art of Diplomacy: How War and Hubris Determined the Rise and Fall of the French Empire*, New York: Savas Beattie, 2012.

Nester, William R., *Hearts, Minds and Hydras: Fighting Terrorism in Afghanistan, Pakistan, America and Beyond, Dilemmas and Lessons*, Washington D.C.: Potomac Books, 2012.

Nester, William R., *The Hamiltonian Vision: The Art of American Power in the Early Republic, 1789-1800*, Washington D.C.: Potomac Books, 2012.

Nester, William R., *The Jeffersonian Vision, The Art of American Power during the Early Republic, 1801-1815*, Washington D.C.: Potomac Books, 2013.

Nester, William R., *Titan: The Art of British Power in the Age of Revolution and Napoleon*, Norman: University of Oklahoma Press, 2016.

Nester, William R., 'Why Did Napoleon Do It?: The Matrix of Character, Circumstance and Choice', *The Journal of International Diplomacy*, vol. 24, no. 3 (Fall 2013), 353–64.
Nicolson, Harold, *The Congress of Vienna: A Study in Allied Unity, 1812-1822*, New York: Grove Press, 1946.
Oman, Carola, *Napoleon's Viceroy: Eugène de Beauharnais*, London: Hodder and Stoughton, 1966.
Pagé, Sylvain, *Le Mythe Napoleonien: De Las Cases à Victor Hugo*, Paris: CNRS Editions, 2013.
Palmer, Alan, *Napoleon and Marie Louise: The Emperor's Second Wife*, New York: St. Martin's Press, 2001.
Palmer, R.R., *Twelve Who Ruled: The Year of Terror in the French Revolution*, Princeton, N.J.: Princeton University Press, 1941.
Paret, Peter, *The Cognitive Challenge of War: Prussia 1806*, Princeton, N.J.: Princeton University Press, 2009.
Parkinson, Northcote, *Britannia Rules: The Classic Age of Naval History, 1793-1815*, London: Royal Naval Museum, 1994.
Pasquino, Pasquale, *Sieyès et l'Invention de la Constitution en France*, Paris: Jacob, 1998.
Passano, Pierre de, *Histoire de l'Annexion de la Corse*, Paris; Horvath, 1990.
Petre, F. Loraine, *Napoleon's Conquest of Prussia, 1806*, London: Greenhill, 1993.
Petre, F. Loraine, *Napoleon at Bay 1814*, London: Greenhill, 1994.
Petre, F. Loraine, *Napoleon's Campaign, 1806-1807*, London: Greenhill, 2001.
Petre, F. Loraine, *Napoleon's Last Campaign in Germany, 1813*, New York: Forgotten Books, 2017.
Pflund, Rosalynd, *Talleyrand and His World*, Afton, Minn.: Afton Press, 2010.
Pichichero, Christy, *The Military Enlightenment: War and Culture in the French Empire, From Louis XIV to Napoleon*, Ithaca, N.Y.: Cornell University Press, 2017.
Plessis, Alain, *Histoires de la Banque de France*, Paris: Albin Michel, 1998.
Pocock, Tom, *A Thirst for Glory: The Life of Admiral Sir Sidney Smith*, London: Thistle, 2013.
Polnay, Peter de, *Napoleon's Police*, New York: W.H. Allen, 1970.
Price, Munro, *Napoleon: The End of Glory*, New York: Oxford University Press, 2014.
Ragsdale, Hugh, ed., *Paul I: A Reassessment of his Life and Reign*, Pittsburgh: University of Pittsburgh Press, 1979.
Ray, Marie-Pierre, *Alexander I: The Tsar Who Defeated Napoleon*, Dekalb: Northern Illinois University Press, 2012.

Reilly, Robin, *William Pitt the Younger*, New York: Putnam's Sons, 1978.
Riall, Lucy, *Risorgimento: The History of Italy from Napoleon to Nation-State*, New York: Palgrave Macmillan, 2008.
Riehn, Richard K., *1812: Napoleon's Russian Campaign*, New York: McGraw Hill, 1991.
Riley, Jonathan, *Napoleon and the World War of 1813: Lessons in Coalition Warfighting*, London: Frank Cass, 2000.
Riley, Jonathan, *Napoleon as a General*, London: Hambledon Continuum, 2007.
Riley, Jonathan, *1813: Empire at Bay, The Sixth Coalition and the Downfall of Napoleon*, London: Pen and Sword, 2013.
Roberts, Andrew, *Napoleon: A Life*, New York: Viking, 2014.
Ros, Martin, *Night of Fire: The Black Napoleon and the Battle for Haiti*, New York: Da Capo, 1994.
Rothenberg, Gunther, *The Art of Warfare in the Age of Napoleon*, Bloomington: University of Indiana Press, 1981.
Rothenberg, Gunther, *Napoleon's Great Adversary: Archduke Charles and the Austrian Army, 1792-1814*, New York: Sarpedon, 1995.
Saul, Norman, *Russia and the Mediterranean, 1797-1807*, Chicago: University of Chicago Press, 1970.
Schama, Simon, *Citizens: A Chronicle of the French*, New York: Vintage, 1990.
Schneid, Frederick, *Napoleon's Italian Campaigns, 1805-1815*, Westport, Conn.: Praeger, 2002.
Schneid, Frederick, *Napoleon's Conquest of Europe: The War of the Third Coalition*, Westport, Conn.: Praeger, 2005.
Schom, Alan, *Trafalgar: Countdown to Battle, 1803-1805*, New York: Oxford University Press, 1990.
Schom, Alan, *One Hundred Days: Napoleon's Road to Waterloo*, New York: Oxford University Press, 1992.
Schom, Alan, *Napoleon Bonaparte*, New York: Harper Collins, 1997.
Secher, Reynald, *A French Genocide: The Vendée*, South Bend, Ind.: Notre-Dame University Press, 2003.
Shaw, Stanford, *Between Old and New: The Ottoman Empire under Selim III, 1789-1806*, Cambridge, Mass.: Harvard University Press, 1971.
Sherwig, John M., *Guineas and Gunpowder: British Aid in the Wars with France, 1793-94*, Cambridge, Mass.: Harvard University Press, 1969.
Sibalis, Michael, 'The Napoleonic Police State', in Philip Dwyer, ed., *Napoleon and Europe*, New York: Routledge, 2001.
Smith, Digby, *The Greenhill Napoleonic Wars Data Book*, London: Greenhill Press, 1998.

Smith, Digby, *1813 Leipzig: Napoleon and the Battle of Nations*, London: Greenhill, 2006.
Smith, Digby, *Murat's Army: The Army of the Kingdom of Italy, 1806-1815*, London: Helion, 2018.
Sparrow, Elizabeth, *Secret Service: British Agents in France, 1792-1815*, London: Boydell Press, 1999.
Strathern, Paul, *Napoleon in Egypt*, New York: Bantam, 2009.
Stinchcombe, William, *The XYZ Affair*, New York: Praeger, 1980.
Storozynski, Alex, *The Peasant Prince: Thaddeus Kosciusko and the Age of Revolution*, New York: St. Martins Griffin, 2010.
Stuart, Andrea, *The Rose of Martinique: A Life of Napoleon's Josephine*, New York: Grove Press, 2003.
Sutherland, Christine, *Marie Walewska: Napoleon's Great Love*, New York: Viking, 1979.
Swartz, Bernard, ed., *The Code Napoleon and the Common Law World*, New York: Lawbook Exchange, 1998.
Tackett, Timothy, *The Coming of the French Revolution*, Cambridge, Mass.: Harvard University Press, 2017.
Thiers, Adolphe, *Histoire du Consulat et empire*, 12 vols, Paris: Paulin, 1845–62.
Thiers, Adolphe, *History of the Consulate and the Empire of France under Napoleon*, vol. 1, New York: Palata Press, 2015.
Thrasher, Peter, *Pasquale Paoli: An Enlightened Hero*, New York: Archon Books, 1970.
Tilly, Charles, *The Vendée*, Cambridge, Mass.: Harvard University Pres, 1964.
Trinder, Barrie, *Britain's Industrial Revolution: The Making of a Manufacturing People*, New York: Carnegie Publishing, 2014.
Tulard, Jean, *Napoleon ou le Mythe du Sauveur*, Paris: Fayard, 1987.
Uffindell, Andrew, *Napoleon 1814: The Defence of France*, London: Pen and Sword, 2009.
Verge-Franceshi, Michel, *La Marine Française au XVIII Siècle*, Paris: Sedes, 1996.
Verge-Franceschi, Michel, *Pasquale Paoli: Un Corse de Lumières*, Paris: Fayard, 2005.
Wagner, Chip, *Double Emperor: The Life and Times of Francis of Austria*, New York: Hamilton Books, 2018.
Waresquiel, Emmanuel de, *Talleyrand: Le Prince Immobile*, Paris: Fayard, 2003.
Weiner, Margery, *The Parvenu Sisters: Elisa, Pauline and Caroline Bonaparte*, London: Murray, 1964.

Whaley, Leigh Ann, *The Impact of Napoleon, 1800-1815*, Lanham, Maryland: Scarecrow Press, 1997.
Williams, Kate, *Ambition and Desire: The Dangerous Life of Josephine Bonaparte*, New York: Ballantine Books, 2014.
Winegarten, Renee, *Germaine de Staël and Benjamin Constant: A Duel Biography*, New Haven, Conn.: Yale University Press, 2008.
Woloch, Isser, *Napoleon and His Collaborators: The Making of a Dictatorship*, New York: W.W. Norton, 2001.
Wood, Dennis, *Benjamin Constant: A Biography*, New York: Routledge, 1993.
Woronoff, Denis, *The Thermidorean Regime and the Directory, 1794-1799*, New York: Cambridge University Press, 1984.
Wright, D.G., *Napoleon and Europe*, New York: Pearson, 1984.
Zamoyski, Adam, *Moscow 1812: Napoleon's Fatal March*, New York: Harper Collins, 2004.
Zamoyski, Adam, *Rites of Peace: The Fall of Napoleon and the Congress of Vienna*, New York: Harper Press, 2007.

Index

Acton, John 146, 148
Adams, John 131
Addington, Henry 123
Alembert, Jean d' 289
Alexander I 120, 121, 150, 151, 169, 175, 186, 190, 192, 193, 194–5, 202, 205, 214, 223–6, 253, 256, 258, 263, 302–03, 310, 311, 313–17, 321, 322, 323, 329, 332, 333, 343, 347, 373, 384, 385
Alexander the Great 3, 23, 71, 311–12, 389
Ali Pasha 73
Allemand, Zacherie 182, 205
Alquier, Charles 148, 281, 282
Alvinczy, Joseph 61, 62
Andreossy, André 150, 213
Antraigues, Louis de Launay, Count d' 67, 162
Argenteau, Eugene 52
Augereau, Charles 6, 50–1, 52, 53, 56, 60, 67, 98, 154, 157, 172, 187, 193, 209, 215, 218, 219–20, 319, 347, 350, 374
Austria 22, 26, 28, 29, 40, 44, 51, 52–69, 71, 74, 93, 109, 112–18, 146, 147, 148, 150, 160, 164, 177, 181–96, 197, 202, 205, 213, 221–2, 225–6, 254, 255, 258, 261–74, 282, 286, 296, 301, 302, 303, 306, 309, 324, 352, 353, 358, 367, 381, 382, 387, 388, 392, 393
Austrian Netherlands 40, 68

Babeuf, François 97
Bachmann, Niklaus 360
Baciocchi, Felix 227, 239
Bagration, Peter 193, 319, 321
Baird, David 257, 258
Barbé-Marbois, François 127, 136, 173, 191, 198, 356
Barclay de Tolly, Michael 319, 320, 360
Barras, Paul 46–7, 48, 49, 55, 68, 98–9
Barthélemy, Balthazar 97
battles and sieges
　Abensburg 265
　Aboukir 94, 138
　Acre 90–3, 380
　Alexandria 77–8
　Arcis-sur-Aube 345, 380
　Arcole 61
　Aspern-Essling 4, 268–9, 380, 382–3
　Austerlitz 194–5, 215, 294, 311, 333, 380

Bailen 252
Bassano 61, 380
Bautzen 334
Berezina 326
Biberach 114
Biezun 215
Borodino 322–3, 333, 382, 385
Breslau/Wroclaw 219
Brienne 343
Cairo 88
Caldiero 61, 191
Calliano 61
Capri 307
Castiglione 6, 60
Castle Bolognese 66
Ceva 53
Champaubert 343
Château-Thierry 343
Chobrakhyr 80
Copenhagen 120, 390
Corunna 259
Craone 345
Czarnowo 215
Damanhur 80
Danzig 219, 221, 222
Dego 53, 54
Dennewitz 337
Dilligen 114
Dresden 337, 385
Durrenstein 190
Eckmühl 265, 381
El Arish 90
Elchingen 189
Elvas 129
Engen 114
Eylau 7, 219–20, 222, 310, 382
Feldkirch 118
Fort Bard 115
Fort Mulgrave 43
Friedland 222–3, 333, 361
Genoa 114, 115
Gradisca 63
Grodchno 268
Grossberen 337
Gundelfingen 114
Gunzburg 189
Haifa 92
Hamburg 334
Hanau 338
Harburg 118
Haslach 189
Heilsberg 222
Hochstadt 114
Hohenlinden 118, 147
Jaffa 90–1, 389–90
Jena-Auerstadt 25, 209–10, 333, 380
Katzbach 337
Kirchberg 114
Klagenfurt 63
Krasnoi 326
Kulm 337
La-Fère-Champenoise 346
La Rothière 343, 380
La Souffel 364
Landshut 118, 265
Lâon 345, 380
Launingenn 114
Leipzig 337–8, 380, 382, 385, 386
Ligny 361–2, 386
Lodi 56
Lonato 60
Lützen 332–3
Madelene Island 40
Mainz 48
Malta 75–7, 118, 119, 120, 381
Mantua 56, 60, 62
Marengo 112, 116–17, 121, 128, 138, 147, 222, 361
Maloyarslavets 325
Medina del Rio Seco 252
Memmingen 114, 189

Messina 307–08
Millesimo 53, 54
Moesskirch 114, 138
Mogilev 321
Mondovi 53, 54
Monte-Legino 53
Monte Nave 115
Montebello 115
Montenotte 53
Montereau 343
Montmirail 343
Mount Tabor 92, 138
Nangis 343
Nile/Aboukir Bay 6, 82–3, 110
Nordlingen 118
Oberhausen 118
Obidos 252
Ocksay 63
Paris Mob 46–7
Paris (1814) 346
Piave 267
Pultusk 215
Pyramids, the 81, 138
Quatre Bras 361–2, 386
Raab 267–8
Ratisbonne/Regensburg 3, 265, 382
Rausnitz 193
Raszyn 268
Rivoli 62, 138
Roliça 252
Roveredo 61
Saalfeld 209
Sacile 267
Saint Dizier 346
Schewennigen 114
Schweidnitz 221
Sediman 82
Smolensk 321–2
Soldau 215
Stockach 114

Stralsund 219, 266
Toulon 3, 41–3, 47
Toulouse 237
Trafalgar 191–2, 298, 389
Turbigo 115
Ulm 189, 380
Valutino-Gora 322
Vauchamps 343
Viazma 325
Vimiero 252
Vitoria 335
Wagram 270–1, 382
Waterloo 23, 25, 362–4, 380, 382
Wertigen 189
Wischau 193
Worgel 266
Znaim 271
Bavaria 22
Beauchamp, Pierre 75
Beauharnais, Alexandre 48
Beauharnais, Augusta 227, 230–1
Beauharnais, Eugène 28, 48, 75, 95, 160, 161, 186, 187, 199, 214, 227, 230–2, 258, 264, 266, 267, 268, 270, 294, 318, 329, 330, 332, 333, 338, 344, 347, 356
Beauharnais, Stephanie 232, 240–1, 303
Beaulieu, Jean 52, 55, 56, 60
Beethoven, Ludwig van 294
Bellegarde, Heinrich 265, 268, 339
Belveder, Fernando 257
Bennigsen, Levin von 186, 214–15, 219–20, 222–3, 319, 336
Berg, Friedrich von 333
Bernadotte, Jean-Baptiste 73, 98, 99, 100, 172, 187, 188, 192, 194, 195, 202, 209, 210, 218, 219–20, 270, 271, 310–11, 317, 336, 337
Bernier, Étienne 122

Berthier, Alexandre 51, 69, 75, 82, 95, 112, 128, 154, 172, 173, 303, 322, 330, 347, 359, 368, 382
Berthollet, Claude 75, 84, 95
Bertrand, Henri 220, 268, 332, 333, 355, 368
Bessières, Jean 9, 95, 165, 187, 209, 251, 252, 257, 258, 264, 270, 271, 318, 333
Biennais, Martine 294
Biran, Maine de 293
Blake, Joaquin 252, 257
Blücher, Gebhard von 332, 333, 336, 337, 339, 342–6, 360–5, 386–7
Bon, Louis 75, 78, 89, 92
Bonaparte, Alexandrine 242
Bonaparte, Carlo 33–5, 36, 39
Bonaparte, Caroline 33, 201–02, 227, 229, 234–5, 238, 286, 303, 307–08, 347, 351, 356, 358
Bonaparte, Catherine 172, 227, 237
Bonaparte, Elisa 3, 33, 227, 228, 229, 231, 238, 239, 279, 286, 347, 356
Bonaparte, Elizabeth Patterson 236
Bonaparte, Hortense Beauharnais 48, 152, 183, 227, 232, 233–4, 235, 291, 301, 303, 356
Bonaparte, Jérôme 3, 172, 218, 219, 221, 224, 225, 227, 236–7, 238, 263, 266, 286, 306, 318, 320, 347, 356, 363
Bonaparte, Joseph 16, 20, 30, 33, 34, 39, 45, 74, 96, 98, 99, 100, 108, 118, 119, 122, 131, 200, 204, 217, 225, 227, 229, 235–6, 242–3, 249, 250, 252, 253, 256, 259, 286, 292, 294, 301, 307, 308–09, 311, 335, 344, 346, 347, 356, 365
Bonaparte, Josephine 7, 10, 36, 47–9, 51, 55–6, 62, 82, 96, 107, 114, 127, 145, 152, 176, 182, 215, 216, 223, 230, 234, 256, 297, 300–02, 304, 351, 368
Bonaparte, Julie Clary 45, 236, 311
Bonaparte, Letizia Ramolino 33, 34, 36–7, 356
Bonaparte, Louis 33, 75, 95, 208, 210, 225, 227, 229, 232, 233–4, 235, 286, 289, 294, 297, 301, 305, 306, 347
Bonaparte, Louis Napoleon 232
Bonaparte, Lucien 33, 35, 39, 41, 96, 98, 101, 102, 108, 128, 130, 227, 228, 229, 241–3, 245, 301, 356
Bonaparte, Marie Louise 284, 303–04, 309, 317–18, 331–2, 346, 347, 348, 352, 359
Bonaparte, Napoleon
  beliefs 11–12, 38–9, 275–8, 295
  character 2–32, 35–6, 229–303, 370–1, 393
  childhood 33–5
  Continental System 19, 211, 296–7, 299, 300, 304–05, 314–15, 379, 388
  coup 97–101
  economic policies 16–19, 141, 198–9, 288–9, 300
  education 34–5
  Elba 285, 347, 348, 355, 368
  Emperor 9, 170–8, 179–96, 197–226, 227–49, 250–9, 260–74, 275–85, 286–312, 313–27, 328–48, 349–67
  espionage 21–2
  First Consul 9, 100–08, 109–24, 125–37, 138–43, 144–58, 159–69
  generalship 23–30, 380–7

propaganda/public relations 22, 105
reforms 16–19, 138–43, 199, 278–80, 287–90, 294–6, 377–8
Saint Helena 3, 31, 49, 134, 313, 355, 367, 368–96
statesmanship 12–16, 20–3, 54–5, 63, 64–5, 101–08, 370–80
writings 36–7
young officer 35–41
Bonaparte, Napoleon Charles 183, 232, 233, 234, 236, 301, 347
Bonaparte, Napoleon François 304
Bonaparte, Napoleon Louis 232
Bonaparte, Pauline 9, 33, 132, 227, 238, 239–40, 243, 301, 339, 351, 356
Borghese, Camille 227, 240, 243
Bourbon de Conde, Louis 168
Bourcet, Pierre de 24
Bourrienne, Louis 8, 70
Brissot, Jacques 125
Britain 8, 17, 18, 19, 20, 26, 29, 40, 41, 42, 43, 69, 72, 75, 83, 90, 106, 107, 109, 110, 112, 117, 118, 120–1, 123–4, 126, 128, 130, 131, 134, 135, 144, 150, 151, 153–8, 161–4, 165–7, 169, 174, 177, 178, 180, 181, 183, 187, 191, 192, 200, 201–02, 204, 205, 211–12, 224, 255, 261, 263, 271, 280, 284, 297, 298, 303, 306, 315, 333, 352, 353–67, 375, 379–80, 387, 389, 390–1, 393
Britain – Empire
  Ceylon 123
  Gibraltar 156
  India 90, 389, 390
  Ireland 154, 155, 375
  Trinidad 123
Brogniart, Alexandre 288

Brueys, François 6, 64, 73, 74, 79, 82–3
Bruix, Eustache 110–11, 112, 156
Brune, Guillaume 107, 117–18, 119, 172, 185, 187, 364
Brunswick, Frederick Duke of 208–10
Bubna, Ferdinand 273
Buchotte, Jean-Baptiste 43
Bülow von Dennewitz, Friedrich 332, 334, 337, 339, 360
Bunbury, Henry 367
Burrand, Harry 252–3
Buttafoco, Matteo 36, 39
Buxhowden, Friedrich von 186, 192

Cadore, Jean Champagny, Duke 173, 226, 243, 255, 268, 271, 272–3, 274, 289
Cadoudal, Georges 107, 162, 165–7, 169, 170
Caesar, Julius 3, 23, 71
Caivagnac, François 308
Cambacérès, Jean 18, 96, 98, 103, 104, 108, 127, 139, 140, 163, 167, 173, 260, 289, 290, 327, 332, 338, 355
Campbell, James 308
Campbell, Neil 349, 351, 353, 357
campaigns
  Austria (1805) 24, 186–96, 380
  Austria (1809) 261–74, 314, 380
  Chouans 41, 46, 106–07, 157, 160
  Egyptian 3, 10, 71–95, 99, 121, 380
  France (1814) 24, 25, 338, 380
  Germany (1813) 24, 25, 285, 328–38, 380, 385–6
  Italian (1795) 44, 45

Italian (1796–7) 7, 10, 24, 25, 27, 50–70, 99, 380, 381
Italian (1800) 112–18
naval 111–12, 180–1, 187–8, 191–2, 205, 217, 298
Palestine 89–93, 389–90
Peninsula 3, 31, 250–4, 257–9, 313, 315, 330, 335, 338, 380, 383–4
Poland 212–26, 289
Portugal 129
Prussia 25, 206–12, 289
Rhône 41
Russian 3, 31, 284, 290, 312, 313–27, 380, 381, 383–5
Saint Domingue/Haiti 132–5, 389
Vendée 41, 46, 106–07, 157, 359
Walcheren 271–2
Waterloo 359–66, 380, 386–7
Canning, George 255
Caprara, Gian 178
Carnot, Lazare 112, 118
Carteaux, Jean-Baptiste 42, 43
Castanos, Francisco 252, 257
Castlereagh, Robert Stewart 343
Catharine Princess 303, 314
Caucault, François 122
Caulaincourt, Armand 21, 168, 172, 258, 262, 317, 334, 336, 341–2, 344–5, 347, 355, 357, 358, 370, 377
Cervellon, Felipe 252
Chabulon, Édouard Fleury de 353
Chalgrin, Jean 288
Championnet, Jean 146–7
Chaptal, Jean-Antoine 5, 8, 12, 19, 104, 122–3, 141, 143, 173, 372
Charlemagne 3, 23, 175, 281, 282, 294, 388, 395

Charles, Archduke 62–3, 186, 191, 193, 261–2, 263, 264, 265, 269, 270–1, 382–3
Charles, Count d'Artois 150
Charles Augustus of Saxe-Weimar 219
Charles of Baden 240–1
Charles III 292
Charles IV 119, 128, 129, 145, 146, 156–7, 179, 219, 243, 244–9
Charles XIII 310
Charles Emmanuel IV 145
Charles Frederick 168, 241
Charles, Hippolyte 55
Chasteler de Courcelles, Jean 265, 266
Chateaubriand, René 293
Chatham, John Pitt, Earl 271
Chauvet, Felix 87
Chichagov, Vassilivich 325, 326
Christian VII 120
Christophe, Henri 134
Clarke, Henri 6, 26, 66, 67, 68, 146, 212, 258, 299, 330, 338
Clary, Désirée 45–6, 311
Clausel, Bertrand 360
Clisson, Simon 75
Cobenzl, Johann 66
Cobenzl, Louis 20, 68, 74, 118, 119, 183
Colbert, Auguste 151
Colbert, Jean-Baptiste 17
Colleredo, Josef 364
Colli-Marchini, Michelangelo 52–3, 54
Collot, George 135
Condorcet, Antoine 125
Congress of Rastadt 68, 69, 74
Congress of Vienna 352, 353, 357–8, 393

INDEX

Consalvi, Hercule 122, 280, 285
Constant, Benjamin 164, 356
Constant, Louis 9
Constantine, Grand Duke 186
Conté, Nicolas 75
Corsica 4, 11, 33, 36, 38–9, 41
Corvisart, Jean 301
Cromwell, Oliver 234, 242
Cuesta, Gregorio 252, 253
Czartoryski, Adam 214

D'Affry, Louis 153
Dalberg, Charles 203
Dallemagne, Claude 56
Dalmatia/Ragusa 214
Dalrymple, Hew 252–3
Daru, 294
Daure, Jean 308
David, Jacques Louis 176, 294
Davie, William 131–2
Davout, Louis 75, 162, 166, 172, 187, 192, 193, 194, 195, 209–10, 213, 215, 218, 258, 264, 265, 269, 270, 271, 318, 323, 332, 334, 336, 356, 359, 382, 385, 386
De La Tour, Victor 59
Decean, Charles 360
Decrès, Denis 135, 154, 155, 167, 173, 180–1, 182, 205, 217, 253, 298, 356
Dejean, Jean 173
Delaroche, Paul 294
Denmark 120, 225, 331, 335, 390
Denon, Dominque 75, 95, 138
Desaix, Louis 75, 78, 82, 94, 116
Despinoy, Hyacinthe 58
Dessalines, Jean 134
Djezzar Pasha 73, 86, 87, 89, 90–3
Dolgorouski, Peter 193

Dombrowski, Henri 213, 221
Dommartin, Eleazar 75
Doppet, François 42, 43
Drake, Francis 162, 163
Du Teil, Jean 41
Du Teil, Pierre 37
Dubois, Louis 105, 287
Ducos, Pierre 98, 99, 100, 101
Dugommier, Jacques 43
Duhesme, Philibert 115, 251, 252
Dumas, Thomas 75
Dumerbion, Pierre 44
Dumouriez, Charles 168
Dumuy, Jean-Baptiste 79
Dupont, Pierre 251, 252
Dupuy, Dominque 88
Duroc, Christophe 9, 118, 120–1, 172, 185, 188, 189, 230–1, 232, 333
Durosnel, Antoine 159

Ellsworth, Oliver 131–2
Elphinstone, George Keith 367
Emmet, Robert 154
Enghien, Louis de Bourbon, Duke d' 168–9, 170, 211
Erlon, Jean-Baptiste Drouet, Count 361, 362, 363, 364, 386
Essen, Hans von 325
Europe 3, 4, 11, 14, 19, 29, 30–1, 59, 110, 313, 391–3

Fain, Agathon 13
Falga, Louis Cafferelli du 74, 75
Ferdinand, Grand Duke 119, 145, 146, 186, 188, 189, 196, 202, 204, 264, 268
Ferdinand IV 146–7, 148, 177, 199–201, 217, 225, 282, 352
Ferdinand VII 244–8, 257, 341

Fesch, Joseph 172, 200, 240, 280
Fontaine, Pierre 288
Forfait, Pierre 112, 127
Fouché, Joseph 15, 22, 98, 99, 100,
    159, 163, 164, 169, 173, 174,
    189, 212, 241–2, 258, 260–1,
    272, 279, 290, 291, 293, 295,
    306, 356, 366, 372, 373, 374
Fox, Charles James 204, 205
France 3, 11, 15, 16, 29, 33,
    38–9, 110
  cultural and economic
    institutions 138–43
  Girondins 41
  Jacobins 38, 40–1, 100, 162,
    165, 291
  political systems 18, 37–8, 40,
    44, 46–7, 97–8, 101–08, 126,
    170–6, 228, 288–9, 341, 351–2,
    355–7, 365–6
  Revolution 3, 23, 37–8, 40,
    97–8, 110, 126, 138, 171,
    198, 213, 291
France – Overseas Empire
  Destrade 124
  Guadeloupe 125, 126, 134, 205
  Guyana 67, 125, 126, 133, 161,
    165, 298
  Les Saintes 125, 126
  Louisiana 128–9
  Marie Galante 125
  Martinique 48, 125, 126, 127, 205
  Saint Domingue/Haiti 124, 125,
    126, 132–5, 240, 298
  Saint Lucia 125, 126, 134
  Saint Martin 125
  Senegal 298
  Tobago 125, 126
Francis II/I 66–7, 68, 109, 117, 118,
    119, 150, 176, 186, 192, 193,
    195, 219, 254, 255, 261, 266,
    272, 273, 302, 328, 329, 335,
    343, 356
Frederick of Saxe-Hildburghausen
    219
Frederick of Württemberg 237,
    254, 264
Frederick II the Great 8, 23, 24,
    190, 206, 210–11
Frederick VI 331
Frederick Augustus III 208, 214,
    226, 265–6, 327
Frederick William III 121, 150, 151,
    154, 175, 185, 190, 192, 201–02,
    206, 207–10, 220, 221, 222,
    223–6, 310, 328, 330, 343
Frimont, Johann 360, 364
Fulton, Robert 289

Galitzin, André 215
Gallitzin, Dmitri 268
Gallo, Marzio Mastrilli, Duke 63,
    66, 67, 200
Ganteaume, Honoré 27, 83, 95, 132
Gaudin, Martin 112, 173, 198, 357
George III 109, 123, 150, 152, 153,
    154, 177, 204, 255
George, Prince Regent/IV 366
German states and associations
  Baden 69, 168, 184, 187, 196, 202,
    203, 204
  Bavaria 69, 109, 162, 163, 183,
    184, 186, 187, 188, 189, 196,
    202, 203–04, 264, 267, 273,
    274, 303
  Berg and Cleves 201–02, 204,
    234–5, 286
  Confederation of the Rhine
    22, 203–04, 208, 225, 237,
    254, 258, 264, 286, 296, 314,
    333, 392
  Frankfurt 69, 168

Hamburg 163–4, 168, 314
Hanover 69, 153, 154, 183, 185, 187, 188, 190, 196, 201, 202, 205
Hesse-Cassel 210, 219
Hesse-Darmstadt 69, 184, 202, 204
Holy Roman Empire 68, 69, 184, 202–03
Mainz 69
Oldenburg 314, 315
Saxony 69, 203, 208, 210, 214, 266, 327
Westphalia 203, 224, 225, 236–7, 263, 286, 306
Württemberg 184, 187, 196, 202, 203, 204, 237, 254, 264
Germany 392–3
Godoy, Manuel 128, 130, 156, 179–80, 244, 245–9
Goethe, Johann Wolfgang 36, 255
Gohier, Louis 98, 99, 100
Gottorp-Holstein, George 314
Gourgaud, Gaspard 368
Gouvion St Cyr, Laurent 114, 130, 135, 172, 187, 191, 199–200, 257, 280, 318, 325, 332, 337, 385
Gravina, Charles 111
Grawert, Julius 319
Gregoire, Henri 125, 126
Grenier, Paul 307–08
Grenville, William 204
Gribeauval, Jean-Baptiste 26
Grouchy, Emmanuel de 172, 359, 361, 365, 386–7
Guibert, Jacques Antoine, de 24
Gustav IV 120, 190, 209, 310

Hamilton, William 146
Hannibal 3, 23, 294, 395

Hardenberg, Karl von 201, 202, 221, 310
Hatzfeld, Franz von 211
Haugwitz, Christian 192, 201, 202, 207
Haussmann, Georges 287
Hauy, René 139
Hawkesbury, Robert 123, 169
Haydn, Joseph 165
Hedouville, Gabriel 107–08, 169
Hill, Rowland 360
Hiller, Johann von 265, 269
Hobbes, Thomas 13
Hofer, Andreas 266
Hogendorp, Thierry 320
Hohenlohe, Frederick 208–10
Hohenzollern, Friedrich 269
Hompesch, Ferdinand von 76
Hood, Samuel 42
Hulin, Pierre 168–9
Humboldt, Wilhelm 336
Hussein Mustafa 94

Ibrahim Pasha 73, 81, 82, 89
Industrial Revolution 17, 18
Islam 72, 82, 86, 89–90
Italian states
  Cisalpine Republic 64–5, 115, 119, 123, 144
  Cispadane Republic 64–5, 66
  Elba 3, 60, 128, 145, 151
  Genoa/Ligurian Republic 14, 38, 45, 51–2, 55, 58–9, 60, 65, 113, 119, 123, 150, 198, 289–90
  Italian Republic/Kingdom 144, 148, 149, 150, 177, 191, 196, 198, 200, 224, 225, 231–2, 286, 296, 392
  Lombardy 52, 57
  Lucca and Piombino 52, 129, 238, 286

Naples/Two Sicilies/
  Parthenopean Republic 22,
  43, 51, 52, 57, 60, 83, 109, 123,
  146–8, 150, 151, 177, 184, 191,
  199–201, 204, 205, 217, 225,
  280, 296, 299, 307–08, 352,
  358–9, 387
Papal States 52, 59, 66, 122, 123,
  146–7, 150, 153, 205, 281, 282,
  284
Parma 52, 55, 57, 58, 128,
  198, 199
Piedmont-Sardinia 43, 51, 52,
  53, 54, 55, 59, 145, 151, 201
Tuscany/Etruria 6, 52, 57, 58, 60,
  83, 118, 128, 129, 145, 146, 147,
  198, 238–9, 286
Venice/Venetia 52, 59, 62, 63–4,
  118, 119, 183
Italy 392–3

Jefferson, Thomas 135–6
John, Archduke 186, 264, 265,
  267, 270
John, Regent/VI 129, 130, 153,
  157, 219, 243
Joubert, Barthelemy 64
Jourdan, Jean-Baptiste 98, 100,
  172, 187, 309
Junot, Andoche 9, 54, 75, 82,
  92, 179, 199, 243–4, 251,
  252–3, 383

Kehr, Abou 79
Kellermann, François 52, 57, 193,
  263, 271
Kilmaine, Charles 63–4
Kléber, Jean-Baptiste 75, 78, 79, 87,
  92, 95
Kleist, Friedrich von 221
Kienmayer, Michael von 265

Knobelsdorf, Wilhelm von 207
Kollowrat-Krakowsky, Karl 265
Kosciusko, Thaddeus 214
Kray, Paul 113, 114
Kutuzov, Mikhail 186, 189–90, 192,
  319, 322–7, 329, 332, 385

La Bouillerie, François 218–19
La Rochefoucauld, Adelaide 215
Lacrosse, Jean 111, 112, 134
Lacuée, Jean 330
Lafayette, Joseph Marquis 125, 365
Laforest, Antoine 206
Lagrange, Joseph 219
Laharpe, Amédée 52, 56
Laine, Joseph 341
Lamarque, Jean 360, 364
Lancret, Jean-Baptiste 75
Langara, Juan 42
Lannes, Jean 9, 21, 75, 115, 116,
  130, 172, 187, 190–1, 192, 194,
  195, 209, 215, 218, 222–3, 257,
  264, 269
Lariboisière, Jean 318
Larrey, Jean 75
Las Cases, Emmanuel 368, 369, 370
Lauderdale, James Maitland 205
Lauriston, Jacques 206, 324
Lauzun, Armand Biron,
  Duke 40, 41
League of Armed Neutrality, the
  120, 121
Lebrun, Charles 103, 104
Lebrun, Ponce 139
Leclerc, Victor 75, 82, 129, 132, 133,
  134, 239–40
Lecourbe, Claude 114, 360, 364
Lefebrve, François 172, 193,
  209, 219, 221, 257, 258, 264,
  266, 359
Lemarois, Jean 281

Lemercier, Pierre 99
Lepère, Jean-Baptiste 75
Lestocq, Anton 214–15, 223
Levasseur, Pierre 294
Level, Jean 168
Liechtenstein, Johann 195, 265, 271, 273
Lisle, Claude Rouget de 139
Lithuania 320, 384
Livingston, Robert 135–6
Livingstone, Edward 139
Lobau, Georges Mouton, Count 361, 364
Louis, Archduke 264, 265
Louis, Prince of Baden 227
Louis I 129, 145–6, 238–9
Louis II 146
Louis XIII 17
Louis XIV 17, 394
Louis XVI 37, 40, 97, 303, 374
Louis XVIII/Count of Provence 107–08, 120, 150, 160, 162, 175, 176, 351–2, 355, 366, 373, 374, 375
Louise, Queen 190, 201, 224, 310
Lowe, Hudson 369
Lucchesini, Girolamo di 206–07

Macdonald, Étienne 98, 172, 267, 270, 319, 322, 329, 337, 347, 359
Machiavelli, Nicolo 13, 231
Mack, Karl von 146, 188, 189
MacPherson, James 36
Madison, James 135
Maitland, Frederick 366
Malet, Claude 290, 325–6, 372
Malta 72, 75, 111, 118, 119, 120, 123, 150, 151, 152, 153, 183, 390
Manin, Ludovico 63–4

Marbeuf, Louis 34
Marchand, Louis 368
Maret de Bassano, Hugues 320, 321, 336, 355
Maria Carolina 146–7, 148, 177, 184, 199–201, 217
Maria Luiza 244, 248
Maria Theresa 303
Marie I 129
Marie Antoinette 148, 303
Marie Louise of Spain/Tuscany 119, 145, 146, 239, 242
Markov, Arkadi 151, 174
Marlborough, John Churchill, Duke 92
Marmont, Auguste 66, 67, 75, 95, 157, 166, 172, 187, 193, 206, 214, 218, 258, 264, 267, 270, 271, 321, 346, 359
Martiniani, Carlo 121
Masséna, André 50, 52, 53, 56, 112–13, 114, 115, 172, 187, 191, 193, 200, 264, 269, 270, 271, 359
Mathis, Christine 301, 302
Mattei, Alessandro 66
Maximilian Joseph 22, 189, 230–1
Melas, Michael 112–13, 114, 115, 116, 117
Melo e Castro, Joao de Alameda 157
Melzi d'Eril, Francesco 144
Menou, Jacques 75, 78, 79–80, 95, 121
Merveldt de Courelles, Johann von 63, 66, 67
Metternich, Clemens von 5, 6, 261, 268, 271, 273, 309, 333, 335, 336, 342, 357–8
Meynier, Jean-Baptiste 52, 56
Miollis, Alexandre 282–3, 284

Mirabeau, Honoré 125
Missiessey, Édouard 180–1
Mollien, Nicolas 264, 330, 355
Moncey, Adrien 115, 172, 251, 252, 347
Monge, Gaspard 69, 75, 84, 95
Monroe, James 136
Montesquieu, Anatole 355
Moore, John 257, 258, 259
Moreau, Jean 98, 99, 100, 113, 114, 118, 165, 166–7, 372
Mortier, Adolphe 153, 154, 172, 185, 190, 193, 219, 223, 318, 325, 346, 359
Moulin, Jean 98, 99
Moutholon-Semonville, Charles 368, 370
Murad Bey 80, 81, 82
Murat, Joachim 22, 46–7, 75, 92, 95, 101, 115, 116, 147, 172, 188, 189, 190–1, 192, 194, 195, 201–02, 209, 215, 219–20, 222–3, 227, 232, 235, 245, 248, 250, 260, 283, 284, 294, 307, 321, 322, 326, 339, 344, 351, 352, 354, 358–9, 372, 374
Murray, William 131–2
Mustafa IV 206

Najac, Benoit 73
Narbonne, Louis 317
Neckar, Jacques 37
Neipperg, Adam von 352, 359
Nelson, Horatio 78–9, 83, 110, 146, 191–2
Netherlands/Batavian Republic 40, 110, 123, 153, 155, 157, 158, 163, 180, 200, 205, 225, 228, 232, 233, 235, 286, 305–06, 314, 342, 355
Neufchâteau, François 74

Newton, Isaac 381
Ney, Michel 148–9, 172, 187, 193, 209, 215, 218, 219–20, 223, 257, 318, 332, 333, 334, 337, 347, 354, 355, 359, 361–5, 386–7
Nitot, Étienne 294
Norry, Charles 75
Nouet, Nicolas 75

O'Hara, Charles 43
O'Meara, Barry 368
Onasco, Louis 364
Ordener, Michel 168
Oriani, Barnaba 59
Osterman-Tolstoy, Alexander 215, 337
Ott, Peter 115
Otto, Louis 123, 163, 188
Ottoman Empire 71, 72, 73, 75, 79, 83, 87, 94–5, 123, 149, 151, 185, 205–06, 217–18, 221, 225, 256, 315, 380, 387
 Albania 77
 Algiers 77, 79, 149
 Barbary States 149, 150
 Egypt 57, 72, 77–95, 111, 123, 142, 149, 387, 389
 Janina 73
 Palestine 73, 86, 89, 149
 Scutari 73, 77
 Syria 86, 89
 Tripoli 77, 149
 Tunis 73, 77, 79
Oubril, Peter 151, 169, 174, 202, 204
Oudinot, Nicolas 172, 264, 269, 270, 305–06, 318, 332, 333, 334, 336, 337, 347, 359
Ouvrand, Gabriel 140, 306

Pacca, Bartolomeo 283, 285
Palafox, Jose 252, 257

Palm, Johann 292
Paoli, Pasquale 39, 40, 41
Paradis, Jean 75
Pasha Abdallah 86, 92
Pasquier, Etienne 287, 290
Paul I 77, 119–20
Perceval, François 75, 95
Percier, Charles 288
Perignon, Dominque 172
Perrée, Jean-Baptiste 80
Persia 185, 217, 222
Peter of Holstein-Gottorp 314
Peter I the Great 314
Peter III 314
Phéllippeaux, Louis 92, 93
Pichegru, Charles 67, 165–7
Pirch, Georg 360, 362
Pius VI 66, 121
Pius VII 121, 122, 146, 147, 150, 153, 175–7, 280, 281, 283–5, 341
Pitt, William 119, 123, 204
Poland 212–15, 232, 384
    Grand Duchy of Warsaw 225, 226, 264, 265, 270, 273, 274, 286, 296, 314, 315, 333, 336
Poniatowski, Josef 172, 214, 221, 265, 268, 318
Portugal 19, 21, 129–31, 153, 155, 157, 180, 225, 239, 243–4, 251, 252–3, 255, 299, 379, 383–4, 387
    Brazil 244, 251
Prometheus 3
Prussia 40, 109, 120, 150, 154, 175, 183, 185, 188, 190, 196, 201–02, 206–15, 237, 261, 264, 292, 296, 302, 309, 310, 324, 329–47, 352, 353–67, 387, 388, 392, 393

Radet, Étienne 283
Rapp, Jean 149, 360, 364
Real, Pierre 98, 100, 290
Reding, Teodoro 257
Redouté, Henri 75
Regnaud, Michel 98
Regnier, Claude 122, 159, 173
Reich, Marie 168
Reille, Honoré 361
Reuss, Heinrich 269
Reynier, Jean 75, 318, 325
Richepanse, Antoine 134
Robespierre, Augustine 44
Robespierre, Maximilien 44
Rocca, Pierre 40
Rochambeau, Jean 134
Roederer, Pierre 98, 131
Romanzov, Nicolas 255
Rosenberg, Franz 265, 269
Rosey, François 163
Rosily-Mesros, François 188
Rostopchin, Fyodor 323
Rousseau, Jean Jacques 13, 36, 376
Ruchel, Ernst von 208–09
Ruffin, Pierre 87
Ruffo, Fabrizio 147
Rumbold, George 161
Rumford, Benjamin Thompson Count 139
Russia 3, 19, 83, 93, 119–20, 146, 151, 169, 174, 178, 181–96, 200, 202, 205, 206, 212–26, 258, 261, 262–3, 273, 274, 280, 292, 296, 298, 302, 310, 311, 313–27, 328–47, 352, 353, 367, 379, 387, 388, 389, 392, 393

Saint Aignan, Louis 340
Saint Hilaire, Louis 75, 106
Saint Julian, Francis 118
Saint-Méry, Mérédic Moreau 145–6
Saliceti, Antoine 42, 44, 200

Savary, Jean 9, 159, 192, 193, 251, 347
Say, Jean-Baptiste 17
Schill, Ferdinand von 266
Schimmelpennick, Roger 157, 163, 180, 233
Schwarzenberg, Karl von 303, 319, 322, 325, 329, 336, 337, 338, 342–6, 360, 364, 365
Sebastiani, Horace 149, 206, 217
Ségur, Louis 172, 355
Seid Mohammad el-Koraim 78
Selim III 73, 77, 86, 87, 149, 185, 186, 206, 217–18
Serbelloni, Galleazzo 65
Sérurier, Jean 52, 53, 56, 60, 61, 172, 346
Seven Islands Republic 121, 149, 178, 204
Shah Feth Ali 186, 222
Sieyès, Emmanuel 98, 99, 100, 101, 102
Siniavin, Dmitri 244
Sisyphus 3
Smith, Adam 17
Smith, Spencer 168
Smith, Sydney 92, 93, 94–5, 110, 390
Soult, Nicholas 114, 166, 170–1, 172, 192, 194, 209, 218, 219–20, 222–3, 254, 257, 258, 259, 339, 347, 359, 365, 386
Spain 19, 31, 42, 43, 109, 110, 111, 119, 126, 128–30, 135, 155, 156–7, 158, 179, 180, 187, 238–9, 243–9, 250–9, 263, 286, 296, 298, 299, 309, 314, 352, 379, 383–4, 387, 390
Spain – Empire
  Cuba 111
  Santo Domingo 111, 126
Spina, Joseph 121, 122

Sprengsporten, Joram 120
Stadion, Johann 261
Staël, Germaine de 14, 164, 293, 375
Stein, Heinrich von 310
Suchet, Louis 114, 115, 172, 359, 360, 364
Sully, Maximilien Bethune, Duke 17
Suvorov, Alexander 380–1
Sweden 120, 174, 181, 209, 225, 310, 311, 317, 336, 352, 387
Switzerland/Helvetia 113, 123, 148–9, 150, 151, 153, 158, 183, 200

Talleyrand-Perigord, Charles 11, 12, 20, 65, 69–70, 72, 79, 98, 100, 109–10, 118, 119, 121–2, 123, 127, 129, 131, 136–7, 145, 146, 152, 157, 160, 163, 164, 168–9, 172, 173, 174, 182, 183, 192, 193, 203, 204, 207, 216, 222, 223, 225, 227, 229, 234, 249, 260–1, 302, 332, 346, 352, 356, 372, 373, 374
Tchernitchev, Alexander 315
terrorism 22, 30
Thevenard, Antoine 11
Thielemann, Johann 360, 362
Thugut, Johann 66–7, 68, 118
Thurreau, Louis 115
Tippo-Sahib 90
Tormazov, Alexander 319, 325
Touche, Jean Méhée de la 162
Toussaint-Louverture, Pierre 126, 127–8, 132–3, 134
Tracy, Destrutt 293
treaties and armistices
  Alexandria 117
  Amiens 123–4, 144, 150, 151, 152, 157, 387
  Andujar 252, 243

Aranjuez 128, 238
Badajoz 129, 130
Basel 126
Bucharest 316
Campo Formio 68, 69, 74, 97, 117, 118, 272, 286, 387
Cherasco 53
Cintra 252–3
Concordat 121–3, 278, 280
Dresden 226
Erfurt 256, 310
Feldsdorf 118
Final Act 358
Florence 147
Fontainebleau 239, 243–4
Fontainebleau (1813) 284
Fontainebleau (1814) 347–8, 351, 352, 353
Hohenlinden 118
Ildefonso 128
Judenburg 63
Kalisch 330
Königsberg 226
Leoben 63
Louisiana Purchase 135–7, 393
Lunéville 118–19, 144, 147, 202, 272, 273, 387
Mortefontaine 132
Paris (1801) 121
Paris (1803) 158
Paris (1814) 351–2
Paris (1815) 394
Pressburg 196, 387
Reichenbach 335
Rheims 345
San Ildefonso 128, 238
Schonbrunn 196, 201, 274, 387
Steyr 119
Tilsit 221–6, 237, 309, 387, 388
Tolentino 66, 122
Trevise 119

Venice 64
Vienna 272
Znaim 272

United States 11, 111, 131–2, 135–7, 316–17, 366, 389, 393
American Revolution 213

Vandamme, Dominique 219, 221, 264, 318, 337, 361
Vaudois, Claude 61, 77
Verdier, Jean 251, 252
Victor Amadeus 54
Victor Emmanuel IV 145, 146
Victor, Claude 66, 115, 116, 172, 223, 257, 319, 324
Villaret-Joyeuse, Louis 132
Villeneuve, Pierre 180–1, 182, 188, 191–2
Villoteau, Guillaume 75
Vives, Juan 257

Walewska, Marie 216, 226, 301, 302, 351
Washington, George 10–11, 131, 214
wars
  1812, of 316–17
  American Independence, of 37, 51, 110
  Cold War 393
  First World War 393
  Quasi 131
  Second World War 393
  Seven Years War 37, 52, 128
Wellington, Arthur Wellesley, Duke of 3, 252–3, 259, 335, 338, 339, 360–5, 380, 386–7, 389, 390
West Indies/Caribbean 123
Whitworth, Charles 150, 152, 153

Wieland, Christophe 255
William, Prince of Orange 360
Winzingerode, Ferdinand von
Wittgenstein, Peter 319, 325, 326, 332, 334
Wrede, Karl von 270, 336–7, 338
Wurmser, Dagobert 60

Uxbridge, Henry Paget, Earl of 360

Xenophon 3

Yarmouth, Francis, Lord Seymour 204
Yorck, Johann 329, 333
Youssef Pasha 94–5

Zastrow, Friedrich 221
Zayonchek, Joseph 221
Ziethen, Hans 360, 361